FAB 4 Features

AF668185

NCERT Tracker
Every topic is tagged with NCERT page numbers for better syncing with NCERT.

TOPIC 1

Sets and Their Representation

NCERT Pg 1-5

1. Which of the following collections are sets?

(i) A collection of all natural numbers less than 50 ________

(ii) The collection of good hockey players in India ________

(iii) The collection of difficult topics in Mathematics ________

(iv) A collection of most dangerous animals of the world ________

***36.** Find the domain of the following functions.

(i) Exponential function (a^x) ________

(ii) Logarithm function $(\log_e x)$ ________

(iii) $f(x) = \dfrac{1}{\sqrt{x + [x]}}$ ________

***40.** Given that $f(x) = x^2 - 4$ and $g(x) = x + 2$, find the domain of $f + g$, $f - g$, fg and f/g.

Important Concept Tagging
Every question which is based on the important concept from JEE & CUET point of view is marked with*.

COMPETITION CONNECT

Topic 1. Power Set [NCERT (Old) Pg. 12]

Competition Connect
Supplement Containing related portions of old NCERT which are present in JEE/CUET syllabus but removed from latest NCERT.

***1.** The total number of subsets of a finite set containing n elements is ________ .

***2.** Two finite sets have m and n elements. The total number of subsets of the first set is 56 more than the total number of subsets of the second set. Find the values of m and n.

3. Let A be a set. Then, the collection of all subsets of A is called ________ of A.

4. If $A = \{a, \{b\}\}$, then $P(A) = \{\phi, \{a\},$ ________ $, \{a,$ ___ $\}\}$.

5. Power set of a given set is always non-empty.

True ☐ False ☐

COMPETITION EDGE UP

1. Let $A = \{n \in [100, 700] \cap N : n$ is neither a multiple of 3 nor a multiple of 4$\}$. Then, the number of elements in A is [JEE Main 2024]

(a) 300 ☐ (b) 280 ☐

(c) 310 ☐ (d) 290 ☐

2. Let $S = \{x \in R : (\sqrt{3} + \sqrt{2})^x + (\sqrt{3} - \sqrt{2})^x = 10\}$. Then, the number of elements in S, is [JEE Main 2024]

(a) 0 ☐

(b) 1 ☐

(c) 4 ☐

(d) 2 ☐

passed in Physics, 16 students passed in Chemistry, atmost 11 students passed in both Mathematics and Physics, atmost 15 students passed in both Physics and Chemistry, atmost 15 students passed in both Mathematics and Chemistry. The maximum number of students passed in all the three subjects is .... [JEE Main 2024]

6. An organisation awarded 48 medals in event A, 25 in event B and 18 in event C. If these medals went to total 60 men and only five men got medals in all the three events, then how many received medals in exactly two of three events? [JEE Main 2023]

(a) 10 ☐ (b) 9 ☐

Competition edge up
Selected PYQs in Sync with NCERT Chapter.

CONTENTS

NCERT MATHEMATICS

REVISION WORK BOOK

Most Effective Revision
& Concept Zipper for >>>>

JEE & CUET

Vol 1 CLASS XI

Authors
Naveen Kumar
Sandeep Singh

arihant
SUCCESS AND NOTHING LESS

arihant
SUCCESS AND NOTHING LESS

ARIHANT PRAKASHAN SERIES, MEERUT

Administrative & Production Offices

Regd. Office
'Ramchhaya' 4577/15, Agarwal Road, Darya Ganj, New Delhi -110002
Tele: 011- 47630600, 43518550

Head Office
Kalindi, TP Nagar, Meerut (UP) - 250002
Tel: 0121-7156203, 7156204

Sales & Support Offices
Agra, Ahmedabad, Bengaluru, Bareilly, Chennai, Delhi, Guwahati, Hyderabad, Jaipur, Jhansi, Kolkata, Lucknow, Nagpur & Pune.

PRICE ₹310.00

PO No : TXT-59-T064854-05-25

Published by Arihant Publications (India) Ltd.

For further information about the books published by Arihant, log on to www.arihantbooks.com or e-mail at info@arihantbooks.com

Follow us on

Super 6

ADVANTAGES OF REVISION WORK BOOKS

1. Learn with fun while practicing with Self Assessment.
2. Different question types are helpful in increasing the learning and understanding about **Core Concepts** and **Conceptual Applications**.
3. Small methodical question using real life situation also help in **enhancing visualisation**.
4. Innovative style of practice in Workbook manner helps in breaking the monotonicity of subject.
5. Complete sync with NCERT along with **Competition Connect** and **Competition Edge Up** helps in building the foundation for the preparation of competitions like JEE and CUET.
6. Questions with one word or maximum one sentence long answers are very helpful in **Faster Revision** and **Confidence Boost Up**.

Chapter 01

Sets

Scan and take Chapter Test

TOPIC 1

Sets and Their Representation

NCERT Pg 1-5

1. Which of the following collections are sets?

(i) A collection of all natural numbers less than 50 ____________

(ii) The collection of good hockey players in India ____________

(iii) The collection of difficult topics in Mathematics ____________

(iv) A collection of most dangerous animals of the world ____________

***2.** **Statement I** Every set is a collection.

Statement II Every collection is a set.

(a) Both statements are correct

(b) Both statements are incorrect

(c) Statement I is correct but Statement II is incorrect

(d) Statement I is incorrect but Statement II is correct

____

3. If $A = \{0, 1, 2, 3, 4, 5, 6, 7, 8, 9, 10\}$, then

(i) $12 \in A$

True ☐ False ☐

(ii) $2(\max A) - 15 \in A$

True ☐ False ☐

(iii) $5(\min A) - 2 \notin A$

True ☐ False ☐

(iv) $3 + 3(\min A)(\max A) = 33$

True ☐ False ☐

*Concepts of all questions bearing * are important for JEE & CUET*

4. Write down another two elements of the sets.

(i) $A = \{2, 4, 6, 8 \,..........\}$ ____________

(ii) $B =$ {Sunday, Monday, Tuesday, ...} ____________

(iii) $Q = \{x : 2x + 3 < 24, x \in N\}$ ____________

(iv) $R = \{y : 3y - 1 < 8, y \in N\}$ ____________

(v) $S = \{x = -1 < x < 5, x \in Z\}$ ____________

5. State True or False.

(i) The set of all vowels in the word 'EQUATION' can be written in roster form as {A, E, I, O, U}.

True ☐ False ☐

(ii) The set of all natural numbers less than 7 can be written in roster form as {0, 1, 2, 3, 4, 5, 6}.

True ☐ False ☐

(iii) The set of all vowels in English alphabet which precedes *s*, is {a, e, i, o}.

True ☐ False ☐

(iv) The set of all irrational numbers can be written as $\{x : x$ is real and irrational$\}$.

True ☐ False ☐

6. Write the set of all integers, whose cube is an even integer.

____

7. State True or False.

(i) Solution set of $\{x : x$ is a positive integer and divisor of $9\}$ in roster form is $\{1, 3, 9\}$.

True ☐ False ☐

(ii) Solution set of the equation $x^2 + x - 2 = 0$ in roster form is $\{-1, 2\}$.

True ☐ False ☐

(iii) Solution set of $\{x : x$ is a letter of the word 'PROPORTION'$\}$ in roster form is {P, R, O, T, I, N}.

True ☐ False ☐

(iv) Solution set of $\{x : x \in Z, x^2 < 20\}$ in roster form is $\{-4, -3, -2, -1, 0, 1, 2, 3, 4\}$.

True ☐ False ☐

8. Write the following sets in roster form.

(i) $A = \{x : x$ is a prime number and $x < 11\}$ ____________

(ii) $B = \left\{x : x = \dfrac{n}{n^2 + 1} \text{ and } 1 \le n \le 3, \text{ where } n \in N\right\}$ ____________

(iii) $C = \{a_n : n \in N, a_{n+2} = a_{n+1} + a_n, a_1 = a_2 = 1\}$ ____________

(iv) $D = \{a_n : n \in N, a_{n+2} = a_{n+1} \cdot a_n, a_1 = a_2 = 1\}$ ____________

(v) $E = \{a_n : n \in N, a_{n+2} = a_{n+1} \cdot a_n, a_1 = a_2 = -2\}$ ____________

9. Write the following sets in tabular form.

(i) $P = \{a : a \in N, a < 10, a \text{ is odd}\}$ ______

(ii) $Q = \{x : x \in I, 2x^2 + x - 6 = 0\}$ ______

(iii) $R = \{x : x \text{ is a month of a year not having 31 days}\}$ ______

10. Match each of the set on the left described in the roster form with the same set on the right described in the set-builder form.

	Column I		Column I
A.	{P, R, I, N, C, A, L}	1.	$\{x : x$ is a positive integer and is a divisor of 18$\}$
B.	{0}	2.	$\{x : x$ is an integer and $x^2 - 9 = 0\}$
C.	{1, 2, 3, 6, 9, 18}	3.	$\{x : x$ is an integer and $x + 1 = 1\}$
D.	{− 3, 3}	4.	$\{x : x$ is a letter of the word 'PRINCIPAL'$\}$

(a) $A \to 4, B \to 1, C \to 2, D \to 3$
(b) $A \to 4, B \to 3, C \to 1, D \to 2$
(c) $A \to 4, B \to 2, C \to 1, D \to 3$
(d) $A \to 4, B \to 3, C \to 2, D \to 1$

11. Write the following sets in set-builder form.

(i) $X = \left\{1, \frac{1}{4}, \frac{1}{9}, \frac{1}{16}, \frac{1}{25}, \ldots\right\}$ ______

(ii) If n is replaced with $\frac{1}{n+1}$ in obtained set builder form of part (i), then write the roster form now ______

(iii) $\left\{\frac{1}{2}, \frac{2}{3}, \frac{3}{4}, \frac{4}{5}, \frac{5}{6}, \frac{6}{7}, \frac{7}{8}, \frac{8}{9}, \frac{9}{10}\right\}$ ______

TOPIC 2

Types of Sets

NCERT Pg. 5-9

12. The set A given by $A = \{x : x \text{ is an even prime number greater than } 2\}$ is a/an ______ set.

13. Which of the following set is an empty set?

(i) $A = \{x : x^2 - 3 = 0 \text{ and } x \text{ is rational}\}$ ______

(ii) $B = \{x : x \text{ is an even prime number}\}$ ______

(iii) $C = \{x : 4 < x < 5, x \in R\}$ ______

(iv) $D = \{x : x^2 = 25 \text{ and } x \text{ is an odd integer}\}$ ______

(v) $E = \{x : x^2 = -2, x \in R\}$ ______

14. State True or False.

(i) $A = \{5\}$ is a singleton set.

True ☐ False ☐

(ii) $B = \{x : x \in N \text{ and } x^2 = 9\}$ is a singleton set equal to $\{3, -3\}$.

True ☐ False ☐

(iii) $C = \{x : x^2 = 4, x \text{ is odd}\}$ is a singleton set.

True ☐ False ☐

(iv) $A = \{x : x \in Z \text{ and } x^2 - 5x + 6 = 0\}$ is a finite set.

True ☐ False ☐

15. Identify the type of the following sets

(i) $A = \{x : x \in Z \text{ and } x > -10\}$ ________________

(ii) $B = \{x : x \in Z \text{ and } -10 < x < -7\}$ ________________

(iii) $C = \{x : x \in Z \text{ and } -7 < x < -5\}$ ________________

(iv) $D = \{x : x \in N \text{ and } x < -5\}$ ________________

16. Which of the following set is an infinite set or finite set?

(i) $\{x : x \in N \text{ and } (x-1)(x-2) = 0\}$ ________________

(ii) $\{x : x \in N \text{ and } x^2 = 4\}$ ________________

(iii) $\{x : x \in N \text{ and } 2x - 1 = 0\}$ ________________

(iv) $\{x : x \in N \text{ and } x \text{ is prime}\}$ ________________

17. Infinite set can be described in roster form.

True ☐ False ☐

18. Match the following

	Column I		Column II
A.	$\{x \in N, 5 < x < 6\}$	1.	Finite set
B.	$\{x : x \in N \text{ and } x \text{ is odd}\}$	2.	Void set
C.	$\{x : x \in Z \text{ and } x^2 = 36\}$	3.	Singleton set
D.	$\{x : x - 5 = 0\}$	4.	Infinite set

Choose the correct option?

(a) A $\rightarrow$ 1, B $\rightarrow$ 4, C $\rightarrow$ 3, D $\rightarrow$ 2

(b) A $\rightarrow$ 3, B $\rightarrow$ 4, C $\rightarrow$ 1, D $\rightarrow$ 2

(c) A $\rightarrow$ 2, B $\rightarrow$ 4, C $\rightarrow$ 1, D $\rightarrow$ 3

(d) A $\rightarrow$ 4, B $\rightarrow$ 2, C $\rightarrow$ 3, D $\rightarrow$ 1

____

19. If $A = \{1, 2, 3, 4\}$ and $B = \{x : -5 < x < 5, x \in N\}$, then A and B are ____________ sets.

20. If A and B are unequal sets, then it can be written as $A \not\subset B$.

True ☐ False ☐

21. $A = \{x : x$ is a letter in the word 'LOYAL'$\}$,
$B = \{x : x$ is a letter in the word 'ALLOY'$\}$. Then,
$A = B$ is true?

Yes ☐ No ☐

22. $A = \{0\}$, $B = \{x : x > 15$ and $x < 5\}$, $C = \{x : x - 5 = 0\}$, $D = \{x : x^2 = 25\}$ and $E = \{x : x$ is an integral positive roots of the equation $x^2 - 2x - 15 = 0\}$

(a) $A = \phi$ (b) $D = \{5\}$
(c) $A = B$ (d) $C = E$

---

23. $A = \{x : x \in Z$ and $x^2 \le 8\}$ and $B = \{x : x \in R$ and $x^2 - 4x + 3 = 0\}$ are equal sets.

True ☐ False ☐

TOPIC 3

Subset and Universal Set

NCERT Pg 9-13

24. If every element of A is an element of B, then A is called __________________ of B.

***25.** If $A \subseteq B$ and $A \ne B$, then

Statement I A is proper subset of B.
Statement II B is super set of A
Statement III $x \in B$, then $x \notin A$
Statement IV $A \subset B$

Which of the following statement/statements is/are correct?

(a) Only I (b) Only IV
(c) II and III (d) I, II, III and IV

---

26. State True or False.

(i) Empty set is a subset of every set.

True ☐ False ☐

(ii) Empty set has no elements.

True ☐ False ☐

(iii) $A \subset \phi \Rightarrow A = \phi$

True ☐ False ☐

(iv) If $A = \{1, 2, \{3, 4,\}, 5\}$, then $\{3, 4\} \subset A$.

True ☐ False ☐

(v) Let A, B and C be three sets of $A \in B$ and $B \subset C$, then $A \subset C$.

True ☐ False ☐

(vi) If $x \in A$ and $A \in B$, then $x \in B$.

True ☐ False ☐

(vii) If $A \subset B$ and $B \in C$, then $A \in C$.

True ☐ False ☐

27. If P is the set of natural numbers less than 50, then

(i) list the subset Q of even numbers ______________________

(ii) list the subset R of odd numbers ______________________

(iii) list the subset S of prime numbers______________________

(iv) list the subset T of numbers divisible by 5 ______________________

28. State True or False.

(i) {mango, banana} $\subset$ {fruit}.

True ☐ False ☐

(ii) {potatoes, carrots} $\subset$ {vegetables}.

True ☐ False ☐

(iii) $\{4, 6\} \not\subset \{1, 2, 4, 6, 10\}$.

True ☐ False ☐

(iv) $\{1, 2, 3, 4\} \subset$ {natural numbers}.

True ☐ False ☐

____

29. $[a, b]$ can be grouped as

(a) 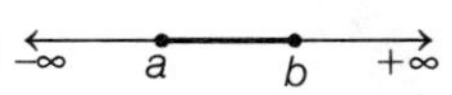

(b) 

(c) 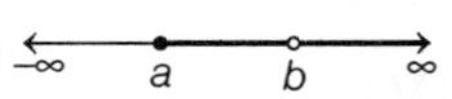

(d) 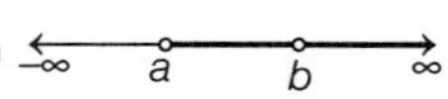

____

30. Write $\{x : x \in R, -4 < x \leq 6\}$ as intervals.

____

31. $[-20, 3)$ in set-builder form is

(a) $\{x : x \in R \text{ and } -20 \leq x \leq 3\}$

(b) $\{x : x \in R \text{ and } -20 < x < 3\}$

(c) $\{x : x \in R \text{ and } -20 \leq x < 3\}$

(d) $\{x : x \in R \text{ and } -20 < x \leq 3\}$

____

32. A set that contains all sets in a given context is called universal set

True ☐ False ☐

33. If $A = \{1, 2, 3\}$, $B = \{2, 4, 5, 6\}$ and $C = \{1, 3, 5, 7\}$. Find the universal set.

____

TOPIC 4

Venn Diagrams, Operations of Sets and Complement of a Set

NCERT Pg 13-20

34. In venn diagram, universal set is represented by ______________________

35. $A \cup B = \{x : x \in A \text{ and } x \in B\}$.

True ☐ False ☐

36. $A \cap B = \{x : x \in A$ ______________ $x \in B\}$.

***37.** Let $P = \{a, b, c, d\}$, $Q = \{a, c, g\}$ and $R = \{c, g, m, n, p\}$, then

(i) $P \cup Q =$ ______________________

(ii) $P \cup R =$ ______________________

(iii) $Q \cup R =$ ______________________

(iv) $P \cap Q =$ ______________________

(v) $P \cap R =$ ______________________

(vi) $Q \cap R =$ ______________________

(vii) $P \cap (Q \cup R) =$ ______________________

(viii) $(P \cap Q) \cup R =$ ______________________

(ix) $(P \cup Q) \cap R =$ ______________________

(x) $(P \cap Q) \cup (P \cap R) =$ ______________________

38. If $A = \{1, 2, 3, 4, 5, 6, 7\}$, $B = \{2, 4, 6, 8, 10\}$ and $C = \{4, 6, 7, 8, 9, 10, 11\}$, then

(i) $A \cap B = \{2, 4, 6\}$

True ☐ False ☐

(ii) $A \cap B \cap C = \{2, 4, 6\}$

True ☐ False ☐

***39.** If $A = \{x : x = 2n, n \in Z\}$ and $B = \{x : x = 3n, n \in Z\}$, then $A \cap B =$ ______________ .

40. If $a \in N$ such that $aN = \{ax : x \in N\}$, then $3N \cap 7N = 21N$.

True ☐ False ☐

41. $A \cup (A \cap B) =$ ______________________

42. If $A = \{1, 2\}$, $B = \{1, 4, 8\}$ and $C = \{2, 4, 6, 8\}$, then

(i) $B - A =$ ______________________

(ii) $A \cup B =$ ______________________

(iii) $C - (A \cup B) =$ ______________________

43. $A' = \{x \in U : x$ __________ $A\}$.

(a) $\in$ (b) $\notin$ (c) $\subseteq$ (d) $\subset$

---

44. **Statement I** $U' = \phi$

Statement II $\phi' = U$

Given both the statements are correct.

True ☐ False ☐

45. $A \cup A' =$ __________

(a) ϕ (b) A (c) A' (d) U

***46.** Observe the diagram and complete the following statements

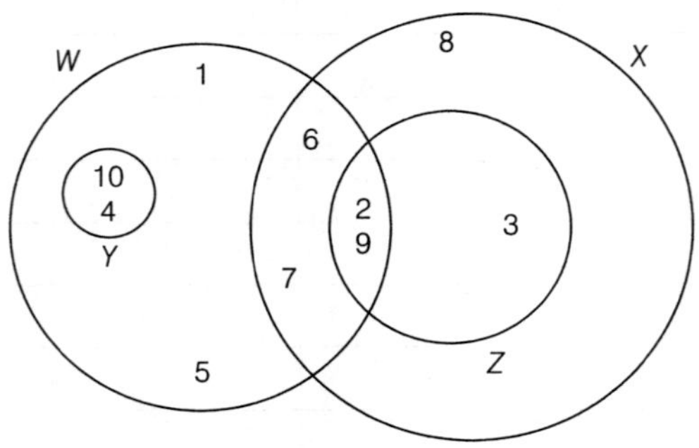

(i) $W = \{$ __________ $\}$

(ii) $X = \{$ __________ $\}$

(iii) $Y = \{$ __________ $\}$

(iv) $Z = \{$ __________ $\}$

(v) $W \cap Y = \{$ __________ $\}$

(vi) $W \cap Z = \{$ __________ $\}$

(vii) $Y \cap Z = \{$ __________ $\}$

(viii) $W \cap X = \{$ __________ $\}$

***47.** Choose the correct venn diagram for $A' \cap B'$.

(a) 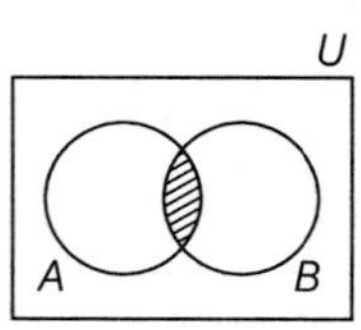

(b) 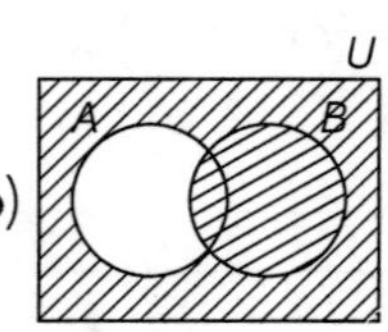

(c) 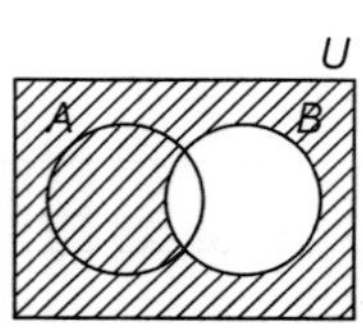

(d) 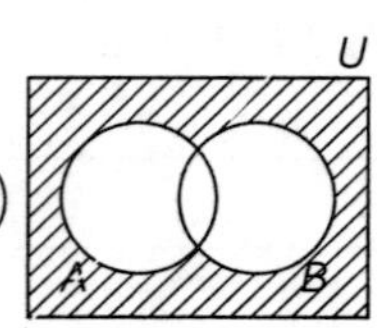

---

48. Draw venn diagram for following

(i) $A' \cup B'$ ______

(ii) $A \cup (B \cap C)$ ______

(iii) $A \cap (B \cup C)$ ______

(iv) $(A \cup B) \cap (A \cup C)$ ______

(v) $(A \cap B) \cup (A \cap C)$ ______

(vi) $A' \cap (B \cup C)$ ______

(vii) $A' \cap (C - B)$ ______

49. If $U = \{1, 2, 3, 4, 5, 6, 7, 8, 9\}$, $A = \{1, 2, 3, 4\}$ and $B = \{2, 4, 6, 8\}$, then find

(i) $A \cup B$ ______

(ii) $(A \cup B)'$ ______

(iii) $A \cap B$ ______

(iv) $(A \cap B)'$ ______

50. If $A = \{1, 3, 5, 7, 9, 11, 13, 15, 17\}$, $B = \{2, 4, 6, \dots, 18\}$ and N is the universal set, then $A' \cup \{(A \cup B) \cap B'\} = \phi$

True ☐ False ☐

51. If A and B are two sets, then $(A \cup B) \cap (A \cup B') =$ ______

52. **Statement I** $(A')' = A$

Statement II $A \cap B = \phi \Rightarrow A \subseteq B'$

Statement III $A' - B' = B - A$

Which of the following statement/statements is/are correct?

(a) Only I (b) Only III

(c) I and III (d) I, II and III

______

53. For three sets A, B and C, $A \cap B = A \cap C$ ______ $B = C$.

(a) $\Rightarrow$ (b) $\Leftrightarrow$

(c) $\not\Rightarrow$ (d) None of these

______

54. If A and B are sets, then mention among $A - B$, $A \cap B$ and $B - A$ which of the pairs represents disjoint sets ______

Assertion-Reason Questions

The following questions consist of two statements – Assertion (A) and Reason (R). Answer these questions by selecting the appropriate option given below.
(a) Both (A) and (R) are true and (R) is correct explanation of (A)
(b) Both (A) and (R) are true but (R) is not the correct explanation of (A)
(c) (A) is true but (R) is false
(d) (A) is false but (R) is true

1. **Assertion** (A) The set $A = \{4, 7, 2, 1, 3\}$ is a finite set.

Reason (R) The set $B = \{ x : x \in R \text{ and } x \in (0, 1)\}$ is a finite set.

(a) ☐ (b) ☐ (c) ☐ (d) ☐

2. **Assertion** (A) Set of all real numbers less than or equal to 0 is $(-\infty, 0)$.

Reason (R) Set of all real numbers less than 3 can be written as $(-\infty, 3)$.

(a) ☐ (b) ☐ (c) ☐ (d) ☐

3. **Assertion** (A) $\{x : x \in N \text{ and } x^2 - 3x + 2 = 0\}$ is a finite set.

Reason (R) A set which consist of a definite number of elements is called a finite set.

(a) ☐ (b) ☐ (c) ☐ (d) ☐

4. **Assertion** (A) The set $P = \{x : x$ is a prime number which is divisor of $20\}$ in roaster form is $\{1, 2, 5\}$.

Reason (R) The set $Q = \{$the set of all letters in the word 'ENVIRONMENT'$\}$ in roaster form is $\{E, N, V, I, R, O, M, T\}$.

(a) ☐ (b) ☐ (c) ☐ (d) ☐

5. **Assertion** (A) Set of English alphabets is the universal set U, then the set of vowels V in english alphabet is subset of U.

Reason (R) The set of vowels is subset of consonants in english alphabets.

(a) ☐ (b) ☐ (c) ☐ (d) ☐

6. **Assertion** (A) Let $A = \{1, 2, 3, 4, 5\}$, $B = \{2, 4, 5\}$. Then, $A - B = \{1, 3\}$.

Reason (R) $A - B$ is set of elements which belongs to A but not to B.

(a) ☐ (b) ☐ (c) ☐ (d) ☐

7. **Assertion** (A) Set of even prime numbers greater than 2 is ϕ.

Reason (R) 2 is only even prime number.

(a) ☐ (b) ☐ (c) ☐ (d) ☐

8. **Assertion** (A) If A, B and C are respectively set of parallelograms, rectangles and squares. Then, $B \subseteq A$ and $B \subseteq C$.

Reason (R) A set A is called a subset of another set B, if all elements of A are also in B.

(a) ☐ (b) ☐ (c) ☐ (d) ☐

9. **Assertion** (A) The set $A = \{x : x^2 = 4 \text{ and } x \text{ is odd}\}$ is an empty set.

Reason (R) As the equation $x^2 = 4$ is not satisfied by any odd value of x, so set A is an empty set.

(a) ☐ (b) ☐ (c) ☐ (d) ☐

10. **Assertion** (A) If $n(A) = 4$, $n(B) = 5$ and $A \cap B = \phi$, then number of elements in $A \cup B = 9$.

Reason (R) If A and B are disjoint, then $n(A \cup B)$ is $n(A) + n(B)$.

(a) ☐ (b) ☐ (c) ☐ (d) ☐

11. **Assertion** (A) The set $\{x : 2, 5, 10, 17, \ldots 101\}$ in set builder form is $\{x : x = n^2 + 1$, where $n \in N$ and $1 \le n \le 10\}$.

Reason (R) In roaster form, the order in which the elements are listed is immaterial.

(a) ☐ (b) ☐ (c) ☐ (d) ☐

12. **Assertion** (A) Let $A = \{1, 2\}$ and $B = \{1, 2, 3\}$. Then, $A \not\subset B$.

Reason (R) If $A \subset B$, then $A \cup B = B$.

(a) ☐ (b) ☐ (c) ☐ (d) ☐

13. **Assertion** (A) The collection of all odd natural number less than 50 is a set.

Reason (R) A set is a well defined collection of distinct objects.

(a) ☐ (b) ☐ (c) ☐ (d) ☐

14. **Assertion** (A) Let A and B be sets, if $A \cap X = B \cap X = \phi$ and $A \cup X = B \cup X$ for some set X, then $A \subset B$.

Reason (R) $A \cap (A \cup X) = A$

(a) ☐ (b) ☐ (c) ☐ (d) ☐

Case Based Questions

Case 1 Two brothers Ram and Shyam were discussing 'set' based problem. Shyam asked questions from Ram. If $A = \{x : x$ is set of letters need to spell 'PARABOLA'$\}$ and $B = \{x : x$ is set of letters need to spell 'PORBAL'$\}$

Based on information given above answer, the questions asked by Shyam.

(i) Which of the following is true?

(a) $A = B$ ☐ (b) $A \subset B$ ☐

(c) $B \subset A$ ☐ (d) None of these ☐

(ii) $A \cup B$ is equal to

(a) B ☐ (b) ϕ ☐

(c) A' ☐ (d) None of these ☐

(iii) $A \cap B$ is not equal to

(a) A ☐ (b) ϕ ☐

(c) B ☐ (d) $A \cup B$ ☐

(iv) $(A - B)$ is equal to

(a) A ☐ (b) B ☐

(c) $A \cap B$ ☐ (d) ϕ ☐

Case 2 A bookstore is categorising its inventory based on genres and language. The store manager needs to manage sets of books for efficient organisation and customer service.

Answer the following questions.

(i) Consider the following sets

A = {Mystery novels}; B = {Books in French}; C = {Hardcover books}

Which set represents the intersection of sets A, B and C?

(a) Mystery novels in French ☐

(b) Hardcover mystery novels ☐

(c) Hardcover books in French ☐

(d) Mystery novels that are not in French ☐

(ii) Let D = {Books published in 2023} and

E = {Books in English}

What is the complement of set E, denoted as E'?

(a) Books are not published in English ☐

(b) Books published in English ☐

(c) Books are not published in 2023 ☐

(d) Books published in 2023 ☐

(iii) If set F represents all books in the store and G represents Science fiction books, which of the following statements about the union of sets F and G, denoted as $F \cup G$, is true?

(a) $F \cup G$ includes all books in the store ☐

(b) $F \cup G$ includes only Science fiction books ☐

(c) $F \cup G$ includes Science fiction books and books are not categorised as Science fiction ☐

(d) $F \cup G$ includes only books that is not Science fiction ☐

(iv) Suppose set H = {Books by author A}
and set I = {Books by author B}
What is the cardinality of the intersection of set H and I, denoted as $|H \cap I|$?
(a) 0 ☐
(b) 1 ☐
(c) 2 ☐
(d) None of the above ☐

COMPETITION CONNECT

Topic 1. Power Set [NCERT (Old) Pg. 12]

***1.** The total number of subsets of a finite set containing n elements is ________.

***2.** Two finite sets have m and n elements. The total number of subsets of the first set is 56 more than the total number of subsets of the second set. Find the values of m and n.

3. Let A be a set. Then, the collection of all subsets of A is called ________ of A.

4. If $A = \{a, \{b\}\}$, then $P(A) = \{\phi, \{a\},$ ________, $\{a,$ ___$\}\}$.

5. Power set of a given set is always non-empty.

True ☐ False ☐

---

6. Power subset of $A = \{1, 2\}$ is
(a) $P(A) = \{\phi, \{1\}, \{2\}\}$ ☐
(b) $P(A) = \{\{1\}, \{2\}\}$ ☐
(c) $P(A) = \{1, 2\}$ ☐
(d) $P(A) = \{\phi, \{1\}, \{2\}, \{1, 2\}\}$ ☐

7. For any two sets A and B, $P(A) = P(B) \Rightarrow A \subset B$.

True ☐ False ☐

Topic 2. Application of Set Theory [NCERT (Old) Pg. 21-24]

8. If X and Y are two sets such that $n(X) = 17$, $n(Y) = 23$ and $n(X \cup Y) = 38$, then $n(X \cap Y) =$
(a) 2 ☐ (b) 4 ☐ (c) 6 ☐ (d) 8 ☐

9. In a group of 800 people, 550 can speak Hindi and 450 can speak English.
Statement I 180 persons can speak both Hindi and English.
Statement II 250 persons can speak both Hindi and English.

(a) Statement I is correct but Statement II is incorrect
(b) Statement I is incorrect but Statement II is correct.
(c) Both statements are correct.
(d) Both statements are incorrect.

---

10. In a class of 35 students, 24 like to play cricket and 16 like to play football. Also, each student likes to play atleast one of the two games. How many students like to play both cricket and football?

---

11. **Assertion (A)** In a group of 50 people, 35 speak Hindi, 25 speak both English and Hindi and all the people speak atleast one of the two languages. Then, 15 people speak English but not Hindi.

Reason (R) If A and B are finite sets, then $n(A \cup B) = n(A) + n(B) - n(A \cap B)$.

(a) Assertion (A) is correct and Reason (R) is the correct explanation of Assertion (A).
(b) Assertion (A) is correct and Reason (R) is not the correct explanation of Assertion (A).
(c) Assertion (A) is incorrect but Reason (R) is correct.
(d) Both Assertion (A) and Reason (R) are incorrect.

---

12. If A, B and C are three sets and U is the universal set such that

$$n(U) = 700,\ n(A) = 200,\ n(B) = 300 \text{ and } n(A \cap B) = 100, \text{ then } n(A' \cap B') =$$

---

13. In a survey of 700 students in a college, 180 were listed as drinking Limca, 275 as drinking Mirinda and 95 were listed as both drinking Limca as well as Mirinda. Then, number of students drinking neither Limca nor Mirinda is

(a) 380 ☐ (b) 360 ☐ (c) 340 ☐ (d) 320 ☐

14. Out of 500 car owners investigated, 400 owned Maruti car, 200 owned Hyundai car and 50 owned both cars.

True ☐ False ☐

---

15. A market research group conducted a survey of 2000 consumers and reported that 1720 consumers liked product P_1 and 1450 consumers liked product P_2.

Statement I 1160 consumers liked both the product.

Statement II Atleast 1170 consumers liked both the product.

(a) Statement I is correct but Statement II is incorrect.
(b) Statement I is incorrect but Statement II is correct.
(c) Both statements are correct.
(d) Both statements are incorrect.

COMPETITION EDGE UP

1. Let $A = \{n \in [100, 700] \cap N : n$ is neither a multiple of 3 nor a multiple of 4$\}$. Then, the number of elements in A is **[JEE Main 2024]**

(a) 300
(b) 280
(c) 310
(d) 290

2. Let $S = \{x \in R : (\sqrt{3} + \sqrt{2})^x + (\sqrt{3} - \sqrt{2})^x = 10\}$. Then, the number of elements in S, is **[JEE Main 2024]**

(a) 0
(b) 1
(c) 4
(d) 2

3. Let A and B be two finite sets with m and n elements, respectively. The total number of subsets of the set A is 56 more than the total number of subsets of B. Then, the distance of the point P(m, n) from the point Q(− 2, − 3) is **[JEE Main 2024]**

(a) 6
(b) 10
(c) 4
(d) 8

4. In a survey of 220 students of a higher secondary school, it was found that atleast 125 and atmost 130 students studied Mathematics; atleast 85 and atmost 95 studied Physics; atleast 75 and atmost 90 studied Chemistry; 30 studied both Physics and Chemistry; 50 studied both Chemistry and Mathematics; 40 studied both Mathematics and Physics and 10 studied none of these subjects. Let m and n respectively be the least and the most number of students who studied all the three subjects. Then, m + n is equal to .... **[JEE Main 2024]**

5. A group of 40 students appeared in an examination of 3 subjects — Mathematics, Physics and Chemistry. It was found that all students passed in atleast one of the subjects, 20 students passed in Mathematics, 25 students passed in Physics, 16 students passed in Chemistry, atmost 11 students passed in both Mathematics and Physics, atmost 15 students passed in both Physics and Chemistry, atmost 15 students passed in both Mathematics and Chemistry. The maximum number of students passed in all the three subjects is .... **[JEE Main 2024]**

6. An organisation awarded 48 medals in event A, 25 in event B and 18 in event C. If these medals went to total 60 men and only five men got medals in all the three events, then how many received medals in exactly two of three events? **[JEE Main 2023]**

(a) 10
(b) 9
(c) 21
(d) 15

7. The number of elements in the set $\{n \in N : 10 \le n \le 100$ and $3^n - 3$ is a multiple of 7$\}$ is .... **[JEE Main 2023]**

8. Let $\lambda \in R$ and let the equation E be $|x|^2 - 2|x| + |\lambda - 3| = 0$. Then, the largest element in the set $S = \{x + \lambda : x$ is an integer solution of E$\}$ is .... **[JEE Main 2023]**

9. Let $A = \{x \in R : |x + 1| < 2\}$ and $B = \{x \in R : |x - 1| \ge 2\}$. Then, which one of the following statements is not true? **[JEE Main 2022]**

(a) $A - B = (-1, 1)$
(b) $B - A = R - (-3, 1)$
(c) $A \cap B = (-3, -1]$
(d) $A \cup B = R - [1, 3)$

10. Let $S = \left\{x \in [-6, 3] - \{-2, 2\} : \dfrac{|x + 3| - 1}{|x| - 2} \ge 0\right\}$ and $T = \{x \in Z : x^2 - 7|x| + 9 \le 0\}$. Then, the number of elements in $S \cap T$ is **[JEE Main 2022]**

(a) 7 ☐
(b) 5 ☐
(c) 4 ☐
(d) 3 ☐

11. Let $S = \{4, 6, 9\}$ and $T = \{9, 10, 11, \ldots, 1000\}$. If $A = \{a_1 + a_2 + \ldots + a_k : k \in N, a_1, a_2, a_3, \ldots, a_k \in S\}$, then the sum of all the elements in the set $T - A$ is equal to .... **[JEE Main 2022]**

12. Let $A = \{1, 2, 3, 4, 5, 6, 7\}$ and $B = \{3, 6, 7, 9\}$, Then, the number of elements in the set $\{C \subseteq A : C \cap B \neq \phi\}$ is .... **[JEE Main 2022]**

13. Let $A : \{1, 2, 3, 4, 5, 6, 7\}$. Define $B = \{T \subseteq A : \text{either } 1 \notin T \text{ or } 2 \in T\}$ and $C = \{T \subseteq A : T$ the sum of all the elements of T is a prime number $\}$. Then, the number of elements in the set $B \cup C$ is .... **[JEE Main 2022]**

14. Let $A = \{n \in N : HCF(n, 45) = 1\}$ and $B = \{2k : k \in \{1, 2, \ldots, 100\}\}$. Then, the sum of all the elements of $A \cap B$ is .... **[JEE Main 2022]**

15. The sum of all the elements of the set $\{\alpha \in \{1, 2, \ldots, 100\}: HCF(\alpha, 24) = 1\}$ is .... **[JEE Main 2022]**

Chapter 02

Relations and Functions

Scan and take Chapter Test

TOPIC 1

Ordered Pairs

NCERT Pg. 24-27

1. Find the values of a and b in the following questions.

(i) $(3a-2, b+3)=(2a-1, 3)$ ______

(ii) $(a+2, 3b-2)=(0, 1)$ ______

(iii) $(2a+1, 3b)=(2b, 2a+1)$ ______

2. State True or False.

(i) If $A=\phi$ or $B=\phi$, then $A \times B=\phi$.

True ☐ False ☐

(ii) If $P=\{a, b, c\}$ and $Q=\{r\}$ form the sets $P \times Q$ and $Q \times P$. Then, $P \times Q=Q \times P$.

True ☐ False ☐

(iii) Let A and B be two non-empty sets having n elements in common, then $A \times B$ and $B \times A$ have n^2 elements in common.

True ☐ False ☐

3. If $A=\{2, 4, 6\}$ and $B=\{1, 2\}$, then

(i) $A \times B=$ ______

(ii) $B \times A=$ ______

(iii) $B \times B=$ ______

(iv) $A \times A=$ ______

(v) $n(A \times B)=n(B \times A)$? ______

4. Let $A=\{1, 2, 3\}$ and $B=\{x: x \in N, x$ is prime less than $5\}$. Then, $A \times B$ is equal to

______

5. If $A \times B=\{(a, 1), (a, 5), (a, 2), (b, 2), (b, 5), (b, 1)\}$, then find $B \times A$.

______

*Concepts of all questions bearing * are important for JEE & CUET*

6. If $A = \{1, 2, 3\}$, $B = \{3, 4\}$ and $C = \{1, 3, 5\}$, then find

(i) $A \times (B \cup C)$ ______

(ii) $A \times (B \cap C)$ ______

(iii) $(A \times B) \cap (A \times C)$ ______

(iv) $(A \times B) \cup (A \times C)$ ______

7. If $A = \{1, 2\}$, $B = \{3, 4\}$ and $C = \{4, 5, 6\}$, then find $A \times B \times C$.

______

8. Let A and B be two sets such that $A \times B$ consists of 6 elements. If three elements of $A \times B$ are $(1, 4)$, $(2, 6)$, $(3, 6)$. Then, $B \times A = \{(1, 4), (1, 6), (2, 4), (2, 6), (3, 4), (3, 6)\}$.

True ☐ False ☐

9. The cartesian product $A \times A$ has 9 elements among which are found $(-1, 0)$ and $(0, 1)$. Then, $A =$ ______

10. Let A and B be two sets such that $n(A) = 5$ and $n(B) = 2$. If a, b, c, d, e are distinct and $(a, 2)$, $(b, 3)$, $(c, 2)$, $(d, 3)$, $(e, 2)$ are in $A \times B$, then find A and B.

______

TOPIC 2

Relations

NCERT Pg. 28-30

11. If $A = \{1, 2, 3\}$ and $B = \{a, b, c\}$, then $R = \{(1, b), (2, c), (1, a), (3, a)\}$ is a relation from A to B.

True ☐ False ☐

12. If $A = \{1, 2, 3\}$ and $B = \{4, 5, 6\}$, are the following a relation from A to B?

(i) $R_1 = \{(1, 4), (1, 5), (1, 6)\}$ ______

(ii) $R_2 = \{(1, 5), (2, 4), (3, 6)\}$ ______

(iii) $R_3 = \{(1, 4), (1, 5), (3, 6), (2, 6), (3, 4)\}$ ______

(iv) $R_4 = \{(4, 2), (2, 6), (5, 2), (2, 4)\}$ ______

13. Depict this relationship using an arrow diagram.

(i) Relation $R = \{(1, 2,), (2, 4), (3, 2), (1, 3), (3, 4)\}$ from set $A = \{1, 2, 3, 4, 5\}$ to set $B = \{2, 3, 4, 5, 6, 7\}$ ______

(ii) Let $A = \{1, 2, 3, 4, \ldots, 14\}$. Define a relation on a set A by

$R = \{(x, y) : 3x - y = 0, \text{ where } x, y \in A\}$ ______

14. Find domain and range of the following relations.

(i) If $A = \{1, 3, 5, 7\}$, $B = \{2, 4, 6, 8, 10\}$ and let $R = \{(1, 8), (3, 6), (5, 2), (1, 4)\}$ be a relation from A to B ______

(ii) Let $A = \{1, 3, 5, 7\}$ and $B = \{2, 4, 6, 8\}$ be two sets and let R be a relation from A to B defined by the phrase $(x, y) \in R \Leftrightarrow x > y$ ____________

(iii) If R is a relation from set $A = \{2, 4, 5\}$ and set $B = \{1, 2, 3, 4, 6, 8\}$ defined by $x\ R\ y \Leftrightarrow x$ divides y ____________

(iv) If $R = \{(x, x+5) : x \in \{0, 1, 2, 3, 4, 5\}\}$ ____________

(v) If $S = \{(a, b) : b = |a-1|, a \in Z \text{ and } |a| \le 3\}$ ____________

15. If $A = \{1, 2, 3, 4, 5 \ldots\ldots\}$, $B = \left\{1, \frac{1}{2}, \frac{1}{3}, \frac{1}{4}, \frac{1}{5}, \frac{1}{6}, \ldots\right\}$ and R is a relation from A to B given by

$R = \left\{(1, 1), \left(2, \frac{1}{2}\right), \left(3, \frac{1}{3}\right), \left(4, \frac{1}{4}\right), \left(5, \frac{1}{5}\right) \ldots\ldots\right\}$, then R in set-builder can be described as

$R = \left\{(a, b) : a \in A, b \in B \text{ and } b = \frac{1}{a}\right\}$.

True ☐ False ☐

16. If R is a relation from set $A = \{-2, -1, 0, 1, 2\}$ to set $B = \{0, 1, 4, 9, 10\}$ by the rule $a\ R\ b \Leftrightarrow a^2 = b$. Then, R can be described in roster form as $R =$ ____________

17. The given figure shows a relationship between the sets P and Q.

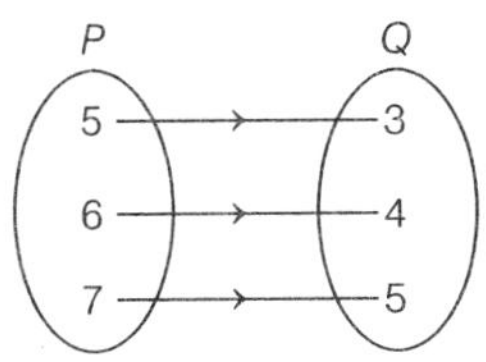

(i) Write this relation in set-builder form ____________

(ii) Write this relation in roster form ____________

18. Let R be a relation on N defined by $R = \{(a, b) : a, b \in N \text{ and } a = b^2\}$, then the statement

(i) $(a, a) \in R\ \forall\ a \in N$ is

True ☐ False ☐

(ii) $(a, b) \in R \Rightarrow (b, a) \in R$ is

True ☐ False ☐

(iii) $(a, b) \in R, (b, c) \in R \Rightarrow (a, c) \in R$ is

True ☐ False ☐

(iv) For the relation R_1 defined on R by the rule $(a, b) \in R_1 \Leftrightarrow 1 + ab > 0$
$(a, b) \in R_1$ and $(b, c) \in R_1 \Rightarrow (a, c) \in R_1$ is not true for all $a, b, c \in R$.

True ☐ False ☐

(v) Dom (R) = Range (R^{-1}) and Range (R) = Dom (R^{-1}).

True ☐ False ☐

19. Let $A = \{1, 2, 3\}$ and $B = \{a, b, c, d\}$ be two sets and let $R = \{(1, a), (1, c), (2, d), (2, c)\}$ be a relation from A to B. Find R^{-1}.

____

20. Let A be the set of first five natural numbers and R be a relation on A defined as follows $(x, y) \in R \Leftrightarrow x \leq y$, then

(i) $R =$ ____________________________

(ii) $R^{-1} =$ ____________________________

(iii) Domain of $R^{-1} =$ ____________________________

(iv) Range of $R^{-1} =$ ____________________________

TOPIC 3
Functions

NCERT Pg. 30-42

21. Let $A = \{1, 2, 3, 4\}$, $B = \{1, 5, 9, 11, 15, 16\}$ and $f = \{(1, 5), (2, 9), (3, 1), (4, 5), (2, 11)\}$.

Are the following true? Justify your answer in each case.

(i) f is a relation from A to B ____________________________

(ii) f is a function from A to B ____________________________

22. Which of the following relations are functions. Give Reason (R)s. If it is a function determine its domain and range.

(i) $R = \{(2, 1), (3, 1), (4, 2)\}$ is a function ____________________________

(ii) $R = \{(2, 2), (2, 4), (3, 3), (4, 4)\}$ is a function ____________________________

(iii) $R = \{(1, 2), (2, 3), (3, 4), (4, 5), (5, 6), (6, 7)\}$ is a function ____________________________

23. Is the following a function? If not, why? If yes, find its domain and range.

(i) 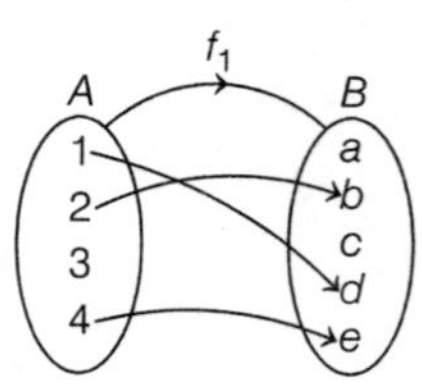

____

(ii) 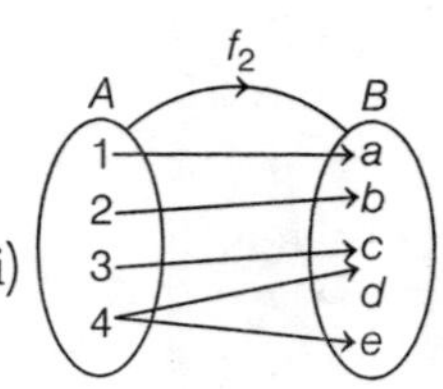

____

(iii) 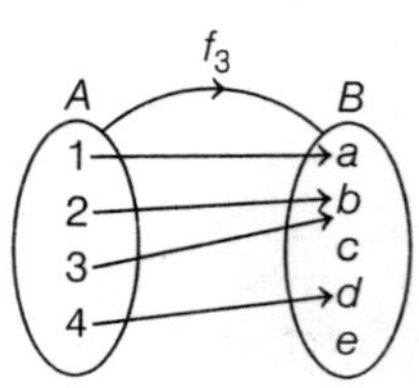

____

(iv) 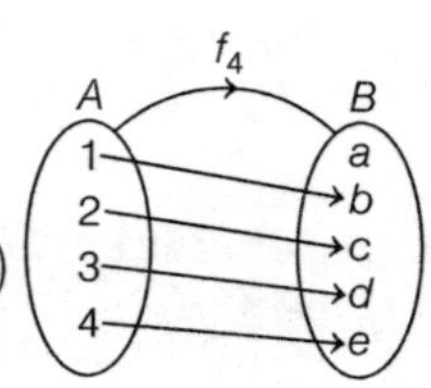

____

24. If $f: R \to R$ is defined as follows

$$f(x)=\begin{cases}1, & \text{if } x \in Q\\ -1, & \text{if } x \notin Q\end{cases}$$

	Column I		Column II
A.	$f\left(\frac{1}{2}\right)$	1.	$\{1, -1\}$
B.	$f(\pi)$	2.	$R-Q$
C.	Range of f	3.	1
D.	Pre-image of -1	4.	-1

Choose the correct option?

(a) A $\to$ 3, B $\to$ 4, C $\to$ 1, D $\to$ 2
(b) A $\to$ 4, B $\to$ 3, C $\to$ 1, D $\to$ 2
(c) A $\to$ 4, B $\to$ 3, C $\to$ 2, D $\to$ 1
(d) A $\to$ 3, B $\to$ 4, C $\to$ 2, D $\to$ 1

25. If $f: A \to R$, $f(x)=x^2+1$, where $A=\{-1, 0, 2, 4\}$. Find range of f.

---

26. State True or False.

(i) Let f be a subset of $Z \times Z$ defined by $f=\{(ab, (a+b)): a, b \in Z\}$. Then, f is a function from Z into Z.

True ☐ False ☐

(ii) Let $f: R \to R$ be such that $f(x)=2^x$. Then, $f(x+y)=f(x)\cdot f(y)$.

True ☐ False ☐

(iii) Let $f: R-\{2\} \to R$ be defined by $f(x)=\dfrac{x^2-4}{x-2}$ and $g: R \to R$ be defined by $g(x)=x+2$. Then, $f=g$

True ☐ False ☐

(iv) A function which has either R or one of its subsets as its range is called a real valued function.

True ☐ False ☐

***27.** Find the domain for which the functions $f(x)=2x^2-1$ and $g(x)=1-3x$ are equals.

---

28. Let f be defined by $f(x)=x-4$ and g be defined by

$$g(x)=\begin{cases}\dfrac{x^2-16}{x+4}, & x \neq -4\\ \lambda, & x=-4\end{cases}$$

The value of λ such that $f(x)=g(x)$ for all x is

(a) 8 (b) -8 (c) 4 (d) -4

---

29. Identify the type of function.

*(i) 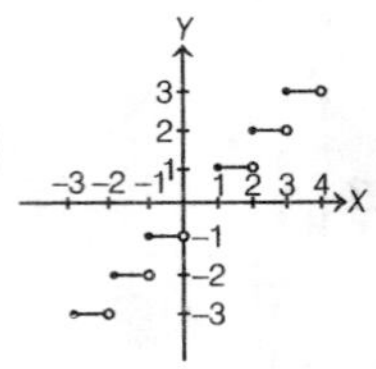

(ii) 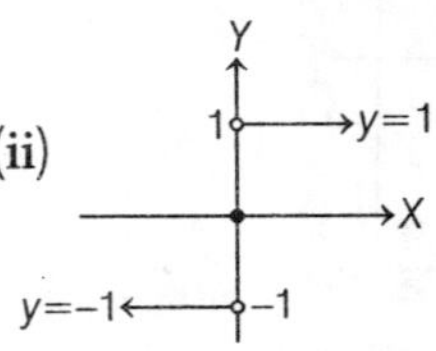

(iii) 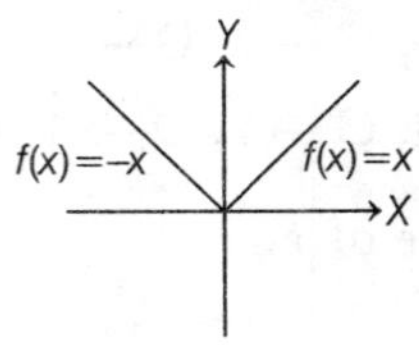

(iv) 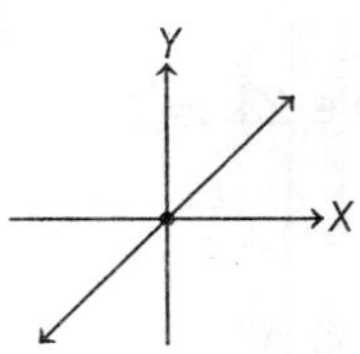

(v) 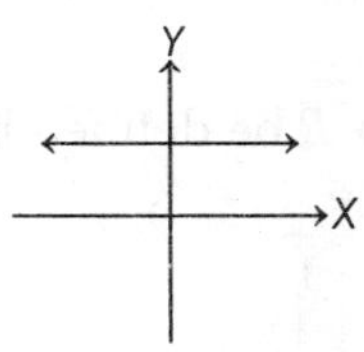

30. A function f is defined by $f(x) = \frac{2x}{5} + 11$. Write down the values of

(i) $f(0)$ ________________

(ii) $f(10)$ ________________

(iii) $f(-1)$ ________________

(iv) $f\left(-\frac{3}{2}\right)$ ________________

31. If $f(x) = 3x^4 - 5x^2 + 9$, then find $f(x-1)$ ________________.

32. Match the following functions with their graph.

	Column I		Column II
A.	$f(x)=\frac{1}{x}$	1.	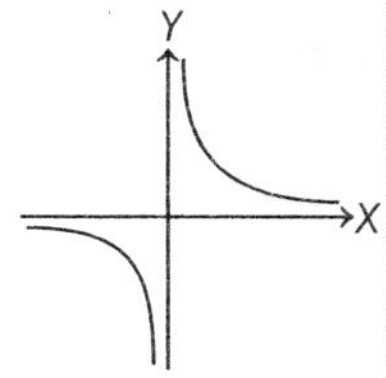
B.	$f(x)=\sqrt{x}$	2.	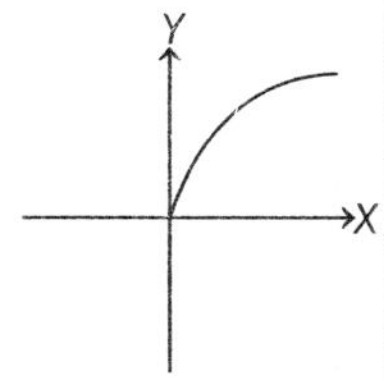
C.	$f(x)=x^2$	3.	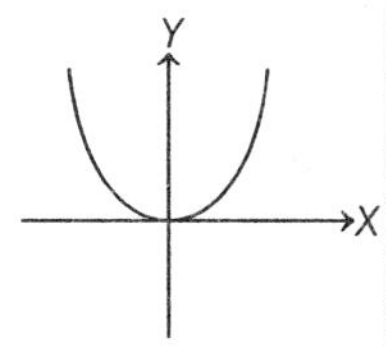
D.	$f(x)=x^3$	4.	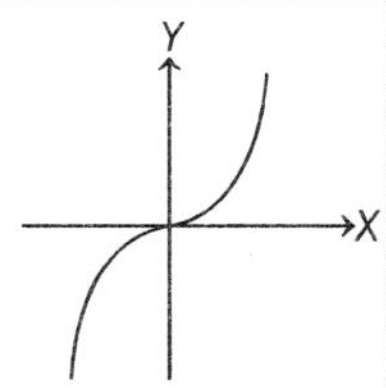

Choose the correct option?

(a) $A \to 1, B \to 2, C \to 3, D \to 4$
(b) $A \to 4, B \to 1, C \to 3, D \to 2$
(c) $A \to 3, B \to 1, C \to 4, D \to 2$
(d) $A \to 3, B \to 4, C \to 2, D \to 1$

33. The function t which maps temperature in degree celsius into temperature in degree fahrenheit is defined by $t(c)=\frac{9c}{5}+32$. Find the value of c, when $t(c)=212$.

____

34. Let f be the exponential function and g be the logarithm function. Then,

(i) $(3f)(1)=$ ____________________

(ii) $(5g)(1)=$ ____________________

***35.** Find the domain of each of the following functions.

(i) $f(x)=\frac{x-1}{x-3}$ ____________________

(ii) $f(x)=\frac{2x-3}{x^2-3x+2}$ ____________________

(iii) $f(x)=\sqrt{4-x^2}$ ____________________

(iv) $f(x)=\sqrt{4-x}+\frac{1}{\sqrt{x^2-1}}$ ____________________

***36.** Find the domain of the following functions.

(i) Exponential function (a^x) ____________________

(ii) Logarithm function $(\log_e x)$ ____________________

(iii) $f(x) = \dfrac{1}{\sqrt{x + [x]}}$ ____________________

37. Find the value of greatest integer function.

(i) If $-1 \le x < 0$, then $[x] =$ ____________________

(ii) If $0 \le x < 1$, then $[x] =$ ____________________

(iii) If $1 \le x < 2$, then $[x] =$ ____________________

(iv) If $2 \le x < 3$, then $[x] =$ ____________________

38. State True or False.

(i) $[x + k] = [x] + k$, for any integer k.

True ☐ False ☐

(ii) $[x] + [-x] = \begin{cases} -1, & \text{if } x \notin Z \\ 0, & \text{if } x \in Z \end{cases}$

True ☐ False ☐

(iii) $\sqrt{x^2} = |x|$

True ☐ False ☐

(iv) $a^2 \le x^2 \le b^2 \Leftrightarrow a \le |x| \le b \Leftrightarrow x \in [-b, -a] \cup [a, b]$

True ☐ False ☐

(v) $|x + y| \le |x| + |y|$

True ☐ False ☐

(vi) $|x - y| \le ||x| - |y||$

True ☐ False ☐

39. Let $f(x) = x^2$ and $g(x) = 2x + 1$ be two real functions. Then, find the following functions.

(i) $(f + g)(x) =$ ____________________

(ii) $(f - g)(x) =$ ____________________

(iii) $fg(x) =$ ____________________

(iv) $\left(\dfrac{f}{g}\right)(x) =$ ____________________

***40.** Given that $f(x) = x^2 - 4$ and $g(x) = x + 2$, find the domain of $f + g$, $f - g$, fg and f/g.

____

41. Find the range of each of the following functions.

(i) $f(x) = 3x$, x is a real number ______

(ii) $f(x) = x^2 - 1$, $x \in R$ ______

(iii) $f(x) = \dfrac{1}{\sqrt{x-5}}$ ______

Assertion-Reason Questions

The following questions consist of two statements – Assertion (A) and Reason (R).
Answer these questions by selecting the appropriate option given below.
(a) Both (A) and (R) are true and (R) is correct explanation of (A)
(b) Both (A) and (R) are true but (R) is not the correct explanation of (A)
(c) (A) is true but (R) is false
(d) (A) is false but (R) is true

1. **Assertion** (A) If $(x-2, y+1) = (3, 1)$, then $x = 5$ and $y = 0$.

Reason (R) Two ordered pairs are equal, if their corresponding elements are equal.

(a) ☐ (b) ☐ (c) ☐ (d) ☐

2. **Assertion** (A) Let $A = \{2, 3, 4\}$ and $B = \{5, 6\}$. Then, number of relations from A to B is 64.

Reason (R) If $n(A) = p$ and $n(B) = q$,then number of relations is 2^{pq}.

(a) ☐ (b) ☐ (c) ☐ (d) ☐

3. **Assertion** (A) The range of function $f(x) = 4 + x^2$ is $[4, \infty)$.

Reason (R) Range of x^2 is $(-\infty, \infty)$.

(a) ☐ (b) ☐ (c) ☐ (d) ☐

4. **Assertion** (A) The domain of the real function defined by $f(x) = \sqrt{x-5}$, is $R - \{5\}$.

Reason (R) The range of function defined by $f(x) = \sqrt{x-5}$ is $[0, \infty)$.

(a) ☐ (b) ☐ (c) ☐ (d) ☐

5. **Assertion** (A) The following arrow diagram represents a function.

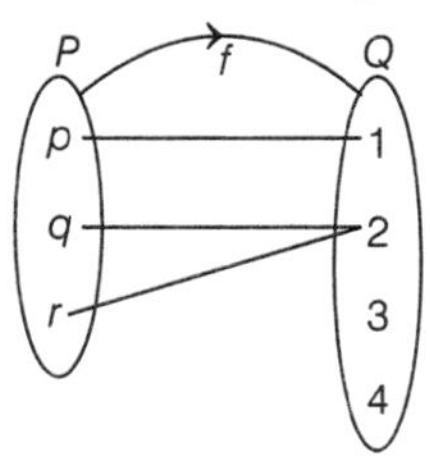

Reason (R) A function f from a set A to a set B is a specific type of relation for which every element x of set A has one and only one image y in set B.

(a) ☐ (b) ☐ (c) ☐ (d) ☐

6. **Assertion** (A) Let $f : R-\{3\} \rightarrow R$ be defined by $f(x) = \dfrac{x^2 - 9}{x - 3}$ and $g : R \rightarrow R$ be defined by $g(x) = x + 4$. Then, $f = g$

Reason (R) The domain of $f(x)$ is any real number other than 3.

(a) ☐ (b) ☐ (c) ☐ (d) ☐

7. **Assertion** (A) Let $A = \{1, 2, 3, 4\}$, $B = \{5, 4, 7\}$ and $R = \{(x, y) : |x - y| \text{ is odd}, x \in A, y \in B\}$. Then, domain of R is $\{1, 2, 3, 4\}$.

Reason (R) $|x|$ is always positive, $\forall\ x \in R$.

(a) ☐ (b) ☐ (c) ☐ (d) ☐

8. Consider the following figure

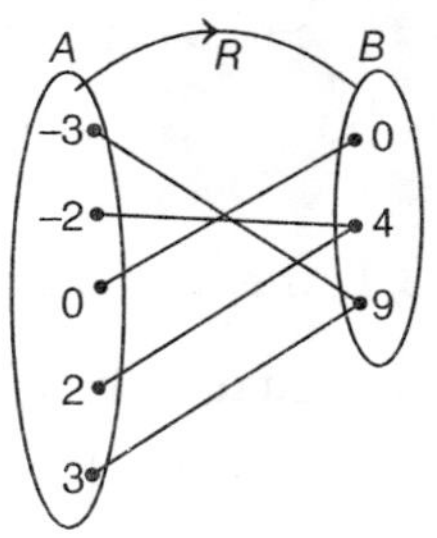

Assertion (A) The figure shows a relationship between the sets A and B. Then, the relation in Set-builder form is $\{(x, y) : y = x^2 \text{ and } x, y \in N\}$

Reason (R) The above relation in Roaster form is $\{(-3, 9), (-2, 4), (0, 0), (2, 4), (3, 9)\}$.

(a) ☐ (b) ☐ (c) ☐ (d) ☐

9. **Assertion** (A) Let R be a relation from Q to Q defined by $R = \{(a, b) : a, b \in Q$ and $a - b \in Z\}$. Then, $(a, a) \in R,\ \forall\ a \in Q$.

Reason (R) Since, $a - a = 0$ and $0 \in Z \Rightarrow (a, a) \in R$.

(a) ☐ (b) ☐ (c) ☐ (d) ☐

10. **Assertion** (A) If $P = \{1, 2\}$ and $Q = \{4, 5, 6\}$, then $P \times Q = \{(1, 4), (1, 5), (1, 6), (2, 4), (2, 5)\}$.

Reason (R) $A \times B$ of two sets A and B is given by $A \times B = \{(a, b); a \in A, b \in B\}$.

(a) ☐ (b) ☐ (c) ☐ (d) ☐

11. **Assertion** (A) Let function f is defined by $f(x) = 2x - 3$, then value of $f(1) = -1$.

Reason (R) A real function has the set of real numbers or one of its subsets both as its domain and as its range.

(a) ☐ (b) ☐ (c) ☐ (d) ☐

Case Based Questions

Case 1 A relation f from a non-empty set A to a non-empty set B is said to be a function, if every element of set A has one and only one image in set B.

In other words, we say that a function f is a relation from a non-empty set A to a non-empty set B such that domain of f is A and no two distinct ordered pairs in f have the same first element or component.

If f is a function from a set A to a set B, then we write $f : A \to B$

Based on information given above, answer the following questions.

(i) The given curve is a

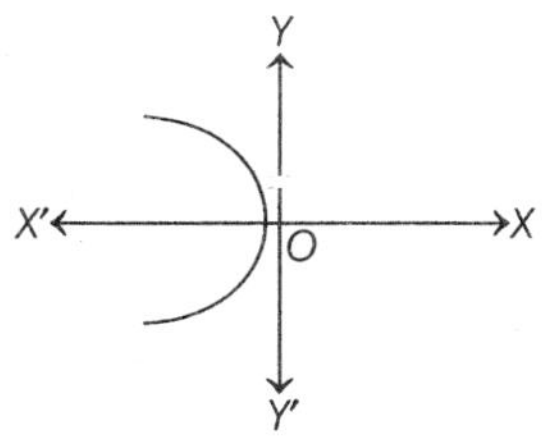

(a) relation ☐ (b) function ☐

(c) cannot say anything ☐ (d) data not sufficient ☐

(ii)

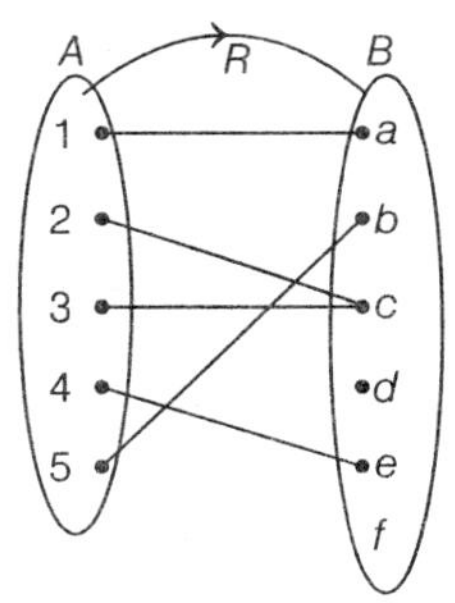

The given arrow diagram is

(a) function ☐ (b) cannot say anything ☐

(c) relation ☐ (d) data not sufficient ☐

*(iii) If $f(x) = \dfrac{1}{\sqrt{2x-1}}$, then domain of $f(x)$ is equal to

(a) $\left[\dfrac{1}{2}, \infty\right)$ ☐ (b) $R - \left\{\dfrac{1}{2}\right\}$ ☐

(c) $\left(\dfrac{1}{2}, \infty\right)$ ☐ (d) R ☐

Case 2 Read the text carefully and answer the questions. Method to find the sets when cartesian product is given.For finding these two sets, we write first element of each ordered pair in first set P and corresponding second element in second set Q (say).

Number of elements in cartesian product of two sets : If there are a elements in set P and b elements in set Q, then these will be ab elements in $P \times Q$ i.e. if $n(P) = a$ and $n(Q) = b$, then $n(P \times Q) = ab$.

(i) The cartesian product $A \times A$ has 16 elemetns among which are found $(x, 1)$ and $(y, 2)$. Then, the set A is

(a) $\{1, 2\}$ ☐ (b) $\{x, y\}$ ☐
(c) $\{x, y, 1, 2\}$ ☐ (d) None of these ☐

(ii) If set A has 3 elements and set B has 2 elements, then number of elements in $A \times B$ is

(a) 0 ☐ (b) 4 ☐
(c) 12 ☐ (d) 6 ☐

(iii) If $A \times B = \{(a, 2), (b, 4), (a, 4), (b, 2)\}$. Then, set A and B respectively are

(a) $(a, b), (2, 4)$ ☐ (b) $(4, a), (b, 2)$ ☐
(c) $(a, 2), (b, 4)$ ☐ (d) None of these ☐

COMPETITION EDGE UP

1. If $S = \{a \in R : |2a - 1| = 3[a] + 2\{a\}\}$, where $[t]$ denotes the greatest integer less than or equal to t and $\{t\}$ represents the fractional part of t, then $72 \sum_{a \in S} a$ is equal to .... **[JEE Main 2024]**

2. Let $A = \{1, 2, 3, ..., 7\}$ and let $P(A)$ denotes the power set of A. If the number of functions $f : A \to P(A)$ such that $a \in f(a), \forall a \in A$ is $m^n \cdot m$ and $n \in N$ and m is least, then $m + n$ is equal to .... **[JEE Main 2024]**

3. If the domain of the function

$$f(x) = \frac{\sqrt{x^2 - 25}}{(4 - x^2)} + \log_{10}(x^2 + 2x - 15)$$

is $(-\infty, \alpha) \cup [\beta, \infty)$, then $\alpha^2 + \beta^3$ is equal to **[JEE Main 2024]**

(a) 175 ☐
(b) 150 ☐
(c) 125 ☐
(d) 140 ☐

4. The domain of the function

$$f(x) = \frac{1}{\sqrt{[x]^2 - 3[x] - 10}}$$ is

(where, $[x]$ denotes the greatest integer less than or equal to x) **[JEE Main 2023]**

(a) $(-\infty, -2) \cup (5, \infty)$ ☐
(b) $(-\infty, -3] \cup [6, \infty)$ ☐
(c) $(-\infty, -3] \cup (5, \infty)$ ☐
(d) $(-\infty, -2) \cup [6, \infty)$ ☐

5. Let $f : R - \{2, 6\} \to R$ be real valued function defined as $f(x) = \frac{x^2 + 2x + 1}{x^2 - 8x + 12}$.

Then, range of f is **[JEE Main 2023]**

(a) $\left(-\infty, -\frac{21}{4}\right] \cup [1, \infty)$ ☐
(b) $\left(-\infty, -\frac{21}{4}\right] \cup [0, \infty)$ ☐
(c) $\left(-\infty, -\frac{21}{4}\right] \cup \left[\frac{21}{4}, \infty\right)$ ☐
(d) $\left(-\infty, -\frac{21}{4}\right) \cup (0, \infty)$ ☐

6. The number of functions

$f : \{1, 2, 3, 4\} \to \{a \in Z, |a| \le 8\}$

satisfying $f(n) + \frac{1}{n} f(n+1) = 1$,

$\forall\ n \in \{1, 2, 3\}$ is **[JEE Main 2023]**

(a) 3
(b) 2
(c) 1
(d) 4

7. Let $f : R - \{0, 1\} \to R$ be a function such that $f(x) + f\left(\frac{1}{1-x}\right) = 1 + x$. Then, $f(2)$ is equal to **[JEE Main 2023]**

(a) $\frac{9}{2}$
(b) $\frac{9}{4}$
(c) $\frac{7}{3}$
(d) $\frac{7}{4}$

8. Consider a function $f : N \to R$, satisfying

$f(1) + 2f(2) + 3f(3) + \ldots + xf(x)$

$= x(x+1) f(x);\ x \ge 2$ with $f(1) = 1$.

Then, $\frac{1}{f(2022)} + \frac{1}{f(2028)}$ is equal to

[JEE Main 2023]

(a) 8200
(b) 8000
(c) 8400
(d) 8100

9. Let $f(x) = 2x^n + \lambda, \lambda \in R, n \in N$ and $f(4) = 133, f(5) = 255$. Then, the sum of all the positive integer divisors of $(f(3) - f(2))$ is **[JEE Main 2023]**

(a) 60
(b) 59
(c) 58
(d) 61

10. If $f(x) = \frac{2^{2x}}{2^{2x} + 2}, x \in R$, then

$f\left(\frac{1}{2023}\right) + f\left(\frac{2}{2023}\right) + \ldots + f\left(\frac{2022}{2023}\right)$ is equal to **[JEE Main 2023]**

(a) 2010
(b) 2011
(c) 1011
(d) 1010

11. Let the sets A and B denote the domain and range respectively of the function $f(x) = \frac{1}{\sqrt{[x] - x}}$, where $[x]$ denotes the smallest integer greater than or equal to x. Then, among the statements **[JEE Main 2023]**

S1 $A \cap B = (1, \infty) - N$ and

S2 $A \cup B = (1, \infty)$

(a) Both S1 and S2 are true
(b) Neither S1 nor S2 is true
(c) Only S1 is true
(d) Only S2 is true

12. Let $A = \{1, 2, 3, 5, 8, 9\}$. Then, the number of possible functions $f : A \to A$ such that $f(m \cdot n) = f(m) \cdot f(n), \forall\ m, n \in A$ with $m \cdot n \in A$ is equal to .... **[JEE Main 2023]**

13. If the domain of the function $f(x) = \frac{[x]}{1 + x^2}$, where $[x]$ is greatest integer $\le x$, is $[2, 6)$, then its range is **[JEE Main 2023]**

(a) $\left(\frac{5}{37}, \frac{2}{5}\right] - \left\{\frac{9}{29}, \frac{27}{109}, \frac{18}{89}, \frac{9}{53}\right\}$
(b) $\left(\frac{5}{26}, \frac{2}{5}\right] - \left\{\frac{9}{29}, \frac{27}{109}, \frac{18}{89}, \frac{9}{53}\right\}$
(c) $\left(\frac{5}{26}, \frac{2}{5}\right]$
(d) $\left(\frac{5}{37}, \frac{2}{5}\right]$

Chapter 03

Trigonometric Functions

Scan and take Chapter Test

TOPIC 1

Measure of an Angle

NCERT Pg 43-49

1. Find the degree measures corresponding to the following radian measures.

(i) $(6)^c$ ________________

(ii) $\left(\frac{5\pi}{3}\right)^c$ ________________

(iii) $(-2)^c$ ________________

(iv) $\left(\frac{11}{16}\right)^c$ ________________

(v) $(8)^c$ ________________

2. Find the radian measures corresponding to the following degree measures.

(i) $7°30'$ ________________

(ii) $-47°\ 30'$ ________________

(iii) $48°37'\ 30''$ ________________

(iv) $340°$ ________________

(v) $40°20'$ ________________

3. Fill in the blanks.

(i) The angles of a triangle are in AP such that the greatest is 5 times the least. The least angles in radian is ________________

(ii) A wheel makes 360 revolutions per minutes. The radians turns in one second is

____

(iii) The radius of a circle is 30 cm. The length of an arc of this circle if the length of the chord of arc is 30 cm, is ________________

(iv) The radius of the circle whose arc length is 15π cm makes an angle of $\frac{3\pi}{4}$ radian at the centre is ________________

(v) A horse is tied to a post by a rope. If the horse moves along a circular path always keeping the rope tight and describes 66 m, when it has traced out 60° at the centre, then the length of the rope is ________________

*Concepts of all questions bearing * are important for JEE & CUET*

4. State True or False.

(i) The ratio of radii in two circles is 5 : 4, when arc of the same length subtend angles 60° and 75° at the centre.

True ☐ False ☐

(ii) The length of an arc of a circle of radius 7 cm subtending a central angle 45° is 6.5 cm.

True ☐ False ☐

TOPIC 2

Trigonometric Functions

NCERT Pg 49-57

***5.** Fill in the blanks.

(i) If $\cos\theta = -\frac{1}{2}$ and $\pi < \theta < \frac{3\pi}{2}$, then the value of $4\tan^2\theta - 3\operatorname{cosec}^2\theta$ is equal to ________

(ii) If $\sin\theta = \frac{12}{13}$ and $\frac{\pi}{2} < \theta < \pi$, then the value of $\sec\theta + \tan\theta$ is equal to ________

(iii) If $\cos\theta = -\frac{3}{5}$ and $\pi < \theta < \frac{3\pi}{2}$, then the value of $\frac{\operatorname{cosec}\theta + \cot\theta}{\sec\theta - \tan\theta}$ is equal to ________

(iv) If $\sin\theta = -\frac{3}{5}$ and $\frac{3\pi}{2} < \theta < 2\pi$, then the value of $\frac{1 + \tan\theta + \operatorname{cosec}\theta}{1 + \cot\theta - \operatorname{cosec}\theta}$ is equal to ________

(v) If $\operatorname{cosec}\theta + \cot\theta = \frac{11}{2}$, $0 < \theta < \frac{\pi}{2}$, then $\tan\theta$ is equal to ________

6. Find the value of following trigonometric functions.

(i) $\tan\frac{11\pi}{6}$ ________

(ii) $\cos 855°$ ________

(iii) $\sin 1845°$ ________

(iv) $\tan(-585°)$ ________

(v) $\sin(-4530°)$ ________

7. State True or False.

(i) If $\cos\theta + \sin\theta = \sqrt{2}\cos\theta$, then $\cos\theta - \sin\theta = \sqrt{2}\sin\theta$.

True ☐ False ☐

(ii) If $\sec\theta + \tan\theta = P$, then $\tan\theta = \frac{P^2 - 1}{P^2 + 1}$.

True ☐ False ☐

(iii) $\sec^2\theta + \operatorname{cosec}^2\theta \geq 4$

True ☐ False ☐

(iv) The value of $3(\sin\theta - \cos\theta)^4 + 6(\sin\theta + \cos\theta)^2 + 4(\sin^6\theta + \cos^6\theta)$ is 12.

True ☐ False ☐

(v) If $\sin\theta + \cos\theta = 0$ and θ lies in fourth quadrant, then the value of $\cos\theta = \frac{1}{\sqrt{2}}$.

True ☐ False ☐

8. Find the value of the following questions.

(i) $\tan 720° - \cos 270° - \sin 150° \cos 120°$ ______

(ii) $\sin^2\frac{\pi}{18} + \sin^2\frac{\pi}{9} + \sin^2\frac{7\pi}{18} + \sin^2\frac{4\pi}{9}$ ______

(iii) $\sin^2 5° + \sin^2 10° + \sin^2 15° + \ldots + \sin^2 85°$ ______

(iv) $\cos 1° \cdot \cos 2° \cdot \cos 3° \ldots \cos 179°$ ______

(v) $\tan 1° \cdot \tan 2° \ldots \tan 89°$ ______

TOPIC 3

Trigonometric Function of Sum and Difference of Two Angles

NCERT Pg 57-68

9. If $\sin\theta = \frac{15}{17}$ and $\cos\phi = \frac{12}{13}$, where θ and ϕ both lie in first quadrant, then which of the following is True or False.

*(i) $\sin(\theta + \phi) = \frac{220}{221}$

True ☐ False ☐

(ii) $\cos(\theta - \phi) = -\frac{71}{221}$

True ☐ False ☐

*(iii) $\tan(\theta + \phi) = \frac{220}{21}$

True ☐ False ☐

10. Simplify the following.

(i) $\sqrt{2}\cos\left(\theta + \frac{\pi}{4}\right)$ ______

(ii) $2\cos\left(\theta - \frac{\pi}{3}\right)$ ______

(iii) $\cos(\alpha + \beta) - \cos(\alpha - \beta)$ ______

***11.** If $\tan(A + B) = \frac{3}{5}$ and $\tan B = \frac{2}{3}$, then the value of $\tan A$ is ______.

***12.** If $\sqrt{3}\sin x + \cos x = k\sin(x+b)$, for $k > 0$ and $0 < b < 2\pi$, then find the value of

(i) k __________

(ii) b __________

13. Find the value of the following questions.

*(i) $\sin 75°$ __________

*(ii) $\tan 15°$ __________

(iii) $\cos 105°$ __________

(iv) $\cot 75°$ __________

*(v) $\sin\left(\frac{13\pi}{12}\right)$ __________

14. State True or False.

*(i) If $\cos(\alpha+\beta) = \frac{4}{5}$ and $\sin(\alpha-\beta) = \frac{5}{13}$, where α, β lie between 0 and $\frac{\pi}{4}$, then $\tan 2\alpha = \frac{56}{33}$.

True ☐ False ☐

*(ii) If $\tan A = \frac{5}{6}$ and $\tan B = \frac{1}{11}$, then $A + B = \frac{\pi}{6}$.

True ☐ False ☐

(iii) The value of $\cos^2\frac{\pi}{4} - \sin^2\frac{\pi}{12}$ is $\frac{\sqrt{3}}{2}$.

True ☐ False ☐

*(iv) The value of $\tan 69° + \tan 66° - \tan 69° \tan 66°$ is 1.

True ☐ False ☐

*(v) $\tan 56° = (-)\frac{\cos 11° + \sin 11°}{\cos 11° - \sin 11°}$.

True ☐ False ☐

(vi) $\frac{\cos 4x + \cos 3x + \cos 2x}{\sin 4x + \sin 3x + \sin 2x} = \cot 4x$

True ☐ False ☐

15. Choose the correct option.

*(i) $\tan 70°$ is equal to

(a) $\tan 20° + 2\tan 60°$
(b) $\tan 30° + 3\tan 50°$
(c) $\tan 20° + 3\tan 60°$
(d) $\tan 20° + 2\tan 50°$

____

(ii) $\frac{\sin x}{1+\cos x}$ is equal to

(a) $\tan\frac{x}{3}$
(b) $\tan\frac{x}{2}$
(c) $\tan\frac{2x}{3}$
(d) $\tan\frac{x}{4}$

____

16. Find the value of the following functions.

(i) $\tan\frac{\pi}{8}$ ______

(ii) $\sin\frac{\pi}{24}$ ______

(iii) $\cot\frac{\pi}{24}$ ______

17. If $\tan x = \frac{3}{4}, \pi < x < \frac{3\pi}{2}$, then find the value of the following functions.

(i) $\sin\frac{x}{2}$ ______

(ii) $\cos\frac{x}{2}$ ______

(iii) $\tan\frac{x}{2}$ ______

18. If $5(\tan^2 x - \cos^2 x) = 2\cos 2x + 9$, then the value of $\cos 4x$ is ______ .

19. State True or False.

(i) $\cos x \cos\left(\frac{\pi}{3} - x\right)\cos\left(\frac{\pi}{3} + x\right) = \frac{1}{4}\cos 3x$

True ☐ False ☐

*(ii) $\tan x + \tan\left(\frac{\pi}{3} + x\right) - \tan\left(\frac{\pi}{3} - x\right) = \tan 3x$

True ☐ False ☐

*(iii) $\tan x \tan\left(\frac{\pi}{3} - x\right)\tan\left(\frac{\pi}{3} + x\right) = \tan 3x$

True ☐ False ☐

20. If $\sin x = \frac{3}{5}, x \in \left(0, \frac{\pi}{2}\right)$, then find the value of the following functions.

(i) $\cos 2x$ ______

(ii) $\sin 3x$ ______

*(iii) $\tan 3x$ ______

21. Simplify the following.

(i) $\frac{\sin 2\theta}{1 + \cos 2\theta} - \tan\theta$ ______

(ii) $\tan\theta + \cot 2\theta$ ______

(iii) $\frac{\sin 2\theta}{\sin\theta} - \frac{\cos 2\theta}{\cos\theta}$ ______

Assertion-Reason Questions

The following questions consist of two statements – Assertion (A) and Reason (R). Answer these questions by selecting the appropriate option given below.
(a) Both (A) and (R) are true and (R) is correct explanation of (A)
(b) Both (A) and (R) are true but (R) is not the correct explanation of (A)
(c) (A) is true but (R) is false
(d) (A) is false but (R) is true

1. **Assertion** (A) The degree measure corresponding to (2) radian is$114°19$ min.

Reason (R) The degree measure of a given radian measure $= \frac{180}{\pi} \times$ Radian measure.

(a) ☐ (b) ☐ (c) ☐ (d) ☐

2. **Assertion** (A) $\sin^2 75 + \cos^2 75 = 1$

Reason (R) For any value of θ, $\sin^2 \theta + \cos^2 \theta = 1$

(a) ☐ (b) ☐ (c) ☐ (d) ☐

3. **Assertion** (A) cosec x is negative in third and fourth quadrants.

Reason (R) $\tan x$ decreases from 0 to $-\infty$ in first quadrant and increases from 0 to ∞ in third quadrant.

(a) ☐ (b) ☐ (c) ☐ (d) ☐

4. **Assertion** (A) If $f(x) = \cos^2 x + \sec^2 x$, then $f(x) \geq 2$.

Reason (R) The value of $\sin x$ is reciprocal of $\sec x$.

(a) ☐ (b) ☐ (c) ☐ (d) ☐

5. **Assertion** (A) The ratio of the radii of two circles at the centres of which two equal arcs subtend angles 65° and 110° is 22 : 13.

Reason (R) Number of radians in an angle subtended at the centre of a circle by an arc is equal to the ratio of the length of the arc to the radius of the circle.

(a) ☐ (b) ☐ (c) ☐ (d) ☐

6. **Assertion** (A) Radian measure for the angle 55° is $\frac{5\pi}{12}$.

Reason (R) Radian measure = Degree measure $\times \frac{\pi}{180°}$.

(a) ☐ (b) ☐ (c) ☐ (d) ☐

7. **Assertion** (A) The function $\sin x$ is negative in third and fourth quadrant.

Reason (R) The function $\sin x$ is decresing in the interval $0 \leq x \leq \frac{\pi}{2}$.

(a) ☐ (b) ☐ (c) ☐ (d) ☐

8. **Assertion** (A) The value of $2\cos\frac{\pi}{13}\cos\frac{9\pi}{13}+\cos\frac{3\pi}{13}+\cos\frac{5\pi}{13}$ is 0.

Reason (R) $\sin(A+B)=\sin A\cos B+\cos A\sin B$

(a) ☐ (b) ☐ (c) ☐ (d) ☐

9. **Assertion** (A) If $\cos x=-\frac{1}{3}$ and x lies in 3rd quadrant, then the value of $\sin x=\frac{-2\sqrt{2}}{3}$.

Reason (R) If the value of $\cos x$ is positive and $\sin x$ is negative, then $x\in\left(\frac{3\pi}{2},2\pi\right)$.

(a) ☐ (b) ☐ (c) ☐ (d) ☐

10. **Assertion** (A) The value of $\sin 930°$ is $-\frac{1}{4}$.

Reason (R) $\sin(180°-Q)=\sin\theta$, where θ is an acute angle.

(a) ☐ (b) ☐ (c) ☐ (d) ☐

Case Based Questions

Case 1 Aman construct two right angled triangles in the fourth quadrant in such a way that the measure of triangle gives $\cos A=\frac{4}{5}$ and $\cos B=\frac{12}{13}$, where $\frac{3\pi}{2}<A$ and $B>2\pi$.

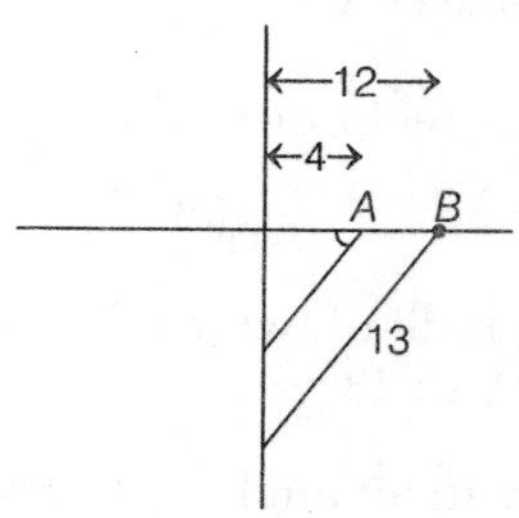

Based on the above information, answer the following questions.

(i) Find the value of $\sec(A+B)$.

(ii) Find the value of $\operatorname{cosec}(A-B)$.

(iii) Find the value of $\cot(A+B)$.

Case 2 Consider $A+B=\frac{\pi}{4}$, where A and B are acute angles.

Based an the above information, answer the following questions.

(i) Find the value of $(1+\tan A)(1+\tan B)$.

(ii) Find the value of $(\cot A-1)(\cot B-1)$.

(iii) Find the value of $\sin(A+B)-\cos(A+B)+\tan(A+B)$.

COMPETITION EDGE UP

1. If $\sin x = \frac{-3}{5}$, where $\pi < x < \frac{3\pi}{2}$, then $80(\tan^2 x - \cos x)$ is equal to **[JEE Main 2024]**

(a) 108 ☐
(b) 109 ☐
(c) 18 ☐
(d) 19 ☐

2. Let $f(x) = \frac{1}{7 - \sin 5x}$ be a function defined on R. Then, the range of the function $f(x)$ is equal to **[JEE Main 2024]**

(a) $\left[\frac{1}{7}, \frac{1}{6}\right]$ ☐
(b) $\left[\frac{1}{7}, \frac{1}{5}\right]$ ☐
(c) $\left[\frac{1}{8}, \frac{1}{6}\right]$ ☐
(d) $\left[\frac{1}{8}, \frac{1}{5}\right]$ ☐

3. For $\alpha, \beta \in \left(0, \frac{\pi}{2}\right)$, let $3 \sin(\alpha + \beta) = 2 \sin(\alpha - \beta)$ and a real number k be such that $\tan \alpha = k \tan \beta$. Then, the value of k is equal to **[JEE Main 2024]**

(a) $\frac{-2}{3}$ ☐
(b) -5 ☐
(c) $\frac{2}{3}$ ☐
(d) 5 ☐

4. Let $|\cos\theta \cos(60 - \theta) \cos(60 + \theta)| \le \frac{1}{8}$, $\theta \in [0, 2\pi]$. Then, the sum of all $\theta \in [0, 2\pi]$, where $\cos 3\theta$ attains its maximum value, is **[JEE Main 2024]**

(a) 9π ☐
(b) 6π ☐
(c) 15π ☐
(d) 18π ☐

5. If the value of $\frac{3 \cos 36° + 5 \sin 18°}{5 \cos 36° - 3 \sin 18°}$ is $\frac{a\sqrt{5} - b}{c}$, where a, b, c are natural numbers and $\gcd(a, c) = 1$, then $a + b + c$ is equal to **[JEE Main 2024]**

(a) 40 ☐
(b) 50 ☐
(c) 54 ☐
(d) 52 ☐

6. If $\tan A = \frac{1}{\sqrt{x(x^2 + x + 1)}}$,

$\tan B = \frac{\sqrt{x}}{\sqrt{x^2 + x + 1}}$ and

$\tan C = (x^{-3} + x^{-2} + x^{-1})^{\frac{1}{2}}$, $0 < A, B, C < \frac{\pi}{2}$, then $A + B$ is equal to **[JEE Main 2024]**

(a) $\frac{\pi}{2} - C$ ☐
(b) C ☐
(c) $\pi - C$ ☐
(d) $2\pi - C$ ☐

7. The value of $36(4\cos^2 9° - 1)(4\cos^2 27° - 1)(4\cos^2 81° - 1)(4\cos^2 243° - 1)$ is **[JEE Main 2023]**

(a) 27 ☐
(b) 36 ☐
(c) 18 ☐
(d) 54 ☐

8. Let

$S = \left\{x \in \left(-\frac{\pi}{2}, \frac{\pi}{2}\right) : 9^{1 - \tan^2 x} + 9^{\tan^2 x} = 10\right\}$

and $\beta = \sum_{x \in S} \tan^2\left(\frac{x}{3}\right)$, then $\frac{1}{6}(\beta - 14)^2$ is equal to **[JEE Main 2023]**

(a) 8 ☐
(b) 16 ☐
(c) 64 ☐
(d) 32 ☐

11. If $\cot \alpha = 1$ and $\sec \beta = -\frac{5}{3}$, where $\pi < \alpha < \frac{3\pi}{2}$ and $\frac{\pi}{2} < \beta < \pi$, then the value of $\tan(\alpha + \beta)$ and the quadrant in which $\alpha + \beta$ lies, respectively are **[JEE Main 2022]**

(a) $-\frac{1}{7}$ and IVth quadrant ☐

(b) 7 and Ist quadrant ☐

(c) -7 and IVth quadrant ☐

(d) $\frac{1}{7}$ and Ist quadrant ☐

12. $16 \sin(20^\circ) \sin(40^\circ) \sin(80^\circ)$ is equal to **[JEE Main 2022]**

(a) $\sqrt{3}$ ☐

(b) $2\sqrt{3}$ ☐

(c) 3 ☐

(d) $4\sqrt{3}$ ☐

13. $\alpha = \sin 36^\circ$ is a root of which of the following equation? **[JEE Main 2022]**

(a) $16x^4 - 10x^2 - 5 = 0$ ☐

(b) $16x^4 + 20x^2 - 5 = 0$ ☐

(c) $16x^4 - 20x^2 + 5 = 0$ ☐

(d) $16x^4 - 10x^2 + 5 = 0$ ☐

14. The value of $\cos\left(\frac{2\pi}{7}\right) + \cos\left(\frac{4\pi}{7}\right) + \cos\left(\frac{6\pi}{7}\right)$ is equal to **[JEE Main 2022]**

(a) -1 ☐

(b) $-\frac{1}{2}$ ☐

(c) $-\frac{1}{3}$ ☐

(d) $-\frac{1}{4}$ ☐

15. The value of $2 \sin(12^\circ) - \sin(72^\circ)$ is **[JEE Main 2022]**

(a) $\frac{\sqrt{5}(1-\sqrt{3})}{4}$ ☐

(b) $\frac{1-\sqrt{5}}{8}$ ☐

(c) $\frac{\sqrt{3}(1-\sqrt{5})}{2}$ ☐

(d) $\frac{\sqrt{3}(1-\sqrt{5})}{4}$ ☐

16. $2 \sin\left(\frac{\pi}{22}\right) \sin\left(\frac{3\pi}{22}\right) \sin\left(\frac{5\pi}{22}\right) \sin\left(\frac{7\pi}{22}\right) \sin\left(\frac{9\pi}{22}\right)$ is equal to **[JEE Main 2022]**

(a) 3/16 ☐

(b) 1/16 ☐

(c) 1/32 ☐

(d) 9/32 ☐

Chapter 04

Complex Numbers and Quadratic Equations

TOPIC 1

Introduction to Iota and Complex Numbers

NCERT Pg 76-77

Scan and take Chapter Test

1. Evaluate the following:

(i) $\sqrt{-144} =$ ______

(ii) $(\sqrt{-2})(\sqrt{-3}) =$ ______

(iii) $\sqrt{-4} \times \sqrt{\frac{-9}{4}} =$ ______

(iv) $(5i)\left(-\frac{3}{5}i\right) =$ ______

(v) $(-i)(2i)\left(-\frac{1}{8}i\right)^3 =$ ______

2. State True or False.

(i) $z_1 = z_2 \Leftrightarrow \text{Re}(z_1) = \text{Re}(z_2)$ and $\text{Im}(z_1) = \text{Im}(z_2)$.

True ☐ False ☐

(ii) If $z_1 = 2 - iy$ and $z_2 = x + 3i$ are equal, then $x = 2$ and $y = -3$.

True ☐ False ☐

3. Find the value of x and y in the following equality.

(i) $x + \sqrt{2}\,i = -\frac{7}{2} + iy$ ______

(ii) $4x + i(3x - y) = 3 + i(-6)$ ______

(iii) $(1 - i)x + (1 + i)y = 1 - 3i$ ______

(iv) $(x + iy)(2 - 3i) = 4 + i$ ______

*Concepts of all questions bearing * are important for JEE & CUET*

(v) $(1+i)y^2 + (6+i) = (2+i)x$ __________

(vi) $(x^4 + 2xi) - (3x^2 + iy) = (3-5i) + (1+2iy)$ __________

(vii) $(x+y) - i(3x+2y) = 5+2i$ __________

(viii) $(3x-7) + 2iy = -5y + (5+x)i$ __________

(ix) $\frac{x-1}{3+i} + \frac{y-1}{3-i} = i$ __________

4. Simplify the following:

(i) i^2 __________

(ii) i^{19} __________

(iii) i^{135} __________

(iv) i^{528} __________

(v) i^{-39} __________

(vi) i^{-58} __________

(vii) i^{-999} __________

(viii) $i^9 + i^{19}$ __________

(ix) $i^{30} + i^{40} + i^{60}$ __________

(x) $i^{49} + i^{68} + i^{89} + i^{110}$ __________

(xi) $(i^{77} + i^{70} + i^{87} + i^{414})^3$ __________

(xii) $(1-i)^4$ __________

(xiii) $\left\{i^{19} + \left(\frac{1}{i}\right)^{25}\right\}^2$ __________

(xiv) $\left\{i^{17} - \left(\frac{1}{i}\right)^{34}\right\}^2$ __________

(xv) $\left\{i^{18} + \left(\frac{1}{i}\right)^{24}\right\}^3$ __________

5. State whether the statement is True or False.

(i) $i^n + i^{n+1} + i^{n+2} + i^{n+3} = 0$ for all $n \in N$.

True ☐ False ☐

(ii) $(-\sqrt{-1})^{4n+3} = i$ for all $n \in N$

True ☐ False ☐

TOPIC 2

Algebra of Complex Number

NCERT Pg 77-81

6. State True or False.

(i) If $z_1 = 6 + \sqrt{-9}$ and $z_2 = -2 - 6i$, then $z_1 + z_2 = 4 - 3i$.

True ☐ False ☐

(ii) In complex number, real and imaginary parts are added separately.

True ☐ False ☐

7. Evaluate $z_1 - z_2$:

(i) $z_1 = 6 + \sqrt{-25}$ and $z_2 = -2 + 3i$ __________

(ii) $z_1 = (1 - i)$ and $z_2 = (-1 + 6i)$ __________

(iii) $z_1 = \left(\frac{1}{5} + \frac{2}{5}i\right)$ and $z_2 = \left(4 + \frac{5}{2}i\right)$ __________

8. Solve $\left\{\left(\frac{1}{3} + \frac{7}{3}i\right) + \left(4 + \frac{1}{3}i\right)\right\} - \left(-\frac{4}{3} + i\right)$ __________

9. Convert the following in $a + ib$ form.

(i) $(-5i)\left(\frac{1}{8}i\right)$ __________

(ii) $3(7 + 7i) + i(7 + 7i)$ __________

(iii) $(-\sqrt{3} + \sqrt{-2})(2\sqrt{3} - i)$ __________

(iv) $(5 - 3i)^3$ __________

(v) $\left(\frac{1}{3} + 3i\right)^3$ __________

(vi) $\left(-2 - \frac{i}{3}\right)^3$ __________

10. If $z_1 = 2 - 6i$, $z_2 = 3 + 5i$ and $z_3 = 9 + 2i$, then the value of $z_1(z_2 + z_3)$ is

(a) $66 - 58i$ (b) $58 - 66i$ (c) $24 - 100i$ (d) $100i - 24$

____

11. Find the value of $\frac{z_1}{z_2}$.

(i) $z_1 = 6 + 3i$ and $z_2 = 2 - i$ __________

(ii) $z_1 = 2 + \sqrt{2}i$ and $z_2 = \sqrt{2} + i$ __________

(iii) $z_1 = 6 - 5i$ and $z_2 = \frac{24 - 20i}{4}$ __________

12. If $z_1 = 2 + i$ and $z_2 = -1 + 2i$, then find

(i) $\text{Im}(4z_1 - 3z_2)$ __________

(ii) $\text{Re}(z_1 z_2)$ __________

(iii) $\text{Im}(iz_1^2)$ __________

(iv) $\text{Re}\left(\dfrac{z_1}{z_2}\right)$ __________

13. $(x + 1 + i)(x + 1 - i)(x - 1 + i)(x - 1 - i) = x^4 + 4.$

True ☐ False ☐

14. If $(x + iy)^{1/3} = a + ib, x, y, a, b \in R$, then $\dfrac{x}{a} + \dfrac{y}{b} = 4(a^2 + b^2)$.

True ☐ False ☐

15. Fill in the blanks :

(i) If $x = -5 + 2\sqrt{-4}$, then $x^4 + 9x^3 + 35x^2 - x + 4 =$ __________ .

(ii) If $x = 1 + 2i$, then $x^3 + 7x^2 - x + 16 =$ __________ .

16. Find the multiplicative inverse of the following complex numbers.

(i) $3 + 2i$ __________

(ii) $a + ib$ __________

(iii) $(2 + \sqrt{3}i)^2$ __________

TOPIC 3

Modulus and Conjugate of a Complex Number

NCERT Pg 81-82

***17.** Find the modulus ($|z|$) of the following complex numbers.

(i) $z = 5 + 6i$ __________

(ii) $z = 12 - 5i$ __________

(iii) $z = -13 - \sqrt{7}i$ __________

(iv) $z = -\sqrt{2} + \sqrt{2}i$ __________

(v) $iz^3 + z^2 - z + i = 0$ __________

18. The sum and product of two complex numbers are real if and only if they are conjugate of each other.

True ☐ False ☐

19. Find the conjugate of the following complex numbers.

(i) $\dfrac{1}{3+4i}$ ____________

(ii) $\dfrac{1-i}{1+i}$ ____________

(iii) $\dfrac{(1+i)^2}{3-i}$ ____________

(iv) $\dfrac{(2+3i)^2}{2-i}$ ____________

20. Find the value of the given expressions :

(i) If $\dfrac{(a+i)^2}{2a-i} = p + iq$, then $p^2 + q^2 =$ ____________

(ii) If $a + ib = \dfrac{(x+i)^2}{2x^2+1}$, then $a^2 + b^2 =$ ____________

(iii) If $x + iy = \sqrt{\dfrac{a+ib}{c+id}}$, then $(x^2 + y^2)^2 =$ ____________

(iv) If $\dfrac{a+ib}{c+id} = x + iy$, then $x^2 + y^2 =$ ____________

21. If z_1, z_2 are $1-i$, $-2+4i$ respectively, then the value of $\text{Im}\left(\dfrac{z_1 z_2}{\bar{z}_1}\right)$ is

(a) $4i$ (b) $-4i$ (c) $-2+4i$ (d) 2

____

22. The real value of y for which the complex numbers $-3 + ix^2y$ and $x^2 + y + 4i$ are conjugate of each other, is -4.

True ☐ False ☐

***23.** Find non-zero integral solutions of $|1-i|^x = 1$.

____

24. The least positive value of n if $\left(\dfrac{1+i}{1-i}\right)^n = 1$, is

(a) 1 (b) 2 (c) 3 (d) 4

____

25. Express following in the form of $a + ib$.

(i) $\dfrac{3-\sqrt{-16}}{1-\sqrt{-9}}$ ____________

(ii) $\dfrac{2-\sqrt{-25}}{1-\sqrt{-16}}$ ______

(iii) $\dfrac{1}{1-\cos\theta+2i\sin\theta}$ ______

(iv) $\dfrac{1}{-11+2i}$ ______

(v) $\dfrac{(3+i\sqrt{5})(3-i\sqrt{5})}{(\sqrt{3}+\sqrt{2}i)-(\sqrt{3}-i\sqrt{2})}$ ______

(vi) $\left(\dfrac{2+3i}{3+4i}\right)\left(\dfrac{2-3i}{3-4i}\right)$ ______

(vii) $\left(\dfrac{3+2i}{2-3i}\right)+\left(\dfrac{3-2i}{2+3i}\right)$ ______

(viii) $\dfrac{(3-2i)(2+3i)}{(1+2i)(2-i)}$ ______

(ix) $\dfrac{1}{-2+\sqrt{-3}}$ ______

(x) $\dfrac{5+4i}{4+5i}$ ______

(xi) $\dfrac{(1+i)^2}{3-i}$ ______

(xii) $\dfrac{1}{3-4i}$ ______

(xiii) $\left(\dfrac{1}{1-2i}+\dfrac{3}{1+i}\right)\left(\dfrac{3+4i}{2-4i}\right)$ ______

26. If $a+ib=\dfrac{c+i}{c-i}$, where c is real, then

(a) $a^2+b^2=1$ (b) $\dfrac{b}{a}=\dfrac{2c}{c^2-1}$ (c) Both (a) and (b) (d) None of these

______

***27.** If z is a complex number such that $|z|=1$, then $\left(\dfrac{z-1}{z+1}\right)$ is purely imaginary.

True ☐ False ☐

***28.** Find real θ such that $\dfrac{3+2i\sin\theta}{1-2i\sin\theta}$ is purely real.

______

29. If α and β are different complex numbers with $|\beta| = 1$, then $\left|\dfrac{\beta - \alpha}{1 - \bar{\alpha}\beta}\right|^2$ is equal to

(a) 0 (b) 1 (c) 2 (d) 3

---

30. (i) If $(a + ib)(c + id)(e + if)(g + ih) = A + iB$, then

$$(a^2 + b^2)(c^2 + d^2)(e^2 + f^2)(g^2 + h^2) = A^2 + B^2.$$

True ☐ False ☐

(ii) If $(1 + i)(1 + 2i)(1 + 3i) \ldots\ldots\ldots (1 + ni) = (x + iy)$, then $2 \cdot 5 \cdot 10 \ldots (1 + n^2) = x^2 + y^2$.

True ☐ False ☐

***31.** If z_1 and z_2 are complex numbers such that $\dfrac{2z_1}{3z_2}$ is purely imaginary numbers, then $\left|\dfrac{z_1 - z_2}{z_1 + z_2}\right|$ is equal to

(a) 0 (b) 1 (c) 2 (d) 3

---

32. If $|z_1| = |z_2| = \ldots. = |z_n| = 1$, then $|z_1 + z_2 + z_3 + \ldots + z_n| = \left|\dfrac{1}{z_1} + \dfrac{1}{z_2} + \dfrac{1}{z_3} + \ldots. + \dfrac{1}{z_n}\right|$.

True ☐ False ☐

TOPIC 4

Argand Plane and Polar Representation

NCERT Pg 83-84

33. Represent the following complex numbers on argand plane.

(i) $-1 + i\sqrt{3}$ ________________ .

(ii) $-\sqrt{5} + i$ ________________ .

34. Argument of $z\,\{\arg(z)\} = x + iy$ and α be an acute angle satisfying $\tan\alpha = \left|\dfrac{y}{x}\right|$, when

	Column I		Column II {arg = (z)}
A.	$x > 0$ and $y > 0$	1.	$\pi - \alpha$
B.	$x < 0$ and $y > 0$	2.	α
C.	$x < 0$ and $y < 0$	3.	$-\alpha$
D.	$x > 0$ and $y < 0$	4.	$\alpha - \pi$

Which one is the correct option?

(a) A → 2, B → 4, C → 1, D → 3
(b) A → 2, B → 1, C → 4, D → 3
(c) A → 3, B → 4, C → 1, D → 2
(d) A → 3, B → 1, C → 4, D → 2

35. Consider the following complex numbers

$z_1 = \sqrt{3}, z_2 = \frac{1}{\sqrt{3}} + i, z_3 = 2, z_4 = -1 + \sqrt{3}i, z_5 = 2\sqrt{3} + 5i, z_6 = 3\sqrt{3} + 6i,$

$z_7 = \sqrt{3} - 4i, z_8 = \sqrt{3} + 2i, z_9 = 1 + i, z_{10} = 1 - i, z_{11} = 1, z_{12} = 1 + i$

Now, find the argument of the following:

(i) $z_1 z_2$ ______

(ii) $z_3 z_4$ ______

(iii) $z_5 - z_6$ ______

(iv) $z_7 + z_8$ ______

(v) $\frac{z_9}{z_{10}}$ ______

(vi) $\frac{z_{11}}{z_{12}}$ ______

36. Find the principal argument of the following complex numbers.

(i) -4 ______

(ii) $-2i$ ______

37. For any complex number z, $|\text{Re}(z)| + |\text{Im}(z)| \leq \sqrt{2}\,|z|$.

True ☐ False ☐

38. Let $|z| = r$ and α be the acute angle given by $\tan^{-1}\left(\frac{y}{x}\right)$. Then, polar form of $z = x + iy$ is

	Column I		Column II
A.	$x > 0$ and $y > 0$	1.	$z = r(-\cos\alpha + i\sin\alpha)$
B.	$x < 0$ and $y > 0$	2.	$z = r(\cos\alpha + i\sin\alpha)$
C.	$x < 0$ and $y < 0$	3.	$z = r(\cos\alpha - i\sin\alpha)$
D.	$x > 0$ and $y < 0$	4.	$z = r(-\cos\alpha - i\sin\alpha)$

Which one is the correct option?

(a) A → 1, B → 2, C → 3, D → 4
(b) A → 1, B → 2, C → 4, D → 3
(c) A → 2, B → 1, C → 3, D → 4
(d) A → 2, B → 1, C → 4, D → 3

39. Convert the following complex numbers into polar form.

(i) $-1 - i$ ______

(ii) $1 - i$ ______

(iii) $-3\sqrt{2} + 3\sqrt{2}\,i$ ______

(iv) $1 + i$ ______

(v) $\frac{1+i}{1-i}$ ______

(vi) $\frac{2 + 6\sqrt{3}i}{5 + \sqrt{3}i}$ ______

40. Put the following in the form $r(\cos\theta + i\sin\theta)$, where r is a positive real number and $-\pi < \theta \leq \pi$: $\dfrac{1+7i}{3-4i}$

____

41. State True or False.

(i) Modulus of $\dfrac{1+2i}{1-3i}$ is $\dfrac{1}{\sqrt{2}}$.

True ☐ False ☐

(ii) Argument of $\dfrac{i-1}{\cos\dfrac{\pi}{3} + i\sin\dfrac{\pi}{3}}$ is $\dfrac{5\pi}{12}$.

True ☐ False ☐

(iii) Polar form of $\dfrac{1+3i}{1-2i}$ is $\sqrt{2}\left(\cos\dfrac{3\pi}{4} + i\sin\dfrac{3\pi}{4}\right)$.

True ☐ False ☐

42. Evaluate the following :

(i) If $z = -\sqrt{3} + i$, then

(a) modulus of z = ______________________________

(b) argument of z = ______________________________

(c) polar form of z = ______________________________

(ii) If $z = \dfrac{-4}{1+i\sqrt{3}}$, then

(a) modulus of z = ______________________________

(b) argument of z = ______________________________

(c) polar form of z = ______________________________

43. Simplify:

(i) $\sqrt{7-24i}$ ______________________________

(ii) $\sqrt{5+12i}$ ______________________________

(iii) $\sqrt{-15-8i}$ ______________________________

(iv) $\sqrt{i}$ ______________________________

Assertion-Reason Questions

The following questions consist of two statements – Assertion (A) and Reason (R). Answer these questions by selecting the appropriate option given below.
(a) Both (A) and (R) are true and (R) is correct explanation of (A)
(b) Both (A) and (R) are true but (R) is not the correct explanation of (A)
(c) (A) is true but (R) is false
(d) (A) is false but (R) is true

1. **Assertion** (A) The imaginary part of the complex number $26+\sqrt{-17}$ is $\sqrt{17}$.

Reason (R) Let $z = a + ib$ be a complex number, then a is called real part and b is called imaginary part of z.

(a) ☐ (b) ☐ (c) ☐ (d) ☐

2. **Assertion** (A) Let $z_1 = 2-7i$ and $z_2 = 3+3i$ be any two complex numbers. Then, $z_1 + z_2 = 5-4i$ is also a complex number.

Reason (R) The sum of two complex numbers is a complex number.

(a) ☐ (b) ☐ (c) ☐ (d) ☐

3. **Assertion** (A) If $z_1 = 5+2i$ and $z_2 = -1+4i$, then $z_1 - z_2 = 4-2i$.

Reason (R) If $z_1 = a+ib$ and $z_2 = c+id$, then $z_1 - z_2 = (a-c)+i(b-d)$.

(a) ☐ (b) ☐ (c) ☐ (d) ☐

4. **Assertion** (A) Simplest form of i^{-37} is i.

Reason (R) Additive inverse of $(1-i)$ is equal to $(-1+i)$.

(a) ☐ (b) ☐ (c) ☐ (d) ☐

5. **Assertion** (A) Let $z_1 = 2+3i$ and $z_2 = 3-4i$ be two complex numbers, then $z_1 + z_2$ is equal to $5-i$.

Reason (R) If z_1 and z_2 be two complex numbers, then $z_1 + z_2 = z_2 + z_1$.

(a) ☐ (b) ☐ (c) ☐ (d) ☐

6. **Assertion** (A) Conjugate of complex number $z_1 = 4-2i$ is $4+2i$.

Reason (R) The conjugate of a complex number z, is obtained by changing the sign of real part of z.

(a) ☐ (b) ☐ (c) ☐ (d) ☐

7. **Assertion** (A) If $x+iy = \sqrt{\frac{3+i}{1+3i}}$, then $(x^2+y^2)^2$ is equal to 1.

Reason (R) The distance of the complex number $z = a+ib$ from origin, is called the modulus of z.

(a) ☐ (b) ☐ (c) ☐ (d) ☐

8. Assertion (A) If $z = 3 + 3i$ is a complex number and its conjugate is $\bar{z} = 3 - 3i$, then $(3, -3)$ is the mirror image of z.

Reason (R) The mirror image of the complex number $z = a + ib$ is called the conjugate of z which is represented by the ordered pair $(a, -b)$.

(a) ☐ (b) ☐ (c) ☐ (d) ☐

9. Assertion (A) The argument of a complex number $-2\sqrt{3} + 2i$ is $\frac{\pi}{4}$.

Reason (R) Let $z = -a + ib$ is a complex number, where $\text{Re}(z) = -a < 0$ and $\text{Im}(z) = b > 0$, then argument of z is $\pi - \theta$, where $\theta = \tan^{-1}\left(\frac{b}{-a}\right)$

(a) ☐ (b) ☐ (c) ☐ (d) ☐

Case Based Questions

Case 1 We have, $i = \sqrt{-1}$. So, we can write the higher powers of i as follows

(i) $i^2 = -1$

(ii) $i^3 = i^2 \cdot i = (-1) \cdot i = -i$

(iii) $i^4 = (i^2 \cdot i^2) = (-1)^2 = 1$

(iv) $i^5 = i^{4+1} = i^4 \cdot i = 1 \cdot i = i$

(v) $i^6 = i^{4+2} = i^4 \cdot i^2 = 1 \cdot i^2 = -1$

In order to compute i^n for $n > 4$, write $i^n = i^{4q+r}$ for some $q, r \in N$ and $0 \le r \le 3$.

Then, $i^n = i^{4q} \cdot i^r = (i^4)^q \cdot i^r = (1)^q \cdot i^r = i^r$

In general, for any integer k, $i^{4k} = 1$, $i^{4k+1} = i$, $i^{4k+2} = -1$, $i^{4k+3} = -i$.

On the basis of above information, answer the following questions

(i) The value of i^{33} is equal to

(a) i ☐ (b) $-i$ ☐ (c) 1 ☐ (d) -1 ☐

(ii) The value of $(\sqrt{-1})^{-30}$ is equal to

(a) i ☐ (b) $-i$ ☐ (c) 1 ☐ (d) -1 ☐

(iii) The value of $\left[i^{17} - \left(\frac{1}{i}\right)^{34}\right]^2$ is equal to

(a) i ☐ (b) $2i$ ☐ (c) -1 ☐ (d) -2 ☐

(iv) The value of $i^{107} + i^{112} + i^{122} + i^{117}$ is equal to

(a) 0 ☐ (b) 1 ☐ (c) i ☐ (d) -1 ☐

(v) If $z = i^{100} + i^{107}$, then z is equal to

(a) $1+i$ ☐ (b) $-1-i$ ☐ (c) $1-i$ ☐ (d) $-1+i$ ☐

Case 2 The conjugate of a complex number z is the complex number, obtained by changing the sign of imaginary part of z. It is denoted by $\bar{z}$. The modulus (or absolute value) of a complex number, $z = a + ib$ is defined as the non-negative real number $\sqrt{a^2 + b^2}$. It is denoted by $|z|$ i.e. $|z| = \sqrt{a^2 + b^2}$.

Multiplicative inverse of z is $\frac{\bar{z}}{|z|^2}$. It is also called reciprocal of z . $z\bar{z} = |z|^2$.

On the basis of above information, answer the following questions

(i) If $z = 4 + 5i$, then $\frac{z + \bar{z}}{2}$ is equal to

(a) 1 ☐ (b) 2 ☐ (c) 3 ☐ (d) 4 ☐

(ii) The value of $(z + 3)(\bar{z} + 3)$ is equivalent to

(a) $|z + 3|^2$ ☐ (b) $|z - 3|$ ☐ (c) $z^2 + 3$ ☐ (d) $-z + 3$ ☐

(iii) If $z_1 = 2 - 4i$ and $z_2 = -4 + 3i$, then $|z_1 + z_2|$ is equal to

(a) 5 ☐ (b) $\sqrt{5}$ ☐ (c) $\sqrt{3}$ ☐ (d) 2 ☐

(iv) Multiplicative inverse of $z = 5 - 3i$ is equal to

(a) $\frac{5}{34} + \frac{3}{34}i$ ☐ (b) $\frac{5}{34} - \frac{3}{34}i$ ☐ (c) $\frac{-5}{34} - \frac{3}{34}i$ ☐ (d) $-\frac{5}{34} + \frac{3}{34}i$ ☐

(v) If $z = 3 + 4i$, then $|z|^2$ is equal to

(a) 12 ☐ (b) 24 ☐ (c) 25 ☐ (d) −7 ☐

COMPETITION CONNECT

Quadratic Equations [NCERT (Old) Pg. 108-109]

1. Find roots of the following quadratic equations.

(i) $x^2 + 2 = 0$ ______

(ii) $x^2 + 4ix - 4 = 0$ ______

(iii) $x^2 - \sqrt{2}\,ix + 12 = 0$ ______

(iv) $3x^2 + 7ix + 6 = 0$ ______

(v) $x^2 - (3\sqrt{2} + 2i)\,x + 6\sqrt{2}i = 0$ ______

(vi) $x^2 + x + 1 = 0$ ______

(vii) $\sqrt{5}\,x^2 + x + \sqrt{5} = 0$ ______

(viii) $25x^2 - 30x + 11 = 0$ ______

(ix) $x^2 - 5ix - 6 = 0$ ______

(x) $x^2 - (3\sqrt{2} - 2i)x - 6\sqrt{2}i = 0$ ______

(xi) $2x^2 + 3ix + 2 = 0$ ______

(xii) $2x^2 - (3 + 7i)x - (3 - 9i) = 0$ ______

(xiii) $x^2 - (7 - i)\,x + (18 - i) = 0$ ______

(xiv) $2x^2 - 4x + 3 = 0$ ______

COMPETITION EDGE UP

1. Let z be a complex number such that the real part of $\frac{z-2i}{z+2i}$ is zero. Then, the maximum value of $|z-(6+8i)|$ is equal to **[JEE Main 2024]**

(a) 10 ☐
(b) 8 ☐
(c) 12 ☐
(d) ∞ ☐

2. The sum of all possible value of $\theta \in [-\pi, 2\pi]$, for which $\frac{1+i\cos\theta}{1-2i\cos\theta}$ is purely imaginary, is equal to **[JEE Main 2024]**

(a) 4π ☐
(b) 5π ☐
(c) 3π ☐
(d) 2π ☐

3. Let z be a complex number such that $|z+2|=1$ and $\text{Im}\left(\frac{z+1}{z+2}\right)=\frac{1}{5}$. Then, the value of $|\text{Re}\,(\overline{z+2})|$ is **[JEE Main 2024]**

(a) $\frac{24}{5}$ ☐
(b) $\frac{2\sqrt{6}}{5}$ ☐
(c) $\frac{1+\sqrt{6}}{5}$ ☐
(d) $\frac{\sqrt{6}}{5}$ ☐

4. If $z=x+iy, xy\neq 0$, satisfies the equation $z^2+i\bar{z}=0$, then $|z^2|$ is equal to **[JEE Main 2024]**

(a) 4 ☐
(b) $\frac{1}{4}$ ☐
(c) 9 ☐
(d) 1 ☐

5. If $z=\frac{1}{2}-2i$ is such that $|z+1|=\alpha z+\beta(1+i), i=\sqrt{-1}$ and $\alpha, \beta \in R$, then $\alpha+\beta$ is equal to **[JEE Main 2024]**

(a) -4 ☐
(b) -1 ☐
(c) 2 ☐
(d) 3 ☐

6. If the set $R=\{(a,b): a+5b=42, a, b \in N\}$ has m elements and $\sum_{n=1}^{m}(1-i^{n!})=x+iy$, where $i=\sqrt{-1}$, then the value of $m+x+y$ is **[JEE Main 2024]**

(a) 12 ☐
(b) 5 ☐
(c) 4 ☐
(d) 8 ☐

7. Let α and β be the sum and the product of all the non-zero solutions of the equation $(\bar{z})^2+|z|=0, z\in C$. Then, $4(\alpha^2+\beta^2)$ is equal to **[JEE Main 2024]**

(a) 6 ☐
(b) 2 ☐
(c) 4 ☐
(d) 8 ☐

8. Let $S=\{z\in C: |z-1|=1$ and $(\sqrt{2}-1)(z+\bar{z})-i(z-\bar{z})=2\sqrt{2}\}$. Let $z_1, z_2 \in S$ be such that $|z_1|=\max_{z\in S}|z|$ and $|z_2|=\min_{z\in S}|z|$. Then, $|\sqrt{2}z_1-z_2|^2$ equals **[JEE Main 2024]**

(a) 4 ☐
(b) 3 ☐
(c) 2 ☐
(d) 1 ☐

9. Let z_1 and z_2 be two complex numbers such that $z_1+z_2=5$ and $z_1^3+z_2^3=20+15i$. Then, $|z_1^4+z_2^4|$ equals **[JEE Main 2024]**

(a) 75 ☐
(b) $25\sqrt{3}$ ☐
(c) $30\sqrt{3}$ ☐
(d) $15\sqrt{15}$ ☐

10. If z_1 and z_2 are two distinct complex number such that $\left|\dfrac{z_1 - 2z_2}{\frac{1}{2} - z_1\bar{z}_2}\right| = 2$, then **[JEE Main 2024]**

(a) both z_1 and z_2 lie on the same circle. ☐

(b) z_1 lies on a circle of radius $\frac{1}{2}$ and z_2 lies on a circle of radius 1. ☐

(c) either z_1 lies on a circle of radius $\frac{1}{2}$ or z_2 lies on a circle of radius 1. ☐

(d) either z_1 lies on a circle of radius 1 or z_2 lies on a circle of radius $\frac{1}{2}$. ☐

11. If z is a complex number such that $|z| \geq 1$, then the minimum value of $\left|z + \frac{1}{2}(3 + 4i)\right|$ is **[JEE Main 2024]**

(a) $\frac{5}{2}$ ☐

(b) 3 ☐

(c) 2 ☐

(d) $\frac{3}{2}$ ☐

12. If $S = \{z \in C : |z - i| = |z + i| = |z - 1|\}$, then $n(S)$ is **[JEE Main 2024]**

(a) 0 ☐

(b) 2 ☐

(c) 1 ☐

(d) 3 ☐

13. Let $S_1 = \{z \in C : |z| \leq 5\}$,

$S_2 = \left\{z \in C : \text{Im}\left(\dfrac{z + 1 - \sqrt{3}i}{1 - \sqrt{3}i}\right) \geq 0\right\}$ and

$S_3 = \{z \in C : \text{Re}(z) \geq 0\}$. Then, the area of the region $S_1 \cap S_2 \cap S_3$ is **[JEE Main 2024]**

(a) $\frac{125\pi}{24}$ ☐

(b) $\frac{125\pi}{12}$ ☐

(c) $\frac{125\pi}{4}$ ☐

(d) $\frac{125\pi}{6}$ ☐

14. The area (in sq units) of the region $S = \{z \in C : |z - 1| \leq 2; (z + \bar{z}) + i(z - \bar{z}) \leq 2, \text{Im}(z) \geq 0\}$ is **[JEE Main 2024]**

(a) $\frac{7\pi}{4}$ ☐

(b) $\frac{3\pi}{2}$ ☐

(c) $\frac{17\pi}{8}$ ☐

(d) $\frac{7\pi}{3}$ ☐

15. If 2 and 6 are the roots of the equation $ax^2 + bx + 1 = 0$, then the quadratic equation whose roots are $\frac{1}{2a + b}$ and $\frac{1}{6a + b}$, is **[JEE Main 2024]**

(a) $x^2 + 8x + 12 = 0$ ☐

(b) $2x^2 + 11x + 12 = 0$ ☐

(c) $x^2 + 10x + 16 = 0$ ☐

(d) $4x^2 + 14x + 12 = 0$ ☐

16. Let S be the set of positive integral values of a for which $\dfrac{ax^2 + 2(a + 1)x + 9a + 4}{x^2 - 8x + 32} < 0$, $\forall\, x \in R$. Then, the number of elements in S is **[JEE Main 2024]**

(a) 1 ☐

(b) 3 ☐

(c) ∞ ☐

(d) 0 ☐

Chapter 05

Linear Inequalities

Scan and take Chapter Test

TOPIC 1
Inequalities

NCERT Pg. 89-90

1. State whether the statement is True or False.

(i) $5x < 40$ is an example of the equation.

True ☐ False ☐

(ii) Two real numbers or two algebraic expressions related by the symbol '>', '<', '≤' or '≥' form an inequality.

True ☐ False ☐

2. Write these two statements in one statement

$$8x + 7y < 10$$
$$8x + 7y = 10$$

---

3. State whether the statement is True or False.

(i) Is it necessary that the numerical inequality contains only numbers?

True ☐ False ☐

(ii) $-3 < 5$ is an example of numerical inequality.

True ☐ False ☐

(iii) $y \leq 5$ is an literal inequality.

True ☐ False ☐

(iv) $2x + 5 > 0$ is an example of strict inequality.

True ☐ False ☐

(v) $2x + 8y \leq 8$ is a slack inequality.

True ☐ False ☐

(vi) $2x^2 + x \leq 0$ is a slack inequality.

True ☐ False ☐

(vii) $5x^2 + 7x + 9 > 0$ is a strict inequality.

True ☐ False ☐

*Concepts of all questions bearing * are important for JEE & CUET*

(viii) If $b = 0$, then $ax + by < c$ is a linear inequality in one variable x.

True ☐ False ☐

4. Fill in the blanks based on the type inequality.

(i) The ______________________ inequality is $17 < 20$.

(ii) $-4 \leq x < 10$ is an example of ______________________ inequality.

(iii) $3x + 4y \geq 5$ is known as ______________________ inequality.

5. Match the following columns.

	Column I		Column II
A.	Literal inequality	1.	$6x^2 + 8x + 9 > 0$
B.	Quadratic inequality	2.	$-2 < y \leq 6$
C.	Double inequality	3.	$x \geq 7$
D.	Strict inequality	4.	$2x + 5 < 0$

Which one is correct option?

(a) $A \rightarrow 4, B \rightarrow 2, C \rightarrow 1, D \rightarrow 3$
(b) $A \rightarrow 3, B \rightarrow 1, C \rightarrow 2, D \rightarrow 4$
(c) $A \rightarrow 3, B \rightarrow 2, C \rightarrow 1, D \rightarrow 4$
(d) $A \rightarrow 4, B \rightarrow 1, C \rightarrow 2, D \rightarrow 3$

TOPIC 2

Algebraic Solutions of Linear Inequalities in one variable and their Graphical Representation

NCERT Pg 91-94

6. For the given value of x, state whether the following inequality is True or False.

(i) When $x = 15$, $3x < 50$.

True ☐ False ☐

(ii) When $x = 0$, $15x - 7 > 8$.

True ☐ False ☐

(iii) When $x = 4$, $\frac{2}{x} + 4 \leq 5x$.

True ☐ False ☐

7. ________ are the solution set of $2x + y \leq 6$ inequality, where $x = 0$ and y is whole number.

8. State whether the statement is True or False.

(i) Equal numbers may be added to both sides of an inequality without affecting the sign of inequality.

True ☐ False ☐

(ii) When we subtract 2 from both sides in the inequality $2x - \frac{3}{5}x \geq 9$, then the inequality sign remains same.

True ☐ False ☐

(iii) When both sides of an inequality multiplied by a negative number, then the inequality is reversed.

True ☐ False ☐

(iv) When we multiply (-5) in the following inequality $2x - 4 < 7x$, then the inequality becomes $5x > (-4)$.

True ☐ False ☐

9. Find the solution set of the following inequalities.

(i) $9x + 9 < 5x + 5$ ________________.

(ii) $\frac{2x-1}{3} \geq \left(\frac{3x-2}{4}\right) - \left(\frac{2-x}{5}\right)$ ________________.

(iii) $8 + 2x \geq \frac{5x+19}{3}$ ________________.

(iv) $|x - 1| > 5$ ________________.

(v) $|x + 2| \leq 9$ ________________.

(vi) $\left|\frac{2}{x-4}\right| > 1$, where $x \neq 4$ ________________.

10. Match the following column.

	Column I		Column II
A.	$2 + x > 2$	1.	$x \in (-\infty, 2)$
B.	$5x > -5$	2.	$x > 0 \; \forall \; x \in N$
C.	$2x > -12$	3.	$x > -1 \; \forall \; x \in W$
D.	$24 \geq 12x$	4.	$x \in (-6, \infty)$

Which one is correct option?

(a) A → 1, B → 2, C → 3, D → 4

(b) A → 4, B → 1, C → 2, D → 3

(c) A → 3, B → 4, C → 1, D → 2

(d) A → 2, B → 3, C → 4, D → 1

11. A solution is to be kept between 68°F and 77°F. The range of temperature in degree celsius (°C) is between 20°C and 25°C, if $F = \frac{9}{5}C + 32$.

True ☐ False ☐

12. Solve the following inequalities.

(i) $3x - 19 < 50$ ____

(ii) $\frac{9x+5}{2} < \frac{7x+21}{3}$ ____

(iii) $-2 + \frac{7x}{21} \le \frac{8}{7}$ ____

(iv) $\frac{9x}{2} \le \frac{5-2x}{3} + 2$ ____

(v) $9x + 2 < \frac{4x}{5} - 1$ ____

(vi) $8 < \frac{-9x+5}{2} < -1$ ____

(vii) $2 \le \frac{-9x+8}{5} \le 3$ ____

13. Which one is the graphical representation of $x < -5$?

(a) 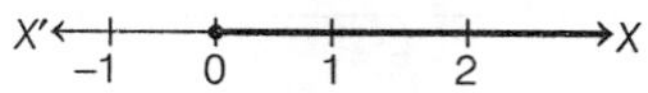

(b) 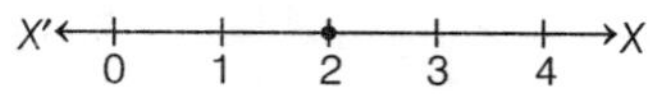

(c) 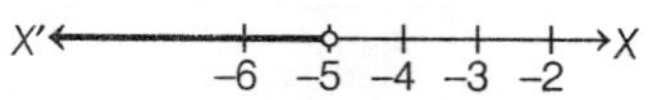

(d) 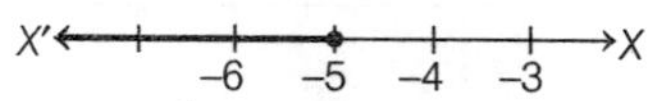

____

14. Solution of the following number line is

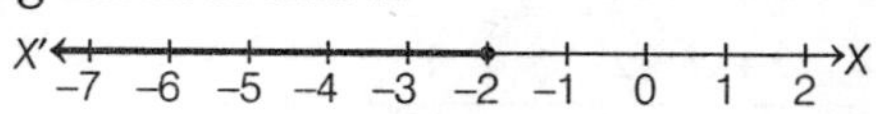

(a) $x > -2$ (b) $x < 2$ (c) $x \ge -2$ (d) $x \le -2$

____

15. Solution of the following number line is

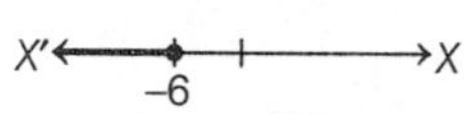

(a) $x \in (-\infty, -6)$ (b) $x \in (-\infty, -6]$ (c) $x \in [-6, \infty)$ (d) $x \in (-6, \infty)$

____

16. Represent the following inequality on number line.

(i) $7x + 3 < 5x + 9$ ____

(ii) $\frac{5-2x}{3} \le \frac{x}{6} - 5$ ____

(iii) $\frac{x}{2} \ge \frac{(5x-2)}{3} - \frac{(7x-3)}{5}$ ____

17. (i) Rohit obtained 20 and 35 marks out of 50 in first two unit test. Find the minimum marks, he should get in third test to have an average of atleast 25 marks.

(ii) Mohit buys x pens of ₹ 20 and y registers of ₹ 40. The total amount spent by him is ₹ 190. How to represent given statement in linear inequality?

(iii) Find the inequality, when a boy wants to cut three lengths from a single ribbon of length 51 cm. The second length is to be 3 cm longer than the shortest and the third length is to be 5 times of the shortest.

(iv) Find all pairs of consecutive even positive integers, both of which are larger than 3 such that their sum is less than 20.

(v) A manufacturer has 500 L of a 28% solution of acid. How many litres of a 10% acid solution must be added to it so that acid content in the resulting mixture will be more than 20%?

Assertion-Reason Questions

The following questions consist of two statements – Assertion (A) and Reason (R). Answer these questions by selecting the appropriate option given below.

(a) Both (A) and (R) are true and (R) is correct explanation of (A)

(b) Both (A) and (R) are true but (R) is not the correct explanation of (A)

(c) (A) is true but (R) is false

(d) (A) is false but (R) is true

1. **Assertion** (A) The inequality $ax + by < 0$ is strict inequality.

Reason (R) The inequality $ax + b \geq 0$ is slack inequality.

(a) ☐ (b) ☐ (c) ☐ (d) ☐

2. **Assertion** (A) For $x \in R$ and $x < 4$, then $x - 4 < 0$.

Reason (R) A number can be added or subtracted from both sides of an inequality without changing its sign.

(a) ☐ (b) ☐ (c) ☐ (d) ☐

3. **Assertion** (A) If $a < b, c < 0$, then $\frac{a}{c} < \frac{b}{c}$.

Reason (R) If both sides are divided by the same negative quantity, then the inequality is reversed.

(a) ☐ (b) ☐ (c) ☐ (d) ☐

4. **Assertion** (A) Solution set of the inequality $x - 3 \le 4, x \in N$ is $\{1, 2, 3, 4, 5, 6, 7\}$.

Reason (R) Solution set of an inequality in x is the set of all values of x satisfying the inequality.

(a) ☐ (b) ☐ (c) ☐ (d) ☐

5. **Assertion** (A) $|3x - 5| > 10 \Rightarrow x \in \left(-\infty, \frac{-5}{3}\right) \cup (5, \infty)$

Reason (R) The region containing all the solutions of an inequality is called the solution region.

(a) ☐ (b) ☐ (c) ☐ (d) ☐

6. **Assertion** (A) The inequality $4x + 3y \ge 8$ is the linear inequality.

Reason (R) The solution of $4x + 3 > 15$, when $x \in R$, is $(3, \infty)$.

(a) ☐ (b) ☐ (c) ☐ (d) ☐

7. **Assertion** (A) Graphical solution set of the inequality $x - 4 < 3, x \in R$ is

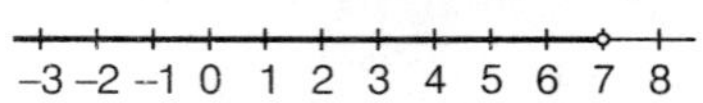

Reason (R) Inequality $2x + 5 < 6$ is a slack inequality.

(a) ☐ (b) ☐ (c) ☐ (d) ☐

8. **Assertion** (A) If $3x + 8 > 20$, then $x \in \{5, 6, 7, 8, \ldots\}$, where x is an integer.

Reason (R) The solution set of the inequality $5x + 4 < 6x + 8, \forall\, x \in R$ is $[4, \infty)$.

(a) ☐ (b) ☐ (c) ☐ (d) ☐

9. **Assertion** (A) $6x < 42$ is an example of the equation.

Reason (R) Two real numbers or two algebraic expressions related by the symbol '>', '<', '≤' or '≥' form an inequality.

(a) ☐ (b) ☐ (c) ☐ (d) ☐

10. **Assertion** (A) When we multiply (-4) in the following inequality $3x - 2 < 2x$, then the inequality becomes $x < 2$.

Reason (R) When both sides of an inequality multiplied by a negative number, then the inequality is reversed.

(a) ☐ (b) ☐ (c) ☐ (d) ☐

11. **Assertion** (A) When we subtract 4 from both sides in the inequality $3x - \frac{6}{5}x > 8$, then the inequality sign changes.

Reason (R) Equal numbers may be added or subtracted to both sides of an inequality without affecting the sign of inequality.

(a) ☐ (b) ☐ (c) ☐ (d) ☐

Case Based Questions

Case 1 A manufacturing company produces certain goods.The company manager used to record data on daily basis about the cost and revenue of these goods separately. The cost and revenue function of a product are given by $C(x) = 20x + 7000$ and $R(x) = 80x + 1000$ respectively, where x is the number of goods produced and sold.

Based on the above information, answer the following questions.

(i) How many goods must be sold to realise some profit?

(a) $x < 10$ ☐ (b) $x \geq 10$ ☐

(c) $x > 10$ ☐ (d) $x \leq 10$ ☐

(ii) If the cost and revenue functions of a product are given by $C(x) = 4x + 400$ and $R(x) = 6x + 50$ respectively, where x is the number of items produced by the manufacturer, then how many items must be sold to realise some profit?

(a) $x > 175$ ☐ (b) $x < 175$ ☐

(c) $x \geq 175$ ☐ (d) $x \leq 175$ ☐

(iii) If x and b are real numbers. If $b > 0$ and $x < b$, then

(a) x is always positive ☐ (b) x is real number ☐

(c) x is always negative ☐ (d) None of these ☐

Case 2 Shweta is a Psychology student and now a days she is learning about Intelligence Quotient (IQ). She knows the result

$$\text{Intelligence Quotient (IQ)} = \frac{\text{Mental Age (MA)}}{\text{Chronological Age (CA)}} \times 100$$

Based on the above information, answer the following questions.

(i) What could be the range of mental age if a group of children with chronological age of 15 years have the IQ range as $90 \leq \text{IQ} \leq 150$?

(ii) What could be the range of IQ if a group of children with age of 10 years have the mental age range as $8 \leq \text{MA} \leq 16$?

(iii) Find the solution set of the inequality $3x - 5 < x + 7$, where x is a whole number.

Chapter 06

Permutations and Combinations

Scan and take Chapter Test

TOPIC 1

Fundamental Principle of Counting

NCERT Pg 100-104

1. Consider the given problem

Mohan has 3 pants and 2 shirts. How many different pairs of a pant and a shirt can he dress up with? The above problem can be solved using which principle?

____

2. If an event can occur in m different ways and if following it, a second event can occur in n different ways, then the two events in succession can occur in ______________ different ways.

3. Meera has 3 school bags, 4 tiffin boxes and 3 water bottles. In how many ways can she share these items?

(a) 10 ways (b) 4 ways

(c) 36 ways (d) 16 ways

____

4. Which of the following best replaces the 'A' in the below statement?

If two events can exclusively occur in exact m ways and n ways respectively, then either of the two events can occur in $\underline{A}$ ways.

(a) $(m \times n)$ ways (b) $(m - n)$ ways

(c) $(m \div n)$ ways (d) $(m + n)$ ways

____

5. In a cinema hall, there are three entrance doors and two exit doors. In how many ways can a person enter the hall and then come out?

____

*Concepts of all questions bearing * are important for JEE & CUET*

6. The flag of a newly formed forum is in the form □ □ □ of three blocks, each to be coloured differently. If there are six different colours on the whole to choose from, how many such designs are possible?

(a) 120 (b) 576 (c) 6 (d) 320

---

7. State which of the statement is True or False.

(i) There are 10 two digit even numbers, can be formed from the digits 1, 2, 3, 4 and 5, if the digits can be repeated.

True □ False □

(ii) There are 10 two digit even numbers, can be formed from the digits 1, 2, 3, 4 and 5, if the digits cannot be repeated.

True □ False □

8. How many words (with or without) meaning of three distinct letters of the English alphabets are there?

---

9. There are 10 buses running between Delhi and Agra. The number of ways by which a man can go from Delhi to Agra and return by a different bus is

(a) 10 (b) 20 (c) 75 (d) 90

---

10. Match the following column.

Column I		Column II
A. Total 3-digit numbers with no digit repeated.	1.	4536
B. Total 4-digit numbers with distinct digits	2.	36
C. Total 4-digits numbers	3.	648
D. Total 2-digit even numbers not having 0 at unit's place	4.	9000

Choose the correct option?

(a) A → 1, B → 3, C → 2, D → 4

(b) A → 4, B → 3, C → 2, D → 1

(c) A → 1, B → 2, C → 3, D → 4

(d) A → 3, B → 1, C → 4, D → 2

11. A coin is tossed 3 times and the outcomes are recorded. How many possible outcomes are there?

TOPIC 2

Permutation

NCERT Pg 104-114

12. State whether the statement is True or False.

$n(n-1)(n-2)....(n-r+1)$ can be denoted by ^nP_r.

True ☐ False ☐

13. State whether the statement is True or False.

$n! = 1 \times 2 \times 3 \times ..... (n-1) \times n$

True ☐ False ☐

14. Evaluate

(i) $0!$ ________

(ii) $5!$ ________

(iii) $6!$ ________

(iv) $7! - 2!$ ________

(v) $\frac{5!}{2!}$ ________

(vi) $\frac{10!}{8!\,2!}$ ________

15. If $n! : 5! :: n(n-1)(n-2)! : \underline{A}$, which of the following best replaces $\underline{A}$?

(a) $5(5-1)(5-2)!$

(b) $5 \times 4!$

(c) $5 \times 4 \times 3 \times 2 \times 1$

(d) $5 \times 4 \times 3 \times 2!$

____

16. What will be the value of $\frac{n!}{r!(n-r)!}$ if $n = 4$ and $r = 2$?

(a) 3 (b) 4 (c) 6 (d) 5

____

17. Find the value of x if

(i) $\frac{1}{6!} + \frac{1}{8!} = \frac{x}{10!}$ ________

(ii) $10! \times (x) + 9! \times (x) = 12!$ ________

18. Find the value of n such that

(i) $^{2n}P_3 = 100 \times {}^nP_2$ ________

(ii) $^{20}P_n = 13 \times {}^{20}P_{n-1}$ ________

(iii) $^nP_5 = 42\ {}^nP_3,\ n > 4$ ________

(iv) $\frac{^{n}P_4}{^{n-1}P_4} = \frac{5}{3}, n > 4$ ______

(v) $\frac{^{15}P_{n-1}}{^{16}P_{n-2}} = \frac{3}{4}$ ______

19. What are the number of ways in which a chairman and a vice-chairman can be chosen from against a group of 12 persons, assuming that one person cannot hold more than one position (repetition not allowed).

(a) 154 (b) 120 (c) 132 (d) 160

______

20. The number of permutations of n objects, where P_1 objects are of one kind, P_2 are of second kind, ... P_k are of kth kind and the rest, if any, are of different kind, is

(a) $\frac{n}{P_1 P_2 \dots P_k}$

(b) $\frac{n!}{P_1! P_2! \dots P_k!}$

(c) $n(n-1)(n-2) \dots nk$

(d) $n(n-2)(n-4) \dots n2k$

______

***21.** What is the required number of permutations for the letters of the word 'ROOT' if the permutation for both O taken as same O for both places?

______

22. The total number of different permutations for the word 'INSTITUTE' will be

(a) 34040 (b) 32161

(c) 36234 (d) 30240

______

***23.** How many words with or without meaning can be formed by using the letters of the word 'DELHI', using each letter exactly once?

______

***24.** The number of different 4 letter words (may be meaningless) that can be formed from the letters of the word 'NUMBERS', is

(a) 812 (b) 840

(c) 807 (d) 842

______

25. In how many ways can 5 children stand in a queue?

______

26. Match the following columns.

	Column I		Column II
A.	Permutations of 7 objects taken 3 at a time	1.	60480
B.	Permutations of 4 objects taken 2 at a time	2.	840
C.	Permutations of 9 objects taken 6 at a time	3.	12
D.	Permutations of 7 objects taken 4 at a time	4.	210

Choose the correct option?

(a) $A \to 4, B \to 3, C \to 2, D \to 1$

(b) $A \to 2, B \to 1, C \to 3, D \to 4$

(c) $A \to 4, B \to 3, C \to 1, D \to 2$

(d) $A \to 1, B \to 2, C \to 3, D \to 4$

27. In how many ways can 10 books be arranged on a shelf so that a particular pair of books shall be

(i) always together? ____________________

(ii) never together? ____________________

28. There are 6 English, 4 Sanskrit and 5 Hindi books. In how many ways can they be arranged on a shelf, so as to keep all the books of the same language together?

(a) $6 \times 360 \times 12 \times 75$

(b) $6 \times 720 \times 12 \times 10$

(c) $6 \times 120 \times 12 \times 75$

(d) $6 \times 720 \times 24 \times 120$

____

***29.** How many permutations can be made out of the letters of the word 'TRIANGLE' which begin with T and end with E?

____

***30.** In how many ways can the letters of the word 'PENCIL' be arranged so that N is always next to E?

(a) 20 ways (b) 60 ways

(c) 120 ways (d) 40 ways

____

31. How many permutations can be formed by the letters of the word 'VOWELS', when

(i) all vowels come together? ____________________

(ii) all consonants come together? ____________________

TOPIC 3

Combination

NCERT Pg 114-119

32. ${}^4P_2 = {}^4C_2 \times \underline{A}$

A can be best replaced by

(a) 4! (b) 2! (c) 3! (d) 1!

____

***33.** If ${}^nP_r = 840$ and ${}^nC_r = 35$, then find r.

(a) 4 (b) 2 (c) 1 (d) 5

____

34. ${}^nC_{n-r} = \frac{A}{B} = \frac{C}{D} = \underline{E}$

i.e. selecting r objects out of n objects is same as rejecting $(n-r)$ objects.

$A =$ ______________________________

$B =$ ______________________________

$C =$ ______________________________

$D =$ ______________________________

$E =$ ______________________________

35. Evaluate the following

(i) ${}^{14}C_3$ ______________________________

(ii) ${}^{100}C_{99}$ ______________________________

(iii) ${}^{35}C_{35}$ ______________________________

(iv) ${}^{30}C_0$ ______________________________

36. If $\frac{{}^{2n}C_3}{{}^nC_3} = \frac{11}{1}$, then find the value of n.

____

37 Choose the correct option.

(i) ${}^nC_r + {}^nC_{r-1}$ is equal to

(a) ${}^{n-1}C_r$ (b) ${}^{2n+1}C_r$ (c) ${}^{n+1}C_r$ (d) ${}^nC_r$

____

(ii) ${}^{13}C_6 + {}^{13}C_5$ is equal to

(a) 2002 (b) 3003 (c) 3000 (d) 3001

____

38. Answer the following :

(i) If ${}^nC_{16} = {}^nC_{14}$, then find ${}^nC_{27}$.

(ii) If ${}^nC_{10} = {}^nC_{12}$, then find ${}^{23}C_n$.

***39.** What is the value of n and r, if ${}^nC_r : {}^{n-1}C_{r-1} = 6 : 3$ and ${}^{n+1}C_{r+1} : {}^nC_r = 11 : 6$?

40. The number of ways in which 3 black and 3 red balls can be selected from a bag containing 6 black and 5 red balls, is

(a) 100 (b) 150 (c) 200 (d) 50

41. In how many ways 2 cards can be chosen from a pack of 52 playing cards, so as to get face cards as result?

42. If there are 10 persons in a meeting and if each two of them shake hands with each other. How many hand shakes happen in the party?

(a) 40 (b) 45 (c) 50 (d) 44

43. In how many ways can a cricket team of 11 players be selected out of 15 players if two particular players are always be included?

***44.** What is the number of ways of choosing 6 cards from a pack of 52 playing cards? In how many of these three are red cards and three are black cards?

(a) 6850000 (b) 683200 (c) 6760000 (d) 5760000

45. A committee of 5 is chosen from 10 men and 6 women. Determine the number of ways of selecting the committee if

(i) there are no restrictions

(ii) it must contain 3 men and 2 women

(iii) it must contain all men

(iv) it must contain atleast 3 men

(v) it must contain atleast one of each sex

46. Find the number of ways of selecting 6 balls from 5 red balls, 6 white balls and 4 blue balls if each selection consists of 2 balls of each colour.

***47.** A committee of 4 members has to be formed from 5 boys and 5 girls. In how many ways can this be done when the committee consists of exactly 2 girls?

(a) 100 (b) 200 (c) 50 (d) 10

48. How many diagonals are there in a polygon of n sides?

49. In how many ways can 4 people be selected from 10 if

(i) one person is always in the selection? ______

(ii) 2 are excluded from every selection? ______

(iii) 1 is always included and 2 are always excluded? ______

50. The number of ways in which 5 white balls and 3 black balls be arranged in a row so that no two black balls are together, are

51. A man has 6 friends. In how many ways can be invite one or more to a party?

(a) 62 (b) 61 (c) 63 (d) 69

52. There are 12 distinct points $A, B, C, D, \ldots, L$ on a circle. Lines are drawn between each pair of points.

(i) How many lines

(a) are there in total? ______

(b) pass through B? ______

(ii) How many triangles

(a) are determined by the lines? ______

(b) have one vertex B? ______

53. There are four types of cards in the pack of 52 cards. Two types in black colour and other two types in red colour.

In the four types (heart, diamond, club and spade) we will have 13 cards in each type.

It consists of 26 black cards, 26 red cards, 4 ace cards, 4 jack cards, 4 queeen cards, 4 king cards and 12 face cards.

On the basis of above information, answer the following questions.

(i) Find the number of ways of choosing 4 cards of the same suit.

(a) 2860 (b) 2800 (c) 3800 (d) 2855

(ii) Find the number of ways of choosing 4 cards that belong to four different suits.

(a) 13^1 (b) 13^2 (c) 13^3 (d) 13^4

(iii) Find the number of ways of choosing 4 face cards.

(a) 499 (b) 495 (c) 490 (d) 300

(iv) Find the number of ways of choosing 4 cards in which two are red and two are black cards.

(a) 105625 (b) 105600 (c) 10500 (d) 60051

(v) Find the number of ways of choosing 4 cards of the same colour.

(a) 29900 (b) 2900 (c) 29990 (d) 2899

Assertion-Reason Questions

The following questions consist of two statements – Assertion (A) and Reason (R). Answer these questions by selecting the appropriate option given below.

(a) Both (A) and (R) are true and (R) is correct explanation of (A)

(b) Both (A) and (R) are true but (R) is not the correct explanation of (A)

(c) (A) is true but (R) is false

(d) (A) is false but (R) is true

1. **Assertion** (A) If $P(9, r) = 3024$, then the value of r is 4.

Reason (R) $P(n, r) = {}^nP_r = \frac{n!}{(n-r)!}, 0 \le r \le n.$

(a) ☐ (b) ☐ (c) ☐ (d) ☐

2. **Assertion** (A) If ${}^{2n}C_3 : {}^nC_3$ is equal to 11 : 1, then the value of $n = 5$.

Reason (R) ${}^nC_r = \frac{n!}{r!(n-r)!}$

(a) ☐ (b) ☐ (c) ☐ (d) ☐

3. **Assertion** (A) A five digit number divisible by 3 is to be formed using the digits 0, 1, 2, 3, 4 and 5 with repetition. The total numbers formed are 216.

Reason (R) If the sum of digits of any number is divisible by 3, then the number must be divisible by 3.

(a) ☐ (b) ☐ (c) ☐ (d) ☐

4. **Assertion** (A) If the letters W, I, F, E are arranged in a row in all possible ways and the words (with or without meaning) so formed are written as in a dictionary, then the word WIFE occurs in the 24th position.

Reason (R) The number of ways of arranging four distinct objects taken all at a time is $C(4, 4)$.

(a) ☐ (b) ☐ (c) ☐ (d) ☐

5. **Assertion** (A) The number of ways of disturbing 10 identical balls in 4 distinct boxes such that no box is empty is ${}^9C_3$.

Reason (R) The number of ways of choosing any 3 places from 9 different places is ${}^9C_3$.

(a) ☐ (b) ☐ (c) ☐ (d) ☐

6. **Assertion** (A) Product of five consecutive natural numbers is divisible by 4!.

Reason (R) Product of n consecutive natural numbers is divisible by $(n+1)!$.

(a) ☐ (b) ☐ (c) ☐ (d) ☐

7. **Assertion** (A) If a polygon has 44 diagonals, then the number of its sides is 11.

Reason (R) When diagonals are formed by joining any two non-adjacent vertices of a polygon. Then, the total number of diagonals is ${}^nC_2 - n$.

(a) ☐ (b) ☐ (c) ☐ (d) ☐

8. **Assertion** (A) Total number of three digit numbers formed using the digits 1, 2, 3, 4 and 5, when repetition is allowed, is 125.

Reason (R) Total number of three digit even numbers formed using the digits 1, 2, 3, 4 and 5, when repetition is allowed, is 50.

(a) ☐ (b) ☐ (c) ☐ (d) ☐

9. **Assertion** (A) If ${}^nC_{15} = {}^nC_5$, then $n = 20$.

Reason (R) ${}^nC_p = {}^nC_q$, if and only if $p = q$ or $n = p + q$.

(a) ☐ (b) ☐ (c) ☐ (d) ☐

10. **Assertion** (A) Total number of lines formed using 10 points and no three of which are collinear, is 40.

Reason (R) Selection of r different things out of n things can be done in ${}^nC_r$ ways.

(a) ☐ (b) ☐ (c) ☐ (d) ☐

Case Based Questions

Case 1 Five students Aman, Ram, Shiva, Vijay and Surya are sitting in a play ground in a line.

Based on the above information, answer the following questions.

(i) Total number of ways of sitting arrangement of five students is

(a) 240 ☐ (b) 160 ☐ (c) 120 ☐ (d) None of these ☐

(ii) Total number of arrangements of sitting if Aman and Shiva sit together, is

(a) 48 ☐ (b) 60 ☐ (c) 72 ☐ (d) 120 ☐

(iii) Total number of arrangements if Ram is sitting in the middle, is

(a) 6 ☐ (b) 12 ☐ (c) 24 ☐ (d) 36 ☐

Case 2 Two friends Rahul and Chetan have just learnt the concept of permutations and combinations. They started playing games on the same place. They are asking each other some questions.

(i) If all the letters in the word 'GAME' are arranged as in a dictionary, then what would be the rank of the word 'MEGA'?

(ii) If all the letters of the word 'SUCCESS' are arranged as in a dictionary, what would be the word at 361th rank?

(iii) How many ways are there to arrange the letters in the word 'GARDEN' with the vowels in alphabetical order?

COMPETITION EDGE UP

1. Number of ways of arranging 8 identical books into 4 identical shelves, where any number of shelves may remain empty is equal to **[JEE Main 2024]**
   (a) 12 ☐
   (b) 16 ☐
   (c) 15 ☐
   (d) 18 ☐

2. Let $\alpha = \dfrac{(4!)!}{(4!)^{3!}}$ and $\beta = \dfrac{(5!)!}{(5!)^{4!}}$. Then, **[JEE Main 2024]**
   (a) $\alpha \in N$ and $\beta \in N$ ☐
   (b) $\alpha \notin N$ and $\beta \notin N$ ☐
   (c) $\alpha \in N$ and $\beta \notin N$ ☐
   (d) $\alpha \notin N$ and $\beta \in N$ ☐

3. If all the words with or without meaning made using all the letters of the word 'NAGPUR' are arranged as in a dictionary, then the word at 315 th position in this arrangement is **[JEE Main 2024]**
   (a) NRAGUP ☐
   (b) NRAPUG ☐
   (c) NRAPGU ☐
   (d) NRAGPU ☐

4. All the letters of the word 'GTWENTY' are written in all possible ways with or without meaning and these words are written as in a dictionary. The serial number of the word 'GTWENTY' is .... **[JEE Main 2024]**

5. The number of ways five alphabets can be chosen from the alphabets of the word MATHEMATICS, where the chosen alphabets are not necessarily distinct, is equal to **[JEE Main 2024]**
   (a) 177 ☐
   (b) 181 ☐
   (c) 179 ☐
   (d) 175 ☐

6. If n is the number of ways five different employees can sit into four indistinguishable offices where any office may have any number of persons including zero, then n is equal to **[JEE Main 2024]**
   (a) 51 ☐
   (b) 43 ☐
   (c) 53 ☐
   (d) 47 ☐

7. The number of ways in which 21 identical apples can be distributed among three children such that each child gets at least 2 apples, is **[JEE Main 2024]**
   (a) 130 ☐
   (b) 406 ☐
   (c) 136 ☐
   (d) 142 ☐

8. Let $0 \le r \le n$. If ${}^{n+1}C_{r+1} : {}^{n}C_{r} : {}^{n-1}C_{r-1} = 55 : 35 : 21$, then $2n + 5r$ is equal to **[JEE Main 2024]**
   (a) 62 ☐
   (b) 60 ☐
   (c) 50 ☐
   (d) 55 ☐

9. If for some $m, n : {}^6C_m + 2({}^6C_{m+1}) + {}^6C_{m+2} > {}^8C_3$ and ${}^{n-1}P_3 : {}^nP_4 = 1 : 8$, then ${}^nP_{m+1} + {}^{n+1}C_m$ is equal to **[JEE Main 2024]**

(a) 372
(b) 376
(c) 380
(d) 384

10. ${}^{n-1}C_r = (k^2 - 8)\,{}^nC_{r+1}$, if and only if **[JEE Main 2024]**

(a) $2\sqrt{2} < k \le \sqrt{3}$
(b) $2\sqrt{3} < k \le 3\sqrt{2}$
(c) $2\sqrt{2} < k < 2\sqrt{3}$
(d) $2\sqrt{3} < k < 3\sqrt{3}$

11. The number of triangles whose vertices are at the vertices of a regular octagon but none of whose sides is a side of the octagon, is **[JEE Main 2024]**

(a) 16
(b) 56
(c) 24
(d) 48

12. The number of 3-digit numbers, formed using the digits 2, 3, 4, 5 and 7. When the repetition of digits is not allowed and which are not divisible by 3 is equal to …….. . **[JEE Main 2024]**

13. The total number of words (with or without meaning) that can be formed out the letters of the word 'DISTRIBUTION' taken four at a time, is equal to ……… **[JEE Main 2024]**

14. The total number of three-digit numbers, divisible by 3, which can be formed using the digits 1, 3, 5, 8, if repetition of digits is allowed, is **[JEE Main 2023]**

(a) 22
(b) 18
(c) 20
(d) 21

15. The number of five digit numbers, greater than 40000 and divisible by 5, which can be formed using the digits 0, 1, 3, 5, 7 and 9 without repetition, is equal to **[JEE Main 2023]**

(a) 72
(b) 132
(c) 96
(d) 120

16. The number of arrangements of the letters of the word 'INDEPENDENCE' in which all the vowels always occur together is **[JEE Main 2023]**

(a) 16800
(b) 33600
(c) 18000
(d) 14800

17. The number of integers, greater than 7000 that can be formed, using the digits 3, 5, 6, 7, 8 without repetition, is **[JEE Main 2023]**

(a) 120
(b) 220
(c) 48
(d) 168

18. All words, with or without meaning, are made using all the letters of the word MONDAY. These words are written as in a dictionary with serial numbers. The serial number of the word MONDAY is **[JEE Main 2023]**

(a) 327
(b) 328
(c) 324
(d) 326

19. If the letters of the word MATHS are permuted and all possible words so formed are arranged as in a dictionary with serial numbers, then the serial number of the word THAMS is **[JEE Main 2023]**

(a) 104
(b) 102
(c) 103
(d) 101

20. If the number of words, with or without meaning, which can be made using all the letters of the word MATHEMATICS in which C and S do not come together, is $(6!)k$, then k is equal to **[JEE Main 2023]**

(a) 5670
(b) 1890
(c) 945
(d) 2835

Chapter 07

Binomial Theorem

Scan and take Chapter Test

TOPIC 1

Binomial Theorem for Positive Index

NCERT Pg 126-132

1. Using the observation of Pascal's triangle,

$$(a+b)^7 = {}^7C_0 a^7 + {}^7C_1 a^6 b + {}^7C_2 a^5 b^2 + {}^7C_3 a^4 b^3 + A + {}^7C_5 a^2 b^5 + {}^7C_6 ab^6 + B$$

A and B can be best replaced by

(a) $A = {}^7C_2 a^2 b^5$ and $B = {}^7C_3 a^3 b^4$

(b) $A = {}^7C_4 a^3 b^4$ and $B = {}^7C_7 b^7$

(c) $A = {}^7C_4 a^4 b^2$ and $B = {}^7C_6 a^4 b^4$

(d) $A = {}^7C_4 a^3 b^2$ and $B = {}^7C_5 b^7$

____

2. The number of terms in the expansion of

(i) $(1+2x+x^2)^{20}$ is ______________________________

(ii) $\left(x - \frac{1}{3x}\right)^9$ is ______________________________

(iii) $(4+x^2-4x)^4$ is ______________________________

3. If $(x+y)^n = {}^nC_0 x^n + {}^nC_1 x^{n-1} y + {}^nC_2 x^{n-2} y^2 + \dots + {}^nC_{n-1} x y^{n-1} + {}^nC_n y^n$, then what is the value of $(x-y)^n$? ______________________________

4. Replacing x by 1 and y by x in binomial expansion of $(x+y)^n$, we have $(1+x)^n =$

______________________________.

5. The binomial expansion $(1+x)^n = {}^nC_0 + {}^nC_1 x + {}^nC_2 x^2 + \dots\dots + {}^nC_n x^n$

If $x = 1$, then $2^n = {}^nC_0 + {}^nC_1 + {}^nC_2 + \dots + {}^nC_n$.

True ☐ False ☐

Concepts of all questions bearing * are important for JEE & CUET

6. Using binomial theorem, expand the following expressions.

(i) $\left(x^2 - \frac{2}{x}\right)^3$ ________________

(ii) $(x^2 + 2y)^5$ ________________

(iii) $(2x - 3y)^4$ ________________

(iv) $\left(x + \frac{1}{x}\right)^4$ ________________

(v) $(2 - x^2)^6$ ________________

(vi) $(2x^2 - ax + 2a^2)^3$ ________________

7. Find the values of the following expressions.

(i) $(99)^4$ ________________

(ii) $(10.1)^5$ ________________

8. The value of $(0.98)^{-3}$ upto 4 decimal places is

(a) 1.0624 (b) 10.6240 (c) 1.0240 (d) 1.2640

____

9. State True or False.

(i) $(1.01)^{1000000} > 10000$

True ☐ False ☐

(ii) $(101)^{50} > (100)^{50} + (99)^{50}$

True ☐ False ☐

10. Evaluate the following

(i) Expand $(a+b)^3 - (a-b)^3$. Hence, evaluate $(\sqrt{5}+\sqrt{3})^3 - (\sqrt{5}-\sqrt{3})^3$ ____________.

(ii) Expand $(x+y)^6 - (x-y)^6$. Hence, evaluate $(\sqrt{2}+1)^6 - (\sqrt{2}-1)^6$ ____________.

(iii) Evaluate $(\sqrt{2}-1)^5 + (\sqrt{2}+1)^5$ ____________.

11. What will be the remainder left, when $6^n - 5n$ is divided by 25? [use binomial theorem]

____

12. If a and b are two distinct integers, then $a^n - b^n$ is divisible by $(a-b) \ \forall \ n \in N$.

True ☐ False ☐

13. Choose the correct answer.

$$\sum_{r=0}^{n} 3^r \cdot {}^nC_r = A$$

Which correct replaces A.

(a) 2^n (b) $2! \, 4^n$ (c) $3! \, 2^n$ (d) 4^n

____

Assertion-Reason Questions

The following questions consist of two statements – Assertion (A) and Reason (R). Answer these questions by selecting the appropriate option given below.
(a) Both (A) and (R) are true and (R) is correct explanation of (A)
(b) Both (A) and (R) are true but (R) is not the correct explanation of (A)
(c) (A) is true but (R) is false
(d) (A) is false but (R) is true

1. **Assertion** (A) $(x+2)^7 = {}^7C_0x^7 + 2\,{}^7C_1x^6 + 4\,{}^7C_2x^5 + 8\,{}^7C_3x^4 + 16\,{}^7C_4x^3 + 32\,{}^7C_5x^2 + 64\,{}^7C_6x^1 + 128\,{}^7C_7$

   Reason (R) $(a+b)^n = \sum_{r=0}^{n} {}^nC_r a^{n-r} b^r$

   (a) ☐ (b) ☐ (c) ☐ (d) ☐

2. **Assertion** (A) Coefficient of the 10th term in the expansion of $\left(\frac{x}{2}+\frac{2}{x}\right)^{12}$ is $64\ {}^{12}C_9$.

   Reason (R) $(a+b)^n = \sum_{r=0}^{n} {}^nC_r a^r b^{n-r}$

   (a) ☐ (b) ☐ (c) ☐ (d) ☐

3. **Assertion** (A) ${}^nC_0 + {}^nC_1 + {}^nC_2 + \dots + {}^nC_n = 2^n$

   Reason (R) Coefficient of x^{10} in the expansion of $(1+x)^{15}$ is ${}^{15}C_9$.

   (a) ☐ (b) ☐ (c) ☐ (d) ☐

4. **Assertion** (A) $\sum_{r=0}^{n} r \cdot {}^nC_r = n2^{n-1}$

   Reason (R) $\sum_{r=0}^{n} r \cdot {}^nC_r x^r = n(1+x)^{n-1}x$

   (a) ☐ (b) ☐ (c) ☐ (d) ☐

5. **Assertion** (A) The number of terms in the expansion $(a+b)^{13}$ is 13.

   Reason (R) The number of terms in the binomial expansion of $(x+y)^n$ is equal to $n+1$.

   (a) ☐ (b) ☐ (c) ☐ (d) ☐

6. **Assertion** (A) The expansion of $\left(x^2+\frac{3}{x}\right)^4$, $x \neq 0$ is $x^8 + 12x^5 + 54x^2 + \frac{108}{x} + \frac{81}{x^4}$.

   Reason (R) The array in which coefficients of the binomial expansions are arranged is called Pascal's triangle.

   (a) ☐ (b) ☐ (c) ☐ (d) ☐

7. Assertion (A) The 3rd term in $(2x-y)^7$ is $672x^5y^2$.

Reason (R) If n is odd, then $C_0 - C_1 + C_2 - \dots + (-1)^n C_n = 0$.

(a) ☐ (b) ☐ (c) ☐ (d) ☐

8. Assertion (A) The value of $(a-b)^n$ is ${}^nC_0 a^n - {}^nC_1 a^{n-1}b + {}^nC_2 a^{n-2}b^2 - \dots + (-1)^n\, {}^nC_n b^n$.

Reason (R) $(a+b)^n = {}^nC_0 a^n + {}^nC_1 a^{n-1}b + {}^nC_2 a^{n-2}b^2 + \dots + {}^nC_{n-1} ab^{n-1} + {}^nC_n b^n$.

(a) ☐ (b) ☐ (c) ☐ (d) ☐

9. Assertion (A) If p and q are two distinct integers, then $p^n - q^n$ is divisible by $(p-q)$, $\forall\, n \in N$.

Reason (R) In the expansion of $(x+a)^n$, the 4th term from the end is ${}^nC_{n-3} x^3 a^{n-3}$.

(a) ☐ (b) ☐ (c) ☐ (d) ☐

Case Based Questions

Case 1 An algebraic expression, $(a+b)^n$ containing two terms is called a binomial expression. The number of terms in a binomial expansion is always one greater than index.

On the basis of the above information, answer the following questions.

(i) The number of terms in the expansion of $(1-x)^5$ is

(a) 6 ☐ (b) 5 ☐ (c) 10 ☐ (d) 4 ☐

(ii) The number of terms in the expansion of $(4+x^2+4x)^3$ is

(a) 5 ☐ (b) 6 ☐ (c) 7 ☐ (d) 8 ☐

(iii) The number of terms in the expansion of $(1+14x+49x^2)^{60}$

(a) 22 ☐ (b) 101 ☐ (c) 121 ☐ (d) 300 ☐

Case 2 Two friends Aman and Utkarsh have just learnt the concept of Binomial expansion and its properties. They started asking questions to each other.

Based on the above information, answer the following questions.

(i) Find the coefficient of y in the expansion of $\left(y^2 + \frac{c}{y}\right)^5$.

____

(ii) Find the coefficient of x^3y^4 in $(2x+3y^2)^5$.

____

(iii) Find the number of terms in the binomial expansion of $(1+3x+3x^2+x^3)^5$.

____

COMPETITION CONNECT

General and Middle Terms [NCERT (Old) Pg. 167-170]

1. Determine the following terms.

   (i) General term in the expansion of $\left(y-\frac{1}{y}\right)^{30}$ is ________

   (ii) The 6th term in the expansion of $\left(\frac{4x}{5}-\frac{5}{2x}\right)^{9}$ is ________

   (iii) The 10th term in the binomial expansion of $\left(2x^2+\frac{1}{x}\right)^{12}$ is ________

2. If $a=1$ in the expansion of $(2+a)^{50}$, then which terms will give equal value?

   (a) 15th and 16th terms
   (b) 16th and 17th terms
   (c) 17th and 18th terms
   (d) 19th and 20th terms

   ____

3. If the value of x, a and n are 1, 2 and 7 respectively in the expansion of $(x+a)^n$, then match the following columns.

Column I		Column II	
(A)	T_3	1.	14
(B)	T_4	2.	280
(C)	T_5	3.	560
(D)	T_2	4.	84

   Which one is the correct option?

   (a) A → 4, B → 3, C → 2, D → 1
   (b) A → 1, B → 2, C → 3, D → 4
   (c) A → 4, B → 2, C → 3, D → 1
   (d) A → 4, B → 1, C → 3, D → 2

4. If the 6th, 7th and 8th terms in the expansion of $(x+a)^n$ are respectively 112, 7 and $\frac{1}{4}$. Find x, a and n.

   ____

5. In the binomial expansion $(a+b)^n$, the coefficients of the 5th and 9th terms are equal to each other. The value of n is ________

*6. Using binomial expansion, find the particular coefficient in the following.

   (i) The coefficient of x^6y^2 in the expansion of $(x+y)^8$ is ________

   (ii) The coefficient of x^{10} in the binomial expansion of $\left(2x^2-\frac{3}{x}\right)^{11}$ is ________

   (iii) The coefficient of a^6b^5 in the expansion of $(3a-2b)^{11}$ is ________

***7.** Find the coefficient a of the following term in the expansion of the binomial. [answer without simplifying a]

	Binomial	Term	a
(i)	$(x+3)^{12}$	ax^5	________
(ii)	$(x-2y)^{10}$	ax^8y^2	________
(iii)	$(z^2-t)^{10}$	az^4t^8	________
(iv)	$(3x-4y)^8$	ax^6y^2	________

8. In the expansion of $(3+x)^6$, find the following.

(i) General term ________

(ii) Total number of terms in the expansion ________

(iii) Middle term in the expansion ________

(iv) Coefficient of 3rd term ________

***9.** If a, b, c and d in any binomial expansion be the 6th, 7th, 8th and 9th terms respectively, then $\dfrac{b^2-ac}{c^2-bd}=\dfrac{A}{B}$.

Replace A and B with which suits best.

(a) $A = 4a$ and $B = 2c$
(b) $A = 3a$ and $B = 4c$
(c) $A = 4a$ and $B = 3c$
(d) $A = 4c$ and $B = 3a$

____

10. Answer the following.

(i) If the middle term of $\left(\dfrac{1}{x}+x\sin x\right)^{10}$ is equal to $7\dfrac{7}{8}$, then the value of x is

____

(ii) If the middle term in the expansion of $\left(\dfrac{P}{2}+2\right)^8$ is 1120, then the value of P is

____

*(iii) If the coefficients of $(2r+1)$th and $(r+2)$th terms in the expansion of $(1+x)^{43}$ are equal, then value of r is ________

(iv) If the coefficients of $(2r+4)$th and $(r-2)$th terms in the expansion of $(1+x)^{18}$ are equal, then the value of r is ________

***11.** In the binomial expansion of $(1+x)^n$, the coefficient of 5th, 6th and 7th terms are in AP. Find all the values of n for which this can happen.

____

***12.** If a and b denote respectively, the coefficients of x^m and x^n in the expansion of $(1+x)^{m+n}$, then the relation between a and b is

(i) $a \neq b$

Yes ☐ No ☐

(ii) $a = b$

Yes ☐ No ☐

***13.** The positive value of m is 3 for which the coefficient of x^2 in the expansion of $(1+x)^m$ is 3.

True ☐ False ☐

14. For what value of a, the coefficients of x^2 and x^3 in the expansion of $(3+ax)^9$ are equal.

***15.** If n is a positive integer, what is the coefficient of x^{-1} in the expansion of $(1+x)^n\left(1+\frac{1}{x}\right)^n$?

***16.** If in the expansion of $(1-x)^{2n-1}$, the coefficient of x^r is denoted by a_r, then the value of $a_{r-1} + a_{2n-r}$ will be

(a) 2 (b) 1 (c) 0 (d) -1

***17.** What is the coefficient of x^5 in the expansion of $(1+2x)^6(1-x)^7$?

***18.** If in the expansion of $(1+x)^n$, the coefficients of pth and qth terms are equal, then what is the relation between p, q and n?

(a) $p+q=n$ (b) $p+q=n+2$

(c) $p-q=n+1$ (d) $p-q+n=2$

***19.** If in the expansion of $(1+x)^n$,

(i) the coefficients of three consecutive terms are 56, 70 and 56, then find the position of the terms of these coefficients. ______

(ii) the coefficients of three consecutive terms are 76, 95 and 76, then find the relation between n and r. ______

20. In the expansion of $(x+a)^n$,

(i) rth term from the end is ${}^nC_{n-r}x^{r-1}a^{n-r+1}$

True ☐ False ☐

(ii) 4th term from the end is ${}^nC_{n-2}x^2a^{n-2}$

True ☐ False ☐

21. What will be the ratio of 5th term from the beginning to the 5th term from the end in the expansion of $\left(\sqrt[4]{2}+\frac{1}{\sqrt[4]{3}}\right)^{10}$?

(a) $\sqrt{6}:1$ (b) $1:\sqrt{6}$ (c) $2:\sqrt{3}$ (d) $\sqrt{3}:2$

COMPETITION EDGE UP

1. If the term independent of x in the expansion of $\left(\sqrt{a}x^2 + \frac{1}{2x^3}\right)^{10}$ is 105, then a^2 is equal to **[JEE Main 2024]**

(a) 6 ☐
(b) 4 ☐
(c) 2 ☐
(d) 9 ☐

2. If the constant term in the expansion of $\left(\frac{\sqrt[5]{3}}{x} + \frac{2x}{\sqrt[3]{5}}\right)^{12}$, $x \neq 0$, is $\alpha \times 2^8 \times \sqrt[5]{3}$, then 25α is equal to **[JEE Main 2024]**

(a) 724 ☐
(b) 742 ☐
(c) 639 ☐
(d) 693 ☐

3. Let m and n be the coefficients of seventh and thirteenth terms respectively in the expansion of $\left\{\frac{1}{3}x^{1/3} + \frac{1}{2x^{2/3}}\right\}^{18}$. Then, $\left(\frac{n}{m}\right)^{1/3}$ is **[JEE Main 2024]**

(a) $\frac{9}{4}$ ☐
(b) $\frac{1}{9}$ ☐
(c) $\frac{4}{9}$ ☐
(d) $\frac{1}{4}$ ☐

4. If A denotes the sum of all the coefficients in the expansion of $(1 - 3x + 10x^2)^n$ and B denotes the sum of all the coefficient in the expansion of $(1 + x^2)^n$, then **[JEE Main 2024]**

(a) $B = A^3$ ☐
(b) $A = 3B$ ☐
(c) $3A = B$ ☐
(d) $A = B^3$ ☐

5. The coefficient of x^{70} in $x^2(1 + x)^{98} + x^3(1 + x)^{97} + x^4(1 + x)^{96} + \dots + x^{54}(1 + x)^{46}$ is ${}^{99}C_p - {}^{46}C_q$. Then, a possible value of $p + q$ is **[JEE Main 2024]**

(a) 61 ☐
(b) 55 ☐
(c) 83 ☐
(d) 68 ☐

6. The sum of all rational terms in the expansion of $(2^{1/5} + 5^{1/3})^{15}$ is equal to **[JEE Main 2024]**

(a) 931 ☐
(b) 633 ☐
(c) 3133 ☐
(d) 6131 ☐

7. Suppose $2 - p, p, 2 - \alpha, \alpha$ are the coefficients of four consecutive terms in the expansion of $(1 + x)^n$. Then, the value of $p^2 - \alpha^2 + 6\alpha + 2p$ equals **[JEE Main 2024]**

(a) 8 ☐
(b) 6 ☐
(c) 10 ☐
(d) 4 ☐

8. If the coefficients of x^4, x^5 and x^6 in the expansion of $(1 + x)^n$ are in the arithmetic progression, then the maximum value of n is **[JEE Main 2024]**

(a) 21 ☐
(b) 14 ☐
(c) 7 ☐
(d) 28 ☐

9. The sum of the coefficients of $x^{2/3}$ and $x^{-2/5}$ in the binomial expansion of $\left(x^{2/3} + \frac{1}{2}x^{-2/5}\right)^9$ is **[JEE Main 2024]**

(a) 19/4 ☐
(b) 21/4 ☐
(c) 69/16 ☐
(d) 63/16 ☐

10. If the second, third and fourth terms in the expansion of $(x + y)^n$ are 135, 30 and $\frac{10}{3}$ respectively, then $6(n^3 + x^2 + y)$ is equal to .... **[JEE Main 2024]**

11. If the constant term in the expansion of $(1+2x-3x^3)\left(\frac{3}{2}x^2-\frac{1}{3x}\right)^9$ is p, then 108 p is equal to .... **[JEE Main 2024]**

12. Let $a = 1 + \frac{{}^2C_2}{3!} + \frac{{}^3C_2}{4!} + \frac{{}^4C_2}{5!} + \ldots,$

$b = 1 + \frac{{}^1C_0 + {}^1C_1}{1!} + \frac{{}^2C_0 + {}^2C_1 + {}^2C_2}{2!} + \frac{{}^3C_0 + {}^3C_1 + {}^3C_2 + {}^3C_3}{3!} \ldots$ Then, $\frac{2b}{a^2}$ is equal to .... **[JEE Main 2024]**

13. If the coefficient of x^{30} in the expansion of $\left(1+\frac{1}{x}\right)^6 (1+x^2)^7 (1-x^3)^8$; $x \neq 0$ is α, then $|\alpha|$ equals .... **[JEE Main 2024]**

14. Let the coefficient of x^r in the expansion of $(x+3)^{n-1} + (x+3)^{n-2}(x+2) + (x+3)^{n-3}(x+2)^2 + \ldots + (x+2)^{n-1}$ be α_r. If $\sum_{r=0}^{n} \alpha_r = \beta^n - \gamma^n$, $\beta, \gamma \in N$, then the value of $\beta^2 + \gamma^2$ equals .... **[JEE Main 2024]**

15. In the expansion of $(1+x)(1-x^2)\left(1+\frac{3}{x}+\frac{3}{x^2}+\frac{1}{x^3}\right)^5$, $x \neq 0$, the sum of the coefficients of x^3 and x^{-13} is equal to .... **[JEE Main 2024]**

16. Number of integral terms in the expansion of $\left\{7^{\left(\frac{1}{2}\right)} + 11^{\left(\frac{1}{6}\right)}\right\}^{824}$ is equal to .... **[JEE Main 2024]**

17. Remainder, when $64^{32^{32}}$ is divided by 9 is equal to ... . **[JEE Main 2024]**

18. The coefficient of x^{2012} in the expansion of $(1-x)^{2008}(1+x+x^2)^{2007}$ is equal to .... **[JEE Main 2024]**

19. Fractional part of the number $\frac{4^{2022}}{15}$ is equal to **[JEE Main 2023]**

(a) $\frac{8}{15}$ ☐

(b) $\frac{1}{15}$ ☐

(c) $\frac{14}{15}$ ☐

(d) $\frac{4}{15}$ ☐

20. Let the number $(22)^{2022} + (2022)^{22}$ leave the remainder α when divided by 3 and β when divided by 7. Then, $(\alpha^2 + \beta^2)$ is equal to **[JEE Main 2023]**

(a) 13 ☐

(b) 5 ☐

(c) 10 ☐

(d) 20 ☐

Chapter 08

Sequence and Series

Scan and take Chapter Test

TOPIC 1

Geometric Progression

NCERT Pg 139-145

1. Find the common ratio of the following GP's.

(i) 1, 4, 16, ____________________

(ii) 5, 25, 125, 625, ____________________

***2.** If the number $-\frac{2}{7}$, k and $-\frac{7}{2}$ are in GP, then find the value of k.

____

3. State True or False.

(i) If a, b, c, d and p are different numbers such that $(a^2+b^2+c^2)p^2-2(ab+bc+cd)\,p+(b^2+c^2+d^2)\leq 0$, then a, b, c and d are in GP.

True ☐ False ☐

(ii) If 4th, 10th and 16th terms of the GP are x, y and z, respectively and then x, y and z are in GP.

True ☐ False ☐

4. 10th term and nth term of the GP $-\frac{3}{4}, \frac{1}{2}, -\frac{1}{3},$ are ____________________.

5. Find the term

(i) Which term of the GP 5, 10, 20, 40, ... is 5120 ____________________

(ii) 131072 is which term of the GP 2, 8, 32, ____________________

(iii) $\frac{1}{128}$ is which term of the GP 2, 1, $\frac{1}{2}, \frac{1}{4},$ ____________________

(iv) Which term of the GP 2, $2\sqrt{2}$, 4, ... is 128 ____________________

(v) Which term of the GP 3, 6, 12, 24, ... is 3072 ____________________

____

*Concepts of all questions bearing * are important for JEE & CUET*

6. If the 8th term of a GP is 192 with the common ratio 2, then the 12th term is 3071.

True ☐ False ☐

7. In a GP,

(i) the sum of first three terms is $\frac{39}{10}$ and their product is 1. The first term is

____

(ii) the sum of three numbers is 65 and product is 3375. Three numbers are

____

***8.** If the 5th term of a GP is 2, then the product of its 9 terms are ________________ .

***9.** If 5th, 8th and 11th terms of a GP are p, q and s respectively, then relation between p, q and s is

____

10. The number of bacteria in a certain culture doubles every hour. If there were 30 bacteria present in the culture originally, how many bacteria will be present at the end of 4th hour?

(a) 500 (b) 486 (c) 490 (d) 480

____

11. Consider the following statements and select an appropriate answer.

Statement I $x^3, x^5, x^7,$ ____________________ are in GP, then $a_n = x^{2n+1}$.

Statement II The sum of $x^3, x^5, x^7, \ldots$ is $\frac{x^3(1-x^{2n})}{1-x^2}$.

(a) Both statements are true

(b) Both statements are false

(c) Statement I is false but Statement II is true

(d) Statement II is false but Statement I is true

____

12. Answer the following :

*(i) Find the number of terms of GP $3, 3^2, 3^3, \ldots\ldots\ldots\ldots\ldots\ldots$ which are needed to give the sum of 120.

____

*(ii) The number of terms of the GP $3, \frac{3}{2}, \frac{3}{4}, \ldots\ldots\ldots\ldots\ldots$ which are needed to give the sum $\frac{3069}{512}$.

____

***13.** The sum of the sequence 8,88,888,8888, ... is

(a) $\frac{80}{81}(10^n - 1) - \frac{8}{9}n$ (b) $\frac{80}{81}(10^n + 1) - \frac{8}{9}n$

(c) $\frac{80}{81}(10^n - 1) + \frac{8}{9}n$ (d) $\frac{80}{81}(10^n + 1) + \frac{8}{9}n$

---

14. A person has 2 parents, 4 grandparents, 8 great grandparents and so on. Then, the number of ancestors during the ten generations preceding his own is 2046.

True ☐ False ☐

15. Consider $0.\overline{3} = \frac{3}{10} + \frac{3}{100} + \frac{3}{1000} + \ldots$ which is an infinite geometric series.

(i) Find a ____________________

(ii) Find r ____________________

(iii) Find the sum ____________________

16. A ball takes 1 s to hit the ground when dropped. It then takes 90% of this time to rebound to its new height and this continues until the ball comes to rest.

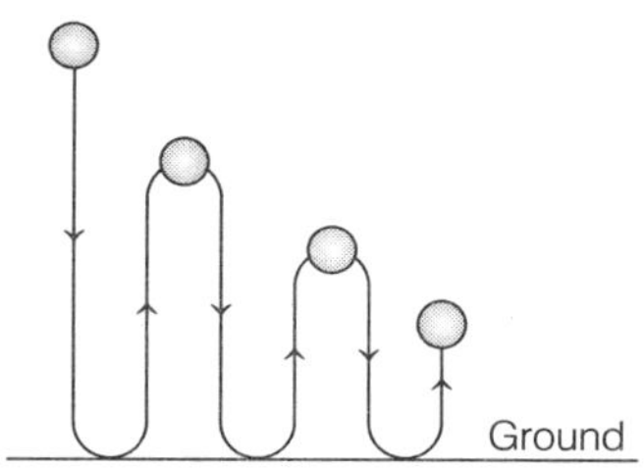

Find the total time of motion ____________________.

17. **Statement I** The two numbers between 3 and 81 so that the resulting sequence is a GP are 9, 27.

Statement II The common ratio r when we insert GM between two numbers a and b, is $r = \left(\frac{b}{a}\right)^n$.

(a) Both statements are true

(b) Both statements are false

(c) Statement I is false but the Statement II is true

(d) Statement II is false but Statement I is true

---

18. The value of n so that $\frac{a^{n+1} + b^{n+1}}{a^n + b^n}$ may be the geometric mean between a and b is

____________________.

***19.** If AM and GM of two positive numbers a and b are 10 and 8 respectively, then numbers are ____________________.

20. State True or False.

(i) The quadratic equation with AM and GM is given by $x^2 - 2\text{AM}x + \text{GM}^2 = 0$.

True ☐ False ☐

(ii) If AM and GM of roots of quadratic equation are 8 and 5 respectively, then the quadratic equation is $x^2 - 16x + 25 = 0$.

True ☐ False ☐

21. State True or False.

(i) The sum of two numbers is 6 times their geometric mean, then the numbers are in the ratio is $(3 + 2\sqrt{2}) : (3 - 2\sqrt{2})$.

True ☐ False ☐

(ii) If A and G be AM and GM, respectively between two positive numbers, then the numbers are $A \pm \sqrt{(A+G)(A-G)}$.

True ☐ False ☐

22. Match the columns.

	Column I		Column II
A.	The geometric mean of a and b	1.	$\sqrt{ab}$
B.	$1^3 + 2^3 + 3^3 \ldots. + n^3$	2.	$\frac{n^2(n+1)^2}{4}$
C.	$1^2 + 2^2 + 3^2 \ldots + n^2$	3.	$\frac{n(n+1)(2n+1)}{6}$
D.	$1 + 2 + 3 + \ldots + n$	4.	$\frac{n(n+1)}{2}$

Which one is the correct option?

(a) A → 2, B → 3, C → 4, D → 1
(b) A → 1, B → 2, C → 3, D → 4
(c) A → 3, B → 1, C → 2, D → 4
(d) A → 1, B → 2, C → 4, D → 3

23. The sum to n terms of the series whose nth term is $n(n + 3)$, is __________.

***24.** The sum to n terms of the series $1 \times 2 + 2 \times 3 + 3 \times 4 +$ __________ is

(a) $\frac{n(n+1)(n+2)}{6}$ (b) $\frac{n(n+3)(n+2)}{3}$

(c) $\frac{n(n+1)(n+2)}{3}$ (d) $\frac{n(n+1)(n+3)}{6}$

Assertion-Reason Questions

The following questions consist of two statements – Assertion (A) and Reason (R). Answer these questions by selecting the appropriate option given below.
(a) Both (A) and (R) are true and (R) is correct explanation of (A)
(b) Both (A) and (R) are true but (R) is not the correct explanation of (A)
(c) (A) is true but (R) is false
(d) (A) is false but (R) is true

1. **Assertion** (A) For $x = \pm 1$, the numbers $-\frac{2}{7}, x, -\frac{7}{2}$ are in G.P.

Reason (R) Three numbers a, b, c are in GP, if $b^2 = ac$.

(a) ☐ (b) ☐ (c) ☐ (d) ☐

2. **Assertion** (A) Sum to n terms of the geometric progression $x^3, x^5, x^7, \ldots (x \neq \pm 1)$ is $\frac{x^3(1-x^{2n})}{(1-x^2)}$.

Reason (R) If a is the first term and r is common ratio of a GP, then sum to n terms is given as $S_n = \frac{a(r^n - 1)}{r-1}, r \neq 1$.

(a) ☐ (b) ☐ (c) ☐ (d) ☐

3. **Assertion** (A) If each term of a GP is multiplied or divided by some fixed non-zero number, the resulting sequence is also a GP.

Reason (R) If A and G are the AM and GM of two positive real numbers a and b, then $A \geq G$.

(a) ☐ (b) ☐ (c) ☐ (d) ☐

4. **Assertion** (A) If the third term of a GP is 4, then the product of its first five terms is 4^5.

Reason (R) Product of first five terms of a GP is given as $a \cdot ar \cdot ar^2 \cdot ar^3 \cdot ar^4$.

(a) ☐ (b) ☐ (c) ☐ (d) ☐

5. **Assertion** (A) If a, b, c are in AP, then $b + c, c + a, a + b$ are in AP.

Reason (R) if a, b, c are in AP, then $10^a, 10^b, 10^c$ are in GP.

(a) ☐ (b) ☐ (c) ☐ (d) ☐

6. **Assertion** (A) If $\frac{2}{3}, k, \frac{5}{8}$ are in AP, then the value of k is $\frac{31}{48}$.

Reason (R) Three numbers a, b, c are in AP, iff $2b = a + c$.

(a) ☐ (b) ☐ (c) ☐ (d) ☐

7. **Assertion** (A) The product of the terms equidistant from the beginning and the end in a geometric progression is always the same.

Reason (R) In a geometric progression, each term is a constant multiple of the previous term.

(a) ☐ (b) ☐ (c) ☐ (d) ☐

8. **Assertion** (A) The arithmetic mean (AM) between two numbers is 34 and their geometric mean is 16, then the numbers are 4 and 64.

Reason (R) For two numbers a and b, $AM = \frac{a+b}{2}$ and $GM = \sqrt{ab}$.

(a) ☐ (b) ☐ (c) ☐ (d) ☐

9. **Assertion** (A) The sum of the series $3 + \frac{3}{2} + \frac{3}{4} + \frac{3}{8}$ is $\frac{45}{8}$.

Reason (R) If the fourth term of a GP is 5, then the product of its first seven terms is 7^5.

(a) ☐ (b) ☐ (c) ☐ (d) ☐

10. **Assertion** (A) In a GP, the product of first n terms is equal to the nth power of the geometric mean of the first and the last term.

Reason (R) In a geometric progression, the ratio of successive terms is constant.

(a) ☐ (b) ☐ (c) ☐ (d) ☐

Case Based Questions

Case 1 Population growth, a small town has a population that follows a geometric progression. The population of the town in the year 2010 was 5000. It is observed that the population doubles every 5 years.

(i) Determine the population in the year 2020.

____

(ii) If this trend continuous, what will be the population in the year 2030?

____

(iii) What will be the population after 25 years from 2010?

____

Case 2 During covid-19, a pharmaceutical company decides to make anti-viral pills at the rate of 1.5 times the pills made every last week.

Based on the above information, answer the following questions.

(i) If they have prepared, 6750 pills in fourth week, then how many pills they have made in first week?

(ii) How many pills will be prepared in nth week?

(iii) In which week they might have prepared 10125 pills?

COMPETITION CONNECT

Topic-1. *n*th Term of an AP [NCERT (Old) Pg. 181-182]

1. Find the first five terms of the sequence if

(i) $a_1 = 3, a_n = 3a_{n-1} + 2, \forall\, n > 1$ ________________.

(ii) $a_n = (-1)^{n-1} 5^{n+1}$ ________________.

2. Find the indicated terms of the sequences.

(i) If *n*th term of the sequence is $a_n = \frac{n^2}{2^n}$, then 7th term is ________________.

(ii) If *n*th term of the sequence is $a_n = \frac{n(n-2)}{n+3}$, then its 20th term is ________________.

(iii) If *n*th term of the sequence is $a_n = \frac{n+1}{n^3}$, then 8th term is ________________.

3. A sequence is defined by $a_n = 3n - 2$.

(i) This is an ________________ sequence.

(ii) Find the first term and common difference ________________

(iii) Find the 50th term ________________

(iv) Find the least term of the sequence, which is greater than 450 ________________

4. If $a_1 = 1$ and $a_n = a_{n-1} + 2, \forall\, n \geq 2$, then the series is

____

5. If *a*, *b* and *c* are in AP, then the value of $(a + 2b - c)(2b + c - a)(a + 2b + c)$ is 16 *abc*.

True ☐ False ☐

6. Find the number of terms in the following.

(i) All natural numbers lying between 100 and 1000, which are multiples of 5 is

____

(ii) The number of odd integers from 1 to 2001 is ________________

(iii) Number of two digit numbers divisible by 3 is ________________

7. Consider the sequence 7, 10, 13, ...

(i) The sequence is an ________________ sequence. (arithmetic/geometric)

(ii) Find the formula for its general term ________________

(iii) Find its 50th term ________________

(iv) Is 68 a member? ________________

8. In an AP, if *m*th term is *n* and *n*th term is *m*, where $m \neq n$, then *p*th term is

(a) $m + n - p$ (b) $m - n + p$ (c) $n - m + p$ (d) $m + n + p$

____

9. 12th term from the end of the sequence 3, 5, 7, 9 ......, 201, is 178.

True ☐ False ☐

____

10. If sum of n terms of an AP is $nP + \frac{1}{2}n(n-1)Q$, then the common difference is Q.

True ☐ False ☐

____

11. Find the numbers.

(i) If the sum of the three numbers in an AP is 24 and the product is 440.

____

(ii) Three numbers are in AP. If the sum of these numbers be 27 and the product is 648.

____

Topic-2. Sum of an Arithmetic Progression [NCERT (Old) Pg. 182-183]

12. Express each of these sums in sigma notation.

(i) 4 + 8 + 12 + 16 + 20 ______________

(ii) 1 + 3 + 5 + 7 + 9 + 11 + 13 ______________

(iii) 9 + 13 + 17 + 21 + 25 ______________

13. In an AP,

(i) if kth term is $5k + 1$, then the sum of first n terms is ______________

(ii) the sum $\sum_{k=1}^{130}(4k+5)$ is ______________

14. If the sum of n terms of an AP is $3n^2 + 5n$ and its mth term is 164, then the value of m is

(a) 25 (b) 26 (c) 24 (d) 27

____

15. The sum of $(m + n)$th and $(m - n)$th terms of an AP is equal to ______________ the mth terms.

16. Find the sum of the given numbers :

(i) The sum of all numbers between 200 and 400 which are divisible by 7.

____

(ii) The sum of integers from 1 to 100 that are divisible by 2 or 5.

____

17. Consider the following statements and choose the appropriate answer.

Statement I If the sum of n terms of an AP is $(pn + qn^2)$, where p and q are constant, then the common difference, $d = 2q$.

Statement II If sum of the AP 25, 22, 19, ______________ is 116, then the number of terms is 9.

(a) Both statements are true
(b) Both statements are false
(c) Statement I is true but Statement II is false
(d) Statement II is true but Statement I is false

---

18. Let the sum of n, $2n$ and $3n$ terms of an AP be S_1, S_2 and S_3, respectively. Then, $3(S_2 - S_1)$ is equal to ______________.

19. If the sum of first p terms of an AP is equal to the sum of first q terms, then the sum of first $(p+q)$ terms is

(a) -1 (b) 0
(c) 1 (d) None of these

---

20. Answer the following :

(i) The sum of n terms of two arithmetic progressions is in the ratio $(3n+8):(7n+15)$. The ratio of their 12th term is ______________

(ii) The sum of n terms of two arithmetic progressions is in the ratio $5n+4:9n+6$. The ratio of their 18th term is ______________

(iii) The ratio of the sum of m and n terms of an AP is $m^2 : n^2$. The ratio of mth and nth terms is ______________

21. **Assertion** The difference between any two consecutive interior angles of a polygon is 5°. If the smallest angle is 120°, then the number of the sides of the polygon is 9.

Reason Sum of all angles of a polygon with n sides is $(n-2)\times 180°$.

(a) Both Assertion and Reason are true and Reason is the correct explanation of Assertion
(b) Both Assertion and Reason are true but Reason is not the correct explanation of Assertion
(c) Assertion is true but Reason is false
(d) Assertion is false but Reason is true

---

22. The income of a person is ₹ 300000 in the first year and he receives an increase of ₹ 10000 to his income per year for the next 19 yr. Find the total amount, he received in 20 yr.

---

23. A man starts repaying a loan as first installment of ₹ 100. If he increases the installment by ₹ 5 every month, then the amount he will pay in the 30 installments, is

(a) ₹ 2450 (b) ₹ 2500 (c) ₹ 5175 (d) ₹ 2650

---

24. A man saved ₹ 16500 in 10 yr. In each year after the first, he saved ₹ 100 more than he did in the preceding year. How much did he save in the first year?

Topic-3. Arithmetic Mean [NCERT (Old) Pg. 183-184]

25. If $\dfrac{a^n + b^n}{a^{n-1} + b^{n-1}}$ is the AM between a and b, then the value of n is 1.

True ☐ False ☐

26. Answer the following :

(i) Three arithmetic means between 4 and 16 are ______________

(ii) The five numbers between 8 and 26 such that resulting sequence is an AP are ______________.

COMPETITION EDGE UP

1. A software company sets up m number of computer systems to finish an assignment in 17 days. If 4 computer systems crashed on the start of the second day, 4 more computer systems crashed on the start of the third day and so on, then it took 8 more days to finish the assignment. The value of m is equal to **[JEE Main 2024]**

(a) 125 ☐
(b) 180 ☐
(c) 160 ☐
(d) 150 ☐

2. For $x \geq 0$, the least value of K, for which $4^{1+x} + 4^{1-x}, \dfrac{K}{2}, 16^x + 16^{-x}$ are three consecutive terms of an AP, is equal to **[JEE Main 2024]**

(a) 10 ☐
(b) 16 ☐
(c) 4 ☐
(d) 8 ☐

3. Let S_n denote the sum of the first n terms of an arithmetic progression. If $S_{10} = 390$ and the ratio of the tenth and the fifth terms is 15 : 7, then $S_{15} - S_5$ is equal to **[JEE Main 2024]**

(a) 690 ☐
(b) 790 ☐
(c) 890 ☐
(d) 800 ☐

4. Let S_n denote the sum of first n terms of an arithmetic progression. If $S_{20} = 790$ and $S_{10} = 145$, then $S_{15} - S_5$ is **[JEE Main 2024]**

(a) 403 ☐
(b) 390 ☐
(c) 410 ☐
(d) 395 ☐

5. If $\log_e a, \log_e b, \log_e c$ are in AP and $\log_e a - \log_e 2b, \log_e 2b - \log_e 3c, \log_e 3c - \log_e a$ are also in an AP, then a : b : c is equal to **[JEE Main 2024]**

(a) 16 : 4 : 1 ☐
(b) 9 : 6 : 4 ☐
(c) 25 : 10 : 4 ☐
(d) 6 : 3 : 2 ☐

6. The 20th term from the end of the progression $20, 19\frac{1}{4}, 18\frac{1}{2}, 17\frac{3}{4}, \ldots, -129\frac{1}{4}$ is **[JEE Main 2024]**

(a) – 110 ☐
(b) – 115 ☐
(c) – 118 ☐
(d) – 100 ☐

7. The number of common terms in the progressions 4, 9, 14, 19, ..., up to 25th term and 3, 6, 9, 12, ..., up to 37th term is **[JEE Main 2024]**

(a) 5 ☐
(b) 8 ☐
(c) 9 ☐
(d) 7 ☐

8. If the sum of the series

$$\frac{1}{1\cdot(1+d)}+\frac{1}{(1+d)(1+2d)}+\ldots+\frac{1}{(1+9d)(1+10d)}$$ is equal to 5, then

50d is equal to **[JEE Main 2024]**

(a) 15 ☐
(b) 20 ☐
(c) 5 ☐
(d) 10 ☐

9. If $\frac{1}{\sqrt{1}+\sqrt{2}}+\frac{1}{\sqrt{2}+\sqrt{3}}+\ldots+\frac{1}{\sqrt{99}+\sqrt{100}}=m$ and

$\frac{1}{1\cdot 2}+\frac{1}{2\cdot 3}+\ldots+\frac{1}{99\cdot 100}=n$, then

the point (m, n) lies on the line **[JEE Main 2024]**

(a) $11x-100y=0$ ☐
(b) $11(x-2)-100(y-1)=0$ ☐
(c) $11(x-1)-100(y-2)=0$ ☐
(d) $11(x-1)-100y=0$ ☐

10. The sum of the series

$$\frac{1}{1-3\cdot 1^2+1^4}+\frac{2}{1-3\cdot 2^2+2^4}+\frac{3}{1-3\cdot 3^2+3^4}+\ldots$$ up to 10terms is

[JEE Main 2024]

(a) $\frac{45}{109}$ ☐
(b) $-\frac{55}{109}$ ☐
(c) $\frac{55}{109}$ ☐
(d) $-\frac{45}{109}$ ☐

11. If $\left(\frac{1}{\alpha+1}+\frac{1}{\alpha+2}+\ldots+\frac{1}{\alpha+1012}\right)-\left(\frac{1}{2\cdot 1}+\frac{1}{4\cdot 3}+\frac{1}{6\cdot 5}+\ldots+\frac{1}{2024\cdot 2023}\right)=\frac{1}{2024}$, then α is equal to ....

[JEE Main 2024]

12. If a function f satisfies $f(m+n)=f(m)+f(n)$ for all $m, n\in N$ and $f(1)=1$, then the largest natural number λ such that $\sum_{k=1}^{2022} f(\lambda+k)\le(2022)^2$ is equal to .... **[JEE Main 2024]**

13. An arithmetic progression is written in the following way

```
                2
            5       8
        11      14      17
    20      23      26      29
    ---------------------------
  -------------------------------
```

The sum of all the terms of the 10th row is _______ . **[JEE Main 2024]**

14. Let the positive integers be written in the form :

```
              1
          2       3
      4       5       6
  7       8       9       10
 .                          .
.                            .
```

If the kth row contain exactly k numbers for every natural number k, then the row in which the number 5310 will be, is .... **[JEE Main 2024]**

15. Let $a_1, a_2, a_3, \ldots$ be in an arithmetic progression of positive terms. Let $A_k=a_1^2-a_2^2+a_3^2-a_4^2+\ldots+a_{2k-1}^2-a_{2k}^2$. If $A_3=-153$, $A_5=-435$ and $a_1^2+a_2^2+a_3^2=66$, then $a_{17}-A_7$ is equal to .... **[JEE Main 2024]**

16. Let 3, a, b, c be in AP and 3, $a-1$, $b+1$, $c+9$ be in GP. Then, the arithmetic mean of a, b and c is **[JEE Main 2024]**

(a) 13 ☐
(b) 11 ☐
(c) -4 ☐
(d) -1 ☐

Chapter 09

Straight Lines

Scan and take Chapter Test

TOPIC 1

A Recall of Coordinate Geometry

NCERT Pg 151-152

1. State whether the statement is True or False.

(i) The point (6, – 3) lies in IIIrd quadrant.

True ☐ False ☐

(ii) The point (–1, 4) lies in IInd quadrant.

True ☐ False ☐

(iii) The point (–2, – 3) lies in IVth quadrant.

True ☐ False ☐

(iv) The point (9, 10) lies in Ist quadrant.

True ☐ False ☐

2. Find the distance between the points

(i) $P(4, 5)$ and $Q(-2, 6)$ __________

(ii) $A(3, 6)$ and $B(7, 5)$ __________

3. (0, – 2) is the point on Y-axis which is equidistant from $A(-4, 3)$ and $B(5, 2)$.

True ☐ False ☐

4. Using distance formula, the points $A(-2, 3)$, $B(1, 2)$ and $C(7, 0)$

(a) forms an isosceles triangle

(b) forms an equilateral triangle

(c) are collinear

(d) forms scalene triangle

____

5. If the line segment joining the points

(i) $A(5, 2)$ and $B(9, 6)$ divided in the ratio 3 : 1, then coordinate of the point is

____

(ii) $A(-4, 2)$ and $B(8, 3)$ divided by the Y-axis in the ratio 1 : 2, then coordinate of the point is __________

*Concepts of all questions bearing * are important for JEE & CUET*

6. In what ratio, the line joining $A(-1, 1)$ and $B(5, 7)$ divided by the line $x + y = 4$?

(a) 1 : 2 (b) 2 : 3 (c) 3 : 4 (d) 4 : 5

7. Find the mid-point of

(i) the line segment joining the points $A(3, 2)$ and $B(5, 3)$ ________

(ii) the line segment joining the points $(x_1, -y_1)$ and $(x_2, -y_2)$ ________

8. The area of triangle whose vertices are

(i) $A(-3, -5)$, $B(5, 2)$ and $C(-9, -3)$ is ________

(ii) $A(6, 3)$, $B(3, 4)$ and $C(2, 7)$ is ________

9. In ΔABC, the mid-point of whose sides AB, BC and CA are $D(3, -1)$, $E(5, 3)$ and $F(1, -3)$, respectively. The area of ΔABC is 8 sq units.

True ☐ False ☐

10. The area of a ΔABC is 0, then three points A, B and C are

(a) parallel (b) in same plane (c) perpendicular (d) collinear

11. State whether the statement is True or False.

Points $A(-5, 1)$, $B(5, 5)$ and $C(10, 7)$ are collinear.

True ☐ False ☐

12. The points $A(-2, 3)$, $B(1, 2)$ and $C(k, 0)$ are collinear, then the value of k is

(a) $k = 3$ (b) $k = 4$ (c) $k = 7$ (d) $k = 8$

TOPIC 2 Slope

NCERT Pg. 152-158

13. Find the slope of the line

(i) which makes an angle of 30° with the positive direction of Y-axis measured anti-clockwise ________

(ii) which makes an angle of 120° with the positive direction of X-axis measured anti-clockwise ________

14. If the slope of a line is positive, then

(a) θ lies between 90° and 180° (b) θ lies between 0 and 90°

(c) θ lies between 180° and 270° (d) θ lies between 270° and 360°

15. Find the slope of

(i) a line parallel to X-axis ______

(ii) a line parallel to Y-axis ______

(iii) the line passes through the points $A(x_1, y_1)$ and $B(x_2, y_2)$ ______

(iv) a line passing through the points (3, – 1) and (3, 2) ______

16. Suppose A (1, 1), B(7, 3) and C(3, 6) are the vertices of a ΔABC. If D is the mid-point of BC and $AL \perp BC$, then match the following.

	Column I		Column II
A.	Slope of AD	1.	$\frac{4}{3}$
B.	Slope of AL	2.	$\frac{7}{8}$
		3.	$\frac{2}{9}$
		4.	$\frac{1}{16}$

Which one is the correct option?

(a) A → 2, B → 4 (b) A → 3, B → 4 (c) A → 1, B → 3 (d) A → 2, B → 1

17. Find the value of x

(i) if 2 is the slope of the line passing through (2, 5) and (x, 3) ______

(ii) if the inclination of the line joining the points (x, – 3) and (2, 5) is 45° ______

***18.** Find the tangent of angle between two lines.

(i) The slope of one line is $\frac{1}{4}$ and slope of the other line is $\frac{1}{3}$ ______

(ii) If $A(-2, -1)$, $B(2, 3)$ and $C(-2, -4)$ are three points, then the angle between BA and BC is ______

(iii) The X-axis and the line joining the points (3, – 1) and (4, – 2) is ______.

(iv) The angle between the lines whose slopes are $\sqrt{3}$ and $\frac{1}{\sqrt{3}}$ is ______.

***19.** State whether the statement is True or False.

If $A(-2, 1)$, $B(2, 3)$, $C(-2, -4)$ are the vertices of a ΔABC, then $\tan B = \frac{2}{3}$.

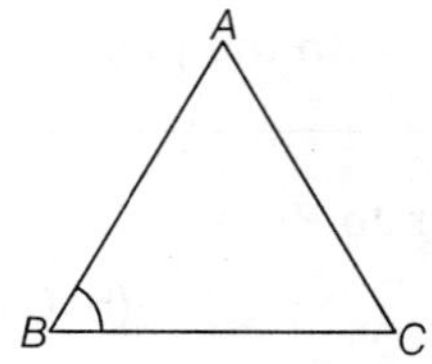

True ☐ False ☐

20. What is the image of a point $P(3, 8)$ with respect to the line $x + 3y = 7$?

---

21. Lines $x + 2y - 9 = 0$ and $2x + 4y + 5 = 0$ are parallel.

True ☐ False ☐

22. If the line through $A(3, y)$ and $B(2, 7)$ is parallel to the line through $C(-1, 4)$ and $D(0, 6)$, then the value of y is

(a) $y = 6$ (b) $y = 15$ (c) $y = 19$ (d) $y = 9$

---

23. Let $A(6, 4)$ and $B(2, 12)$ be two given points. What is the slope of the line perpendicular to AB?

---

24. The line joining $(2, -5)$ and $(-2, 5)$ is parallel to the line joining $(6, 3)$ and $(1, 1)$.

True ☐ False ☐

25. The angles between the lines $\sqrt{3}x + y = 1$ and $x + \sqrt{3}y = 1$ are 60° and 120°.

True ☐ False ☐

TOPIC 3

Various forms of the Equation of a Line

NCERT Pg 159-163

26. Find a given that

(i) $(a, 3)$ lies in the line with equation $y = \frac{x}{2} + \frac{5}{2}$ ____________

(ii) $(-1, a)$ lies in the line with equation $y = x + 2$ ____________

27. Find the equation of the

(i) horizontal line through $(3, -4)$ ____________

(ii) vertical line with x intercept 5 ____________

(iii) vertical line through $(-1, -3)$ ____________

(iv) horizontal line with y intercept 2 ____________

(v) X-axis ____________

(vi) Y-axis ____________

28. Find the equation of the line which satisfy the given conditions.

(i) Passing through the point $(-3, 5)$ and parallel to the axes ____________

(ii) Passing through the point $(3, -4)$ and parallel to the X-axis ____________

(iii) Passing through the point $(2, -5)$ and parallel to the line $2x - 3y = 7$ ____________

29. Write the equation of a line when $\tan\theta = \frac{1}{2}$, where θ is the inclination and

(i) y intercept is $\frac{-5}{4}$ ______

(i) x intercept is 5 ______

30. What is the equation of the line, which makes intercepts 2 and –3 on the X and Y-axes, respectively?

______

31. The intercepts cut-off by the line $2x - y + 16 = 0$ on the coordinate axes are x intercept $= A$ and the y intercept $= B$, then $A + B$ is

______

32. Fill in the blanks.

	Equation of line	Gradient	x intercept	y intercept
(i)	$2x + y = 6$	–	–	–
(ii)	$x - 9y = 22$	–	–	–
(iii)	$11x - 4y = -43$	–	–	–
(iv)	$\sqrt{3}x + y = -2$	–	–	–

33. The equation of the perpendicular bisector of the line joining the points $A(2, 3)$ and $B(6, -5)$ is

(a) $2x - 4y + 5 = 0$ (b) $4x - 9y + 3 = 0$ (c) $2x - 2y + 6 = 0$ (d) $x - 2y - 6 = 0$

______

34. State whether the following statement is True or False.

(i) The reduction of the equation $y + \sqrt{3}x + 2 = 0$ to slope intercept form is $y = -\sqrt{3}x - 2$.

True ☐ False ☐

(ii) The reduction of the equation $3x - 2y + 4 = 0$ to intercept form is $\frac{x}{(-4/3)} + \frac{y}{2} = 1$,

where $a = \left(\frac{-4}{3}\right)$ and $b = 2$.

True ☐ False ☐

35. The equation of the line so that the line segment intercepted between the axes is divided by the point $P(-5, 4)$ in the ratio $1 : 2$ can be given by

(a) $8x - 5y + 60 = 0$ (b) $2x - 3y + 18 = 0$

(c) $3x + 2y - 12 = 0$ (d) $13x + 13y - 6 = 0$

______

36. The perpendicular distance of a line from the origin is 5 units and its slope is – 1. The equation of the line is

(a) $x + y + 5\sqrt{2} = 0$ (b) $x = 5\sqrt{2} + 2y$ (c) $x - y + 5\sqrt{2} = 0$ (d) $x + 2y + 6 = 0$

______

37. State whether the statement is True or False.

(i) The length of perpendicular from the point (a, b) to the line $\frac{x}{a}+\frac{y}{b}=1$ is $\frac{|ab|}{\sqrt{a^2+b^2}}$.

True ☐ False ☐

(ii) The distance of the point $P(-1, 1)$ from the line $12(x+6)=5(y-2)$ is 5 units.

True ☐ False ☐

(iii) The line $5x-2y-1=0$ is the mid-parallel to the lines $5x-2y-9=0$ and $5x-2y+7=0$.

True ☐ False ☐

38. Find the distance between the following parallel lines

(i) $15x+8y-34=0$ and $15x+8y+31=0$

____

(ii) $3x-4y+9=0$ and $6x-8y-17=0$

____

Assertion-Reason Questions

The following questions consist of two statements – Assertion (A) and Reason (R). Answer these questions by selecting the appropriate option given below.

(a) Both (A) and (R) are true and (R) is correct explanation of (A)
(b) Both (A) and (R) are true but (R) is not the correct explanation of (A)
(c) (A) is true but (R) is false
(d) (A) is false but (R) is true

1. **Assertion** (A) Slope of the line $x=2$ is not defined.

Reason (R) Slope of a line making angle θ with positive direction of X-axis is $\tan\theta$.

(a) ☐ (b) ☐ (c) ☐ (d) ☐

2. **Assertion** (A) Slope of the line $2x+4y=5$ is $-\frac{1}{2}$.

Reason (R) Two lines are parallel if and only if their slopes are equal.

(a) ☐ (b) ☐ (c) ☐ (d) ☐

3. **Assertion** (A) Line $3x+5y=10$ is parallel to the line $5x+3y=9$.

Reason (R) Slope of the line joining the points $(2, 3)$ and $(4, -1)$ is -2.

(a) ☐ (b) ☐ (c) ☐ (d) ☐

4. **Assertion** (A) The inclination of the line l may be acute or obtuse.

Reason (R) Slope of X-axis is zero and slope of Y-axis is not defined.

(a) ☐ (b) ☐ (c) ☐ (d) ☐

5. **Assertion** (A) Line $x + y = 8$ has equal intercepts on the axes.

Reason (R) Distance between two parallel lines $3x + 4y = 7$ and $6x + 8y = 10$ is 3 units.

(a) ☐ (b) ☐ (c) ☐ (d) ☐

6. **Assertion** (A) Slope of the line passing through the points (3, – 2) and (3, 4) is 0.

Reason (R) If two lines having the same slope pass through a common point, then these lines will coincide.

(a) ☐ (b) ☐ (c) ☐ (d) ☐

7. **Assertion** (A) The equation of line making intercepts a and b on X and Y-axis, respectively is $\frac{x}{a} + \frac{y}{b} = 1$.

Reason (R) The slope of the line $ax + by + c = 0$ is $\frac{b}{a}$.

(a) ☐ (b) ☐ (c) ☐ (d) ☐

8. **Assertion** (A) The equation of a line parallel to the line $ax + by + c = 0$ is $ax - by - \lambda = 0$, where λ is a constant.

Reason (R) The equation of a line perpendicular to the line $ax + by + c = 0$ is $bx - ay + \lambda = 0$, where λ is a constant.

(a) ☐ (b) ☐ (c) ☐ (d) ☐

9. **Assertion** (A) The distance between the parallel lines $3x - 4y + 9 = 0$ and $6x - 8y - 15 = 0$ is $\frac{33}{10}$.

Reason (R) Distance between the parallel lines $Ax + By + C_1 = 0$ and $Ax + By + C_2 = 0$, is given by $d = \frac{|C_1 - C_2|}{\sqrt{A^2 + B^2}}$.

(a) ☐ (b) ☐ (c) ☐ (d) ☐

10. **Assertion** (A) Equation of the horizontal line having distance a from the X-axis is either $y = a$ or $y = -a$.

Reason (R) Equation of the vertical line having distance b from the Y-axis is either $x = b$ or $x = -b$.

(a) ☐ (b) ☐ (c) ☐ (d) ☐

Case Based Questions

Case 1 Given map is showing Shobha's home and school. Her school is situated at point A and home is at point B. Assuming O is the origin, OA is along X-axis and OB is along Y-axis, answer the following questions.

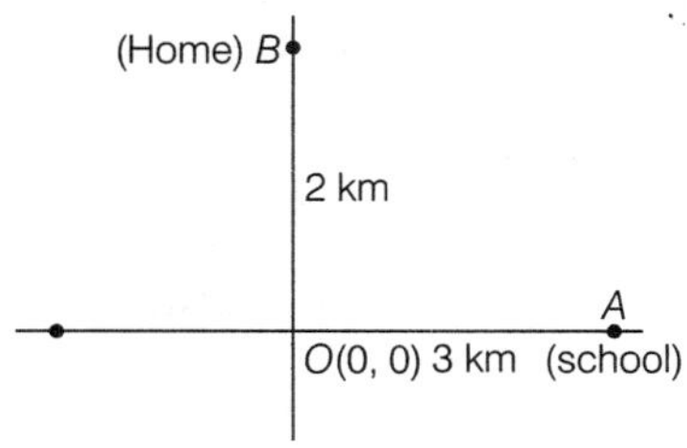

(i) What would be the coordinates of the points A and B?

(a) (0, 3), (2, 0) ☐ (b) (0, 3), (0, 2) ☐

(c) (3, 0), (0, 2) ☐ (d) (3, 0), (2, 0) ☐

(ii) What would be the equation of line passing through the points A and B?

(a) $2x + 3y = 6$ ☐ (b) $3x - 2y = 6$ ☐

(c) $2x - 3y = 6$ ☐ (d) $3x + 2y = 6$ ☐

(iii) A shopping mall is situated at point C. If slope of the line BC is 1, then its equation will be

(a) $x - y + 2 = 0$ ☐ (b) $y = x$ ☐

(c) $x + y = 2$ ☐ (d) $x + y = 0$ ☐

Case 2 Five friends Kanika, Kashvi, Preeti, Priyanka and Manvi have their homes respectively situated at the points A, B, C, D and E. Assuming A is the origin and B, C are on the X-axis and E is on the Y-axis. Based on the above information, answer the following questions.

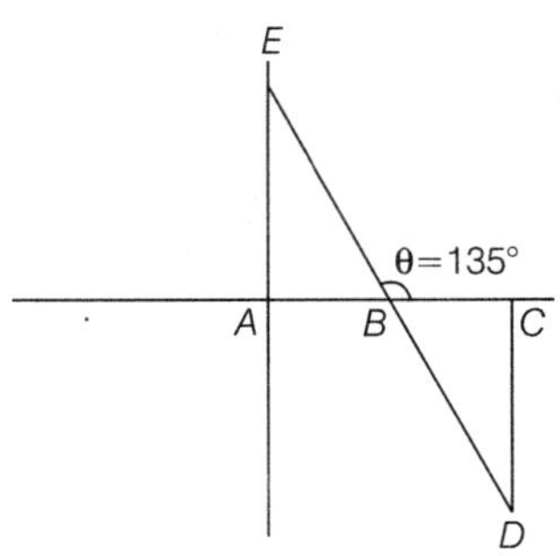

(i) What will be the slope of BE?

(ii) If $AB = BC = AE = 6$ m and $CD = 6$ m, then what would be the equation of the line BE?

(iii) What would be the coordinates of point D?

(iv) What would be the equation of the line BD?

COMPETITION CONNECT

General Equation of a Line [NCERT (Old) Pg. 220-224]

1. What is the equation of the line whose perpendicular distance from the origin is 3 units and the angle between the positive directions of X-axis and the perpendicular is $15°$?

____

2. The reduction of the equation $y + 4 = 0$ to the normal form $x \cos \alpha + y \sin \alpha = p$ and hence the values of α and p are $280°$ and 4, respectively.

True ☐ False ☐

3. The reduction of the equation $\sqrt{3}x + y + 2 = 0$ to the

(i) normal form is ______________________________

(ii) the value of α and β ______________________________

COMPETITION EDGE UP

1. If the locus of the point whose distances from the point $(2, 1)$ and $(1, 3)$ are in the ratio $5 : 4$, is $ax^2 + by^2 + cxy + dx + ey + 170 = 0$, then the value of $a^2 + 2b + 3c + 4d + e$ is equal to **[JEE Main 2024]**

(a) 5 ☐
(b) 37 ☐
(c) 437 ☐
(d) -27 ☐

2. If $x^2 - y^2 + 2hxy + 2gx + 2fy + c = 0$ is the locus of a point, which moves such that it is always equidistant from the lines $x + 2y + 7 = 0$ and $2x - y + 8 = 0$, then the value of $g + c + h - f$ equals **[JEE Main 2024]**

(a) 29 ☐
(b) 14 ☐
(c) 8 ☐
(d) 6 ☐

3. Let $\left(5, \frac{a}{4}\right)$ be the circumcenter of a triangle with vertices $A(a, -2)$, $B(a, 6)$ and $C\left(\frac{a}{4}, -2\right)$. Let α denotes the circumradius, β denotes the area and γ denotes the perimeter of the triangle. Then, $\alpha + \beta + \gamma$ is **[JEE Main 2024]**

(a) 30 ☐
(b) 60 ☐
(c) 53 ☐
(d) 62 ☐

4. Let two straight lines drawn from the origin O intersect the line $3x + 4y = 12$ at the points P and Q such that ΔOPQ is an isosceles triangle and $\angle POQ = 90°$. If $l = OP^2 + PQ^2 + QO^2$, then the greatest integer less than or equal to l is **[JEE Main 2024]**

(a) 44 ☐
(b) 42 ☐
(c) 46 ☐
(d) 48 ☐

5. The distance of the point $(2, 3)$ from the line $2x - 3y + 28 = 0$, measured parallel to the line $\sqrt{3}x - y + 1 = 0$, is equal to **[JEE Main 2024]**

(a) $6\sqrt{3}$ ☐
(b) $3 + 4\sqrt{2}$ ☐
(c) $4\sqrt{2}$ ☐
(d) $4 + 6\sqrt{3}$ ☐

6. Let R be the interior region between the lines $3x - y + 1 = 0$ and $x + 2y - 5 = 0$ containing the origin. The set of all values of a, for which the points $(a^2, a + 1)$ lie in R, is **[JEE Main 2024]**

(a) $(-3,-1)\cup\left(\frac{1}{3},1\right)$ ☐

(b) $(-3,0)\cup\left(\frac{2}{3},1\right)$ ☐

(c) $(-3,-1)\cup\left(-\frac{1}{3},1\right)$ ☐

(d) $(-3,0)\cup\left(\frac{1}{3},1\right)$ ☐

7. The portion of the line $4x+5y=20$ in the first quadrant is trisected by the lines L_1 and L_2 passing through the origin. The tangent of an angle between the lines L_1 and L_2 is **[JEE Main 2024]**

(a) $\frac{25}{41}$ ☐

(b) $\frac{30}{41}$ ☐

(c) $\frac{2}{5}$ ☐

(d) $\frac{8}{5}$ ☐

8. Let a ray of light passing through the point (3, 10) reflects on the line $2x+y=6$ and the reflected ray passes through the point (7, 2). If the equation of the incident ray is $ax+by+1=0$, then a^2+b^2+3ab is equal to .... **[JEE Main 2024]**

9. Let ABC be an isosceles triangle, in which A is at $(-1,0)$, $\angle A=\frac{2\pi}{3}$, $AB=AC$ and B is on the positive X-axis. If $BC=4\sqrt{3}$ and the line BC intersects the line $y=x+3$ at (α,β), then $\frac{\beta^4}{\alpha^2}$ is .... **[JEE Main 2024]**

10. In a ΔABC, suppose $y=x$ is the equation of the bisector of the $\angle B$ and the equation of the side AC is $2x-y=2$. If $2AB=BC$ and the points A and B are (4, 6) and (α,β), respectively then $\alpha+2\beta$ is equal to **[JEE Main 2024]**

(a) 42 ☐

(b) 45 ☐

(c) 48 ☐

(d) 39 ☐

11. If (α,β) is the orthocenter of the ΔABC with vertices $A(3,-7)$, $B(-1,2)$ and $C(4,5)$, then $9\alpha-6\beta+60$ is equal to **[JEE Main 2023]**

(a) 30 ☐

(b) 35 ☐

(c) 40 ☐

(d) 25 ☐

12. If the point $\left(\alpha,\frac{7\sqrt{3}}{3}\right)$ lies on the curve traced by the mid-points of the line segments of the lines $x\cos\theta+y\sin\theta=7$, $\theta\in\left(0,\frac{\pi}{2}\right)$ between the coordinate axes, then α is equal to **[JEE Main 2023]**

(a) $7\sqrt{3}$ ☐

(b) 7 ☐

(c) $-7\sqrt{3}$ ☐

(d) -7 ☐

13. Let $C(\alpha,\beta)$ be the circumcenter of the triangle formed by the lines $4x+3y=69$, $4y-3x=17$ and $x+7y=61$. Then, $(\alpha-\beta)^2+\alpha+\beta$ is equal to **[JEE Main 2023]**

(a) 16 ☐

(b) 17 ☐

(c) 18 ☐

(d) 15 ☐

14. If the orthocentre of the triangle, whose vertices are (1, 2), (2, 3) and (3, 1) is (α,β), then the quadratic equation whose roots are $\alpha+4\beta$ and $4\alpha+\beta$, is **[JEE Main 2023]**

(a) $x^2-20x+99=0$ ☐

(b) $x^2-19x+90=0$ ☐

(c) $x^2-18x+80=0$ ☐

(d) $x^2-22x+120=0$ ☐

Chapter 10

Conic Sections

Scan and take Chapter Test

TOPIC 1 Circle

NCERT Pg. 179-181

***1.** The equation of the circle with

(i) centre (2, – 3) and radius 4 is ____________

(ii) centre $\left(\frac{1}{3}, \frac{1}{2}\right)$ and radius $\frac{1}{6}$ is ____________

(iii) centre $(a\cos\theta, a\sin\theta)$ and radius a is ____________

(iv) centre $(-a, -b)$ and radius $\sqrt{a^2 - b^2}$ is ____________

(v) centre $\left(\frac{a}{b}\cos\theta, \frac{a}{b}\sin\theta\right)$ and radius $\frac{a}{b}$ is ____________

***2.** Find the centre and radius of each of the following circles.

(i) $(x+3)^2 + (y-2)^2 = 16$ ____________

(ii) $\left(x - \frac{1}{4}\right)^2 + \left(y + \frac{1}{5}\right)^2 = \frac{1}{9}$ ____________

(iii) $x^2 + y^2 - 2x + 6y - 2 = 0$ ____________

(iv) $2x^2 + 2y^2 - x = 0$ ____________

(v) $x^2 + y^2 - \frac{16}{5}x - \frac{4}{3}y - \frac{449}{225} = 0$ ____________

3. When a circle touches X-axis, then its radius is equal to the absolute value of the y-coordinate of the centre.

True ☐ False ☐

***4.** The equation of the circle with centre (2, 0) and touching the Y-axis is

(a) $x^2 + y^2 + 4x = 0$

(b) $x^2 + y^2 - 4x = 0$

(c) $x^2 + y^2 + 8x = 0$

(d) $x^2 + y^2 - 8x =$

____

*Concepts of all questions bearing * are important for JEE & CUET*

5. $x^2 + y^2 - 2ax - 2ay + a^2 = 0$ is the equation of the circle when the circle touches both the axes in first quadrant with radius a.

True ☐ False ☐

6. The equation of the circle passing through the points $(1, -2)$ and $(4, -3)$ and whose centre lies on the line $3x + 4y = 7$ is $15x^2 + 15y^2 - 94x + 18y + 55 = 0$.

True ☐ False ☐

7. The equation of a circle of radius 5 units, whose centre lies on the X-axis and which passes through the point $(3, 3)$ is ______________________.

8. If a circle touches a line, then length of the perpendicular from its centre on the given line is equal to the radius of the circle.

True ☐ False ☐

9. Which one is the equation of the circle, passing through the point $(1, 1)$, $(2, 0)$ and $(-6, -6)$.

(a) $x^2 + y^2 + 4x + 6y - 12 = 0$
(b) $x^2 + y^2 + 6x + 4y - 12 = 0$
(c) $x^2 + y^2 + 2x + 3y - 12 = 0$
(d) $x^2 + y^2 + 8x + 12y - 12 = 0$

____

10. The equation of the circle with centre $(9, -4)$ and passes through the point $(2, 3)$ is

____

11. The line $2x + 9y = 0$ is a diameter of the circle $x^2 + y^2 + 6x + 2y = 0$.

True ☐ False ☐

12. The point $(-3.5, 3.5)$ lies ______________________ the circle $x^2 + y^2 = 13$.

TOPIC 2
Parabola

NCERT Pg. 182-187

13. A line through the focus and perpendicular to the directrix is called the ______________ of the parabola.

(a) axis (b) directrix (c) focus (d) vertex

____

14. Equation of a parabola, if the vertex is at the origin, axis symmetry to Y-axis and focus is $(0, a)$ is

(a)
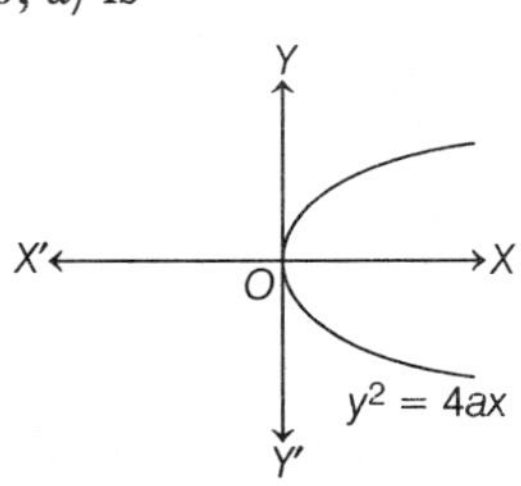

(b)
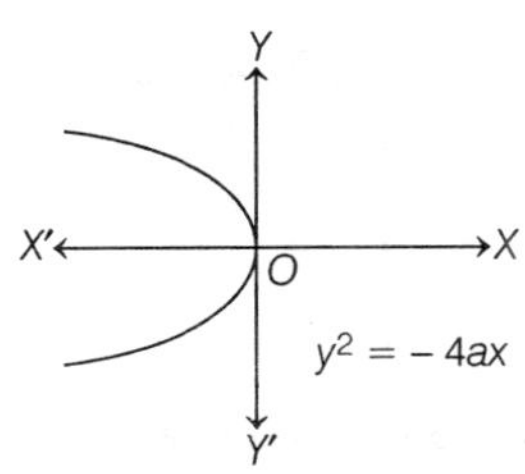

(c) 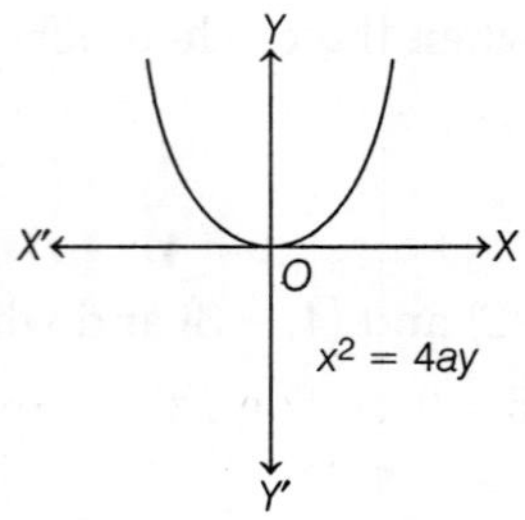

(d) 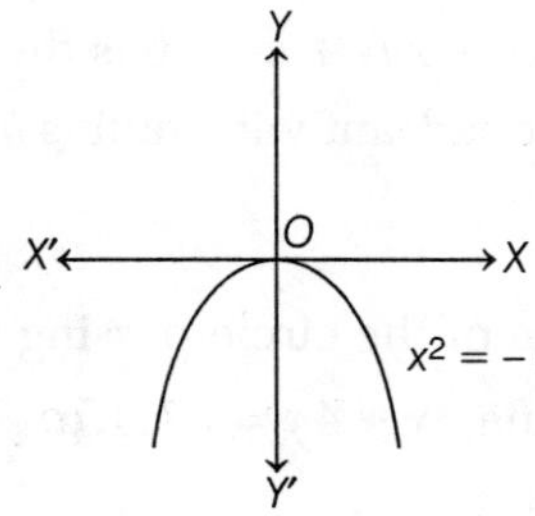

---

15. In each of the following questions, find the coordinates of the focus, axis of the parabola, the equation of the directrix and the length of the latusrectum.

(i) $y^2 = 8x$ ____________________

(ii) $y^2 = -12x$ ____________________

(iii) $x^2 = 14y$ ____________________

(iv) $x^2 = -7y$ ____________________

16. The equation of the parabola that satisfies

(i) focus (4, 0) and directrix, $x = -4$ is $y^2 = 16x$

True ☐ False ☐

(ii) focus (0, – 5) and directrix, $y = 5$ is $x^2 = 10y$

True ☐ False ☐

(iii) vertex (0, 0) and focus (6, 0) is $x^2 = -24y$

True ☐ False ☐

(iv) vertex (0, 0) and focus (0, – 8) is $x^2 = -32y$

True ☐ False ☐

17. In the following figure, the equation of the directrix is

(i)

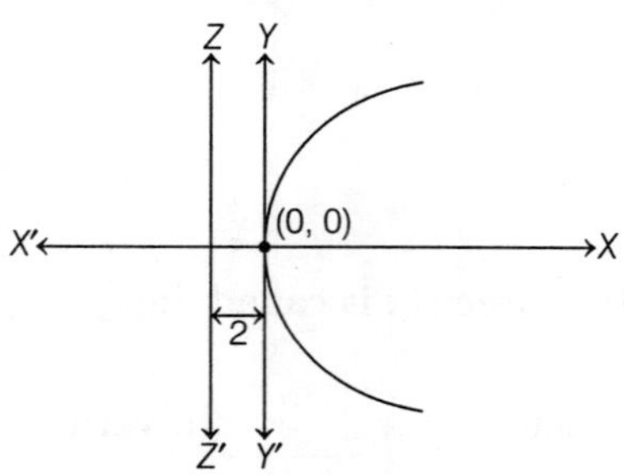

____

(ii)

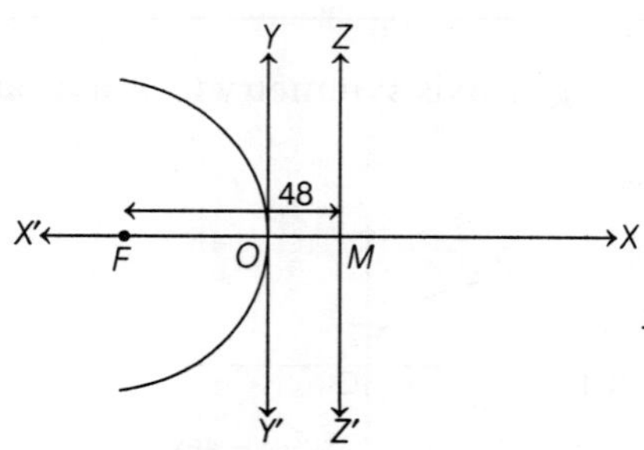

____

18. A chord of the parabola is a ____________________, if it passes through the focus.

19. Find the coordinates of the focus when the equation of the directrix is $y = -4$.

____

***20.** Which of the following is the equation of the parabola, when vertex (0, 0) and the equation of the directrix is $y = 3$?

(a) $x^2 = 12y$ (b) $y^2 = 12x$ (c) $x^2 = -12y$ (d) $y^2 = -12x$

____

21. Coordinates of the focus is $\left(0, \frac{2}{5}\right)$, when the parabola passing through the point $(\sqrt{8}, 5)$ with the vertex (0, 0) and axis is along Y-axis.

True ☐ False ☐

22. Equation of the parabola is ______________ , if it passes through the point (9, 11) with vertex (0, 0) and axis along with X-axis.

23. An equilateral triangle is inscribed in the parabola $y^2 = -4ax$, where one vertex is at the vertex of the parabola. Find the length of the side of the triangle.

____

***24.** Which one of the area of the triangle formed by the line joining the vertex of the parabola $x^2 = -12y$ to the ends of its latus rectum?

(a) 18 sq units (b) 4.5 sq units (c) 12 sq units (d) 6 sq units

____

25. An arch is in the form of a parabola with its axis vertical. The arch is 10 m high and 5 m wide at the base. $\sqrt{5}$ m wide it is 2m from the vertex of the parabola.

True ☐ False ☐

TOPIC 3

Ellipse

NCERT Pg. 187-195

26. Answer the following :

(i) The line segment through the foci of the ellipse is called ______________

(ii) The line segment through the centre and perpendicular to the major axis of the ellipse is called the ______________

(iii) The end points of the major axis of the ellipse are called ______________

27. **Statement I** Relationship between semi-major axis, semi-minor axis and the distance of the focus from the centre of the ellipse is $c = \sqrt{a^2 - b^2}$.

Statement II In $c^2 = a^2 - b^2$, when $c = 0$, then $a^2 = b^2$, so the ellipse becomes the circle.

Statement III When $c = a$, then $b = 0$, the ellipse reduces to the line segment.

(a) Statements I and II are correct
(b) Statements I, II and III are correct
(c) Statements I and II are incorrect
(d) Statements II and III are incorrect

28. Match the following Columns.

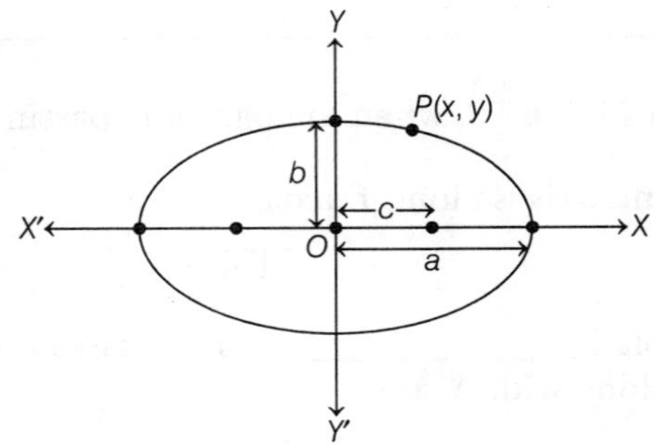

	Column I		Column II
A.	Major axis	1.	$2b$
B.	Minor axis	2.	$2a$
C.	Lactus rectum	3.	$\frac{x^2}{a^2}+\frac{y^2}{b^2}=1$
D.	Equation of the ellipse	4.	$\frac{2b^2}{a}$

Which one is the correct option?
(a) $A \to 2, B \to 1, C \to 4, D \to 3$
(b) $A \to 1, B \to 2, C \to 3, D \to 4$
(c) $A \to 2, B \to 3, C \to 1, D \to 4$
(d) $A \to 2, B \to 4, C \to 1, D \to 3$

***29.** Find the coordinates of the foci, the vertices, the length of major axis, the minor axis, the eccentricity and the length of the latusrectum of the ellipse.

(i) $\frac{x^2}{25}+\frac{y^2}{16}=1$ __________

(ii) $\frac{x^2}{9}+\frac{y^2}{16}=1$ __________

(iii) $9x^2+y^2=144$ __________

(iv) $4x^2+y^2=400$ __________

(v) $3x^2+27y^2=81$ __________

30. If $\left(\pm\frac{9}{2}, 0\right)$ is the end points of the major axis, then the length of the major axis is 3 units.

True ☐ False ☐

31. Major axis of the ellipse $x^2 + 4y^2 = 52$ is along the ________________.

32. The equation of the ellipse in the following figure, is

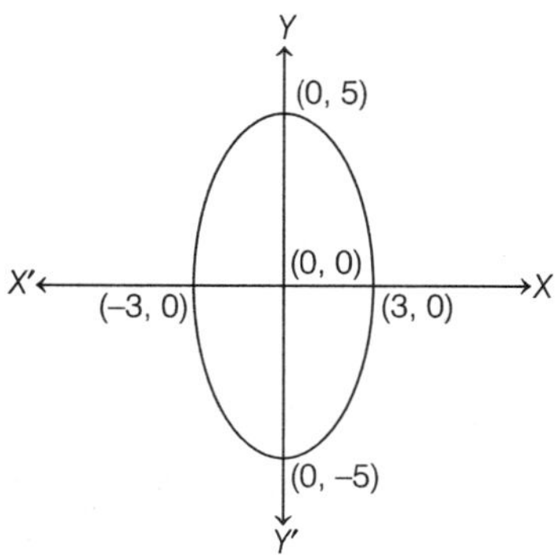

(a) $\frac{x^2}{9} + \frac{y^2}{25} = 1$
(b) $\frac{x^2}{25} - \frac{y^2}{9} = 1$
(c) $\frac{x^2}{25} + \frac{y^2}{9} = 1$
(d) $\frac{x^2}{9} - \frac{y^2}{25} = 1$

***33.** Coordinates of foci are $(0, \pm\sqrt{5})$ and the end points of the major axis are $(0, \pm 9)$, then the value of eccentricity is

(a) $\sqrt{5}/9$
(b) $-5/9$
(c) $-9/5$
(d) $9/\sqrt{5}$

---

34. Length of the major axis is 46 and coordinates of the foci are $(\pm 2, 0)$. What is eccentricity?

***35.** **Statement I** Latus rectum of an ellipse is a line segment passing through any of the foci.

Statement II Latus rectum of an ellipse is perpendicular to the major axis.

(a) Statement I is correct but Statement II is incorrect
(b) Statement I is incorrect but Statement II is correct
(c) Both statements are correct
(d) Both statements are incorrect

---

36. The length of the latus rectum of the following ellipse.

(i) $\frac{x^2}{36}+\frac{y^2}{16}=1$ is ____________

(ii) $4x^2+9y^2=1$ is ____________

(iii) The length of the major and minor axes of the ellipse are 25 and 16, respectively ____________

37. Find the equation for the ellipse that satisfies the given condition.

(i) Vertices $(\pm 13, 0)$ and foci $(\pm 5, 0)$ ____________

(ii) Ends of major axis $(\pm 4, 0)$, end of minor axis $(0, \pm 3)$ ____________

(iii) Foci $(\pm 7, 0)$ and $a = 10$, ____________

(iv) $b = 4$, $c = 5$, centre at origin and foci on the X-axis ____________

(v) Major axis on the X-axis and passes through the points (4, 3) and (6, 2) ____________

***38.** A rod of length 12 cm moves with its ends always touching the coordinates axes, the equation of the locus of a point A on the rod, which is 3 cm from the end in contact with X-axis, is

(a) $\frac{x^2}{9}+\frac{y^2}{81}=1$ (b) $\frac{x^2}{81}-\frac{y^2}{9}=1$ (c) $\frac{x^2}{9}-\frac{y^2}{81}=1$ (d) $\frac{x^2}{81}+\frac{y^2}{9}=1$

____

39. An arch is in the form of a semi-ellipse. It is 10 m wide and 4 m high at the centre. Then, the height of the arch at a point 3 m from one end is ____________.

TOPIC 4

Hyperbola

NCERT Pg 195-202

***40.** **Statement I** The line through foci is called the transverse axis.

Statement II The line through the centre and perpendicular to the transverse axis is called the conjugate axis.

(a) Both statements are correct

(b) Both statements are incorrect

(c) Statement I is correct and but Statement II is incorrect

(d) Statement I is incorrect but Statement II is correct

____

41. The eccentricity of the hyperbola is

(a) $e<1$ (b) $e>1$ (c) $e=1$ (d) $e=0$

____

42. In terms of the eccentricity, the foci are at a distance of _______________ from the centre.

43. A hyperbola in which $a = b$ is called an equilateral hyperbola.

True ☐ False ☐

***44.** Find the coordinates of the foci, the vertices, the eccentricity and the length of the latus rectum of the hyperbolas.

(i) $\frac{x^2}{49} - \frac{y^2}{25} = 1$ _______________

(ii) $\frac{y^2}{16} - \frac{x^2}{36} = 1$ _______________

(iii) $6y^2 - 4x^2 = 36$ _______________

(iv) $9x^2 - 16y^2 = 144$ _______________

45. The distance between the foci is 26 and transverse axis along X-axis with centre (0, 0). Then, the coordinates of the foci is $(\pm 13, 0)$.

True ☐ False ☐

46. The coordinates of the foci of the hyperbola $\frac{x^2}{1600} - \frac{y^2}{81} = 1$ is _______________

47. Coordinates of the vertices, when the equation of the hyperbola is $\frac{x^2}{16} - \frac{y^2}{25} = 1$.

(a) $(\pm 5, 0)$ (b) $(0, \pm 4)$ (c) $(0, \pm 5)$ (d) $(\pm 4, 0)$

____

***48.** If the foci of the hyperbola are $(0, \pm \sqrt{27})$ and the vertices are $(0, \pm 4)$, then the eccentricity is _______________.

***49.** The length of the latus rectum of the hyperbola.

(i) $\frac{x^2}{2304} - \frac{y^2}{196} = 1$ is _______________

(ii) $5y^2 - 9x^2 = 36$ is _______________

50. The equation of the hyperbola satisfying the given conditions.

(i) vertices $\left(0, \pm \frac{\sqrt{11}}{2}\right)$ and foci $(0, \pm 3)$ is _______________

(ii) foci $(\pm 10, 0)$ and the transverse axis is of length 16, is _______________

(iii) foci $(\pm 3\sqrt{5}, 0)$ and the latus rectum is of length 8, is _______________

(iv) vertices $(\pm 7, 0)$ and eccentricity $\frac{4}{3}$ is _______________

(v) vertices $(0, \pm 6)$ and $e = \frac{5}{3}$ is _______________

Assertion-Reason Questions

The following questions consist of two statements – Assertion (A) and Reason (R). Answer these questions by selecting the appropriate option given below.
(a) Both (A) and (R) are true and (R) is correct explanation of (A)
(b) Both (A) and (R) are true but (R) is not the correct explanation of (A)
(c) (A) is true but (R) is false
(d) (A) is false but (R) is true

1. **Assertion** (A) If the coordinates of the end points of the diameter are (1, 5) and (– 1, 3), then the equation of circle is $x^2 + y^2 - 8y + 14 = 0$.

Reason (R) The equation of the circle drawn on the straight line joining two given points (x_1, y_1) and(x_2, y_2) as diameter is $(x - x_1)(x - x_2) + (y - y_1)(y - y_2) = 0$.

(a) ☐ (b) ☐ (c) ☐ (d) ☐

2. **Assertion** (A) The distance between the directrices of the ellipse $\frac{x^2}{16} + \frac{y^2}{8} = 1$ is $4\sqrt{2}$.

Reason (R) The distance between the directrices of the ellipse $\frac{x^2}{a^2} + \frac{y^2}{b^2} = 1$ is $\frac{2a}{e}$.

(a) ☐ (b) ☐ (c) ☐ (d) ☐

3. **Assertion** (A) The equation of the circle with centre (2, – 5) and radius 3 is $x^2 + y^2 - 4x + 10y + 20 = 0$

Reason (R) The equation of a circle with centre (*h*, *k*) and radius *r* is given by $(x - h)^2 + (y - k)^2 = r^2$

(a) ☐ (b) ☐ (c) ☐ (d) ☐

4. **Assertion** (A) Centre and radius of the circle $2x^2 + 2y^2 + 4x + 6y + 1 = 0$ are respectively (– 2, – 3) and $2\sqrt{3}$.

Reason (R) Equation of circle with centre (2, 1) and radius 2 is $(x - 2)^2 + (y - 1)^2 = 4$.

(a) ☐ (b) ☐ (c) ☐ (d) ☐

5. **Assertion** (A) Parabola $y^2 = 12x$ is symmetric about *X*-axis.

Reason (R) Equation of the parabola with focus (0, 3) is $x^2 = 12y$.

(a) ☐ (b) ☐ (c) ☐ (d) ☐

6. **Assertion** (A) Equation of the ellipse with centre at the origin, foci $(\pm 3, 0)$ and 4 as the length of the minor axis is $\frac{x^2}{9}+\frac{y^2}{4}=1$.

Reason (R) Equation of the ellipse $\frac{x^2}{a^2}+\frac{y^2}{b^2}=1$ has its major axis along X-axis, if $a>b$.

(a) ☐ (b) ☐ (c) ☐ (d) ☐

7. **Assertion** (A) Equation of a parabola with focus $(0, -2)$ and directrix $y=2$ is $x^2=-8y$.

Reason (R) Parabola is the locus of a point whose distance from a fixed point and a fixed line are always same. The fixed point is called the focus and the fixed line is called the directrix of the parabola.

(a) ☐ (b) ☐ (c) ☐ (d) ☐

8. **Assertion** (A) Hyperbola $\frac{x^2}{16}-\frac{y^2}{9}=1$ has its foci on X-axis.

Reason (R) Equation of the hyperbola whose centre is at the origin and transverse axis is along X-axis is $\frac{y^2}{b^2}-\frac{x^2}{a^2}=1$.

(a) ☐ (b) ☐ (c) ☐ (d) ☐

9. **Assertion** (A) Eccentricity of conjugate hyperbola is equal to $\sqrt{\frac{b^2+a^2}{b^2}}$.

Reason (R) Equation of directrix of conjugate hyperbola is $y=\pm\frac{b}{e}$.

(a) ☐ (b) ☐ (c) ☐ (d) ☐

10. **Assertion** (A) If major axis is on the Y-axis and ellipse passes through the points $(3, 2)$ and $(1, 6)$, then the equation of ellipse is $\frac{x^2}{10}+\frac{y^2}{40}=1$.

Reason (R) $\frac{x^2}{b^2}+\frac{y^2}{a^2}=1$ is an equation of ellipse if its major axis is along Y-axis.

(a) ☐ (b) ☐ (c) ☐ (d) ☐

Case Based Questions

Case 1 Rohan and Aman have learnt about the equation of circle. The equation of the circle having centre (h, k) and radius r is $(x-h)^2+(y-k)^2=r^2$

$$\Rightarrow \quad x^2+y^2-2hx-2ky+h^2+k^2-r^2=0$$

Which is of the form $x^2+y^2+2gx+2fy+c=0$,

where $g=-h, f=-k$ and $c=h^2+k^2-r^2$

The above equation of a circle is called the general equation of a circle with centre $(-g,-f)$ and radius, $r=\sqrt{h^2+k^2-c}$ or $r=\sqrt{g^2+f^2-c}$.

On the basis of above information, answer the following questions.

(i) If the equation of the circle is $x^2+y^2+6x-4y+4$, then its radius is

(a) 2 units ☐ (b) 4 units ☐
(c) 3 units ☐ (d) 6 units ☐

(ii) If the equation of circle is $x^2+y^2-4x+6y-96=0$, then its centre is

(a) (2, 3) ☐ (b) (2, – 3) ☐
(c) (– 2, 3) ☐ (d) (–2, – 3) ☐

(iii) If the centre of the circle $x^2+y^2-8x-6y+16=0$ is (h, k), then $h-k$ is equal to

(a) 1 ☐ (b) – 1 ☐
(c) 3 ☐ (d) 4 ☐

Case 2 Huma is making a flowerbed in her garden. Surprisingly, the flower bed becomes in the shape of parabola whose equation is $x^2=8y$, the flower bed is shown as in the below figure.

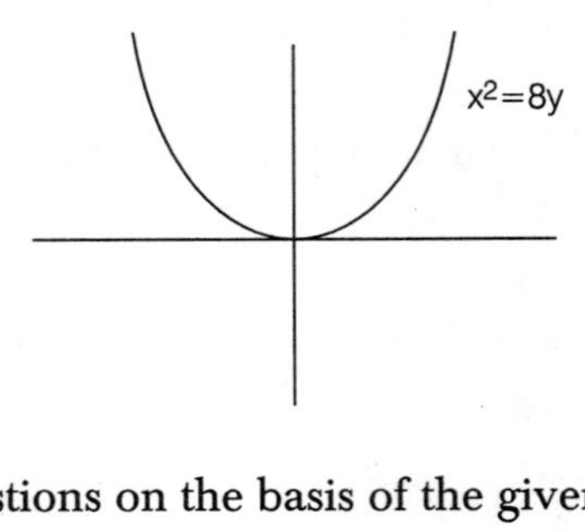

Answer the following questions on the basis of the given figure.

(i) Find the focus of the given parabola.

(ii) Equation of the directrix of the parabola is ____________________

(iii) Find the length of the latus rectum of the parabola.

COMPETITION EDGE UP

1. If $P(6,1)$ be the orthocentre of the triangle whose vertices are $A(5,-2)$, $B(8,3)$ and $C(h,k)$, then the point C lies on the circle **[JEE Main 2024]**

(a) $x^2+y^2-52=0$ ☐

(b) $x^2+y^2-61=0$ ☐

(c) $x^2+y^2-65=0$ ☐

(d) $x^2+y^2-74=0$ ☐

2. Let the circle $C_1: x^2+y^2-2(x+y)+1=0$ and C_2 be a circle having centre at $(-1,0)$ and radius 2. If the line of the common chord of C_1 and C_2 intersects the Y-axis at the point P, then the square of the distance of P from the centre of C_1 is **[JEE Main 2024]**

(a) 2 ☐

(b) 4 ☐

(c) 6 ☐

(d) 1 ☐

3. Let C be a circle with radius $\sqrt{10}$ units and centre at the origin. Let the line $x+y=2$ intersects the circle C at the points P and Q. Let MN be a chord of C of length 2 units and slope -1. Then, a distance (in units) between the chord PQ and the chord MN is **[JEE Main 2024]**

(a) $3-\sqrt{2}$ ☐

(b) $\sqrt{2}-1$ ☐

(c) $2-\sqrt{3}$ ☐

(d) $\sqrt{2}+1$ ☐

4. Let a circle C of radius 1 and closer to the origin be such that the lines passing through the point (3, 2) and parallel to the coordinate axes touch it. Then, the shortest distance of the circle C from the point (5,5) is **[JEE Main 2024]**

(a) $4\sqrt{2}$ ☐

(b) 4 ☐

(c) $2\sqrt{2}$ ☐

(d) 5 ☐

5. Let a variable line passing through the centre of the circle $x^2+y^2-16x-4y=0$, meets the positive coordinate axes at the points A and B. Then, the minimum value of $OA+OB$, where O is the origin is equal to **[JEE Main 2024]**

(a) 18 ☐

(b) 24 ☐

(c) 20 ☐

(d) 12 ☐

6. Let the circles $C_1: (x-\alpha)^2+(y-\beta)^2=r_1^2$ and $C_2: (x-8)^2+\left(y-\frac{15}{2}\right)^2=r_2^2$ touch each other externally at the point (6, 6). If the point (6, 6) divides the line segment joining the centres of the circles C_1 and C_2 internally in the ratio 2 : 1, then $(\alpha+\beta)+4(r_1^2+r_2^2)$ equals **[JEE Main 2024]**

(a) 125 ☐

(b) 145 ☐

(c) 110 ☐

(d) 130 ☐

7. Let a circle passing through (2, 0) have its centre at the point (h, k). Let (x_c, y_c) be the point of intersection of the lines $3x+5y=1$ and $(2+c)x+5c^2y=1$. If $h=\lim_{c\to 1} x_c$ and $k=\lim_{c\to 1} y_c$, then the equation of the circle is **[JEE Main 2024]**

(a) $5x^2+5y^2-4x-2y-12=0$ ☐

(b) $25x^2+25y^2-2x+2y-60=0$ ☐

(c) $25x^2+25y^2-20x+2y-60=0$ ☐

(d) $5x^2+5y^2-4x+2y-12=0$ ☐

8. A square is inscribed in the circle $x^2+y^2-10x-6y+30=0$. One side of this square is parallel to $y=x+3$. If (x_i, y_i) are the vertices of the square, then $\Sigma(x_i^2+y_i^2)$ is equal to **[JEE Main 2024]**

(a) 156 ☐

(b) 152 ☐

(c) 148 ☐

(d) 160 ☐

9. Let PQ be a chord of the parabola $y^2 = 12x$ and the mid-point of PQ be at (4, 1). Then, which of the following point lies on the line passing through the points P and Q? [JEE Main 2024]

(a) $\left(\frac{3}{2}, -16\right)$ ☐

(b) $\left(\frac{1}{2}, -20\right)$ ☐

(c) (3, −3) ☐

(d) (2, −9) ☐

10. If the shortest distance of the parabola $y^2 = 4x$ from the centre of the circle $x^2 + y^2 - 4x - 16y + 64 = 0$ is d, then d^2 is equal to [JEE Main 2024]

(a) 24 ☐

(b) 16 ☐

(c) 20 ☐

(d) 36 ☐

11. Let P be a parabola with vertex (2, 3) and directrix $2x + y = 6$. Let an ellipse $E : \frac{x^2}{a^2} + \frac{y^2}{b^2} = 1, a > b$, of eccentricity $\frac{1}{\sqrt{2}}$ pass through the focus of the parabola P. Then, the square of the length of the latus rectum of E, is [JEE Main 2024]

(a) $\frac{385}{8}$ ☐

(b) $\frac{512}{25}$ ☐

(c) $\frac{656}{25}$ ☐

(d) $\frac{347}{8}$ ☐

12. Consider the circle $C : x^2 + y^2 = 4$ and the parabola $P : y^2 = 8x$. If the set of all value of α, for which three chords of the circle C on three distinct lines passing through the point (α, 0) are bisected by the parabola P is the interval (p, q), then $(2q - p)^2$ is equal to .... [JEE Main 2024]

13. Let a line perpendicular to the line $2x - y = 10$ touch the parabola $y^2 = 4(x - 9)$ at the point P.

The distance of the point P from the centre of the circle $x^2 + y^2 - 14x - 8y + 56 = 0$ is ...... [JEE Main 2024]

14. Suppose AB is a focal chord of the parabola $y^2 = 12x$ of length l and slople $m < \sqrt{3}$. If the distance of the chord AB from the origin is d, then ld^2 is equal to .... [JEE Main 2024]

15. If the length of the minor axis of an ellipse is equal to half of the distance between the foci, then the eccentricity of the ellipse is [JEE Main 2024]

(a) $\frac{\sqrt{3}}{2}$ ☐

(b) $\frac{2}{\sqrt{5}}$ ☐

(c) $\frac{1}{\sqrt{3}}$ ☐

(d) $\frac{\sqrt{5}}{3}$ ☐

16. Let P be a point on the ellipse $\frac{x^2}{9} + \frac{y^2}{4} = 1$. Let the line passing through P and parallel to Y-axis meet the circle $x^2 + y^2 = 9$ at point Q such that P and Q are on the same side of the X-axis. Then, the eccentricity of the locus of the point R on PQ such that PR : RQ = 4 : 3 as P moves on the ellipse is [JEE Main 2024]

(a) $\frac{11}{19}$ ☐

(b) $\frac{13}{21}$ ☐

(c) $\frac{\sqrt{139}}{23}$ ☐

(d) $\frac{\sqrt{13}}{7}$ ☐

17. Let the line $2x + 3y - k = 0, k > 0$, intersect the X-axis and Y-axis at the points A and B, respectively. If the equation of the circle having the line segment AB as a diameter is $x^2 + y^2 - 3x - 2y = 0$ and the length of the latus rectum of the ellipse $x^2 + 9y^2 = k^2$ is $\frac{m}{n}$, where m and n are coprime, then $2m + n$ is equal to

[JEE Main 2024]

(a) 13 ☐
(b) 12 ☐
(c) 11 ☐
(d) 10 ☐

18. Let P be a point on the hyperbola $H : \frac{x^2}{9} - \frac{y^2}{4} = 1$ in the first quadrant such that the area of triangle formed by P and the two foci of H is $2\sqrt{13}$. Then, the square of the distance of P from the origin is **[JEE Main 2024]**

(a) 20 ☐
(b) 26 ☐
(c) 22 ☐
(d) 18 ☐

19. Let the foci of a hyperbola H coincide with the foci of the ellipse $E : \frac{(x-1)^2}{100} + \frac{(y-1)^2}{75} = 1$ and the eccentricity of the hyperbola H be the reciprocal of the eccentricity of the ellipse E. If the length of the transverse axis of H is α and the length of its conjugate axis is β, then $3\alpha^2 + 2\beta^2$ is equal to

[JEE Main 2024]

(a) 242 ☐
(b) 205 ☐
(c) 237 ☐
(d) 225 ☐

20. Let $H : \frac{-x^2}{a^2} + \frac{y^2}{b^2} = 1$ be the hyperbola, whose eccentricity is $\sqrt{3}$ and the length of the latus rectum is $4\sqrt{3}$. Suppose the point $(\alpha, 6), \alpha > 0$ lies on H. If β is the product of the focal distances of the point $(\alpha, 6)$, then $\alpha^2 + \beta$ is equal to **[JEE Main 2024]**

(a) 172 ☐
(b) 169 ☐
(c) 171 ☐
(d) 170 ☐

Chapter 11

Introduction To 3D

Scan and take Chapter Test

TOPIC 1

Cartesian Coordinate System

NCERT Pg 209-211

1. Name the octants in which the following points lie.

(i) (– 3, 2, 5) ____________

(ii) (2, – 3, – 4) ____________

(iii) (7, – 9, 2) ____________

(iv) (5, 7, 6) ____________

(v) (–20, –45, 30) ____________

2. Answer the following :

(i) A point lies on the Y-axis. It's

x-coordinate is ____________

z-coordinate is ____________

(ii) A point lies on the Z-axis. It's

x-coordinate is ____________

y-coordinate is ____________

3. Match the following points with their correct plane in which they lie.

	Points		Planes
A.	(3, – 4, 0)	1.	YZ-plane
B.	(– 5, 0, – 6)	2.	XY-plane
C.	(0, 4, – 2)	3.	XZ-plane

Choose the correct option?

(a) A → 3, B → 1, C → 2

(b) A → 2, B → 3, C → 1

(c) A → 1, B → 2, C → 3

(d) A → 1, B → 3, C → 2

____

*Concepts of all questions bearing * are important for JEE & CUET*

4. State True or False.

(i) The X-axis and Y-axis taken together determine a plane known as XY-plane.

True ☐ False ☐

(ii) The coordinate of a point in the XY-plane are of the form $(0, 0, z)$.

True ☐ False ☐

(iii) Coordinate planes divide the space into six octants.

True ☐ False ☐

(iv) The equation of the plane $z = 6$ represents a plane perpendicular to the XY-plane having a z intercept of 6 units.

True ☐ False ☐

(v) The equation of the plane $x = 4$ represents a plane parallel to YZ-plane having a x intercept of 4 units.

True ☐ False ☐

5. Two distinct lines intersecting each other in a plane can have ______________ point in common.

TOPIC 2

Distance Formula

NCERT Pg 211-213

6. If the distance between the points $(a, 0, 1)$ and $(0, 1, 2)$ is $\sqrt{27}$, then the value of a is

(a) 5
(b) ± 5
(c) -5
(d) None of these

---

7. Fill in the blanks.

(i) The length of foot of perpendicular drawn from the point $P(5, 7, 9)$ on Y-axis is ______________

(ii) The length of foot of perpendicular drawn from the point $Q(1, 2, 3)$ on X-axis is ______________

(iii) The length of foot of perpendicular drawn from the point $R(5, 1, 6)$ on Z-axis is ______________

(iv) The point on Z-axis which are at a distance $\sqrt{21}$ from the point $(1, 2, 3)$ is ______________

8. Let $(-1, 4, 3)$ and $(1, -2, 3)$ be end points of a diameter of circle. Then, radius of circle is equal to

(a) $\sqrt{10}$
(b) $\sqrt{20}$
(c) $\sqrt{40}$
(d) $\sqrt{80}$

---

9. State True or False.

(i) The following points $P(0, 7, -7)$, $Q(1, 4, -5)$ and $R(-1, 10, -9)$ are collinear.

True ☐ False ☐

(ii) Points $A(2, -4, 1)$, $B(-3, -2, 1)$ and $C(-1, 3, 4)$ are the vertices of right angled triangle.

True ☐ False ☐

(iii) The tetrahedron with vertices at the points $O(0, 0, 0)$, $A(0, 1, 1)$, $B(1, 0, 1)$ and $C(1, 1, 0)$ is a regular one.

True ☐ False ☐

(iv) Points $(-1, 2, 1)$, $(1, -2, 5)$, $(4, -7, 8)$ and $(2, -3, 4)$ are vertices of parallelogram.

True ☐ False ☐

(v) Points $(5, -1, 1)$, $(7, -4, 7)$, $(1, -6, 10)$ and $(-1, -3, 4)$ are vertices of rhombus.

True ☐ False ☐

10. The equation of set of points R such that $RA^2 + RB^2 = 2K^2$, where A and B are points $(-3, -2, 1)$ and $(1, 4, -3)$, respectively.

____

11. The coordinate of a point equidistant from the four points $O(0, 0, 0)$, $A(\alpha, 0, 0)$, $B(0, \beta, 0)$ and $C(0, 0, \gamma)$ is ______________________________.

12. Two vertices of an equilateral triangle are (2, 1, 5) and (3, 2, 3), then its third vertex is

(a) 2, 3, 4 (b) 4, 0, 4 (c) 0, 4, – 4 (d) 4, 4, 1

____

13. The point which is equidistant from points (– 1, 1, 3), (2, 1, 2), (0, 5,6) and (3, 2, 2) is

______________________________.

Assertion-Reason Questions

The following questions consist of two statements – Assertion (A) and Reason (R). Answer these questions by selecting the appropriate option given below.

(a) Both (A) and (R) are true and (R) is correct explanation of (A)

(b) Both (A) and (R) are true but (R) is not the correct explanation of (A)

(c) (A) is true but (R) is false

(d) (A) is false but (R) is true

1. **Assertion** (A) Vertices of a triangle are $A(1, 2, -1)$, $B(3, 2, 1)$ and $C(-4, 0, 2)$. Its side BC has length $3\sqrt{6}$ units.

Reason (R) Distance between the points $P(x_1, y_1, z_1)$ and $Q(x_2, y_2, z_2)$ is $\sqrt{(x_2 - x_1)^2 + (y_2 - y_1)^2 + (z_2 - z_1)^2}$

(a) ☐ (b) ☐ (c) ☐ (d) ☐

2. **Assertion** (A) The points $A(3, -1, 2)$, $B(1, 2, -4)$, $C(-1, 1, 2)$ and $D(1, -2, 8)$ are the vertices of a parallelogram $ABCD$.

Reason (R) $AB = CD$, $BC = DA$ and $AC \neq BD$.

(a) ☐ (b) ☐ (c) ☐ (d) ☐

3. **Assertion** (A) Vertices of a ΔABC are $A(-1, 3, 2)$, $B(2, 3, 5)$, and $C(3, 5, -2)$. $\angle A = 90°$.

Reason (R) $AB^2 + CA^2 = BC^2$.

(a) ☐ (b) ☐ (c) ☐ (d) ☐

4. **Assertion** (A) Three points $P(0, 0, 4)$, $Q(6, 2, 4)$, and $R(-9, -3, 4)$ are collinear.

Reason (R) Three points A, B and C are collinear if B divides the line segment AC in the ratio $1:1$.

(a) ☐ (b) ☐ (c) ☐ (d) ☐

5. **Assertion** (A) The points $A(2, 9, 12)$, $B(1, 8, 8)$, $C(2, 11, 8)$ and $D(1, 12, 12)$ are the vertices of a rhombus.

Reason (R) $AB = BC = CD = DA$ and $AC = BD$.

(a) ☐ (b) ☐ (c) ☐ (d) ☐

6. **Assertion** (A) The point $P(0, 4, 0)$ lies on Y-axis.

Reason (R) The x and z coordinate of a point on Y-axis is zero.

(a) ☐ (b) ☐ (c) ☐ (d) ☐

7. **Assertion** (A) The points $(-3, 5, 4)$ and $(4, -5, 3)$ are at different positions in the coordinate plane.

Reason (R) The position of (x, y, z) in the cartesian coordinate is different from the position of (z, y, x).

(a) ☐ (b) ☐ (c) ☐ (d) ☐

8. **Assertion** (A) Distance of the point $(2, 3, 5)$ from the ZX-plane is 5 units.

Reason (R) Coordinates a, b and c of a point $A(a, b, c)$ are respectively its distance from YZ-plane, ZX-plane and XY-plane respectively.

(a) ☐ (b) ☐ (c) ☐ (d) ☐

9. **Assertion** (A) The point $(-5, 0, 0)$ lies on Y-axis, $(0, 0, -8)$ on X-axis and $(0, -3, 0)$ on Z-axis.

Reason (R) Every point on X, Y and Z-axis have zero unit distance from X, Y and Z-axis, respectively.

(a) ☐ (b) ☐ (c) ☐ (d) ☐

10. **Assertion** (A) Point (3, 1, 0) lies on the XY-plane.

Reason (R) Point (0, 0, 2) lies on the Z-axis.

(a) ☐ (b) ☐ (c) ☐ (d) ☐

Case Based Questions

Case 1 A three dimensional cartsian coordinate system is formed by a point called the origin (denoted by O) and a basis consisting of three mutually perpendicular vectors. These vectors define the three coordinate axes: X, Y and Z axes. Those are also known as abscissa, ordinate and applicate axis, respectively.

The coordinate of any point in the space is determined by three real numbers x, y and z. The planes known as coordinate planes divide the space into octants.

Below shown figure depicts a rectangular parallelopiped. Based on the above information answer the questions below:

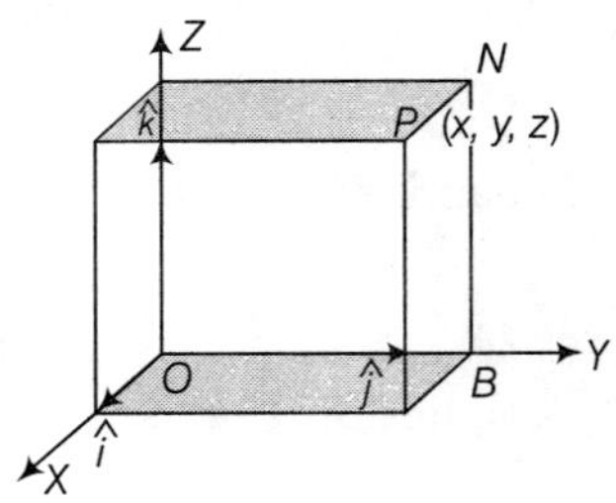

(i) If point P represents the coordinate (3, 6, 5), the coordinates of point N will be

(a) (3, 0, 5) ☐ (b) (0, 6, 5) ☐

(c) (3, 6, 0) ☐ (d) (0, 0, 0) ☐

(ii) In which octant does the point (3, −2, −5) lies?

(a) II ☐ (b) VI ☐

(c) VIII ☐ (d) IV ☐

(iii) From the figure above, the coordinates of point B will be

(a) (0, 6, 0) ☐ (b) (0, 0, 5) ☐

(c) (0, 6, 5) ☐ (d) (3, 6, 0) ☐

(iv) If a point lies on Z-axis, then the coordinates of the points are

(a) (x, y, z) ☐ (b) $(x, y, 0)$ ☐

(c) $(0, y, 0)$ ☐ (d) $(0, 0, z)$ ☐

Case 2 The equation of motions of a missile are $x = 3t$, $y = -4t$ and $z = t$, where the time t is given in seconds and the distance is measured in kilo meters.

(i) What is the path of missile?

(a) Straight line ☐ (b) Parabola ☐

(c) Circle ☐ (d) Ellipse ☐

(ii) Which of the following points lie on the path of the missile?

(a) (6, 8, 2) ☐ (b) (6, – 8, – 2) ☐

(c) (6, – 8, 2) ☐ (d) (– 6, – 8, 2) ☐

(iii) At what distance will the rocket from the starting point (0, 0, 0) in 5 seconds?

(a) $\sqrt{550}$ kms ☐ (b) $\sqrt{650}$ kms ☐

(c) $\sqrt{450}$ kms ☐ (d) $\sqrt{750}$ kms ☐

(iv) If the position of rocket at a certain instant of time is (5, –8, 10), then what will be the height of the rocket from the ground? (The ground is considered as the XY-plane).

(a) 12 km ☐ (b) 11 km ☐

(c) 20 km ☐ (d) 10 km ☐

COMPETITION CONNECT

Section Formula [NCERT (Old) Pg. 273-276]

1. Find the coordinates of the point which divides the join of

(i) $P(4, -3, 2)$ and Q (2, 3, – 4) in the ratio 5 : 4 ______________.

(ii) $P(2, -1, 4)$ and Q (4, 3, 1) in the ratio of 3 : 4 externally ______________.

(iii) $P(-3, 5, 2)$ and Q (1, 4, – 3) in the ratio of 3 : 2 internally ______________.

2. Find the coordinates of the points which trisect the line segment AB given that A (– 3, 1, 2) and B (3, – 8, 5).

____

3. A point R with x-coordinate 4 lies on the line segment joining the points P (2, – 3, 1) and Q (7, 9, 5). What is the coordinate of point R?

(a) $\frac{2}{5}$, 6, 4 (b) 4, $\frac{9}{5}$, $\frac{13}{5}$ (c) – 3, 4, 2 (d) – 5, 4, 1

____

4. Three vertices of a parallelogram $ABCD$ are A(1, 2, – 4), B(3, 2, – 1) and C (1, 4, 3). What is the coordinate of fourth vertex D?

(a) 2, 4,– 3 (b) – 3, 2, 1 (c) 4, – 2, 3 (d) – 1, 4, 0

____

5. Using section formula, state True or False.

(i) The points $A(5, 3, -2)$, $B(3, 2, 1)$ and $C(-1, 0, 7)$ are collinear.

True ☐ False ☐

(ii) The coordinate of the point of division in which line joining the points (1, 2, 3) and $(-3, 4, -5)$ is divided by XY-plane, is $-\frac{1}{2}, \frac{11}{4}, 0$.

True ☐ False ☐

(iii) The ratio in which the plane $2x + 3y + 6z = 1$ divide the line segment joining the points (7, 0, 5) and $(1, -3, 2)$, is $-31 : 4$.

True ☐ False ☐

6. Fill in the blanks.

(i) Given that $P(1, 2, 3)$, $Q(4, 5, 6)$ and $R(7, 8, 9)$ are collinear. The ratic in which Q divides PR is ________________

(ii) The centroid of ΔABC is at the point (1, 1, 1). If the coordinates at A and B are $(4, 2, -6)$ and $(3, -5, 8)$, respectively. The coordinates of point C are ________

(iii) The coordinates of A and B are $(1, -2, 3)$ and $(3, 4, -5)$ and the centroid of ΔABC is at point (2, 2, 2). Then, coordinates of C are ____________

7. Choose the correct option.

(i) The centroid of a ΔABC is at point (1, 1, 1) and the coordinates of A and B are $(2, -3, 5)$ and $(-1, -4, 3)$, respectiverly. The coordinates of point C are

(a) $1, 4, -5$ (b) $7, -10, 3$ (c) $2, 10, -5$ (d) $2, -5, 4$

____

(ii) What is the ratio in which the line joining the points (4, 5,6) and $(-1, -2, -3)$ is divided by XY-plane?

(a) 2 : 3 (b) 1 : 2 (c) 2 : 1 (d) 3 : 4

____

(iii) What is the image of $(-8, 0, 0)$ in XY-plane?

(a) 8, 0, 0 (b) $-8, 0, 0$ (c) $0, -8, 0$ (d) $0, 0, -8$

____

Chapter 12

Limits and Derivatives

Scan and take Chapter Test

TOPIC 1

Limits

NCERT Pg. 220-228

1. If $f(x)=\begin{cases}1, & x\le 0\\ 2, & x>0\end{cases}$, then the left hand limit of $f(x)$ at 0 is ____________________.

2. Evaluate the following limits.

(i) $\lim_{x\to 0^+}\dfrac{|10x|}{x}$ ____________________.

(ii) $\lim_{x\to -2^+}\dfrac{x^2-1}{x+2}$ ____________________.

(iii) $\lim_{x\to 0^+}\dfrac{\sqrt{x^5}}{x^{1/2}}$ ____________________.

3. Choose the correct option.

*(i) Let $f(x)=\begin{cases}x^3+8x^2+3x+1, & \text{if } x\le 1\\ 16x+5, & \text{if } x>1\end{cases}$, then $\lim_{x\to 1^+} f(x)$ is

(a) 21

(b) 13

(c) 34

(d) Limit does not exist

____

*(ii) Let $f(x)=\begin{cases}\cos x+1, & x\ge 0\\ x+k, & x<0\end{cases}$

Find the value of k given that $\lim_{x\to 0} f(x)$ exist.

(a) 0 (b) 1 (c) – 1 (d) 2

____

*Concepts of all questions bearing * are important for JEE & CUET*

(iii) Let $f(x)=\begin{cases} x^3+1, & 0<x<1 \\ 2x+1, & 1\le x<2 \end{cases}$, the quadratic equation whose roots are $\lim_{x\to 1^-} f(x)$ and $\lim_{x\to 1^+} f(x)$, is

(a) $x^2-6x+9=0$

(b) $x^2-5x+6=0$

(c) $x^2-x+6=0$

(d) $x^2-10x+21=0$

(iv) If f is a function such that $f(-x)=-f(x)$ and $\lim_{x\to 0} f(x)$ exists, then $\lim_{x\to 0} f(x)$ is equal to

(a) 0 (b) 1 (c) 2 (d) – 2

---

*(v) If $f(x)=\begin{cases} |x-1|-1, & x<1 \\ ax+b, & x=1 \\ |x-1|+1, & x>1 \end{cases}$

For what values of a and b does $\lim_{x\to 1} f(x)=f(1)$?

(a) $a=1$ and $b=0$

(b) $a=0$ and $b=-1$

(c) $a=0$ and $b=0$

(d) no such values of a and b

---

*(vi) Suppose $f(x)=\begin{cases} ax^2+b, & x<0 \\ 2, & x=0 \\ a+b(x+1), & x>0 \end{cases}$ and if $\lim_{x\to 0} f(x)=f(0)$, then the value of $10-ab$ is

(a) 2 (b) 10 (c) 4 (d) None of these

(vii) Let f be a function defined by $f(x)=\begin{cases} \dfrac{ax}{|x|-bx^2}, & x\ne 0 \\ 0, & x=0 \end{cases}$. Then, $\lim_{x\to 0} f(x)$ is

(a) 0 (b) a (c) $-a$ (d) Does not exist

---

*(viii) If $f(x)=\begin{cases} ax^3+b, & x<0 \\ a+bx, & 0\le x<1 \\ ax^2-bx+1, & x>1 \end{cases}$

If both $\lim_{x\to 0} f(x)$ and $\lim_{x\to 1} f(x)$ exist, then the values of a and b are

(a) $a=2$ and $b=1$

(b) $a=1$ and $b=-2$

(c) $a=b=1$

(d) $a=b=\dfrac{1}{2}$

TOPIC 2

Limits of Polynomials and Rational Functions

NCERT Pg 228-233

4. Evaluate the limit of following polynomial functions.

(i) $\lim_{x \to -1} \sqrt{5}x^6 + \sqrt{3}x^3 + x^2 + x$

(a) 0 (b) $\frac{2}{(\sqrt{5}+\sqrt{3})}$ (c) $\sqrt{5}+\sqrt{3}$ (d) None of these

(ii) $\lim_{x \to \sqrt{3}} \frac{2}{3}x^2 + \sqrt{3}x - 5$

(a) 0 (b) 1 (c) 2 (d) 3

(iii) $\lim_{x \to 5}(x^3 - 3x^2 + 5x + 1)$

(a) 70 (b) 76 (c) 50 (d) 55

(iv) $\lim_{x \to -1}(x^4 + 3x^3 + 2x^2 + x - 1)$

(a) − 2 (b) − 1 (c) 0 (d) 5

***5.** Evaluate the limit of following rational functions.

(i) $\lim_{x \to 1} \frac{x^3 - 3x^2 + 3x - 1}{x - 1}$

(ii) $\lim_{a \to 1} \frac{a^3 - 3a^2 + 2a}{a - 1}$

(iii) $\lim_{x \to 1} \frac{x^3 - 6x^2 + 11x - 6}{x^2 - 3x + 2}$

(iv) $\lim_{x \to 2} \frac{x^6 - 24x - 16}{x^3 + 2x - 12}$

6. State True or False.

(i) $\lim_{x \to 0} \frac{1}{\sqrt{x^2+1} - \sqrt{x^2-1}} = \frac{(1+i)}{2}$

True ☐ False ☐

(ii) $\lim_{x \to 0} \frac{\sqrt{1+x} - \sqrt{1-x}}{x} = -1$

True ☐ False ☐

(iii) $\lim_{x \to 0} \frac{\sqrt{x^2 + a^2} - a}{\sqrt{x^2 + b^2} - b} = \frac{b}{a}$

True ☐ False ☐

7. Answer the following questions.

*(i) $\lim_{x \to 1} \frac{x^5 - 1}{x^3 - 1}$ is equal to ____________

*(ii) Find the positive integer n such that

$\lim_{x \to 2} \frac{x^n - 2^n}{x - 2} = 192$ ____________

*(iii) $\lim_{x \to 0} \frac{(1+x)^n - 1}{x}$ is equal to ____________

*(iv) Let $f(x) = x^6 + x^5 + 2x^3 + x^2 + 4, x \in R$, then the natural number n for which

$\lim_{x \to 1} \frac{x^n f(1) - 3\{f(0) - 1\}}{x - 1} = 45$, then n is equal to ____________

TOPIC 3

Limits of Trigonometric Functions

NCERT Pg 234-237

8. Evaluate the following limits.

(i) $\lim_{x \to 0} \frac{\sin 3x}{x}$ ____________

(ii) $\lim_{x \to 0} \left[\frac{\sin mx}{x} + \frac{\sin^2 2x}{x^2}\right]$ ____________

(iii) $\lim_{x \to 0} \left[\frac{1 - \cos 2x}{x} + \cos^2 x + 1\right]$ ____________

9. Choose the correct option.

(i) $\lim_{x \to 0} x \cos \frac{1}{x}$ is equal to

(a) 0 (b) 1 (c) $\frac{1}{2}$ (d) Does not exist

____

(ii) $\lim_{x \to 0} \left(\frac{x}{\tan x} + \sqrt{x} + 3 \right)$ is equal to

(a) 3 (b) 4
(c) 5 (d) Cannot be determined

(iii) The value of limit of function $f(x)$ as $x \to 0$, where $f(x) = \frac{\sqrt{\frac{1}{2}(1 - \cos 2x)}}{x}$, is

(a) 1 (b) 2 (c) –1 (d) –2

---

*(iv) Let $f(x) = \begin{cases} \frac{k \sin\left(x - \frac{\pi}{2}\right)}{\pi - 2x}, & x \neq \frac{\pi}{2} \\ 2, & x = \frac{\pi}{2} \end{cases}$ and if $\lim_{x \to \frac{\pi}{2}} f(x) = f\left(\frac{\pi}{2}\right)$, then the value of k is

(a) 1 (b) $\frac{1}{2}$ (c) – 2 (d) – 4

(v) $\lim_{x \to 0} \frac{\sin ax - \sin bx}{\sqrt{1 - \cos cx}}$ is equal to

(a) $\frac{a^2 - b^2}{c^2}$ (b) $\frac{1}{\sqrt{2}} \left(\frac{a^2 - b^2}{c^2} \right)$ (c) $\frac{a - b}{c}$ (d) $\sqrt{2} \left(\frac{a - b}{c} \right)$

(vi) The limit as x tends to zero of the function $f(x)$, where

$$f(x) = \frac{1}{x} [\cos(a + x) - \cos(a - x)] \text{ is}$$

(a) $2 \sin x$ (b) $\sin a \cdot \cos x$ (c) $2 \cos a$ (d) $-2 \sin a$

(vii) $\lim_{y \to 0} \frac{(x + y) \sec(x + y) - x \sec x}{y}$ is

(a) $\sec x$ (b) $x \tan x$ (c) $1 + x \tan x$ (d) $\sec x + x \tan x \sec x$

---

10. Fill in the blanks.

*(i) If $\lim_{x \to 0} \tan \frac{x}{\sqrt{3}} \cdot \operatorname{cosec} mx = 2$, then m is equal to ________________

(ii) Limit of the function $f(x)$ at x tends to $\frac{\pi}{4}$, where $f(x) = \frac{\cos x - \sin x}{\left(x - \frac{\pi}{4} \right)}$ is __________

TOPIC 4

Derivatives

NCERT Pg 239-248

11. Find $f'(x)$ for the following functions.

(i) $f(x)=\left[\left(1+\frac{1}{x}\right)\left(1-\frac{1}{x}\right)\right]$ ______

(ii) $f(x)=\frac{x^5}{5}-2\sqrt{x}+\frac{7}{x^2}+x$ ______

(iii) $f(x)=\sqrt{x}+\frac{1}{\sqrt{x}}$ ______

(iv) $f(x)=x^{-m}(b+cx^{-n})$ ______

(v) $f(x)=\frac{1}{\sqrt{a^2-x^2}}$ ______

12. Choose the correct option.

(i) If $f(x) = 3x^2 + 6x$, then the value of $f'(-1)$ is

(a) 0 (b) 1 (c) 2 (d) 3

______

(ii) If $f(x) = x^3 + 2x^2 + 3x$, then the value of $f'(1)$ is

(a) 30 (b) 10 (c) 5 (d) 0

______

*(iii) If $f(x) = x^3 - 4x^2 + 5x + 1$, then the value of $3f'(0) - f'(-1) + 2f'(1)$ is

(a) – 1 (b) 1 (c) 0 (d) – 5

______

*(iv) If $f(x) = x^3 + 5x^2 - 3x + 2$, then the value of $f'(0) + 3f(2)$ is

(a) 69 (b) 50 (c) 72 (d) – 72

______

(v) If $f(x) = (1 + ax)(1 + bx^2)(1 + cx^3)$, then $f'(x)$ at $x = 1$ is

(a) $a(1+b)(1+c)+2b(1+a)(1+c)+3c(1+b)(1+a)$

(b) $2a(1+b)(1+c)+3b(1+a)(1+c)+c(1+a)(1+b)$

(c) $2a(1-b)(1-c)+3b(1-a)(1-c)+c(1-a)(1-b)$

(d) $3a(1+b)(1+c)+2b(1+a)(1+c)+a(1+b)(1+c)$

______

13. Find $\frac{dy}{dx}$ in each of the following functions.

(i) If $y = \frac{x-1}{x^2-3}$ ________________________________

(ii) If $y = \frac{x}{\sqrt{1+x^2}}$ ________________________________

(iii) If $y = \frac{1+\frac{1}{\sqrt{x}}}{1-\frac{1}{\sqrt{x}}}$ ________________________________

*(iv) If $y = \frac{ax^2+bx+c}{rx^2+sx+t}$ at $x = 0$ ________________________________

14. Find the derivatives of the following functions.

(i) $\sin x + \cos x$ ________________________________

(ii) $3\sec x + 2\tan x$ ________________________________

(iii) $5\cot x + 2\sin x$ ________________________________

(iv) $3\operatorname{cosec} x + 2\tan x$ ________________________________

(v) $\sec x + \tan x - \sin x$ ________________________________

(vi) $\tan x \cdot \cot x$ ________________________________

15. Choose the correct derivative of the following functions.

(i) $y = \frac{1}{\sqrt{1+\tan^2 x}}$

(a) $\cos x$ (b) $-\sin x$ (c) $\sec x$ (d) $\tan x$

____

(ii) $y = \sqrt{1+\sin 2x}$

(a) $\cos x - \sin x$ (b) $\cos x + \sin x$

(c) $\sin x - \cos x$ (d) None of these

____

(iii) $y = x^2 \sin x$

(a) $2x\sin x + x^2\cos x$ (b) $x\sin x + \cos x$

(c) $\cos x + \sin x$ (d) None of these

____

16. Fill in the blanks

(i) If $f(x) = x\cos x$, then $f'(\pi)$ is ________________________________

(ii) Let $f(x) = (3x^2+2x+5)(x\sin x + \tan x)$, then $f'(x)$ is ________________________________

17. State True or False.

(i) Derivative of $\sqrt{x \tan x}$ is $\dfrac{1}{2\sqrt{x \tan x}}(\tan x + x \sec^2 x)$.

True ☐ False ☐

*(ii) If $f(x) = x^n \tan^2 x + \sec x + 1$, then the value of $xf'(0)$ is 0.

True ☐ False ☐

18. Choose the correct option.

(i) If $xy + 1 = -\cos(xy)$, then $\dfrac{dy}{dx}$ at $x = \dfrac{\pi}{2}$ and $y = 0$ is

(a) 1
(b) -1
(c) 0
(d) Cannot be determined

(ii) Differentiate the function with respect to x, where $f(x) = \sin^2 2x \cdot \cos^4 4x + x^3 + 1$, is

(a) $2 \sin 2x \cos^4 4x + 3x^2$

(b) $2 \sin 2x \cos^4 4x + 4 \cos 4x \sin + 3x^2$

(c) $2 \sin 4x \cos^4 4x + 3x^2 - 16 \sin^2 2x \sin 4x \cos^3 4x$

(d) None of the above

(iii) $\dfrac{d}{dx}\left(\dfrac{x}{\sin x}\right)$ is

(a) $\dfrac{\cos x + x \sin x}{\sin^2 x}$
(b) $\dfrac{1}{\cos x}$
(c) $-\dfrac{1}{\cos x}$
(d) $\dfrac{\sin x - x\cos x}{\sin^2 x}$

*(iv) If $y = \dfrac{\sin x + \cos x}{\sin x - \cos x}$, then $\dfrac{dy}{dx}$ at $x = \dfrac{\pi}{2}$ is

(a) 1
(b) 0
(c) -2
(d) 2

19. Fill in the blanks.

(i) If $y = (x + \sin x)(1 - \tan x)$, then $\dfrac{dy}{dx}$ is ______________

(ii) The derivative of $\dfrac{1 - \sin x}{\cos x}$ is equal to ______________

20. Derivative of $\dfrac{\sin ax}{1 + \cos bx}$ at $x = 0$ is $\dfrac{a}{2}$.

True ☐ False ☐

21. Fill in the blanks with suitable answer.

(i) If $y = \cos(\sqrt{\sin\sqrt{x}})$, then $\frac{dy}{dx}$ = ____________________

(ii) If $y = \sqrt{\frac{1-\tan x}{1+\tan x}}$, then $\frac{dy}{dx}$ = ____________________

(iii) If $y = \sqrt{1+\sin x} + \sqrt{\frac{1-x^2}{1+x^2}}$, then $\frac{dy}{dx}$ = ____________________

Assertion-Reason Questions

The following questions consist of two statements – Assertion (A) and Reason (R). Answer these questions by selecting the appropriate option given below.
(a) Both (A) and (R) are true and (R) is correct explanation of (A)
(b) Both (A) and (R) are true but (R) is not the correct explanation of (A)
(c) (A) is true but (R) is false
(d) (A) is false but (R) is true

1. **Assertion** (A) $\lim_{x \to 0} \frac{\cos 2x - 1}{\cos x - 1} = 4$

Reason (R) $\cos x = 1 - 2\sin^2 \frac{x}{2}$

(a) ☐ (b) ☐ (c) ☐ (d) ☐

2. **Assertion** (A) $\lim_{x \to 0} \frac{(x+2)^3 - 8}{x} = 12$

Reason (R) For the function $f(x) = \begin{cases} 3x-2, & x \le 1 \\ 3(x-1), & x > 1 \end{cases}$, $\lim_{x \to 1} f(x)$ does not exist.

(a) ☐ (b) ☐ (c) ☐ (d) ☐

3. **Assertion** (A) $\lim_{x \to 0} \frac{\sqrt{1-\cos x}}{x}$ does not exist.

Reason (R) $\lim_{x \to 0} \frac{e^{\sin x} - 1}{x}$ is equal to 1.

(a) ☐ (b) ☐ (c) ☐ (d) ☐

4. **Assertion** (A) $\lim_{x \to 0} \frac{\sin 3x}{\sin 2x}$ is equal to $\frac{3}{2}$.

Reason (R) $\lim_{x \to 0} \frac{\sin x}{x(1+\cos x)}$ is not defined.

(a) ☐ (b) ☐ (c) ☐ (d) ☐

5. **Assertion** (A) $\lim_{x \to 1} \frac{ax^2 + bx + c}{cx^2 + bx + a}$ is equal to 1, where $a + b + c \neq 0$.

Reason (R) $\lim_{x \to -2} \frac{\frac{1}{x} + \frac{1}{2}}{x + 2}$ is equal to $\frac{1}{4}$.

(a) ☐ (b) ☐ (c) ☐ (d) ☐

6. **Assertion** (A) If $\lim_{x \to a} f(x) = L$, then $f(a) = L$

Reason (R) The limit of a function as x approaches a is the value of the function at a.

(a) ☐ (b) ☐ (c) ☐ (d) ☐

7. **Assertion** (A) $\lim_{x \to a} (x^3 - a^3) = 0$

Reason (R) $\lim_{x \to a} x^3 = a^3$

(a) ☐ (b) ☐ (c) ☐ (d) ☐

8. **Assertion** (A) If $f(x) = x^2$, then $f'(x) = 2x$.

Reason (R) The derivative of x^n is nx^{n-1}.

(a) ☐ (b) ☐ (c) ☐ (d) ☐

9. **Assertion** (A) The derivative of $f(x) = x^2$ at $x = 2$ is 4.

Reason (R) The derivative of $f(x) = \sin x + \cos x$ is $\sin x - \cos x$.

(a) ☐ (b) ☐ (c) ☐ (d) ☐

10. **Assertion** (A) The $\lim_{x \to 1} \frac{x^2 - 1}{x - 1}$ exists.

Reason (R) $\frac{x^2 - 1}{x - 1} = x + 1$

(a) ☐ (b) ☐ (c) ☐ (d) ☐

Case Based Questions

Case 1 A function f is said to be rational function, if $f(x) = \frac{g(x)}{h(x)}$, where $g(x)$ and $h(x)$ are polynomial functions such that $h(x) \neq 0$.

Then, $\lim_{x \to a} f(x) = \lim_{x \to a} \frac{g(x)}{h(x)} = \frac{\lim_{x \to a} g(x)}{\lim_{x \to a} h(x)}$

However, if $h(a) = 0$, then there are two cases arise.

(i) $g(a) \neq 0$ (ii) $g(a) = 0$

In the first case, we say that the limit does not exist.

In the second case, we can find limit.

Based on above information, answer the following questions.

(i) $\lim_{x \to -1} \left(\frac{x^{10} + x^5 + 1}{x - 1} \right)$ is equal to

(a) $\frac{1}{2}$ ☐ (b) $-\frac{1}{2}$ ☐ (c) 2 ☐ (d) $\frac{3}{2}$ ☐

(ii) $\lim_{x \to -1} \frac{(x-1)^2 + 3x^2}{(x^4 + 1)^2}$ is equal to

(a) $\frac{7}{4}$ ☐ (b) $\frac{6}{5}$ ☐ (c) $\frac{4}{7}$ ☐ (d) $\frac{3}{4}$ ☐

(iii) The value of $\lim_{x \to 2} \left[\frac{x^2 - 4}{x^3 - 4x^2 + 4x} \right]$ is

(a) 0 ☐ (b) 1 ☐ (c) 2 ☐ (d) does not exist ☐

(iv) $\lim_{x \to 0} \frac{\sqrt{1 + x^3} - \sqrt{1 - x^3}}{x^2}$ is equal to

(a) 1 ☐ (b) 0 ☐ (c) -1 ☐ (d) 2 ☐

Case 2 Three important limits are

(i) $\lim_{x \to 0} \frac{\sin x}{x} = 1$ (ii) $\lim_{x \to 0} \frac{1 - \cos x}{x} = 0$ (iii) $\lim_{x \to 0} \frac{\tan x}{x} = 1$

Based on above information, answer the following questions.

(i) $\lim_{x \to 0} \frac{\sin 4x}{8x}$ is equal to

(a) $\frac{2}{5}$ ☐ (b) $\frac{1}{2}$ ☐ (c) $\frac{1}{4}$ ☐ (d) $\frac{3}{4}$ ☐

(ii) $\lim_{\theta \to b} \frac{\tan (\theta - b)}{\theta - b}$ is equal to

(a) 0 ☐ (b) 1 ☐ (c) 2 ☐ (d) 3 ☐

(iii) $\lim_{x \to 0} \frac{\tan 2x - \sin 2x}{x^3}$ is equal to

(a) 4 ☐ (b) 3 ☐ (c) 2 ☐ (d) 1 ☐

(iv) $\lim_{x \to 0} \frac{2 \sin x - \sin 2x}{x^2}$ is equal to

(a) 0 ☐ (b) -1 ☐ (c) 2 ☐ (d) 3 ☐

COMPETITION EDGE UP

1. $\lim_{x \to 0} \dfrac{e - (1+2x)^{\frac{1}{2x}}}{x}$ is equal to **[JEE Main 2024]**

(a) 0 ☐

(b) e ☐

(c) $e - e^2$ ☐

(d) $\dfrac{-2}{e}$ ☐

2. $\lim_{n \to \infty} \left\{ \left(2^{\frac{1}{2}} - 2^{\frac{1}{3}}\right)\left(2^{\frac{1}{2}} - 2^{\frac{1}{5}}\right) \ldots \left(2^{\frac{1}{2}} - 2^{\frac{1}{2n-1}}\right) \right\}$

is equal to **[JEE Main 2023]**

(a) $1/\sqrt{2}$ ☐

(b) $\sqrt{2}$ ☐

(c) 0 ☐

(d) 1 ☐

3. The set of all values of a for which $\lim_{x \to \infty} [x - 5] - [2x + 2] = 0$, where $[\alpha]$ denotes the greatest integer less than or equal to α is equal to **[JEE Main 2023]**

(a) $[-7.5, -6.5)$ ☐

(b) $(-7.5, -6.5)$ ☐

(c) $(-7.5, -6.5]$ ☐

(d) $[-7.5, -6.5]$ ☐

4. $\lim_{n \to \infty} \dfrac{(1^2 - 1)(n-1) + (2^2 - 2)(n-2) + \ldots ((n-1)^2 - (n-1)) \cdot 1}{(1^3 + 2^3 + \ldots + n^3) - (1^2 + 2^2 + \ldots + n^2)}$

is equal to **[JEE Main 2024]**

(a) $\dfrac{3}{4}$ ☐

(b) $\dfrac{1}{3}$ ☐

(c) $\dfrac{1}{2}$ ☐

(d) $\dfrac{2}{3}$ ☐

5. The value of

$$\lim_{n \to \infty} \frac{(1+2-3) + (4+5-6) + \ldots + (3n-2) + (3n-1) - 3n}{\sqrt{2n^4 + 4n + 3} - \sqrt{n^4 + 5n + 4}}$$ is **[JEE Main 2023]**

(a) $\dfrac{3}{2}(\sqrt{2} + 1)$ ☐

(b) $\dfrac{3}{2\sqrt{2}}$ ☐

(c) $3(\sqrt{2} + 1)$ ☐

(d) $\dfrac{\sqrt{2} + 1}{2}$ ☐

6. $\lim_{x \to \infty} \dfrac{(\sqrt{3x+1} + \sqrt{3x-1})^6 + (\sqrt{3x+1} - \sqrt{3x-1})^6}{(x + \sqrt{x^2 - 1})^6 + (x - \sqrt{x^2 - 1})^6} x^3$ **[JEE Main 2023]**

(a) is equal to $\dfrac{27}{2}$ ☐

(b) does not exist ☐

(c) is equal to 27 ☐

(d) is equal to 9 ☐

7. If $\lim_{x \to 0} \dfrac{ax^2e^x - b\log_e(1+x) + cxe^{-x}}{x^2 \sin x} = 1$, then $16(a^2 + b^2 + c^2)$ is equal to .... **[JEE Main 2024]**

8. Let $\sum_{n=0}^{\infty} \dfrac{n^3((2n)!) + (2n-1)(n!)}{(n!)((2n)!)} = ae + \dfrac{b}{e} + c$, where $a, b, c \in Z$ and $e = \sum_{n=0}^{\infty} \dfrac{1}{n!}$. Then, $a^2 - b + c$ is equal to .... **[JEE Main 2023]**

9. $\lim_{x \to 0} \dfrac{e^{2|\sin x|} - 2|\sin x| - 1}{x^2}$ **[JEE Main 2024]**

(a) does not exist ☐

(b) is equal to -1 ☐

(c) is equal to 1 ☐

(d) is equal to 2 ☐

10. $\lim_{x \to \infty}\left(\left(\dfrac{1-\cos^2(3x)}{\cos^3(4x)}\right)\left(\dfrac{\sin^3(4x)}{(\log_e(2x+1))^5}\right)\right)$ is equal to .... **[JEE Main 2023]**

(a) 24 ☐

(b) 9 ☐

(c) 18 ☐

(d) 15 ☐

12. If

$$\lim_{x \to 0}\frac{3+\alpha \sin x+\beta \cos x+\log_e(1-x)}{3\tan^2 x}$$

$= \frac{1}{3}$, then $2\alpha - \beta$ is equal to **[JEE Main 2024]**

(a) 2 ☐

(b) 5 ☐

(c) 7 ☐

(d) 1 ☐

11. $\lim_{t \to 0}\left(1^{\frac{1}{\sin^2 t}} + 2^{\frac{1}{\sin^2 t}} + \ldots + n^{\frac{1}{\sin^2 t}}\right)^{\sin^2 t}$

is equal to **[JEE Main 2023]**

(a) $\dfrac{n(n+1)}{2}$ ☐

(b) n ☐

(c) $n^2 + n$ ☐

(d) n^2 ☐

13. If $\lim_{x \to 0}\dfrac{e^{ax} - \cos(bx) - \dfrac{cxe^{-cx}}{2}}{1-\cos(2x)} = 17,$

then $5a^2 + b^2$ is equal to

[JEE Main 2023]

(a) 76 ☐

(b) 72 ☐

(c) 64 ☐

(d) 68 ☐

14. Let $x = 2$ be a root of the equation $x^2 + px + q = 0$ and

$f(x) =$

$$\begin{cases} \dfrac{1-\cos(x^2-4px+q^2+8q+16)}{(x-2p)^4}, & x \neq 2p \\ 0, & x = 2p \end{cases}$$

Then, $\lim_{x \to 2p^+}[f(x)]$, where $[\,.\,]$ denotes greatest integer function, is **[JEE Main 2023]**

(a) 1 ☐

(b) – 1 ☐

(c) 2 ☐

(d) 0 ☐

Chapter 13

Statistics

Scan and take Chapter Test

TOPIC 1

Introduction to Measures of Central Tendency

NCERT Pg 257-258

1. What is the mean of the following data?

(i) 2, 9, 5, 6, 4 ______

(ii) 7, 17, 9, 10, 8, 13, 6 ______

(iii) 9, 13, 4, 11, 20, 16, 10, 5 ______

(iv) 1, 0, 1, –1, 2, 3 ______

2. State True or False.

(i) The median of the data 63, 80, 56, 163, 124, 180 and 72 is 80.

True ☐ False ☐

(ii) The median of the data 24, 69, 57 and 102 is 69.

True ☐ False ☐

3. The median of the run made by a player in five T20 matches are 44, 21, 35, 55 and 45 is

(a) 34 (b) 44 (c) 68 (d) 70

______

4. The sum of median and mean of the data 14, 12, 56, 60, 72, 80 and 126 is ______ .

TOPIC 2

Measures of Dispersion and Range

NCERT Pg 259

5. Which of the following are measures of dispersion? (Yes/No)

(i) Range

Yes ☐ No ☐

(ii) Mean deviation

Yes ☐ No ☐

*Concepts of all questions bearing * are important for JEE & CUET*

(iii) Standard deviation

Yes ☐ No ☐

(iv) Quartile deviation

Yes ☐ No ☐

6. The range of a series is given by minimum value – maximum value.

True ☐ False ☐

7. Find the range of the given sets of the following data.

(i) – 1, 0, – 1, 0, – 2, 2, 3, 4 ____________________

(ii) 47, 95, 96, 42, 48, 54, 2, 78 and 80 ____________________

(iii) 2, 4, 9, 0, 2, – 1, – 1, 0, 4, 6, 8 ____________________

(iv) 101, 102, 103, 100, 101, 104, 101, 100, 103 ____________________

TOPIC 3

Mean Deviation

NCERT Pg 259-270

8. What will be the absolute values of deviation for the following data about the mean?

(i) 6, 10, 12, 14, 5, 7 ____________________

(ii) 15, 8, 7, 4, 6, 11, 5, 16 ____________________

***9.** Find the mean deviation about the mean of the following data.

(i) 2, 5, 2, 3, – 4, – 2 ____________________

(ii) – 1, 0, 2, 3, – 1, 1, 0, 2, 3, 1 ____________________

(iii) 5, 8, 10, 13, 4, 6, 9, 17, 18 ____________________

***10.** Find the mean deviation about the median of the following data.

(i) 1, 1, 1, – 1, 2, – 2 ____________________

(ii) 4, 6, 7, 21, 14, 19, 12, 8, 9, 10, 18 ____________________

***11.** Calculate the mean deviation about the mean of the following data.

(i)

x_i	2	6	0	– 5	2
f_i	4	3	9	2	2

(ii)

x_i	3	5	2	8	10	18
f_i	4	8	20	6	7	5

12. State True or False.

(i) The mean deviation about the median of the following data is 2.13.

Weight (in kg)	2	4	1	3
Items	2	4	6	3

True ☐ False ☐

(ii) The mean deviation about the median of the following data is 1.86 cm.

Height (in cm)	147	148	150	152	155
Number of students	8	12	15	10	5

True ☐ False ☐

***13.** Find the mean deviation about the mean for the following data.

(i)

Distance (in km)	0-5	5-10	10-15	15-20
Number of people	4	2	4	2

(ii)

Classes	30-40	40-50	50-60	60-70	70-80
Frequency	2	4	3	2	1

***14.** Calculate the mean deviation about the mean for the following data. (using shortcut method)

Age group	10-20	20-30	30-40	40-50	50-60	60-70
Number of people	5	12	7	8	6	2

(a) 12.8 (b) 12.4 (c) 13.8 (d) 12.2

***15.** Find the mean deviation about the median of the following data.

(i)

Quantity of students	0-10	10-20	20-30	30-40	40-50
School buses	3	2	1	1	1

(ii)

Marks obtained	15-25	25-35	35-45	45-55	55-65	65-75
Number of students	9	13	25	30	13	10

***16.** Find the mean deviation about the median of the following data.

(i)

Age	1-5	6-10	11-15	16-20
Student	2	5	1	3

(ii)

Class	56-60	61-65	66-70	71-75	76-80
Frequency	8	6	12	28	16

17. The sum of absolute value of deviation from the mean is always more than the sum of deviation from median.

True ☐ False ☐

TOPIC 4

Variance and Standard Deviation

NCERT Pg 271-281

18. Evaluate the following statements.

(i) The variance of first n natural numbers 1, 2, 3, ... n is ______

(ii) The variance of first n natural numbers is 10 and the variance of first m even natural numbers is 16, then what will be the sum of m and n is ______

19. If the observation $x_1, x_2, x_3 \dots x_n$ is increased by a, where a is a negative or positive integer, then the variance will get changed.

True ☐ False ☐

20. The variance of first 10 multiples of 4 is 136.

True ☐ False ☐

***21.** The mean and variance of seven observation are 10 and 16, respectively, if five of these are 7, 8, 12, 13 and 17, then the remaining two observation will be ______ and ______.

***22.** The mean and variance of six observation are 7 and 14, respectively. Each observation is multiplied by 3. What will be the new mean and new variance of observation?

(a) 20, 125 (b) 21, 126 (c) 21, 142 (d) 25, 142

23. What is the variance and standard deviation of the following data

4, 6, 8, 10, 12, 14, 16, 18, 20 and 22?

(i) Variance ______

(ii) Standard deviation ______

24. State True or False based on given data.

Size of item	4.5	5.5	6.5	7.5	8.5	9.5	10.5
Frequency	4	8	23	62	85	32	11

(i) The variance of the observation is 2.45

True ☐ False ☐

(ii) The standard deviation of the observation is 1.2.

True ☐ False ☐

(iii) The standard deviation of the observation is 4.5.

True ☐ False ☐

(iv) The variance of the observation is 1.45.

True ☐ False ☐

25. The standard deviation for the following distribution

66, 68, 58, 46, 48, 55, 60, 72, 80 and 37 is

(a) 11.48 (b) 10.44 (c) 7.89 (d) 12.38

26.

x	5.5	15.5	25.5	35.5	45.5	55.5	65.5
f	2	6	13	23	18	10	5

The standard deviation for the given observation is 14.03.

True ☐ False ☐

27.

Marks	10-20	20-30	30-40	40-50	50-60	60-70	70-80
Number of students	4	7	12	16	14	6	5

Which of the following statement is true?

(a) The variance for the given observation is 218.23

(b) The standard deviation of the observation is 14.75

(c) The variance of the observation is 204.82

(d) None of the above

28. Fill in the blanks.

2, 4, 6, 8, 10 and 12

(i) Mean ____________

(ii) Variance ____________

(iii) Standard deviation ____________

29. The mean and standard deviations of 80 observation were calculated as 50 and 5, respectively by a student who took by mistake 40 instead of 30 for one observation. What will be the

(i) correct mean ____________

(ii) correct standard deviation ____________

30. The mean and standard deviation of 10 observation are found to be 10 and 4, respectively. On rechecking it was found that an observation 5 was incorrect. What will be the correct mean and standard deviation, when the wrong item is omitted?

31. If $\sum_{i=1}^{n}(x_i - a) = n$ and $\sum_{i=1}^{n}(x_i - a)^2 = na\ (n, a > 1)$, then the variance of n observation $x_1, x_2 \ldots x_n$ is $a+1$.

True ☐ False ☐

***32.** Let $x_i\ (1 \le i \le 10)$ be 10 observation of a random variable X.

If $\sum_{i=1}^{10} x_i - P = 3$ and $\sum_{i=1}^{10}(x_i - P)^2 = 9$, where $0 \ne P \in R$, then the standard deviation of these observation is

(a) $\frac{8}{10}$ (b) $\frac{9}{10}$ (c) $\frac{7}{12}$ (d) $\frac{8}{16}$

Assertion-Reason Questions

The following questions consist of two statements – Assertion (A) and Reason (R). Answer these questions by selecting the appropriate option given below.
(a) Both (A) and (R) are true and (R) is correct explanation of (A)
(b) Both (A) and (R) are true but (R) is not the correct explanation of (A)
(c) (A) is true but (R) is false
(d) (A) is false but (R) is true

1. **Assertion** (A) In order to find the dispersion of values of x from mean $\bar{x}$, we take absolute measure of dispersion.

Reason (R) Sum of the deviations from mean $\bar{x}$ is zero.

(a) ☐ (b) ☐ (c) ☐ (d) ☐

2. **Assertion** (A) The mean deviation about the mean for the data 4, 7, 8, 9, 10, 12, 13, 17 is 3.

Reason (R) The mean deviation about the mean is $\frac{1}{N}\sum_{i=1}^{n}|x_i - \bar{x}|$.

(a) ☐ (b) ☐ (c) ☐ (d) ☐

3. **Assertion** (A) Consider the following data.

x_i	5	10	15	20	25
f_i	7	4	6	3	5

Then, the mean deviation about the mean is 6.32.

Reason (R) Consider the following data.

x_i	10	30	50	70	90
f_i	4	24	28	16	8

Then, the mean deviation about the mean is 15.

(a) ☐ (b) ☐ (c) ☐ (d) ☐

4. **Assertion** (A) The mean deviation about median calculated for series, where variability is very high, cannot be fully relied.

Reason (R) The median is not a representative of central tendency for the series where degree of variability is very high.

(a) ☐ (b) ☐ (c) ☐ (d) ☐

5. **Assertion** (A) The mean deviation about the mean to find measure of dispersion has certain limitations.

Reason (R) The sum of deviations from the mean is more than the sum of deviations from median. Therefore, the mean deviation about the mean is not very scientific, where degree of variability is very high.

(a) ☐ (b) ☐ (c) ☐ (d) ☐

6. **Assertion** (A) The average marks of boys in a class is 52 and that of girls is 42. The average marks of boys and girls combined is 50. The percentage of boys in the class is 80%.

Reason (R) Mean marks scored by the students of a class is 53. The mean marks of the girls is 55 and the mean marks of the boys is 50. The percentage of girls in the class is 64%.

(a) ☐ (b) ☐ (c) ☐ (d) ☐

7. **Assertion** (A) The weights (in kg) of 15 students are as follows 31, 35, 27, 29, 32, 43, 37, 41, 34, 28, 36, 44, 45, 42, 30. If the weight 44 kg is replaced by 46 kg and 27 kg is by 25 kg, then new median is 35.

Reason (R) The mean deviation from the median of the weights (in kg) 54, 50, 40, 42, 51, 45, 47, 57 is 4.75.

(a) ☐ (b) ☐ (c) ☐ (d) ☐

8. **Assertion** (A) The proper measure of dispersion about the mean of a set of observations i.e. standard deviation is expressed as positive square root of the variance.

Reason (R) The units of individual observations x_i and the unit of their mean are different that of variance. Since, variance involves sum of squares of $(x - \bar{x})$.

(a) ☐ (b) ☐ (c) ☐ (d) ☐

9. Consider the following data.

x_i	4	8	11	17	20	24	32
f_i	3	5	9	5	4	3	1

Assertion (A) The variance of the data is 45.8.

Reason (R) The standard deviation of the data is 6.77.

(a) ☐ (b) ☐ (c) ☐ (d) ☐

10. Consider the following data.

x_i	6	10	14	18	24	28	30
f_i	2	4	7	12	8	4	3

Assertion (A) The mean of the data is 19.

Reason (R) The variance of the data is 43.4.

(a) ☐ (b) ☐ (c) ☐ (d) ☐

11. Consider the following data.

x_i	60	61	62	63	64	65	66	67	68
f_i	2	1	12	29	25	12	10	4	5

Assertion (A) The mean of the data using shortcut method is 32.

Reason (R) The standard deviation of the data using shortcut method is 1.69.

(a) ☐ (b) ☐ (c) ☐ (d) ☐

12. **Assertion** (A) If each of the observations $x_1, x_2, \ldots, x_n$ is increased by a, where a is a negative or positive number, then the variance remains unchanged.

Reason (R) Adding or subtracting a positive or negative number to (or from) each observation of a group does not affect the variance.

(a) ☐ (b) ☐ (c) ☐ (d) ☐

13. If for a distribution $\Sigma(x-5)=3$, $\Sigma(x-5)^2=43$ and the total number of items is 18.

Assertion (A) Mean of the distribution is 4.1666.

Reason (R) Standard deviation of the distribution is 1.54.

(a) ☐ (b) ☐ (c) ☐ (d) ☐

14. **Assertion** (A) The variance of first n even natural numbers is $\frac{n^2-1}{4}$.

Reason (R) The sum of first n natural numbers is $\frac{n(n+1)}{2}$ and the sum of squares of first n natural numbers is $\frac{n(n+1)(2n+1)}{6}$.

(a) ☐ (b) ☐ (c) ☐ (d) ☐

15. **Assertion** (A) If the mean of n observations $1^2, 2^2, 3^2, \ldots. n^2$ is $\frac{46n}{11}$, then n is equal to 11.

Reason (R) For two data sets each of size 5, the variances are given to be 4 and 5 and the corresponding means are given to be 2 and 4, respectively.

The variance of combined data set is $\frac{11}{2}$.

(a) ☐ (b) ☐ (c) ☐ (d) ☐

Case Based Questions

Case 1 You are given some observations as 34, 66, 30, 38, 44, 50, 40, 60, 42, 51.

Based on these observations, answer the following questions.

(i) The mean of the given data is

(a) 40.5 ☐ (b) 45.0 ☐ (c) 45.5 ☐ (d) 50.5 ☐

(ii) The mean deviation about the mean is

(a) 10.0 ☐ (b) 9.5 ☐ (c) 9.1 ☐ (d) 9.0 ☐

(iii) The median of the given data is

(a) 41 ☐ (b) 42 ☐ (c) 43 ☐ (d) 44 ☐

(iv) The mean deviation about the median is

(a) 8.0 ☐ (b) 8.3 ☐ (c) 8.5 ☐ (d) 8.7 ☐

(v) The difference between mean deviation about the mean and mean deviation about the median is

(a) 0.1 ☐ (b) 0.2 ☐ (c) 0.3 ☐ (d) 0.4 ☐

Case 2 Consider the data

x_i	4	8	11	17	20	24	32
f_i	3	5	9	5	4	3	1

Based on above information, answer the following questions.

(i) Mean is calculated by the formula

(a) $\bar{x} = \dfrac{\Sigma f_i x_i}{N}$ ☐ (b) $\bar{x} = \Sigma f_i x_i$ ☐

(c) $\bar{x} = \dfrac{\Sigma f_i x_i^2}{N}$ ☐ (d) None of these ☐

(ii) Variance is calculated by the formula

(a) $\sigma^2 = \dfrac{1}{N} \Sigma f_i (x_i - \bar{x})^2$ ☐ (b) $\sigma^2 = \dfrac{1}{N} \Sigma f_i (x_i + \bar{x})^2$ ☐

(c) $\sigma^2 = \dfrac{1}{N} \Sigma (x_i - \bar{x})$ ☐ (d) None of these ☐

(iii) Mean of the given data is

(a) 10 ☐ (b) 12 ☐ (c) 14 ☐ (d) 15 ☐

(iv) Variance of the given data is

(a) 40 ☐ (b) 45.8 ☐ (c) 41.5 ☐ (d) 39.8 ☐

(v) Standard deviation of the given data is

(a) 6.77 ☐ (b) 5 ☐ (c) 4.8 ☐ (d) 3.19 ☐

COMPETITION CONNECT

Analysis of Frequency Distribution [NCERT (Old) Pg. 372-375]

1. The observation which has greater coefficient of variation has the highest variability and lower coefficient of variation has lowest variability.

True ☐ False ☐

2. For series with equal means, the series with lesser standard deviation is more consistent or less scattered.

Yes ☐ No ☐

3. The coefficient of variation of different distribution is given, which distribution shows the lowest variability.

Distribution	I	II	III	IV
Coefficient of variation	16	21	15.5	14.8

(a) I (b) II (c) III (d) IV

4. An analysis of monthly payout paid to their employee in two firms A and B gives the following results

Firm	A	B
Number of employee	300	250
Mean of monthly payout	₹ 7999	₹ 7999
Variance of payout	144	169

(i) Which firm A or B pays out larger amount as monthly payout? ____________

(ii) Which firm A or B shows greater variability in individual payout? ____________

5. What will be the coefficient of variation if mean is 12 and variance is 9?

(a) 91% (b) 36% (c) 25% (d) None of these

6. The coefficient of variation is 198, when mean is 10, arithmetic sum of squares of the deviation is $(28)^2$ and $N = 2$.

True ☐ False ☐

7. The mean and standard deviations of marks obtained by 40 students of a class in three subjects Mathematics, Physics and Chemistry are given below.

Subject	Mathematics	Physics	Chemistry
Mean	48	80	45
Standard deviation	12	16	15

Which of the following statement is true?

(a) Highest variability in marks is in Physics

(b) Highest variability in marks is in Chemistry

(c) Highest variability in marks is in Mathematics

(d) Lowest variability in marks is in Chemistry

8. Coefficient of variation of two distribution are 80 and 90 respectively and their standard deviation are 40 and 18. Calculate the sum of their means.

9. The time taken in minutes to complete a homework by 8 students in a day, is given by 38, 40, 47, 44, 46, 43, 49 and 53. What will be the coefficient of variation?

(a) 11% (b) 10.07% (c) 9.89% (d) 7.28%

10. The sum and sum of squares corresponding to rupee X and dollar Y of 25 country currencies are given below

$$\sum_{i=1}^{25} x_i = 169, \sum_{i=1}^{25} x_i^2 = 1150, \sum_{i=1}^{25} y_i = 225 \text{ and } \sum_{i=1}^{25} y_i^2 = 2035$$

Which is more varying the rupee or dollar?

11. The following is the record of goals scored by team A in football session

Number of goals scored	0	1	2	3	4
Number of matches	3	8	6	6	2

For the team B, mean number of goals scored per match was 3 with a standard deviation 2.25 goals. Which team may be considered more consistent?

12. Suppose that samples of patient from two hospitals A and B are tested for coronavirus by government. The range of different samples given by are as

Sampling range	**Number of patient**	
	A	***B***
5-10	3	10
10-15	8	12
15-20	30	17
20-25	53	31
25-30	12	28
30-35	4	13

Which set of patient has highest average samples and which has more uniform sampling?

(a) Hospital A, Hospital B

(b) Hospital B, Hospital B

(c) Hospital B, Hospital A

(d) Hospital A, Hospital A

COMPETITION EDGE UP

1. If the variance of the frequency distribution

x	c	$2c$	$3c$	$4c$	$5c$	$6c$
f	2	1	1	1	1	1

is 160, then the value of $c \in N$ is **[JEE Main 2024]**

(a) 8 ☐
(b) 5 ☐
(c) 6 ☐
(d) 7 ☐

2. The frequency distribution of the age of students in a class of 40 students is given below

Age	15	16	17	18	19	20
Number of Students	5	8	5	12	x	y

If the mean deviation about the median is 1.25, then $4x + 5y$ is equal to **[JEE Main 2024]**

(a) 44 ☐
(b) 43 ☐
(c) 46 ☐
(d) 47 ☐

3. Let $a, b, c \in N$ and $a < b < c$. Let the mean, the mean deviation about the mean and the variance of the 5 observations 9, 25, a, b, c be 18, 4 and $\frac{136}{5}$, respectively. Then, $2a + b - c$ is equal to .... **[JEE Main 2024]**

4. The mean and standard deviation of 20 observations are found to be 10 and 2, respectively. On rechecking, it was found that an observation by mistake was taken 8 instead of 12. The correct standard deviation is **[JEE Main 2024]**

(a) 1.8 ☐
(b) $\sqrt{3.96}$ ☐
(c) $\sqrt{3.86}$ ☐
(d) 1.94 ☐

5. Let $\alpha, \beta \in R$. Let the mean and the variance of 6 observations $-3, 4, 7, -6, \alpha, \beta$ be 2 and 23, respectively. The mean deviation about the mean of these 6 observations is **[JEE Main 2024]**

(a) $\frac{16}{3}$ ☐
(b) $\frac{14}{3}$ ☐
(c) $\frac{11}{3}$ ☐
(d) $\frac{13}{3}$ ☐

6. Consider 10 observations $x_1, x_2, \ldots, x_{10}$ such that $\sum_{i=1}^{10}(x_i - \alpha) = 2$ and $\sum_{i=1}^{10}(x_i - \beta)^2 = 40$, where α, β are positive integers. Let the mean and the variance of the observations be $\frac{6}{5}$ and $\frac{84}{25}$, respectively. Then, $\frac{\beta}{\alpha}$ is equal to **[JEE Main 2024]**

(a) 2 ☐
(b) 1 ☐
(c) $\frac{3}{2}$ ☐
(d) $\frac{5}{2}$ ☐

7. Let the median and the mean deviation about the median of 7 observations 170, 125, 230, 190, 210, a, b be 170 and $\frac{205}{7}$, respectively. Then, the mean deviation about the mean of these 7 observations is **[JEE Main 2024]**

(a) 32 ☐
(b) 28 ☐
(c) 30 ☐
(d) 31 ☐

8. Let the mean and the variance of 6 observations a, b, 68, 44, 48, 60 be 55 and 194, respectively. If $a > b$, then $a + 3b$ is **[JEE Main 2024]**

(a) 180 ☐
(b) 190 ☐
(c) 200 ☐
(d) 210 ☐

9. The variance σ^2 of the data

x_i	0	1	5	6	10	12	17
f_i	3	2	3	2	6	3	3

is .... **[JEE Main 2024]**

10. Let M denote the median of the following frequency distribution. **[JEE Main 2024]**

Class	0-4	4-8	8-12	12-16	16-20
Frequency	3	9	10	8	6

Then, 20 M is equal to

(a) 32

(b) 416

(c) 104

(d) 208

11. If the mean and variance of five observations are $\frac{24}{5}$ and $\frac{194}{25}$ respectively and the mean of the first four observations is $\frac{7}{2}$, then the variance of the first four observations is equal to **[JEE Main 2024]**

(a) 4/5

(b) 77/12

(c) 5/4

(d) 105/4

12. If the mean and variance of the data 65, 68, 58, 44, 48, 45, 60, α, β, 60, where $\alpha > \beta$, are 56 and 66.2 respectively, then $\alpha^2 + \beta^2$ is equal to .... **[JEE Main 2024]**

13. The mean and standard deviation of 15 observations were found to be 12 and 3, respectively. On rechecking it was found that an observation was read as 10 in place of 12. If μ and σ^2 denote the mean and variance of the correct observations respectively, then $15(\mu + \mu^2 + \sigma^2)$ is equal to .... **[JEE Main 2024]**

14. Let $a_1, a_2, \ldots, a_{10}$ be 10 observations such that $\sum_{k=1}^{10} a_k = 50$ and $\sum_{\forall k < j} a_k \cdot a_j = 1100$. Then, the standard deviation of $a_1, a_2, \ldots, a_{10}$ is equal to **[JEE Main 2024]**

(a) 10

(b) $\sqrt{5}$

(c) 5

(d) $\sqrt{115}$

Probability

Scan and take Chapter Test

TOPIC 1

Random Experiment and Sample Space

NCERT Pg 289

1. Find the sample space for each of the following, when a coin is tossed.

(i) Once ______

(ii) Twice ______

(iii) Thrice ______

(iv) Four times ______

2. Find the sample space for each of the following.

(i) A die is thrown once ______

(ii) Two dice are thrown together ______

(iii) Roots of the quadratic equation $x^2 - 5x + 6 = 0$ ______

(iv) Roots of the equation $x^3 + 3x^2 + 3x + 1 = 0$ ______

3. Two dice are thrown. Write down the sample spaces that the sum of the faces is equal to 7.

______

4. A reporter is noting down the number of omicron cases in India during a month. Where,

IN = Natural numbers $\{1, 2, 3, ...\}$

7 L = Integers $\{0, \pm 1, \pm 2, ...\}$

IR = Set of real numbers

Then, the required sample space is

(a) IN (b) 7L (c) IR (d) IN $\cup$ $\{0\}$

______

5. A coin is tossed and then a die is rolled only in case a head is shown on the coin. Then, find the sample space of the experiment.

______

*Concepts of all questions bearing * are important for JEE & CUET*

6. A bag contains one white and one red ball. A ball is drawn from the bag. If the ball drawn is white it is replaced in the bag and again a ball is drawn, otherwise a die is tossed. The number of sample point in the sample space of above experiment is

(a) 6 (b) 7 (c) 8 (d) 9

7. An experiment consist of rolling a die and then drawing a ball from a box. Which contains one red, one black and one white ball. If the number on the die is even, then a ball is drawn. If the number on the die is odd, then a coin is tossed. Write the sample space for this experiment.

8. If a coin is tossed six times, then total number of outcomes in sample space is

(a) 6^2 (b) 2^6 (c) 2×6 (d) None of these

9. Two boys B_1, B_2 and one girl G_1 are in room X and two cats C_1, C_2 and one girl G_2 are in room Y, then which of the following is the sample space for the experiment in which a room is selected and then a cat?

(a) $\{XC_1, XC_2\}$ (b) $\{XB_1, XB_2, YC_1, YC_2\}$

(c) $\{YC_1, YC_2, YG_1\}$ (d) $\{YC_1, YC_2\}$

10. A coin is tossed, if it shows a tail, we draw a ball from a box which contains 2 red and 1 black balls. If it shows head, we throw a die. Then, the sample space is $\{TB, H6\}$ of getting a black ball or one face of die is 6.

True ☐ False ☐

11. A box contains 2 white and 3 black balls, find the sample space for the following experiment.

(i) 2 balls are drawn randomly __________

(ii) First ball is drawn and then second is drawn only, if black ball is drawn in the first case, without replacement __________

TOPIC 2 Event

NCERT Pg. 289-294

12. *A* die is thrown. Describe the following events.

(i) A : A prime number __________

(ii) B : A multiple of 4 __________

(iii) C : An odd number less than 5 __________

(iv) D : A number greater than 8 __________

(v) E : A number which is a divisor of 6 __________

13. The experiment of throwing a die and the event 'a number less than or equal to 5' is true, if outcomes are 4 or 5.

True ☐ False ☐

14. Event of getting five kings in a pack of cards, is an example of

(i) Impossible event ☐

(ii) Sure event ☐

15. In an experiment of 'throwing a die once', identify the following events as sure event, impossible event, simple event or compound event.

(i) 'Getting an even number' is ____________

(ii) 'Getting a number greater than 6' is ____________

(iii) 'Getting an even prime number' is ____________

(iv) 'Getting a number more than 0 and less than 7' is ____________

16. Fill in the blanks with the correct events.

{simple event, impossible event, compound event}

Two dice are thrown.

(i) Event A : 'The sum of faces is greater than 13' is ____________

(ii) Event B : 'The sum of faces is 12' is ____________

(iii) Event C : 'The sum of faces is multiple of 2' is ____________

17. A box contains 2 red, 3 white and 5 black balls. Three balls are drawn from the box one by one without replacement. Consider the event A is 'atmost two are black and exactly one is red' and event B is 'atleast two are black and atmost one is red'.

Then, state true or false for $A = B'$.

Where $B' \equiv$ Complementary event of B.

True ☐ False ☐

***18.** Four coins are tossed once. Let E denotes the event 'Three head and one tail appears'. Then, which of the following is correct for the event 'not E'.

(a) $\{HHHT, HHTT, TTHH\}$

(b) $\{HHHH, TTHH, HTHH\}$

(c) $\{HHHH, HHTT, HTTH, TTHH, TTTH\}$

(d) $\{HHHH, HTHT, THHT, THHH\}$

____

***19.** A die is thrown, describe the following events

A : A number less than 7

B : A number greater than 7

$A \cup B =$ ____________ .

***20.** If $A = \{1, 2, 3\}$ and $B = \{6\}$, then $A \cap B$ is ____________ .

***21.** Let S be the sample space associated with the experiment and A, B be any two events space of S, then $A \cap B'$ can be written in the place of $A - B$.

True ☐ False ☐

***22.** An urn contains 2 white balls W and 3 black balls B. Three balls are drawn from the urn one by one and consider the following events.

A : Atleast one ball is white.

B : Exactly one ball is black.

C : Atmost two balls are white and atleast one is black.

Now, find the events.

(i) A' ____________________

(ii) $A \cup B$ ____________________

(iii) $A \cap C$ ____________________

(iv) $A - C$ ____________________

(v) $A \cap B \cap C$ ____________________

(vi) not B ____________________

(vii) not C ____________________

(viii) $A \cap B' \cap C'$ ____________________

***23.** A die is rolled two times consider the following events.

A : Sum of faces is multiple of 5.

B : Sum is greater than 5.

Then, events A and B are mutually exclusive.

True ☐ False ☐

***24.** Two dice are thrown and sum of the numbers which come up on the dice is noted. Consider the following events.

A : Getting an even number on the first die.

B : Sum is atleast 9 and multiple of 4.

C : Sum is even and greater than 8.

D : Getting an odd number on the first die and multiple of 3 on the second.

Verify the following pairs are mutually exclusive or not.

(i) A and C.

Yes ☐ No ☐

(ii) B and C.

Yes ☐ No ☐

(iii) A and D.

Yes ☐ No ☐

(iv) A' and D.

Yes ☐ No ☐

***25.** Three coins are tossed, two events A and B are as follows,

A : Exactly one tail appears.

B : Atleast two tails appears.

Then, events A and B are mutually exclusive and exhaustive.

True ☐ False ☐

26. A coin is tossed three times. Describe.

(i) two events which are mutually exclusive __________

(ii) two events which are not mutually exclusive __________

(iii) three events which are mutually exclusive and exhaustive __________

(iv) two events which are not mutually exclusive and exhaustive __________

27. Three coins are tossed once, let A denotes the event 'three heads show', B denotes the event 'two consecutive heads show', C denotes 'two tails and one head' and D denotes an event 'a head show on the first coin', then mention the following events.

(i) Simple __________

(ii) Compound __________

(iii) Mutually exclusive __________

(iv) Exhaustive event __________

TOPIC 3

Axiomatic Approach to Probability

NCERT Pg 295-305

***28.** A coin is tossed thrice. Find the probability of getting

(i) 3 tails __________

(ii) 2 tails __________

(iii) atleast 2 tails __________

(iv) no head __________

(v) no tail __________

(vi) atmost 2 heads __________

***29.** Four coins are tossed once. The probability of getting atleast three heads is

__________.

***30.** A card is drawn at random from a well-shuffled pack of cards. Then, the probability of getting one ace, one diamond is

(a) $\frac{1}{4}, \frac{2}{13}$ (b) $\frac{1}{4}, \frac{1}{13}$ (c) $\frac{1}{13}, \frac{1}{4}$ (d) $\frac{4}{13}, \frac{4}{52}$

____

31. The probability of having 53 Mondays in randomly selected leap year is

__________.

32. A dart board has 36 sectors labelled 1 to 36, determine the probability that a dart thrown at the centre of the board hits.

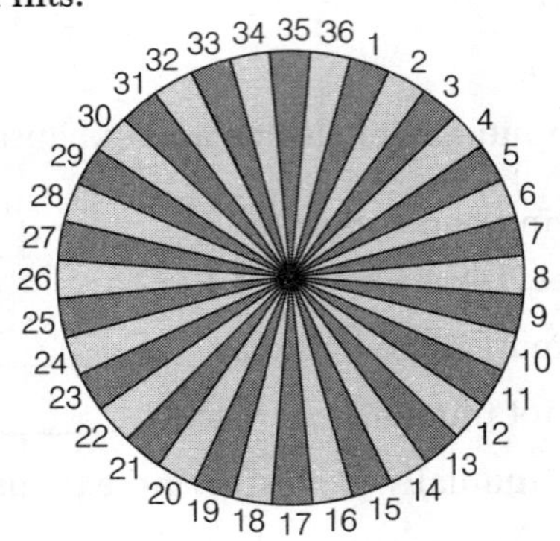

(i) A multiple of 4 ______

(ii) A number greater than 20 ______

(iii) A multiple of 13 ______

(iv) An odd number which is a multiple of 3 ______

(v) A number between 6 and 10 ______

***33.** List the six different orders in which Anuj, Amit and Neha may sit in a row. If the three of them sit randomly in a row, determine the probability that

(i) Anuj sits in the middle ______

(ii) Anuj sits at the left end ______

(iii) Anuj sits at the right end ______

(iv) Amit and Neha are seated together ______

***34.** In an experiment of 'examining three consecutive bulbs produced in a factory' are classified as good (non-defective) and bad (defective).

Find the following probabilities.

(i) Probability of getting exactly one defective bulb ______

(ii) Probability of getting atleast two defective bulbs ______

(iii) Probability of getting no defective bulb ______

35. Two dice are thrown randomly. Then, what is the probability of getting equal faces?

______

36. A coin is tossed 3 times successfully. Then, the probability of getting 2 consecutive heads is

(a) $\frac{3}{8}$ (b) $\frac{1}{8}$ (c) $\frac{2}{8}$ (d) $\frac{5}{8}$

______

***37.** Suppose 3 bulbs are selected at random from a lot. Each bulb is tested and classified as defective D or non-defective N. We may get atmost 3 defective bulbs as result after testing. Then, the probability of getting atleast two defective bulbs is

(a) $\frac{2}{3}$ (b) $\frac{1}{2}$ (c) $\frac{3}{8}$ (d) $\frac{5}{8}$

______

***38.** Two dice are thrown, let A be the event the sum of the faces equal to 6, B be the event sum of the faces is greater than 10 and C be the event sum of faces is even and given probabilities are

I. $\frac{1}{12}$ II. $\frac{5}{36}$ III. $\frac{1}{2}$

Then, which of the following pair is correct ?

(a) A-I, B-II, C-III (b) A-II, B-I, C-III (c) A-III, B-II, C-I (d) A-I, B-III, C-II

---

39. A boy has 1 red, 1 black and 1 blue pens in his pocket. He takes out two pens out of his pocket, one after the other without replacement. Then, the probability of pens out of which one is black and another is red, is $\frac{1}{3}$.

True ☐ False ☐

40. Consider a random experiment in which a coin is tossed repeatedly until a tail comes up. The probability of this experiment is

---

41. Two integers a and b are choosen at random with replacement from first 11 positive integers. The probability that $|a^2 - b^2|$ is divisible by 2, is ________________.

42. If a die is thrown, then the probability of getting a number greater than 4 or getting a number less than 3, is ________________.

43. A in 65% of cases and B in 75% of cases speak the truth. What percentage of cases do they contradict to make the same information statement?

---

44. A and B are events such that $P(A) = \frac{2}{3}$ and $P(B) = \frac{1}{6}$, then the probability of 'not A and not B' is ________________, if $P(A \cap B) = \frac{1}{3}$.

45. A bag contains 6 fruits of which 4 are mangoes and 2 are oranges. One fruit is drawn from the bag. Calculate the probability that it will be

(i) mango ________________

(ii) orange ________________

(iii) either mango or orange________________

(iv) not mango________________

46. For any two events A and B, if $P(A - B) = \frac{1}{3}$, $P(A) = \frac{1}{2}$ and $P(B) = \frac{1}{3}$, then what is the value of $P(A \cap B)$?

---

47. A number is chosen at random from the first 500 natural numbers, the probability that the number is divisible by 4 or 5, is 2/5.

True ☐ False ☐

48. Let A and B be any two events of random experiment, where $P(A) = \frac{3}{4}$ and $P(B) = \frac{5}{8}$. Then, the value of $P(A \cap B)$ will lie between $\frac{3}{8}$ and $\frac{5}{8}$. Justify the statement.

____

49. A die is thrown twice in succession, the probability of obtaining six atleast once is

____________________.

50. Three cards are drawn from a well-shuffled pack of 52 cards, what is the probability of getting atleast one of them is diamond?

____

51. Two players Shivam and Rishi alternately throw a pair of die. Shivam wins if he throws 6 before Rishi throws 7 and Rishi wins if he throws 7 before Shivam throws 6. If Shivam begins, then the probability that Shivam wins, is ____________________.

52. If A and B are two independent events and $P(A) > \frac{1}{2}$, $P(B) > \frac{1}{2}$, $P(A \cap B') = \frac{3}{25}$ and $P(B \cap A') = \frac{8}{25}$. Then, the values of $P(A)$ and $P(B)$ are respectively,

(a) $\frac{4}{5}$ and $\frac{3}{5}$ (b) $\frac{3}{5}$ and $\frac{4}{5}$ (c) $\frac{3}{5}$ and $\frac{2}{5}$ (d) $\frac{2}{5}$ and $\frac{4}{5}$

____

53. A box contains 2 red balls R and 3 white balls W. The balls are drawn from the urn one-by-one and placed on the table in the order drawn. Then, the probability that they are drawn in the order $RWWRW$, is

(a) $\frac{1}{5}$ (b) $\frac{2}{5}$ (c) $\frac{1}{10}$ (d) $\frac{3}{10}$

____

54. 7 boys and 3 girls are placed at random in a row of a group. Find the probability that none of girls are placed consecutively, is ____________________.

55. Three cards are drawn from a well-shuffled pack. What is the probability that atleast one of them is a spade?

____

56. What is the probability that a bridge hand of 13 cards contains one king?

____

57. Two letters are chosen at random from the word 'PROBABILITY', then the probability that atleast one letter is vowel, is ____________________.

58. A packet contains 20 wrist watches in which 5 are defective. If we choose 14 wrist watches randomly, then what is the probability of getting atleast one is defective?

____

59. A group of three members is selected from three boys and two girls. The probability that the group will have

(i) exactly one boy, is ________________

(ii) atleast one boy, is ________________

(iii) atmost two girls, is ________________

60. 13 cards are drawn from a well-shuffled deck of 52 cards. Then, what is the probability of getting all the aces or atleast one ace? [both events are mutually exclusive]

61. A survey regarding liking for Mathematics, Chemistry and Physics among students of a college is made. The survey shows that 20% read Mathematics, 16% read Chemistry, 14% read Physics, 8% read both Mathematics and Chemistry, 6% read Mathematics and Physics, 4% read Chemistry and Physics and 2% read all three. If a student is chosen at random, then find the probability that he/she reads other than Mathematics or Chemistry or Physics.

62. A person writes four letters and the corresponding addresses on envelopes. If he inserts the letters in the envelopes at random irrespective of address, then the probability that all the letters are wrongly placed, is

(a) $\frac{3}{8}$ (b) $\frac{8}{3}$ (c) $\frac{2}{8}$ (d) $\frac{8}{2}$

63. Let S be the associated sample space of any random experiment and let A, B and C be mutually exclusive and exhaustive events. If $P(B) = \frac{5}{4}P(A)$ and $P(C) = \frac{1}{5}P(B)$, then $P(C)$ is equal to

(a) $\frac{1}{6}$ (b) $\frac{1}{5}$ (c) $\frac{1}{10}$ (d) $\frac{4}{5}$

64. Let A, B and C be mutually exclusive and exhaustive events of a sample space S of any random experiment. Then, the following assignments of probabilities to each outcomes are valid or not? Where, $P(A) = 0.38$, $P(B) = 0.30$ and $P(C) = 0.32$.

***65.** Let A, B and C be three events of any random experiment, where $P(A) = 0.4$, $P(B) = 0.5$, $P(C) = 0.3$. If $P(A \cup B) = 0.9$, $P(A \cap C) = 0.2$, $P(A \cap B \cap C) = 0.1$ and $P(A \cup B \cup C) \geq 0.65$, the upper range and lower range of $P(B \cap C)$ are

(a) 0.28 and 0.35 (b) 0.35 and 0.42

(c) 0.45 and 0.1 (d) 0.45 and 0.01

Assertion-Reason Questions

The following questions consist of two statements – Assertion (A) and Reason (R).
Answer these questions by selecting the appropriate option given below.
(a) Both (A) and (R) are true and (R) is correct explanation of (A)
(b) Both (A) and (R) are true but (R) is not the correct explanation of (A)
(c) (A) is true but (R) is false
(d) (A) is false but (R) is true

1. **Assertion** (A) The sample space while a coin is tossed and 0 die is rolled at once is {H1, H2, H3, H4, H5, H6, T1, T2, T3, T4, T5, T6}

Reason (R) The sample space of throwing a die twice is $\{(a, b) : a, b \in \{1, 2, 3, 4, 5,, 6\}\}$

(a) ☐ (b) ☐ (c) ☐ (d) ☐

2. **Assertion** (A) A die is rolled. Two events a prime number appears and an even number appears are independent.

Reason (R) A coin is tossed twice, getting all heads and getting all tails are two mutually exclusive events.

(a) ☐ (b) ☐ (c) ☐ (d) ☐

3. **Assertion** (A) A letter is chosen randomly from the word MATHEMATICS, total outcomes in the sample space are 8.

Reason (R) Probability of getting a single head in two tosses of a coin is $\frac{1}{3}$.

(a) ☐ (b) ☐ (c) ☐ (d) ☐

4. **Assertion** (A) Probability of getting a sum of 10 while rolling a pair of dice is $\frac{1}{12}$.

Reason (R) Probability of occurrence of an even A of a sample space S is $P(A) = \frac{n(A)}{n(S)}$, if all the outcomes of the sample space are equally likely.

(a) ☐ (b) ☐ (c) ☐ (d) ☐

5. **Assertion** (A) For two events A and B of S, $P(A) = \frac{1}{4}$, $P(B) = \frac{2}{5}$ and $P(A \cap B) = \frac{3}{4}$.

Reason (R) For two events A and B of S, $P(A) = \frac{1}{4}$, $P(B') = \frac{2}{5}$, $P(A \cap B') = \frac{3}{20}$ and $P(A \cup B) = \frac{3}{4}$.

(a) ☐ (b) ☐ (c) ☐ (d) ☐

6. **Assertion** (A) Probability of getting a head in a toss of an unbiased coin is $\frac{1}{2}$.

Reason (R) In a simultaneous toss of two coins, the probability of getting 'no tails' is $\frac{1}{4}$.

(a) ☐ (b) ☐ (c) ☐ (d) ☐

7. **Assertion** (A) In tossing a coin, the exhaustive number of cases is 2.

Reason (R) If a pair of dice is thrown, then the exhaustive number of cases is $6 \times 6 = 36$.

(a) ☐ (b) ☐ (c) ☐ (d) ☐

8. **Assertion** (A) A letter is chosen at random from the word 'NAGATATION'. Then, the total number of outcomes is 10.

Reason (R) A letter a chosen at random from the word 'ASSASSINATION'. Then, the number of outcomes is 13.

(a) ☐ (b) ☐ (c) ☐ (d) ☐

9. **Assertion** (A) Two dice are thrown simultaneously. There are 11 possible outcomes and each of them has a probability $\frac{1}{11}$.

Reason (R) Probability of an event (E) is defined as

$$P(E) = \frac{\text{Number of favourable outcomes}}{\text{Total number of possible outcomes}}$$

(a) ☐ (b) ☐ (c) ☐ (d) ☐

Case Based Questions

Case 1 Mohit is the Human Resource manager in a multinational company. For post of two software developers he has resume of 3 men and 2 women.

Based on the above information, answer the following questions.

(i) What will be the probability that only one man will be selected?

(a) $\frac{3}{5}$ ☐ (b) $\frac{2}{5}$ ☐ (c) $\frac{1}{5}$ ☐ (d) $\frac{4}{5}$ ☐

(ii) What will be the probability that no man will be selected?

(a) $\frac{2}{5}$ ☐ (b) $\frac{1}{10}$ ☐ (c) $\frac{1}{5}$ ☐ (d) $\frac{3}{5}$ ☐

(iii) What will be the probability that both men will be selected?

(a) $\frac{1}{10}$ ☐ (b) $\frac{2}{5}$ ☐ (c) $\frac{3}{5}$ ☐ (d) $\frac{3}{10}$ ☐

Case 2 Two students Shikha and Kajal appeared in an examination. The probability that Shikha qualify the examination is 0.05 and that Kajal will qualify the examination is 0.10. The probability that both will qualify the examination is 0.02.

Based on the given information, answer the following questions.

(i) Find the probability that Kajal will not quality the exam.

(ii) Find the probability that atleast one of them will qualify the exam.

(iii) Find the probability that both Shikha and Kajal will not qualify the exam.

COMPETITION EDGE UP

1. If an unbiased dice is rolled thrice, then the probability of getting a greater number in the ith roll than the number obtained in the $(i-1)$th roll, $i = 2, 3$, is equal to [JEE Main 2024]

(a) $\frac{3}{54}$ ☐
(b) $\frac{1}{54}$ ☐
(c) $\frac{2}{54}$ ☐
(d) $\frac{5}{54}$ ☐

2. The coefficients a, b and c in the quadratic equation $ax^2 + bx + c = 0$ are from the set $\{1, 2, 3, 4, 5, 6\}$. If the probability of this equation having one real root bigger than the other is p, then $216p$ equals [JEE Main 2024]

(a) 57 ☐
(b) 38 ☐
(c) 76 ☐
(d) 19 ☐

3. A coin is biased so that a head is twice as likely to occur as a tail. If the coin is tossed 3 times, then the probability of getting two tails and one head is [JEE Main 2024]

(a) $\frac{1}{27}$ ☐
(b) $\frac{2}{9}$ ☐
(c) $\frac{2}{27}$ ☐
(d) $\frac{1}{9}$ ☐

4. Two marbles are drawn in succession from a box containing 10 red, 30 white, 20 blue and 15 orange marbles with replacement being made after each drawing. Then, the probability that first drawn marble is red and second drawn marble is white, is [JEE Main 2024]

(a) $\frac{4}{75}$ ☐
(b) $\frac{2}{3}$ ☐
(c) $\frac{4}{25}$ ☐
(d) $\frac{2}{25}$ ☐

5. A fair die is thrown until 2 appears. Then, the probability that 2 appears in even number of throws, is [JEE Main 2024]

(a) $\frac{5}{11}$ ☐
(b) $\frac{1}{6}$ ☐
(c) $\frac{5}{6}$ ☐
(d) $\frac{6}{11}$ ☐

6. An urn contains 6 white and 9 black balls. Two successive draws of 4 balls are made without replacement. The probability, that the first draw gives all white balls and the second draw gives all black balls, is [JEE Main 2024]

(a) $\frac{5}{256}$ ☐
(b) $\frac{3}{715}$ ☐
(c) $\frac{5}{715}$ ☐
(d) $\frac{3}{256}$ ☐

7. Let the sum of two positive integers be 24. If the probability, that their product is not less than 3/4 times their greatest possible product is $\frac{m}{n}$, where gcd $(m, n) = 1$, then $n - m$ equals [JEE Main 2024]

(a) 8 ☐
(b) 10 ☐
(c) 11 ☐
(d) 9 ☐

8. Two integers x and y are chosen with replacement from the set $\{0, 1, 2, 3, \ldots, 10\}$. Then, the probability that $|x - y| \geq 5$, is [JEE Main 2024]

(a) $\frac{62}{121}$ ☐
(b) $\frac{30}{121}$ ☐
(c) $\frac{60}{121}$ ☐
(d) $\frac{31}{121}$ ☐

9. Let a, b and c denote the outcomes of three independent rolls of a fair tetrahedral die, whose four faces are marked 1, 2, 3, 4. If the probability that $ax^2 + bx + c = 0$ has all real roots is $\frac{m}{n}$, $\gcd(m, n) = 1$, then $m + n$ is equal to .... **[JEE Main 2024]**

10. Let Ajay will not appear in JEE exam with probability $p = \frac{2}{7}$, while both Ajay and Vijay will appear in the exam with probability $q = \frac{1}{5}$. Then, the probability, that Ajay will appear in the exam and Vijay will not appear is **[JEE Main 2024]**

11. An integer is chosen at random from the integers 1, 2, 3, ..., 50. The probability that the chosen integer is a multiple of atleast one of 4, 6 and 7 is **[JEE Main 2024]**

(a) $\frac{8}{25}$ ☐

(b) $\frac{9}{50}$ ☐

(c) $\frac{14}{25}$ ☐

(d) $\frac{21}{50}$ ☐

12. Three dice are rolled. If the probability of getting different numbers on the three ices is $\frac{p}{q}$, where p and q are co-prime, then $q - p$ is equal to

(a) 4 ☐

(b) 3 ☐

(c) 1 ☐

(d) 2 ☐

13. Let Ω be the sample space and $A \subseteq \Omega$ be an event.

Given below are two statements

S1 If $P(A) = 0$, then $A = \phi$

S2 If $P(A) = 1$, then $A = \Omega$.

Then,

(a) only (S2) is true ☐

(b) Both (S1) and (S2) are true ☐

(c) only (S1) is true ☐

(d) Both (S1) and (S2) are false ☐

14. Let N be the sum of the numbers appeared when two fair dice are rolled and let the probability that $N - 2$, $\sqrt{3N}$, $N + 2$ are in geometric progression be $k/48$. Then, the value of k is **[JEE Main 2023]**

(a) 2 ☐

(b) 8 ☐

(c) 16 ☐

(d) 4 ☐

15. A fair $n(n > 1)$ faces die is rolled repeatedly until a number less than n appears. If the mean of the number of tosses required is $n/9$, then n is equal to .... **[JEE Main 2023]**

16. A bag contains six balls of different colours. Two balls are drawn in succession with replacement. The probability that both the balls are of the same colour is p. Next four balls are drawn in succession with replacement and the probability that exactly three balls are of the same colour is q. If $p : q = m : n$, where m and n are coprime, then $m + n$ is equal to .... **[JEE Main 2023]**

17. Let A be the event that the absolute difference between two randomly chosen real numbers in the sample space {0, 60} is less than or equal to a. If $P(A) = \frac{11}{36}$, then a is equal to .... **[JEE Main 2023]**

18. The probability, that in a randomly selected 3-digit number at least two digits are odd, is **[JEE Main 2022]**

(a) $\frac{19}{36}$ ☐

(b) $\frac{15}{36}$ ☐

(c) $\frac{13}{36}$ ☐

(d) $\frac{23}{36}$ ☐

19. Five numbers x_1, x_2, x_3, x_4, x_5 are randomly selected from the numbers 1, 2, 3, ..., 18 and are arranged in the increasing order $(x_1 < x_2 < x_3 < x_4 < x_5)$. The probability that $x_2 = 7$ and $x_4 = 11$ is **[JEE Main 2022]**

(a) $\frac{1}{136}$ ☐

(b) $\frac{1}{72}$ ☐

(c) $\frac{1}{68}$ ☐

(d) $\frac{1}{34}$ ☐

Solutions

Chapter-1
Sets

1. (i) Yes (ii) No (iii) No (iv) No

2. (c) Every set is a collection but a collection is not necessarily a set. Only well defined collections are sets.
e.g. Collection of good cricket players is a collection but it is not a set.

3. (i) False (ii) True (iii) True (iv) False

4. (i) 10, 12
(ii) Wednesday, Thursday
(iii) 1, 2
(iv) 1, 2
(v) 0, 1

5. (i) (True)
Clearly, word 'EQUATION' has following vowels A, E, I, O, U.
So, required set can be described as follows
{A, E, I, O, U}
(ii) (False)
Natural numbers less than 7 are 1, 2, 3, 4, 5 and 6.
Hence, required set can be described as follows
{1, 2, 3, 4, 5, 6}
(iii) (True)
The vowels in English alphabet which precedes, are a, e, i, o. So, the required set is {a, e, i, o}.
(iv) (True)
We know that all rational numbers are expressible as the quotient of two integers. Therefore, the required set of all irrational numbers which can be written as
$\{x : x$ is real and irrational$\}$
or $\{x : x \in R$ but $x \notin Q\}$

6. $\{2n : n \in Z\}$

7. (i) (True)
Since, x is a positive integer and a divisor of 9.
So, x can take values 1, 3 and 9.
$\therefore$ $\{x : x$ is a positive integer and a divisor of $9\} = \{1, 3, 9\}$
(ii) (False)
The given equation can be written as $(x-1)(x+2)=0$
i.e. $x = 1, -2$
$\therefore$ The solution set of the given equation can be written in roster form as $\{1, -2\}$.
(iii) (True)
We find that distinct letters in the word 'PROPORTION' are P, R, O, T, I, N.
So, x can be P, R, O, T, I, N.
Hence, $\{x : x$ is a letter in the word 'PROPORTION'$\}$
= {P, R,O, T, I, N}
(iv) (True)
We observe that the squares of integers $0, \pm 1, \pm 2, \pm 3$ and ± 4 are less than 20.
Therefore, the set A in roster form is
$$A = \{-4, -3, -2, -1, 0, 1, 2, 3, 4\}$$

8. (i) $A = \{2, 3, 5, 7\}$
(ii) We have,
$x = \dfrac{n}{n^2+1}$, where $n \in N$ and
$1 \le n \le 3$
$\therefore$ $x = \dfrac{n}{n^2+1}$, where $n = 1, 2, 3$
$\Rightarrow x = \dfrac{1}{1^2+1}, \dfrac{2}{2^2+1}, \dfrac{3}{3^2+1}$
$\Rightarrow x = \dfrac{1}{2}, \dfrac{2}{5}, \dfrac{3}{10}$
Hence, $B = \left\{\dfrac{1}{2}, \dfrac{2}{5}, \dfrac{3}{10}\right\}$
(iii) We have, $a_1 = 1, a_2 = 1$ and
$a_{n+2} = a_{n+1} + a_n$
Putting $n = 1, 2, 3, 4, \ldots\ldots$ in $a_{n+2} = a_{n+1} + a_n$, we get
$a_3 = a_2 + a_1 = 1 + 1 = 2$
$a_4 = a_3 + a_2 = 2 + 1 = 3$
$a_5 = a_4 + a_3 = 3 + 2 = 5$
$a_6 = a_5 + a_4 = 5 + 3 = 8$ and so on.
Hence,
$C = \{a_1, a_2, a_3, a_4, a_5, a_6 \ldots\ldots\}$
$= \{1, 1, 2, 3, 5, 8 \ldots\ldots\}$
(iv) $a_1 = a_2 = 1$
$a_3 = a_2 . a_1 = 1 \times 1 = 1$
$a_4 = a_3 . a_2 = 1 \times 1 = 1$
$a_5 = a_4 . a_3 = 1 \times 1 = 1$ and so on.
Hence, $D = \{1, 1, 1, 1, 1 \ldots\ldots\}$.
(v) $a_1 = a_2 = -2$
$a_3 = a_2 \cdot a_1 = (-2)(-2) = 4$
$a_4 = a_3 \cdot a_2 = (4)(-2) = -8$
$a_5 = a_4 \cdot a_3 = (-8)(4) = -32$
and so on.
Hence, $E = \{-2, -2, 4, -8, -32, \ldots\ldots\}$.

9. (i) $P = \{1, 3, 5, 7, 9\}$
(ii) Since, $2x^2 + x - 6 = 0$
$\Rightarrow (2x-3)(x+2) = 0$
$\Rightarrow x = -2, \dfrac{3}{2}$
$Q = \left\{-2, \dfrac{3}{2}\right\}$
(iii) R = {February, April, June, September, November}

10. (b) We have,
(A) {P, R, I, N, C, A, L}
= {P, R, I, N, C, I, P, A, L}
= $\{x : x$ is a letter of the word 'PRINCIPAL'$\}$
Hence, A $\to$ 4.
(B) $\{0\} = \{x : x$ is an integer equal to zero$\} = \{x : x$ is an integer and $x + 1 = 1\}$
Hence, B $\to$ 3.
(C) {1, 2, 3, 6, 9, 18} = Set of all positive divisors of 18
$= \{x : x$ is a positive integer and is a divisor of 18$\}$.
Hence, C $\to$ 1.
(D) $\{-3, 3\} = \{x : x$ is an integer and $x^2 - 9 = 0\}$
Hence, D $\to$ 2.

11. (i) We observe that the elements of set X are the reciprocals of the squares of all natural numbers.
So, the set X in set-builder is
$$X = \left\{\frac{1}{n^2} : n \in N\right\}$$
(ii) $X = \left\{\dfrac{1}{n^2} : n \in N\right\}$
$n \to \dfrac{1}{n+1}$
$Y = \{(n+1)^2 : n \in N\}$
In roster form,
$Y = \{4, 9, 16, \ldots\ldots\}$.

(iii) We observe that each element in the given set has the denominator one more than the numerator. Also,the numerator begins from 1 and do not exceed 9. Hence, in the set-builder form the given set can be written as

$$\left\{x : x = \frac{n}{n+1}, n \in N, n \leq 9\right\}$$

12. Since, 2 is the only even prime number.

Hence, set A is empty/null/void set.

13. (i) We know that there is no rational number, whose square is 3. So, $x^2 - 3 = 0$ is not satisfied by any rational number.

Hence, A is an empty set.

(ii) We know that 2 is the only even prime number. Therefore, $B = \{2\}$.

So, B is not an empty set.

(iii) Since, there are infinite real numbers between 4 and 5. So, C is not an empty set.

(iv) Since, $x = 5, -5$ satisfy $x^2 = 25$ and ± 5 are odd integers.

Therefore, $D = \{-5, 5\}$.

Thus, D is a non-empty set.

(v) $x^2 = -2$

$\Rightarrow \quad x = \pm\sqrt{2}i$

But $x \in R$

$\therefore \{x \in R : x^2 = -2\} = \phi$

Hence, E is an empty set.

14. (i) (True)

(ii) (False)

$B = \{x : x \in N \text{ and } x^2 = 9\} = \{3\}$

(iii) (False)

$C = \{x : x^2 = 4, x \text{ is odd}\}$ is an empty set because the equation $x^2 = 4$ is not satisfied by any odd value of x.

(iv) (True)

$A = \{x : x \in Z$ and $x^2 - 5x + 6 = 0\} = \{2, 3\}$

So, A is a finite set.

15. (i) $A = \{x : x \in Z \text{ and } x > -10\}$
$= \{-9, -8, -7, -6, \ldots\}$

Clearly, A is an infinite set.

(ii) $B = \{x : x \in Z$ and $-10 < x < -7\} = \{-9, -8\}$

Hence, B is a finite set.

(iii) $C = \{x : x \in Z$ and $-7 < x < -5\} = \{-6\}$

Hence, C is a singleton set.

(iv) $D = \{x : x \in N$ and $x < -5\} = \phi$

Hence, D is empty set.

16. (i) Given, set $= \{1, 2\}$.

Hence, it is finite.

(ii) Given, set $= \{2\}$.

Hence, it is finite.

(iii) Given, set $= \phi$.

Hence, it is finite.

(iv) The given set is the set of all prime numbers and since set of prime numbers is infinite.

Hence, the given set is infinite.

17. (False)

e.g. Set of real numbers cannot be described in this form because the elements of this set do not follow any particular pattern.

18. (c) (A) $\{x \in N : 5 < x < 6\} = \phi$

So, A $\rightarrow$ 2

(B) $\{x : x \in N$ and x is odd$\}$
$= \{1, 3, 5, 7, 9, \ldots\ldots\}$

So, B $\rightarrow$ 4

(C) $\{x : x \in Z$ and $x^2 = 36\}$
$= \{6, -6\}$

So, C $\rightarrow$ 1

(D) $\{x : x - 5 = 0\} = \{5\}$

So, D $\rightarrow$ 3

19. $A = \{1, 2, 3, 4\}, B = \{1, 2, 3, 4\}$

$\Rightarrow A = B$

A and B are equal sets.

20. (False)

$A \neq B$

21. (Yes)

$A = \{\text{L, O, Y, A, L}\} = \{\text{L,O, Y, A}\}$

$B = \{\text{A, L, L, O, Y}\} = \{\text{L,O, Y, A}\}$

Clearly, $A = B$

22. (d) We have,

$A = \{0\}$

$B = \{x : x > 15 \text{ and } x < 5\} = \phi$

$C = \{x : x - 5 = 0\} = \{5\}$

$D = \{x : x^2 = 25\} = \{-5, 5\}$

$E = \{5\}$

Clearly, $C = E$

23. (False)

$A = \{x : x \in Z \text{ and } x^2 \leq 8\}$
$= \{-2, -1, 0, 1, 2\}$

$B = \{x : x \in R$ and $x^2 - 4x + 3 = 0\} = \{1, 3\}$

Since, $0 \in A$ but $0 \notin B$.

So, $A \neq B$

24. subset

25. (d)

26. (i) (True)

(ii) (True)

(iii) (True)

We know that two sets A and B are equal, iff $A \subset B$ and $B \subset A$. Also, we know that $\phi \subset A$ and $A \subset \phi$ (given)

$\therefore A = \phi$

(iv) (False)

Since, $\{3, 4\}$ is an element of set A.

Therefore, $\{3, 4\} \not\subset A$.

(v) (False)

Consider the following sets

$A = \{a\}, B = \{\{a\}, b\}$ and $C = \{\{a\}, b, c\}$

Clearly, $A \in B$ and $B \subset C$.

But $A \not\subset C$, as $a \in A$ but $a \notin C$.

Thus, the given statement is not true.

(vi) (False)

Consider, $A = \{1\}$ and $B = \{\{1\}, 2\}$

Clearly, $1 \in A$ and $A \in B$ but $1 \notin B$

So, $x \in A$ and $A \in B$ need not imply that $x \in B$.

(vii) (False)

Let $A = \{1\}, B = \{1, 2\}$ and $C = \{\{1, 2\}, 3\}$

Then, we observe that

$A \subset B$ and $B \in C$ but $A \notin C$

Thus, $A \subset B$ and $B \in C$ need not imply that $A \in C$.

27. (i) $Q = \{2, 4, 6, 8 \ldots\ldots, 48\}$

(ii) $R = \{1, 3, 5, 7 \ldots\ldots, 49\}$

(iii) $S = \{2, 3, 5, 7 \ldots\ldots, 47\}$

(iv) $T = \{5, 10, 15, 20 \ldots\ldots, 45\}$

28. (i) True

(ii) True

(iii) False

(iv) True

29. (a) $[a, b] = \{x \in R : a \leq x \leq b\}$

30. $\{x : x \in R, -4 < x \leq 6\} = (-4, 6]$

31. (c)

32. True

33. $U = \{1, 2, 3, 4, 5, 6, 7\}$

34. Rectangle

35. (False)

$\because A \cup B = \{x : x \in A \text{ or } x \in B\}$

36. and

37. $P = \{a, b, c, d\}, Q = \{a, c, g\}$ and $R = \{c, g, m, n, p\}$

(i) $P \cup Q = \{a, b, c, d, g\}$

(ii) $P \cup R = \{a, b, c, d, g, m, n, p\}$

(iii) $Q \cup R = \{a, c, g, m, n, p\}$

(iv) $P \cap Q = \{a, c\}$

(v) $P \cap R = \{c\}$

(vi) $Q \cap R = \{c, g\}$

(vii) $P \cap (Q \cup R) = \{a, b, c, d\} \cap \{a, c, g, m, n, p\} = \{a, c\}$

(viii) $(P \cap Q) \cup R = \{a, c\} \cup \{c, g, m, n, p\} = \{a, c, g, m, n, p\}$

(ix) $(P \cup Q) \cap R = \{a, b, c, d, g\} \cap \{c, g, m, n, p\} = \{c, g\}$

(x) $(P \cap Q) \cup (P \cap R) = \{a, c\} \cup \{c\} = \{a, c\}$

or $P \cap (Q \cup R)$

38. (i) True (ii) False

39. $A \cap B = \{x : x = 2n, n \in Z\} \cap \{x : x = 3n, n \in Z\}$

$= \{......, -4, -2, 0, 2, 4, 6, ...\} \cap \{...... -9, -6, -3, 0, 3, 6, 9, ...\}$

$= \{ ...... -6, 0, 6, 12, ...\}$

$= \{x : x = 6n, n \in Z\}$

40. (True)

We have, $aN = \{ax : x \in N\}$

$\therefore \quad 3N = \{3x : x \in N\} = \{3, 6, 9, 12, ...\}$

and $7N = \{7x : x \in N\} = \{7, 14, 21, 28, ...\}$

Hence, $3N \cap 7N = \{21, 42, ...\} = \{21x : x \in N\} = 21N$

41. $A \cup (A \cap B) = (A \cup A) \cap (A \cup B)$ [$\because \cup$ is distributive over $\cap$]

$= A \cap (A \cup B)$

$= A \quad [\because A \subset A \cup B]$

42. $A = \{1, 2\}, B = \{1, 4, 8\}$ and $C = \{2, 4, 6, 8\}$

(i) $B - A = \{4, 8\}$

(ii) $A \cup B = \{1, 2, 4, 8\}$

(iii) $C - (A \cup B) = \{6\}$

43. (b)

44. (True)

$U' = \{x \in U : x \notin U\} = \phi$

$\phi' = \{x \in U : x \notin \phi\} = U$

45. (d) $A \cup A' = \{x \in U : x \in A\} \cup \{x \in U : x \notin A\} = U$

46. (i) $W = \{1, 10, 4, 5, 6, 7, 2, 9\}$

(ii) $X = \{8, 3, 2, 9, 6, 7\}$

(iii) $Y = \{4, 10\}$

(iv) $Z = \{2, 9, 3\}$

(v) $W \cap Y = \{4, 10\}$

(vi) $W \cap Z = \{2, 9\}$

(vii) $Y \cap Z = \phi$

(viii) $W \cap X = \{2, 9, 6, 7\}$

47. (d)

48. (i)

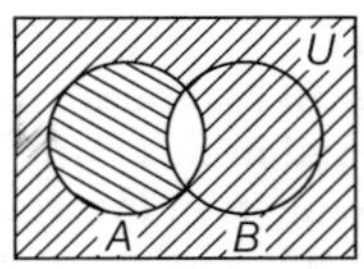

(ii)

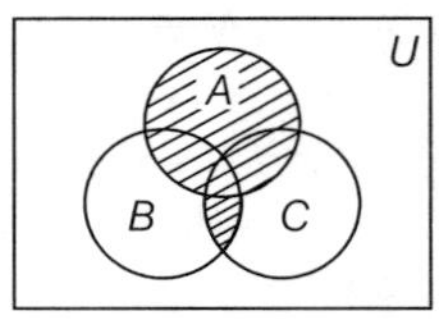

(iii)

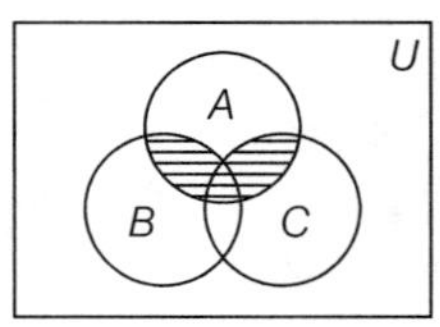

(iv)

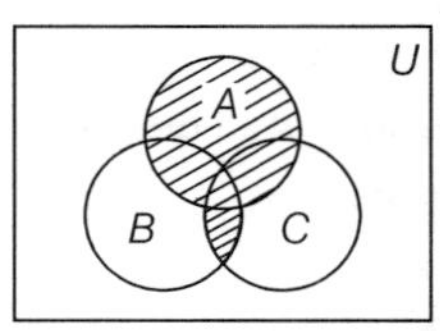

(v)

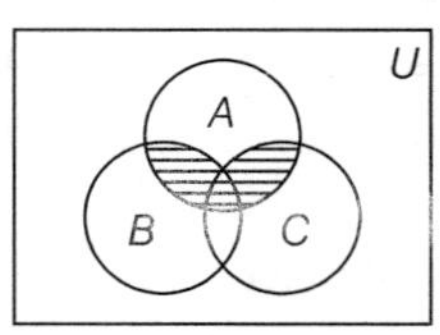

(vi)

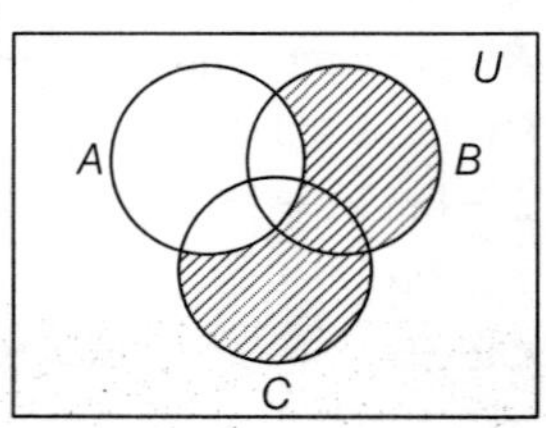

(vii)

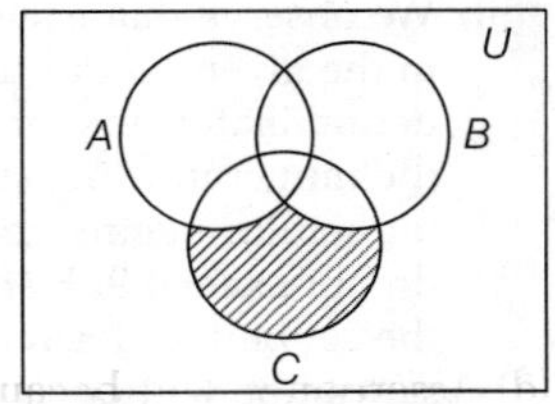

49. (i) $A \cup B = \{1, 2, 3, 4, 6, 8\}$

(ii) $(A \cup B)' = \{5, 7, 9\}$

(iii) $A \cap B = \{2, 4\}$

(iv) $(A \cap B)' = \{1, 3, 5, 6, 7, 8, 9\}$

50. (False)

We have, $(A \cup B) \cap B' = A$ [$\because A$ and B are disjoint sets]

$\therefore A' \cup ((A \cup B) \cap B') = A' \cup A = N$

51. $(A \cup B) \cap (A \cup B')$

$= ((A \cup B) \cap A) \cup ((A \cup B) \cap B'))$

$= A \cup ((A \cup B) \cap B')$

$= A \cup ((A \cap B') \cup (B \cap B'))$

$= A \cup (A \cap B')$

$= A$

52. (d) **Statement I**

$(A')' = \{x \in U : x \notin A'\}$

$= \{x \in U : x \in A\} = A$

Statement II

$x \in A \Rightarrow x \notin B$

$\Rightarrow \quad x \in B'$.

So, $\quad A \subseteq B'$

Statement III

We know that

$X - Y = X \cap Y'$

So, $A' - B' = A' \cap (B')'$

$= A' \cap B$

$= B \cap A'$

$= B - A$

53. (c) Let $A = \{1, 2, 3, 4\}$, $B = \{3, 4, 5, 6\}$

and $C = \{3, 4, 7, 8\}$

$\therefore A \cap B = \{3, 4\} = A \cap C$

But $B \neq C$

Hence, $A \cap B = A \cap C \nRightarrow B = C$

54. We have,

$A - B = \{x : x \in A \text{ and } x \notin B\}$

$B - A = \{x : x \in B \text{ and } x \notin A\}$

$A - B$ and $B - A$ are disjoint sets.

Now, $x \in A - B \Rightarrow x \in A$ and $x \notin B \Rightarrow x \notin A \cap B$

$\therefore (A - B)$ and $(A \cap B)$ are disjoint sets.

Similarly, $B - A$ and $A \cap B$ are disjoint sets.

Assertion-Reason

1. (c) Assertion is true

Reason is false because (0, 1) there exist infinite number of real number, so B was infinitne element.

2. (d) Assertion is false because set of all real numbers less than or equal to 0 is $(-\infty, 0]$.

Reason is true.

3. (a) Assertion is true because $x : x \in N$ and $x^2 - 3x + 2 = 0$

will be $x^2 - 2x - x + 2 = 0$

$$(x-2)(x-1) = 0$$

$$x = 1, 2$$

So, set is {1, 2} that is finite set.

Reason is correct explanation of Assertion.

4. (d) $P = \{x : x \text{ is prime number which is divisor of } 20\}$ in roaster form

$P = \{2, 5\}$

1 will not be included in P because it is not a prime number, so Assertion is wrong.

Reason is true.

5. (c) U set of english alphabets

$U = \{a, b, c, \ldots, z\}$

$V = \{a, e, i, o, u\}$

$V \subset U$

$\Rightarrow$ Assertion is true

$V = \{a, e, i, o, u\}$

consonants $= U - V$

$\Rightarrow$ set of consonant is not a subset of vowels

$\Rightarrow$ Reason is false.

6. (a)

7. (a)

8. (d) $B \subseteq A \Rightarrow$ all rectangles are parallelogram that is true.

$B \subseteq C \Rightarrow$ all rectangles are square that is false.

$\Rightarrow$ Assertion is false.

Reason is true.

9. (a) $A = \{x : x^2 = 4 \text{ and } x \text{ is odd}\}$
$= \{\phi\}$

10. (a)

11. (b)

12. (d) If $A = \{1, 2\}$ and $B = \{1, 2, 3\}$, then $A \subset B$ because all elements of A are contained in B.

13. (a)

14. (a) We have,

$A \cup X = B \cup X$ for some set X

$A \cap (A \cup X) = A \cap (B \cup X)$

$\Rightarrow A = (A \cap B) \cup (A \cap X)$

$[\because A \cap (A \cup X) = A]$

$\Rightarrow A = (A \cap B) \cup \phi$

$[\because A \cap X = \phi \text{ (given)}]$

$\Rightarrow A = A \cap B$

$\Rightarrow A \subset B$

Case Based Questions

Case 1

(i) (a) $A = \{x : x$ is set of letters needs to spell 'PARABOLA'$\}$

Roaster form
$A = \{P, A, R, B, O, L\}$

$B = \{x : x$ is set of letters needs to spell 'PORBAL'$\}$

Roaster form $B = \{P, O, R, B, A, L\}$

$\therefore \quad A = B$

(ii) (a) $A = \{P, A, R, B, O, L\}$

$B = \{P, O, R, B, A, L\}$

$A \cup B = \{P, O, R, B, A, L\} = B$

(iii) (b) $A \cap B = \{P, O, R, B, A, L\}$
$= B = A = A \cup B$

(iv) (d) $A = \{P, A, R, B, O, L\}$

$B = \{P, O, R, B, A, L\}$

$A - B = \phi \qquad [\because A = B]$

Case 2

(i) (b) Hardcover mystery novels represents the intersection of set A, B and C.

(ii) (a) Books are not published in English is the complement of set E.

(iii) (c) $F \cup G$ includes Science fiction books and books not categorised as Science fiction.

(iv) (b) The cardinality of the intersection of set $H \cap I$ is 1.

Competition Connect

1. 2^n

2. Let A and B be two sets having m and n elements, respectively.

Then, number of subsets of set $A = 2^m$

Number of subsets of set $B = 2^n$

It is given that $2^m - 2^n = 56$

$\Rightarrow 2^n(2^{m-n} - 1) = 2^3(2^3 - 1)$

$\Rightarrow n = 3$ and $m - n = 3$

$\Rightarrow n = 3$ and $m = 6$

3. Power set

4. $\{\{b\}\}, \{b\}$

5. (True)

Since, the empty set and the set A itself are subsets of A and are therefore elements of $P(A)$. Thus, the power set of a given set is always non-empty.

6. (d)

7. (True)

Let x be an arbitrary element of A. Then, there exists a subset, say X, of set A such that $x \in X$.

Now, $X \subset A \Rightarrow X \in P(A)$

$\Rightarrow X \in P(B) \qquad [\because P(A) = P(B)]$

$\Rightarrow X \subset B$

$\Rightarrow \quad x \in B \qquad [\because x \in X \text{ and } X \subset B \ \therefore x \in B]$

Thus, $x \in A \Rightarrow x \in B$.

$\therefore A \subset B$

8. (a) We have,

$$n(X \cup Y) = n(X) + n(Y) - n(X \cap Y)$$

$\Rightarrow \qquad 38 = 17 + 23 - n(X \cap Y)$

$\Rightarrow n(X \cap Y) = 40 - 38 = 2$

9. (d) Let H denotes the set of people speaking Hindi and E denotes the set of people speaking English.

We are given that $n(H) = 550$, $n(E) = 450$ and $n(H \cup E) = 800$

We have to find $n(H \cap E)$

We know that

$$n(H \cup E) = n(H) + n(E) - n(H \cap E)$$

$\Rightarrow n(H \cap E) = n(H) + n(E) - n(H \cup E)$

$\Rightarrow n(H \cap E) = 550 + 450 - 800 = 200$

Hence, 200 persons can speak both Hindi and English.

10. Let C be the set of students, who like to play cricket and F be the set of of students, who like to play football. We have,

$n(C) = 24, n(F) = 16$

and $\quad n(C \cup F) = 35$

Now, $n(C \cup F) = n(C) + n(F) - n(C \cap F)$

$\Rightarrow 35 = 24 + 16 - n(C \cap F)$

$\Rightarrow n(C \cap F) = 40 - 35 = 5$

11. (b) Let H denotes the set of people speaking Hindi and E denotes the set of people speaking English. Then,
$n(H \cup E) = 50, n(H) = 35$ and $n(H \cap E) = 25$

Now, $n(E - H) = n(H \cup E) - n(H)$
$= 50 - 35 = 15$

Thus, the number of people who speak english is 15.

12. We have, $A' \cap B' = (A \cup B)'$

$\therefore n(A' \cap B') = n(A \cup B)'$
$= n(U) - n(A \cup B)$
$= n(U) - [n(A) + n(B) - n(A \cap B)]$
$= 700 - (200 + 300 - 100)$
$= 300$

13. (c) Let U be the set of all surveyed students, A denotes the set of students drinking Limca and B be the set of students drinking Mirinda.

It is given that
$n(U) = 700, n(A) = 180, n(B) = 275$ and $n(A \cap B) = 95$

Now, $n(A' \cap B') = n(A \cup B)'$
$= n(U) - n(A \cup B)$
$= n(U) - [n(A) + n(B) - n(A \cap B)]$
$= 700 - [180 + 275 - 95]$
$= 700 - 360$
$= 340$

14. (False)

Let U be the set of all car owners investigated, M be the set of persons who owned Maruti cars and H be the set of persons who owned Hyundai cars.

It is given that
$n(U) = 500, n(M) = 400,$
$n(H) = 200$ and $n(M \cap H) = 50$

$\therefore n(M \cup H) = n(M) + n(H) - n(M \cap H)$
$= 400 + 200 - 50 = 550$

But $M \cup H \subseteq U$.

Therefore, $n(M \cup H) \le n(U)$

$\Rightarrow \quad n(M \cup H) \le 500$

This is a contradiction. So, the given data is incorrect.

15. (b) Let U be the set of all consumers who were surveyed, A be the set of consumers who liked product P_1 and B be the set of consumers who liked the product P_2.

It is given that
$n(U) = 2000, n(A) = 1720$ and $n(B) = 1450$

Now, $n(A \cup B) = n(A) + n(B) - n(A \cap B)$
$= 1720 + 1450 - n(A \cap B)$
$= 3170 - n(A \cap B)$

Since, $A \cup B \subset U$

$\therefore \quad n(A \cup B) \le n(U)$

$\Rightarrow 3170 - n(A \cap B) \le 2000$

$\Rightarrow \quad 3170 - 2000 \le n(A \cap B)$

$\Rightarrow \quad n(A \cap B) \ge 1170$

Hence, the least number of consumers who liked both the products is 1170.

Competition Edge Up

1. (a) Total elements $= 601$
(Natural number between [100, 700])

Let set P denotes number multiple of 3 and set Q denotes number multiple of 4.

Now, according to the question, we need

$n(\overline{P} \cap \overline{Q})$

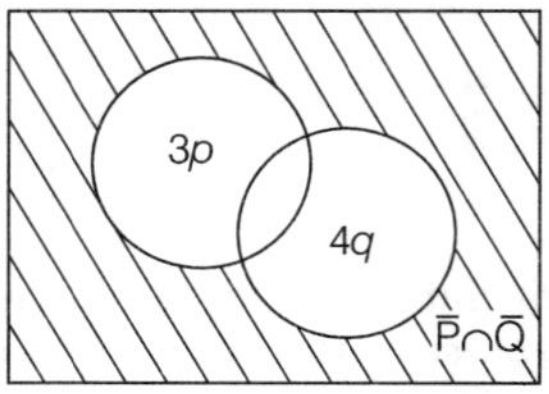

By De-Morgan's law,

$n(\overline{P} \cap \overline{Q}) = n(\overline{P \cup Q})$

Now, $\quad n(P) = 200$

$[\because 700 \ge (102 + (n-1)\,3]$

and $700 \ge (100 + (m-1)\,4))$

$n(Q) = 151$

$n(P \cap Q) = 50$

$[\because 700 \ge (104 + (r-1)12)]$

$\Rightarrow n(P \cup Q) = n(P) + n(Q) - n(P \cap Q)$
$= 200 + 151 - 50$
$= 301$

$\Rightarrow n(\overline{P \cup Q}) = 601 - 301$
$= 300 = n(\overline{P} \cap \overline{Q})$

$\therefore$ Number of elements in set A is 300.

2. (d) Given,
$(\sqrt{3} + \sqrt{2})^x + (\sqrt{3} - \sqrt{2})^x = 10$

Let $(\sqrt{3} + \sqrt{2})^x = t$

$\Rightarrow \quad (\sqrt{3} - \sqrt{2})^x = \dfrac{1}{t}$

$\Rightarrow \quad t + \dfrac{1}{t} = 10$

$\Rightarrow \quad t^2 - 10t + 1 = 0$

$\Rightarrow \quad t = \dfrac{10 \pm \sqrt{96}}{2} = 5 \pm 2\sqrt{6}$

$\Rightarrow \quad (\sqrt{3} + \sqrt{2})^x = (\sqrt{3} \pm \sqrt{2})^2$

$x = \pm 2$

$\therefore$ Number of solutions $= 2$

3. (b) Given, $n(A) = m$ and $n(B) = n$

$\therefore$ Number of subsets of $A = 2^m$

and number of subsets of $B = 2^n$

According to the question,

$2^m - 2^n = 56$

$\Rightarrow \quad 2^m - 2^n = 2^6 - 2^3$

$\Rightarrow \quad m = 6$ and $n = 3$

So, distance between the points $P(m, n)$ i.e. $P(6, 3)$ and $Q(-2, -3)$ is given by

$\sqrt{(6+2)^2 + (3+3)^2} = \sqrt{64 + 36}$
$= \sqrt{100} = 10$

4. (45) According to question,

$125 \le m + 90 - x \le 130$

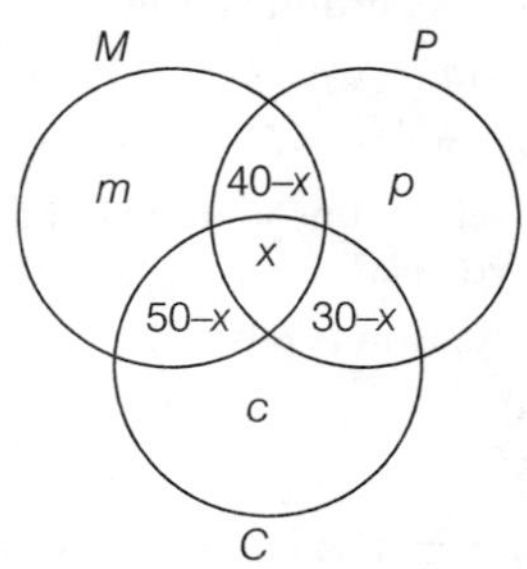

$85 \le p + 70 - x \le 95$

$75 \le c + 80 - x \le 90$

$m + p + c + 120 - 2x = 210$

$\Rightarrow \quad 15 \le x \le 45$

and $\quad 30 - x \ge 0$

$\Rightarrow \quad 15 \le x \le 30$

Hence, $30 + 15 = 45$

5. (10) Given, $n(M \cup P \cup C) = 40$,

We have,

$x = n(P \cap M \cap C)$

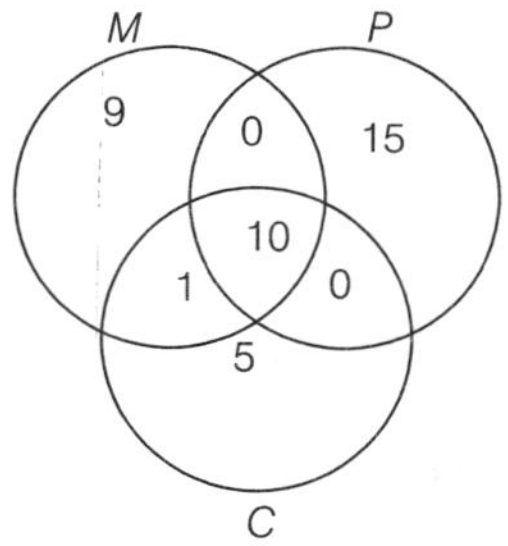

Now, $11 - n(P \cap M \cap C) \geq 0$

$\Rightarrow n(P \cap M \cap C) = 11,$

which does not satisfy the dute

So, $n(P \cap M \cap C) = 10$

Hence, maximum number of students passed in all the three subjects is 10.

6. (c) We have, $n(A) = 48,$

$n(B) = 25, n(C) = 18,$

$n(A \cup B \cup C) = 60$

and $n(A \cap B \cap C) = 5$

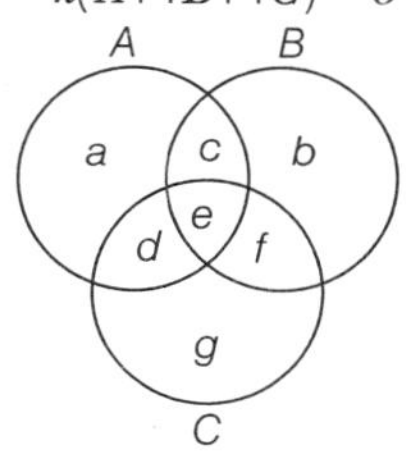

$e = 5,$

$a + c + e + d = 48$

$\Rightarrow a + c + d = 43$ ...(i)

$b + c + e + f = 25$

$\Rightarrow b + c + f = 20$ ...(ii)

$d + e + f + g = 18$

$\Rightarrow d + f + g = 13$ ...(iii)

$a + b + c + d + e + f + g = 60$

$\Rightarrow a + b + c + d + f + g = 55$ ...(iv)

On adding Eqs. (i), (ii) and (iii),

$a + b + 2c + 2d + 2f + g = 76$ ...(v)

Subtract Eq. (iv) from Eq. (v), we get $c + d + f = 21$

$\therefore$ Number of men who received exactly 2 medals $= c + d + f = 21$

7. (15) We have, $n \in N$

$10 \leq n \leq 100$ and $3^n - 3$ is a multiple of 7.

$\therefore 3^n - 3 = 7k, \forall k \in I$

$3^n = 7k + 3$

Now, $3 = 3 \pmod 7$

$3^2 = 2 \pmod 7$

$3^3 = -1 \pmod 7$ or $6 \pmod 7$

$3^6 = 1 \pmod 7$

$3^7 = 3 \pmod 7$

Since, $3^{13} = 3 \pmod 7$

$\vdots$

$\therefore n$ can be 13, 19, ... 97

$\therefore$ Total $n = 15$

8. (5) Given,

$|x|^2 - 2|x| + |\lambda - 3| = 0$

$\Rightarrow |x|^2 - 2|x| + 1 + |\lambda - 3| - 1 = 0$

$\Rightarrow (|x| - 1)^2 + |\lambda - 3| = 1$

Since, $\lambda \in R$

At $\lambda = 3, x = 0, 2$

At $\lambda = 4$ or 2, $x = 1$ or -1

So, maximum value of $x + \lambda = 5$

Hence, the largest element in the set S is 5.

9. (b) For set A, $-2 < x + 1 < 2$

$\Rightarrow -3 < x < 1$

$\Rightarrow x \in (-3, 1)$

For set B, $x - 1 \leq -2$ or $x - 1 \geq 2$

$\Rightarrow x \leq -1$ or $x \geq 3$

$\Rightarrow x \in (-\infty, -1] \cup [3, \infty)$

$A - B = (-1, 1)$

$B - A = R - (-3, 3)$

$A \cap B = (-3, -1]$

$A \cup B = R - [1, 3)$

10. (d) Given,

$$S = \left\{x \in [-6, 3] - \{-2, 2\} : \frac{|x + 3| - 1}{|x| - 2} \geq 0\right\}$$

and

$T = \{x \in Z : x^2 - 7|x| + 9 \leq 0\}$

Here, $x^2 - 7|x| + 9 \leq 0$

$\Rightarrow |x|^2 - 7|x| + 9 \leq 0$ $[\because |x|^2 = x^2]$

$$\Rightarrow \left[|x| - \left(\frac{7 + \sqrt{49 - 36}}{2}\right)\right] \leq 0$$

$$\left[|x| - \left(\frac{7 - \sqrt{49 - 36}}{2}\right)\right] \leq 0$$

$$\Rightarrow |x| \in \left[\frac{7 - \sqrt{13}}{2}, \frac{7 + \sqrt{13}}{2}\right]$$

But x an integer,

$|x| = 2, 3, 4, 5$ and $x = \pm 2, \pm 3, \pm 4, \pm 5$

$T = \{\pm 2, \pm 3, \pm 4, \pm 5\}$

$S \cap T \neq \{\pm 2, 4, 5\}$ as $S \notin \{\pm 2, 4, 5\}$

When $x = -3$, then $\dfrac{|-3 + 3| - 1}{|-3| - 2}$

$= \dfrac{-1}{1} < 0$

When $x = -4$,

then $\dfrac{|-4 + 3| - 1}{|-4| - 2} = 0$

When $x = -5$, then

$\dfrac{|-5 + 3| - 1}{|-5| - 2} = \dfrac{1}{3} \geq 0$

When $x = 3$,

then $\dfrac{|3 + 3| - 1}{|3| - 2} = 5 \geq 0$

Hence, $S \cap T = \{-5, -4, 3\}$

$\Rightarrow n(S \cap T) = 3$

11. (11) $S = \{4, 6, 9\},$

$T = \{9, 10, 11, \ldots, 1000\}$

$A = \{a_1 + a_2 + \ldots a_k : k \in N,$
$a_1, a_2, a_3 \ldots a_k \in S\}$

$A = \{a; a = 4x + 6y + 9z, \; x, y, z \in \{0, 1, 2, \ldots\}\}$

$\therefore A = \{9, 10, 12, 13, 14, 15, 16, 17, 18, \ldots\}$

$T - A = \{11\}$

12. (112) Given, $A = \{1, 2, 3, 4, 5, 6, 7\}$ and $B = \{3, 6, 7, 9\}$

Total number of subset of $A = 2^7 = 128$

As, $C \subseteq A$ and $C \cap B = \phi$, so the set C contains only 4 elements

i.e. $\{1, 2, 4, 5\}$

$\therefore$ The number of elements in the set $\{C \subseteq A : C \cap B \neq \phi\}$

= total number of sets – number of sets, when $C \subseteq A$

and $C \cap B = \phi$

$= 128 - 2^4 = 128 - 16 = 112$

13. (107) Apply De-Morgan's law,

$(B \cup C)' = B' \cap C'$

B' containing subsets of A which do not contains 2 but element 1

and C' is a set containing subsets of A whose sum of elements is not prime.

So, we need to calculate number of subsets of $\{3, 4, 5, 6, 7\}$, whose sum of elements plus 1 is composite.

Number of 5 elements subset = 1

Number of 4 elements subset = 3 (except selecting 3 or 7)

Number of 3 elements subset = 6 (except selecting {3,4,5}, {3,6,7}, {4,5,7} or {5,6,7}

Number of such 2 elements subset = 7 (except selecting, {3,7}, {4,6}, {5,7})

Number of such 1 element subset = 3 (except selecting {4} or {6})

Number of such 0 elements subset = 1

Here,
$n(B'\cap C') = 1+3+6+7+3+1 = 21$
Therefore, $n(B\cup C) = 2^7 - 21 = 107$

14. (5264) $B = \{2, 4, 6, 8, \ldots, 200\}$ and $45 = 3^2 \cdot 5$

n (multiples of 6) = 33
n (multiples of 10) = 20
n (multiples of 30) = 6

Sum = $S_6 = 6\,(1+2+\ldots+33)$
$= \dfrac{6\,(33\times 34)}{2}$
$S_{10} = 10\,(1+2+\ldots+20)$
$= \dfrac{10\,(20\times 21)}{2}$
$S_{30} = 30\,(1+2+\ldots+6)$
$= \dfrac{30\,(6\times 7)}{2}$

Total sum,
$S_{200} = 2\,(1+2+\ldots+100)$
$= \dfrac{2(100\times 101)}{2}$

Sum of elements of $A\cap B$
$= [100\times 101 - 3\times 33\times 34 - 5\times 20\times 21 + 15\times 6\times 7]$
$= 10100 - 3366 - 2100 + 630$
$= 5264$

15. (1633) Let $S(\alpha)$ is the sum of all element of the set.

$S(\alpha) = (\Sigma\alpha) - (\Sigma \text{ multiple of } 2) - (\Sigma \text{ multiple of } 3) + \alpha\,(\Sigma \text{ multiple of } 6)$

Let $S(\alpha)$ is the sum of all elements of the set
$\{\alpha \in \{1, 2, 3, \ldots, 100\};$
HCF $(24, \alpha) = 1\}$

Since, HCF $(24, \alpha) = 1$
$\Rightarrow S(\alpha) = (1+2+3\ldots+100)$
$-S$ (multiple of 3) $- S$(multiple of 2) $+ S$(multiple of 6)
$\Rightarrow S(\alpha) = (1+2+3\ldots+100) - (2+4+6+\ldots+100) - (3+6+9+\ldots+99) + (6+12+18+\ldots 96)$

$\Rightarrow S(\alpha) = \dfrac{100\cdot(100+1)}{2} - 2\cdot(1+2+3+\ldots+50) - 3(1+2+3+\ldots+33) + 6(1+2+3+\ldots 16)$

$= \dfrac{100\cdot 101}{2} - 2\cdot\dfrac{50\cdot(50+1)}{2} - 3\cdot\dfrac{33\cdot(33+1)}{2} + 6\cdot\dfrac{16\cdot(16+1)}{2}$

$= 5050 - 2550 - 1683 + 816$
$= 1633$

Chapter-2

Relations and Functions

1. (i) By the definition of equality of ordered pairs, we have
$(3a-2, b+3) = (2a-1, 3)$
$\Rightarrow 3a - 2 = 2a - 1$ and $b + 3 = 3$
$\Rightarrow a = 1$ and $b = 0$

(ii) $(a+2, 3b-2) = (0, 1)$
$\Rightarrow a + 2 = 0$ and $3b - 2 = 1$
$\Rightarrow a = -2$ and $b = 1$

(iii) $(2a+1, 3b) = (2b, 2a+1)$
$\Rightarrow 2a + 1 = 2b$ and $3b = 2a + 1$
$\Rightarrow\ 2a - 2b + 1 = 0$ ...(i)
and $2a - 3b + 1 = 0$ ...(ii)
On solving Eqs. (i) and (ii), we get
$b = 0$ and $a = -\dfrac{1}{2}$

2. (i) True

(ii) (False)
By definition of the cartesian product,
$P\times Q = \{(a, r), (b, r), (c, r)\}$
and
$Q\times P = \{(r, a), (r, b), (r, c)\}$
Since, by the definition of equality of ordered pairs, the pair (a, r) is not equal to the pair (r, a), we conclude that $P\times Q \neq Q\times P$.

(iii) True

3. (i) $A\times B = \{2, 4, 6\}\times\{1, 2\}$
$= \{(2, 1), (2, 2), (4, 1), (4, 2), (6, 1), (6, 2)\}$

(ii) $B\times A = \{1, 2\}\times\{2, 4, 6\}$
$= \{(1, 2), (1, 4), (1, 6), (2, 2), (2, 4), (2, 6)\}$.

(iii) $B\times B = \{1, 2\}\times\{1, 2\}$
$= \{(1, 1), (1, 2), (2, 1), (2, 2)\}$

(iv) $A\times A = \{2, 4, 6\}\times\{2, 4, 6\}$
$= \{(2, 2,), (2, 4), (2, 6), (4, 2), (4, 4), (4, 6), (6, 2), (6, 4), (6, 6)\}$

(v) Yes, $n(A\times B) = n(A)\times n(B)$
$= 3\times 2 = 6$
$n(B\times A) = n(B)\times n(A)$
$= 2\times 3 = 6$
Hence, $n(A\times B) = n(B\times A)$

4. We have, $A = \{1, 2, 3\}$ and
$B = \{x : x\in N, x$ is prime less than $5\} = \{2, 3\}$
$\therefore\ A\times B = \{1, 2, 3\}\times\{2, 3\}$
$= \{(1, 2), (1, 3), (2, 2), (2, 3), (3, 2), (3, 3)\}$

5. Clearly, $B\times A$ can be obtained from $A\times B$ by interchanging the entries (or components) or ordered pair in $A\times B$.
$\therefore\ B\times A = \{(1, a), (5, a), (2, a), (2, b), (5, b), (1, b)\}$

6. (i) $B\cup C = \{1, 3, 4, 5\}$
$A\times(B\cup C) = \{(1, 1), (1, 3), (1, 4), (1, 5), (2, 1), (2, 3), (2, 4), (2, 5), (3, 1), (3, 3), (3, 4), (3, 5)\}$

(ii) $B\cap C = \{3\}$
$A\times(B\cap C)$
$= \{(1, 3), (2, 3), (3, 3)\}$

(iii) $A\times B = \{(1, 3), (1, 4), (2, 3), (2, 4), (3, 3), (3, 4)\}$
$A\times C = \{(1, 1), (1, 3), (1, 5), (2, 1), (2, 3), (2, 5), (3, 1), (3, 3), (3, 5)\}$
$\therefore\ (A\times B)\cap(A\times C)$
$= \{(1, 3), (2, 3), (3, 3)\}$

(iv) $(A\times B)\cup(A\times C)$
$= \{(1, 1), (1, 3), (1, 4), (1, 5), (2, 1), (2, 3), (2, 4), (2, 5), (3, 1), (3, 3), (3, 4), (3, 5)\}$

7. $A\times B = \{(1, 3), (1, 4), (2, 3), (2, 4)\}$
$A\times B\times C = (A\times B)\times C$
$= \{(1, 3, 4), (1, 3, 5), (1, 3, 6), (1, 4, 4), (1, 4, 5), (1, 4, 6), (2, 3, 4), (2, 3, 5), (2, 3, 6), (2, 4, 4), (2, 4, 5), (2,4, 6)\}$

8. (False)
Since, (1, 4), (2, 6) and (3, 6) are elements of $A\times B$, it follows that 1, 2, 3 are elements of A and 4, 6 are elements of B. It is given that $A\times B$ has 6 elements.

So, $A = \{1, 2, 3\}$ and $B = \{4, 6\}$.

Hence, $B\times A = \{(4,1), (4, 2), (4, 3), (6, 1), (6, 2), (6, 3)\}$.

9. Since, $(-1, 0) \in A \times A$ and $(0, 1) \in A \times A$. Therefore,
$(-1, 0) \in A \times A \Rightarrow -1, 0 \in A$
and $(0, 1) \in A \times A \Rightarrow 0, 1 \in A$
$\therefore -1, 0, 1 \in A$
It is given that A has exactly 3 elements.
Hence, $A = \{-1, 0, 1\}$.

10. Since, $(a, 2), (b, 3), (c, 2), (d, 3)$ and $(e, 2)$ are elements of $A \times B$.
Therefore, $a, b, c, d, e \in A$ and $2, 3 \in B$. It is given that $n(A) = 5$ and $n(B) = 2$
$\therefore a, b, c, d, e \in A$ and $n(A) = 5$
$\Rightarrow A = \{a, b, c, d, e\}$
$2, 3 \in B$ and $n(B) = 2$
$\Rightarrow B = \{2, 3\}$.

11. (True)
Since, $R \subseteq A \times B$

12. (i) (Yes)
Clearly, $R_1 \subseteq A \times B$. So, it is a relation from A to B.
(ii) (Yes)
Clearly, $R_2 \subseteq A \times B$. So, it is a relation from A to B.
(iii) (Yes)
Clearly, $R_3 \subseteq A \times B$. So, it is a relation from A to B.
(iv) (No)
Since, $(4, 2) \in R_4$ but $(4, 2) \notin A \times B$. So, R_4 is not a relation from A to B.

13. (i)

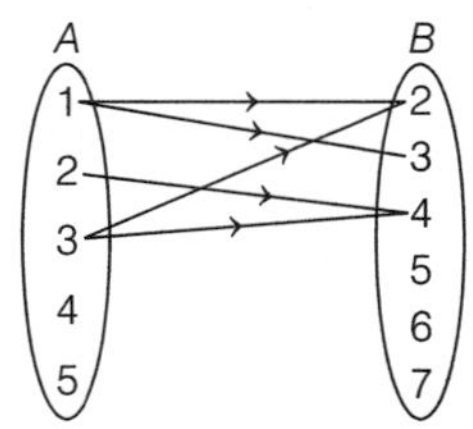

(ii)

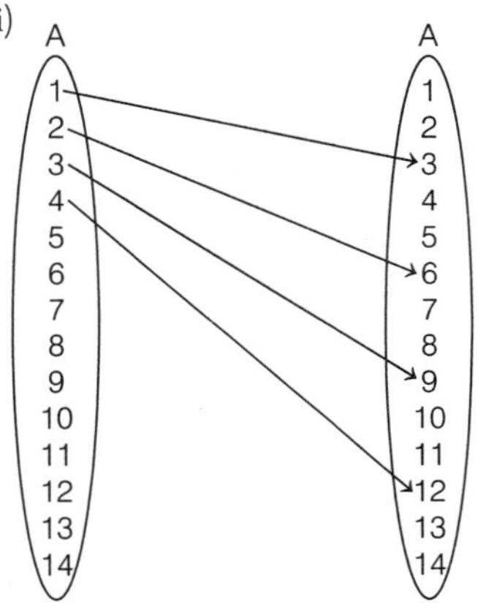

14. (i) Dom $(R) = \{1, 3, 5\}$ and range $(R) = \{8, 6, 2, 4\}$.
(ii) Under this relation R, we have $3R2, 5R2, 5R4, 7R2, 7R4$ and $7R6$
i.e. $R = \{(3, 2), (5, 2), (5, 4), (7, 2), (7, 4), (7, 6)\}$
$\therefore$ Dom $(R) = \{3, 5, 7\}$
and range $(R) = \{2, 4, 6\}$
(iii) Clearly, $2R2, 2R4, 2R6, 2R8, 4R4$ and $4R8$
$\therefore R = \{(2, 2), (2, 4), (2, 6), (2, 8), (4, 4), (4, 8)\}$
Clearly, Dom $(R) = \{2, 4\}$
and range $(R) = \{2, 4, 6, 8\}$
(iv) We have,
$R = \{(0, 5), (1, 6), (2, 7), (3, 8), (4, 9), (5, 10)\}$
Dom $(R) = \{0, 1, 2, 3, 4, 5\}$
$\therefore$Range $(R) = \{5, 6, 7, 8, 9, 10\}$
(v) We have,
$S = \{(-3, 4), (-2, 3), (-1, 2), (0, 1), (1, 0), (2, 1), (3, 2)\}$
$\therefore$ Dom $(S) = \{-3, -2, -1, 0, 1, 2, 3\}$
Range $(S) = \{0, 1, 2, 3, 4\}$

15. True

16. Since, $a\, R\, b \Leftrightarrow a^2 = b$
Then, $0R0, -2R\,4, -1R1, 1R1$ and $2R4$. So, R can be described in roster form as
$R = \{(0, 0), (-1, 1), (-2, 4), (1, 1), (2, 4)\}$

17. (i) $R = \{(x, y) : y = x - 2, x \in P, y \in Q\}$
(ii) $R = \{(5, 3), (6, 4), (7, 5)\}$

18. (i) (False)
We observe that $a = a^2$ is true for $a = 1 \in N$ only.
Therefore, $(1, 1) \in R$.
But $(2, 2), (3, 3), (4, 4)$, etc does not belong to R.
So, $(a, a) \in R$ for all $n \in N$, is not true.
(ii) (False)
We observe that $(4, 2) \in R$, because $4 = 2^2$.
But, $(2,4) \notin R$ as $2 \neq 4^2$
So, $(a, b) \in R \Rightarrow (b, a) \in R$ is not true.
(iii) (False)
We observe that $(16, 4) \in R$ and $(4, 2) \in R$.
However, $(16, 2) \notin R$
So, $(a, b) \in R$ and $(b, c) \in R$
$\Rightarrow (a, c) \in R$ is not true.
(iv) (True)
We have, $\left(1, -\frac{1}{2}\right) \in R_1$
as $1 + \left(-\frac{1}{2}\right) > 0$
and $\left(-\frac{1}{2}, -4\right) \in R_1$
as $1 + \left(-\frac{1}{2}\right)(-4) > 0$
But $1 + 1 \times -4 \not> 0$.
So, $(1, -4) \notin R_1$.
(v) True

19. $R^{-1} = \{(a, 1), (c, 1), (d, 2), (c, 2)\}$

20. We are given the relation as
$(x, y) \in R \Leftrightarrow x \le y$
(i) $R = \{(1, 1), (1, 2), (1, 3), (1, 4), (1, 5), (2, 2), (2, 3), (2, 4), (2, 5), (3, 3), (3, 4), (3, 5), (4, 4), (4, 5), (5, 5)\}$
(ii) $R^{-1} = \{(1, 1), (2, 1), (3, 1), (4, 1), (5, 1), (2, 2), (3, 2), (4, 2), (5, 2), (3, 3), (4, 3), (5, 3), (4, 4), (5, 4), (5, 5)\}$
(iii) Domain of $R^{-1} = \{1, 2, 3, 4, 5\}$
(iv) Range of $R^{-1} = \{1, 2, 3, 4, 5\}$

21. Given, $A = \{1, 2, 3, 4\}$,
$B = \{1, 5, 9, 11, 15, 16\}$
and $f = \{(1, 5), (2, 9), (3, 1), (4, 5), (2, 11)\}$
(i) (Yes)
f is a relation from A to B because relation $f \subseteq A \times B$.
(ii) (No)
f is not a function from A to B because the same first element 2 corresponds to two different images 9 and 11.

22. (i) Since, 2, 3 and 4 are the elements of domain of R having their unique images, this relation R is a function.
$\therefore$ Domain $= \{2, 3, 4\}$
and range $= \{1, 2\}$
(ii) Since, the same first element 2 corresponds to two different images 2 and 4, this relation is not a function.
(iii) Since, every element has one and only one image, this relation is a function.

$\therefore$ Domain $= \{1, 2, 3, 4, 5, 6\}$
and range $= \{2, 3, 4, 5, 6, 7\}$

23. A relation f from set A to set B is said to be a function if every element of set A has one and only one image in set B.

(i) (No)
f_1 is not a function because every element of set A don't have image in set B.

(ii) (No)
f_2 is not a function because element 4 has two images in set B.

(iii) (Yes)
f_3 is a function.
$\therefore$ Dom $(f_3) = \{1, 2, 3, 4\}$
and range $(f_3) = \{a, b, d\}$

(iv) (Yes)
f_4 is a function
$\therefore$ Dom $(f_4) = \{1, 2, 3, 4\}$
and range $(f_4) = \{b, c, d, e\}$

24. (a) (A) Since, $\frac{1}{2} \in Q \Rightarrow f\left(\frac{1}{2}\right) = 1$

(B) Since, $\pi \notin Q \Rightarrow f(\pi) = -1$

(C) We have, range of
$f = \{f(x) : x \in R\}$
Also, by definition $f(x)$ attains values 1 or -1 according as x is rational or irrational and a real number is either rational or irrational.
$\therefore$ Range of $f = \{1, -1\}$

(D) -1 is the image of every real number which is not rational.
$\therefore f^{-1}(-1) = R - Q =$ Set of irrational numbers.

25. We have, $f(-1) = (-1)^2 + 1 = 2$
$f(0) = 0^2 + 1 = 1, f(2) = 2^2 + 1 = 5$
and $f(4) = 4^2 + 1 = 17$
$\therefore f = \{(x, f(x)) : x \in A\}$
$= \{(-1, 2), (0, 1) (2, 5), (4, 17)\}$
Hence, range of $f = \{2, 1, 5, 17\}$

26. (i) (False)
We observe that
$1 \times 6 = 6$ and $2 \times 3 = 6$
$\Rightarrow (1 \times 6, 1 + 6) \in f$
and $(2 \times 3, 2 + 3) \in f$
$\Rightarrow (6, 7) \in f$ and $(6, 5) \in f$
So, f is not a function from Z into Z.

(ii) (True)
We have,
$f(x + y) = 2^{x+y} = 2^x \cdot 2^y$
$= f(x) \cdot f(y)$
$\therefore f(x + y) = f(x) f(y)$ holds true for all $x, y \in R$.

(iii) (False)
Clearly, $f(x) = g(x)$,
$\forall x \in R - \{2\}$
But $f(x)$ and $g(x)$ have different domains. In fact domain of $f = R - \{2\}$ and domain of $g = R$.
Therefore, $f \neq g$.

(iv) (True)

27. We have, $f(x) = g(x)$
$\Rightarrow 2x^2 - 1 = 1 - 3x$
$\Rightarrow 2x^2 + 3x - 2 = 0$
$\Rightarrow (2x - 1)(x + 2) = 0 \Rightarrow x = -2, \frac{1}{2}$
Thus, $f(x)$ and $g(x)$ are equal on the set $\left\{-2, \frac{1}{2}\right\}$.

28. (b) We have, $f(x) = g(x), \forall x \in R$
$\Rightarrow f(-4) = g(-4) \Rightarrow -4 - 4 = \lambda$
$\lambda = -8$

29. *(i) Greatest integer function
(ii) Signum function
(iii) Modulus function
(iv) Identity function
(v) Constant function

30. We have, $f(x) = \frac{2x}{5} + 11$

(i) $f(0) = \frac{2 \times 0}{5} + 11 = 0 + 11 = 11$

(ii) $f(10) = \frac{2 \times 10}{5} + 11$
$= 4 + 11 = 15$

(iii) $f(-1) = \frac{2 \times (-1)}{5} + 11$
$= \frac{-2 + 55}{5} = \frac{53}{5} = 10\frac{3}{5}$

(iv) $f\left(-\frac{3}{2}\right) = \frac{2}{5} \times \left(-\frac{3}{2}\right) + 11$
$= -\frac{3}{5} + 11 = \frac{-3 + 55}{5}$
$= \frac{52}{5} = 10\frac{2}{5}$

31. We have, $f(x) = 3x^4 - 5x^2 + 9$
$\therefore f(x - 1) = 3(x - 1)^4 - 5(x - 1)^2 + 9$
$= 3[(x^2 + 1 - 2x)(x^2 + 1 - 2x)]$
$- 5[x^2 + 1 - 2x] + 9$
$= 3[x^4 + x^2 - 2x^3 + x^2 + 1 - 2x$
$-2x^3 - 2x + 4x^2] - 5x^2 - 5 + 10x + 9$
$= 3x^4 - 12x^3 + 18x^2 - 12x + 3$
$- 5x^2 + 10x + 4$
$= 3x^4 - 12x^3 + 13x^2 - 2x + 7$

32. (a)

33. $\frac{9c}{5} + 32 = 212 \Rightarrow \frac{9c}{5} = 180$
$\Rightarrow 9c = 900 \Rightarrow c = 100$

34. (i) We have,
$(3f)(x) = 3\{f(x)\} = 3e^x$
$\therefore (3f)(1) = 3e^1 = 3e$

(ii) We have,
$(5g)(x) = 5\{g(x)\} = 5\log_e x$
$\therefore (5g)(1) = 5\log_e 1 = 5 \times 0 = 0$

35. (i) Clearly, $f(x)$ assumes real values for all x except for the values of x for which $x - 3 = 0$ i.e. $x = 3$
$\therefore$ Dom $(f) = R - \{3\}$

(ii) Clearly, $f(x)$ assumes real values for all x except for all those values of x for which $x^2 - 3x + 2 = 0$ i.e. $x = 1, 2$.
$\therefore$ Dom $(f) = R - \{1, 2\}$

(iii) Clearly, $f(x)$ assumes real values if
$4 - x^2 \geq 0$
$\Rightarrow -(x^2 - 4) \geq 0$
$\Rightarrow x^2 - 4 \leq 0$
$\Rightarrow (x - 2)(x + 2) \leq 0$
$\Rightarrow x \in [-2, 2]$
$\therefore$ Dom $(f) = [-2, 2]$

(iv) Clearly, $f(x)$ is defined for $4 - x \geq 0$ and $x^2 - 1 > 0$
$\Rightarrow x - 4 \leq 0$ and
$(x - 1)(x + 1) > 0$
$\Rightarrow x \leq 4$ and $(x < -1$ or $x > 1)$
$\Rightarrow x \in (-\infty, -1) \cup (1, 4]$
$\therefore$ Dom $(f) = (-\infty, -1) \cup (1, 4]$

36. (i) We have, $f(x) = a^x$
Domain of $f(x) = R$

(ii) We have, $f(x) = \log_e x$
Domain of $f(x) = (0, \infty)$

(iii) We know that
$x + [x] > 0 \ \forall x > 0$
$\Rightarrow x + [x] = 0$ for $x = 0$ ...(i)
$\Rightarrow x + [x] < 0 \ \forall x < 0$
Also, $f(x) = \frac{1}{\sqrt{x + [x]}}$ is defined for all x satisfying $x + [x] > 0$.
$\therefore$ Dom $(f) = (0, \infty)$
[using Eq. (i)]

37. (i) -1 (ii) 0 (iii) 1 (iv) 2

38. (i) True (ii) True (iii) True (iv) True (v) True (vi) False

39. Given, $f(x)=x^2$ and $g(x)=2x+1$

(i) $f+g(x)=f(x)+g(x)$
$=x^2+2x+1$

(ii) $f-g(x)=f(x)-g(x)$
$=x^2-(2x+1)$
$=x^2-2x-1$

(iii) $fg(x)=f(x)\cdot g(x)$
$=(x^2)\cdot(2x+1)$
$=2x^3+x^2$

(iv) $\dfrac{f}{g}(x)=\dfrac{f(x)}{g(x)}=\dfrac{x^2}{2x+1}$

40. The domain of f is the set of all real numbers. The domain of g is also the set of all real numbers. The domains of $f+g$, $f-g$ and fg are equal to intersection of the domains of f and g, which is again the set of real numbers i.e. R.

Now, for f/g, denominator g can't be zero and $g-2=0$. Hence, we must exclude -2 from R. Thus, the domain of f/g is the set of real numbers excluding -2 i.e.

$R-\{-2\}$ or $(-\infty,-2)\cup(-2,\infty)$.

41. (i) Given, x is a real number
$-\infty<x<\infty$
$\Rightarrow\ -\infty<3x<\infty$
$\Rightarrow\ -\infty<f(x)<\infty$
$\Rightarrow\ f(x)\in R$

(ii) We know,
$x^2\ge 0$
$\Rightarrow\ x^2-1\ge -1\Rightarrow f(x)\ge -1$
Range of $f(x)=[-1,\infty)$

(iii) Clearly, $f(x)$ takes real values if $x-5>0$
$\Rightarrow x>5\Rightarrow x\in(5,\infty)$
$\therefore$ Dom $(f)=(5,\infty)$
For $x>5$, we have
$x-5>0\Rightarrow\sqrt{x-5}>0$
$\Rightarrow\ \dfrac{1}{\sqrt{x-5}}>0\Rightarrow f(x)>0$
Thus, $f(x)$ takes all real values greater than 0.
$\therefore$ Range $(f)=(0,\infty)$

Assertion-Reason

1. (a) $(x-2,y+1)=(3,1)$
$\Rightarrow\ x-2=3\Rightarrow x=5$
$\Rightarrow\ y+1=1\Rightarrow y=0$
So, Assertion is correct and Reason is correct explanation.

2. (a) $A=\{2,3,4\}$
$\Rightarrow\ n(A)=3$
$B=\{5,6\}\Rightarrow n(B)=2$
Number of relation
$=2^{3\times2}=2^6=64$
So, Aassertion is correct and Reason is correct explanation.

3. (c) $f(x)=4+x^2$
$-\infty<x<\infty$
$0\le x^2<\infty$
$4\le x^2+4<\infty$
So, range of x^2+4 is $[4,\infty)$
Assertion is correct but Reason is false.

4. (d) $f(x)=\sqrt{x-5}$
Domain $=x-5\ge 0$
$=x\ge 5\Rightarrow x\in[5,\infty)$
Range $[0,\infty)$
So, Assertion is false and Reason is correct.

5. (a) Since, in set P every element have unique image in Q.
So, relation f is function from P to Q.
So, Assertion is correct and Reason is correct explanation.

6. (d) $f(x)=\dfrac{x^2-9}{x-3}$
Domain of $f(x)$ is $R-\{3\}$
$f(x)=\dfrac{(x+3)(x-3)}{(x-3)}=(x+3)$
and $g(x)=(x+4)$
$g(x)\ne f(x)$
So, Assertion is false and Reason is correct.

7. (b) $A=\{1,2,3,4\}$, $B=\{5,6,7\}$
$R=\{(1,6),(3,6),(2,5),(2,7),(4,5),(4,7)\}$
Domain $=\{1,3,2,4\}$
$|x|$ is always positive.
So, Assertion and Reason are correct but Reason is not correct explanation of Assertion.

8. (d) Relation
$\{(x,y):y=x^2,\ x,y\in N\}$
So, domain of relation $\{1,2,3,\ldots\}$
So, Assertion is false and Reason is correct.

9. (a) $R=\{(a,b):a,b\in Q$ and $a-b\in Z\}$
So, let us take (a,a)
$\Rightarrow\ a-a=0$
$\Rightarrow\ a\in R$
$\Rightarrow\ (a,a)\in R$
So, Assertion is correct and Reason is correction explanation.

10. (d) $P=\{1,2)$ and $Q=\{4,5,6\}$
$P\times Q=\{(1,4),(1,5),(1,6),(2,4),(2,5),(2,6)\}$
So, Assertion is false and Reason is correct.

11. (b) $f(x)=2x-3$
$f(1)=2(1)-3=-1$
and a real function has the set of real numbers or one of its subsets both as its domain and as its range.
So, Assertion and Reason both are correct but Reason is not correct explanation of Assertion.

Case Base

Case 1

(i) (a) Given curve is not a function, because at one x there are two values of y.

(ii) (a) Given relation R is a function because every elemetn in A, have unique image in B.

(iii) (c) $f(x)=\dfrac{1}{\sqrt{2x-1}}$
$2x-1>0$
$\Rightarrow\ 2x>1$
$\Rightarrow\ x>\dfrac{1}{2}$
$\Rightarrow\ x\in\left(\dfrac{1}{2},\infty\right)$

Case 2

(i) (c) $A\times A$ has 16 elements.
Some of which are $(x,1)$ and $(y,2)$
Then, $A=\{1,2,x,y\}$

(ii) (d) $n(A)=p$ and $n(B)=q$,
then $n(A\times B)=pq$
$\Rightarrow\ n(A)=3$ and $n(B)=2$,
then $n(A\times B)=6$

(iii) (a) $A\times B=\{(a,2),(b,4),(a,4),(b,2)\}$.
Then, set $A=\{a,b\}$ and
set $B=\{2,4\}$

Competition Edge Up

1. (18) We have,

$$|2a-1| = 3[a] + 2\{a\}$$
$$\Rightarrow |2a-1| = 3[a] + 2(a-[a])$$
$$\Rightarrow |2a-1| = [a] + 2a$$

When $a > \frac{1}{2}$, then

$$2a - 1 = [a] + 2a$$
$$\Rightarrow [a] = -1$$

$\Rightarrow a \in [-1, 0)$, which is not satisfied.

When $a < \frac{1}{2}$, then

$$-2a + 1 = [a] + 2a$$

On putting $a = I + f$

$$-2(I+f) + 1 = I + 2(I+f)$$
$$\Rightarrow -2I - 2f + 1 = I + 2I + 2f$$
$$\Rightarrow 5I + 4f = 1$$
$$\Rightarrow I = 0, f = \frac{1}{4}$$
$$\therefore a = \frac{1}{4}$$
$$\therefore 72\Sigma a = 72 \times \frac{1}{4} = 18$$

2. (51) Given, $A = \{1, 2, 3, \ldots, 7\}$

Then, $n(P(A)) = 2^7 = 128$

$f: A \to P(A)$

So, number of function $= 128 \times 128 \times \ldots \times 128$

$$= 128^7 = (2^7)^7 = 2^{49}$$
$$\Rightarrow m^n = 2^{49}$$
$$\therefore m = 2 \text{ and } n = 49$$
$$\therefore m + n = 51$$

3. (b) We have, $f(x) = \frac{\sqrt{x^2-25}}{4-x^2} + \log_{10}(x^2+2x-15)$

Now, for $\frac{\sqrt{x^2-25}}{4-x^2}$

$$x^2 - 25 \ge 0$$
$$(x-5)(x+5) \ge 0$$
$$\Rightarrow x \in (-\infty, -5] \cup [5, \infty) \quad \text{...(i)}$$

and $4 - x^2 \ne 0$ ...(ii)

Now, for $\log_{10}(x^2+2x-15)$

$$\Rightarrow x^2 + 2x - 15 > 0$$
$$\Rightarrow (x+5)(x-3) > 0$$
$$\Rightarrow x \in (-\infty, -5) \cup [3, \infty) \quad \text{...(iii)}$$

From Eqs. (i), (ii) and (iii), we get

$$x \in (-\infty, -5) \cup [5, \infty)$$

So, $\alpha = -5, \beta = 5$, then

$$\alpha^2 + \beta^3 = 25 + 125 = 150$$

4. (d) Given, $f(x) = \frac{1}{\sqrt{[x]^2 - 3[x] - 10}}$

For domain of $f(x)$,

$[x]^2 - 3[x] - 10 > 0$

Let $[x] = t$

Then, $t^2 - 3t - 10 > 0$

$$\Rightarrow (t-5)(t+2) > 0$$
$$\Rightarrow t \in (-\infty, -2) \cup (5, \infty)$$
$$\Rightarrow [x] < -2 \text{ or } [x] > 5$$

But $[x]$ is an integer value

$$\Rightarrow x < -2 \text{ or } x \ge 6$$

Hence, domain is

$$x \in (-\infty, -2) \cup [6, \infty).$$

5. (b) Let $y = \frac{x^2+2x+1}{x^2-8x+12}$

$$\Rightarrow (y-1)x^2 - (8y+2)x + 12y - 1 = 0$$

Since, $x \in R$.

$$\therefore D \ge 0$$
$$\Rightarrow (8y+2)^2 - 4(y-1)(12y-1) \ge 0$$
$$\Rightarrow 16y^2 + 8y + 1 - 12y^2 + 12y + y - 1 \ge 0$$
$$\Rightarrow y(4y+21) \ge 0$$
$$\therefore y \in \left(-\infty, \frac{-21}{4}\right] \cup [0, \infty)$$

So, range of f is

$$\left(-\infty, \frac{-21}{4}\right] \cup [0, \infty).$$

6. (b) Given,

$f: \{1, 2, 3, 4\} \to \{a \in Z; |a| \le 8\}$

and $f(n) + \frac{1}{n} f(n+1) = 1$, $\forall n \in \{1, 2, 3\}$

So, let's suppose

$$A = a \in Z; |a| \le 8$$

So, $A = \{-8, -7, -6, \ldots, 7, 8\}$

Now, $f(n) + \frac{1}{n} f(n+1) = 1$

On multiplying n in above equation,

$$nf(n) + f(n+1) = n$$

as, $f(n+1) = n - nf(n)$

Now, for $n = 1$,

$$f(2) = 1 - f(1)$$

For $n = 2$,

$$f(3) = 2 - 2f(2) = 2 - 2(1 - f(1))$$

or $f(3) = 2f(1)$

For $n = 3$,

$$f(4) = 3 - 3f(3) = 3 - 3(2f(1))$$

or $f(4) = 3 - 6f(1)$

We know that

$$f(1) \in \{-8, -7, \ldots, 7, 8\} \quad \text{...(i)}$$

Now, $-8 \le f(2) \le 8$

$$-8 \le 1 - f(1) \le 8$$

Subtract 1 from the inequality,

$$-9 \le -f(1) \le 7$$

Now, multiply (-1) in the inequality,

$$9 \ge f(1) \ge -7$$

or $f(1) \in \{-7, -6, \ldots, 8, 9\}$ ...(ii)

Now, $-8 \le f(3) \le 8$;

$$-8 \le 2f(1) \le 8$$

Divide the inequality by 2

$$-4 \le f(1) \le 4$$

or $f(1) \in \{-4, -3, -2, -1, 0, 1, 2, 3, 4\}$ ...(iii)

Now, $-8 \le f(4) \le 8$

$$-8 \le 3 - 6f(1) \le 8$$

Subtract 3 from inequality,

$$-11 \le -6f(1) \le 5$$

Now, divide the inequality by (-6),

$$\frac{11}{6} \ge f(1) \ge \frac{-5}{6}$$

But $f(1) \in I$

So, $f(1) \in \{0, 1\}$ ...(iv)

From Eqs. (i), (ii), (iii) and (iv),

$$f(1) = 0, 1$$

If $f(1) = 0$, then $f(2) = 1$, $f(3) = 0$, $f(4) = 3$

If $f(1) = 1$, then $f(2) = 0$, $f(3) = 2$, $f(4) = -3$

So, number of such functions = 2

7. (b) We have,

$$f(x) + f\left(\frac{1}{1-x}\right) = 1 + x$$

Put $x = 2$, then

$$f(2) + f(-1) = 3 \quad \text{...(i)}$$

Put $x = 1/2$, then

$$f\left(\frac{1}{2}\right) + f(2) = \frac{3}{2} \quad \ldots\text{(ii)}$$

Put $x = -1$, then

$$f(-1) + f\left(\frac{1}{2}\right) = 0 \quad \ldots\text{(iii)}$$

On subtracting Eq. (iii) from Eq. (i), we get

$$f(2) - f\left(\frac{1}{2}\right) = 3 \quad \ldots\text{(iv)}$$

On adding Eqs. (ii) and (iv), we get

$$2f(2) = \frac{3}{2} + 3$$

$$\Rightarrow \quad 2f(2) = \frac{9}{2} \Rightarrow f(2) = \frac{9}{4}$$

8. (d) Let us consider a function $f : N \to R$ satisfying

$$f(1) + 2f(2) + 3f(3) \ldots + xf(x) = x(x+1)f(x) \quad \ldots\text{(i)}$$

We have, for $x \geq 2$,

$$f(1) + 2f(2) + 3f(3) + \ldots + xf(x) = x(x+1)f(x) \quad \ldots\text{(ii)}$$

Now, we will replace x by $(x+1)$ and subtracting Eq. (i) from Eq. (ii),

$$x(x+1)f(x) + (x+1)f(x+1) = (x+1)(x+2)f(x+1)$$

$$\Rightarrow \quad \frac{x}{f(x+1)} + \frac{1}{f(x)} = \frac{(x+2)}{f(x)}$$

$$\Rightarrow \quad xf(x) = (x+1)f(x+1)$$

For $x \geq 2$, $f(2) = \frac{1}{4}$; $f(4) = \frac{1}{8}$

Now, $f(2022) = \frac{1}{4044}$

Similarly, $f(2028) = \frac{1}{4056}$

So, $\frac{1}{f(2022)} + \frac{1}{f(2028)} = 4044 + 4056 = 8100$

9. (a) Given, $f(x) = 2x^n + \lambda$, $\lambda \in R, n \in N$

and put $x = 4$

$$f(4) = 133, f(5) = 255$$

$$f(4) = 2x^n + \lambda$$

So, $133 = 2(4)^n + \lambda \quad \ldots$(i)

and put $x = 5$

$255 = 2(5)^n + \lambda \quad \ldots$(ii)

On subtracting Eq. (i) from Eq. (ii), we get

$122 = 2[5^n - 4^n]$ or $5^n - 4^n = 61$

By hit and trial method for $n = 3$,

$$5^3 - 4^3 = 61$$

$n = 3$ satisfies the equation

Now, putting the value of n in Eq. (i), we get $133 = 2(4)^3 + \lambda$

$\lambda = 133 - 128 \Rightarrow \lambda = 5$

Now, $f(x) = 2x^3 + 5$

So, $f(3) = 2(3)^3 + 5 = 59$

$f(2) = 2(2)^3 + 5 = 21$

So, $f(3) - f(2) = 59 - 21 = 38$

Positive integer divisor of 38 $= 1, 2, 19, 38$.

So, sum of positive integer divisors $= 1 + 2 + 19 + 38 = 60$

10. (c) Given, $f(x) = \frac{2^{2x}}{2^{2x} + 2}$

$$\therefore f(1-x) = \frac{2^{2(1-x)}}{2^{2(1-x)} + 2} = \frac{\frac{2^2}{2^{2x}}}{\frac{2^2}{2^{2x}} + 2}$$

$$= \frac{4}{4 + 2 \cdot 2^{2x}} = \frac{2}{2 + 2^{2x}}$$

$$\therefore \quad f(x) + f(1-x) = \frac{2^{2x}}{2^{2x} + 2} + \frac{2}{2 + 2^{2x}}$$

$$= \frac{2^{2x} + 2}{2^{2x} + 2} = 1$$

$$\therefore \quad f(x) + f(1-x) = 1$$

$$\therefore \quad f\left(\frac{1}{2023}\right) + f\left(1 - \frac{1}{2023}\right) = 1$$

$$\Rightarrow \quad f\left(\frac{1}{2023}\right) + f\left(\frac{2022}{2023}\right) = 1$$

So, $\left\{f\left(\frac{1}{2023}\right) + f\left(\frac{2022}{2023}\right)\right\} + \left\{f\left(\frac{2}{2023}\right) + f\left(\frac{2021}{2023}\right)\right\} + \ldots 1011$ times

$= 1 + 1 + \ldots\ldots 1011$ times $= 1011$

11. (c) We have, $f(x) = \frac{1}{\sqrt{[x] - x}}$

$\therefore$ Domain of $f(x)$, $A = R - I$ and

Range of $f(x)$, $B = (1, \infty)$

$\therefore A \cap B = (1, \infty) - N$ and $A \cup B \neq (1, \infty)$

$\therefore$ Only S_1 is true.

12. (432) $f(1 \cdot n) = f(1) \cdot f(n)$

$\Rightarrow \quad f(1) = 1$

$f(3.3) = (f(3))^2$

$\Rightarrow \quad f(9) = f(3) \times f(3)$

So, $\quad f(3) = 1$ or 3

$f(2)$, $f(5)$ and $f(8)$ can be chosen in 6 ways each.

Therefore, total number of functions

$$= 1 \times 6 \times 2 \times 6 \times 6 \times 1 = 432$$

13. (d) We have,

$$f(x) = \frac{[x]}{1 + x^2}, 2 \leq x < 6$$

$$= \begin{cases} \frac{2}{1+x^2}, & 2 \leq x < 3 \\ \frac{3}{1+x^2}, & 3 \leq x < 4 \\ \frac{4}{1+x^2}, & 4 \leq x < 5 \\ \frac{5}{1+x^2}, & 5 \leq x < 6 \end{cases}$$

Since, $f(x)$ is a decreasing function.

So, range of $f(x) = (f(6), f(2)]$

Now, $f(2) = \frac{2}{5}$

and $\quad f(6) = \frac{5}{37}$

$\therefore$ Range of $f(x)$ is $\left(\frac{5}{37}, \frac{2}{5}\right]$.

Chapter-3

Trigonometric Functions

1. (i) $(6)^c = \left(6 \times \frac{180}{\pi}\right)^\circ = \left(\frac{180 \times 7 \times 6}{22}\right)^\circ$

$$= \left(\frac{3780}{11}\right)^\circ = \left(343\frac{7}{11}\right)^\circ$$

$$= 343^\circ\left(\frac{7}{11} \times 60\right)'$$

$$= 343^\circ 38'\left(\frac{2}{11} \times 60\right)''$$

$$= 343^\circ 38' 11''$$

(ii) $\left(\frac{5\pi}{3}\right)^c = \left(\frac{5\pi}{3} \times \frac{180}{\pi}\right)^\circ = 300^\circ$

(iii) $(-2)^c = \left(\frac{-2 \times 180}{\pi}\right)^\circ$

$$= \left(\frac{-2 \times 7 \times 180}{22}\right)^\circ$$

$$= -\left(114\frac{6}{11}\right)^\circ$$

$$= -114^\circ\left(\frac{6}{11} \times 60\right)'$$

$$= -114^\circ 32'\left(\frac{8}{11} \times 60\right)''$$

$$= -114^\circ 32' 44''$$

(iv) $\left(\frac{11}{16}\right)^c = \left(\frac{11}{16}\times\frac{180}{\pi}\right)^\circ$

$= \left(\frac{11}{16}\times\frac{7}{22}\times 180\right)^\circ$

$= \left(\frac{315}{8}\right)^\circ$

$= 39^\circ\left(\frac{3}{8}\times 60\right)'$

$= 39^\circ 22'\left(\frac{1}{2}\times 60\right)''$

$= 39^\circ 22' 30''$

(v) 8 rad $= \frac{180}{\pi}\times 8$

$= \frac{1440\times 7}{22} = 458^\circ\frac{4^\circ}{22}$

$= 458^\circ\frac{4\times 60'}{22}$

$= 458^\circ 10'\frac{20'}{22}$

$= 458^\circ 10' 54''$

2. (i) $7^\circ 30' = \left(7\frac{1}{2}\right)^\circ$

$= \left(\frac{15}{2}\right)^\circ = \left(\frac{15}{2}\times\frac{\pi}{180}\right)^c$

$= \left(\frac{\pi}{24}\right)^c$

(ii) $-47^\circ 30' = \left(-47\frac{1}{2}\right)^\circ$

$= \left(-\frac{95}{2}\right)^\circ$

$= \left(-\frac{95}{2}\times\frac{\pi}{180}\right)^c$

$= -\left(\frac{19\pi}{72}\right)^c$

(iii) $1'' = \left(\frac{1}{60}\right)'$

$30'' = \left(\frac{30}{60}\right)' = \left(\frac{1}{2}\right)'$

Total minutes to convert

$37' + \left(\frac{1}{2}\right)' = \left(\frac{74+1}{2}\right)' = \left(\frac{75}{2}\right)'$

$(1') = \left(\frac{1}{60}\right)^\circ$

$\left(\frac{75}{2}\right)' = \left(\frac{75}{2}\times\frac{1}{60}\right)^\circ = \left(\frac{5}{8}\right)^\circ$

Total degree to convert

$48^\circ + \left(\frac{5}{8}\right)^\circ$

$\left(\frac{384+5}{8}\right)^\circ = \left(\frac{389}{8}\right)^\circ$

Radian measure $= \frac{\pi}{180}\times$ degree measure

$\left(\frac{389}{8}\right)^\circ = \frac{\pi}{180}\times\frac{389}{8}$ rad

$= \frac{389\pi}{1440}$ rad

(iv) $340^\circ = \left(340\times\frac{\pi}{180}\right)^c = \left(\frac{17\pi}{9}\right)^c$

(v) $40^\circ 20' = \left(40\frac{1}{3}\right)^\circ = \left(\frac{121}{3}\right)^\circ$

$= \left(\frac{121}{3}\times\frac{\pi}{180}\right)^c = \left(\frac{121\pi}{540}\right)^c$

3. (i) Let the measure of the angles of the triangle are in radian be $a-d$, a and $a+d$. Then,

$a - d + a + a + d = \pi$

$\Rightarrow 3a = \pi \Rightarrow a = \frac{\pi}{3}$

It is given that greatest is 5 times the least.

$\therefore a + d = 5(a - d)$

$\Rightarrow 6d = 4a$

$\Rightarrow d = \frac{4}{6}\times\frac{\pi}{3} = \frac{4\pi}{18} = \frac{2\pi}{9}$

$\therefore$ Least angle $= a - d$

$= \frac{\pi}{3} - \frac{2\pi}{9} = \frac{\pi}{9}$

(ii) Given, 1 min $= 360$ revolutions

60 s $= 360\times 2\pi$ rad

[$\because$ 1 revolution $= 2\pi$ rad]

$\Rightarrow 1\text{ s} = \left(\frac{360\times 2\pi}{60}\right)$ rad

$\Rightarrow 1\text{s} = 12\pi$ rad

(iii) Given, $r = 30$ cm and chord $AB = 30$ cm

$\because \Delta OAB$ is equilateral triangle.

$\therefore \angle AOB = 60^\circ = \frac{\pi}{3}$ rad

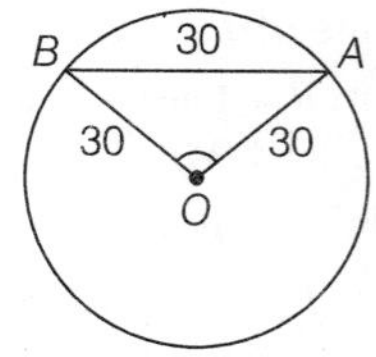

$\therefore$ Length of an arc

$AB = r\times\theta$

$= 30\times\frac{\pi}{3}$

$= 10\pi$ cm

(iv) Given, $l = 15\pi$ cm and $\theta = \frac{3\pi}{4}$

$\therefore r = l/\theta = \frac{15\pi\times 4}{3\pi} = 20$ cm

$\therefore$ Radius of circle is 20 cm

(v) Given, $\theta = 60^\circ$

$\theta = 60\times\frac{\pi}{180}$

$= \frac{\pi}{3}\left[\because 1^\circ = \frac{\pi}{180}\text{ rad}\right]$

$\therefore \theta = \frac{l}{r}$

$\Rightarrow \frac{\pi}{3} = \frac{66}{r}$ [$\because l = 66$ m]

$\Rightarrow r = \frac{66\times 3}{\pi}$

$\Rightarrow r = \frac{198}{\pi} = 63$ m

4. (i) (True)

We know, $\theta = \frac{l}{r}$

For I circle,

$60\times\frac{\pi}{180} = \frac{l}{r_1}$ ...(i)

and for II circle,

$75\times\frac{\pi}{180} = \frac{l}{r_2}$ ...(ii)

Dividing Eq. (i) by Eq. (ii), we get

$\frac{60\times\frac{\pi}{180}}{75\times\frac{\pi}{180}} = \frac{\frac{l}{r_1}}{\frac{l}{r_2}} \Rightarrow \frac{4}{5} = \frac{r_2}{r_1}$

$\therefore \frac{r_1}{r_2} = 5/4$

(ii) (False)

Length of arc,

$l = r\theta$

$= 7\times\frac{45\pi}{180} = \frac{7\pi}{4}$

$= \frac{7\times 22/7}{4} = \frac{22}{4} = 5.5$ cm

5. (i) We have, $\cos\theta = -\frac{1}{2}$,

$\sec\theta = -2$

$\tan^2\theta = \sec^2\theta - 1$

$= (-2)^2 - 1 = 4 - 1 = 3$

and $\sin\theta = -\sqrt{1-\cos^2\theta}$

$= -\sqrt{1-\frac{1}{4}} = -\frac{\sqrt{3}}{2}$

[$\because \sin\theta < 0$ in III quadrant]

$\therefore \operatorname{cosec}\theta = -\frac{2}{\sqrt{3}}$

Now, $4\tan^2\theta - 3\text{cosec}^2\theta$

$$= 4(3) - 3\left(-\frac{2}{\sqrt{3}}\right)^2$$

$$= 12 - 3 \times \frac{4}{3} = 8$$

(ii) We have, $\sin\theta = \frac{12}{13}$,

θ lie in II quadrant.

$\therefore \tan\theta = -\frac{12}{5}$

[$\because \tan\theta < 0$ in II quadrant]

$\sec\theta = -\frac{13}{5}$

[$\because \sec\theta < 0$ in II quadrant]

$$\therefore \sec\theta + \tan\theta = -\frac{13}{5} - \frac{12}{5} = -\frac{25}{5} = -5$$

(iii) We have, $\cos\theta = -\frac{3}{5}$,

θ lie in III quadrant.

$\therefore \quad \sin\theta = -4/5$

Now, $\frac{\text{cosec}\,\theta + \cot\theta}{\sec\theta - \tan\theta}$

$$= \frac{\frac{1}{\sin\theta} + \frac{\cos\theta}{\sin\theta}}{\frac{1}{\cos\theta} - \frac{\sin\theta}{\cos\theta}}$$

$$= \frac{(1+\cos\theta)\cos\theta}{\sin\theta(1-\sin\theta)}$$

$$= \frac{\left(1-\frac{3}{5}\right)\left(-\frac{3}{5}\right)}{-4/5\,(1+4/5)}$$

$$= \frac{2\times 3}{4\times 9} = \frac{1}{6}$$

(iv) We have, $\sin\theta = -\frac{3}{5}$,

θ lie in IV quadrant.

$\therefore \tan\theta = -\frac{3}{4}, \text{cosec}\,\theta = -\frac{5}{3}$

and $\cot\theta = -\frac{4}{3}$

Now, $\frac{1+\tan\theta+\text{cosec}\,\theta}{1+\cot\theta-\text{cosec}\,\theta}$

$$= \frac{1-3/4-5/3}{1-4/3+5/3}$$

$$= \frac{(12-9-20)\times 3}{12(3-4+5)}$$

$$= \frac{-17\times 3}{12\times 4} = -\frac{17}{16}$$

(v) We have,

$$\text{cosec}\,\theta + \cot\theta = \frac{11}{2} \quad \ldots(i)$$

$$\therefore \text{cosec}\,\theta - \cot\theta = \frac{2}{11} \quad \ldots(ii)$$

Subtracting Eq. (ii) from Eq. (i), we get

$$2\cot\theta = \frac{11}{2} - \frac{2}{11} = \frac{121-4}{22} = \frac{117}{22}$$

$$\therefore \quad \cot\theta = \frac{117}{44}$$

$$\tan\theta = \frac{44}{117}$$

6. (i) $\tan\left(\frac{11\pi}{6}\right) = \tan\left(2\pi - \frac{\pi}{6}\right)$

$$= -\tan\frac{\pi}{6} = -\frac{1}{\sqrt{3}}$$

(ii) $\cos(855°) = \cos(900° - 45°)$

$$= -\cos 45° = -\frac{1}{\sqrt{2}}$$

(iii) $\sin(1845°) = \sin(1800° + 45°)$

$$= \sin 45° = \frac{1}{\sqrt{2}}$$

(iv) $\tan(-585°) = -\tan(585°)$

$$= -\tan(540° + 45°)$$

$$= -\tan 45° = -1$$

(v) $\sin(-4530°) = -\sin(4530°)$

$$= -\sin(4500° + 30°)$$

$$= -(-\sin 30°) = \frac{1}{2}$$

7. (i) (True)

We have,

$$\cos\theta + \sin\theta = \sqrt{2}\cos\theta$$

$$\sin\theta = (\sqrt{2}-1)\cos\theta$$

$$\Rightarrow (\sqrt{2}+1)\sin\theta = (\sqrt{2}-1)(\sqrt{2}+1)\cos\theta$$

$$\Rightarrow \sqrt{2}\sin\theta + \sin\theta = \cos\theta$$

$$\Rightarrow \quad \cos\theta - \sin\theta = \sqrt{2}\sin\theta$$

(ii) (False)

We have,

$$\sec\theta + \tan\theta = P \quad \ldots(i)$$

$$\therefore \quad \sec\theta - \tan\theta = \frac{1}{P} \quad \ldots(ii)$$

Subtracting Eq. (ii) from Eq. (i), we get

$$2\tan\theta = P - \frac{1}{P} = \frac{P^2-1}{P}$$

$$\therefore \quad \tan\theta = \frac{P^2-1}{2P}$$

(iii) (True)

$\sec^2\theta + \text{cosec}^2\theta$

$$= 1 + \tan^2\theta + 1 + \cot^2\theta$$

$$= 2 + \tan^2\theta + \cot^2\theta$$

$$= 2 + (\tan\theta - \cot\theta)^2 + 2$$

$$= 4 + (\tan\theta - \cot\theta)^2 \geq 4$$

$$\therefore \sec^2\theta + \text{cosec}^2\theta \geq 4$$

(iv) (False)

We have, $3(\sin\theta - \cos\theta)^4 + 6(\sin\theta + \cos\theta)^2 + 4(\sin^6\theta + \cos^6\theta)$

$$= 3(1 - 2\sin\theta\cos\theta)^2 + 6(1 + 2\sin\theta\cos\theta) + 4[(\sin^2\theta + \cos^2\theta)^3 - 3\sin^2\theta\cos^2\theta(\sin^2\theta + \cos^2\theta)]$$

$$= 3(1 - 4\sin\theta\cos\theta + 4\sin^2\theta\cos^2\theta) + 6 + 12\sin\theta\cos\theta + 4(1 - 3\sin^2\theta\cos^2\theta)$$

$$= 3 - 12\sin\theta\cos\theta + 12\sin^2\theta\cos^2\theta + 6 + 12\sin\theta\cos\theta + 4 - 12\sin^2\theta\cos^2\theta$$

$$= 3 + 6 + 4 = 13$$

(v) (True)

We have, $\sin\theta + \cos\theta = 0$

$\Rightarrow \quad \sin\theta = -\cos\theta$

$\Rightarrow \quad \tan\theta = -1$

$\Rightarrow \quad \cos\theta = \frac{1}{\sqrt{2}}$

8. (i) $\tan 720° - \cos 270° - \sin 150° \cos 120°$

$$= \tan(4\pi) - \cos\frac{3\pi}{2} - \sin\frac{5\pi}{6}\cos\frac{2\pi}{3}$$

$$= 0 - 0 - \sin\left(\pi - \frac{\pi}{6}\right)\cos\left(\pi - \frac{\pi}{3}\right)$$

$$= -\sin\left(\frac{\pi}{6}\right)\left(-\cos\frac{\pi}{3}\right)$$

$$= -\left(\frac{1}{2}\right)\left(-\frac{1}{2}\right) = \frac{1}{4}$$

(ii) $\sin^2\frac{\pi}{18} + \sin^2\frac{\pi}{9} + \sin^2\frac{7\pi}{18} + \sin^2\frac{4\pi}{9}$

$$= \sin^2\frac{\pi}{18} + \sin^2\frac{4\pi}{9} + \sin^2\frac{\pi}{9} + \sin^2\frac{7\pi}{18}$$

$$= \sin^2 \frac{\pi}{18} + \sin^2\left(\frac{\pi}{2} - \frac{\pi}{18}\right) + \sin^2\left(\frac{\pi}{9}\right) + \sin^2\left(\frac{\pi}{2} - \frac{\pi}{9}\right)$$

$$= \sin^2 \frac{\pi}{18} + \cos^2 \frac{\pi}{18} + \sin^2 \frac{\pi}{9} + \cos^2 \frac{\pi}{9}$$

$$= 1 + 1 = 2$$

(iii) $\sin^2 5° + \sin^2 10° + \sin^2 15° + \ldots + \sin^2 85°$

$$= (\sin^2 5° + \sin^2 85°) + (\sin^2 10° + \sin^2 80°) + \ldots + (\sin^2 40° + \sin^2 50°) + \sin^2 45°$$

$$= (\sin^2 5° + \cos^2 5°) + (\sin^2 10° + \cos^2 10°) + \ldots + (\sin^2 40° + \cos^2 40°) + \left(\frac{1}{\sqrt{2}}\right)^2$$

$$= (1 + 1 + \ldots. + 1)8 \text{ times} + \frac{1}{2}$$

$$= 8 + \frac{1}{2} = 17/2$$

(iv) $\cos 1° \cos 2° \cos 3° \ldots \cos 179°$

$$= \cos 1° \cos 2° \cos 3° \ldots \cos 90° \cos 91° \ldots \cos 179°$$

$$= 0$$

(v) $\tan 1° \tan 2°. \tan 3° \ldots. \tan 89°$

$$= (\tan 1° \tan 89°)(\tan 2° \tan 88°) \ldots (\tan 44° \tan 46°) \tan 45°$$

$$= (\tan 1° \cot 1°)(\tan 2° \cot 2°) \ldots (\tan 44° \cot 44°) \times 1$$

$$= 1 \times 1 \times 1 \ldots. \times 1 = 1$$

9. We have,

$$\sin\theta = \frac{15}{17} \text{ and } \cos\phi = \frac{12}{13}$$

$$\therefore \quad \cos\theta = \frac{8}{17}, \tan\theta = \frac{15}{8}$$

$$\text{and } \sin\phi = \frac{5}{13}, \tan\phi = \frac{5}{12}$$

(i) (True)

$$\sin(\theta + \phi) = \sin\theta\cos\phi + \cos\theta\sin\phi$$

$$= \frac{15}{17} \times \frac{12}{13} + \frac{8}{17} \times \frac{5}{13}$$

$$= \frac{180 + 40}{221} = \frac{220}{221}$$

(ii) (False)

$$\cos(\theta - \phi) = \cos\theta\cos\phi + \sin\theta\sin\phi$$

$$= \frac{8}{17} \times \frac{12}{13} + \frac{15}{17} \times \frac{5}{13}$$

$$= \frac{96 + 75}{221} = \frac{171}{221}$$

(iii) (True)

$$\tan(\theta + \phi) = \frac{\tan\theta + \tan\phi}{1 - \tan\theta\tan\phi}$$

$$= \frac{\frac{15}{8} + \frac{5}{12}}{1 - \frac{15}{8} \times \frac{5}{12}}$$

$$= \frac{180 + 40}{96 - 75} = \frac{220}{21}$$

10. (i) $\sqrt{2}\cos\left(\theta + \frac{\pi}{4}\right) = \sqrt{2}$

$$\left[\cos\theta\cos\frac{\pi}{4} - \sin\theta\sin\frac{\pi}{4}\right]$$

$$= \sqrt{2}\left[\frac{1}{\sqrt{2}}\cos\theta - \frac{1}{\sqrt{2}}\sin\theta\right]$$

$$= \cos\theta - \sin\theta$$

(ii) $2\cos\left(\theta - \frac{\pi}{3}\right) = 2$

$$\left[\cos\theta\cos\frac{\pi}{3} + \sin\theta\sin\frac{\pi}{3}\right]$$

$$= 2\left[\frac{1}{2}\cos\theta + \frac{\sqrt{3}}{2}\sin\theta\right]$$

$$= \cos\theta + \sqrt{3}\sin\theta$$

(iii) $\cos(\alpha + \beta) - \cos(\alpha - \beta)$

$$= \cos\alpha\cos\beta - \sin\alpha\sin\beta - \cos\alpha\cos\beta - \sin\alpha\sin\beta$$

$$= -2\sin\alpha\sin\beta$$

11. $\tan(A + B) = \dfrac{\tan A + \tan B}{1 - \tan A \tan B}$

$$\Rightarrow \quad \frac{3}{5} = \frac{x + \frac{2}{3}}{1 - \frac{2x}{3}} \text{ [let } \tan A = x]$$

$$\Rightarrow \quad \frac{3}{5} = \frac{3x + 2}{3 - 2x}$$

$$\Rightarrow \quad 9 - 6x = 15x + 10$$

$$\Rightarrow \quad 9 - 10 = 15x + 6x$$

$$\Rightarrow \quad -1 = 21x$$

$$\Rightarrow \quad x = \frac{-1}{21} \Rightarrow \tan A = \frac{-1}{21}$$

12. We have,

$$\sqrt{3}\sin x + \cos x = k\sin(x + b)$$

$$\Rightarrow 2\left(\frac{\sqrt{3}}{2}\sin x + \frac{1}{2}\cos x\right) = k\sin(x + b)$$

$$\Rightarrow 2\left(\sin x\cos\frac{\pi}{6} + \cos x\sin\frac{\pi}{6}\right) = k\sin(x + b)$$

$$\Rightarrow 2\sin\left(x + \frac{\pi}{6}\right) = k\sin(x + b)$$

$$\Rightarrow \quad k = 2 \text{ and } b = \frac{\pi}{6}$$

13. (i) $\sin 75° = \sin(45° + 30°)$

$$= \sin 45°\cos 30° + \cos 45°\sin 30°$$

$$= \left(\frac{1}{\sqrt{2}} \times \frac{\sqrt{3}}{2}\right) + \left(\frac{1}{\sqrt{2}} \times \frac{1}{2}\right)$$

$$= \frac{\sqrt{3} + 1}{2\sqrt{2}}$$

(ii) $\tan 15° = \tan(45° - 30°)$

$$= \frac{\tan 45° - \tan 30°}{1 + \tan 30°\tan 45°}$$

$$= \frac{1 - 1/\sqrt{3}}{1 + \frac{1}{\sqrt{3}}} = \frac{\sqrt{3} - 1}{\sqrt{3} + 1}$$

$$= \frac{(\sqrt{3} - 1)^2}{(\sqrt{3} + 1)(\sqrt{3} - 1)}$$

$$= 2 - \sqrt{3}$$

(iii) $\cos 105° = \cos(60° + 45°)$

$$= \cos 60°\cos 45° - \sin 60°\sin 45°$$

$$= \frac{1}{2} \times \frac{1}{\sqrt{2}} - \frac{\sqrt{3}}{2} \times \frac{1}{\sqrt{2}}$$

$$= \frac{1 - \sqrt{3}}{2\sqrt{2}}$$

(iv) $\cot 75° = \cot(45° + 30°)$

$$= \frac{\cot 45° \cdot \cot 30° - 1}{\cot 45° + \cot 30°}$$

$$= \frac{\sqrt{3} - 1}{1 + \sqrt{3}}$$

$$= \frac{(\sqrt{3} - 1)^2}{(\sqrt{3} + 1)(\sqrt{3} - 1)}$$

$$= 2 - \sqrt{3}$$

(v) $\sin\left(\frac{13\pi}{12}\right) = \sin\left(\pi + \frac{\pi}{12}\right)$

$$= -\sin\frac{\pi}{12} = -\sin 15°$$

$$= -\sin(45° - 30°)$$

$$= -(\sin 45°\cos 30° - \cos 45°\sin 30°)$$

$$= -\left(\frac{1}{\sqrt{2}} \times \frac{\sqrt{3}}{2} - \frac{1}{\sqrt{2}} \times \frac{1}{2}\right)$$

$$= -\left(\frac{\sqrt{3} - 1}{2\sqrt{2}}\right)$$

14. (i) (True)

We have, $\cos(\alpha + \beta) = 4/5$ and $\sin(\alpha - \beta) = 5/13$

$\therefore \quad \tan(\alpha+\beta)=\frac{3}{4}$

and $\tan(\alpha-\beta)=\frac{5}{12}$

Now, $\tan 2\alpha = \tan(\alpha+\beta+\alpha-\beta)$

$=\frac{\tan(\alpha+\beta)+\tan(\alpha-\beta)}{1-\tan(\alpha+\beta)\tan(\alpha-\beta)}$

$\Rightarrow \tan 2\alpha = \frac{3/4+5/12}{1-\frac{3}{4}\times\frac{5}{12}}$

$=\frac{36+20}{48-15}=\frac{56}{33}$

$\therefore \tan 2\alpha = \frac{56}{33}$

(ii) (False)

We have,

$\tan A = \frac{5}{6}$ and $\tan B = \frac{1}{11}$

$\therefore \tan(A+B)=\frac{\tan A+\tan B}{1-\tan A\tan B}$

$\Rightarrow \tan(A+B)=\frac{5/6+1/11}{1-\frac{5}{6}\times\frac{1}{11}}$

$=\frac{55+6}{66-5}=\frac{61}{61}=1$

$\Rightarrow \tan(A+B)=1 \Rightarrow A+B=\frac{\pi}{4}$

(iii) (False)

We have, $\cos^2\frac{\pi}{4}-\sin^2\frac{\pi}{12}$

$=\cos^2 45^\circ - \sin^2 15^\circ$

$\Rightarrow \cos(45^\circ+15^\circ)\cos(45^\circ-15^\circ)$

$[\because \cos^2 A - \sin^2 B = \cos(A+B)\cos(A-B)]$

$\Rightarrow \cos 60^\circ \cdot \cos 30^\circ = \frac{1}{2}\times\frac{\sqrt{3}}{2}$

$=\frac{\sqrt{3}}{4}$

(iv) (False)

$\tan(135^\circ)=\tan(69^\circ+66^\circ)$

$\therefore \tan 135^\circ = \frac{\tan 69^\circ+\tan 66^\circ}{1-\tan 69^\circ\tan 66^\circ}$

$\Rightarrow \quad -1=\frac{\tan 69^\circ+\tan 66^\circ}{1-\tan 69^\circ\tan 66^\circ}$

$\Rightarrow \quad -1+\tan 69^\circ\tan 66^\circ = \tan 69^\circ+\tan 66^\circ$

$\Rightarrow \quad \tan 69^\circ+\tan 66^\circ - \tan 69^\circ\tan 66^\circ = -1$

(v) (False)

$\tan 56^\circ = \tan(45^\circ+11^\circ)$

$=\frac{\tan 45^\circ+\tan 11^\circ}{1-\tan 45^\circ.\tan 11^\circ}$

$=\frac{1+\tan 11^\circ}{1-\tan 11^\circ}$

$=\frac{\cos 11^\circ+\sin 11^\circ}{\cos 11^\circ-\sin 11^\circ}$

(vi) (False)

$\frac{\cos 4x+\cos 3x+\cos 2x}{\sin 4x+\sin 3x+\sin 2x}$

$=\frac{(\cos 4x+\cos 2x)+\cos 3x}{(\sin 4x+\sin 2x)+\sin 3x}$

$=\frac{2\cos\left(\frac{4x+2x}{2}\right)\cos\left(\frac{4x-2x}{2}\right)+\cos 3x}{2\sin\left(\frac{4x+2x}{2}\right)\cos\left(\frac{4x-2x}{2}\right)+\sin 3x}$

$=\frac{\cos 3x\,(2\cos x+1)}{\sin 3x\,(2\cos x+1)}$

$=\cot 3x$

15. (i) (d) $\tan 70^\circ = \tan(20^\circ+50^\circ)$

$\Rightarrow \tan 70^\circ = \frac{\tan 20^\circ+\tan 50^\circ}{1-\tan 20^\circ\cdot\tan 50^\circ}$

$\Rightarrow \tan 70^\circ - \tan 70^\circ\tan 20^\circ\tan 50^\circ = \tan 20^\circ+\tan 50^\circ$

$\Rightarrow \tan 70^\circ = \tan 20^\circ + 2\tan 50^\circ$

(ii) (b) $\frac{\sin x}{1+\cos x}$

$=\frac{2\sin x/2\cdot\cos x/2}{2\cos^2 x/2}$

$=\tan x/2$

16. (i) $\tan\frac{\pi}{8}=\frac{1-\cos\pi/4}{\sin\pi/4}$

$\left[\because \tan x = \frac{1-\cos 2x}{\sin 2x}\right]$

$\Rightarrow \quad \tan\frac{\pi}{8}=\frac{1-\frac{1}{\sqrt{2}}}{\frac{1}{\sqrt{2}}}=\sqrt{2}-1$

(ii) $\sin\frac{\pi}{24}=\sqrt{\frac{1-\cos\frac{\pi}{12}}{2}}$

$\left[\because \sin x = \sqrt{\frac{1-\cos 2x}{2}}\right]$

$=\sqrt{\frac{1-\cos 15^\circ}{2}}$

$=\sqrt{\frac{1-\frac{\sqrt{3}+1}{2\sqrt{2}}}{2}}$

$\left[\because \cos 15^\circ = \frac{\sqrt{3}+1}{2\sqrt{2}}\right]$

$=\sqrt{\frac{2\sqrt{2}-\sqrt{3}-1}{4\sqrt{2}}}$

$=\frac{\sqrt{4-\sqrt{6}-\sqrt{2}}}{2\sqrt{2}}$

(iii) $\cot\frac{\pi}{24}=\frac{1+\cos\frac{\pi}{12}}{\sin\frac{\pi}{12}}$

$\left[\because \cot x = \frac{1+\cos 2x}{\sin 2x}\right]$

$=\frac{1+\cos 15^\circ}{\sin 15^\circ}=\frac{1+\frac{\sqrt{3}+1}{2\sqrt{2}}}{\frac{\sqrt{3}-1}{2\sqrt{2}}}$

$\left[\because \cos 15^\circ = \frac{\sqrt{3}+1}{2\sqrt{2}} \text{ and } \sin 15^\circ = \frac{\sqrt{3}-1}{2\sqrt{2}}\right]$

$=\frac{2\sqrt{2}+\sqrt{3}+1}{\sqrt{3}-1}$

$=\frac{(2\sqrt{2}+\sqrt{3}+1)(\sqrt{3}+1)}{(\sqrt{3}+1)(\sqrt{3}-1)}$

$=\frac{2\sqrt{6}+2\sqrt{2}+3+\sqrt{3}+\sqrt{3}+1}{3-1}$

$=\frac{2\sqrt{6}+2\sqrt{2}+2\sqrt{3}+2\sqrt{4}}{2}$

$=\sqrt{6}+\sqrt{4}+\sqrt{3}+\sqrt{2}$

$=2+\sqrt{2}+\sqrt{3}+\sqrt{6}$

17. We have, $\tan x = \frac{3}{4}, \pi < x < \frac{3\pi}{2}$

$\therefore \quad \cos x = -\frac{4}{5}$

[x lies in III quadrant]

Now, $\frac{\pi}{2}<\frac{x}{2}<\frac{3\pi}{4}$

[$\therefore \frac{x}{2}$ lies in II quadrant]

(i) $\sin\frac{x}{2}=\sqrt{\frac{1-\cos x}{2}}$

$=\sqrt{\frac{1+4/5}{2}}=\frac{3}{\sqrt{10}}$

(ii) $\cos\frac{x}{2}=-\sqrt{\frac{1+\cos x}{2}}$

$=-\sqrt{\frac{1-4/5}{2}}=-\frac{1}{\sqrt{10}}$

(iii) $\tan\frac{x}{2}=\frac{\sin x/2}{\cos x/2}$

$=\frac{3/\sqrt{10}}{-1/\sqrt{10}}=-3$

18. We have,

$$5(\tan^2 x - \cos^2 x) = 2\cos 2x + 9$$

$$\Rightarrow 5\tan^2 x = 2\cos 2x + 9 + 5\cos^2 x$$

$$\Rightarrow \frac{5(1-\cos 2x)}{1+\cos 2x} = 2\cos 2x + 9 + 5\frac{(1+\cos 2x)}{2}$$

$$\Rightarrow 10 - 10\cos 2x = (9\cos 2x + 23)(1+\cos 2x)$$

$$\Rightarrow 10 - 10\cos 2x = 9\cos^2 2x + 32\cos 2x + 23$$

$$\Rightarrow 9\cos^2 2x + 42\cos 2x + 13 = 0$$

$$\Rightarrow 9\cos^2 2x + 39\cos 2x + 3\cos 2x + 13 = 0$$

$$\Rightarrow (3\cos 2x + 13)(3\cos 2x + 1) = 0$$

$$\Rightarrow \cos 2x = -\frac{1}{3}, \cos 2x \neq -\frac{13}{3}$$

Now, $\cos 4x = 2\cos^2 2x - 1$

$$= 2\left(-\frac{1}{3}\right)^2 - 1$$

$$= \frac{2}{9} - 1 = -\frac{7}{9}$$

19. (i) (True)

$$\cos x \cos\left(\frac{\pi}{3} - x\right)\cos\left(\frac{\pi}{3} + x\right)$$

$$\cos x\left(\cos^2\frac{\pi}{3} - \sin^2 x\right)$$

$[\because \cos(A+B)\cos(A-B) = \cos^2 A - \sin^2 B]$

$$= \cos x\left[\frac{1}{4} - (1-\cos^2 x)\right]$$

$$= \cos x\left[\frac{1}{4} - 1 + \cos^2 x\right]$$

$$= \frac{4\cos^3 x - 3\cos x}{4}$$

$$= \frac{1}{4}\cos 3x$$

(ii) (False)

$$\tan x + \tan\left(\frac{\pi}{3} + x\right) - \tan\left(\frac{\pi}{3} - x\right)$$

$$= \tan x + \frac{\sqrt{3} + \tan x}{1 - \sqrt{3}\tan x} - \frac{\sqrt{3} - \tan x}{1 + \sqrt{3}\tan x}$$

$$= \tan x + \frac{(\sqrt{3} + \tan x)(1 + \sqrt{3}\tan x) - (\sqrt{3} - \tan x)(1 - \sqrt{3}\tan x)}{1 - 3\tan^2 x}$$

$$= \tan x + \frac{8\tan x}{1 - 3\tan^2 x}$$

$$= \frac{9\tan x - 3\tan^3 x}{1 - 3\tan^2 x}$$

$$= \frac{3(3\tan x - \tan^3 x)}{1 - 3\tan^2 x}$$

$$= 3\tan 3x$$

(iii) (True)

$$\tan x \tan\left(\frac{\pi}{3} - x\right)\tan\left(\frac{\pi}{3} + x\right)$$

$$\Rightarrow \tan x\left(\frac{\sqrt{3} - \tan x}{1 + \sqrt{3}\tan x}\right)\left(\frac{\sqrt{3} + \tan x}{1 - \sqrt{3}\tan x}\right)$$

$$\Rightarrow \frac{\tan x(3 - \tan^2 x)}{1 - 3\tan^2 x}$$

$$= \frac{3\tan x - \tan^3 x}{1 - 3\tan^2 x} = \tan 3x$$

20. (i) We have,

$$\sin x = \frac{3}{5}$$

$$\therefore \cos 2x = 1 - 2\sin^2 x$$

$$= 1 - 2 \times \frac{9}{25} = \frac{7}{25}$$

(ii) $\therefore \sin 3x = 3\sin x - 4\sin^3 x$

$$= 3 \times \frac{3}{5} - 4\left(\frac{3}{5}\right)^3$$

$$= \frac{9}{5} - \frac{108}{125}$$

$$= \frac{225 - 108}{125} = \frac{117}{125}$$

(iii) $\because \sin x = \frac{3}{5}$

$$\therefore \tan x = \frac{3}{4}$$

$$\therefore \tan 3x = \frac{3\tan x - \tan^3 x}{1 - 3\tan^2 x}$$

$$= \frac{3\left(\frac{3}{4}\right) - \left(\frac{3}{4}\right)^3}{1 - 3\left(\frac{3}{4}\right)^2}$$

$$= \frac{\frac{9}{4} - \frac{27}{64}}{1 - \frac{27}{16}}$$

$$= \frac{144 - 27}{-44}$$

$$= \frac{-117}{44}$$

21. (i) $\frac{\sin 2\theta}{1 + \cos 2\theta} - \tan\theta$

$$= \frac{2\sin\theta\cos\theta}{2\cos^2\theta} - \tan\theta$$

$$= \tan\theta - \tan\theta = 0$$

(ii) $\tan\theta + \cot 2\theta$

$$= \frac{\sin\theta}{\cos\theta} + \frac{\cos 2\theta}{\sin 2\theta}$$

$$= \frac{\sin\theta}{\cos\theta} + \frac{1 - 2\sin^2\theta}{2\sin\theta\cos\theta}$$

$$= \frac{\sin\theta}{\cos\theta} + \frac{1}{2\sin\theta\cos\theta} - \frac{\sin\theta}{\cos\theta}$$

$$= \frac{1}{\sin 2\theta} = \text{cosec } 2\theta$$

(iii) $\frac{\sin 2\theta}{\sin\theta} - \frac{\cos 2\theta}{\cos\theta}$

$$= \frac{2\sin\theta\cos\theta}{\sin\theta} - \frac{2\cos^2\theta - 1}{\cos\theta}$$

$$= 2\cos\theta - 2\cos\theta + \frac{1}{\cos\theta}$$

$$= \theta$$

Assertion-Reason

1. (d) 2 Radian $= \left(\frac{2\times 180}{\pi}\right)^\circ$

$$= \left(\frac{2\times 7\times 180}{22}\right)^\circ$$

$$= \left(114\frac{6}{11}\right)^\circ$$

$$= 114^\circ\left(\frac{6}{11}\times 60\right)'$$

$$= 114^\circ\, 32'\left(\frac{8}{11}\times 60\right)''$$

$$= 114^\circ\, 32'\, 44''$$

$\therefore$ Assertion is false and Reason is true.

2. (a) We know that

$\sin^2\theta + \cos^2\theta = 1$

So, $\sin^2 75^\circ + \cos^2 75 = 1$

Satisfies the above identity.

3. (c) We know that cosec x is negative in third and fourth quadrant.

$\therefore$ Assertion is true.

Also, $\tan x$ increases from 0 to ∞ in first quadrant and third quadrant.

$\therefore$ Reason is false.

4. (c) We have,

$$f(x) = \cos^2 x + \sec^2 x$$

we know that AM $\geq$ GM

$$\Rightarrow \frac{\cos^2 x + \sec^2 x}{2} \geq \sqrt{\cos^2 x \sec^2 x}$$

$$\Rightarrow \frac{\cos^2 x + \sec^2 x}{2} \geq \sqrt{\cos^2 x \cdot \frac{1}{\cos^2 x}}$$

$$\Rightarrow \frac{\cos^2 x + \sec^2 x}{2} \geq 1$$

$$\Rightarrow \cos^2 x + \sec^2 x \geq 2$$

$$\Rightarrow f(x) \geq 2$$

$\therefore$ Assertion is correct.

We know that the value of sin x is reciprocal of cosec x.

$\therefore$ Reason is false.

5. (a) Let r_1 and r_2 be the radii of the circles.

Here, $\theta_1 = 65°, \theta_2 = 110°$.

It is given that the arc length are equal.

So, $s_1 = s_2$

$$\Rightarrow r_1\theta_1 = r_2\theta_2$$

$$\Rightarrow \frac{r_1}{r_2} = \frac{\theta_2}{\theta_1} = \frac{110°}{65°} = \frac{22}{13}$$

$\therefore$ Assertion is correct.

We know that

$$\theta = \frac{l}{r}$$

$\therefore$ Reason is true.

6. (d) We know that

Radian measure = Degree Measure $\times \frac{\pi}{180°}$

So, $55^c = 55° \times \frac{\pi}{180°} = \frac{11\pi}{36°}$

$\therefore$ Assertion is false.

and Reason is true.

7. (c) We know that sin x is negative in third and fourth quadrant.

$\therefore$ Assertion is true.

Also, the function sin x is increasing in the interval $0 \leq x \leq \frac{\pi}{2}$.

$\therefore$ Reason is false.

8. (b) $2\cos\frac{\pi}{13}$

$$\cos\frac{9\pi}{13} + \cos\frac{3\pi}{13} + \cos\frac{5\pi}{13}$$

$$= \cos\left(\frac{10\pi}{13}\right) + \cos\left(\frac{-8\pi}{13}\right) + \cos\left(\pi - \frac{10\pi}{13}\right) + \cos\left(\pi - \frac{8\pi}{13}\right)$$

$$= \cos\frac{10\pi}{13} + \cos\frac{8\pi}{13} - \cos\frac{10\pi}{13} - \cos\frac{8\pi}{13} = 0$$

$\therefore$ Assertion is true.

and Reason is true.

9. (b) Given, $\cos x = -\frac{1}{3}$

So, $\sin x = \pm\sqrt{1 - \cos^2 x}$

$$= \pm\sqrt{1 - \left(-\frac{1}{3}\right)^2}$$

$$= \pm\sqrt{1 - \frac{1}{9}}$$

$$= \pm\frac{2\sqrt{2}}{3}$$

Since, x lies in third quadrant

$$\therefore \quad \sin x = -\frac{2\sqrt{2}}{3}$$

$\therefore$ Assertion is true and Reason is true.

10. (d)

$$\sin(930°) = \sin(3 \times 360° - 150°)$$

$$= -\sin 150° \quad [\because \sin(n \times 360° - \theta) = -\sin\theta, n \in Z]$$

$$= -\sin(180° - 30°)$$

$$= -\sin 30° \quad [\because \sin(180° - \theta)] = \sin\theta]$$

$$= -\frac{1}{2}$$

Case Based

Case 1 Given, $\cos A = \frac{4}{5}$, where

$$\frac{3\pi}{2} < A < 2\pi$$

$$\therefore \quad \sin A = -\sqrt{1 - \cos^2 A} = -\frac{3}{5}$$

[$\because$ A lies in IVth quadrant]

and $\cos B = \frac{12}{13}$, where

$$\frac{3\pi}{2} < B < 2\pi$$

$$\therefore \quad \sin B = -\sqrt{1 - \cos^2 B} = -\frac{5}{13}$$

[$\because$ B lies in IVth quadrant]

(i) $\cos(A + B)$

$$= \frac{4}{5} \times \frac{12}{13} - \left(-\frac{3}{5}\right)\left(-\frac{5}{13}\right)$$

[$\because \cos(A + B) = \cos A \cos B - \sin A \sin B$]

$$= \frac{48}{65} - \frac{15}{65} = \frac{33}{65}$$

$$\Rightarrow \sec(A + B) = \frac{65}{33}$$

(ii) $\sin(A - B)$

$$= \left(-\frac{3}{5}\right) \times \frac{12}{13} - \frac{4}{5}\left(-\frac{5}{13}\right)$$

[$\because \sin(A - B) = \sin A \cos B - \cos A \sin B$]

$$= -\frac{36}{65} + \frac{20}{65} = -\frac{16}{65}$$

$$\Rightarrow \text{cosec}(A - B) = -\frac{65}{16}$$

(iii) $\therefore \sin(A + B) = \left(-\frac{3}{5}\right) \cdot \left(\frac{12}{13}\right) + \left(\frac{4}{5}\right) \cdot \left(-\frac{5}{13}\right)$

[$\because \sin(A + B) = \sin A \cos + \cos A \sin B$]

$$= \frac{-36 - 20}{5 \times 13} = -\frac{56}{65}$$

$$\therefore \tan(A + B) = \frac{-\frac{56}{65}}{\frac{33}{65}} = -\frac{56}{33}$$

$$\left[\because \tan(A + B) = \frac{\sin(A + B)}{\cos(A + B)}\right]$$

$$\Rightarrow \cot(A + B) = \frac{-33}{56}$$

Case 2 (i) We have,

$$A + B = \frac{\pi}{4}$$

$$\Rightarrow \tan(A + B) = \tan\frac{\pi}{4}$$

$$\Rightarrow \frac{\tan A + \tan B}{1 - \tan A \tan B} = 1$$

$$\Rightarrow \tan A + \tan B = 1 - \tan A \tan B$$

$$\Rightarrow \tan A + \tan B + \tan A \tan B = 1 \quad \ldots\text{(i)}$$

On adding 1 both sides of Eq. (i), we get

$$1 + \tan A + \tan B + \tan A \tan B = 2$$

$$\Rightarrow (1 + \tan A) + \tan B(1 + \tan A) = 2$$

$$\Rightarrow (1 + \tan A)(1 + \tan B) = 2$$

(ii) On dividing both sides of Eq. (i) by $\tan A \tan B$, we get

$$\frac{\tan A+\tan B+\tan A\tan B}{\tan A\tan B}=\frac{1}{\tan A\tan B}$$

$\Rightarrow \cot A+\cot B+1=\cot A\cot B$

$\Rightarrow \cot A\cot B-\cot A-\cot B=1$

$\Rightarrow \cot A\cot B-\cot A-\cot B+1=2$

$\Rightarrow \cot A(\cot B-1)-(\cot B-1)=2$

$\Rightarrow \quad (\cot B-1)(\cot A-1)=2$

(iii) Given, $A+B=\frac{\pi}{4}$

$\therefore \quad \sin(A+B)=\sin\frac{\pi}{4}=\frac{1}{\sqrt{2}}$

$\cos(A+B)=\cos\frac{\pi}{4}=\frac{1}{\sqrt{2}}$

and $\tan(A+B)=\tan\frac{\pi}{4}=1$

$\therefore \sin(A+B)-\cos(A+B)+\tan(A+B)$

$$=\frac{1}{\sqrt{2}}-\frac{1}{\sqrt{2}}+1=1$$

Competition Edge Up

1. (b) $\sin x=-\frac{3}{5}$ and $\pi<x<\frac{3\pi}{2}$

So, $\cos x=-\frac{4}{5}$ and $\tan x=\frac{3}{4}$

Then, $80(\tan^2 x-\cos x)$

$$=80\left[\left(\frac{3}{4}\right)^2-\left(-\frac{4}{5}\right)\right]$$

$$=80\left[\frac{9}{16}+\frac{4}{5}\right]=80\left[\frac{45+64}{80}\right]$$

$$=80\times\frac{109}{80}=109$$

2. (c) We know, $-1\le \sin nx\le 1$

So, $\quad -1\le\sin 5x\le 1$

Multiplying -1, $-1\le-\sin 5x\le 1$

Adding 7, $6\le 7-\sin 5x\le 8$

Now, taking reciprocal

$$\frac{1}{8}\le\frac{1}{7-\sin 5x}\le\frac{1}{6}$$

$\therefore \quad$ Range $=\left[\frac{1}{8},\frac{1}{6}\right]$

3. (b) Given, $3\sin(\alpha+\beta)=2\sin(\alpha-\beta)$

$\Rightarrow 3\sin\alpha\cos\beta+3\cos\alpha\sin\beta$

$=2\sin\alpha\cos\beta-2\cos\alpha\sin\beta$

$\Rightarrow \quad \sin\alpha\cos\beta=-5\cos\alpha\sin\beta$

$\Rightarrow \quad \tan\alpha=-5\tan\beta$

On comparing,

$\tan\alpha=k\tan\beta\Rightarrow k=-5$

4. (b) As, we know that

$\cos\theta\cdot\cos(60^\circ-\theta)\cdot\cos(60^\circ+\theta)$

$$=\frac{1}{4}\cos 3\theta$$

So, given equation reduces to

$$\left|\frac{1}{4}\cos 3\theta\right|\le\frac{1}{8}$$

$\Rightarrow \quad |\cos 3\theta|\le\frac{1}{2}$

$\Rightarrow \quad -\frac{1}{2}\le\cos 3\theta\le\frac{1}{2}$

So, maximum value of $\cos 3\theta=\frac{1}{2}$

$\Rightarrow \quad 3\theta=2n\pi\pm\frac{\pi}{3}, n\in I$

$\Rightarrow \quad \theta=\frac{2n\pi}{3}\pm\frac{\pi}{9}, n\in I$

As, $\theta\in[0,2\pi]$, possible values are

$$\theta=\left\{\frac{\pi}{9},\frac{5\pi}{9},\frac{7\pi}{9},\frac{11\pi}{9},\frac{13\pi}{9},\frac{17\pi}{9}\right\}$$

and its sum $=\frac{54\pi}{9}=6\pi$

5. (d) $\frac{3\cos 36^\circ+5\sin 18^\circ}{5\cos 36^\circ-3\sin 18^\circ}$

$$=\frac{3\left(\frac{\sqrt{5}+1}{4}\right)+5\left(\frac{\sqrt{5}-1}{4}\right)}{5\left(\frac{\sqrt{5}+1}{4}\right)-3\left(\frac{\sqrt{5}-1}{4}\right)}$$

$$=\frac{3\sqrt{5}+3+5\sqrt{5}-5}{5\sqrt{5}+5-3\sqrt{5}+3}=\frac{8\sqrt{5}-2}{2\sqrt{5}+8}$$

$$=\frac{4\sqrt{5}-1}{\sqrt{5}+4}\times\frac{\sqrt{5}-4}{\sqrt{5}-4}$$

$$=\frac{20-16\sqrt{5}-\sqrt{5}+4}{-11}$$

$$=\frac{24-17\sqrt{5}}{-11}=\frac{17\sqrt{5}-24}{11}$$

Now, $\frac{17\sqrt{5}-24}{11}=\frac{a\sqrt{5}-b}{c}$

$a=17$, $b=24$ and $c=11$

Therefore, $a+b+c=52$

6. (b) Given, $\tan A=\frac{1}{\sqrt{x(x^2+x+1)}}$,

$\tan B=\frac{\sqrt{x}}{\sqrt{x^2+x+1}}$,

and $\tan C=\sqrt{\left(\frac{1}{x^3}+\frac{1}{x^2}+\frac{1}{x}\right)}$

$$=\sqrt{\frac{1+x+x^2}{x^3}}$$

$$\tan C=\frac{\sqrt{x^2+x+1}}{x\sqrt{x}}$$

$$\tan(A+B)=\frac{\tan A+\tan B}{1-\tan A\tan B}$$

$$=\left(\frac{\frac{1}{\sqrt{x}\sqrt{x^2+x+1}}+\frac{\sqrt{x}}{\sqrt{x^2+x+1}}}{1-\frac{1}{\sqrt{x}\sqrt{x^2+x+1}}\cdot\frac{\sqrt{x}}{\sqrt{x^2+x+1}}}\right)$$

$$=\left(\frac{1+x}{x^2+x+1-1}\right)\frac{\sqrt{x^2+x+1}}{\sqrt{x}}$$

$$=\frac{(1+x)\sqrt{x^2+x+1}}{x(x+1)\sqrt{x}}=\frac{\sqrt{x^2+x+1}}{x\sqrt{x}}$$

$\tan(A+B)=\tan C$

$\therefore \quad A+B=C$

7. (b) $4\cos^2\theta-1=4-4\sin^2\theta-1$

$=3-4\sin^2\theta$

$$=\frac{3\sin\theta-4\sin^3\theta}{\sin\theta}=\frac{\sin 3\theta}{\sin\theta}$$

$\therefore$ Given expression

$$=36\cdot\frac{\sin(3\times 9^\circ)}{\sin 9^\circ}\times\frac{\sin(3\times 27^\circ)}{\sin 27^\circ}\times\frac{\sin(3\times 81^\circ)}{\sin 81^\circ}\times\frac{\sin(3\times 243^\circ)}{\sin 243^\circ}$$

$$=36\cdot\frac{\sin 729^\circ}{\sin 9^\circ}$$

$$=36\times\frac{\sin(2\times 360^\circ+9^\circ)}{\sin 9^\circ}$$

$$=36\times\frac{\sin 9^\circ}{\sin 9^\circ}=36$$

8. (d) We have,

$$S=\left\{x\in\left(-\frac{\pi}{2},\frac{\pi}{2}\right):9^{1-\tan^2 x}+9^{\tan^2 x}=10\right\}$$

and $\beta=\sum_{x\in S}\tan^2\left(\frac{x}{3}\right)$

Now, $9^{1-\tan^2 x}+9^{\tan^2 x}=10$

$$\frac{9}{9^{\tan^2 x}}+9^{\tan^2 x}=10$$

Let $\quad 9^{\tan^2 x}=t$

$$\frac{9}{t}+t=10$$

$\Rightarrow t^2-10t+9=0\Rightarrow \quad t=9$ or 1

If $\quad t=9, 9^{\tan^2 x}=9\Rightarrow x=\pm\frac{\pi}{4}$

If $t=1, 9^{\tan^2 x}=1\Rightarrow x=0$

Also, $\beta = \sum_{x \in S} \tan^2\left(\frac{x}{3}\right)$

$= \tan^2\left(\frac{0}{3}\right) + \tan^2\left(\frac{\pi}{12}\right) + \tan^2\left(-\frac{\pi}{12}\right)$

$= 0 + 2\tan^2\frac{\pi}{12} = 2[2-\sqrt{3}]^2$

$= 2[4+3-4\sqrt{3}] = 14 - 8\sqrt{3}$

So, $\frac{1}{6}(\beta - 14)^2$

$= \frac{1}{6}[14 - 8\sqrt{3} - 14]^2$

$= \frac{1}{6} \times 64 \times 3 = 32$

9. (b) Let $A = 96\cos\frac{\pi}{33}\cos\frac{2\pi}{33}\cos\frac{4\pi}{33}\cos\frac{8\pi}{33}\cos\frac{16\pi}{33}$

$\Rightarrow 2A = 96 \times 2\left(\cos\frac{\pi}{33}\cos\frac{2\pi}{33}\cos\frac{4\pi}{33}\cos\frac{8\pi}{33}\cos\frac{16\pi}{33}\right)$

$\Rightarrow 2A \times \sin\frac{\pi}{33} = 96 \times \left(2\sin\frac{\pi}{33}\cos\frac{\pi}{33}\cos\frac{2\pi}{33}\cos\frac{4\pi}{33}\cdot\cos\frac{8\pi}{33}\cos\frac{16\pi}{33}\right)$

$\Rightarrow 2A \times \sin\frac{\pi}{33} = 6 \times \sin\frac{32\pi}{33}$

$= 6 \times \sin\frac{\pi}{33}$

$\Rightarrow 2A = 6 \Rightarrow A = 3$

Thus, the required answer is 3.

10. (4) Given,

$\tan 9° - \tan 27° - \tan 63° + \tan 81°$

$= \tan 9° + \tan(90° - 9°) - \tan 27° - \tan(90° - 27°)$

$= \tan 9° + \cot 9° - \tan 27° - \cot 27°$

$= \frac{\sin 9°}{\cos 9°} + \frac{\cos 9°}{\sin 9°} - \left(\frac{\sin 27°}{\cos 27°} + \frac{\cos 27°}{\sin 27°}\right)$

$= \frac{\sin^2 9° + \cos^2 9°}{\sin 9° \cos 9°} - \left(\frac{\sin^2 27° + \cos^2 27°}{\cos 27° \sin 27°}\right)$

$= \frac{2}{\sin 18°} - \frac{2}{\sin 54°}$

$= \frac{2\times 4}{\sqrt{5}-1} - \frac{2\times 4}{\sqrt{5}+1}$

$= 8\left(\frac{\sqrt{5}+1-\sqrt{5}+1}{5-1}\right) = 4$

11. (a) Given, $\cot\alpha = 1, \alpha \in \left(\pi, \frac{3\pi}{2}\right)$

Then, $\tan\alpha = 1$

and $\sec\beta = \frac{-5}{3}, \beta \in \left(\frac{\pi}{2}, \pi\right)$

Then, $\tan\beta = -\frac{4}{3}$

$\therefore \quad \tan(\alpha+\beta) = \frac{\tan\alpha + \tan\beta}{1 - \tan\alpha\cdot\tan\beta}$

$= \frac{1-\frac{4}{3}}{1+\frac{4}{3}} = -\frac{1}{7}$

$\alpha + \beta \in (3\pi/2, 2\pi)$ i.e. fourth quadrant.

12. (b) $16\sin 20°\sin 40°\sin 80°$

We know that

$\sin\theta\sin(60°-\theta)\sin(60°+\theta) = \frac{1}{4}\sin 3\theta$

In the given question, let $\theta = 20°$

$\therefore 16\sin 20°\sin(60°-20°)\sin(60°+20°)$

$= 16 \times \frac{1}{4}\sin 60° = \frac{4\sqrt{3}}{2} = 2\sqrt{3}$

13. (c) Given,

$\alpha = \sin 36° = \frac{\sqrt{10-2\sqrt{5}}}{4}$

$\Rightarrow (4\alpha)^2 = 10 - 2\sqrt{5}$

$\Rightarrow (16\alpha^2 - 10)^2 = (-2\sqrt{5})^2 = 20$

$\Rightarrow 4(8\alpha^2 - 5)^2 = 20$

$\Rightarrow 64\alpha^4 - 80\alpha^2 + 25 = 5$

$\Rightarrow 64\alpha^4 - 80\alpha^2 + 20 = 0$

$\Rightarrow 16\alpha^4 - 20\alpha^2 + 5 = 0$

$\therefore \alpha$ is a root of the equation

$16x^4 - 20x^2 + 5 = 0$

14. (b) $\cos\frac{2\pi}{7} + \cos\frac{4\pi}{7} + \cos\frac{6\pi}{7}$

On applying sum formula of cos series,

$$\frac{\cos\left(\frac{\frac{2\pi}{7}+\frac{6\pi}{7}}{2}\right)\sin\left(3\times\frac{2\pi/7}{2}\right)}{\sin\left(\frac{2\pi/7}{2}\right)}$$

$= \frac{\sin\frac{3\pi}{7}\cos\frac{4\pi}{7}}{\sin\frac{\pi}{7}}$

$= \frac{\sin\left(\pi - \frac{4\pi}{7}\right)\cos\frac{4\pi}{7}}{\sin\frac{\pi}{7}}$

$= \frac{2\sin\frac{4\pi}{7}\cos\frac{4\pi}{7}}{2\sin\frac{\pi}{7}} = \frac{\sin\frac{8\pi}{7}}{2\sin\frac{\pi}{7}}$

$= \frac{\sin\left(\pi + \frac{\pi}{7}\right)}{2\sin\frac{\pi}{7}} = \frac{-\sin\frac{\pi}{7}}{2\sin\frac{\pi}{7}} = \frac{-1}{2}$

15. (d) $2\sin(12°) - \sin(72°)$

$= \sin 12° + \sin 12° - \sin 72°$

$= \sin 12° + 2\cos 42°\sin(-30°)$

$= \sin 12° - 2 \times \frac{1}{2}\cos 42°$

$= \sin 12° - \sin 48°$

$[\because \sin(\theta) = \cos(90° - \theta)]$

$= 2\cos 30°\sin(-18°)$

$= -\frac{2\sqrt{3}}{2} \times \left[\frac{\sqrt{5}-1}{4}\right]$

$= \frac{\sqrt{3}(1-\sqrt{5})}{4}$

16. (b) $2\sin\frac{\pi}{22}\cdot\sin\frac{3\pi}{22}\cdot\sin\frac{5\pi}{22}\cdot\sin\frac{7\pi}{22}\cdot\sin\frac{9\pi}{22}$

$= 2\sin\left(\frac{\pi}{2} - \frac{10\pi}{22}\right)\sin\left(\frac{\pi}{2} - \frac{8\pi}{22}\right)\sin\left(\frac{\pi}{2} - \frac{6\pi}{22}\right)\sin\left(\frac{\pi}{2} - \frac{4\pi}{22}\right)\sin\left(\frac{\pi}{2} - \frac{2\pi}{22}\right)$

$= 2\cdot\cos\frac{10\pi}{22}\cdot\cos\frac{8\pi}{22}\cos\frac{6\pi}{22}\cdot\cos\frac{4\pi}{22}\cdot\cos\frac{2\pi}{22}$

$= 2\cdot\cos\frac{\pi}{11}\cdot\cos\frac{2\pi}{11}\cos\frac{3\pi}{11}\cdot\cos\frac{4\pi}{11}\cdot\cos\frac{5\pi}{11}$

On multiplying and dividing by $\sin\left(\frac{\pi}{11}\right)$, we get

$\frac{2\sin\frac{32\pi}{11}}{2^5\sin\frac{\pi}{11}}$

$\left[\because \cos\left(\frac{3\pi}{11}\right) = -\cos\left(\frac{8\pi}{11}\right), \cos\left(\frac{5\pi}{11}\right) = -\cos\left(\frac{16\pi}{11}\right)\right.$ and $\left.\sin 2\theta = 2\sin\theta\cos\theta\right]$

$= \frac{2}{32}\frac{\sin\left(3\pi - \frac{\pi}{11}\right)}{\sin\frac{\pi}{11}} = \frac{1}{16}$

Chapter-4

Complex Numbers and Quadratic Equations

1. (i) $\sqrt{-144} = \sqrt{-1 \times 144}$

$= \sqrt{-1} \times \sqrt{144} = 12i$

(ii) $(i\sqrt{2})(i\sqrt{3}) = i^2\sqrt{6} = -\sqrt{6}$

(iii) $\sqrt{-4} \times \sqrt{\frac{-9}{4}} = (2i)\left(\frac{3i}{2}\right)$

$= 3i^2 = -3$

(iv) $-3i^2 = 3$

(v) $-2i^2 \times \left(-\frac{1}{512}i^3\right)$

$= \frac{1}{256} \times i^2 \times i^3 = \frac{i}{256}$

2. (i) True

(ii) (True)

$z_1 = z_2$

$\Rightarrow 2 - iy = x + 3i$

Equating the real and imaginary parts, we get

$2 = x$ and $-y = 3$

$\Rightarrow \quad x = 2$ and $y = -3$

3. (i) Equating the real and imaginary parts, we get

$x = \frac{-7}{2}$ and $y = \sqrt{2}$

(ii) $4x + i(3x - y) = 3 + i(-6)$

Equating the real and imaginary parts, we get

$4x = 3$

$\Rightarrow \quad x = \frac{3}{4}$

$\Rightarrow \quad 3x - y = -6$

$\Rightarrow \quad 3 \times \frac{3}{4} + 6 = y$

$\therefore \quad y = \frac{33}{4}$

(iii) $(1 - i)x + (1 + i)y = 1 - 3i$

$\Rightarrow (x + y) + i(-x + y) = 1 - 3i$

$\Rightarrow x + y = 1$ and $-x + y = -3$

$\Rightarrow \quad x = 2$ and $y = -1$

(iv) $(x + iy)(2 - 3i) = 4 + i$

$\Rightarrow (2x + 3y) + i(-3x + 2y) = 4 + i$

$\Rightarrow \quad 2x + 3y = 4$ and $-3x + 2y = 1$

$\Rightarrow \quad x = \frac{5}{13}$ and $y = \frac{14}{13}$

(v) $(1 + i)y^2 + (6 + i) = (2 + i)x$

$\Rightarrow (y^2 + 6) + i(y^2 + 1) = 2x + ix$

$\Rightarrow y^2 + 6 = 2x$ and $y^2 + 1 = x$

$\Rightarrow x = 5$ and $y = \pm 2$

(vi) $(x^4 + 2xi) - (3x^2 + iy) = (3 - 5i) + (1 + 2iy)$

$\Rightarrow x^4 - 3x^2 = 4$

and $2x - y = 2y - 5$

$\Rightarrow \quad x = 2$ and $y = 3$

or $\quad x = -2$ and $y = \frac{1}{3}$

(vii) $(x + y) - i(3x + 2y) = 5 + 2i$

$\Rightarrow x + y = 5$ and $-(3x + 2y) = 2$

$\Rightarrow \quad x = -12$ and $y = 17$

(viii) $(3x - 7) + 2iy = -5y + (5 + x)i$

$\Rightarrow 3x - 7 = -5y$ and $2y = 5 + x$

$\Rightarrow 3x + 5y = 7$ and $x - 2y = -5$

$\Rightarrow \quad x = -1, y = 2$

(ix) $\frac{x - 1}{3 + i} + \frac{y - 1}{3 - i} = i$

$\Rightarrow \frac{(3x + 3y - 6) + i(y - x)}{9 - i^2} = i$

$\Rightarrow \frac{3x + 3y - 6}{10} = 0$

and $\quad \frac{y - x}{10} = 1$

$\Rightarrow \quad x + y - 2 = 0$

and $\quad y - x = 10$

$\Rightarrow \quad x = -4$ and $y = 6$

4. (i) $i^2 = -1$

(ii) $i^{19} = i^3 = -i$

(iii) $i^{135} = i^3 = -i$

(iv) $i^{528} = (i^2)^{264} = (-1)^{264} = 1$

(v) $i^{-39} = (i^4)^{-10} i = i$

(vi) $i^{-58} = \frac{1}{i^{58}} = \frac{1}{(i^2)^{29}}$

$= \frac{1}{(-1)^{29}} = \frac{1}{(-1)} = -1$

(vii) $i^{-999} = \frac{1}{i^{999}} = \frac{1}{i^3} = \frac{i}{i^4} = \frac{i}{1} = i$

(viii) $i^9 + i^{19} = (i^4)^2 i + (i^4)^4 i^3$

$= i + i^3 = i - i = 0$

(ix) $i^{30} + i^{40} + i^{60}$

$= (i^2)^{15} + (i^2)^{20} + (i^2)^{30}$

$= (-1)^{15} + (-1)^{20} + (-1)^{30}$

$= -1 + 1 + 1 = 1$

(x) $(i^{49} + i^{68} + i^{89} + i^{110})$

$= (i^2)^{24} i + (i^2)^{34} + (i^2)^{44} i + (i^2)^{55}$

$= i + 1 + i - 1 = 2i$

(xi) $(i^{77} + i^{70} + i^{87} + i^{414})^3$

$= \{(i^2)^{38} i + (i^2)^{35} + (i^2)^{43} . i + (i^2)^{207}\}^3$

$= \{i - 1 - i - 1\}^3 = -8$

(xii) $(1 - i)^4 = (1 - 2i + i^2)^2$

$= (-2i)^2 = -4$

(xiii) $\left\{i^{19} + \left(\frac{1}{i}\right)^{25}\right\}^2 = \left\{i^{19} + \frac{1}{i^{25}}\right\}^2$

$= \left\{i^3 + \frac{1}{i}\right\}^2 = \left\{-i + \frac{i^3}{i^4}\right\}^2$

$= \{-i + i^3\}^2 = (-i - i)^2$

$= 4i^2 = -4$

(xiv) $\left\{i^{17} - \frac{1}{i^{34}}\right\}^2 = \left\{i - \frac{1}{i^2}\right\}^2$

$= (i + 1)^2 = 2i$

(xv) $\left\{i^{18} + \frac{1}{i^{24}}\right\}^3 = (i^2 + 1)^3$

$= (-1 + 1)^3 = 0$

5. (i) (True)

$i^n + i^{n+1} + i^{n+2} + i^{n+3}$

$= i^n(1 + i - 1 - i)$

$= i^n(0) = 0$

(ii) (True)

$(-\sqrt{-1})^{4n+3} = (-i)^{4n+3}$

$= (-i)^{4n}(-i)^3$

$= \{(-i)^4\}^n(-i^3)$

$= 1 \times -i^3 = i$

6. (i) (True)

$z_1 + z_2 = 6 + \sqrt{-9} + (-2 - 6i)$

$= 6 + 3i - 2 - 6i$

$= 6 - 2 + (3 - 6)i$

$= 4 - 3i$

(ii) True

7. (i) Given, $z_1 = 6 + 5i$

$z_2 = -2 + 3i$

Then,

$z_1 - z_2 = 6 + 5i - (-2 + 3i)$

$= 6 + 5i + 2 - 3i$

$= 8 + 2i$

(ii) $(1 - i) - (-1 + 6i)$

$= 1 - i + 1 - 6i$

$= 2 - 7i$

(iii) $\left(\frac{1}{5} + \frac{2}{5}i\right) - \left(4 + \frac{5}{2}i\right)$

$= \left(\frac{1}{5} - 4\right) + \frac{2i}{5} - \frac{5i}{2}$

$= -\frac{19}{5} - \frac{21}{10}i$

8. $\left\{\left(\frac{1}{3}+\frac{7}{3}i\right)+\left(4+\frac{1}{3}i\right)\right\}-\left\{-\frac{4}{3}+i\right\}$

$=\frac{17}{3}+\frac{5}{3}i$

9. (i) $(-5i)\left(\frac{1}{8}i\right)=\frac{-5}{8}i^2=-\frac{5}{8}\times-1$

$=\frac{5}{8}=\frac{5}{8}+0i$

(ii) $3(7+7i)+i(7+7i)$

$=21+21i+7i-7$

$=14+28i$

(iii) $(-\sqrt{3}+\sqrt{-2})(2\sqrt{3}-i)$

$=-6+\sqrt{3}i+2\sqrt{6}i-\sqrt{2}\,i^2$

$=(\sqrt{2}-6)+(\sqrt{3}+2\sqrt{6})i$

(iv) $(5-3i)^3=125+27i$

$-225i-135$

$=-10-198i$

(v) $\left(\frac{1}{3}+3i\right)^3=\frac{1}{27}+27i^3$

$+3i\left(\frac{1}{3}+3i\right)$

$=\frac{1}{27}-27i+i-9$

$=\frac{-242}{27}-26i$

(vi) $\left(-2-\frac{i}{3}\right)^3=-8-\frac{1}{27}i^3$

$+2i\left(-2-\frac{i}{3}\right)$

$=-8+\frac{1}{27}i-4i+\frac{2}{3}$

$=-\frac{22}{3}-\frac{107}{27}i$

10. (a) $z_1(z_2+z_3)=(2-6i)$

$(3+5i+9+2i)$

$=(2-6i)(12+7i)$

$=24+14i-72i-42i^2$

$=24+14i-72i+42$

$=66-58i$

11. (i) Given, $z_1=6+3i$

and $z_2=2-i$

$\therefore\quad \frac{z_1}{z_2}=\left((6+3i)\times\frac{1}{2-i}\right)$

$=\frac{(6+3i)}{2-i}$

$=(6+3i)\left(\frac{2+i}{5}\right)$

$=\frac{1}{5}(9+12i)$

(ii) We have,

$z_1=2+\sqrt{2}i$

$=\sqrt{2}(\sqrt{2}+i)$

and $z_2=\sqrt{2}+i$

$\therefore\quad \frac{z_1}{z_2}=\frac{\sqrt{2}(\sqrt{2}+i)}{\sqrt{2}+i}=\sqrt{2}$

(iii) We have, $z_1=6-5i$

and $z_2=\frac{24-20i}{4}=6-5i$

$\therefore\quad \frac{z_1}{z_2}=\frac{6-5i}{6-5i}=1$

12. (i) $4z_1-3z_2$

$=8+4i-(-3+6i)$

$=8+4i+3-6i=11-2i$

$\therefore \text{Im}(4z_1-3z_2)=-2$

(ii) $z_1z_2=(2+i)(-1+2i)$

$=-2+4i-i-2$

$=-4+3i$

$\therefore \text{Re}(z_1z_2)=-4$

(iii) $iz_1^2=i(2+i)^2=i(4+i^2+4i)$

$=4i-i-4=-4+3i$

$\therefore \text{Im}(iz_1^2)=3$

(iv) $\frac{z_1}{z_2}=\frac{2+i}{-1+2i}\times\frac{-1-2i}{(-1-2i)}=-i$

$\therefore \text{Re}\left(\frac{z_1}{z_2}\right)=0$

13. (True)

$(x+1+i)(x+1-i)(x-1+i)$

$(x-1-i)$

$=\{(x+1)^2-i^2\}\cdot\{(x-1)^2-i^2\}$

$=\{x^2+2x+2\}\{x^2-2x+2\}$

$=(x^2+2)^2-(2x)^2=x^4+4$

14. (False)

$x+iy=(a+ib)^3$

$\Rightarrow\quad x=a^3-3ab^2$

and $\quad y=3a^2b-b^3$

$\Rightarrow\quad \frac{x}{a}=a^2-3b^2$

and $\quad \frac{y}{b}=3a^2-b^2$

$\Rightarrow \frac{x}{a}+\frac{y}{b}=4(a^2-b^2)$

15. (i) $\quad x=-5+2\sqrt{-4}$

$\Rightarrow\quad x+5=4i$

$\Rightarrow (x+5)^2=16i^2$

$\Rightarrow x^2+10x+41=0$

We have,

$x^4+9x^3+35x^2-x+4$

$=x^2(x^2+10x+41)$

$-x(x^2+10x+41)$

$+4(x^2+10x+41)-160$

$=-160$

(ii) $\quad x=1+2i$

$\Rightarrow\quad x-1=2i$

$\Rightarrow\quad (x-1)^2=4i^2$

$\Rightarrow x^2-2x+5=0$

We have,

x^3+7x^2-x+16

$=x(x^2-2x+5)$

$+9(x^2-2x+5)$

$+(12x-29)$

$=12x-29$

$=-17+24i$

16. (i) Let $z=3+2i$

$\frac{1}{z}=\frac{1}{3+2i}\times\frac{3-2i}{3-2i}$

$=\frac{3}{13}-\frac{2}{13}i$

(ii) $z=a+ib$

$z^{-1}=\frac{1}{z}=\frac{1}{a+ib}$

$=\frac{1}{a+ib}\times\frac{a-ib}{a-ib}$

$=\frac{a-ib}{a^2+b^2}$

$=\frac{a}{a^2+b^2}-i\frac{b}{a^2+b^2}$

(iii) $z=(2+\sqrt{3}i)^2=1+4\sqrt{3}\,i$

$\frac{1}{z}=\frac{1}{1+4\sqrt{3}\,i}\times\frac{1-4\sqrt{3}\,i}{1-4\sqrt{3}\,i}$

$=\frac{1}{49}-\frac{4\sqrt{3}\,i}{49}$

17. (i) $|z|=|5+6i|$

$=\sqrt{5^2+6^2}=\sqrt{61}$

(ii) $|z|=|12-5i|$

$=\sqrt{12^2+5^2}=13$

(iii) $|z|=|-13-\sqrt{7}\,i|$

$=\sqrt{(-13)^2+(-\sqrt{7})^2}$

$=\sqrt{176}$

(iv) $|z|=|-\sqrt{2}+\sqrt{2}i|$

$=\sqrt{(-\sqrt{2})^2+(\sqrt{2})^2}=2$

(v) $\quad iz^3+z^2-z+i=0$

$\Rightarrow z^3-iz^2+iz+1=0$

$\Rightarrow\quad (z-i)(z^2+i)=0$

$\Rightarrow\quad z=i \text{ or } z^2=-i$

$\Rightarrow\quad |z|=1 \text{ and } |z^2|=1=|z|^2$

Hence, $|z|=1$

18. True

19. (i) $z=\frac{1}{3+4i}\times\frac{3-4i}{3-4i}=\frac{3}{25}-\frac{4}{25}i$

$\therefore\ \bar{z}=\frac{3}{25}+\frac{4}{25}i$

(ii) $z=\frac{1-i}{1+i}\times\frac{1-i}{1-i}$

$=\frac{1-2i-1}{1+1}=-i$

$\therefore\ \bar{z}=i$

(iii) $z=\frac{(1+i)^2}{3-i}\times\frac{3+i}{3+i}=\frac{6i+2i^2}{9-i^2}$

$=-\frac{1}{5}+\frac{3}{5}i$

$\therefore\ \bar{z}=-\frac{1}{5}-\frac{3}{5}i$

(iv) $z=\frac{(2+3i)^2}{2-i}\times\frac{2+i}{2+i}$

$=\frac{-22+19i}{4-i^2}=-\frac{22}{5}+\frac{19}{5}i$

$\therefore\ \bar{z}=-\frac{22}{5}-\frac{19}{5}i$

20. (i) $\frac{(a+i)^2}{2a-i}=p+iq$

$\Rightarrow \frac{(a-i)^2}{2a+i}=p-iq$

$\Rightarrow \frac{(a+i)^2}{2a-i}\times\frac{(a-i)^2}{2a+i}=(p+iq)(p-iq)$

$\Rightarrow \frac{(a^2+1)^2}{4a^2+1}=p^2+q^2$

(ii) $a+ib=\frac{(x+i)^2}{2x^2+1}$

$\Rightarrow a-ib=\frac{(x-i)^2}{2x^2+1}$

$\Rightarrow (a+ib)(a-ib)=\frac{(x+i)^2}{2x^2+1}\times\frac{(x-i)^2}{2x^2+1}$

$\Rightarrow a^2+b^2=\frac{(x^2+1)^2}{(2x^2+1)^2}$

(iii) $x+iy=\sqrt{\frac{a+ib}{c+id}}$

$\Rightarrow\ x-iy=\sqrt{\frac{a-ib}{c-id}}$

$\Rightarrow\ (x+iy)(x-iy)=\sqrt{\frac{a+ib}{c+id}\times\frac{a-ib}{c-id}}$

$\Rightarrow x^2+y^2=\sqrt{\frac{a^2+b^2}{c^2+d^2}}$

$\Rightarrow (x^2+y^2)^2=\frac{a^2+b^2}{c^2+d^2}$

(iv) We have,

$\frac{a+ib}{c+id}=x+iy$

and $\frac{a-ib}{c-id}=x-iy$

$\Rightarrow \frac{a+ib}{c+id}\times\frac{a-ib}{c-id}=(x+iy)(x-iy)$

$\Rightarrow \frac{a^2+b^2}{c^2+d^2}=x^2+y^2$

21. (d) $\frac{z_1 z_2}{\bar{z}_1}=\frac{(1-i)(-2+4i)}{1+i}$

$=\frac{2+6i}{1+i}\times\frac{1-i}{1-i}=4+2i$

$\therefore\ \text{Im}\left(\frac{z_1 z_2}{\bar{z}_1}\right)=2$

22. (True)

$-3+ix^2y=x^2+y-4i$

$\Rightarrow\ -3=x^2+y$ and $x^2y=-4$

$\Rightarrow\ x=\pm 1$ and $y=-4$

23. $|1-i|^x=1$

$\Rightarrow(\sqrt{2})^x=1$

$\Rightarrow\ 2^{x/2}=1=2^0$

$\Rightarrow\ \frac{x}{2}=0$

$\Rightarrow\ x=0$

$\therefore$ No, non-zero integral solution.

24. (d) $\frac{1+i}{1-i}\times\frac{1+i}{1+i}=\frac{1+2i-1}{1+1}=i$

Since, $\left(\frac{1+i}{1-i}\right)^n=1$

$\Rightarrow i^n=1 \Rightarrow n$ is a multiple of 4.

25. (i) $\frac{3-\sqrt{-16}}{1-\sqrt{-9}}=\frac{3-4i}{1-3i}\times\frac{1+3i}{1+3i}$

$=\frac{3}{2}+\frac{1}{2}i$

(ii) $\frac{2-\sqrt{-25}}{1-\sqrt{-16}}=\frac{2-5i}{1-4i}\times\frac{1+4i}{1+4i}$

$=\frac{22}{17}+\frac{3}{17}i$

(iii) $\frac{1}{1-\cos\theta+2i\sin\theta}\times\frac{1-\cos\theta-2i\sin\theta}{1-\cos\theta-2i\sin\theta}$

$=\frac{1-\cos\theta-2i\sin\theta}{(1-\cos\theta)^2+4\sin^2\theta}$

$=\frac{1-\cos\theta-2i\sin\theta}{2-2\cos\theta+3\sin^2\theta}$

$=\left(\frac{1-\cos\theta}{2-2\cos\theta+3\sin^2\theta}\right)+i\left(\frac{-2\sin\theta}{2-2\cos\theta+3\sin^2\theta}\right)$

(iv) $\frac{1}{-11+2i}=\frac{1}{-11+2i}\times\frac{(-11-2i)}{(-11-2i)}$

$=\frac{-11}{125}-\frac{2}{125}i$

(v) $\frac{(3+i\sqrt{5})(3-i\sqrt{5})}{(\sqrt{3}+\sqrt{2}i)-(\sqrt{3}-i\sqrt{2})}$

$=\frac{(9+5)}{2\sqrt{2}i}=\frac{7}{\sqrt{2}}i$

(vi) $\left(\frac{2+3i}{3+4i}\right)\left(\frac{2-3i}{3-4i}\right)$

$=\frac{4-9i^2}{9-16i^2}=\frac{13}{25}$

(vii) $\left(\frac{3+2i}{2-3i}\right)+\left(\frac{3-2i}{2+3i}\right)$

$=\frac{(3+2i)(2+3i)}{4-9i^2}+\frac{(3-2i)(2-3i)}{4-9i^2}=0$

(viii) $\frac{(3-2i)(2+3i)}{(1+2i)(2-i)}$

$=\frac{12+5i}{4+3i}\times\frac{4-3i}{4-3i}$

$=\frac{63}{25}-\frac{16}{25}i$

(ix) $\frac{1}{-2+\sqrt{-3}}=\frac{1}{-2+i\sqrt{3}}\times\frac{-2-i\sqrt{3}}{-2-i\sqrt{3}}$

$=-\frac{2}{7}-\frac{\sqrt{3}}{7}i$

(x) $\frac{5+4i}{4+5i}\times\frac{4-5i}{4-5i}=\frac{40-9i}{16-25i^2}$

$=\frac{40}{41}-\frac{9}{41}i$

(xi) $\frac{(1+i)^2}{3-i}\times\frac{3+i}{3+i}=\frac{6i+2i^2}{9-i^2}$

$=-\frac{1}{5}+\frac{3}{5}i$

(xii) $\frac{1}{3-4i}=\frac{1}{3-4i}\times\frac{3+4i}{3+4i}$

$=\frac{3+4i}{9-16i^2}$

$=\frac{3}{25}+\frac{4}{25}i$

(xiii) $\left(\frac{1}{1-2i}+\frac{3}{1+i}\right)\left(\frac{3+4i}{2-4i}\right)$

$$=\frac{4-5i}{3-i}\times\frac{3+4i}{2-4i}$$

$$=\frac{32+i}{2-14i}\times\frac{2+14i}{2+14i}$$

$$=\frac{1}{4}+\frac{9}{4}i$$

26. (c) $a+ib=\frac{c+i}{c-i}\times\frac{c+i}{c+i}$

$$=\frac{c^2-1}{c^2+1}+\frac{i2c}{c^2+1}$$

$$\Rightarrow \quad a=\frac{c^2-1}{c^2+1} \text{ and } b=\frac{2c}{c^2+1}$$

$$a^2+b^2=\frac{(c^2-1)^2}{(c^2+1)^2}+\frac{4c^2}{(c^2+1)^2}$$

$$=\frac{c^4+1-2c^2+4c^2}{(c^2+1)^2}$$

$$=\frac{c^4+1+2c^2}{(c^2+1)^2}$$

$$=\frac{(c^2+1)^2}{(c^2+1)^2}=1$$

and $\frac{b}{a}=\frac{2c}{c^2+1}\times\frac{c^2+1}{c^2-1}=\frac{2c}{c^2-1}$

27. (True)

Let $z=x+iy \Rightarrow |z|=1$

$$\Rightarrow \quad x^2+y^2=1$$

$$\frac{z-1}{z+1}=\frac{(x-1)+iy}{(x+1)+iy}\times\frac{(x+1)-iy}{(x+1)-iy}$$

$$=\frac{(x^2+y^2-1)+2iy}{(x+1)^2+y^2}$$

$$=\frac{2iy}{(x+1)^2+y^2}$$

28. $\frac{3+2i\sin\theta}{1-2i\sin\theta}\times\frac{1+2i\sin\theta}{1+2i\sin\theta}$

$$=\frac{3-4\sin^2\theta}{1+4\sin^2\theta}+\frac{i8\sin\theta}{1+4\sin^2\theta}$$

$$\therefore \quad \frac{8\sin\theta}{1+4\sin^2\theta}=0$$

$$\Rightarrow \quad \sin\theta=0 \Rightarrow \theta=n\pi, n\in Z$$

29. (b) $\left|\frac{\beta-\alpha}{1-\bar{\alpha}\beta}\right|^2=\left(\frac{\beta-\alpha}{1-\bar{\alpha}\beta}\right)\left(\overline{\frac{\beta-\alpha}{1-\bar{\alpha}\beta}}\right)$

$$=\frac{(\beta-\alpha)(\bar{\beta}-\bar{\alpha})}{(1-\bar{\alpha}\beta)(1-\alpha\bar{\beta})}$$

$$=\frac{|\beta|^2-\alpha\bar{\beta}-\bar{\alpha}\beta+|\alpha|^2}{1-\alpha\bar{\beta}-\bar{\alpha}\beta+(\alpha\bar{\alpha})(\beta\bar{\beta})}$$

$$=\frac{|\alpha|^2-\alpha\bar{\beta}-\bar{\alpha}\beta+1}{1-\alpha\bar{\beta}-\bar{\alpha}\beta+|\alpha|^2}=1$$

$$\Rightarrow \left|\frac{\beta-\alpha}{1-\bar{\alpha}\beta}\right|^2=1$$

30. (i) (True)

$$|(a+ib)(c+id)(e+if)(g+ih)|=|A+iB|$$

$$\Rightarrow |a+ib||c+id||e+if||g+ih|=|A+iB|$$

$$\Rightarrow \sqrt{a^2+b^2}\sqrt{c^2+d^2}\sqrt{e^2+f^2}\sqrt{g^2+h^2}=\sqrt{A^2+B^2}$$

$$\Rightarrow (a^2+b^2)(c^2+d^2)(e^2+f^2)(g^2+h^2)=A^2+B^2$$

(ii) (True)

$$|(1+i)(1+2i)(1+3i)\ldots(1+ni)|=|x+iy|$$

$$\Rightarrow |1+i||1+2i||1+3i|\ldots|1+ni|=|x+iy|$$

$$\Rightarrow \sqrt{1+1}\sqrt{1+4}\ldots\sqrt{1+n^2}=\sqrt{x^2+y^2}$$

$$\Rightarrow 2\cdot5\cdot10\ldots(1+n^2)=(x^2+y^2)$$

31. (b) $\frac{2z_1}{3z_2}=\lambda i$ for some $\lambda\in R$

$$\therefore \left|\frac{z_1-z_2}{z_1+z_2}\right|=\left|\frac{\frac{z_1}{z_2}-1}{\frac{z_1}{z_2}+1}\right|$$

$$=\left|\frac{\frac{3}{2}\lambda i-1}{\frac{3}{2}\lambda i+1}\right|=\left|\frac{3\lambda i-2}{3\lambda i+2}\right|$$

$$=\frac{\sqrt{4+9\lambda^2}}{\sqrt{4+9\lambda^2}}=1$$

32. (True)

$|z_1+z_2+z_3+\ldots+z_n|$

$$=\left|\frac{z_1\bar{z}_1}{\bar{z}_1}+\frac{z_2\bar{z}_2}{\bar{z}_2}+\frac{z_3\bar{z}_3}{\bar{z}_3}+\ldots+\frac{z_n\bar{z}_n}{\bar{z}_n}\right|$$

$$=\left|\frac{|z_1|^2}{\bar{z}_1}+\frac{|z_2|^2}{\bar{z}_2}+\frac{|z_3|^2}{\bar{z}_3}+\ldots+\frac{|z_n|^2}{\bar{z}_n}\right|$$

$$=\left|\overline{\left(\frac{1}{z_1}+\frac{1}{z_2}+\frac{1}{z_3}+\ldots+\frac{1}{z_n}\right)}\right|$$

$$=\left|\frac{1}{z_1}+\frac{1}{z_2}+\frac{1}{z_3}+\ldots+\frac{1}{z_n}\right|$$

33. (i) Given, $z=-1+i\sqrt{3}$

$\therefore$ The point $(x, y)=(-1, \sqrt{3})$

and $|z|=\sqrt{(-1)^2+(\sqrt{3})^2}=2$

Geometrical representation

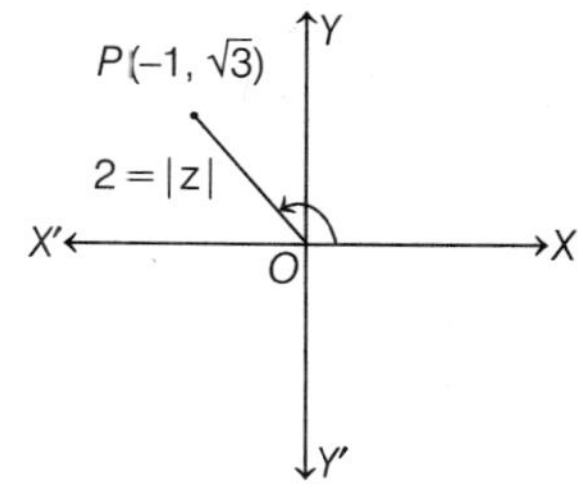

(ii) Given, $z=-\sqrt{5}+i$

$\therefore$ The point $P(x, y)=(-\sqrt{5}, 1)$

and $|z|=\sqrt{(-\sqrt{5})^2+1}$

$$=\sqrt{5+1}=\sqrt{6}$$

Geometrical representation

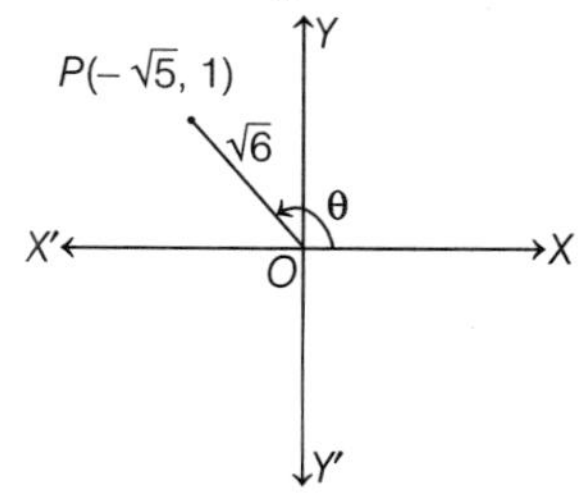

34. (b)

35. (i) $z=z_1z_2=\sqrt{3}\left(\frac{1}{\sqrt{3}}+i\right)$

$$=1+\sqrt{3}i$$

$$\alpha=\tan^{-1}\left|\frac{\text{Im}(z)}{\text{Re}(z)}\right|$$

$$=\tan^{-1}\left|\frac{\sqrt{3}}{1}\right|=\frac{\pi}{3}$$

Since, $\text{Re}(z)>0$ and $\text{Im}(z)>0$

$\therefore \arg(z)=\alpha=\frac{\pi}{3}$

(ii) $z=z_3z_4=2(-1+\sqrt{3}i)$

$$=-2+2\sqrt{3}i$$

$$\alpha=\tan^{-1}\left|\frac{2\sqrt{3}}{-2}\right|$$

$$=\tan^{-1}(\sqrt{3})=\frac{\pi}{3}$$

$\therefore \arg(z)=\pi-\alpha=\frac{2\pi}{3}$

(iii) $z = z_5 - z_6$
$= 2\sqrt{3} + 5i - 3\sqrt{3} - 6i$
$= -\sqrt{3} - i$

$\alpha = \tan^{-1}\left|\frac{-1}{-\sqrt{3}}\right| = \frac{\pi}{6}$

$\therefore \arg(z) = -(\pi - \alpha) = -\frac{5\pi}{6}$

(iv) $z = z_7 + z_8$
$= \sqrt{3} - 4i + \sqrt{3} + 2i$
$= 2\sqrt{3} - 2i$

$\alpha = \tan^{-1}\left|\frac{-2}{2\sqrt{3}}\right| = \frac{\pi}{6}$

$\therefore \arg(z) = -\alpha = -\frac{\pi}{6}$

(v) $z = \frac{z_9}{z_{10}} = \frac{1+i}{1-i}$

$z = \frac{1+i}{1-i} \times \frac{1+i}{1+i} = i$

$\Rightarrow \tan\alpha = \infty \Rightarrow \alpha = \frac{\pi}{2}$

$\therefore \arg(z) = \alpha = \frac{\pi}{2}$

(vi) $z = \frac{z_{11}}{z_{12}} = \frac{1}{1+i}$

$z = \frac{1}{1+i} \times \frac{1-i}{1-i} = \frac{1}{2} - \frac{1}{2}i$

$\Rightarrow \tan\alpha = \left|\frac{-\frac{1}{2}}{\frac{1}{2}}\right| = 1 \Rightarrow \alpha = \frac{\pi}{4}$

$\therefore \arg(z) = -\alpha = -\frac{\pi}{4}$

36. (i) Point $(-4, 0)$ representing $z = -4 + 0i$ lies on the negative side of real axis.
$\therefore$ Principal argument of z is π.

(ii) Clearly, the point $(0, -2)$ representing $z = -2i$ lies on the negative side of imaginary axis.
$\therefore$ Principal argument of z is $-\frac{\pi}{2}$.

37. (True)
Let $z = r(\cos\theta + i\sin\theta)$
$\Rightarrow |z| = r$ and $\arg(z) = \theta$
$|\text{Re}(z)| + |\text{Im}(z)| = |r\cos\theta| + |r\sin\theta|$
$\Rightarrow \{|\text{Re}(z)| + \text{Im}(z)|\}^2 = r^2\{|\cos\theta| + |\sin\theta|\}^2$
$= r^2\{1 + |\sin 2\theta|\}$
$= 2r^2 \quad [\because |\sin 2\theta| \le 1]$
$\therefore |\text{Re}(z)| + |\text{Im}(z)| \le \sqrt{2}\, r$

38. (d)

39. (i) $r = |z| = \sqrt{(-1)^2 + (-1)^2} = \sqrt{2}$

$\tan\alpha = \left|\frac{-1}{-1}\right| = 1 \Rightarrow \alpha = \frac{\pi}{4}$

$\Rightarrow \quad \theta = -(\pi - \alpha) = \frac{-3\pi}{4}$

Polar form
$z = \sqrt{2}\left(\cos\frac{3\pi}{4} - i\sin\frac{3\pi}{4}\right)$

(ii) $r = |z| = \sqrt{1^2 + (-1)^2} = \sqrt{2}$

$\tan\alpha = \left|\frac{-1}{1}\right| = 1 \Rightarrow \alpha = \frac{\pi}{4}$

$\Rightarrow \quad \theta = -\alpha = -\frac{\pi}{4}$

$\therefore$ Polar form
$z = \sqrt{2}\left(\cos\frac{\pi}{4} - i\sin\frac{\pi}{4}\right)$

(iii) Let $z = -3\sqrt{2} + 3\sqrt{2}i$
$r = |z| = \sqrt{(-3\sqrt{2})^2 + (3\sqrt{2})^2}$
$= 6$

$\tan\alpha = 1 \Rightarrow \alpha = \frac{\pi}{4}$

$\theta = \pi - \alpha = \pi - \frac{\pi}{4} = \frac{3\pi}{4}$

$\therefore$ Polar form
$z = 6\left(\cos\frac{3\pi}{4} + i\sin\frac{3\pi}{4}\right)$

(iv) Let $z = 1 + i$
$r = |z| = \sqrt{2}$
and $\tan\alpha = \left|\frac{1}{1}\right| = 1 \Rightarrow \alpha = \frac{\pi}{4}$

Thus, the polar form of z is
$\sqrt{2}\left(\cos\frac{\pi}{4} + i\sin\frac{\pi}{4}\right)$.

(v) $z = \frac{1+i}{1-i} \times \frac{1+i}{1+i} = i$

$r = |z| = 1$

$\arg(z) = \frac{\pi}{2}$

$\therefore \quad z = \cos\frac{\pi}{2} + i\sin\frac{\pi}{2}$

(vi) $\quad z = \frac{2 + 6\sqrt{3}\,i}{5 + \sqrt{3}\,i} \times \frac{5 - \sqrt{3}i}{5 - \sqrt{3}i}$
$= 1 + i\sqrt{3}$
$r = |z| = 2$

$\theta = \tan^{-1}\left(\frac{\sqrt{3}}{1}\right) = \frac{\pi}{3}$

$\therefore z = 2\left(\cos\frac{\pi}{3} + i\sin\frac{\pi}{3}\right)$

40. $z = \frac{1+7i}{3-4i} \times \frac{3+4i}{3+4i} = -1 + i$

$r = |z| = \sqrt{2}$

$\alpha = \tan^{-1}\left|\frac{1}{-1}\right| = \frac{\pi}{4}$

$\theta = \arg(z) = \pi - \alpha = \frac{3\pi}{4}$

$\therefore z = \sqrt{2}\left(\cos\frac{3\pi}{4} + i\sin\frac{3\pi}{4}\right)$

41. (i) (True)
$z = \frac{1+2i}{1-3i} \times \frac{1+3i}{1+3i} = \frac{-1}{2} + \frac{1}{2}i$

$\therefore |z| = \sqrt{\left(-\frac{1}{2}\right)^2 + \left(\frac{1}{2}\right)^2} = \frac{1}{\sqrt{2}}$

(ii) (True)
$z = \frac{i-1}{\cos\frac{\pi}{3} + i\sin\frac{\pi}{3}} = \frac{i-1}{\frac{1}{2} + i\frac{\sqrt{3}}{2}}$
$= \left(\frac{\sqrt{3}-1}{2}\right) + i\left(\frac{\sqrt{3}+1}{2}\right)$

$\therefore \tan\alpha = \frac{\sqrt{3}+1}{\sqrt{3}-1}$

$= \frac{\tan\frac{\pi}{4} + \tan\frac{\pi}{6}}{1 - \tan\frac{\pi}{4}\tan\frac{\pi}{6}}$

$= \tan\left(\frac{\pi}{4} + \frac{\pi}{6}\right)$

$= \tan\frac{5\pi}{12}$

$\because \quad \alpha = \frac{5\pi}{12}$

$\therefore \arg(z) = \frac{5\pi}{12}$

(iii) (True)
$z = \frac{1+3i}{1-2i} \times \frac{1+2i}{1+2i}$
$= -1 + i$
$r = |z| = \sqrt{2}$

$\alpha = \tan^{-1}\left|\frac{1}{-1}\right| = \frac{\pi}{4}$

$\arg(z) = \pi - \alpha = \frac{3\pi}{4}$

$\therefore$ Polar form
$z = \sqrt{2}\left(\cos\frac{3\pi}{4} + i\sin\frac{3\pi}{4}\right)$

42. (i) Given, $z = -\sqrt{3} + i$

$\Rightarrow r\cos\theta = -\sqrt{3}$ and $r\sin\theta = 1$

On squaring and adding, we get

$$r^2(\cos^2\theta + \sin^2\theta) = 4$$

$$\Rightarrow r = 2 \quad [\because \cos^2\theta + \sin^2\theta = 1]$$

Hence, modulus of $z = 2$.

$\therefore \cos\theta = \frac{-\sqrt{3}}{2}$ and $\sin\theta = \frac{1}{2}$

$$\Rightarrow \theta = \frac{5\pi}{6}$$

Hence, argument of $z = \frac{5\pi}{6}$

$\therefore$ Polar form

$$= 2\left(\cos\frac{5\pi}{6} + i\sin\frac{5\pi}{6}\right)$$

(ii) Given, $z = \frac{-4}{1 + i\sqrt{3}}$

$$= \frac{-4}{1 + i\sqrt{3}} \times \frac{1 - i\sqrt{3}}{1 - i\sqrt{3}}$$

$$= \frac{4(-1 + i\sqrt{3})}{4}$$

$$= -1 + i\sqrt{3}$$

$\Rightarrow r\cos\theta = -1$ and $r\sin\theta = \sqrt{3}$

On squaring and adding, we get

$$r^2(\cos^2\theta + \sin^2\theta) = 4$$

$$\Rightarrow r = 2 \ [\because \sin^2\theta + \cos^2\theta = 1]$$

Hence, modulus of $z = 2$.

$$\therefore \cos\theta = -\frac{1}{2}$$

and $\sin\theta = \frac{\sqrt{3}}{2} \Rightarrow \theta = \frac{2\pi}{3}$

$\therefore$ Polar form

$$= 2\left(\cos\frac{2\pi}{3} + i\sin\frac{2\pi}{3}\right)$$

43. (i) Let $z = 7 - 24i$

$\Rightarrow \text{Re}(z) = 7$

and $|z| = \sqrt{49 + 576} = 25$

Since, $\sqrt{7 - 24i}$

$$= \pm\left\{\sqrt{\frac{|z| + \text{Re}(z)}{2}} - i\sqrt{\frac{|z| - \text{Re}(z)}{2}}\right\}$$

$$= \pm(4 - 3i)$$

(ii) Let $z = 5 + 12i$

$\Rightarrow \text{Re}(z) = 5$ and

$|z| = \sqrt{25 + 144} = 13$

$$\therefore \sqrt{5 + 12i} = \pm\left\{\sqrt{\frac{13+5}{2}} + i\sqrt{\frac{13-5}{2}}\right\}$$

$$= \pm(3 + 2i)$$

(iii) Let $z = -15 - 8i$

$\Rightarrow \text{Re}(z) = -15$

and $|z| = \sqrt{225 + 64} = 17$

$\therefore \sqrt{-15 - 8i}$

$$= \pm\left\{\sqrt{\frac{17-15}{2}} - i\sqrt{\frac{17+15}{2}}\right\}$$

$$= \pm(1 - 4i)$$

(iv) Let $z = i$

$\Rightarrow \text{Re}(z) = 0$ and $|z| = 1$

$$\therefore \sqrt{i} = \pm\left\{\sqrt{\frac{1+0}{2}} + i\sqrt{\frac{1-0}{2}}\right\}$$

$$= \pm\frac{1}{\sqrt{2}}(1 + i)$$

Assertion Reason

1. (a) Given complex number is $26 + \sqrt{-17}$ which can be written as $26 + \sqrt{17}i$, its imaginary part is $\sqrt{17}$.

$\because$ We know that for any complex number $z = a + ib$, a is real part and b is imaginary part of z.

$\therefore$ Both Assertion and Reason are correct and Reason is the corerct explanation of Assertion.

2. (a) Given, $z_1 = 2 - 7i$ and $z_2 = 3 + 3i$ are two complex numbers.

$\because$ Sum of two complex numbers is a complex number.

$\therefore z_1 + z_2 = 5 - 4i$ is a complex number.

Hence, both Assertion and Reason are correct and Reason is the correct explanation of Assertion.

3. (d) $\because$ If $z_1 = a + ib$ and $z_2 = c + id$.

Then, $z_1 - z_2 = (a - c) + i(b - d)$

$\therefore$ Reason is correct.

We have, $z_1 = 5 + 2i$ and

$z_2 = -1 + 4i$, then $z_1 - z_2 = 6 - 2i$

$\therefore$ Assertion is incorrect.

4. (d) **Assertion** We have,

$$i^{-37} = \frac{1}{i^{37}} = \frac{1}{i^{36}i} = \frac{1}{(i^4)^9 \cdot i} = \frac{1}{i}$$

$\therefore$ Assertion is incorrect

Reason Let $z = 1 - i$

Additive inverse of $z = -1 + i$

$\therefore$ Reason is correct.

5. (b) Both Assertion and Reason are correct, but Reason is not the correct explanation of Assertion

$\because z_1 = 2 + 3i$ and $z_2 = 3 - 4i$,

then $z_1 + z_2 = 5 - i$.

6. (c) We know that the conjugate of a complex number is obtained by changing the sign of imaginary part of z.

$\therefore$ Conjugate of $z_i = 4 - 2i$ is $4 + 2i$.

Assertion is correct and Reason is incorrect.

7. (b) Given, $x + iy = \sqrt{\frac{3+i}{1+3i}}$

$$x - iy = \sqrt{\frac{3-i}{1-3i}}$$

Then,

$$(x + iy)(x - iy) = \sqrt{\frac{3+i}{1+3i}} \times \sqrt{\frac{3-i}{1-3i}}$$

$$\Rightarrow x^2 + y^2 = \sqrt{\frac{(3+i)(3-i)}{(1+3i)(1-3i)}} = 1$$

$$\therefore (x^2 + y^2)^2 = (1)^2 = 1$$

Thus, Assertion is correct.

The distance of the complex number $z = a + ib$ from origin is $\sqrt{a^2 + b^2}$, which is called the modulus of z.

Thus, Reason is correct but it is not the explanation of Assertion.

8. (a) Given $z = 3 + 3i$ and $\bar{z} = 3 - 3i$.

Mirror image of z is $\bar{z}$ which is represented by ordered pair $(3, -3)$.

$\therefore$ Both A and R are correct and R is the correct explanation of A.

9. (d) Let $z = -2\sqrt{3} + 2i$

$$\theta = \tan^{-1}\left(\frac{2}{-2\sqrt{3}}\right) = \tan^{-1}\left(\frac{1}{-\sqrt{3}}\right)$$

$\because$ Complex number is in 2nd quadrant, (where real part is negative and imaginary part is positive).

We need to add 'π' to this angle to get the correct argument.

$$\therefore \arg(z) = \pi - \frac{\pi}{6} = \frac{5\pi}{6}.$$

$\therefore$ Reason is correct but Assertion is incorrect.

Case Based

Case 1 (i) (a) $i^{33} = i^{32} \cdot i$

$= (i^4)^8 \cdot i$

$= (1)^8 \cdot i \quad (\because i^4 = 1)$

$= i$

(ii) (d) $(\sqrt{-1})^{-30} = i^{-30}$

$= \frac{1}{i^{30}}$

$= \frac{1}{(i^2)^{15}} = \frac{1}{(-1)^{15}} = -1$

(iii) (b) $\left\{i^{17} - \left(\frac{1}{i}\right)^{34}\right\}^2$

$= \left\{i^{16} \cdot i - \left(\frac{1}{i^2}\right)^{17}\right\}^2$

$= \{(i^2)^8 i - (-1)^{17}\}^2$

$= (i+1)^2 = 2i$

(iv) (a) $i^{107} + i^{112} + i^{122} + i^{117}$

$= i^{106} \cdot i + i^{112} + i^{122} + i^{116} \cdot i$

$= (i^2)^{53} \cdot i + (i^2)^{56} + (i^2)^{61} + (i^2)^{58} \cdot i$

$= (-1)^{53} \cdot i + (-1)^{56} + (-1)^{61} + (-1)^{58} \cdot i$

$= -i + 1 - 1 + i(-1)^{56}$

$= 0$

(v) (c) $z = i^{100} + i^{107}$

$= (i^2)^{50} + (i^2)^{53} \cdot i$

$= (-1)^{50} + (-1)^{53} i$

$= 1 - i$

Case 2 (i) (d) Given, $z = 4 + 5i$

$\Rightarrow \bar{z} = 4 - 5i$

$\Rightarrow \frac{z + \bar{z}}{2} = \frac{4 + 5i + 4 - 5i}{2} = 4$

(ii) (a) Let $z = x + iy$, $\bar{z} = x - iy$

$\therefore (z+3)(\bar{z}+3) = (x + iy + 3)(x - iy + 3)$

$= ((x+3) + iy)((x+3) - iy)$

$= (x+3)^2 + y^2$

$= |z+3|^2$

(iii) (b) Given, $z_1 = 2 - 4i$ and $z_2 = -4 + 3i$

$\Rightarrow z_1 + z_2 = 2 - 4i - 4 + 3i$

$= -2 - i$

$\therefore |z_1 + z_2| = \sqrt{4+1} = \sqrt{5}$

(iv) (a) Given, $z = 5 - 3i$

$\Rightarrow \frac{1}{z} = \frac{1}{5-3i} \times \frac{5+3i}{5+3i}$

$= \frac{5+3i}{34} = \frac{5}{34} + \frac{3}{34} i$

Hence, Multiplicative inverse of z is $\frac{5}{34} + \frac{3}{34} i$

(v) (c) Given, $z = 3 + 4i$, then $\bar{z} = 3 - 4i \Rightarrow |z|^2 = z\bar{z}$

$= (3+4i)(3-4i) = 9 + 16 = 25$

Competition Connect

1. (i) $x^2 + 2 = 0$

$\Rightarrow x^2 = -2$

$\Rightarrow x = \pm \sqrt{2}\, i$

(ii) $x^2 + 4ix + 4i^2 = 0$

$\Rightarrow (x + 2i)^2 = 0$

$\Rightarrow x = -2i, -2i$

(iii) $x^2 - 3\sqrt{2}\, ix + 2\sqrt{2}\, i\, x - 12i^2 = 0$

$\Rightarrow (x - 3\sqrt{2}\, i)(x + 2\sqrt{2} i) = 0$

$\Rightarrow x = 3\sqrt{2}\, i$ or $x = -2\sqrt{2}\, i$

(iv) $3x^2 + 9ix - 2ix - 6i^2 = 0$

$\Rightarrow (x + 3i)(3x - 2i) = 0$

$\Rightarrow x = -3i$ or $x = \frac{2}{3} i$

(v) $(x^2 - 3\sqrt{2}x) - (2ix - 6\sqrt{2}i) = 0$

$\Rightarrow (x - 2i)(x - 3\sqrt{2}) = 0$

$\Rightarrow x = 2i, 3\sqrt{2}$

(vi) $b^2 - 4ac = 1^2 - 4(1)(1) = -3$

$\therefore x = \frac{-1 \pm \sqrt{3}\, i}{2}$

(vii) $b^2 - 4ac = 1^2 - 4(\sqrt{5})(\sqrt{5})$

$= -19$

$\therefore x = \frac{-1 \pm \sqrt{19}\, i}{2\sqrt{5}}$

(viii) $b^2 - 4ac = 900 - 1100 = -200$

$\therefore x = \frac{30 \pm 10\sqrt{2}i}{50} = \frac{3}{5} \pm \frac{\sqrt{2}}{5} i$

(ix) $b^2 - 4ac = -25 - 4(-6)$

$= -25 + 24 = -1$

$\therefore x = \frac{5i \pm i}{2} = 3i, 2i$

(x) $b^2 - 4ac$

$= (3\sqrt{2} - 2i)^2 + 4(6\sqrt{2}i)$

$= (3\sqrt{2} + 2i)^2$

$\therefore x = \frac{(3\sqrt{2} - 2i) \pm (3\sqrt{2} + 2i)}{2}$

$\Rightarrow x = 3\sqrt{2}, -2i$

(xi) $b^2 - 4ac = 9i^2 - 16 = -25$

$\therefore x = \frac{-3i \pm 5i}{4} = \frac{i}{2}, -2i$

(xii) $b^2 - 4ac = (3 + 7i)^2 + 8(3 - 9i)$

$= -16 - 30i$

$\therefore x = \frac{(3+7i) \pm (3 - 5i)}{4}$

$= \frac{3}{2} + \frac{1}{2} i, 3i$

(xiii) $b^2 - 4ac = (7 - i)^2 - 4(18 - i)$

$= -24 - 10i$

$\therefore x = \frac{(7 - i) \pm (1 - 5i)}{2}$

$= 4 - 3i, 3 + 2i$

(xiv) $b^2 - 4ac = (-4)^2 - 4(2)(3)$

$= 16 - 24 = -8$

$\Rightarrow x = \frac{4 \pm 2\sqrt{2}\, i}{4} = 1 \pm \frac{1}{\sqrt{2}} i$

Competition Edge Up

1. (c) $\text{Re}\left(\frac{z - 2i}{z + 2i}\right) = 0$

$\Rightarrow \frac{z - 2i}{z + 2i} + \left(\overline{\frac{z - 2i}{z + 2i}}\right) = 0$

$\Rightarrow \frac{(z - 2i)(\bar{z} - 2i) + (z + 2i)(\bar{z} + 2i)}{(z + 2i)(\bar{z} - 2i)} = 0$

$\Rightarrow z\bar{z} - 2i\bar{z} - 2iz - 4 + z\bar{z} + 2iz + 2\bar{z}i - 4 = 0$

$\Rightarrow 2|z|^2 = 8 \Rightarrow |z|^2 = 4 \Rightarrow |z| = 2$

$\therefore \quad |z - (6 + 8i)|_{\min} = 10 + 2 = 12$

2. (c) $z = \frac{1 + i\cos\theta}{1 - 2i\cos\theta}$

$= \frac{1 + i\cos\theta}{1 - 2i\cos\theta} \times \frac{1 + 2i\cos\theta}{1 + 2i\cos\theta}$

$= \frac{1 + 2i\cos\theta + i\cos\theta - 2\cos^2\theta}{1 + 4\cos^2\theta}$

$= \frac{1 - 2\cos^2\theta}{1 + 4\cos^2\theta} + i\frac{3\cos\theta}{1 + 4\cos^2\theta}$

$\because z$ is purely imaginary

So, $\frac{1 - 2\cos^2\theta}{1 + 4\cos^2\theta} = 0$

$1 - 2\cos^2\theta = 0 \quad [\because 1 + 4\cos^2\theta \neq 0]$

$\Rightarrow \cos\theta = \pm\frac{1}{\sqrt{2}}$

So, $\theta = -\frac{3\pi}{4}, -\frac{\pi}{4}, \frac{\pi}{4}, \frac{3\pi}{4}, \frac{5\pi}{4}, \frac{7\pi}{4}$

Sum of all values $= \frac{12\pi}{4} = 3\pi$

3. (b) Let $z = x + iy$

Given, $I_m = \left(\frac{z+1}{z+2}\right) = \frac{1}{5}$

$$\text{Im}\left(\frac{(x+1)+iy}{(x+2)+iy}\right) = \frac{1}{5}$$

$$\Rightarrow \text{Im}\left(\frac{((x+1)+iy)\times((x+2)-iy)}{((x+2)+iy)((x+2)-iy)}\right) = \frac{1}{5}$$

$$\Rightarrow \frac{y(x+2)-y(x+1)}{(x+2)^2+y^2} = \frac{1}{5}$$

and $|z+2| = 1$

$\Rightarrow (x+2)^2 + y^2 = 1$

So, $y(x+2) - y(x+1) = \frac{1}{5}$

$\Rightarrow y = \frac{1}{5}$

$\because (x+2)^2 + y^2 = 1$

$\Rightarrow (x+2)^2 = 1 - \frac{1}{25} = \frac{24}{25}$

$\Rightarrow x + 2 = \frac{2\sqrt{6}}{5}$ ...(i)

$|\text{Re}(\overline{z+2})| = |\text{Re}(\bar{z}+2)| = (x+2)$

Using Eq. (i),

$$|\text{Re}(\overline{z+2})| = \frac{2\sqrt{6}}{5}$$

4. (d) We have,

$$z^2 + i\bar{z} = 0$$

$\Rightarrow z^2 = -i\bar{z} \Rightarrow |z^2| = |-i\bar{z}|$

$\Rightarrow |z^2| = |z|$

$\therefore |z|^2 - |z| = 0$

$\Rightarrow |z|(|z| - 1) = 0$

$|z| = 0$ (not comparable)

$\therefore |z| = 1$

So, $|z^2| = 1$

5. (d) We have, $z = \frac{1}{2} - 2i$

and $|z+1| = \alpha z + \beta(1+i)$

$\Rightarrow \left|\frac{1}{2} - 2i + 1\right| = \alpha\left(\frac{1}{2} - 2i\right) + \beta(1+i)$

$\Rightarrow \left|\frac{3}{2} - 2i\right| = \frac{\alpha}{2} - 2\alpha i + \beta + \beta i$

$\Rightarrow \left|\frac{3}{2} - 2i\right| = \left(\frac{\alpha}{2} + \beta\right) + (\beta - 2\alpha)i$

$\Rightarrow \sqrt{\frac{9}{4} + 4} = \left(\frac{\alpha}{2} + \beta\right) + (\beta - 2\alpha)i$

$\Rightarrow \beta - 2\alpha = 0$ and $\frac{\alpha}{2} + \beta = \frac{5}{2}$

$\Rightarrow \beta = 2\alpha$ and $\frac{\alpha}{2} + 2\alpha = \frac{5}{2} \Rightarrow \alpha = 1$

Also, $\beta = 2$

$\therefore \alpha + \beta = 1 + 2 = 3$

6. (a) $a + 5b = 42 \Rightarrow b = \frac{42-a}{5}$

So, $(a, b) = \{(2, 8), (7, 7), (12, 6), (17, 5), (22, 4), (27, 3), (32, 2) (37, 1)\} \Rightarrow 8$ pairs

So, $m = 8$

$\therefore, \sum_{n=1}^{8}(1 - i^{n!}) = \sum_{n=1}^{8} 1 - \sum_{n=1}^{8} i^{n!}$

$= 8 - (i + (-1) + (-1) + 1 + 1 + 1 + 1 + 1)$

$= 8 - (i + 3) = 5 - i = x + iy$

So, $x = 5, y = -1$

Therefore,
$x + y + m = 5 - 1 + 8 = 12$

7. (c) Given, $(\bar{z})^2 + |z| = 0$ ... (i)

Let $z = x + iy$
So, $\bar{z} = x - iy$
From Eq. (i),
$(x - iy)^2 + |x + iy| = 0$

$\Rightarrow (x^2 - y^2) + \sqrt{x^2 + y^2} - 2xyi = 0$

On equating real and imaginary parts from both sides, we get

$2xy = 0$ ... (ii)

and $x^2 - y^2 + \sqrt{x^2 + y^2} = 0$ ... (iii)

From Eq. (i), there are two cases arises

Case I when $x = 0$ and $y \neq 0$

From Eq. (iii),
$-y^2 + |y| = 0 \Rightarrow |y| = y^2 = |y|^2$

$\Rightarrow y = 0, \pm 1$ but $y \neq 0$

So, $y = \pm 1$

$\therefore z = 0 + i$ or $z = 0 - i$ i.e. $z = i$ or $z = -i$

Case II when $x \neq 0$ and $y = 0$

From Eq. (iii), $x^2 + |x| = 0$

$\Rightarrow x = 0$ only which is not possible because $x \neq 0$.

Hence, $z = \pm i$ (finally)

Now, $\alpha = i - i = 0$ and
$\beta = (i)(-i) = -i^2 = -(-1) = 1$

Therefore,

$4(\alpha^2 + \beta^2) = 4(0 + 1) = 4$

8. (c) Given $|z - 1| = 1$

$(x-1)^2 + y^2 = 1$ ...(i)

and $(\sqrt{2} - 1)(z + \bar{z}) - i(z - \bar{z}) = 2\sqrt{2}$

$(\sqrt{2} - 1)(2x) - i(2iy) = 2\sqrt{2}$

$[\because z + \bar{z} = 2x, z - \bar{z} = 2yi]$

$2(\sqrt{2} - 1)x + 2y = 2\sqrt{2}$

$(\sqrt{2} - 1)x + y = \sqrt{2}$ ...(ii)

On solving Eqs. (i) and (ii), we get

$$x = 1, \frac{1}{2 - \sqrt{2}}$$

when $x = 1$, then $y = 1$

$\therefore z_2 = 1 + i$

and when $x = \frac{1}{2-\sqrt{2}}$, then

$$y = \sqrt{2} - \frac{1}{\sqrt{2}}$$

$\therefore z_1 = 1 + \frac{1}{\sqrt{2}} + \frac{i}{\sqrt{2}}$

$\therefore |\sqrt{2}z_1 - z_2|^2$

$= z\left|\sqrt{2}\left(1 + \frac{1}{\sqrt{2}}\right) + i - 1 - i\right|^2$

$= (\sqrt{2})^2 = 2$

9. (a) Given, $z_1 + z_2 = 5$

$z_1^3 + z_2^3 = 20 + 15i$

$\Rightarrow z_1^3 + z_2^3 = (z_1 + z_2)((z_1 + z_2)^2 - 3z_1z_2)$

$\Rightarrow 20 + 15i = 5(5^2 - 3z_1z_2)$

$\Rightarrow 4 + 3i = 25 - 3z_1z_2$

$\Rightarrow z_1z_2 = 7 - i$

$z_1 + z_2 = 5$

$\Rightarrow (z_1 + z_2)^2 = 5^2$

$z_1^2 + z_2^2 + 2z_1z_2 = 25$

$z_1^2 + z_2^2 + 14 - 2i = 25$

$z_1^2 + z_2^2 = 11 + 2i$

On squaring both sides,

$(z_1^2 + z_2^2)^2 = (11 + 2i)^2$

$z_1^4 + z_2^4 + 2(z_1z_2)^2 = 121 - 4 + 44i$

$z_1^4 + z_2^4 + 2(7 - i)^2 = 117 + 44i$

$z_1^4 + z_2^4 + 2(49 - 1 - 14i) = 117 + 44i$

$z_1^4 + z_2^4 = 21 + 72i$

$\therefore |z_1^4 + z_2^4| = \sqrt{21^2 + 72^2} = 75$

10. (d) According to the question,

$$\left|\frac{z_1 - 2z_2}{\frac{1}{2} - z_1\bar{z}_2}\right| = 2 \Rightarrow \frac{|z_1 - 2z_2|}{\left|\frac{1}{2} - z_1\bar{z}_2\right|} = 2$$

($\because$ modulus is distributive)

$$\Rightarrow |z_1 - 2z_2| = 2\left|\frac{1}{2} - z_1\bar{z}_2\right|$$

On squaring both sides,

$$|z_1 - 2z_2|^2 = |1 - 2z_1\bar{z}_2|^2$$

$$\Rightarrow (z_1 - 2z_2)(\bar{z}_1 - 2\bar{z}_2) = (1 - 2z_1\bar{z}_2)(1 - 2\bar{z}_1 z_2)$$

($\because |z|^2 = z\bar{z}$)

$$\Rightarrow |z_1|^2 + 4|z_2|^2 - 2\bar{z}_1 z_2 - 2z_1\bar{z}_2 = 1 - 2\bar{z}_1 z_2 - 2z_1\bar{z}_2 + 4|z_1|^2|z_2|^2$$

$$\Rightarrow |z_1|^2 + 4|z_2|^2 - 4|z_1|^2|z_2|^2 - 1 = 0$$

$$\Rightarrow (|z_1|^2 - 1)(1 - 4|z_2|^2) = 0$$

$$\Rightarrow |z_1| = 1 \text{ and } |z_2| = \frac{1}{2}$$

11. (d) If $|z| \geq 1$

$\Rightarrow z$ lie out side or on circle

$$|z| = 1$$

$$\left|z + \frac{3}{2} + 2i\right|$$

$\Rightarrow$ distance of z from $\left(-\frac{3}{2}, -2\right)$

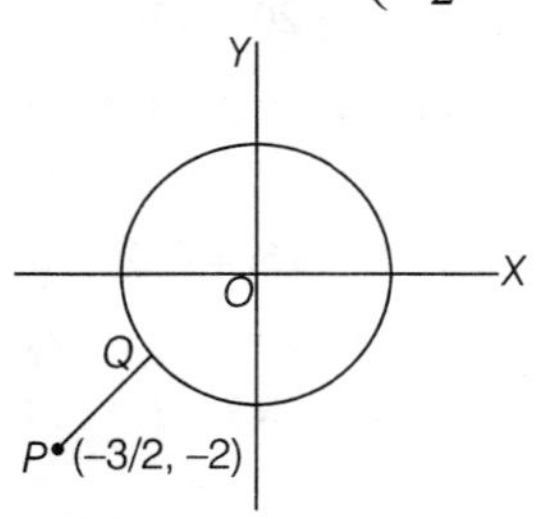

So, minimum value of PQ

$$= PO - QO$$

$$= \sqrt{\left(\frac{-3}{2} - 0\right)^2 + (-2-0)^2} - 1$$

$$= \sqrt{\frac{9}{4} + 4} - 1 \qquad [\because \cos\theta = 1]$$

$$= \sqrt{\frac{25}{4}} - 1 = \frac{5}{2} - 1 = \frac{3}{2}$$

So, minimum value of $\left|z + \frac{1}{2}(3 + 4i)\right|$ is $\frac{3}{2}$.

12. (c) Given, $|z - i| = |z + i|$

$$= |z - 1| \qquad \text{...(i)}$$

From Eq. (i), we observe that geometrically, z will be circumcentre of triangle with vertices $A(1)$, $B(i)$, $C(-i)$ as shown in figure below

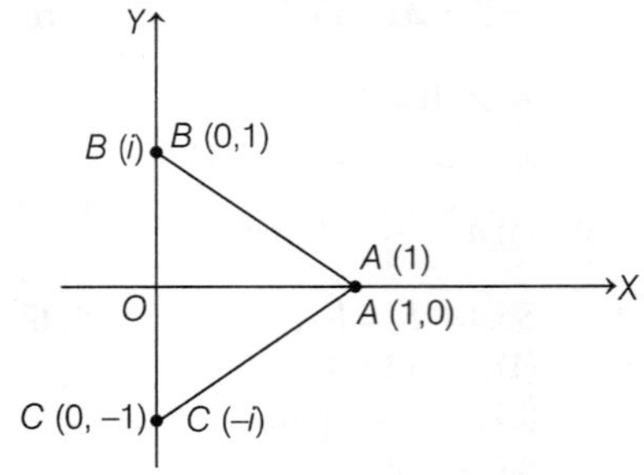

So, only one element exists in the set S.

Hence, $n(S) = 1$

13. (b) $S_1 = \{z \in C : |z| \leq 5\}$

$$\Rightarrow x^2 + y^2 \leq 25$$

$$S_2 = \left\{z \in C : \text{Im}\frac{(z + 1 - \sqrt{3}i)}{1 - \sqrt{3}i} \geq 0\right\}$$

$$\text{Im}\left(\frac{z}{1 - \sqrt{3}i} + \frac{(1 - \sqrt{3}i)}{1 - \sqrt{3}i}\right) \geq 0$$

$$\text{Im}\left(\frac{z}{1 - \sqrt{3}i} + 1\right) \geq 0$$

$$\text{Im}\left(\frac{z}{1 - \sqrt{3}i} \times \frac{1 + \sqrt{3}i}{1 + \sqrt{3}i}\right) \geq 0$$

$$\text{Im}(x + iy)(1 + \sqrt{3}i) \geq 0$$

$$\Rightarrow \sqrt{3}x + y \geq 0, \theta \Rightarrow 120°$$

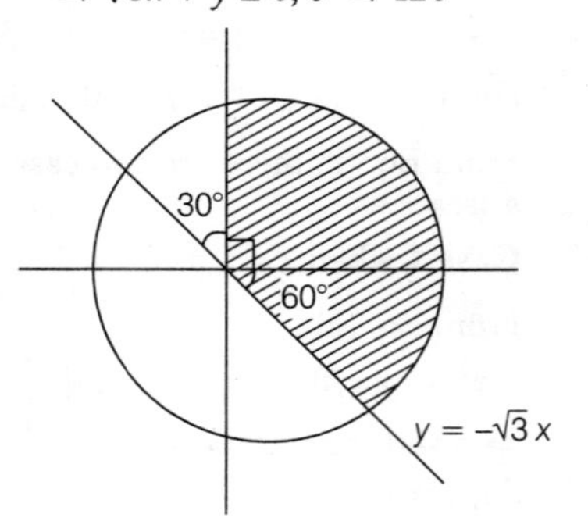

$$S_3 = z \in C : \text{Re}(z) \geq 0\} \Rightarrow x \geq 0$$

$$\therefore \text{Area} = \frac{\pi r^2(150°)}{360}$$

$$= \pi \times \frac{5 \times 5 \times 150}{360}$$

$$= \pi\,\frac{5 \times 5 \times 5}{12} = \frac{125\pi}{12}$$

14. (b) $|z - 1| \leq 2$,

$$z + \bar{z} + i(z - \bar{z}) \leq 2, \text{Im}(z) \geq 0$$

Let $z = x + iy$ and $\bar{z} = x - iy$

$$|(x - 1) + iy| \leq 2$$

$$(x - 1)^2 + y^2 = 4$$

Centre of circle (1, 0)

Radius = 2;

$$\text{Im } z + \bar{2} + i(z - \bar{2}) \leq 2$$

$$\Rightarrow 2x + i(2iy) \leq 2 \Rightarrow 2x - 2y \leq 2$$

$$\Rightarrow x - y \leq 1 \text{ and Im}(z) \geq 0, y \geq 0$$

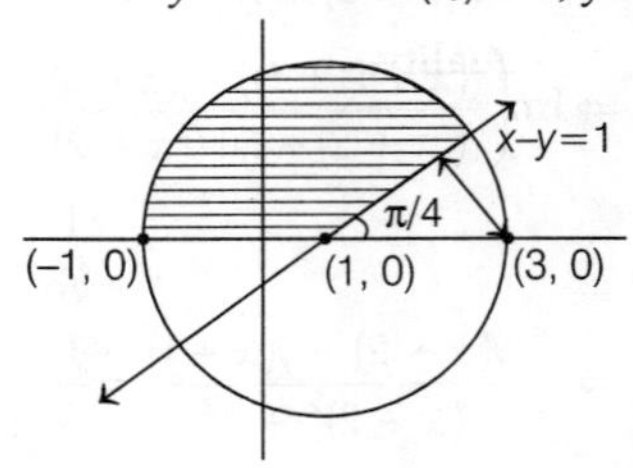

$\therefore$ Required area = Area of semicircle – Area of sector

$$= \frac{\pi(r^2)}{2} - \frac{\pi r^2\theta}{360}$$

$$= \frac{\pi(2)^2}{2} - \frac{\pi(2)^2 \times 45°}{360°}$$

$$= 2\pi - \frac{\pi}{2} = \frac{3\pi}{2} \text{ sq. units}$$

15. (a) Given, 2 and 6 are the roots of the equation $ax^2 + bx + 1 = 0$

$$\therefore \text{Sum of roots} = -\frac{b}{a} = 8$$

$$\text{Product of roots} = \frac{1}{a} = 12$$

$$\Rightarrow \quad a = \frac{1}{12} \text{ so, } b = -\frac{2}{3}$$

Now, $2a + b = \frac{2}{12} - \frac{2}{3} = -\frac{1}{2}$

and $6a + b = \frac{6}{12} - \frac{2}{3} = -\frac{1}{6}$

Now,

$$\frac{1}{2a + b} + \frac{1}{6a + b} = -2 - 6 = -8$$

and $\left(\frac{1}{2a + b}\right)\left(\frac{1}{6a + b}\right) = 12$

$\therefore$ Required quadratic equation is

$$x^2 + 8x + 12 = 0$$

16. (d) $\dfrac{ax^2 + 2(a + 1)x + 9a + 4}{x^2 - 8x + 32} < 0, \quad \forall x \in R$

$$\Rightarrow \frac{ax^2 + 2(a + 1)x + 9a + 4}{(x - 4)^2 + 16} < 0, \quad \forall x \in R$$

$$\Rightarrow ax^2 + 2(a + 1)x + 9a + 4 < 0, \quad \forall x \in R$$

coefficient of $x^2 < 0$ and $D < 0$

$a < 0$ and $D < 0$

$\therefore$ No positive integral values of a.

Hence, $|S| = 0$

Chapter-5

Linear Equations

1. (i) (False)

It does not involve the sign of equality.

(ii) True

2. $8x + 7y \le 10$

3. (i) (True)

Becuase numerical inequality contains only numerical values.

(ii) (True)

Because numerical inequality contains only numerical values.

(iii) True

(iv) True

(v) True

(vi) True

(vii) True

(viii) (True)

$$ax + by < c$$
$$ax + 0 \cdot y < c$$
$$ax < c$$

$\Rightarrow$ Linear inequality in one variable x.

4. (i) Numerical

(ii) Double

(iii) Slack

5. (b)

6. (i) (True)

For $x = 15$,

$3 \times 15 < 50$

$45 < 50$, true

(ii) (False)

When $x = 0$,

$0 - 7 > 8$

$-7 > 8$ (not true)

(iii) (True)

When $x = 4$,

$\frac{2}{4} + 4 \le 20$

$\frac{9}{2} \le 20$

(true) $\left[\because \frac{9}{2} < 20\right]$

7. For $x = 0$,

$y \le 6$

Thus, (0, 0), (0, 1), (0, 2), (0, 3), (0, 4), (0, 5) and (0, 6) are the solution sets.

8. (i) True

(ii) (True)

Inequality sign remains same when we do addition or subtraction in any inequality.

(iii) (True)

When we multiply or divide by a negative number, then the inequality will be reversed.

(iv) (True)

$$(-5)(2x - 4) > 7x(-5)$$
$$\Rightarrow -10x + 20 > (-35)x$$
$$\Rightarrow 35x - 10x > (-20)$$
$$\Rightarrow 25x > (-20)$$
$$\Rightarrow 5x > (-4)$$

9. (i) Given, $9x + 9 < 5x + 5$

$\Rightarrow 4x < -4 \Rightarrow x < -1$,

$\forall x \in R, x \in (-\infty, -1)$

(ii) Given,

$$\frac{2x - 1}{3} \ge \left(\frac{3x - 2}{4}\right) - \left(\frac{2 - x}{5}\right)$$
$$\Rightarrow \frac{2x - 1}{3} \ge \frac{15x - 10 - 8 + 4x}{4 \times 5}$$
$$\Rightarrow 40x - 20 \ge 57x - 54$$
$$\Rightarrow -17x \ge -34$$
$$x \le 2$$

$\therefore$ Solution set is $(-\infty, 2]$.

(iii) Given, $8 + 2x \ge \frac{5x + 19}{3}$

$$\Rightarrow 3(8 + 2x) \ge 5x + 19$$
$$\Rightarrow 24 + 6x \ge 5x + 19$$
$$\Rightarrow x \ge -5$$

Thus, the solution set is $[-5, \infty)$.

(iv) Given, $|x - 1| > 5$

$\Rightarrow (x - 1) > 5$

and $(x - 1) < (-5)$

$\Rightarrow x > 6$ and $x < (-4)$

Thus, the solution set is $(-\infty, -4) \cup (6, \infty)$.

(v) Given, $|x + 2| \le 9$

$$\Rightarrow -9 \le x + 2 \le 9$$
$$\Rightarrow -11 \le x \le 7$$
$$x \in [-11, 7]$$

(vi) We have,

$$\Rightarrow \frac{2}{x - 4} < -1 \text{ and } \frac{2}{x - 4} > 1$$
$$\Rightarrow \frac{2}{x - 4} + 1 < 0$$
$$\text{and } \frac{2}{x - 4} - 1 > 0$$
$$\Rightarrow \frac{-2 + x}{x - 4} < 0 \text{ and } \frac{6 - x}{x - 4} > 0$$

$x < 2$, $x < 6$ and $x \ne 4$ (given)

$\Rightarrow x < 2$

Thus, the solution set is $(-\infty, 2)$.

10. (d)(A) $2 + x > 2$

$\Rightarrow x > 0, \forall x \in N$

(B) $5x > -5$

$\Rightarrow x > -1, \forall x \in W$

(C) $2x > -12$

$x > -6$

$\Rightarrow x \in (-6, \infty)$

(D) $24 > 12x$

$2 > x \Rightarrow x \in (-\infty, 2)$

11. (True)

We have, $68° < F < 77°$

On putting $F = \frac{9}{5}C + 32$,

$$68 < \frac{9}{5}C + 32 < 77$$
$$\Rightarrow 36 < \frac{9}{5}C < 45$$
$$\Rightarrow 20 < C < 25$$
$$\text{or } 20° < C < 25°$$

12. (i) Given, $3x - 19 < 50$

$$\Rightarrow 3x < 50 + 19$$
$$\Rightarrow 3x < 69$$
$$\Rightarrow x < 23$$

(ii) Given, $\frac{9x + 5}{2} < \frac{7x + 21}{3}$

$$\Rightarrow 3(9x + 5) < 2(7x + 21)$$
$$\Rightarrow 27x + 15 < 14x + 42$$
$$\Rightarrow 13x < 27$$
$$\Rightarrow x < \frac{27}{13}$$

(iii) We have,

$$-2 + \frac{7x}{21} \le \frac{8}{7}$$
$$\Rightarrow -2 + \frac{x}{3} \le \frac{8}{7}$$
$$\Rightarrow 7(-6 + x) \le 24$$
$$\Rightarrow -42 + 7x \le 24$$
$$\Rightarrow 7x \le 66$$
$$\Rightarrow x \le \frac{66}{7}$$

(iv) We have, $\frac{9x}{2} \le \frac{5 - 2x + 6}{3}$

$$\Rightarrow 3 \times 9x \le 2(11 - 2x)$$
$$\Rightarrow 27x \le 22 - 4x$$
$$\Rightarrow 31x \le 22$$
$$\Rightarrow x \le \frac{22}{31}$$

(v) We have, $9x + 2 < \frac{4x - 5}{5}$

$$\Rightarrow 45x + 10 < 4x - 5$$

$\Rightarrow \quad 41x < -15$

$\Rightarrow \quad x < -\frac{15}{41}$

(vi) We have,

$$8 < \frac{-9x+5}{2} < -1$$

$\Rightarrow \quad 16 < -9x + 5 < -2$

$\Rightarrow \quad 11 < -9x < -7$

$\Rightarrow -11 > 9x > 7$

$\Rightarrow -\frac{11}{9} > x > \frac{7}{9}$

(vii) We have,

$$2 \times 5 \le -9x + 8 \le 3 \times 5$$

$\Rightarrow \quad 10 \le -9x + 8 \le 15$

$\Rightarrow \quad 2 \le -9x \le 7$

$\Rightarrow -2 \ge 9x \ge -7$

$\Rightarrow -\frac{2}{9} \ge x \ge -\frac{7}{9}$

13. (c)

14. (d) On the number line, all the points less than and including (–2) are satisfying option (d).

15. (b) – 6 is also included.

16. (i) We have, $7x + 3 < 5x + 9$

$\Rightarrow \quad 7x - 5x < 9 - 3$

$\Rightarrow \quad 2x < 6 \Rightarrow x < 3$

Graphical representation

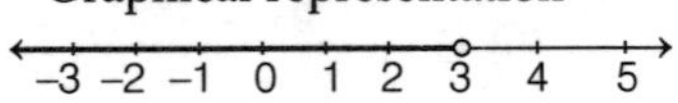

(ii) We have,

$$\frac{5-2x}{3} \le \frac{x}{6} - 5$$

$\Rightarrow \quad \frac{5-2x}{3} \le \frac{x-30}{6}$

$\Rightarrow \quad 10 - 4x \le x - 30$

$\Rightarrow \quad 40 \le 5x$

$\Rightarrow \quad x \ge 8$

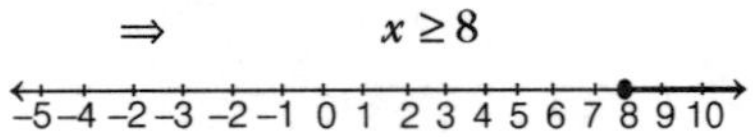

(iii) We have,

$$\frac{x}{2} \ge \frac{(5x-2)}{3} - \frac{(7x-3)}{5}$$

$$\frac{x}{2} \ge \frac{25x - 10 - 21x + 9}{15}$$

$\Rightarrow 15x \ge 2(4x - 1)$

$\Rightarrow 15x \ge 8x - 2$

$\Rightarrow 15x - 8x \ge (-2)$

$\Rightarrow \quad 7x \ge -2$

$\Rightarrow \quad x \ge -\frac{2}{7}$

Thus, the graphical representation is

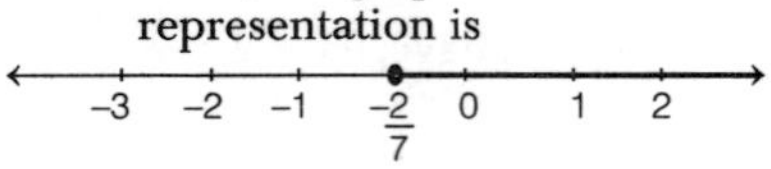

17. (i) Let x be the marks obtained in third unit test.

According to the question,

$$\frac{20 + 35 + x}{3} \ge 25$$

$\Rightarrow \quad 55 + x \ge 75$

$\Rightarrow \quad x \ge 20$

Thus, Rohit must obtain 20 marks minimum.

(ii) x pens of ₹ 20 i.e. $20x$

y registers of ₹ 40 i.e. $40y$

Then, the inequality is

$$20x + 40y \le 190$$

(iii) Let x be the shortest length.

According to question,

Lengths are x, $(x + 3)$, $5x$.

Thus, the inequality is

$x + (x + 3) + 5x \le 51$

$7x + 3 \le 51$

(iv) Let x and $x + 2$ are two consecutive even positive integers.

Since, both are larger than 3.

$\Rightarrow \quad x > 3 \quad \ldots$(i)

According to the question,

$x + x + 2 < 20$

$\Rightarrow \quad 2x + 2 < 20$

$\Rightarrow \quad 2x < 20 - 2$

$\Rightarrow \quad 2x < 18$

$\Rightarrow \quad x < 9 \quad \ldots$(ii)

From Eqs. (i) and (ii), we get

$$3 < x < 9$$

Since, x is an even number

$\Rightarrow \quad x = 4, 6, 8$

Thus, the required possible pairs are

(4, 6), (6, 8) and (8, 10).

(v) Let x L of 10% acid solution is required to be added.

Then, total mixture

$= (x + 500)$ L

$\Rightarrow$ 10% x + 28% of 500 > 20% of $(x + 500)$

$\Rightarrow \frac{x}{10} + \frac{28}{100} \times 500 > \frac{20}{100}(x + 500)$

$\Rightarrow \frac{x}{10} + 140 > \frac{x + 500}{5}$

$\Rightarrow x + 1400 > 2(x + 500)$

$\Rightarrow x + 1400 > 2x + 1000$

$\Rightarrow \quad x < 400$

Assertion-Reason

1. (b) Let us consider some inequalities

$ax + b < 0 \quad \ldots$(i)

$ax + b > 0 \quad \ldots$(ii)

$ax + b \le 0 \quad \ldots$(iii)

$ax + b \ge 0 \quad \ldots$(iv)

$ax + by > c \quad \ldots$(v)

$ax + by \le c \quad \ldots$(vi)

$ax^2 + bx + c > 0 \quad \ldots$(vii)

$ax^2 + bx + c \le 0 \quad \ldots$(viii)

Inequalities (i), (ii), (v) and (vii) are strict inequalities, while inequalities (iii), (iv), (vi) and (viii) are slack inequalities.

∴ Both Assertion and Reason are correct but Reason is not the correct explanation of Assertion.

2. (a) We have, for $x \in R$ and $x < 4$

Now, subtract 4 from both sides, we get

$$x - 4 < 4 - 4 \Rightarrow x - 4 < 0$$

∴ Both Assertion and Reason are true and Reason is the correct explanation of Assertion.

3. (d) We have, $a < b$ and $c < 0$

$\Rightarrow \quad \frac{a}{c} > \frac{b}{c}$

∴ Assertion is false but Reason is true.

4. (a) We have,

$$x - 3 \le 4$$

On adding 3 both sides, we get

$x - 3 + 3 \le 4 + 3$

$\Rightarrow \quad x \le 7$

$\Rightarrow \quad x \in \{1, 2, 3, 4, 5, 6, 7\}$

∴ {1, 2, 3, 4, 5, 6, 7} is the solution set of the given inequality.

∴ Both Assertion and Reason are true and Reason is the correct explanation of Assertion.

5. (b) We have, $|3x - 5| > 10$

$\Rightarrow \quad 3x - 5 < -10$ or $3x - 5 > 10$

$\Rightarrow \quad 3x < -5$ or $3x > 15$

$\Rightarrow \quad x < \frac{-5}{3}$ or $x > 5$

$\therefore \quad x \in \left(-\infty, -\frac{5}{3}\right) \cup (5, \infty)$

∴ Both Assertion and Reason are true but Reason is not the correct explanation of Assertion.

6. (b) We have,

$4x+3>15$

$\Rightarrow \quad 4x>12$

$\Rightarrow \quad x>3$

$\therefore \quad x \in (3, \infty)$

$\therefore$ Both Assertion and Reason are true but Reason is not the correct explanation of Assertion.

7. (c) We have, $x-4<3$

$\Rightarrow \quad x<7$

Graphical solution set is given by

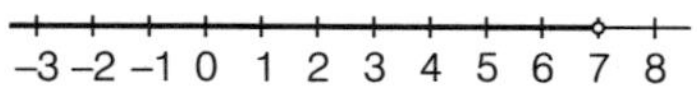

$\therefore$ Assertion is true.

Here, $2x+5<6$ is not a slack inequality.

$\therefore$ Reason is false.

8. (c) We have, $3x+8>20$

$\Rightarrow \quad 3x>20-8$

$\Rightarrow \quad 3x>12$

$\Rightarrow \quad x>4$

$\Rightarrow \quad x \in \{5, 6, 7, 8, \dots\}$

$\therefore$ Assertion is true.

Now, we have,

$5x+4<6x+8$

$\Rightarrow \quad 5x-6x<8-4$

$\Rightarrow \quad -x<4$

$\Rightarrow \quad x>-4$

$\Rightarrow \quad x \in (-4, \infty)$

$\therefore$ Reason is false.

9. (d) We have, $6x<42$, which represents an inequality.

$\therefore$ Assertion is false.

10. (a) We have, $3x-2<2x$

Multiplying (-4) on both sides, we get

$(-4)(3x-2)>(-4)(2x)$

$\Rightarrow \quad -12x+8>-8x$

$\Rightarrow \quad 8>-8x+12x$

$\Rightarrow \quad 8>4x$

$\Rightarrow \quad 2>x$

$\therefore$ Both Assertion and Reason are true and Reason is the correct explanation of Assertion.

11. (d) Inequality sign remains same when we do addition or subtraction in any inequality.

$\therefore$ Assertion is false but Reason is true.

Case Based

1. (i) (c) We know that

Profit = Revenue − Cost

$\therefore$ In order to realise some profit, revenue should be greater than the cost.

Thus, we should have $R(x)>C(x)$

$\Rightarrow \quad 80x+1000>20x+7000$

$\Rightarrow \quad 80x+1000-20x>20x+7000-20x$

$\Rightarrow \quad 60x+1000>7000$

$\Rightarrow \quad 60x+1000-1000>7000-1000$

$\Rightarrow \quad 60x>6000 \Rightarrow x>10$

Hence, the manufacturer must sell more than 10 items to realise some profit.

(ii) (a) In order to realise some profit, we should have

$R(x)>C(x)$

$\Rightarrow \quad 6x+50>4x+400$

$\Rightarrow \quad 6x-4x>400-50$

$\Rightarrow \quad 2x>350$

$\Rightarrow \quad x>175$

(iii) (d) We have, $b>0$ and $x<b$

It means x is always less than some positive quantity.

$\therefore x$ may be a real number.

2. (i) Given, $90 \le IQ \le 150$

$\Rightarrow \quad 90 \le \frac{MA}{15} \times 100 \le 150$

$\Rightarrow \quad \frac{90\times15}{100} \le MA \le \frac{150\times15}{100}$

$\Rightarrow \quad \frac{27}{2} \le MA \le \frac{45}{2}$

$\Rightarrow \quad 13\frac{1}{2} \le MA \le 22\frac{1}{2}$

$\therefore$ Range of MA is $13\frac{1}{2} \le MA \le 22\frac{1}{2}$.

(ii) Given, $IQ = \frac{MA}{CA} \times 100$

$\Rightarrow \quad MA = \frac{IQ \times CA}{100}$

and $8 \le MA \le 16$

$8 \le \frac{IQ \times 10}{100} \le 16$

$\Rightarrow \quad \frac{8\times100}{10} \le IQ \le \frac{16\times100}{10}$

$\Rightarrow \quad 80 \le IQ \le 160$

$\therefore$ Range of IQ is $80 \le IQ \le 160$

(iii) We have, $3x-5<x+7$

$\Rightarrow \quad 3x-5+5<x+7+5$

$\Rightarrow \quad 3x<x+12$

$\Rightarrow \quad 3x-x<x+12-x$

$\Rightarrow \quad 2x<12$

$\Rightarrow \quad \frac{2x}{2}<\frac{12}{2}$

$\Rightarrow \quad x<6$

$\because \quad x$ is a whole number

$\therefore \quad x \in \{0, 1, 2, 3, 4, 5\}$

Chapter-6

Permutations and Combinations

1. Fundamental principle of counting, $3\times2=6$ pairs of a pant and a shirt.

2. $m \times n$

3. (c) 3 school bags can be shared in 3 ways.

4 tiffin boxes can be shared in 4 ways and 3 water bottles can be shared in 3 ways.

$\therefore$ Total numbers of ways

$=4\times3\times3=36$ ways

4. (d) $(m+n)$ ways

5. Number of ways a person can enter the hall and then come out

$=3\times2=6$ ways

6. (a) | A | B | C |

Flag A to be coloured in 6 ways

Flag B to be coloured in 5 ways

Flag C to be coloured in 4 ways.

$\therefore$ Total number of ways

$=6\times5\times4=120$

7. (i) True (ii) False

8. In a three letter word, let the first letter be taken from any of 26 alphabets.

So, there are 26 alphabets/ways.

In second letter, there are 25 ways. Similarly, in the third letter there are 24 ways.

$\therefore$ Total number of ways/words

$=26\times25\times24=15600$

9. (d) A man can go Delhi to Agra by choosing any of the 10 buses.

So, for travelling Delhi to Agra, he has 10 ways.

In case of returning, he will have one way less i.e. the way in which he travelled.

So, in returning, he has 9 ways.

$\therefore$ Total number of ways

$=10\times9=90$ ways

10. (d)

11. Total number of possible outcomes can be 8.
First coin will give either H or T (2 ways)
Second coin will give either H or T (2 ways)
Third coin will give either H or T (2 ways)
So, total ways $= 2\times 2\times 2 = 8$ ways

12. True **13.** True

14. (i) $0! = 1$
(ii) $5! = 5\times4\times3\times2\times1 = 120$
(iii) $6! = 6\times5\times4\times3\times2\times1 = 720$
(iv) $7! - 2! = 7\times5\times4\times3\times2! - 2!$
$= 2!(35\times12 - 1)$
$= 2!\times 419 = 838$
(v) $\dfrac{5!}{2!} = \dfrac{5\times4\times3\times2!}{2!} = 60$
(vi) $\dfrac{10!}{8!2!} = \dfrac{10\times9\times8!}{8!\times2!} = \dfrac{90}{2} = 45$

15. (a)

16. (c) $\dfrac{4!}{2!(4-2)!} = \dfrac{4\times3\times2!}{2!\times2!} = \dfrac{12}{2} = 6$

17. (i) $\dfrac{1}{6!} + \dfrac{1}{8\times7\times6!}$
$= \dfrac{x}{10\times9\times8\times7\times6!}$
$\Rightarrow \dfrac{1}{6!}\left[\dfrac{1}{1} + \dfrac{1}{56}\right] = \dfrac{x}{6!\times90\times56}$
$\Rightarrow \dfrac{57}{56} = \dfrac{x}{90\times56}$
$\Rightarrow x = 57\times90$
$\Rightarrow x = 5130$
(ii) $10!\times x + 9!\times x = 12!$
$\Rightarrow 10\times9!\times x + 9!\times x$
$= 12\times11\times10\times9!$
$\Rightarrow 9![10x + x] = 1320\times9!$
$\Rightarrow 11x = 1320$
$\Rightarrow x = \dfrac{1320}{11} = 120$

18. (i) ${}^{2n}P_3 = 100\times{}^{n}P_2$
$\Rightarrow \dfrac{2n!}{(2n-3)!} = 100\times\dfrac{n!}{(n-2)!}$
$\Rightarrow 2n(2n-1)(2n-2)$
$= 100\times n(n-1)$
$\Rightarrow 2(2n-1)\,2(n-1)$
$= 100(n-1)$
$\Rightarrow 2n - 1 = 25$
$\Rightarrow n = 13$

(ii) ${}^{20}P_n = 13\times{}^{20}P_{n-1}$
$\Rightarrow \dfrac{20!}{(20-n)!}$
$= 13\times\dfrac{20!}{(20-n+1)!}$
$\Rightarrow \dfrac{1}{(20-n)!}$
$= \dfrac{13}{(20-n+1)(20-n)!}$
$\Rightarrow 20 - n + 1 = 13$
$\Rightarrow n = 8$

(iii) ${}^{n}P_5 = 42\times{}^{n}P_3$
$\Rightarrow \dfrac{n!}{(n-5)!} = 42\times\dfrac{n!}{(n-3)!}$
$\Rightarrow \dfrac{1}{(n-5)!}$
$= \dfrac{42}{(n-3)(n-4)(n-5)!}$
$\Rightarrow n^2 - 7n + 12 = 42$
$\Rightarrow n^2 - 7n - 30 = 0$
$(n-10)(n+3) = 0$
$\Rightarrow n = 10, -3$
$n = 10$ $[\because n > 4]$

(iv) $\dfrac{{}^{n}P_4}{{}^{n-1}P_4} = \dfrac{5}{3}$
$\Rightarrow \dfrac{n!}{(n-4)!}\times\dfrac{(n-1-4)!}{(n-1)!} = \dfrac{5}{3}$
$\Rightarrow \dfrac{n(n-1)!\times(n-5)!}{(n-4)(n-5)!(n-1)!} = \dfrac{5}{3}$
$\Rightarrow 3n = 5n - 20$
$\Rightarrow n = 10$

(v) $\dfrac{{}^{15}P_{n-1}}{{}^{16}P_{n-2}} = \dfrac{3}{4}$
$\dfrac{15!}{(15-n+1)!}\times\dfrac{(16-n+2)!}{16!} = \dfrac{3}{4}$
$\Rightarrow \dfrac{15!}{16\times15!}\times\dfrac{(18-n)!}{(16-n)!} = \dfrac{3}{4}$
$\Rightarrow \dfrac{1}{16}\times\dfrac{(18-n)(17-n)}{1} = \dfrac{3}{4}$
$\Rightarrow 306 - 35n + n^2 = 12$
$\Rightarrow n^2 - 35n + 294 = 0$
$\Rightarrow n^2 - 21n - 14n + 294 = 0$
$\Rightarrow n(n-21) - 14(n-21) = 0$
$\Rightarrow (n-21)(n-14) = 0$
$\Rightarrow n = 14$
but $n \neq 21$
$[\because (n-1)$ cannot be more than 15 here$]$

19. (c) Number of ways $= {}^{12}P_2$
$= \dfrac{12!}{10!} = 132$

20. (b) $\dfrac{n!}{P_1!P_2!\ldots P_k!}$

21. 'ROOT' word can be arranged in 4! ways and permutation for O taken as same O for both places by 2! ways
$\therefore$ Required number of permutations $= \dfrac{4!}{2!} = 4\times3 = 12$

22. (d) 'INSTITUTE' word can be written in 9! ways.
I appears two times i.e. 2! ways
T appears three times i.e. 3! ways
$\therefore$ Total number of ways
$= \dfrac{9!}{2!3!}$
$= \dfrac{9\times8\times7\times6\times5\times4\times3!}{2!\times3!}$
$= 72\times42\times10 = 72\times420$
$= 30240$

23. Number of ways $= 5!$
$= 5\times4\times3\times2\times1$
$= 120$

24. (b) Number of 4 letter words
$= {}^{7}P_4 = \dfrac{7!}{3!} = 840$

25. Number of ways in which 5 children stand in a queue
$= 5! = 5\times4\times3\times2\times1$
$= 120$

26. (c)

27. (i) $2!\times9!$
(ii) $10! - 2!\times9!$
$= 10\times9! - 2\times9!$
$= 8\times9!$

28. (d) English, Sanskrit and Hindi books can be placed by 3! ways
$= 6$ ways
Among them 6 English books can be placed as 6! ways
$= 720$ ways
4 Sanskrit books can be placed as 4! ways $= 24$ ways
5 Hindi books can be placed as 5! ways $= 120$ ways
$\therefore$ Total number of ways
$= 6\times720\times24\times120$

29. In the word 'TRIANGLE'
If T and E are fixed, then 6 letters are arranged among themselves in 6! ways
$= 6 \times 5 \times 4 \times 3 \times 2 \times 1$
$= 720$

30. (c) If NE is letters together in 'PENCIL', then there are 5! ways to arrange it.
∴ Total number of ways
$= 5!$ ways
$= 5 \times 4 \times 3 \times 2 \times 1$
$= 120$ ways

31. (i) If vowels come together, then O and E will be together, then OE will be taken as one element.
∴ Total number of ways in which 'VOWELS' can be arranged = 5! ways
OE can be arranged in 2 ways among themselves
Total ways = $5! \times 2$
$= 5 \times 4 \times 3 \times 2 \times 1 \times 2$
$= 120 \times 2 = 240$ ways

(ii) If consonants come together, then VWLS will be taken as one element and 'VOWELS' can be arranged in 3! ways
$= 3 \times 2 \times 1 = 6$ ways
VWLS among themselves can be arranged in 4! ways
$= 4 \times 3 \times 2 \times 1$
$= 24$ ways
∴ Total number of ways
$= 24 \times 6 = 144$ ways

32. (b) $^4P_2 = \frac{4!}{2!}$
$= \frac{4!}{2! \times 2!} \times 2!$
$= \frac{4!}{2!(4-2)!} \times 2!$
$= {}^4C_2 \times 2!$

33. (a) We know that
$^nP_r = {}^nC_r \times r!$
$\therefore \; 840 = 35 \times r!$
$\Rightarrow \; r! = \frac{840}{35} = 24 = 4! \Rightarrow r = 4$

34. $A = n!$
$B = (n-r)![n-(n-r)]!$
$C = n!$
$D = (n-r)!\,r!$
$E = {}^nC_r$

35. (i) $^{14}C_3 = \frac{14!}{3!(14-3)!} = \frac{14!}{3! \times 11!}$
$= \frac{14 \times 13 \times 12 \times 11!}{(3 \times 2 \times 1) \times 11!}$
$= 14 \times 13 \times 2 = 364$

(ii) $^{100}C_{99} = \frac{100!}{99!(100-99)!}$
$= \frac{100!}{99! \times 1!}$
$= \frac{100 \times 99!}{99!} = 100$

(iii) $^{35}C_{35} = 1$

(iv) $^{30}C_0 = 1$

36. $\because \frac{^{2n}C_3}{^nC_3} = \frac{11}{1}$

$$\Rightarrow \frac{\frac{2n(2n-1)(2n-2)}{3 \cdot 2 \cdot 1}}{\frac{n(n-1)(n-2)}{3 \cdot 2 \cdot 1}} = \frac{11}{1}$$

$$\Rightarrow \frac{2n(2n-1)2(n-1)}{3 \cdot 2 \cdot 1} \times \frac{3 \cdot 2 \cdot 1}{n(n-1)(n-2)} = \frac{11}{1}$$

$\Rightarrow \frac{4(2n-1)}{n-2} = \frac{11}{1}$
$\Rightarrow \; 8n - 4 = 11n - 22$
$\Rightarrow \; 18 = 3n \Rightarrow n = 6$

37. (i) (c)
(ii) (b) $\because {}^nC_r + {}^nC_{r-1} = {}^{n+1}C_r$
$\Rightarrow {}^{13}C_6 + {}^{13}C_5 = {}^{14}C_6$
$= \frac{14!}{6!(14-6)!}$
$= \frac{14!}{6! \times 8!}$
$= \frac{14 \times 13 \times 12 \times 11 \times 10 \times 9 \times 8!}{6 \times 5 \times 4 \times 3 \times 2 \times 1 \times 8!}$
$= 7 \times 13 \times 11 \times 3 = 3003$

38. (i) We know that
$^nC_x = {}^nC_y$
$\Rightarrow x + y = n$ or $x = y$
Here, $x \neq y$, so $x + y = n$
$\Rightarrow n = 16 + 14 = 30$
Now, $^nC_{27} = {}^{30}C_{27} = {}^{30}C_{30-27}$
$= {}^{30}C_3 = \frac{30 \cdot 29 \cdot 28}{3 \cdot 2 \cdot 1} = 4060$

(ii) Here $x \neq y$, so $x + y = n$
$\Rightarrow \; n = 10 + 12 = 22$
Now, $^{23}C_n = {}^{23}C_{22} = {}^{23}C_{23-22}$
$= {}^{23}C_1 = 23$

39. $\frac{^nC_r}{^{n-1}C_{r-1}} = \frac{6}{3}$

$$\Rightarrow \frac{\frac{n!}{r!(n-r)!}}{\frac{(n-1)!}{(r-1)!(n-1-r+1)!}} = \frac{6}{3}$$

$\Rightarrow \frac{n!}{r!(n-r)!} \times \frac{(r-1)!(n-r)!}{(n-1)!} = \frac{6}{3}$

$\Rightarrow \frac{n \times (n-1)! \times (r-1)! \times (n-r)!}{r(r-1)! \times (n-r)!(n-1)!} = 2$

$\Rightarrow n = 2r$

Also, $\frac{^{n+1}C_{r+1}}{^nC_r} = \frac{11}{6}$

$$\frac{\frac{(n+1)!}{(r+1)!(n+1-r-1)!}}{\frac{n!}{r!(n-r)!}} = \frac{11}{6}$$

$\Rightarrow \frac{(n+1)\,n!}{(r+1)\,r!(n-r)!} \times \frac{(n-r)!\,r!}{n!} = \frac{11}{6}$

$\Rightarrow \frac{n+1}{r+1} = \frac{11}{6}$
$\Rightarrow \; 6n + 6 = 11r + 11$
$\Rightarrow 6n - 11r = 5$
$\Rightarrow 12r - 11r = 5$
$\Rightarrow \; r = 5$
$n = 2 \times 5 = 10$

40. (c) The required number of ways
$= {}^6C_3 \times {}^5C_3$
$= \frac{6 \times 5 \times 4}{3 \times 2 \times 1} \times \frac{5 \times 4 \times 3}{3 \times 2 \times 1}$
$= 20 \times 10$
$= 200$

41. There are 12 face cards and 2 are to be selected out of these 12 cards. This can be done in $^{12}C_2$ ways.
∴ Required number of ways
$= {}^{12}C_2$
$= \frac{12!}{2!10!}$
$= \frac{12 \times 11 \times 10!}{2 \times 10!}$
$= 66$ ways

42. (b) The required number of ways
$= {}^{10}C_2$
$= \frac{10 \times 9}{2 \times 1} = 45$

43. $\because$ Two particular players are always included. So, we have to select 9 players out of 13 players. This can be done in $^{13}C_9$ ways.

Hence, required number of ways

$$= {}^{13}C_9 = {}^{13}C_4$$

44. (c) There are 26 red cards and 26 black cards.

Required number of ways

$$= {}^{26}C_3 \times {}^{26}C_3 = ({}^{26}C_3)^2$$

$$= \left(\frac{26!}{3!\,23!}\right)^2$$

$$= \left(\frac{26 \times 24 \times 25}{3 \times 2}\right)^2$$

$$= (26 \times 100)^2 = 6760000$$

45. (i) $({}^{10}C_5) + ({}^{10}C_4 \times {}^6C_1) + ({}^{10}C_3 \times {}^6C_2) + ({}^{10}C_2 \times {}^6C_3) + ({}^{10}C_1 \times {}^6C_4) + ({}^6C_5)$

$= 252 + 1260 + 1800 + 900 + 150 + 6$

$= 4368$

(ii) ${}^{10}C_3 \times {}^6C_2 = 1800$

(iii) ${}^{10}C_5 = 252$

(iv) $({}^{10}C_3 \times {}^6C_2) + ({}^{10}C_4 \times {}^6C_1) + ({}^{10}C_5)$

$= 1800 + 1260 + 252$

$= 3312$

(v) $({}^{10}C_1 \times {}^6C_4) + ({}^{10}C_2 \times {}^6C_3) + ({}^{10}C_3 \times {}^6C_2) + ({}^{10}C_4 \times {}^6C_1)$

$= 150 + 900 + 1800 + 1260$

$= 4110$

46. The required number of ways

$$= {}^5C_2 \times {}^6C_2 \times {}^4C_2$$

$$= \frac{5 \times 4}{2 \times 1} \times \frac{6 \times 5}{2 \times 1} \times \frac{4 \times 3}{2 \times 1}$$

$$= 5 \times 2 \times 3 \times 5 \times 2 \times 3$$

$$= 900$$

47. (a) The required number of ways

$$= {}^5C_2 \times {}^5C_2$$

$$= \frac{5 \times 4}{2 \times 1} \times \frac{5 \times 4}{2 \times 1}$$

$$= 10 \times 10 = 100$$

48. Number of diagonals

= Number of lines − number of sides

$$= {}^nC_2 - n = \frac{n(n-3)}{2}$$

49. (i) $${}^9C_3 = \frac{9!}{3!\,6!} = \frac{9 \times 8 \times 7 \times 6!}{3 \times 2 \times 6!} = 84$$

(ii) $${}^8C_4 = \frac{8!}{4!\,4!} = \frac{8 \times 7 \times 6 \times 5 \times 4!}{4 \times 3 \times 2 \times 1 \times 4!} = 70$$

(iii) $${}^7C_3 = \frac{7!}{3!\,4!} = \frac{7 \times 6 \times 5 \times 4!}{3 \times 2 \times 1 \times 4!} = 35$$

50. $W \times W \times W \times W \times W \times$

Number of ways $= {}^6C_3 = \dfrac{6!}{3!\,3!}$

$$= \frac{6 \times 5 \times 4 \times 3!}{3! \times 3!} = \frac{120}{3 \times 2} = 20$$

51. (c) Number of ways

$$= {}^6C_1 + {}^6C_2 + {}^6C_3 + {}^6C_4 + {}^6C_5 + {}^6C_6$$

$$= \frac{6!}{1!\,5!} + \frac{6!}{2!\,4!} + \frac{6!}{3!\,3!} + \frac{6!}{4!\,2!} + \frac{6!}{5!\,1!} + \frac{6!}{6!\,0!}$$

$$= 63$$

52. (i) (a) ${}^{12}C_2 = 66$

(b) ${}^{11}C_1 = 11$

(ii) (a) ${}^{12}C_3 = 220$

(b) ${}^{11}C_2 = 55$

53. (i) (a) The required number of ways

$$= {}^{13}C_4 + {}^{13}C_4 + {}^{13}C_4 + {}^{13}C_4$$

$$= 2860$$

(ii) (d) The required number of ways

$$= {}^{13}C_1 \times {}^{13}C_1 \times {}^{13}C_1 \times {}^{13}C_1$$

$$= 13^4$$

(iii) (b) The required number of ways $= \dfrac{12!}{4!\,8!} = 495$

(iv) (a) The required number of ways

$$= {}^{26}C_2 \times {}^{26}C_2$$

$$= 105625$$

(v) (a) The required number of ways

$$= {}^{26}C_4 + {}^{26}C_4$$

$$= 29900$$

Assertion-Reason

1. (a) We have, $P(9, r) = 3024$

$\Rightarrow \quad {}^9P_r = 3024$

$\Rightarrow \quad \dfrac{9!}{(9-r)!} = 3024$

$\Rightarrow \quad \dfrac{9!}{(9-r)!} = 9 \times 336$

$\Rightarrow \quad \dfrac{9!}{(9-r)!} = 9 \times 8 \times 7 \times 6$

$\Rightarrow \quad \dfrac{9!}{(9-r)!} = \dfrac{9 \times 8 \times 7 \times 6 \times 5!}{5!}$

[multiply numerator and denominator by 5!]

$\Rightarrow \quad \dfrac{9!}{(9-r)!} = \dfrac{9!}{5!}$

$\Rightarrow \quad (9-r)! = 5!$

On comparing, we get

$9 - r = 5$

$\Rightarrow \quad r = 4$

$\therefore$ Assertion is true and Reason is also true and Reason is the correct explanation of Assertion.

2. (d) We have, ${}^{2n}C_3 : {}^nC_3 = 11 : 1$

$\Rightarrow \quad \dfrac{{}^{2n}C_3}{{}^nC_3} = \dfrac{11}{1}$

$$\Rightarrow \quad \frac{\dfrac{2n(2n-1)(2n-2)}{3 \cdot 2 \cdot 1}}{\dfrac{n(n-1)(n-2)}{3 \cdot 2 \cdot 1}} = \frac{11}{1}$$

$$\Rightarrow \frac{2n(2n-1)2(n-1)}{3 \cdot 2 \cdot 1} \times \frac{3 \cdot 2 \cdot 1}{n(n-1)(n-2)} = \frac{11}{1}$$

$\Rightarrow \quad \dfrac{4(2n-1)}{n-2} = \dfrac{11}{1}$

$\Rightarrow \quad 8n - 4 = 11n - 22$

$\Rightarrow \quad 18 = 3n \Rightarrow n = 6$

Hence, the value of n is 6.

$\therefore$ Assertion is false but Reason is true.

3. (d) Number formed using 1, 2, 3, 4, 5 = 5! = 120

Number formed using 0, 1, 2, 4, 5

4	4	3	2	1

Total number formed, divisible by 3 (taking numbers without repetition) = 216

$\therefore$ Assertion is false but Reason is true.

4. (c) When W, I, F, E are arranged in all possible ways, then number of words formed is $4! = 24$ and WIFE occurs last of all as its letters are against alphabetical order.

Number of ways of arranging four distinct objects in a line is

$^4P_4 = 4! = 24$

$\therefore$ Assertion is true but Reason is false.

5. (a) Let the number of ways of distributing n identical objects among r persons such that each person gets atleast one object is same as the number of ways of selecting $(r-1)$ places out of $(n-1)$ different places i.e. $^{n-1}C_{r-1}$.

$\therefore$ Assertion is true and Reason is also true and Reason is the correct explanation of Assertion.

6. (c) Product of n consecutive natural numbers

$$= (m+1)(m+2)(m+3)\ldots(m+n), \quad [m \in \text{whole numbers}]$$

$$= \frac{(m+n)!}{m!} = \frac{(m+n)!}{m!n!} \times n!$$

$$= n!\, ^{m+n}C_n!$$

Product is divisible by $n!$, then it is always divisible by $(n-1)!$ but not by $(n+1)!$.

$\therefore$ Assertion is true but Reason is false.

7. (a) Let n be the number of sides of a polygon.

Then, number of vertices of polygon $= n$

Now, number of diagonals

$$= {^nC_2} - n = 44$$

[$\because$ diagonal will be formed by joining any two non-adjacent vertices of the polygon, therefore total number of diagonals is $^nC_2 - n$]

$$\Rightarrow \frac{n(n-1)}{2} - n = 44$$

$$\Rightarrow n^2 - 3n - 88 = 0$$

$$\Rightarrow n = -8 \text{ or } 11 \Rightarrow n = 11$$

[$\because n$ cannot be negative]

$\therefore$ Assertion is true and Reason is also true and Reason is the correct explanation of Assertion.

8. (a) Total number of three digit numbers formed using the digits 1, 2, 3, 4 and 5, when repetition is allowed $= 5 \times 5 \times 5 = 125$

Total number of even numbers formed using the digits 1, 2, 3, 4 and 5, when repetition is allowed $= 5 \times 5 \times 2 = 50$.

$\therefore$ Assertion is true and Reason is also true and Reason is the correct explanation of Assertion.

9. (a) We know that $^nC_p = {^nC_q}$, if and only if $p = q$ or $n = p + q$

$$\Rightarrow {^nC_{15}} = {^nC_5}, \text{ then } = 15 + 5$$

$$\Rightarrow n = 20$$

$\therefore$ Assertion is true and Reason is also true and Reason is the correct explanation of Assertion.

10. (d) We have to choose 2 points among 10.

Total number of lines formed using 10 points, no three of which are collinear $= {^{10}C_2}$

$$= \frac{10!}{2!8!} = 45$$

$\therefore$ Assertion is false but Reason is true.

Case Based

1. (i) (c) We have five students.

$\therefore$ Total number of arrangements is $5! = 120$

(ii) (a) Given, Aman and Shiva sit together.

$\therefore$ Total number of arrangements

$$= 4! \times 2!$$

$$= 24 \times 2 = 48$$

(iii) (c) Number of arrangements if Ram sits in middle $= 4! = 24$

2. (i) Letters of word 'GAME' arranged in dictionary is

A, E, G, M.

Number of words starting with

$$A = {^3P_3} = 3! = 6$$

Number of words starting with

$$E = {^3P_3} = 3! = 6$$

Number of words starting with

$$G = {^3P_3} = 3! = 6$$

Total number of words

$$= 6 + 6 + 6 = 18$$

So, 19th word is MAEG

20th word is MAGE

21st word is MEAG

22nd word is MEGA

$\therefore$ Rank of word 'MEGA' is 22nd.

(ii) Number of words starting with

$$C = \frac{6!}{3!} = 120$$

Number of words starting with

$$E = \frac{6!}{2!3!} = 60$$

Number of words starting with

$$S = \frac{6!}{2!2!} = 180$$

Total number of words = 360

$\therefore$ 361th word will be UCCESSS.

(iii) Given word is GARDEN.

Total number of ways in which all letters can be arranged in alphabetical order $= 6!$.

There are 2 vowels in the word GARDEN i.e. A and E.

So, the total number of ways in which these two vowels can be arranged $= 2!$

Hence, required number of ways

$$= \frac{6!}{2!} = 360$$

EDGE UP

1. (c) 8 identical objects into 4 identical shelves, where any number of shelves may remain empty is given by

0008, 0017, 0026, 0035, 0044 = 5

$$\left.\begin{matrix} 0 & 1 & 1 & 6 \\ 0 & 1 & 2 & 5 \\ 0 & 1 & 3 & 4 \\ 0 & 2 & 2 & 4 \\ 0 & 2 & 3 & 3 \end{matrix}\right] = 5$$

$$\left.\begin{matrix} 1 & 1 & 1 & 5 \\ 1 & 1 & 2 & 4 \\ 1 & 1 & 3 & 3 \\ 1 & 2 & 2 & 3 \end{matrix}\right] = 4$$

$$\left.\begin{matrix} 2 & 2 & 2 & 2 \end{matrix}\right] = 1$$

Total = 15

2. (a) Let 24 distinct objects are divided into 6 groups of 4 objects on each group.

Number of ways of formation of group

$$= \frac{24!}{(4!)^6 \cdot 6!} \in N$$

Similarly,

let 120 distinct objects are divided into 24 groups of 5 objects in each group.

$\therefore$ Number of ways of formation of groups $= \dfrac{(120)!}{(5!)^{24} \cdot 24!} \in N$

Hence, $\alpha \in N$ and $\beta \in N$.

3. (c) NAGPUR can be arranged alphabetically as A G N P R U

Now, we need to find 315th word

So, total words starting with

$A = A\ 5\ 4\ 3\ 2\ 1 = 5! = 120$

Total words starting with

$G = G\ 5\ 4\ 3\ 2\ 1 = 5! = 120$

Total words starting with

$N = N\ 5\ 4\ 3\ 2\ 1 = 5! = 120$

Total words

$= 120 + 120 + 120 = 360$

So, 315th words starts with N.

Now, words with N as first letter, and A as second letter

$= N\ A\ 4\ 3\ 2\ 1 = 4! = 24$

G as second letter

$= N\ G\ 4\ 3\ 2\ 1 = 4! = 24$

P as second letter

$= N\ P\ 4\ 3\ 2\ 1 = 4! = 24$

Total words so far

$= 240 + 24 \times 3 = 312$

So, we have to find next 3 words

$\Rightarrow$ N R A G P U

$\Rightarrow$ N R A G U P

$\Rightarrow$ N R A P G U $\rightarrow$ 315th word

4. (553) Given word GTWENTY

Words start with E $= \dfrac{6!}{2!} = 360$

Words start with GE $= \dfrac{5!}{2!} = 60$

Words start with GN $= \dfrac{5!}{2!} = 60$

Words start with GTE $= 4! = 24$

Words start with GTN $= 4! = 24$

Words start with GTT $= 4! = 24$

$\therefore$ Serial number of the word GTWENTY

$= 360 + 60 + 60 + 24 + 24 + 24 + 1$

$= 553$

5. (c) AA, MM, TT, H, I, C, S, E

(a) All distinct $= {}^8C_5 = \dfrac{8 \cdot 7 \cdot 6}{3 \cdot 2 \cdot 1} = 56$

(b) 2 same 1st kind, 2 same 2nd kind, 1 different

$= {}^3C_2 \times {}^6C_1 = 3 \times 6 = 18$

(c) 2 same, 3 different

$= {}^3C_1 \times {}^7C_4 = 3 \times \dfrac{7 \cdot 6 \cdot 5}{3 \cdot 2 \cdot 1} = 105$

Hence, the total

$= 56 + 18 + 105 = 179$

6. (a) Since, office are identical so we can distributes in following ways.

I	II	III	IV	
0	0	0	5	$1 = 1$
0	0	1	4	$\dfrac{5!}{4!1!} = 5$
0	1	1	3	$\dfrac{5!}{3!\,2!} = 10$
0	1	2	2	$\dfrac{5!}{2!2!2!} = 15$
1	1	1	2	$\dfrac{5!}{1!1!2!} \times \dfrac{1}{3!} = 10$
0	0	2	3	$\dfrac{5!}{3!2!} = 10$

$\therefore$ Total

$1 + 5 + 10 + 15 + 10 + 10 = 51$

7. (c) Remaining apples after distributing 2 apples to each of three child

$= 21 - 6 = 15$

Number of ways $= {}^{15+3-1}C_{3-1}$

$= {}^{17}C_2 = \dfrac{17 \times 16}{2}$

$= 17 \times 8 = 136$

8. (c) Given, $\dfrac{{}^{n+1}C_{r+1}}{{}^nC_r} = \dfrac{55}{35}$ ...(i)

and $\dfrac{{}^nC_r}{{}^{n-1}C_{r-1}} = \dfrac{35}{21}$ ...(ii)

Now, using property,

$${}^nC_r = \frac{n}{r}\,{}^{n-1}C_{r-1}$$

Using Eq. (i),

$\dfrac{n+1}{r+1} \times \dfrac{{}^nC_r}{{}^nC_r} = \dfrac{55}{35} \Rightarrow \dfrac{n+1}{r+1} = \dfrac{11}{7}$

$\Rightarrow 7n + 7 = 11r + 11$

$\Rightarrow 7n = 11r + 4$ ...(iii)

Using Eq. (ii),

$\dfrac{n}{r}\dfrac{{}^{n-1}C_{r-1}}{{}^{n-1}C_{r-1}} = \dfrac{35}{21}$

$\Rightarrow \dfrac{n}{r} = \dfrac{5}{3} \Rightarrow 3n = 5r$ ...(iv)

Using Eqs. (iii) and (iv),

$n = 10$ and $r = 6$

$\Rightarrow 2n + 5r = 2 \times 10 + 5 \times 6 = 50$

9. (a) Given,

$${}^6C_m + 2({}^6C_{m+1}) + {}^6C_{m+2} > {}^8C_3$$

$\Rightarrow ({}^6C_m + {}^6C_{m+1}) + ({}^6C_{m+1} + {}^6C_{m+2}) > {}^8C_3$

$\Rightarrow {}^7C_{m+1} + {}^7C_{m+2} > {}^8C_3$

${}^8C_{m+2} > {}^8C_3$

$m = 2$ and $\dfrac{{}^{n-1}P_3}{{}^nP_4} = \dfrac{1}{8}$

$$\frac{\dfrac{(n-1)!}{(n-4)!}}{\dfrac{n!}{(n-4)!}} = \frac{1}{8}$$

$\Rightarrow \dfrac{1}{n} = \dfrac{1}{8} \Rightarrow n = 8$

${}^nP_{m+1} + {}^{n+1}C_m = {}^8P_3 + {}^9C_2$

$= 8 \times 7 \times 6 + \dfrac{9 \times 8}{2}$

$= 336 + 36 = 372$

10. (a) Given, ${}^{n-1}C_r = (k^2 - 8)\,{}^nC_{r+1}$ ...(i)

$\Rightarrow {}^{n-1}C_r = (k^2 - 8)\dfrac{n}{r+1} \cdot {}^{n-1}C_r$

$\left[\because {}^nC_r = \dfrac{n}{r}\,{}^{n-1}C_{r-1}\right]$

$\Rightarrow \dfrac{1}{k^2 - 8} = \dfrac{n}{r+1}$ ...(ii)

From Eq. (i) to defined ${}^nC_{r+1}$,

$n \ge r + 1 \Rightarrow \dfrac{n}{r+1} \ge 1$

$\Rightarrow \dfrac{1}{k^2 - 8} \ge 1$

$\Rightarrow \dfrac{1 - (k^2 - 8)}{k^2 - 8} \ge 0$

$\Rightarrow \dfrac{k^2 - 9}{k^2 - 8} \le 0$

$\Rightarrow \dfrac{(k-3)(k+3)}{(k - 2\sqrt{2})(k + 2\sqrt{2})} \le 0$

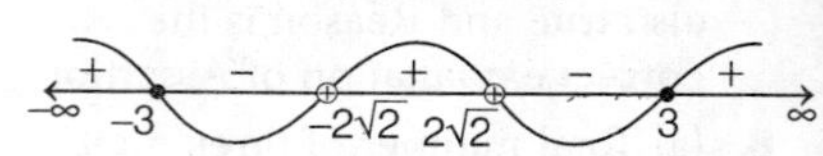

$\Rightarrow k \in [-3, -2\sqrt{2}) \cup (2\sqrt{2}, 3]$

So, $k \in (2\sqrt{2}, \sqrt{3}]$ [by given option]

11. (a) Total triangle formed with vertices of octagon = ${}^8C_3$

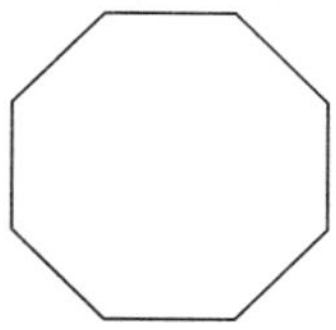

Now, one condition is given that no side of triangle coincides with side of octagon.

Case I Number of triangle with all sides coincides with octagon = 0

Case II Number of triangle with 2 sides coincides with octagon = ${}^8C_1$

[∵ from one vertex two adjacent sides are originating]

Case III Number of triangle with 1 side coincides with octagon

$= {}^8C_1 \times {}^4C_1$

[∵ when we select one side, we have to leave adjacent sides also of selected side, so remaining vertices will be 4]

∴ Total triangles with no sides coinciding with octagon is

$= {}^8C_3 - 0 - {}^8C_1 - {}^8C_1 \times {}^4C_1$

$= 56 - (0 + 8 + 32) = 16$

12. (36) Given digits = 2, 3, 4, 5, 7

Total 3-digit numbers = ${}^5C_3 \times 3! = 60$

Now, 3-digit numbers that are divisible by 3

234, 237, 345, 357

↓ ↓ ↓ ↓

$3! + 3! + 3! + 3! = 24$

Hence, three digit numbers that are not divisible by 3

= Total – Divisible by 3

$= 60 - 24 = 36$

13. (3734) DISTRIBUTION

3I, 2T, 1D, 1S, 1R, 1B, 1U, 1O, 1N

Number of words taken 4 at time.

Case	Number of words
1. All are different	${}^9C_4 \times 4! = 3024$
2. 1 Pair + 2 different	${}^2C_1 \times {}^8C_2 \times \frac{4!}{2!} = 672$
3. 2 Pairs	${}^2C_2 \times \frac{4!}{2!2!} = 6$
4. 1 triplet + 1 Different	${}^1C_1 \times {}^8C_1 \times \frac{4!}{3!} = 32$
Total	**3734**

14. (a) **I** All three digits are alike

111, 333, 555, 888 → 4

II 2 digits are alike

$558 \rightarrow \frac{3!}{2!} = 3;$

$885 \rightarrow \frac{3!}{2!} = 3$

III All three digits are different

1, 3, 5 → 6; 1, 3, 8 → 6

∴ Total numbers = 22

15. (d) Since, number is divisible by 5, so units digit can be 0 or 5.

Case 1 Units digit = 0

Since, number is greater than 40000 and digits can not be repeated, the leading digit has only 3 options (5 or 7 or 9) Remaining digits can be filled in 4 and 3 and 2 ways.

Number of ways $= 4! \times 3$

Case 2 Units digit = 5

Here, leading digit has 2 options (7 or 9). Remaining digits can be filled in 4 and 3 and 2 ways. So, number of ways $= 4! \times 2$

Total numbers

$= 4! \times 3 + 4! \times 2 = 120$

16. (a) Vowels – I, EEEE

Consonants – N, D, P, N, D, N, C

Number of ways in which vowels are always occur together

$= \frac{8!}{3! \times 2!} \times \frac{5!}{4!}$

$= 16800$

17. (d) Given, digits are 3, 5, 6, 7, 8.

Since, there is no any repetition and number greater than 7000 will be of 4 and 5 digits.

For 4-digit number, the first place will contain 2 ways and the remaining will be arranged in ${}^4P_3$ ways.

∴ Number of ways

$= 2 \times {}^4P_3$

$= 2 \times 24 = 48$

Also, 5-digit number will be arranged in ${}^5P_5$ ways

$= 5! = 120$ ways

∴ Total number of ways

$= 120 + 48$

$= 168$ ways

18. (a) First arrange the letters of the word MONDAY in alphabetical order i.e. ADMNOY

A - - - - - = 5!

D - - - - - = 5!

(M) A - - - - = 4!

(M) D - - - - = 4!

(M) (N) - - - - = 4!

(M) (O) A - - - = 3!

(M) (O) D - - - = 3!

(M) (O) (N) A - - = 2!

(M) (O) (N) (D) (A) (Y) = 327

Rank = 327

19. (c) To find the rank of word 'THAMS'

We know that according to dictionary the letters would appear as A, H, M, S, T.

Words starting with letter 'A'- - - -

$= 4! = 24$

Words starting with letter 'H'- - - -

$= 4! = 24$

Words starting with letter 'M' - - - -

$= 4! = 24$

Words starting with letter 'S' - - - -

$= 4! = 24$

Words starting with letter TA - - -

$= 3! = 6$

Words starting with letter THAMS = 1

Rank = 103

Hence, rank of word 'THAMS'

= 103

20. (a) Total number of words

$= \frac{11!}{2!2!2!}$

C and S come together in

$\frac{10!}{2!2!2!} \times 2!$ words

∴ Required number of words

$= \frac{11!}{(2!)^3} - \frac{10!}{(2!)^2}$

$= \frac{10!}{(2!)^2}\left(\frac{11}{2} - 1\right)$

$= \frac{10! \times 9}{8}$

$= 10 \times 9 \times 8 \times 7 \times 6! \times \frac{9}{8}$

$= 6! \times 5670$

$\Rightarrow k = 5670$

Chapter-7

Binomial Theorem

1. (b)

2. (i) $(1+2x+x^2)^{20} = \{(1+x)^2\}^{20}$
$= (1+x)^{40}$
$\therefore$ Number of terms $= (n+1)$
$= 40+1 = 41$

(ii) Since, $n = 9$.
$\therefore$ Number of terms
$= 9+1 = 10$

(iii) $(4+x^2-4x)^4 = [(x-2)^2]^4$
$= (x-2)^8$
Here, $n+1 = 8+1 = 9$

3. $(x-y)^n = {}^nC_0x^n - {}^nC_1x^{n-1}y + {}^nC_2x^{n-2}y^2 + \dots + (-1)^n\,{}^nC_ny^n$

4. ${}^nC_0 + {}^nC_1x + {}^nC_2x^2 + \dots\ {}^nC_nx^n$

5. True

6. (i) $\left(x^2-\frac{2}{x}\right)^3 = {}^3C_0(x^2)^3 + {}^3C_1(x^2)^2\left(-\frac{2}{x}\right) + {}^3C_2\,(x^2)\left(-\frac{2}{x}\right)^2 + {}^3C_3\left(-\frac{2}{x}\right)^3$
$= x^6 + 3x^4\left(-\frac{2}{x}\right) + 3x^2\left(\frac{4}{x^2}\right) + \left(-\frac{8}{x^3}\right)$
$= x^6 - 6x^3 + 12 - \frac{8}{x^3}$

(ii) $(x^2+2y)^5 = {}^5C_0(x^2)^5 + {}^5C_1(x^2)^4(2y) + {}^5C_2(x^2)^3(2y)^2 + {}^5C_3(x^2)^2(2y)^3 + {}^5C_4x^2(2y)^4 + {}^5C_5(2y)^5$
$= x^{10} + 10x^8y + 40x^6y^2 + 80x^4y^3 + 80x^2y^4 + 32y^5$

(iii) $(2x-3y)^4 = [2x+(-3y)]^4$
$= {}^4C_0(2x)^4(-3y)^0 + {}^4C_1(2x)^3(-3y) + {}^4C_2(2x)^2(-3y)^2 + {}^4C_3(2x)^1(-3y)^3 + {}^4C_4(-3y)^4$
$= 16x^4 - 96x^3y + 216x^2y^2 - 216xy^3 + 81y^4$

(iv) $\left(x+\frac{1}{x}\right)^4 = {}^4C_0(x)^4 + {}^4C_1(x)^3\left(\frac{1}{x}\right)^1 + {}^4C_2(x)^2\left(\frac{1}{x}\right)^2 + {}^4C_3(x)\left(\frac{1}{x}\right)^3 + {}^4C_4\left(\frac{1}{x}\right)^4$
$= 1\times x^4 + 4\times x^2 + 6\times x^0 + 4\times\frac{1}{x^2} + 1\times\frac{1}{x^4}$
$= x^4 + 4x^2 + 6 + \frac{4}{x^2} + \frac{1}{x^4}$

(v) $(2-x^2)^6 = {}^6C_0 2^6 + {}^6C_1 2^5(-x^2) + {}^6C_2 2^4(-x^2)^2 + {}^6C_3 2^3(-x^2)^3 + {}^6C_4 2^2(-x^2)^4 + {}^6C_5 2^1(-x^2)^5 + {}^6C_6(-x^2)^6$
$= 1\times 64 + 6\times 32\,(-x^2) + 15\times 16\,(x^4) + 20\times 8\,(-x^6) + 15\times 4(x^8) + 6\times 2(-x^{10}) + 1\times(x^{12})$
$= 64 - 192x^2 + 240x^4 - 160x^6 + 60x^8 - 12x^{10} + x^{12}$

(vi) Given, $[(2x^2-ax)+2a^2]^3$
$= {}^3C_0(2x^2-ax)^3 + {}^3C_1(2x^2-ax)^2(2a^2)^1 + {}^3C_2(2x^2-ax)(2a^2)^2 + {}^3C_3(2a^2)^3$
$= (2x^2-ax)^3 + 3(4x^4+a^2x^2-4ax^3)(2a^2) + 3\,(2x^2-ax)\,(4a^4) + 8a^6$
$= (2x^2-ax)^3 + 24x^4a^2 + 6a^4x^2 - 24a^3x^3 + 24x^2a^4 - 12a^5x + 8a^6$ ...(i)

Again, using binomial theorem, we get
$(2x^2-ax)^3 = {}^3C_0(2x^2)^3 + {}^3C_1(2x^2)^2(-ax) + {}^3C_2\,(2x^2)(-ax)^2 + {}^3C_3\,(-ax)^3$
$= 8x^6 - 12x^5a + 6a^2x^4 - a^3x^3$ ... (ii)

From Eqs. (i) and (ii),
$(2x^2-ax+2a^2)^3$
$= 8x^6 - 12x^5a + 6a^2x^4 - a^3x^3 + 24x^4a^2 + 6a^4x^2 - 24a^3x^3 + 24x^2a^4 - 12a^5x + 8a^6$
$= 8x^6 - 12x^5a + 30a^2x^4 - 25a^3x^3 + 30x^2a^4 - 12a^5x + 8a^6$

7. (i) $(99)^4 = (100-1)^4$
$= {}^4C_0\times(100)^4 - {}^4C_1(100)^3 + {}^4C_2\times(100)^2\times(1)^2 - {}^4C_3\times 100\times 1^3 + {}^4C_4\times(1)^4$
$= 96059601$

(ii) $(10.1)^5 = (10+0.1)^5$
$= {}^5C_0\times(10)^5\times(0.1)^0 + {}^5C_1\times(10)^4\times(0.1) + {}^5C_2\times(10)^3\times(0.1)^2 + {}^5C_3\times(10)^2\times(0.1)^3 + {}^5C_4\times(10)^1\times(0.1)^4 + {}^5C_5(10)^0\times(0.1)^5$
$= 100000 + 5000 + 100 + 1 + 0.005 + 0.00001$
$= 105101.00501$

8. (a) Given, $(0.98)^{-3}$
$= (1-0.02)^{-3}$
$= 1 + (-3)\cdot(-0.02) + \frac{(-3)(-4)}{2!}(-0.02)^2 + \dots$
$= 1 + 0.06 + 0.0024 + \dots = 1.0624$

9. (i) (True)
$(1.01)^{1000000}$
$= (1+0.01)^{1000000}$
$= {}^{1000000}C_0 + {}^{1000000}C_1(0.01)$ + other positive terms
$= 1 + 1000000\times 0.01$ + other positive terms
> 10000
$\therefore (1.01)^{1000000} > 10000$

(ii) (True)
Let $x = (101)^{50}$ and
$y = (100)^{50} + (99)^{50}$
Then, $x - y = (101)^{50} - (99)^{50} - (100)^{50}$ ... (i)
$\Rightarrow\ (101)^{50} = (100+1)^{50}$
$= {}^{50}C_0 100^{50} + {}^{50}C_1 100^{49} + {}^{50}C_2 100^{48} + \dots + {}^{50}C_{50}\cdot 100^0$
Now, $(99)^{50} = (100-1)^{50}$
$= {}^{50}C_0 100^{50} - {}^{50}C_1 100^{49} + {}^{50}C_2\,100^{48} - \dots + {}^{50}C_{50}$
Then, $(101)^{50} - (99)^{50}$
$= 2\,[{}^{50}C_1 100^{49} + {}^{50}C_3\,100^{47} + \dots + {}^{50}C_{49}\,100^1]$
$= 2\times 50\times 100^{49} + 2\,[{}^{50}C_3 100^{47} + \dots + {}^{50}C_{49}\cdot 100^1]$
$= 100^{50} + 2\,[{}^{50}C_3 100^{47} + \dots + {}^{50}C_{49}\cdot 100^1]$ ...(ii)

By putting the value into Eq. (i) from Eq. (ii), we get

$x - y = 2\,[{}^{50}C_3 100^{47} + \ldots + {}^{50}C_{49} \cdot 100^1] > 0$

$\Rightarrow \quad x > y$

$\Rightarrow 101^{50} > 100^{50} + 99^{50}$

10. Using binomial theorem,

(i) $(a+b)^3 = {}^3C_0 a^3 b^0 + {}^3C_1 a^2 b^1 + {}^3C_2 a^1 b^2 + {}^3C_3 a^0 b^3$

$(a-b)^3 = {}^3C_0 a^3 (-b)^0 + {}^3C_1 a^2 (-b)^1 + {}^3C_2 a^1 (-b)^2 + {}^3C_3 a^0 (-b)^3$

$\therefore (a+b)^3 - (a-b)^3 = 2[{}^3C_1 a^2 b + b^3]$

$= 2b\,[3a^2 + b^2]$

On putting $a = \sqrt{5}$ and $b = \sqrt{3}$, we obtain

$(\sqrt{5}+\sqrt{3})^3 - (\sqrt{5}-\sqrt{3})^3 = 2(\sqrt{3})\,[3 \times 5 + 3]$

$= 2\sqrt{3}\,[15 + 3] = 36\sqrt{3}$

(ii) $(x+y)^6 - (x-y)^6$

$= {}^6C_0 x^6 + {}^6C_1 x^5 y + {}^6C_2 x^4 y^2 + {}^6C_3 x^3 y^3 + {}^6C_4 x^2 y^4 + {}^6C_5 x y^5 + {}^6C_6 y^6 - [{}^6C_0 x^6 + {}^6C_1 x^5 (-y)^1 + {}^6C_2 x^4 (-y)^2 + {}^6C_3 x^3 (-y)^3 + {}^6C_4 x^2 (-y)^4 + {}^6C_5 x (-y)^5 + {}^6C_6 (-y)^6]$

$= 2\,(6x^5 y + 20x^3 y^3 + 6xy^5)$

$= 4xy\,(3x^4 + 10x^2 y^2 + 3y^4)$

On substituting $x = \sqrt{2}$ and $y = 1$, we get

$(\sqrt{2}+1)^6 - (\sqrt{2}-1)^6 = (4 \times \sqrt{2} \times 1)$

$[3(\sqrt{2})^4 + 10(\sqrt{2})^2 (1)^2 + 3(1)^4]$

$= 4\sqrt{2}\,(12 + 20 + 3)$

$= 140\sqrt{2}$

(iii) $(x-y)^5 + (x+y)^5$, where $x = \sqrt{2}$ and $y = 1$

$= [{}^5C_0 x^5 - {}^5C_1 x^4 y + {}^5C_2 x^3 y^2 - {}^5C_3 x^2 y^3 + {}^5C_4 x y^4 - {}^5C_5 y^5] + [{}^5C_0 x^5 + {}^5C_1 x^4 y + {}^5C_2 x^3 y^2 + {}^5C_3 x^2 y^3 + {}^5C_4 x y^4 + {}^5C_5 y^5]$

$= 2\,[{}^5C_0 x^5 + {}^5C_2 x^3 y^2 + {}^5C_4 x y^4]$

$= 2[(\sqrt{2})^5 + 10(\sqrt{2})^3 \cdot 1^2 + 5(\sqrt{2}) \cdot 1^4]$

$= 2[4\sqrt{2} + 20\sqrt{2} + 5\sqrt{2}]$

$= 58\sqrt{2}$

11. $6^n - 5n = (1+5)^n - 5n$

$\Rightarrow 6^n - 5n = {}^nC_0 \times 5^0 + {}^nC_1 \times 5^1 + {}^nC_2 \times 5^2 + {}^nC_3 \times 5^3 + \ldots + {}^nC_n \times 5^n - 5n$

$= 1 + 5n + {}^nC_2 \times 5^2 + {}^nC_3 \times 5^3 + \ldots\ldots + {}^nC_n \times 5^n - 5n$

$\Rightarrow 6^n - 5n = 25 \times \text{an integer} + 1$

$\therefore 6^n - 5n$ leaves the remainder 1, when divided by 25.

12. (True)

$a^n = [(a-b) + b]^n$

$a^n = {}^nC_0 (a-b)^n + {}^nC_1 (a-b)^{n-1} b^1 + {}^nC_2 (a-b)^{n-2} b^2 + \ldots + {}^nC_{n-1} (a-b) b^{n-1} + {}^nC_n b^n$

$a^n - b^n = (a-b)\{(a-b)^{n-1} + {}^nC_1 (a-b)^{n-2} b + {}^nC_2 (a-b)^{n-3} b^2 + \ldots + {}^nC_{n-1} b^{n-1}\}$

13. (d) $\because \sum_{r=0}^{n} {}^nC_r a^{n-r} b^r = (a+b)^n$

On putting $b = 3$ and $a = 1$, we get

$\sum_{r=0}^{n} {}^nC_r 1^{n-r} 3^r = (1+3)^n$

$\sum_{r=0}^{n} 3^r \cdot {}^nC_r = (4)^n$

Assertion-Reason

1. (a) $(x+2)^7 = {}^7C_0 x^7 2^0 + {}^7C_1 x^6 2^1 + {}^7C_2 x^5 2^2 + \ldots {}^7C_7 x^0 2^7$

$= {}^7C_0 x^7 + 2 \cdot {}^7C_1 x^6 + 4 \cdot {}^7C_2 x^5 + \ldots 128\,{}^7C_7$

Both Assertion and Reason are true and Reason is the correct explanation of Assertion.

2. (c) We know that

$$(a+b)^n = \sum_{r=0}^{n} {}^nC_r a^{n-r} b^r$$

$\Rightarrow \quad T_{r+1} = {}^nC_r a^{n-r} b^r$

Here, $r = 9, n = 12$

$\Rightarrow T_{10} = {}^{12}C_9 \left(\frac{x}{2}\right)^3 \left(\frac{2}{x}\right)^9$

$= {}^{12}C_9 \frac{x^3}{2^3} \times \frac{2^9}{x^9}$

$= {}^{12}C_9 2^{9-3} x^{3-9}$

$= {}^{12}C_9 2^6 x^{-6}$

$= 64\,{}^{12}C_9 x^{-6}$

Thus, the coefficient of 10th term is $64\,{}^{12}C_9$.

Assertion is true but Reason is false.

3. (c) We know that

${}^nC_0 + {}^nC_1 + {}^nC_2 + \ldots {}^nC_n = 2^n$

Here, in the expansion of $(1+x)^n$, the coefficient of x^r is given by

$T_{r+1} = {}^{15}C_r x^r$

$\Rightarrow \quad T_{11} = {}^{15}C_{19} \cdot x^{10}$

$\therefore$ The coefficient of x^{10} is ${}^{15}C_{10}$.

Assertion is true but Reason is false.

4. (a) We have,

$\sum_{r=0}^{n} r\,{}^nC_r x^r = \sum_{r=0}^{n} r \frac{n}{r}\,{}^{n-1}C_{r-1} x^{r-1} \times x$

$\Rightarrow \sum_{r=0}^{n} r\,{}^nC_r x^r = nx \sum_{r=1}^{n} {}^{n-1}C_{r-1} x^{r-1}$

$\Rightarrow \sum_{r=0}^{n} r\,{}^nC_r x^r = nx(1+x)^{n-1} \quad \ldots(i)$

Replacing x by r in Eq. (i), we get

$\sum_{r=0}^{n} r\,{}^nC_r = n2^{n-1}$

Both Assertion and Reason are true and Reason is the correct explanation of Assertion.

5. (d) We know that the number of terms in the binomial expansion of $(x+y)^n$ is equal to $n+1$.

So, the number of terms in the expansion of $(x+y)^{13}$ is $(13+1)$ i.e. 14.

Assertion is false but Reason is true.

6. (b) Using binomial theorem, we get

$\left(x^2 + \frac{3}{x}\right)^4 = {}^4C_0 (x^2)^4 + {}^4C_1 (x^2)^3 \left(\frac{3}{x}\right) + {}^4C_2 (x^2)^2 \left(\frac{3}{x}\right)^2 + {}^4C_3 (x^3) \left(\frac{3}{x}\right)^3 + {}^4C_4 \left(\frac{3}{x}\right)^4$

$$= x^8 + 4x^6 \cdot \frac{3}{x} + 6x^4 \cdot \frac{9}{x}$$
$$+ 4x^2 \cdot \frac{27}{x^3} + \frac{81}{x^4}$$
$$= x^8 + 12x^5 + 54x^2 + \frac{108}{x} + \frac{81}{x^4}$$

Both Assertion and Reason are true but Reason is not the correct explanation of Assertion.

7. (b) Here, $r = 2$, $a = 2x$, $b = -y$ and $n = 7$

$\therefore \quad T_3 = T_{2+1}$
$$= {}^7C_2\,(2x)^{7-2}(-y)^2 = 672x^5y^2$$

Both Assertion and reason are true.

8. (a) We know that

$$(a+b)^n = {}^nC_0a^n + {}^nC_1a^{n-1}b + {}^nC_2a^{n-2}b^2 + \dots + {}^nC_{n-1}ab^{n-1} + {}^nC_nb^n$$
$$(a+(-b))^n = {}^nC_0\,a^n + {}^nC_1a^{n-1}(-b) + {}^nC_2a^{n-2}(-b)^2 + \dots + {}^nC_{n-1}a(-b)^{n-1} + {}^nC_n(-b)^n$$
$$= {}^nC_0\,a^n - {}^nC_1a^{n-1}b + {}^nC_2a^{n-2}b^2 + \dots + (-1)^n\,{}^nC_nb^n$$

Both Assertion and Reason are true and Reason is the correct explanation of Assertion.

9. (b) $p^n = [(p-q)+q]^n$

$$\Rightarrow p^n = {}^nC_0\,(p-q)^n + {}^nC_1(p-q)^{n-1}q + {}^nC_2(p-q)^{n-2}q^2 + \dots + {}^nC_{n-1}(p-q)(q)^{n-1} + {}^nC_nq^n$$
$$p^n - q^n = (p-q)\,\{(p-q)^{n-1} + {}^nC_1(p-q)^{n-2}q + {}^nC_2(p-q)^{n-3}q^2 + \dots + {}^nC_{n-1}q^{n-1}$$

$\therefore p^n - q^n$ is divisible by $(p-q)$, $\forall\, n \in N$.

Hence, Assertion is true.

Now, 4th term from end

$$= T_{(n-4+1)+1}$$
$$= {}^nC_{n-4+1}x^{4-1}a^{n-4+1}$$
$$= {}^nC_{n-3}x^3a^{n-3}$$

Hence, Reason is true.

Case Base

Case 1 (i) (a) We know that there are $(n+1)$ terms in the binomial expansion of $(a+b)^n$.

So, the expansion of $(1-x)^5$ has $(5+1)$ terms i.e. 6 terms.

(ii) (c) We have,
$$(4 + x^2 + 4x)^3 = ((x+2)^2)^3 = (x+2)^6$$

So, the expansion of $(x+2)^6$ has 7terms

(iii) (c) We have,
$$(1 + 14x + 49x^2)^{60} = [(1+7x)^2]^{60} = (1+7x)^{120}$$

$\therefore$ The number of terms
$$= 120 + 1 = 121$$

Case 2 (i) Given, binomial expression is $\left(y^2 + \frac{c}{y}\right)^5$

$$\text{Now, } T_{r+1} = {}^5C_r \times (y^2)^{5-r} \times \left(\frac{c}{y}\right)^r$$
$$= {}^5C_r y^{10-3r} \times c^r$$

Now, $10 - 3r = 1$

$\Rightarrow \quad 3r = 9 \Rightarrow r = 3$

$\therefore$ The coefficient of
$$y = {}^5C_3c^3 = 10c^3.$$

(ii) Given, $(2x + 3y^2)^5$

Therefore, the general form for the expression $(2x+3y^2)^5$ is $T_{r+1} = {}^5C_r\,(2x)^r(3y^2)^{5-r}$

Hence,
$$T_{3+1} = {}^5C_3(2x)^3 \cdot (3y^2)^{5-3}$$
$$\Rightarrow \quad T_4 = {}^5C_3\,(2x)^3\,(3y^2)^2$$
$$\Rightarrow \quad T_4 = {}^5C_3 8x^3 9y^4$$
$$= 720x^3y^4$$

$\therefore$ The coefficient of x^3y^4 in $(2x+3y^2)^5$ is 720.

(iii) We have, $(1 + 3x + 3x^2 + x^3)^5$

$$\Rightarrow \quad (1 + 3x + 3x^2 + x^3)^5 = [(x+1)^3)^5] = (x+1)^{15}$$

$\therefore$ Number of terms
$$= 15 + 1 = 16$$

Competition Connect

1. (i) $T_{r+1} = {}^{30}C_r(y)^{30-r}\left(-\frac{1}{y}\right)^r$
$$= {}^{30}C_r\,(y)^{30-2r}(-1)^r.$$

(ii) $T_6 = T_{5+1}$
$$= {}^9C_5\left(\frac{4x}{5}\right)^{9-5}\left(\frac{-5}{2x}\right)^5$$
$$= -\,{}^9C_4\left(\frac{4x}{5}\right)^4\left(\frac{5}{2x}\right)^5$$
$$= \frac{-9\times 8\times 7\times 6}{4\times 3\times 2\times 1}\left(\frac{2^8x^4}{5^4}\right) \times \left(\frac{5^5}{2^5 \times x^5}\right)$$
$$= -\frac{5040}{x}$$

(iii) $T_{10} = T_{9+1}$
$$= {}^{12}C_9(2x^2)^{12-9}\left(\frac{1}{x}\right)^9$$
$$= {}^{12}C_3\,\frac{8}{x^3}$$
$$= \frac{12\times 11\times 10}{3\times 2\times 1} \times \frac{8}{x^3}$$
$$= \frac{1760}{x^3}$$

2. (c) 17th and 18th terms
$$T_{17} = {}^{50}C_{16}\,2^{34}(1)^{16}$$
$$T_{18} = {}^{50}C_{17}2^{33}(1)^{17}$$

3. (c) $T_{r+1} = {}^nC_rx^{n-r}a^r$
$$= {}^7C_r2^r$$

(A) $T_3 = T_{2+1} = {}^7C_22^2$
$$= 21 \times 4 = 84$$

(B) $T_4 = T_{3+1} = {}^7C_32^3$
$$= 35 \times 8 = 280$$

(C) $T_5 = T_{4+1} = {}^7C_42^4$
$$= 35 \times 16 = 560$$

(D) $T_2 = T_{1+1} = {}^7C_12^1$
$$= 7 \times 2 = 14$$

4. $T_6 = {}^nC_5x^{n-5}a^5 = 112 \quad \dots\text{(i)}$

$T_7 = {}^nC_6x^{n-6}a^6 = 7 \quad \dots\text{(ii)}$

$T_8 = {}^nC_7x^{n-7}a^7 = \frac{1}{4} \quad \dots\text{(iii)}$

On dividing Eq. (ii) by Eq. (i), we get
$$\frac{{}^nC_6x^{n-6}a^6}{{}^nC_5x^{n-5}a^5} = \frac{7}{112}$$
$$\Rightarrow \frac{n-6+1}{6}\,x^{-1}a = \frac{1}{16}$$
$$\Rightarrow \quad \frac{a}{x} = \frac{3}{8n-40} \quad \dots\text{(iv)}$$

On dividing Eq. (iii) by Eq. (ii), we get
$$\frac{{}^nC_7x^{n-7}a^7}{{}^nC_6x^{n-6}a^6} = \frac{1/4}{7}$$

$\Rightarrow \frac{n-7+1}{7} x^{-1} a = \frac{1}{28}$

$\Rightarrow \frac{a}{x} = \frac{1}{4n-24}$ ...(v)

From Eqs. (iv) and (v), we get

$n = 8$

Also, $x = 8a$

Now, $a = \frac{1}{2}$ from Eq. (ii),

Therefore, $x = 4$

5. Coefficient of 5th term

= Coefficient of 9th term

$\Rightarrow {}^nC_4 = {}^nC_8$

$\Rightarrow n = 12$ $[\because {}^nC_x = {}^nC_y;$ $\therefore x = y$ or $x + y = n]$

6. (i) Suppose x^6y^2 occurs in the $(r+1)$th term of the expansion $(x+y)^8$.

$T_{r+1} = {}^8C_r\, x^{8-r}(y)^r$

$= {}^8C_r x^{8-r} y^r$

On putting $r = 2$, we get

Coefficient of x^6y^2

$= {}^8C_2$

$= 28$

(ii) $T_{r+1} = {}^{11}C_r(2x^2)^{11-r}\left(\frac{-3}{x}\right)^r$

$= (-1)^r\, {}^{11}C_r(2)^{11-r} \cdot 3^r \cdot x^{22-3r}$

If T_{r+1} contains x^{10}, then

$22 - 3r = 10 \Rightarrow r = 4$

So, $(4+1)$th term

i.e. 5th term contains x^{10}

On putting $r = 4$, we get

$T_5 = (-1)^4\, {}^{11}C_4 2^{11-4} \times 3^4 \times x^{10}$

$= {}^{11}C_4 \times 2^7 \times 3^4 \times x^{10}$

Coefficient of $x^{10} = {}^{11}C_4 \times 2^7 \times 3^4$

(iii) $T_{r+1} = {}^{11}C_r(3a)^{11-r}(-2b)^r$

$= {}^{11}C_r(3)^{11-r}(2)^r (a)^{11-r}(b)^r(-1)^r$

For the coefficient of a^6b^5, put $r = 5$

$T_{5+1} = {}^{11}C_5 3^6 \cdot 2^5 \cdot a^6 \cdot b^5(-1)^5$

$= [-\,{}^{11}C_5 \cdot 3^6 \cdot 2^5]\, a^6b^5$

The coefficient of a^6b^5

$= -\,{}^{11}C_5 \cdot 3^6 \cdot 2^5$

7. (i) $T_{r+1} = {}^{12}C_r x^{12-r} 3^r$

For x^5, put $12 - r = 5$ i.e. $r = 7$

$T_{7+1} = {}^{12}C_7 x^5 3^7 = {}^{12}C_7 \cdot 3^7 \cdot x^5$

$a = {}^{12}C_7 3^7$

(ii) $T_{r+1} = {}^{10}C_r x^{10-r}(-2y)^r$

$= {}^{10}C_r x^{10-r} 2^r y^r(-1)^r$

For x^8y^2, put $r = 2$

$\Rightarrow T_{2+1} = {}^{10}C_2 x^8 2^2 y^2 \times 1$

$= {}^{10}C_2 2^2 \cdot x^8y^2$

$a = {}^{10}C_2 \cdot 2^2$

(iii) $T_{r+1} = {}^{10}C_r(z^2)^{10-r}(-t)^r$

$= {}^{10}C_r z^{20-2r} t^r(-1)^r$

For z^4t^8, put $r = 8$

$T_{8+1} = {}^{10}C_8 z^{20-2\times 8} t^8 \times 1$

$= {}^{10}C_8 z^4 t^8$

$a = {}^{10}C_8$

(iv) $T_{r+1} = {}^8C_r(3x)^{8-r}(-4y)^r$

$= {}^8C_r 3^{8-r} 4^r x^{8-r} y^r(-1)^r$

For x^6y^2, put $r = 2$

$T_{2+1} = {}^8C_2 3^6 \cdot 4^2 x^6y^2 \times 1$

$= {}^8C_2 3^6 4^2 x^6 y^2$

$a = {}^8C_2 \cdot 3^6 \cdot 4^2$

8. In the expansion of $(3+x)^6$

(i) $T_{r+1} = {}^6C_r 3^{6-r} \cdot x^r$

(ii) We have, $n = 6$

Total number of terms

$= n + 1 = 6 + 1 = 7$

(iii) Total terms = 7

Middle term = 4th term

$= T_{3+1}$

$= {}^6C_3(3)^{6-3}x^3$

$= \frac{6!}{3!3!} \times (3)^3 x^3$

$= 27 \times \frac{6\times5\times4}{3\times2} x^3$

$= 540\,x^3$

(iv) $T_{2+1} = {}^6C_2\, 3^{6-2} x^2$

$\Rightarrow T_3 = {}^6C_2 \cdot 3^4 \cdot x^2$

Coefficient of third term

$= \frac{6\cdot5}{2\cdot1} \times 81 = 1215$

9. (c) $A = 4a$ and $B = 3c$

$T_6 = {}^nC_5 x^{n-5} y^5 = a$

$T_7 = {}^nC_6 x^{n-6} y^6 = b$

$T_8 = {}^nC_7 x^{n-7} y^7 = c$

$T_9 = {}^nC_8\, x^{n-8} y^8 = d$

$\frac{b^2 - ac}{c^2 - bd} = \frac{4a}{3c}$

$\frac{b^2 - ac}{a} = \frac{4}{3}\left[\frac{c^2 - bd}{c}\right]$

$\Rightarrow \frac{1}{b}\left[\frac{b^2 - ac}{a}\right] = \frac{4}{3}\left[\frac{c^2 - bd}{bc}\right]$

$\Rightarrow \frac{b}{a} - \frac{c}{b} = \frac{4}{3}\left[\frac{c}{b} - \frac{d}{c}\right]$

$\because \frac{n-5}{6} - \frac{n-6}{7} = \frac{4}{3}\left[\frac{n-6}{7} - \frac{n-7}{8}\right]$

$\frac{n+1}{42} = \frac{n+1}{42}$

10. (i) Here, $n = 10$, which is an even number.

$\therefore$ Middle term is given by $\left(\frac{10}{2} + 1\right)$th term i.e. 6th term.

Let T_{r+1} be its general term. Then,

$T_{r+1} = {}^{10}C_r\left(\frac{1}{x}\right)^{10-r}(x \sin x)^r$

$= {}^{10}C_r x^{r-10+r} \sin^r x$

$= {}^{10}C_r x^{2r-10} \sin^r x$

Now, $T_6 = T_{5+1}$

$= {}^{10}C_5 x^{10-10} \sin^5 x$

$= {}^{10}C_5 \sin^5 x$

$\because$ Middle term $= 7\frac{7}{8}$

$\therefore {}^{10}C_5 \sin^5 x = \frac{63}{8}$

$\Rightarrow \sin^5 x = \frac{63}{8 \times 252}$

$= \frac{1}{8\times4} = \frac{1}{32}$

$\Rightarrow \sin x = \frac{1}{2}$

$\Rightarrow \sin x = \sin\frac{\pi}{6}$

$\therefore x = n\pi + (-1)^n \frac{\pi}{6}$

(ii) Middle term $= \left(\frac{8}{2} + 1\right)$

= 5th term

$T_5 = {}^8C_4\left(\frac{P}{2}\right)^{8-4} 2^4$

$\Rightarrow 1120 = {}^8C_4 P^4$

$\Rightarrow 1120 = 7 \times 2 \times 5 \times P^4$

$\Rightarrow P^4 = \frac{1120}{70}$

$P^4 = 16$

$\Rightarrow P = \pm 2$

(iii) In the expansion of $(1+x)^{43}$,

$T_{r+1} = {}^{43}C_r x^r$

$T_{2r+1} = {}^{43}C_{2r} x^{2r}$

and $T_{r+2} = {}^{43}C_{r+1} x^{r+1}$

According to the statement,

${}^{43}C_{2r} = {}^{43}C_{r+1}$

$\Rightarrow \quad 2r = r+1$

or $\quad 43 = 2r + r + 1$

$\Rightarrow \quad r = 1$ or $r = 14$

(iv) ${}^{18}C_{2r+3} = {}^{18}C_{r-3}$

$\Rightarrow (2r+3) + (r-3) = 18$

$\Rightarrow \quad r = 6$

11. Coefficient of 5th, 6th and 7th terms are ${}^nC_4$, ${}^nC_5$ and ${}^nC_6$.

$\because$ They are in AP.

$\therefore {}^nC_5 - {}^nC_4 = {}^nC_6 - {}^nC_5$

$\Rightarrow \quad 2\cdot {}^nC_5 = {}^nC_6 + {}^nC_4$

$\Rightarrow \quad 2 = \dfrac{{}^nC_6}{{}^nC_5} + \dfrac{{}^nC_4}{{}^nC_5}$

$\Rightarrow \quad 2 = \dfrac{n-5}{6} + \dfrac{5}{n-4}$

$\Rightarrow \quad 2 = \dfrac{30 + (n-4)(n-5)}{6(n-4)}$

$\Rightarrow 12n - 48 = 30 + n^2 - 9n + 20$

$\Rightarrow \quad n = 7, 14$

12. Option (ii) is correct.

$T_{r+1} = {}^{m+n}C_r x^r$

$T_{n+1} = {}^{m+n}C_n x^n$

$\Rightarrow$ Coefficient of $x^n = {}^{m+n}C_n = a$

$T_{m+1} = {}^{m+n}C_m x^m$

$\Rightarrow$ Coefficient of $x^m = {}^{m+n}C_m = b$

${}^{m+n}C_n = {}^{m+n}C_{[(m+n)-n]} = {}^{m+n}C_m$

$\Rightarrow \quad a = b$

13. (True)

${}^mC_2 = 3$

$\Rightarrow \quad \dfrac{m(m-1)}{2!} = 3$

$\Rightarrow \quad m^2 - m - 6 = 0$

$\Rightarrow \quad m^2 + 2m - 3m - 6 = 0$

$\Rightarrow m(m+2) - 3(m+2) = 0$

$\Rightarrow \quad (m-3)(m+2) = 0$

$\because \quad m \neq -2$

$\therefore \quad m = 3$

14. $(3+ax)^9 = {}^9C_0 \times 3^9 + {}^9C_1 \times 3^8 \times (ax)^1 + {}^9C_2 \times 3^7 \times (ax)^2 + {}^9C_3 \times 3^6 \times (ax)^3 + \dots + {}^9C_9 (ax)^9$

$\Rightarrow {}^9C_2 \times 3^7 \times a^2 = {}^9C_3 \times 3^6 \times a^3$

$\Rightarrow \quad a = \dfrac{36 \times 3^7}{84 \times 3^6} = \dfrac{9}{7}$

15. $(1+x)^n \left(1 + \dfrac{1}{x}\right)^n$

$= \dfrac{(1+x)^n (1+x)^n}{x^n} = \dfrac{(1+x)^{2n}}{x^n}$

Coefficient of x^{-1}

$=$ Coefficient of x^{-1} in $\dfrac{(1+x)^{2n}}{x^n}$

$=$ Coefficient of x^{n-1} in $(1+x)^{2n}$

$= {}^{2n}C_{n-1}$

16. (c) $a_{r-1} =$ Coefficient of x^{r-1} in $(1-x)^{2n-1}$

$= (-1)^{r-1}\, {}^{2n-1}C_{r-1}$

$a_{2n-r} =$ Coefficient of x^{2n-r} in $(1-x)^{2n-1}$

$= (-1)^{2n-r}\, {}^{2n-1}C_{2n-r}$

$a_{r-1} + a_{2n-r}$

$= \left\{(-1)^{r-1} + \dfrac{1}{(-1)^r}\right\} {}^{2n-1}C_{2n-r}$

$= \dfrac{-1+1}{(-1)^r}\, {}^{2n-1}C_{2n-r} = 0$

17. $[1 + {}^6C_1(2x) + {}^6C_2\cdot(2x)^2 + {}^6C_3(2x)^3 + {}^6C_4(2x)^4 + {}^6C_5(2x)^5 + \dots]$
$\times [1 - {}^7C_1 x + {}^7C_2 x^2 - {}^7C_3 x^3 + {}^7C_4 x^4 - {}^7C_5 x^5 + \dots]$

$= [1 + 12x + 60x^2 + 160x^3 + 240x^4 + 192x^5 + \dots]$
$\times [1 - 7x + 21x^2 - 35x^3 + 35x^4 - 21x^5 + \dots]$

$\therefore$ Coefficient of x^5 in the product
$= [1 \times (-21) + (12 \times 35) + 60 \times (-35) + 160 \times 21 + 240 \times (-7) + 192 \times 1]$

$= 171$

18. (b) $\dfrac{n!}{(n-q+1)!(q-1)!}$

$= \dfrac{n!}{(n-p+1)!(p-1)!}$

$\Rightarrow (n-p+1)!(p-1)!$

$= (n-q+1)! \times (q-1)!$

$\because \quad p \neq q$

$(q-1)! \neq (p-1)!$

$(q-1)! = (n-p+1)!$

$\therefore \quad q - 1 = n - p + 1$

$\Rightarrow \quad p + q = n + 2$

19. (i) Let the coefficient of rth, $(r+1)$th and $(r+2)$th terms are 56, 70 and 56. Then,

${}^nC_{r-1} = 56$, ${}^nC_r = 70$ and ${}^nC_{r+1} = 56$

$\Rightarrow {}^nC_{r-1} = {}^nC_{r+1}$

$\Rightarrow \quad r - 1 = n - (r+1)$

$\Rightarrow \quad n = 2r$

Now, $\dfrac{{}^nC_{r-1}}{{}^nC_r} = \dfrac{56}{70}$

$\Rightarrow \quad \dfrac{r}{n-r+1} = \dfrac{4}{5} \Rightarrow \dfrac{r}{r+1} = \dfrac{4}{5}$

$\Rightarrow \quad r = 4, n = 8$

$\therefore$ Required positions are 4th, 5th and 6th.

(ii) $\because {}^nC_{r-1} = {}^nC_{r+1}$

$\therefore n = 2r$

20. (i) (False)

Since, there are $(n+1)$ terms.
1st term from the end is the $(n+1)$th term of the expansion and $n+1 = (n+1) - (1-1)$
2nd term from the end is the nth term and $n = (n+1) - (2-1)$
3rd term from the end is the $(n-1)$th term and $n - 1 = (n+1) - (3-1)$ and so on.
Thus, rth term from the end will be term number $(n+1) - (r-1) = (n-r+2)$ of the expansion and $(n-r+2)$th term is ${}^nC_{n-r+1}\, x^{r-1} a^{n-r+1}$

(ii) (False)

4th term from the end

$= T_{(n-4+1)+1}$

$= {}^nC_{n-4+1}\, x^{4-1}\, a^{n-4+1}$

$= {}^nC_{n-3}\, x^3 a^{n-3}$

21. (a) 5th term from the beginning

$= {}^{10}C_4 (\sqrt[4]{2})^6 \left(\dfrac{1}{\sqrt[4]{3}}\right)^4$

$= {}^{10}C_4 \times \dfrac{2\sqrt{2}}{3}$

5th term from the end

$= {}^{10}C_6 (\sqrt[4]{2})^4 \left(\dfrac{1}{\sqrt[4]{3}}\right)^6$

$= {}^{10}C_4 \times \dfrac{2}{3} \times \dfrac{1}{\sqrt{3}}$

$\therefore$ Required ratio $= \sqrt{6} : 1$

Competition Edge Up

1. (b) $\left(\sqrt{a}x^2 + \frac{1}{2x^3}\right)^{10}$

General term

$= {}^{10}C_r(\sqrt{a}x^2)^{10-r}\left(\frac{1}{2x^3}\right)^r$

For the term independent of x,

$2(10-r) - 3r = 0 \Rightarrow r = 4$

Put $r = 4$,

${}^{10}C_4(\sqrt{a}x^2)^6\left(\frac{1}{2x^3}\right)^4$

$= \frac{10\cdot 9\cdot 8\cdot 7}{4\cdot 3\cdot 2\cdot 1} \times a^3 \times \frac{1}{2^4}$

$= 210a^3 \times \frac{1}{16}$

Now, $210a^3 \times \frac{1}{16} = 105$

$\Rightarrow \quad a^3 = 8 \Rightarrow a^2 = 4$

2. (d) For $\left(\frac{\sqrt[5]{3}}{x} + \frac{2x}{\sqrt[3]{5}}\right)^{12}$

$T_{r+1} = {}^{12}C_r\left(\frac{3^{1/5}}{x}\right)^{12-r}\left(\frac{2x}{5^{1/3}}\right)^r$

$= {}^{12}C_r\, 3^{\frac{12-r}{5}} \cdot 5^{-\frac{r}{3}} \cdot 2^r \cdot x^{r-12+r}$

For constant term,

$r - 12 + r = 0 \Rightarrow r = 6$

$T_7 = {}^{12}C_6 \cdot 3^{6/5} \cdot 5^{-2} \cdot 2^6$

$= \frac{9\times 11\times 7}{25} \times 2^8 \times 3^{1/5}$

On comparing, $\alpha = \frac{9\times 11\times 7}{25}$

$\Rightarrow \quad 25\alpha = 693$

3. (c) We have, $\left(\frac{1}{3}x^{1/3} + \frac{1}{2x^{2/3}}\right)^{18}$

Given, coefficients of $T_7 = m$

and coefficients of $T_{13} = n$

Now, $\frac{m}{n} = \frac{{}^{18}C_6\left(\frac{1}{3}\right)^{12}\cdot\left(\frac{1}{2}\right)^6}{{}^{18}C_{12}\left(\frac{1}{3}\right)^6\cdot\left(\frac{1}{2}\right)^{12}}$

$[\because {}^nC_r = {}^nC_{n-r}]$

$\Rightarrow \left(\frac{m}{n}\right)^{1/3} = \left(\frac{1}{3^{12}}\times 3^6 \times \frac{1}{2^6}\times 2^{12}\right)^{1/3}$

$= \left(\frac{2^6}{3^6}\right)^{1/3} = \frac{4}{9}$

$\therefore \left(\frac{m}{n}\right)^{1/3} = \frac{4}{9}$

4. (d) Given, A = sum of all the coefficients in the expansion of $(1-3x+10x^2)^n$

B = sum of all the coefficient in the expansion of $(1+x^2)^n$.

Put $x = 1$ in $(1-3x+10x^2)^n$ to get A and in similar way you can find B also.

So, $A = (8)^n$ and $B = 2^n$

Hence, $A = (2^n)^3 = B^3$

5. (c) Coefficient of x^{70} in $x^2(1+x)^{98} + x^3(1+x)^{97}$ $+ x^4(1+x)^{96} + \dots + x^{54}(1+x)^{46}$ is

$= {}^{98}C_{68} + {}^{97}C_{67} + {}^{96}C_{66} + \dots$
$+ {}^{47}C_{17} + {}^{46}C_{16}$

$= {}^{46}C_{30} + {}^{47}C_{30} + \dots + {}^{98}C_{30}$

$= ({}^{46}C_{31} + {}^{46}C_{30}) + {}^{47}C_{30} + \dots$
$+ {}^{98}C_{30} - {}^{46}C_{31}$

$= {}^{47}C_{31} + {}^{47}C_{30} + \dots\dots {}^{98}C_{30} - {}^{46}C_{31}$

$= {}^{99}C_{31} - {}^{46}C_{31} = {}^{99}C_p - {}^{46}C_q$

$\therefore$ Possible values of $(p+q)$ are 62, 83.

$\therefore \quad p + q = 83$

6. (c) General term

$T_{r+1} = {}^{15}C_r\left(5^{\frac{1}{3}}\right)^r\left(2^{\frac{1}{5}}\right)^{15-r}$

$= {}^{15}C_r 5^{\frac{r}{3}} \cdot 2^{\frac{15-r}{5}}, r \in \{0, 1, 2, \dots, 15\}$

For rational terms,

$\frac{r}{3} \in$ integer and $\frac{r}{5} \in$ integer

$\Rightarrow$ 3 and 5 divides r

$\Rightarrow$ 15 divides r

$\Rightarrow$ $r = 0$ and 15

Hence, only two rational terms

i.e. ${}^{15}C_0 2^3 + {}^{15}C_{15}(5)^5$

$= 8 + 3125 = 3133$

7. (*) Binomial coefficients of 4 consecutive terms of $(1+x)^n$ are ${}^nC_r, {}^nC_{r+1}, {}^nC_{r+2}, {}^nC_{r+3}$, respectively.

Given, ${}^nC_r = 2 - p$,

${}^nC_{r+2} = 2 - \alpha$,

${}^nC_{r+1} = p$, ${}^nC_{r+3} = \alpha$

$\therefore {}^nC_r + {}^nC_{r+1} = 2$

and ${}^nC_{r+2} + {}^nC_{r+3} = 2$

$\Rightarrow \quad {}^{n+1}C_{r+1} = 2$

and $\quad {}^{n+1}C_{r+3} = 2$

$\therefore \quad {}^{n+1}C_{r+1} = {}^{n+1}C_{r+3}$

$\Rightarrow \quad r + 1 + r + 3 = n + 1$

$\Rightarrow \quad 2r + 4 = n + 1$

$\Rightarrow \quad n = 2r + 3$

Now, ${}^{n+1}C_{r+1} = 2$

${}^{2r+4}C_{r+1} = 2$

Not such value possible.

8. (b) For $(1+x)^n$

Coefficient of $x^4 \Rightarrow {}^nC_4$

Coefficient of $x^5 = {}^nC_5$

Coefficient of $x^6 = {}^nC_6$

$\because \quad {}^nC_4, {}^nC_5, {}^nC_6 \to$ AP

$\Rightarrow \quad 2.{}^nC_5 = {}^nC_4 + {}^nC_6$

$2 \times \frac{n!}{(n-5)!\,5!}$

$= \frac{n!}{(n-4)!\,4!} + \frac{n!}{(n-6)!\,6!}$

$\Rightarrow \frac{2}{(n-5)\cdot 5} = \frac{1}{(n-4)(n-5)}$

$+ \frac{1}{6\times 5}$

$\Rightarrow n^2 - 21n + 98 = 0$

$\Rightarrow \quad n = 14, 7$

$\therefore$ Maximum value of $n = 14$

9. (b) In the expansion of

$\left(x^{\frac{2}{3}} + \frac{x^{-\frac{2}{5}}}{2}\right)$

$T_{r+1} = {}^9C_r\left(x^{\frac{2}{3}}\right)^{9-r}\left(\frac{x^{-\frac{2}{5}}}{2}\right)^r$

$= {}^9C_r \cdot \frac{1}{2^r} \cdot x^{\frac{18-2r}{3} - \frac{2r}{5}}$

For coefficient of $x^{\frac{2}{3}}$,

$\frac{18-2r}{3} - \frac{2r}{5} = \frac{2}{3}$

$\Rightarrow \quad 5(9-r) - 3r = 5$

$\Rightarrow \quad 45 - 8r = 5$

$r = 5$

Coefficient of $x^{\frac{2}{3}} = \frac{{}^9C_5}{2^5}$

For coefficient of $x^{-\frac{2}{5}}$

$$\frac{18-2r}{3}-\frac{2r}{5}=\frac{-2}{5}$$

$$\Rightarrow \quad 5(9-r)-3r=-3$$

$$45-8r=-3$$

$$r=6$$

Coefficient of $x^{-\frac{2}{5}}=\frac{{}^9C_6}{2^6}$

$$\therefore \text{ Sum}=\frac{{}^9C_5}{2^5}+\frac{{}^9C_6}{2^6}=\frac{21}{4}$$

10. (806) $(x+y)^n={}^nC_0x^ny^0 + {}^nC_1x^{n-1}y^1+{}^nC_2x^{n-2}y^2 + \ldots + {}^nC_nx^0y^n$

Now, second term,

$$T_2={}^nC_1x^{n-1}y=135 \quad \ldots(\text{i})$$

Third term,

$$T_3={}^nC_2x^{n-2}y^2=30 \quad \ldots(\text{ii})$$

Fourth term,

$$T_4={}^nC_3x^{n-3}y^3=\frac{10}{3} \quad \ldots(\text{iii})$$

By Eqs. (i) and (ii),

$$\frac{{}^nC_1x^{n-1}y}{{}^nC_2x^{n-2}y^2}=\frac{135}{30}$$

$$\Rightarrow \quad \frac{2n}{n(n-1)}\cdot\frac{x}{y}=\frac{9}{2}$$

$$\Rightarrow \quad \frac{1}{n-1}\cdot\frac{x}{y}=\frac{9}{4} \quad \ldots(\text{iv})$$

From Eqs. (ii) and (iii),

$$\frac{{}^nC_2x^{n-2}y^2}{{}^nC_3x^{n-3}y^3}=\frac{30\times 3}{10}$$

$$\Rightarrow \quad \frac{n(n-1)}{2\times 1}\times\frac{3\times2\times1}{n(n-1)(n-2)}\times\frac{x}{y}=9$$

$$\Rightarrow \quad \frac{1}{(n-2)}\frac{x}{y}=3 \quad \ldots(\text{v})$$

From Eqs. (iv) and (v),

$$\frac{\frac{1}{n-1}\cdot\frac{x}{y}}{\frac{1}{(n-2)}\frac{x}{y}}=\frac{\frac{9}{4}}{\frac{3}{1}} \Rightarrow \frac{n-2}{n-1}=\frac{3}{4}$$

$$\Rightarrow \quad 4n-8=3n-3 \Rightarrow n=5$$

Now, if $n=5$, then

Eq. (i) will become ${}^5C_1x^4y=135$

$$\Rightarrow \quad x^4y=27$$

and Eq. (v) will become $x=9y$

Using both $\Rightarrow (9y)^4\cdot y=27$

$$\Rightarrow \quad y^5=\frac{3^3}{3^8}=\frac{1}{3^5}\Rightarrow y=\frac{1}{3}$$

and $\quad x=9\times\frac{1}{3}=3$

$$\therefore 6(n^3+x^2+y)=6\left(125+9+\frac{1}{3}\right)$$

$$=806$$

11. (54) We have,

$$(1+2x-3x^2)\left(\frac{3}{2}x^2-\frac{1}{3x}\right)^9$$

Here, general term of

$$\left(\frac{3}{2}x^2-\frac{1}{3x}\right)^9$$

$$={}^9C_r\left(\frac{3}{2}x^2\right)^{9-r}(-1)^r\left(\frac{1}{3x}\right)^r$$

$$={}^9C_r\frac{(3)^{9-r}}{(2)^{9-r}}(x^2)^{9-r}(-1)^r(3x)^{-r}$$

$$={}^9C_r\frac{3^{9-2r}}{2^{9-r}}(-1)^r x^{18-3r}$$

For constant term, put $18-3r=0$

$$\Rightarrow \quad r=6$$

On putting $r=6$, we get

Coefficient of $x^0={}^9C_6\frac{1}{216}x^0$

$$=\frac{7}{18}x^0$$

On putting $r=7$, we get

Coefficient of

$$x^{-3}={}^9C_7\frac{3^{-5}}{2^2}(-1)^7x^{-3}$$

$$=-{}^9C_7\frac{1}{3^5\cdot 2^2}x^{-3}=-\frac{1}{27}x^{-3}$$

$$\therefore (1+2x-3x^3)\left(\frac{7}{18}x^0-\frac{1}{27}x^{-3}\right)$$

$$\text{Constant term}=\frac{7}{18}+\frac{3}{27}$$

$$=\frac{7+2}{18}=\frac{1}{2}$$

$$\therefore \quad p=\frac{1}{2}$$

$$\therefore \; 108p=108\times\frac{1}{2}$$

$$=54$$

12. (8) Since,

$$e^{1+x}=1+\frac{(1+x)}{1!}+\frac{(1+x)^2}{2!}+\frac{(1+x)^3}{3!}+\ldots$$

$$\Rightarrow \quad \frac{e^{1+x}}{1+x}=\frac{1}{1+x}+1+\frac{(1+x)}{2!}+\frac{(1+x)^2}{3!}+\frac{(1+x)^3}{4!}+\ldots$$

Now, coefficient of x^2 in RHS is

$$1+\frac{{}^2C_2}{3}+\frac{{}^3C_2}{4}+\ldots=a$$

and coefficient of x^2 in LHS

$$e\left(1+x+\frac{x^2}{2!}\right)\ldots\left(1-x+\frac{x^2}{2!}+\ldots\right)$$

is $\quad e-e+\frac{e}{2!}=a$

$$b=1+\frac{2}{1!}+\frac{2^2}{2!}+\frac{2^3}{3!}+\ldots=e^2$$

$$\therefore \quad \frac{2b}{a^2}=8$$

13. (678) Coefficient of x^{30} in

$$\frac{(x+1)^6(1+x^2)^7(1-x^3)^8}{x^6}$$

Coefficient of x^{36} in

$(1+x)^6(1+x^2)^7(1-x^3)^8$

General term,

$${}^6C_{r_1}\,{}^7C_{r_2}\,{}^8C_{r_3}(-1)^{r_3}x^{r_1+2r_2+3r_3}$$

$$r_1+2r_2+3r_3=36$$

$r_1+2r_2=12$ [taking $r_3=8$]

Case I

r_1	r_2	r_3
0	6	8
2	5	8
4	4	8
4	3	8

Case II

r_1	r_2	r_3
1	7	7
3	6	7
5	5	7

$r_1+2r_2=15$ [taking $r_3=7$]

Case III

r_1	r_2	r_3
4	7	6
6	6	6

$r_1+2r_2=18$ [taking $r_3=6$]

Coefficient

$= 7 + (25 \times 21) + (15 \times 35) + (35) - (6 \times 8) - (20 \times 7 \times 8) - (6 \times 21 \times 8) + (15 \times 28) + (7 \times 28)$

$= -678 = \alpha$

Hence, $|\alpha| = 678$

14. (25) $(x+3)^{n-1} + (x+3)^{n-2}(x+2) + (x+3)^{n-3}(x+2)^2 + \ldots + (x+2)^{n-1}$

$$= (x+3)^{n-1}\left[\frac{\left(\frac{x+2}{x+3}\right)^n - 1}{\frac{x+2}{x+3} - 1}\right]$$

$$= (x+3)^{n-1}\left[\frac{\frac{(x+2)^n}{(x+3)^n} - 1}{\frac{-1}{x+3}}\right]$$

$= (x+3)^n - (x+2)^n$

Coefficient of

$x^r = {}^nC_r 3^r - {}^nC_r 2^r = \alpha_r$

$$\sum_{r=0}^{n} \alpha_r = \sum_{r=0}^{n} {}^nC_r 3^r - \sum_{r=0}^{n} {}^nC_r 2^r$$

$= (1+3)^n - (1+2)^n$

$= 4^n - 3^n = \beta^n - \gamma^n$

$\beta = 4, \gamma = 3$ and $\beta^2 + \gamma^2 = 25$

15. (118) Expansion of $(1+x)(1-x^2)\left(1 + \frac{3}{x} + \frac{3}{x^2} + \frac{1}{x^3}\right)^5$

$$= (1+x)(1-x^2)\left[\left(1+\frac{1}{x}\right)^3\right]^5$$

$$= (1+x)(1-x^2)\frac{(1+x)^{15}}{x^{15}}$$

$$= \frac{(1+x)^{16}(1+x)(1-x)}{x^{15}}$$

$$= \frac{(1+x)^{17}(1-x)}{x^{15}}$$

$$\text{Expansion} = \frac{(1+x)^{17}}{x^{15}} - \frac{x(1+x)^{17}}{x^{15}}$$

Coefficient of x^3 in expansion is equal to coefficient of x^{18} in the expansion

$= 0 - 1 = -1$

and coefficient of x^{-13} in the expansion is equal to coefficient of x^2 in the expansion

$= {}^{17}C_2 - {}^{17}C_1$

$= 17 \times 8 - 17$

$= 17 \times 7$

$= 119$

$\therefore$ Sum $= -1 + 119 = 118$

16. (138) We have,

$$T_{n+1} = {}^nC_r 11^{r/6} \cdot 7^{\frac{824-r}{2}}$$

For integral term 6 should divided r

and $\frac{824-r}{2}$ must be integer

$\Rightarrow$ 2 must divide r

$\Rightarrow r$ divisible by 6

$\Rightarrow$ Possible values of

$r \in \{0, 1, 2, \ldots, 824\}$

$\Rightarrow$ For integer terms,

$r \in \{0, 6, 12, \ldots, 822\}$

$\therefore \quad 822 = 0 + (n-1)6$

$\Rightarrow \quad n = 138$

Hence, number of integral term is 138 term.

17. (1) $(64)^P = (9 \times 7 + 1)^P = (9\lambda + 1)^P$;

$P = 32^{32}$

${}^PC_0(9\lambda)^P + {}^PC_1(9\lambda)^{P-1} + \ldots\ldots + {}^PC_{P-1}(9\lambda) + {}^PC_P 1.$

$= M(a) + {}^PC_P 1 = M(9) + 1$

$\therefore$ Remainder $= 1$

18. (0) Since,

$(1-x^3) = (1-x)(1+x+x^2)$

$\Rightarrow (1-x^3)^{2007} = (1-x)^{2007}(1+x+x^2)^{2007}$

Now, coefficient of x^{2012} in $(1-x)^{2008}(1+x+x^2)^{2007}$

$=$ Coefficient of x^{2012} in $(1-x^3)^{2007}(1-x)$

$=$ Coefficient of x^{2012} in ${}^{2007}C_{r_1}(-x^3)^{r_1} + {}^{2007}C_{r_2}(-1)^{r_2} \cdot x^{3r_2+1}$

$\because 3r_1 = 2012$, which is not possible for any $r_1 \in W$

and $3r_2 + 1 = 2012$ also not possible for any $r_2 \in W$

Hence, no any term containing x^{2012}.

Thus, coefficient of x^{2012} is zero.

19. (b) $\frac{4^{2022}}{15} = \frac{4^{2(1011)}}{15}$

$$= \frac{(16)^{1011}}{15} = \frac{(15+1)^{1011}}{15} = \frac{15K+1}{15}$$

$$\therefore \left\{\frac{4^{2022}}{15}\right\} = \left\{\frac{15K+1}{15}\right\} = \frac{1}{15}$$

20. (b) We have, $(22)^{2022} + (2022)^{22}$

As 2022 is completely divisible by 3, so $(2022)^{22}$ is also divisible by 3

$(22)^{2022} = (21+1)^{2022}$

$= (3 \times 7 + 1)^{2022} = 3m + 1$

$\Rightarrow (22)^{2022}$ leaves a remainder 1, when divided by 3.

$\therefore (22)^{2022} + (2022)^{22}$ leaves a remainder 1 when divided by 3.

$\therefore \quad \alpha = 1$

$(22)^{2022} + (2022)^{22} = (21+1)^{2022} + (2023-1)^{22}$

$= 7K + 1 + 7\mu + 1 = 7(K+\mu) + 2$

$\Rightarrow (22)^{2022} + (2022)^{22}$

leaves a remainder 2, when divided by 7.

$\therefore \quad \beta = 2$

Hence, $\alpha^2 + \beta^2 = 1^2 + 2^2 = 5$

Chapter-8

Sequence and Series

1. (i) $r = \frac{4}{1} = \frac{16}{4} = 4$

(ii) $r = \frac{25}{5} = \frac{125}{25} = 5$

2. The numbers $-\frac{2}{7}$, k and $-\frac{7}{2}$ are in GP.

Then, $\frac{k}{-2/7} = \frac{-7/2}{k}$

$\Rightarrow \quad k^2 = -\frac{7}{2} \times -\frac{2}{7} = 1$

$\Rightarrow \quad k = \pm 1$

3. (i) (True)

Given, $(a^2 + b^2 + c^2)p^2 - 2(ab + bc + cd)p + (b^2 + c^2 + d^2) \le 0 \quad \ldots$(i)

But LHS $= (a^2p^2 + b^2 - 2abp) + (b^2p^2 + c^2 - 2bcp) + (c^2p^2 + d^2 - 2cdp)$

which gives

$(ap-b)^2 + (bp-c)^2 + (cp-d)^2 \ge 0 \quad \ldots$(ii)

Since, the sum of squares of real numbers is non-negative. Therefore, from Eqs. (i) and (ii), we get

$$(ap-b)^2+(bp-c)^2+(cp-d)^2=0$$

$$\Rightarrow ap-b=0,\ bp-c=0,\ cp-d=0$$

This implies that

$$\frac{b}{a}=\frac{c}{b}=\frac{d}{c}=p$$

Hence, a, b, c and d are in GP.

(ii) (True)

Given, $a_4=x$

$$\Rightarrow \quad ar^3=x \quad \ldots(\text{i})$$

$$a_{10}=y\Rightarrow ar^9=y \quad \ldots(\text{ii})$$

$$a_{16}=z\Rightarrow ar^{15}=z \quad \ldots(\text{iii})$$

On dividing Eq. (ii) by Eq. (i) and Eq. (iii) by Eq. (ii) and equating them, we get

$$\frac{y}{x}=\frac{z}{y}=r^6$$

This means x, y and z are in GP.

4. We have, $a=-\dfrac{3}{4}$

and $r=\dfrac{1/2}{-3/4}=-\dfrac{2}{3}$

$$\therefore\ a_{10}=ar^9$$

$$a_{10}=-\frac{3}{4}\times\left(-\frac{2}{3}\right)^9=\frac{1}{2}\left(\frac{2}{3}\right)^8$$

and $a_n=ar^{n-1}=-\dfrac{3}{4}\times\left(-\dfrac{2}{3}\right)^{n-1}$

$$=-\frac{3}{4}\times\left(-\frac{3}{2}\right)\left(-\frac{2}{3}\right)^n$$

$$=\frac{3^2}{2^3}\times\left(\frac{2}{3}\right)^n(-1)^n=(-1)^n\cdot\frac{2^{n-3}}{3^{n-2}}$$

5. (i) We have, first term, $a=5$ and common ratio, $r=2$

$$a_n=5120$$

$$\Rightarrow ar^{n-1}=5120$$

$$\Rightarrow 5(2)^{n-1}=5120$$

$$\Rightarrow \quad 2^{n-1}=1024$$

$$\Rightarrow \quad 2^{n-1}=2^{10}$$

$$\Rightarrow \quad n-1=10$$

$$\Rightarrow \quad n=11$$

Hence, 11th term of the given GP is 5120.

(ii) We have, first term, $a=2$ and common ratio, $r=4$

$$a_n=131072$$

$$\Rightarrow \quad ar^{n-1}=131072$$

$$\Rightarrow 2(4)^{n-1}=131072$$

$$\Rightarrow \quad 4^{n-1}=65536$$

$$\Rightarrow \quad 4^{n-1}=4^8$$

$$\Rightarrow \quad n-1=8$$

$$\Rightarrow \quad n=9$$

Hence, 131072 is 9th term of the GP.

(iii) We have, first term, $a=2$ and common ratio, $r=\dfrac{1}{2}$

$$a_n=\frac{1}{128}$$

$$\Rightarrow \quad ar^{n-1}=\frac{1}{128}$$

$$\Rightarrow 2\left(\frac{1}{2}\right)^{n-1}=\frac{1}{128}$$

$$\Rightarrow \left(\frac{1}{2}\right)^{n-1}=\left(\frac{1}{2}\right)^8$$

$$\Rightarrow \quad n-1=8$$

$$\Rightarrow \quad n=9$$

Hence, $\dfrac{1}{128}$ is 9th term of the GP.

(iv) We have, first term, $a=2$ and common ratio, $r=\sqrt{2}$

$$a_n=128$$

$$\Rightarrow \quad ar^{n-1}=128$$

$$\Rightarrow (2)(\sqrt{2})^{n-1}=128$$

$$\Rightarrow \quad (\sqrt{2})^{n-1}=64$$

$$\Rightarrow \quad (\sqrt{2})^{n-1}=2^6$$

$$\Rightarrow \quad (\sqrt{2})^{n-1}=(\sqrt{2})^{12}$$

$$\Rightarrow \quad n-1=12$$

$$\Rightarrow \quad n=13$$

Hence, 13th term of the GP is 128.

(v) We have, first term, $a=3$ and common ratio, $r=2$

$$a_n=3072$$

$$\Rightarrow \quad ar^{n-1}=3072$$

$$\Rightarrow 3(2)^{n-1}=3072$$

$$\Rightarrow (2)^{n-1}=1024$$

$$\Rightarrow (2)^{n-1}=2^{10}$$

$$\Rightarrow (n-1)=10$$

$$\Rightarrow \quad n=11$$

Hence, 11th term of the GP is 3072.

6. (False)

Given, $a_8=192\Rightarrow ar^7=192$

$$\Rightarrow a\times 2^7=192\Rightarrow a=\frac{192}{2^7}$$

The 12th term is

$$a_{12}=ar^{11}=\frac{192}{2^7}\times 2^{11}=3072$$

7. (i) Let the three terms are $\dfrac{a}{r}$, a and ar.

Then, product $=\dfrac{a}{r}\times a\times ar=1$

$$\Rightarrow \quad a^3=1$$

$$\Rightarrow \quad a=1$$

(ii) Let the three terms are $\dfrac{a}{r}$, a and ar.

Then, product

$$=\frac{a}{r}\times a\times ar=3375$$

$$\Rightarrow \quad a^3=3375\Rightarrow a=15$$

$$\text{Sum}=\frac{a}{r}+a+ar=65$$

$$\Rightarrow \quad \frac{15}{r}+15+15r=65$$

$$\Rightarrow \quad \frac{15}{r}+15r=50$$

$$\Rightarrow \quad r+\frac{1}{r}=\frac{10}{3}$$

Gives, $r=3$

The numbers are 5, 15 and 45.

8. Given, 5th term = 2 i.e. $ar^4=2$

Product of 9 terms

$$=a\times ar\times ar^2\times ar^3\times\ldots\times ar^8$$

$$=a^9r^{1+2+3+\ldots+8}=a^9r^{36}$$

$$=(ar^4)^9=2^9=512$$

9. Given, $a_5=p\Rightarrow ar^4=p \quad \ldots(\text{i})$

$$a_8=q\Rightarrow ar^7=q \quad \ldots(\text{ii})$$

$$a_{11}=s\Rightarrow ar^{10}=s \quad \ldots(\text{iii})$$

On dividing Eq. (ii) by Eq. (i) and Eq. (iii) by Eq. (ii), we get

$$\frac{ar^7}{ar^4}=\frac{q}{p}\ \text{and}\ \frac{ar^{10}}{ar^7}=\frac{s}{q}$$

$$\Rightarrow \quad r^3=\frac{q}{p}\ \text{and}\ r^3=\frac{s}{q}$$

$$\Rightarrow \quad \frac{q}{p}=\frac{s}{q}$$

$$\Rightarrow \quad q^2=ps$$

10. (d) It is given that number of bacteria double every hour. Therefore, number of bacteria after every hour forms a GP.

Here, $a = 30$ and $r = 2$

The number of bacteria at the end of 4th hour is

$$a_5 = ar^4 = 30 \times 2^4 = 480$$

11. (a) Here, $r = \frac{x^5}{x^3} = x^2$, then

$$a_n = x^3(x^2)^{n-1}$$
$$= x^{3+2n-2} = x^{2n+1}$$

Sum, $S_n = \frac{a[1-(x^2)^n]}{1-x^2}$

$$= \frac{x^3(1-x^{2n})}{1-x^2}$$

12. (i) Given,

$$S_n = 120$$
$$\therefore \frac{a(r^n-1)}{r-1} = 120$$
$$\Rightarrow \frac{3(3^n-1)}{3-1} = 120$$
$$\Rightarrow (3^n-1) = \frac{120 \times 2}{3} = 80$$
$$\Rightarrow 3^n = 81 = 3^4, \text{ gives}$$
$$n = 4$$

(ii) Here, $S_n = \frac{3069}{512}$

$$\Rightarrow \frac{a(1-r^n)}{1-r} = \frac{3069}{512}$$
$$\Rightarrow \frac{3\left(1-\frac{1}{2^n}\right)}{1-\frac{1}{2}} = \frac{3069}{512}$$
$$\Rightarrow 6\left(1-\frac{1}{2^n}\right) = \left(\frac{3069}{512}\right)$$
$$\Rightarrow \frac{3069}{3072} = 1 - \frac{1}{2^n}$$
$$\Rightarrow 1 - \frac{3069}{3072} = \frac{1}{2^n}$$
$$\Rightarrow 2^n = 1024 = 2^{10}$$

So, $n = 10$

13. (a) $S = 8 + 88 + 888 + \ldots$

$$\therefore S = \frac{8}{9}[9 + 99 + 999 + \ldots + \text{to } n \text{ terms}]$$
$$= \frac{8}{9}[(10-1) + (10^2-1) + (10^3-1) + \ldots + \text{to } n \text{ terms}]$$
$$= \frac{8}{9}[(10 + 10^2 + 10^3 + \ldots \text{to } n \text{ terms}) - (1 + 1 + 1 + \ldots + n \text{ terms})]$$
$$= \frac{8}{9}\left[\frac{10(10^n-1)}{9} - n\right]$$
$$\Rightarrow S = \frac{80}{81}(10^n-1) - \frac{8}{9}n$$

14. (True)

Here, $a = 2$ and $r = 2$

We have to find the number of ancestors in ten generations,

$$S_n = \frac{a(r^n-1)}{r-1}$$
$$\Rightarrow S_{10} = \frac{2(2^{10}-1)}{2-1}$$
$$= 2 \times 1023 = 2046$$

15. We have,

$$0.\overline{3} = \frac{3}{10} + \frac{3}{100} + \frac{3}{1000} + \ldots$$

(i) $a = \frac{3}{10} = 0.3$

(ii) $r = \frac{3}{100} \times \frac{10}{3} = \frac{1}{10} = 0.1$

(iii) Required sum

$$= \frac{a}{1-r} = \frac{0.3}{1-0.1} = \frac{0.3}{0.9} = \frac{1}{3}$$

16. The total time of motion is given by

$$1 + 2(0.9) + 2(0.9)^2 + 2(0.9)^3 + \ldots$$
$$= 1 + 2\left[\frac{(0.9)}{1-0.9}\right]$$
$$= 1 + \frac{1.8}{0.1}$$
$$= 1 + 18 = 19 \text{ s}$$

17. (d) Let 3, G_1, G_2 and 81 are in GP.

Then, $a_4 = 81$

$$ar^3 = 81$$
$$3 \times r^3 = 81$$
$$r^3 = 27 \Rightarrow r = 3$$

So, $G_1 = ar = 9$

$$G_2 = ar^2 = 27$$

The numbers are 9 and 27.

The common ratio when we insert GM between two numbers is $r = \left(\frac{b}{a}\right)^{\frac{1}{n+1}}$.

18. We have,

$$\sqrt{ab} = \frac{a^{n+1} + b^{n+1}}{a^n + b^n}$$
$$\Rightarrow ab(a^n + b^n)^2 = (a^{n+1} + b^{n+1})^2$$
$$\Rightarrow ab(a^{2n} + 2a^nb^n + b^{2n})$$
$$= (a^{2n+2} + 2a^{n+1}b^{n+1} + b^{2n+2})$$
$$\Rightarrow a^{2n+1}b + 2a^{n+1}b^{n+1} + ab^{2n+1} = a^{2n+2} + 2a^{n+1}b^{n+1} + b^{2n+2}$$
$$\Rightarrow ab^{2n+1} - b^{2n+2} = a^{2n+2} - a^{2n+1}b$$
$$\Rightarrow b^{2n+1}(a-b) = a^{2n+1}(a-b)$$
$$\Rightarrow \left(\frac{a}{b}\right)^{2n+1} = 1 = \left(\frac{a}{b}\right)^0$$
$$\Rightarrow 2n + 1 = 0$$
$$\therefore n = -1/2$$

19. Given,

$$\frac{a+b}{2} = 10$$
$$\Rightarrow a + b = 20 \text{ and } \sqrt{ab} = 8$$
$$ab = 64$$

From $a + b = 20$

$$\Rightarrow b = 20 - a$$

So, $a(20-a) = 64$

$$\Rightarrow 20a - a^2 = 64$$
$$\Rightarrow a^2 - 20a + 64 = 0$$
$$\Rightarrow (a-16)(a-4) = 0$$
$$a = 16, 4$$

Then, $b = 4, 16$

So, numbers are 4 and 16.

20. (i) (True)

We have,

$a + b = 2\text{AM}$ and $\sqrt{ab} = \text{GM}$

$a + b = 2\text{AM}$ and $ab = \text{GM}^2$

$\therefore$ Quadratic equation is

$x^2 -$ (sum of zeroes) x + product of zeroes = 0

$$x^2 - 2\text{AM}x + \text{GM}^2 = 0$$

(ii) (True)

Given, AM = 8 means

$$a + b = 16$$

GM = $\sqrt{ab} = 5$ means

$$ab = 25$$

Then, quadratic equation is

$$x^2 - 2 \times 8x + 25 = 0$$
$$\Rightarrow x^2 - 16x + 25 = 0$$

21. (i) (True)

Given, $a+b=6\sqrt{ab}$ ...(i)

$(a+b)^2=36ab$

Also, $(a-b)^2=(a+b)^2-4ab$

$(a-b)^2=36ab-4ab=32ab$

$a-b=4\sqrt{2}\cdot\sqrt{ab}$ ...(ii)

On adding Eqs. (i) and (ii), we get

$2a=(6+4\sqrt{2})\sqrt{ab}$

$\Rightarrow\quad a=(3+2\sqrt{2})\sqrt{ab}$

From Eq. (i),

$b=6\sqrt{ab}-(3+2\sqrt{2})\sqrt{ab}$

$\Rightarrow b=(3-2\sqrt{2})\sqrt{ab}$

Now, $\frac{a}{b}=\frac{(3+2\sqrt{2})\sqrt{ab}}{(3-2\sqrt{2})\sqrt{ab}}$

$=\frac{(3+2\sqrt{2})}{(3-2\sqrt{2})}$

(ii) (True)

$a+b=2A$ ...(i)

and $ab=G^2$ ...(ii)

We have,

$(a-b)^2=(a+b)^2-4ab$

$\Rightarrow(a-b)^2=4A^2-4G^2$

$=4(A^2-G^2)$

$(a-b)^2=4(A+G)(A-G)$

$a-b=2\sqrt{(A+G)(A-G)}$ ...(iii)

On adding Eqs. (i) and (iii), we get

$a=A+\sqrt{(A+G)(A-G)}$

Then,

$b=A-\sqrt{(A+G)(A-G)}$

By combining these two equations, hence numbers are $A\pm\sqrt{(A+G)(A-G)}$

22. (b)

23. Given, $a_n=n(n+3)=n^2+3n$

$\therefore S_n=\Sigma a_n=\Sigma n^2+\Sigma 3n$

$\Rightarrow S_n=\frac{n(n+1)(2n+1)}{6}+3\frac{n(n+1)}{2}$

$\Rightarrow S_n=\frac{n(n+1)(n+5)}{3}$

24. (c) Given series

$1\times2+2\times3+3\times4+\dots$

nth term, $a_n=n(n+1)$

$S_n=\Sigma a_n=\Sigma n^2+\Sigma n$

$\Rightarrow S_n=\Sigma a_n=\frac{n(n+1)(2n+1)}{6}+\frac{n(n+1)}{2}$

$\Rightarrow S_n=\frac{n(n+1)}{2}\left(\frac{2n+1}{3}+1\right)$

$=\frac{n(n+1)}{2}\left(\frac{2n+4}{3}\right)$

$\therefore S_n=\frac{n(n+1)(n+2)}{3}$

Assertion Reason

1. (a) We know that if a, b, c are in GP, then $b^2=ac$.

Here, $-\frac{2}{7}, x, -\frac{7}{2}$ are in GP

$\Rightarrow\quad x^2=\left(-\frac{2}{7}\right)\left(-\frac{7}{2}\right)$

$\Rightarrow\quad x^2=1\Rightarrow x=\pm1$

$\therefore$ Both Assertion and Reason are correct and Reason is the correct explanation of Assertion.

2. (a) Given, GP is

$x^3, x^5, x^7, \dots (x\neq\pm1)$

We know that sum to n terms of a GP is given by

$S_n=\frac{a(r^n-1)}{r-1}$, $r\neq1$, where a is the first term and r is the common ratio.

Here, $a=x^3, r=x^2$

$\therefore\quad S_n=\frac{x^3((x^2)^n-1)}{x^2-1}$

$=\frac{x^3(1-x^{2n})}{1-x^2}$

$\therefore$ Both Assertion and Reason are correct and Reason is the correct explanation of Assertion.

3. (b) Let, a, ar, ar^2 are in GP and let P be the fixed non-zero number.

So, ap, arp, ar^2p will also be in GP with first term ap and common ratio r.

Also, $A=\frac{a+b}{2}$ and $G=\sqrt{ab}$

So, $A-G=\frac{a+b}{2}-\sqrt{ab}$

$=\frac{a+b-2\sqrt{ab}}{2}$

$=\frac{(\sqrt{a}-\sqrt{b})^2}{2}\geq0$

$\therefore\ A\geq G$

$\therefore$ Both Assertion and Reason are correct but Reason is not the correct explanation of Assertion.

4. (a) Given, $ar^2=4$

$\therefore$ Product of first five terms

$=a(ar)(ar^2)(ar^3)(ar^4)$

$=a^5r^{10}$

$=(ar^2)^5=4^5$

$\therefore$ Both Assertion and Reason are correct and Reason is the correct explanation of Assertion.

5. (b) Given, a, b, c are in A.P.

$\therefore\quad 2b=a+c$

Now, if $b+c, c+a, a+b$ are in AP.

$\Rightarrow\quad 2(c+a)=(b+c)+(a+b)$

$\Rightarrow\quad 2c+2a=2b+a+c$

$\Rightarrow\quad a+c=2b$

Here, a, b, c are in AP

$\Rightarrow\quad b-a=c-b$

$\Rightarrow\quad 10^{(b-a)}=10^{(c-b)}$

$\Rightarrow\quad 10^b=\sqrt{10^a\cdot10^c}$

$\therefore\quad 10^a, 10^b, 10^c$ are in GP

$\therefore$ Both Assertion and Reason are correct but Reason is not the correct explanation of Assertion.

6. (a) Since, $\frac{2}{3}, k, \frac{5}{8}$ are in AP

$\Rightarrow\quad 2k=\frac{2}{3}+\frac{5}{8}$

[$\because$ if a, b, c are in AP, then $2b=a+c$]

$\Rightarrow\quad 2k=\frac{31}{24}$

$\Rightarrow\quad k=\frac{31}{48}$

$\therefore$ Both Assertion and Reason are correct and Reason is the correct explanation of Assertion.

7. (b) Let, first term of a GP be a and common ratio be r

nth term of the GP is given by,

$T_n=ar^{n-1}$

Now, consider terms equidistant from the beginning and the end in the GP.

Let's take the kth term from the beginning and the kth term from the end. If the total number of terms is n, then $\underset{\text{(from the beginning)}}{T_k} = ar^{k-1}$

$\underset{\text{(from the end)}}{T_k} = ar^{n-k}$

The product of these terms

$= (ar^{k-1}) \cdot (ar^{n-k})$

$= a^2 r^{n-1}$

Since, this expression is the same for any k, the product of the terms equidistant from the beginning and the end in a GP is indeed always the same, proving that Assertion is true.

The Reason is a true statement, but it does not directly explain why the product of terms equidistant from the beginning and the end is always the same.

$\therefore$ Both Assertion and Reason are true but Reason is not the correct explanation of Assertion.

8. (a) We know that for two numbers a and b,

$AM = \frac{a+b}{2}$ and $GM = \sqrt{ab}$

Here, $a = 4$ and $b = 64$

$\therefore AM = \frac{4+64}{2} = \frac{68}{2} = 34$

and $GM = \sqrt{4 \times 64} = 16$

$\therefore$ Both Assertion and Reason are correct and Reason is the correct explanation of Assertion.

9. (c) Given, $a = 3$ and $r = \frac{1}{2}$, $x = 4$

$$S_4 = \frac{3\left(\left(\frac{1}{2}\right)^4 - 1\right)}{\frac{1}{2} - 1}$$

$$= \frac{3\left(\frac{1}{16} - 1\right)}{-\frac{1}{2}}$$

$$= \frac{3\left(-\frac{15}{16}\right)}{-\frac{1}{2}} = \frac{45}{8}$$

$\therefore$ Assertion is correct.

Given, $ar^3 = 5$

$\therefore$ Product of first seven terms

$= a\,(ar)\,(ar^2)(ar^3)(ar^4)(ar^5)(ar^6)$

$= a^7 r^{21}$

$= (ar^3)^7$

$= 5^7$

$\therefore$ Reason is incorrect.

10. (b) In a GP with the first term a and common ratio r, the nth term

$T_n = ar^{n-1}$

The product of the first n terms,

$P_n = a \cdot ar \cdot ar^2 \ldots\ldots ar^{n-1}$

$\Rightarrow P_n = a^n \cdot r^{0+1+2+3+\ldots\ldots+(n-1)}$

Using formula for the sum of the first n natural numbers,

$0 + 1 + 2 + 3 + \ldots\ldots + (n-1)$

$= \frac{(n-1)n}{2}$

$\Rightarrow \quad P_n = a^n \cdot r^{\frac{(n-1)n}{2}}$

The geometric mean of the first term a and the nth term ar^{n-1} is

$GM = \sqrt{a \cdot ar^{n-1}}$

$= \sqrt{a^2 r^{n-1}}$

$= ar^{(n-1)/2}$

The nth power of this GM is

$(ar^{(n-1)/2})^n = a^n r^{(n-1)^{n/2}}$

Thus, the product of the first n terms P_n is indeed equal to the nth power of the GM of the first and the nth term.

Now, In a GP, the ratio of successive terms is constant and equal to the common ratio.

$\therefore$ Both Assertion and Reason are true but Reason is not correct explanation of Assertion.

Case Based

Case 1 Given, population in the year

2010 = 5000

$\therefore \quad a = 5000$

$\because$ Population doubles every 5 yr, so in 10 yr (2 periods of 5 yr)

$\therefore \quad r = 2$ (it is common ratio)

(i) $n = 3$

$\therefore$ Population in the year 2020

$= \frac{a(r^n - 1)}{r - 1}$

$\Rightarrow$ population in the year 2020

$= \frac{5000((2)^3 - 1)}{2 - 1}$

$\Rightarrow$ population in the year 2020

$= 35000$

(ii) From 2010 to 2030 is 20 yr, which is 4 periods of 5 yr.

So, $n = 5$

$\therefore$ Population in the yr 2030

$= \frac{a(r^n - 1)}{r - 1}$

$\Rightarrow$ population in the yr 2030

$= \frac{5000((2)^5 - 1)}{2 - 1}$

$\Rightarrow$ population in the yr 2030

$= 155000$

(iii) After 25 yr corresponds to 5 periods of 5 yr.

So, $n = 6$

$\therefore$ Population after 25 yr

$= \frac{a(r^n - 1)}{r - 1}$

$\Rightarrow$ population after 25 yr

$= \frac{5000(2^6 - 1)}{(2 - 1)}$

$\Rightarrow$ population after 25 yr

$= 315000$

Case 2 (i) Let number of pills made in first week, $a_1 = a$.

Given, $a_4 = 6750$ and $r = 1.5$

$\Rightarrow \quad ar^3 = 6750 \; [\because a_n = ar^{n-1}]$

$\Rightarrow a(1.5)^3 = 6750$

$\Rightarrow \quad a = \frac{6750}{(1.5)^3} = 2000$

Hence, number of pills made in first week are 2000.

(ii) We know that $a_n = ar^{n-1}$

$\Rightarrow \quad a_n = 2000\;(1.5)^{n-1}$

$[\because a = 2000$ and $r = 1.5]$

Hence, number of pills prepared in n th week will be $2000\,(1.5)^{n-1}$

(iii) Given, $a_k = 10125$, where k is the kth week

$\Rightarrow 2000(1.5)^{k-1} = 10125$

$[\because a_n = a(r)^{n-1}$ and $a = 2000, r = 1.5]$

$\Rightarrow \quad (1.5)^{k-1} = \frac{10125}{2000}$

$\Rightarrow \quad \left(\frac{3}{2}\right)^{k-1} = \frac{81}{16}$

$\Rightarrow \quad \left(\frac{3}{2}\right)^{k-1} = \left(\frac{3}{2}\right)^4$

$\Rightarrow \quad k - 1 = 4$

$\Rightarrow \quad k = 5$

Hence, in 5th week 10125 pills might have been prepared.

Competition Connect

1. (i) $a_2 = 3a_1 + 2$

$\Rightarrow a_2 = 3 \times 3 + 2 = 11$

$a_3 = 3a_2 + 2$

$\Rightarrow a_3 = 3 \times 11 + 2 = 35$

Similarly, $a_4 = 107$, $a_5 = 323$

First five terms are 3, 11, 35, 107, and 323.

(ii) $a_n = (-1)^{n-1} 5^{n+1}$ gives,

$a_1 = (-1)^{1-1} 5^{1+1} = 25$

$a_2 = (-1)^{2-1} 5^{2+1} = -125$

$a_3 = (-1)^{3-1} 5^{3+1} = 625$

$a_4 = (-1)^{4-1} 5^{4+1} = -3125$

$a_5 = (-1)^{5-1} 5^{5+1} = 15625$

First five terms are 25, –125, 625, –3125 and 15625.

2. (i) We have, $a_n = \frac{n^2}{2^n}$,

then $a_7 = \frac{7^2}{2^7} = \frac{49}{128}$

(ii) $a_{20} = \frac{20(20-2)}{20+3} = \frac{360}{23}$

(iii) $a_8 = \frac{8+1}{8^3} = \frac{9}{512}$

3. (i) We have, $a_n = 3n - 2$

Now, $a_{n+1} - a_n = 3(n+1) - 2 - (3n-2)$

$= 3n + 3 - 2 - 3n + 2 = 3$,

which is a constant.

Hence, the given sequence is an arithmetic sequence.

(ii) $a_1 = 3(1) - 2 = 1$

$a_2 = 3(2) - 2 = 4$

$d = a_2 - a_1 = 4 - 1 = 3$

(iii) $a_{50} = 3 \times 50 - 2$

$= 150 - 2 = 148$

(iv) $a_n > 450$

$\Rightarrow \quad 3n - 2 > 450 \Rightarrow n > 150.66$

$\therefore \quad n = 151$

4. $a_1 = 1$

$a_2 = a_1 + 2 = 3$

$a_3 = a_2 + 2 = 5$ and so on.

The series is $1 + 3 + 5$ ....

5. (True)

$(a + 2b - c)(2b + c - a)(a + 2b + c)$

$= (a + a + c - c)(a + c + c - a)$

$(2b + 2b)$ [$\because 2b = a + c$]

$= 2a \times 2c \times 4b = 16abc$

6. (i) Multiples of 5 are 105, 110, 115, ..., 995

$\Rightarrow \quad a_n = 995$

$\Rightarrow \quad a + (n-1)\,d = 995$

$\Rightarrow 105 + (n-1)\,5 = 995$

$\Rightarrow \quad (n-1) = \frac{890}{5} = 178$

$\therefore \quad n = 179$

(ii) Odd integers from 1 to 2001 are 1, 3, 5, 7, 9, ..., 1999, 2001

Here, $\quad a_n = 2001$

$\Rightarrow \quad a + (n-1)d = 2001$

$\Rightarrow 1 + (n-1) \times 2 = 2001$

$\Rightarrow \quad (n-1)2 = 2000$

$\Rightarrow (n-1) = \frac{2000}{2} = 1000$

$\therefore \quad n = 1000 + 1 = 1001$

(iii) Two digit numbers divisible by 3 are 12, 15, 18, 21, ..., 99

$a_n = 99$

$\Rightarrow \quad a + (n-1)d = 99$

$\Rightarrow \quad 12 + (n-1)3 = 99$

$\Rightarrow \quad n - 1 = 29$

$n = 30$

7. (i) Given sequence is

7, 10, 13, ...

Here, $10 - 7 = 13 - 10 = 3$

$\therefore$ The sequence is an arithmetic sequence.

(ii) Here $a_1 = 7$, $d = 10 - 7 = 3$

$\therefore \quad a_n = 7 + (n-1)\,3$

$= 7 + 3n - 3$

$= 3n + 4$

(iii) $a_{50} = 3(50) + 4 = 154$

(iv) $a + (n-1)d = 68$

$\Rightarrow 7 + (n-1)3 = 68$

$n - 1 = \frac{61}{3} \Rightarrow n = \frac{64}{3}$

$\because$ n is not a natural number.

So, 68 is not a member of the given sequence.

8. (a) We have,

$a_m = a + (m-1)\,d = n \quad$ ...(i)

and $a_n = a + (n-1)d = m \quad$ ...(ii)

On solving Eqs. (i) and (ii), we get

$(m - n)d = (n - m)$

$\Rightarrow \quad d = -1$ and $a = m + n - 1$

Therefore, $a_p = a + (p-1)d$

$\Rightarrow \quad a_p = m + n - 1 + (p-1)(-1)$

$\Rightarrow \quad a_p = n + m - p$

9. (False)

nth term from the end of the AP $= l - (n-1)d$

12th term from the end

$= 201 - (12-1)(2)$

$= 201 - 22 = 179$

10. (True)

$S_n = a_1 + a_2 + a_3 + \ldots + a_n$

$= nP + \frac{1}{2}n(n-1)Q$

Therefore, $S_1 = a_1 = P$

and $S_2 = a_1 + a_2 = 2P + Q$

So, $a_2 = S_2 - S_1 = P + Q$

Hence, the common difference is

$d = a_2 - a_1 = P + Q - P = Q$

11. (i) Let the three numbers in an AP are $a - d$, a, $a + d$.

Then, $a - d + a + a + d = 24$

$\Rightarrow \quad 3a = 24 \Rightarrow a = 8$

and $(a - d)(a)(a + d) = 440$

$\Rightarrow \quad (8 - d)(8)(8 + d) = 440$

$\Rightarrow \quad (8^2 - d^2) = 55$

$\therefore d^2 = 9 \Rightarrow d = \pm 3$

Therefore, when $d = 3$, the numbers are 5, 8 and 11

and when $d = -3$, the numbers are 11, 8 and 5.

Thus, the three numbers are 5, 8 and 11.

(ii) Let the three numbers be $a - d$, a, $a + d$.

Their sum = 27

$\therefore a - d + a + a + d = 27$

$3a = 27$

$\Rightarrow \quad a = 9$

Product,

$(a - d)(a)(a + d) = 648$

$9(9^2 - d^2) = 648$

$(81 - d^2) = 72$

$d^2 = 9$

$d = \pm 3$

When $a = 9$, $d = 3$, we get 6, 9, 12

When $a = 9$, $d = -3$, we get 12, 9, 6

12. (i) $\sum_{k=1}^{5} 4k$

(ii) $\sum_{k=0}^{6} 2k + 1$

(iii) $\sum_{k=2}^{6} 4k + 1$

13. (i) $a_k = 5k + 1$

$a_1 = 6$, $a_2 = 11$, then $d = 5$

$\therefore S_n = \frac{n}{2}[12 + (n-1)5]$

$S_n = \frac{n}{2}[12 + 5n - 5]$

$S_n = \frac{n}{2}[7 + 5n]$

(ii) First few terms of $\sum_{k=1}^{130}(4k+5)$ are

$9+13+17+\dots\dots$

It is an arithmetic series, where $a_1=9$, $d=4$ and $n=130$.

$\therefore S_n=\frac{n}{2}[2a+(n-1)d]$

$S_{130}=\frac{130}{2}[2\times9+(130-1)(4)]$

$=65[18+516]=65\times534$

$=34710.$

14. (d) Given, $S_n=3n^2+5n$

$S_1=3\times1+5\times1=8=a_1$

$S_2=3\times2^2+5\times2=22=a_1+a_2$

$a_2=S_2-S_1=22-8=14$

Common difference,

$d=a_2-a_1=14-8=6$

Now, we have

$a_m=164$

$a+(m-1)d=164$

$8+(m-1)6=164$

$(m-1)6=156$

$(m-1)=26$

$m=27$

15. It is known that $a_k=a+(k-1)d$

Then, $a_{m+n}=a+(m+n-1)d$

and $a_{m-n}=a+(m-n-1)d$

According to the question,

$a_{m+n}+a_{m-n}=a+(m+n-1)d+a+(m-n-1)d$

$a_{m+n}+a_{m-n}=2a+(m+n-1+m-n-1)d$

$a_{m+n}+a_{m-n}=2a+(2m-2)d$

$=2[a+(m-1)d]=2a_m$

Thus, the sum of $(m+n)$th and $(m-n)$th term of an AP is equal to twice the mth term.

16. (i) The numbers lying between 200 and 400, which are divisible by 7, are 203, 210, 217 ..., 399.

Here, $a_n=a+(n-1)d$

$\Rightarrow\quad 399=203+(n-1)7$

$\Rightarrow 399-203=(n-1)7$

$\Rightarrow\quad (n-1)=\frac{196}{7}=28$

$\therefore\quad n=29$

$\therefore\quad S_{29}=\frac{29}{2}(203+399)$

$=8729$

(ii) The integers from 1 to 100, which are divisible by 2, are 2, 4, 6, ..., 100. This forms an AP.

$\therefore 100=2+(n-1)2$

$\Rightarrow\quad n=50$

Thus, $2+4+6+8+\dots+100$

$=\frac{50}{2}(2\times2+49\times2)$

$=25(102)=2550$

The integers from 1 to 100, which are divisible by 5, are 5, 10, 15, ..., 100. This forms an AP.

$\therefore 100=5+(n-1)5$

$\Rightarrow\quad n=20$

Thus,

$5+10+15+20+\dots+100$

$=\frac{20}{2}(2\times5+19\times5)$

$=10(105)=1050$

The integers from 1 to 100, which are divisible by both 2 and 5, are 10, 20, 30 ..., 100. This forms an AP.

$\therefore 100=10+(n-1)10$

$\Rightarrow\quad n=10$

Thus, $10+20+30+40+\dots+100=\frac{10}{2}(2\times10+9\times10)$

$=5(110)=550$

$\therefore$ Required sum

$=2550+1050-550$

$=3050$

17. (c) Given, $S_n=(pn+qn^2)$

$\frac{n}{2}[2a+(n-1)d]=pn+qn^2$

$na+n^2\frac{d}{2}-n\frac{d}{2}=pn+qn^2$

On comparing both sides coefficients of n^2, we get

$\frac{d}{2}=q$

$\Rightarrow\quad d=2q$

and $\quad S_n=116$

$\Rightarrow\quad \frac{n}{2}[2a+(n-1)d]=116$

$\Rightarrow n[2\times25+(n-1)(-3)]=232$

$\Rightarrow\quad 50n-3n^2+3n=232$

$\Rightarrow\quad 3n^2-53n+232=0$

$\Rightarrow\quad (3n-29)(n-8)=0$

Thus, $n=8, n=\frac{29}{3}$,

which is not a natural number. Therefore, number of terms is 8.

18. We have,

$S_1=\frac{n}{2}[2a+(n-1)d]\quad\dots(i)$

$S_2=\frac{2n}{2}[2a+(2n-1)d]$

$=n[2a+(2n-1)d]\quad\dots(ii)$

$S_3=\frac{3n}{2}[2a+(3n-1)d]\dots(iii)$

From Eqs. (i) and (ii), we get

$S_2-S_1=n[2a+(2n-1)d]-\frac{n}{2}[2a+(n-1)d]$

$S_2-S_1=n\left\{\frac{4a+4nd-2d-2a-nd+d}{2}\right\}$

$S_2-S_1=n\left\{\frac{2a+3nd-d}{2}\right\}$

$=\frac{n}{2}[2a+(3n-1)d]$

$\therefore 3(S_2-S_1)=\frac{3n}{2}[2a+(3n-1)d]$

$=S_3$

19. (b) We know that

$S_n=\frac{n}{2}[2a+(n-1)d]$

According to the question,

$S_p=S_q$

$\Rightarrow \frac{p}{2}[2a+(p-1)d]=\frac{q}{2}[2a+(q-1)d]$

$\Rightarrow p[2a+(p-1)d]=q[2a+(q-1)d]$

$\Rightarrow 2ap+pd(p-1)=2aq+qd(q-1)$

$\Rightarrow 2ap-2aq=d[q(q-1)-p(p-1)]$

$\Rightarrow 2a(p-q)=d[q^2-p^2-q+p]$

$\Rightarrow 2a(p-q)=-d[(p-q)(p+q)-(p-q)]$

$\Rightarrow 2a(p-q)=-d(p-q)[(p+q)-1]$

$\Rightarrow 2a(p-q)+d(p-q)[(p+q)-1]=0$

$\Rightarrow\quad (p-q)[2a+d(p+q-1)]=0$

$p-q=0$ or $2a+d(p+q-1)=0$

But $p\neq q$, so $2a+d(p+q-1)=0$

Now, $S_{p+q}=\frac{p+q}{2}[2a+(p+q-1)d]$

$=\frac{p+q}{2}\times0=0$

20. (i) Let a_1, a_2 be the first term and d_1, d_2 be the common differences of the given AP's, respectively.

$$\frac{\text{Sum of } n \text{ terms of first AP}}{\text{Sum of } n \text{ terms of second AP}} = \frac{3n+8}{7n+15}$$

$$\Rightarrow \frac{\frac{n}{2}[2a_1+(n-1)d_1]}{\frac{n}{2}[2a_2+(n-1)d_2]} = \frac{3n+8}{7n+15}$$

$$\Rightarrow \frac{2a_1+(n-1)d_1}{2a_2+(n-1)d_2} = \frac{3n+8}{7n+15}$$

$$\Rightarrow \frac{a_1+\left(\frac{n-1}{2}\right)d_1}{a_2+\left(\frac{n-1}{2}\right)d_2} = \frac{3n+8}{7n+15}$$

Now, replace $\frac{n-1}{2} = 11$

i.e. $n = 2\times11+1 = 23$, we get

$$\frac{a_1+11d_1}{a_2+11d_2} = \frac{3\times23+8}{7\times23+15} = \frac{77}{176}$$

$$\Rightarrow \frac{\text{12th term of first AP}}{\text{12th term of second AP}} = \frac{7}{16}$$

(ii) We have,

$$\frac{a_1+\left(\frac{n-1}{2}\right)d_1}{a_2+\left(\frac{n-1}{2}\right)d_2} = \frac{5n+4}{9n+6}$$

[similar to part (i)]

Now, replace $\frac{n-1}{2} = 17$

i.e. $n = 2\times17+1 = 35$, we get

$$\frac{a_1+17d_1}{a_2+17d_2} = \frac{5\times35+4}{9\times35+6} = \frac{179}{321}$$

$$\Rightarrow \frac{\text{18th term of first AP}}{\text{18th term of second AP}} = \frac{179}{321}$$

(iii) $$\frac{\text{Sum of } m \text{ terms}}{\text{Sum of } n \text{ terms}} = \frac{m^2}{n^2}$$

$$\Rightarrow \frac{\frac{m}{2}[2a+(m-1)d]}{\frac{n}{2}[2a+(n-1)d]} = \frac{m^2}{n^2}$$

$$\Rightarrow \frac{m[2a+(m-1)d]}{n[2a+(n-1)d]} = \frac{m^2}{n^2}$$

$$\Rightarrow \frac{[2a+(m-1)d]}{[2a+(n-1)d]} = \frac{m}{n},$$

Replace $m = 2m-1, n = 2n-1,$

$$\frac{[2a+(2m-2)d]}{[2a+(2n-2)d]} = \frac{2m-1}{2n-1}$$

$$\Rightarrow \frac{2[a+(m-1)d]}{2[a+(n-1)d]} = \frac{2m-1}{2n-1}$$

$$\Rightarrow \frac{[a+(m-1)d]}{[a+(n-1)d]} = \frac{2m-1}{2n-1}$$

$$\frac{m\text{th term of an AP}}{n\text{th term of an AP}} = \frac{2m-1}{2n-1}$$

21. (a) The angles are

$120°, 125°, 130°, \ldots$

and $S_n = (n-2)180°$

$\Rightarrow \frac{n}{2}[2a+(n-1)d] = (n-2)\,180°$

$\Rightarrow n[2\times120+(n-1)5]$

$= (n-2)\times2\times180$

$\Rightarrow 240n+5n^2-5n = 360n-720$

$\Rightarrow 5n^2-125n+720 = 0$

$\Rightarrow n^2-25n+144 = 0$

Factorise $(n-9)(n-16) = 0$ gives

$n = 9$ or 16

But $n = 16$ is not possible because

$a_{16} = a+15d = 120+15\times5$

$= 195° > 180°$

Interior angle of a polygon cannot be more than 180°.

The number of sides of the polygon is 9.

22. Here, $a = 300000$ and $d = 10000$

$S_{20} = \frac{20}{2}[600000+19\times10000]$

$= 7900000$

The person received ₹ 7900000 in 20 yr.

23. (c) The installments are

100, 105, 110, ...

$\because \quad a_n = a+(n-1)d$

$\Rightarrow \quad a_{30} = 100+29\times5 = 245$

Now, $S_n = \frac{n}{2}(a+a_n)$

$\therefore \quad S_{30} = \frac{30}{2}(100+245) = 5175$

24. Let the amount saved by the men in the first year is ₹ A.

$\therefore \quad S_n = \frac{n}{2}[2A+(n-1)d]$

$\Rightarrow \quad S_{10} = \frac{10}{2}[2A+9\times100]$

$\Rightarrow 16500 = 5(2A+900)$

$\Rightarrow 3300 = 2A+900$

$\Rightarrow \quad A = 1200$

25. (True)

Given, $\frac{a^n+b^n}{a^{n-1}+b^{n-1}} = \frac{a+b}{2}$

$\Rightarrow \quad 2a^n+2b^n = a^n+ab^{n-1}+ba^{n-1}+b^n$

$\Rightarrow \quad a^n+b^n = ab^{n-1}+ba^{n-1}$

$\Rightarrow a^n-ba^{n-1} = ab^{n-1}-b^n$

$\Rightarrow a^{n-1}(a-b) = b^{n-1}(a-b)$

$\Rightarrow \quad \left(\frac{a}{b}\right)^{n-1} = 1$

$= \left(\frac{a}{b}\right)^0$

Comparing the exponent,

$n-1 = 0$ gives $n = 1$

26. (i) We have, $a = 4$ and $b = 16$

$d = \frac{b-a}{n+1} = \frac{16-4}{3+1} = 3$

Then, $A_1 = a+d = 4+3 = 7$

$A_2 = a+2d = 4+2\times3 = 10$

and $A_3 = a+3d = 4+3\times3 = 13$

Hence, required three arithmetic means are 7, 10 and 13.

(ii) We have, $a = 8$ and $b = 26$

$d = \frac{b-a}{n+1} = \frac{26-8}{5+1} = 3$

Then,

$A_1 = a+d = 11$

$A_2 = a+2d = 14$

$A_3 = a+3d = 17$

$A_4 = a+4d = 20$

$A_5 = a+5d = 23$

The required five numbers between 8 and 26 are

11, 14, 17, 20 and 23.

(iii) Here, $a = 3$ and $b = 24$

$d = \frac{b-a}{n+1}$

$= \frac{24-3}{6+1} = 3$

Then, $A_1 = a+d = 3+3 = 6$

$A_2 = a+2d = 9$

$A_3 = a+3d = 12$

$A_4 = a+4d = 15$

Similarly,

$A_5 = a+5d = 18$

$A_6 = a+6d = 21$

Required arithmetic means are 6, 9, 12, 15, 18 and 21.

Competition Edge Up

1. (d) $17m = m + (m-4) + (m-4\times 2) + \dots + (m-4\times 24)$

$\Rightarrow 17m = 25m - 4(1+2+\dots+24)$

$\Rightarrow \quad 8m = \dfrac{4\cdot 24\cdot 25}{2} = 150$

2. (a) $4^{1+x}+4^{1-x}, \dfrac{K}{2}, 16^x+16^{-x} \to$ AP

$K = 4^{1+x} + 4^{1-x} + 16^x + 16^{-x}$

$= 4\left(4^x + \dfrac{1}{4^x}\right) + \left(4^{2x} + \dfrac{1}{4^{2x}}\right)$

$\because P + \dfrac{1}{P} \geq 2$, for all $P > 0$

$\therefore \quad K_{min} = 4\times 2 + 2 = 10$

3. (b) Given that

$S_{10} = 390$ and $\dfrac{a_{10}}{a_5} = \dfrac{15}{7}$

$S_{10} = \dfrac{10}{2}[2a+9d] = 390$

$\Rightarrow \quad 2a + 9d = 78 \quad \dots(i)$

$\dfrac{a_{10}}{a_5} = \dfrac{a+9d}{a+4d} = \dfrac{15}{7}$

$\Rightarrow 7a + 63d = 15a + 60d$

$\Rightarrow \quad 8a = 3d \quad \dots(ii)$

On solving Eqs. (i) and (ii), we get

$a = 3, d = 8$

Now, $S_{15} - S_5 = \dfrac{15}{2}[2a+14d] - \dfrac{5}{2}[2a+4d]$

$= \dfrac{5}{2}[6a + 42d - 2a - 4d]$

$= \dfrac{5}{2}[4a + 38d] = 5(2a + 19d)$

$= 5(6 + 19\times 8) = 790$

4. (d) Given that

$S_{20} = 790$ and $S_{10} = 145$

$S_{20} = \dfrac{20}{2}[2a + 19d] = 790$

$\Rightarrow 2a + 19d = 79 \quad \dots(i)$

$\left[\because S_n = \dfrac{n}{2}[2a + (n-1)d]\right]$

and $\quad S_{10} = 145$

$\Rightarrow \dfrac{10}{2}[2a+9d] = 145$

$2a + 9d = 29 \quad \dots(ii)$

On solving Eqs. (i) and (ii),

$a = -8, d = 5$

Now, $S_{15} - S_5$

$= \dfrac{15}{2}[2a+14d] - \dfrac{5}{2}[2a+4d]$

$= \dfrac{15}{2}[-16+70] - \dfrac{5}{2}[-16+20]$

$= 405 - 10 = 395$

5. (b) $\log_e a, \log_e b, \log_e c$ are in AP

$\Rightarrow \quad 2\log b = \log a + \log c$

$\Rightarrow \quad b^2 = ac$

$\because \quad \log_e a - \log_e 2b$,

$\log_e 2b - \log_e 3c, \log_e 3c - \log_e a$ are in AP

$\Rightarrow \log_e \dfrac{a}{2b}, \log_e \dfrac{2b}{3c}, \log_e \dfrac{3c}{a}$ are in AP

$\Rightarrow 2\log_e \dfrac{2b}{3c} = \log_e \dfrac{a}{2b} + \log_e \dfrac{3c}{a}$

$\Rightarrow \quad \left(\dfrac{2b}{3c}\right)^2 = \dfrac{a}{2b} \times \dfrac{3c}{a}$

$\dfrac{4b^2}{9c^2} = \dfrac{3c}{2b}$

$8b^3 = 27c^3$

$2b = 3c$

$\because \quad b^2 : ac$

$\left(\dfrac{3c}{2}\right)^2 : ac$

$\Rightarrow \quad 9c = 4a$

$\therefore \quad a : b : c$

$\dfrac{9c}{4} : \dfrac{3c}{2} : c$

$\Rightarrow \quad 9 : 6 : 4$

6. (b) Given progression is

$20, 19\dfrac{1}{4}, 18\dfrac{1}{2}, 17\dfrac{3}{4}, \dots, \left(-129\dfrac{1}{4}\right)$

i.e. $20, \dfrac{77}{4}, \dfrac{37}{2}, \dfrac{71}{3}, \dots, \left(-\dfrac{517}{4}\right)$

i.e. last term, t_n or $l = -\dfrac{517}{4}$

As, we know that $a + (n-1)d = l$

$\Rightarrow \quad -\dfrac{517}{4} = 20 + (n-1)\left(-\dfrac{3}{4}\right)$

$\Rightarrow \quad -517 = 80 + (-3n + 3)$

$\Rightarrow \quad -600 = -3n \Rightarrow n = 200$

Since, rth term from end $= (n - r + 1)$th term from beginning

$\Rightarrow$ 20th term from end $= (200 - 20 + 1)$th term from beginning

$\Rightarrow$ 20th term from end $=$ 181th term from beginning

Hence, $t_{181} = 20 + (181 - 1)\left(-\dfrac{3}{4}\right)$

$= 20 - 135 = -115$

7. (d) First progression is 4, 9, 14, 19, ... upto 25th term.

Second progression is 3, 6, 9, 12, ... upto 37th term.

Now, T_{25} (for first)

$= 4 + (25-1)\times 5$

$= 4 + 120 = 124$

and T_{37} (for second)

$= 3 + (37-1)\times 3$

$= 3 + 108 = 111$

Let $d_1 =$ common difference of 1st sequence $= 5$

$d_2 =$ common difference of 2nd sequence $= 3$

and first common term $= 9$

So, first common difference $= 15$, (which is LCM of d_1 and d_2)

Hence, common terms are 9, 24, 39, 54, 69, 84, 99.

Thus, total number of common terms $= 7$

8. (c) Given,

$\dfrac{1}{1\cdot(1+d)} + \dfrac{1}{(1+d)(1+2d)} + \dots + \dfrac{1}{(1+9d)(1+10d)} = 5$

$\dfrac{1}{d}\left[\dfrac{(1+d)-1}{1\cdot(1+d)} + \dfrac{(1+2d)-(1+d)}{(1+d)(1+2d)} + \dots + \dfrac{(1+10d)-(1+9d)}{(1+9d)(1+10d)}\right] = 5$

$\Rightarrow \dfrac{1}{d}\left[\left(1 - \dfrac{1}{1+d}\right) + \left(\dfrac{1}{1+d} - \dfrac{1}{1+2d}\right) + \dots + \left(\dfrac{1}{1+9d} - \dfrac{1}{1+10d}\right)\right] = 5$

$\Rightarrow \quad \dfrac{1}{d}\left[1 - \dfrac{1}{1+10d}\right] = 5$

$\Rightarrow \quad \dfrac{10d}{d(1+10d)} = 5$

$\Rightarrow \quad 50d = 5$

9. (a) We have,

$m = \dfrac{1}{\sqrt{1}+\sqrt{2}} + \dfrac{1}{\sqrt{2}+\sqrt{3}} + \dots + \dfrac{1}{\sqrt{99}+\sqrt{100}}$

$\Rightarrow m = \dfrac{\sqrt{2}-\sqrt{1}}{(\sqrt{1}+\sqrt{2})(\sqrt{2}-\sqrt{1})} + \dfrac{\sqrt{3}-\sqrt{2}}{(\sqrt{2}+\sqrt{3})(\sqrt{3}-\sqrt{2})} + \dots + \dfrac{\sqrt{100}-\sqrt{99}}{(\sqrt{99}+\sqrt{100})(\sqrt{100}-\sqrt{99})}$

$$\Rightarrow m = (\sqrt{2} - \sqrt{1}) + (\sqrt{3} - \sqrt{2}) + \ldots.. + (\sqrt{100} - \sqrt{99})$$
$$= \sqrt{100} - \sqrt{1} = 10 - 1 = 9$$

Also, $n = \frac{1}{1 \cdot 2} + \frac{1}{2 \cdot 3} + \ldots + \frac{1}{99 \cdot 100}$

$$n = \frac{2-1}{1 \cdot 2} + \frac{3-2}{2 \cdot 3} + \ldots + \frac{100-99}{99 \cdot 100}$$
$$\Rightarrow \quad n = 1 - \frac{1}{2} + \frac{1}{2} - \frac{1}{3} + \ldots + \frac{1}{99} - \frac{1}{100}$$
$$\Rightarrow \quad n = 1 - \frac{1}{100} = \frac{99}{100}$$
$$\therefore \quad (m, n) = \left(9, \frac{99}{100}\right),$$

which lies on the line

$$11x - 100y = 0$$

10. (b) $S = \frac{1}{1 - 3 \cdot 1^2 + 1^4} + \frac{2}{1 - 3 \cdot 2^2 + 2^4} + \frac{3}{1 - 3 \cdot 3^2 + 3^4} + \ldots 10$

Term, $T_n = \frac{n}{1 - 3n^2 + n^4}$

$$= \frac{n}{(n^2 - n - 1)(n^2 + n - 1)}$$
$$= \frac{1}{2}\left[\frac{1}{n^2 - n - 1} - \frac{1}{n^2 + n - 1}\right]$$
$$S = \sum_{n=1}^{10} T_n$$
$$= \frac{1}{2}\left[\sum_{n=1}^{10} \frac{1}{n^2 - n - 1} - \frac{1}{n^2 + n - 1}\right]$$
$$= \frac{1}{2}\left[\left(\frac{1}{-1} - \frac{1}{1}\right) + \left(\frac{1}{1} - \frac{1}{5}\right) + \left(\frac{1}{5} - \left(-\frac{1}{11}\right)\right) + \ldots \left(\frac{1}{89} - \frac{1}{109}\right)\right]$$
$$= \frac{1}{2}\left(-1 - \frac{1}{109}\right) = \frac{-55}{109}$$

11. (1011) $\left(\frac{1}{\alpha+1} + \frac{1}{\alpha+2} + \ldots + \frac{1}{\alpha+1012}\right) - \left(\frac{1}{2 \cdot 1} + \frac{1}{4 \cdot 3} + \frac{1}{6 \cdot 5} + \ldots - \frac{1}{2024 \cdot 2023}\right) = \frac{1}{2024}$

$$\Rightarrow \left(\frac{1}{\alpha+1} + \frac{1}{\alpha+2} + \ldots + \frac{1}{\alpha+1012}\right) - \left\{\left(\frac{1}{1} - \frac{1}{2}\right) + \left(\frac{1}{3} - \frac{1}{4}\right) + \ldots \left(\frac{1}{2023} - \frac{1}{2024}\right)\right\} = \frac{1}{2024}$$
$$= \left(\frac{1}{\alpha+1} + \frac{1}{\alpha+2} + \ldots \frac{1}{\alpha+1012}\right) - \left\{\left(1 + \frac{1}{2} + \frac{1}{3} + \ldots \frac{1}{2023}\right) - \frac{1}{2024} - 2\left(\frac{1}{2} + \frac{1}{4} + \ldots \frac{1}{2022}\right)\right\} = \frac{1}{2024}$$
$$\Rightarrow \frac{1}{\alpha+1} + \frac{1}{\alpha+2} + \ldots + \frac{1}{\alpha+1012} - \left(\frac{1}{1} + \frac{1}{2} + \ldots + \frac{1}{2023}\right) + \frac{1}{2024} + 2\left(\frac{1}{2} + \frac{1}{4} + \ldots + \frac{1}{2022}\right) = \frac{1}{2024}$$
$$\Rightarrow \frac{1}{\alpha+1} + \frac{1}{\alpha+2} + \ldots + \frac{1}{\alpha+1012} = \frac{1}{1012} + \frac{1}{1013} + \ldots + \frac{1}{2023}$$
$$\therefore \quad \alpha = 1011$$

12. (1010)

Given, $f(m+n) = f(m) + f(n)$

So, $f(x) = mx$

$\because \quad f(1) = 1 \Rightarrow 1 = m \times 1 \Rightarrow m = 1$

$\therefore \quad f(x) = x$

Now, $\sum_{k=1}^{2022} f(\lambda + k) \le (2022)^2$

$$\Rightarrow \sum_{k=1}^{2022} (\lambda + k) \le (2022)^2$$
$$\Rightarrow (\lambda + \lambda + \lambda + \ldots + \lambda) + (1 + 2 + 3 + \ldots + 2022) \le (2022)^2$$

(2022 terms)

$$\Rightarrow 2022\lambda + \frac{2022 \times 2023}{2} \le (2022)^2$$
$$\Rightarrow \lambda \le 2022 - \frac{2023}{2}$$
$$\Rightarrow \lambda \le \frac{2021}{2} = 1010.5$$

$\therefore$ Largest natural number of λ is 1010.

13. (1505)

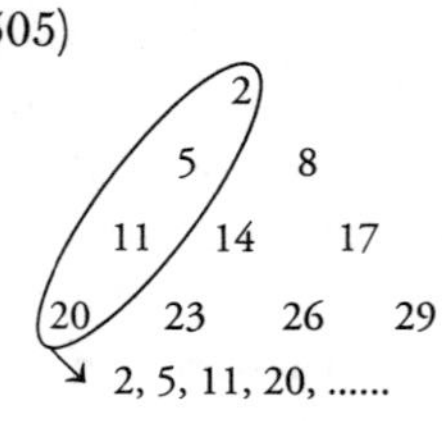

General term $= \frac{3n^2 - 3n + 4}{2}$

$$T_{10} = \frac{3 \times 100 - 3 \times 10 + 4}{2}$$
$$= \frac{300 - 26}{2} = 137$$
$$d = 3$$

So, sum $= \frac{10}{2}[2 \times 137 + 9 \times 3]$

$$= 5(274 + 27) = 1505$$

14. (103) For 5310,

$$\frac{k(k+1)}{2} < 5310 \Rightarrow k(k+1) < 10620$$

For $k = 102$ (maximum value of k),

$$k(k+1) < 10620$$

That means, 5310 will contain in next row.

So, required row $= 102 + 1 = 103$

15. (910) We have,

$$A_k = a_1^2 - a_2^2 + a_3^2 - a_4^2 + a_{2k-1}^2 - a_{2k}^2$$
$$= (-d)(a_1 + a_2 + \ldots + a_{2k})$$
$$= (-d)\left(\frac{2k}{2}\right)(2a_1 + (2k-1)d)$$
$$\Rightarrow \quad A_3 = (-3d)(2a_1 + 5d) = -153$$
$$\Rightarrow \quad (d)(2a_1 + 5d) = 51 \quad \ldots(i)$$

Also, $A_5 = (-5d)(2a_1 + 9d) = -435$

$$= (d)(2a_1 + 9d) = 87 \quad \ldots(ii)$$

From Eqs. (i) and (ii), we get

$$4d^2 = 36 \Rightarrow d = \pm 3$$
$$\therefore \quad 3(2a_1 + 9d) = 87$$
$$\Rightarrow \quad 2a_1 + 9d = 29$$
$$\Rightarrow \quad 2a_1 = 29 - 27 = 2 \Rightarrow a_1 = 1$$
$$\therefore a_{17} - A_7 = (a + 16d) - (-7d)(2 + 13d)$$
$$= (1 + 16 \times 3) - (-7 \times 3)(2 + 13 \times 3)$$
$$= 49 + 7 \times 3(2 + 39)$$
$$= 49 + 21 \times 41 = 910$$

16. (b) Let AP be $3, 3+d, 3+2d, 3+3d$

So, $3 + d = a, 3 + 2d = b, 3 + 3d = c$

Also, let GP be $3, 3r, 3r^2, 3r^3$

So, $3r = a - 1, 3r^2 = b + 1, 3r^3 = c + 9$

On comparing, we get

$$3r = 3 + d - 1$$
$$\Rightarrow \quad d = 3r - 2 \quad \ldots(i)$$

and $3r^2 = 3 + 2d + 1$

$$\Rightarrow \quad 3r^2 = 2d + 4 \quad \ldots(ii)$$

On solving Eqs. (i) and (ii), we get

$r = 2, a = 7, b = 11, c = 15$

Hence, AM of a, b and c

$$= \frac{7 + 11 + 15}{3} = 11$$

Chapter-9

Straight Lines

1. (i) (False)

Since, x-coordinate of point is positive and its y-coordinate is negative, therefore point lies in IVth quadrant.

(ii) (True)

Since, x-coordinate of point is negative and its y-coordinate is positive, therefore point lies in IInd quadrant.

(iii) (False)

Since, both x and y-coordinate are negative, therefore point lies in IIIrd quadrant.

(iv) (True)

Since, both x and y-coordinates are positive, therefore point lies in Ist quadrant.

2. (i) $PQ = \sqrt{(-2-4)^2 + (6-5)^2}$
$= \sqrt{36+1} = \sqrt{37}$ units

(ii) $AB = \sqrt{(7-3)^2 + (5-6)^2}$
$= \sqrt{16+1} = \sqrt{17}$ units

3. (True)

Let the required point be $P(0, y)$.

$\therefore AP = \sqrt{\{0-(-4)\}^2 + (y-3)^2}$
$= \sqrt{16 + y^2 + 9 - 6y}$
$= \sqrt{25 + y^2 - 6y}$

$BP = \sqrt{(0-5)^2 + (y-2)^2}$
$= \sqrt{25 + y^2 + 4 - 4y}$
$= \sqrt{29 + y^2 - 4y}$

$\because AP = BP$

$\Rightarrow 25 + y^2 - 6y = 29 + y^2 - 4y$

$\Rightarrow \quad -2y = 4 \Rightarrow y = -2$

4. (c) $AB = \sqrt{(1+2)^2 + (2-3)^2}$
$= \sqrt{(3)^2 + (-1)^2} = \sqrt{10}$ units

$BC = 2\sqrt{10}$ units

$AC = 3\sqrt{10}$ units

$\therefore AB + BC = AC$

$\therefore$ The points are collinear.

5. (i) $x = \dfrac{(mx_2 + nx_1)}{m+n} = \dfrac{27+5}{4} = 8$

$y = \dfrac{(my_2 + ny_1)}{m+n} = \dfrac{18+2}{4} = 5$

$\therefore$ Required coordinate is (8, 5).

(ii) Let $P(0, y)$ be the point of division and the ratio is 1 : 2.

$\therefore y = \dfrac{1\times 3 + 2\times 2}{1+2} = \dfrac{3+4}{3} = \dfrac{7}{3}$

6. (a) Let line $x + y = 4$ divides the line joining the points $(-1, 1)$ and $(5, 7)$ at C in the ratio $m:1$.

$$C\left(\frac{5m-1}{m+1}, \frac{7m+1}{m+1}\right)$$

This point C must lie on the line $x + y = 4$.

$\therefore \dfrac{5m-1}{m+1} + \dfrac{7m+1}{m+1} = 4 \Rightarrow m = \dfrac{1}{2}$

7. (i) Mid-point of the line segment joining the points (3, 2) and (5, 3) is

$M(x, y) = \left(\dfrac{3+5}{2}, \dfrac{3+2}{2}\right)$
$= \left(4, \dfrac{5}{2}\right)$

(ii) $\left(\dfrac{x_1 + x_2}{2}, \dfrac{-y_1 - y_2}{2}\right)$

8. (i) Area of triangle

$= \dfrac{1}{2}|x_1(y_2 - y_3) + x_2(y_3 - y_1) + x_3(y_1 - y_2)|$

$= \dfrac{1}{2}|-3(2+3) + 5(-3+5) - 9(-5-2)|$

$= \dfrac{1}{2}|-15 + 10 + 63|$

$= \dfrac{58}{2} = 29$ sq. units

(ii) Area of triangle

$= \dfrac{1}{2}|x_1(y_2 - y_3) + x_2(y_3 - y_1) + x_3(y_1 - y_2)|$

$= \dfrac{1}{2}|6(4-7) + 3(7-3) + 2(3-4)|$

$= \dfrac{1}{2}|6(-3) + 3(4) + 2(-1)|$

$= \dfrac{1}{2}|-18 + 12 - 2|$

$= \dfrac{1}{2}|-8| = 4$ sq. units

9. (True)

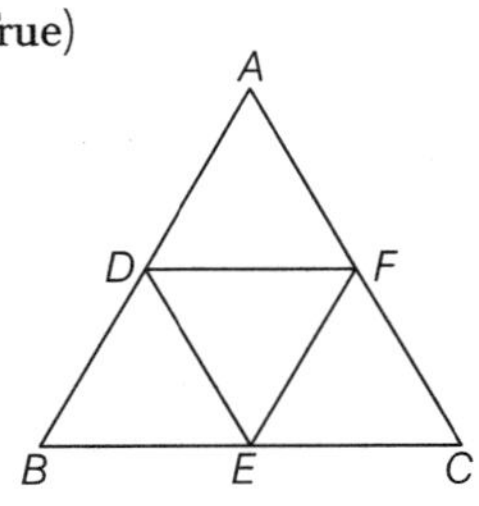

Let ΔABC be given and D, E and F be the mid-points of AB, BC and AC, respectively.

$\therefore$ ar $(\Delta ABC) = 4 \times$ ar (ΔDEF)

ar$(\Delta DEF) = \dfrac{1}{2}|3(3+3) + 5(-3+1) + 1(-1-3)|$

$= \dfrac{1}{2}|18 - 10 - 4|$

$= 2$ sq. units

$\therefore$ ar$(\Delta ABC) = 4 \times 2 = 8$ sq. units

10. (d)

11. (True)

ar$(\Delta ABC) = \dfrac{1}{2}|-5(5-7) + 5(7-1) + 10(1-5)|$

$= \dfrac{1}{2}|10 + 30 - 40|$

ar $(\Delta ABC) = 0$

Hence, the points are collinear.

12. (c) For collinearity

$\Rightarrow |x_1(y_2 - y_3) + x_2(y_3 - y_1) + x_3(y_1 - y_2)| = 0$

$\Rightarrow |-2(2-0) + 1(0-3) + k(3-2)| = 0$

$\Rightarrow \quad |-4 - 3 + 3k - 2k| = 0$

$\Rightarrow \quad |-7 + k| = 0$

$\Rightarrow \quad k = 7$

13. (i)

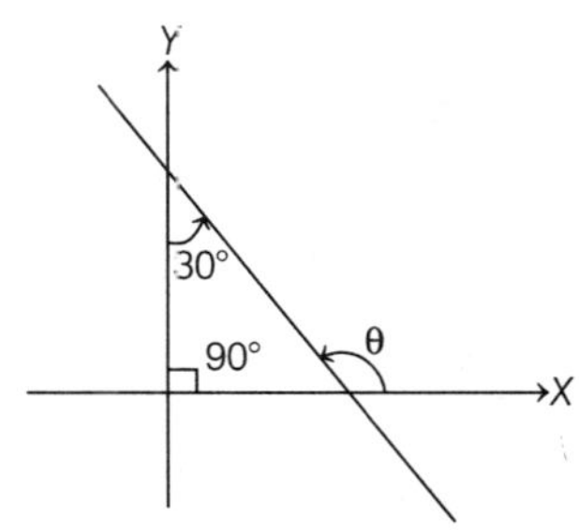

The line makes angle of 30° from positive Y-axis.

Hence, it makes angle of $(90° + 30°)$ i.e. 120° from positive X-axis.

Hence, $\theta = 120°$

Slope, $m = \tan\theta$

$\tan 120° = \tan(180° - 60°)$
$= -\tan 60°$

Therefore, slope of line
$= -\sqrt{3}$

(ii) Slope $= \tan 120°$
$= \tan(180° - 60°)$
$= -\tan 60°$
$= -\sqrt{3}$

14. (b) θ lies between 0° and 90. As θ is an acute angle. θ lies in Ist quadrant. Thus, the slope of line is positive.

15. (i) The X-axis or any line parallel to the X-axis has a slope of zero.

(ii) The Y-axis or any line parallel to the Y-axis has slope undefined.

(iii) Slope $= \dfrac{y_2 - y_1}{x_2 - x_1}$

(iv) Slope $= \dfrac{2-(-1)}{3-3} = \dfrac{3}{0}$
$=$ undefined

16. (d)

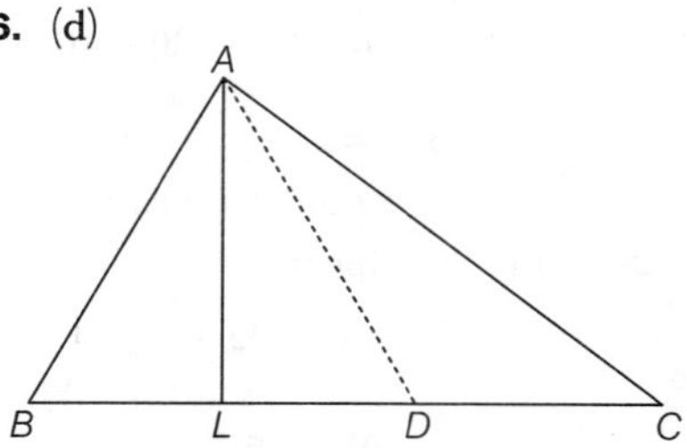

Coordinates of
$$D = \left[\frac{7+3}{2}, \frac{6+3}{2}\right] = \left[5, \frac{9}{2}\right]$$
$$\therefore \text{ Slope of } AD = \frac{\frac{9}{2} - 1}{5-1} = \frac{7}{8}$$
$$\therefore \text{ Slope of } AL = \frac{-1}{\text{Slope of } BC}$$
$$= \frac{-1}{(6-3)} \times (3-7)$$
$$= \frac{4}{3}$$

17. (i) Slope $= 2$
$$\therefore \frac{3-5}{x-2} = 2$$
$\Rightarrow 3 - 5 = 2x - 4$
$\Rightarrow -2 + 4 = 2x$
$\Rightarrow 2x = 2$
$\Rightarrow x = 1$

(ii) $\dfrac{5-(-3)}{2-x} = \tan 45°$
$\Rightarrow \dfrac{8}{2-x} = 1$
$\Rightarrow 8 = 2 - x$
$\Rightarrow x = 2 - 8$
$= -6$

18. (i) $\tan\theta = \left|\dfrac{m_2 - m_1}{1 + m_1 \cdot m_2}\right|$
$$\Rightarrow \tan\theta = \left|\frac{\frac{1}{3} - \frac{1}{4}}{1 + \frac{1}{3}\cdot\frac{1}{4}}\right| = \frac{1}{13}$$

(ii) $m_1(BA) = \dfrac{3-(-1)}{2-(-2)} = \dfrac{4}{4} = 1$
$$m_2(BC) = \frac{-4-3}{-2-2} = \frac{7}{4}$$
$$\therefore \tan\theta = \left|\frac{m_2 - m_1}{1 + m_1 \cdot m_2}\right|$$
$$= \left|\frac{\frac{7}{4} - 1}{1 + \frac{7}{4} \times 1}\right|$$
$$= \frac{3}{11}$$

(iii) Let m_1 be slope of X-axis $= 0$
and $m_2 = \dfrac{-2-(-1)}{4-3} = \dfrac{-1}{1} = -1$
$$\tan\theta = \left|\frac{0-(-1)}{1 + 0\cdot(-1)}\right| = 1$$

(iv) $\tan\theta = \left|\dfrac{m_2 - m_1}{1 + m_1 \cdot m_2}\right|$
$$= \left|\frac{\frac{1}{\sqrt{3}} - \sqrt{3}}{1 + \frac{1}{\sqrt{3}}\cdot\sqrt{3}}\right|$$
$$= \left|\frac{\frac{1-3}{\sqrt{3}}}{2}\right| = \frac{1}{\sqrt{3}}$$

19. (True)
$$m_1 = \text{Slope of } BA = \frac{3-1}{2+2} = \frac{1}{2}$$
$$m_2 = \text{Slope of } BC = \frac{-4-3}{-2-2} = \frac{7}{4}$$
$$\therefore \tan B = \left|\frac{m_2 - m_1}{1 + m_1 \cdot m_2}\right|$$
$$= \left|\frac{\frac{7}{4} - \frac{1}{2}}{1 + \frac{7}{4}\cdot\frac{1}{2}}\right| = \frac{2}{3}$$

20. $x + 3y = 7$ ...(i)
$$\Rightarrow y = -\frac{1}{3}x + \frac{7}{3}$$
Slope of $AB = -\dfrac{1}{3}$
$\therefore m_{PQ} = 3$

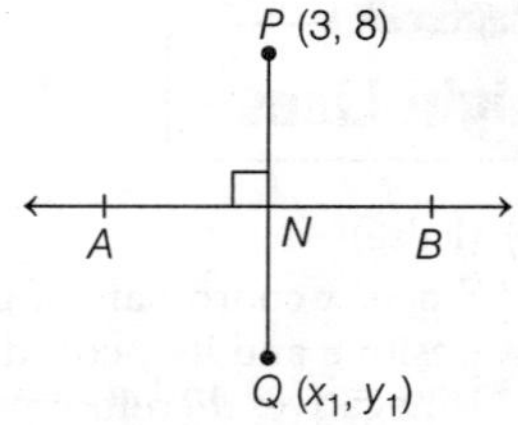

Equation of PQ,
$$\frac{y-8}{x-3} = 3$$
$\Rightarrow 3x - y - 1 = 0$ ...(ii)
On solving Eqs. (i) and (ii), we get
$\therefore x = 1$ and $y = 2$
$\therefore \dfrac{3 + x_1}{2} = 1$ and $\dfrac{8 + y_1}{2} = 2$
[from mid-point formula]
$\Rightarrow x_1 = -1$ and $y_1 = -4$

21. (True)
$x + 2y - 9 = 0$
$\Rightarrow y = -\dfrac{1}{2}x + \dfrac{9}{2}$
$\Rightarrow m_1 = -\dfrac{1}{2}$
$\Rightarrow 2x + 4y + 5 = 0$
$\Rightarrow y = -\dfrac{1}{2}x - \dfrac{5}{4}$
$\Rightarrow m_2 = -\dfrac{1}{2}$
$\therefore m_1 = m_2$

22. (d) $m_1 =$ Slope of AB
$$= \frac{7-y}{2-3} = y - 7$$
$m_2 =$ Slope of CD
$$= \frac{6-4}{0-(-1)} = 2$$
$\because AB \parallel CD$
$\therefore m_1 = m_2$
$\Rightarrow y - 7 = 2$
$\Rightarrow y = 9$

23. $m =$ Slope of $AB = \dfrac{12-4}{2-6} = -2$
Slope of line perpendicular to AB
$$= -\frac{1}{m} = -\left(-\frac{1}{2}\right) = \frac{1}{2}$$

24. (False)
Both the lines will not be parallel as $m_1 \neq m_2$.
$$\left[\because m_1 = -\frac{5}{2} \text{ and } m_2 = \frac{2}{5}\right]$$
They are perpendicular.
$\because m_1 \cdot m_2 = -1$

25. (False)

$\sqrt{3}x + y = 1 \Rightarrow y = -\sqrt{3}x + 1$

and $\quad x + \sqrt{3}y = 1$

$\Rightarrow \quad y = -\frac{1}{\sqrt{3}}x + \frac{1}{\sqrt{3}}$

$m_1 = -\sqrt{3}$ and $m_2 = -\frac{1}{\sqrt{3}}$

$\therefore \tan\theta = \left|\frac{m_2 - m_1}{1 + m_1 \cdot m_2}\right|$

$= \left|\frac{-\frac{1}{\sqrt{3}} + \sqrt{3}}{1 + (-\sqrt{3}) \times \left(-\frac{1}{\sqrt{3}}\right)}\right| = \frac{1}{\sqrt{3}}$

$\theta = 30°$

and $(180° - \theta) = (180° - 30°) = 150°$

26. (i) $\because$ Point $(a, 3)$ lies on the given line.

$\therefore \quad 3 = \frac{a}{2} + \frac{5}{2}$

$\Rightarrow \quad \frac{a}{2} = 3 - \frac{5}{2} = \frac{1}{2} \Rightarrow a = 1$

(ii) $\because$ Point $(-1, a)$ lies on the given line.

$\therefore \quad a = -1 + 2 \Rightarrow a = 1$

27. (i) Equation of the horizontal line through $(3, -4)$ is given by $y = -4$

(ii) Equation of the vertical line with x-intercept 5 is $x = 5$

(iii) Equation of the vertical line through $(-1, -3)$ is given by $x = -1$

(iv) Equation of the horizontal line with y-intercept 2 is $y = 2$

(v) Equation of the X-axis is $y = 0$

(vi) Equation of the Y-axis is $x = 0$

28. (i)

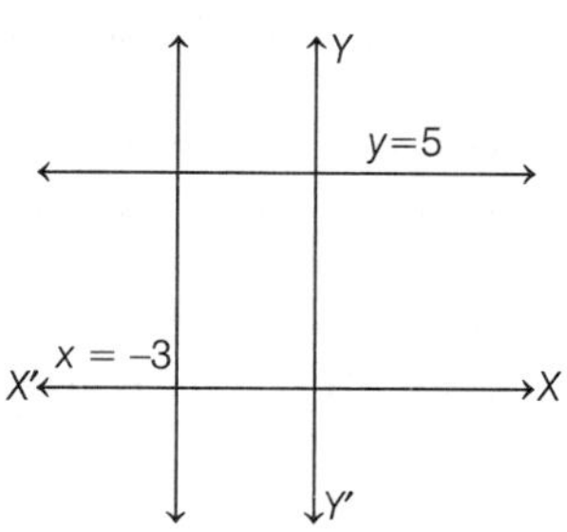

Equation of the line passing through $(-3, 5)$ and parallel to X-axis is $y = 5$.

Equation of the line passing through $(-3, 5)$ and parallel to Y-axis is $x = -3$.

(ii) $\because$ Equation is parallel to X-axis.

$\therefore \quad m = 0$

$\Rightarrow y - y_1 = \frac{y_2 - y_1}{x_2 - x_1}(x - x_1)$

$\Rightarrow y + 4 = 0(x - 3)$

$\Rightarrow y + 4 = 0$

(iii) $\quad y = \frac{2}{3}x - \frac{7}{3}$

Slope $= \frac{2}{3}$

$\therefore$ Equation of line with slope $\frac{2}{3}$ and passing through the point $(2, -5)$ is

$\frac{y - (-5)}{x - 2} = \frac{2}{3}$

$\Rightarrow 2x - 3y - 19 = 0$

29. (i) $m = \frac{1}{2}$ and y intercept, $c = \frac{-5}{4}$

$y = \frac{1}{2}x - \frac{5}{4}$

$4y - 2x + 5 = 0$

(ii) $y = \frac{1}{2}(x - 5)$

$\Rightarrow 2y = x - 5 \Rightarrow x - 2y - 5 = 0$

30. $\quad \frac{x}{2} + \frac{y}{-3} = 1$

$\Rightarrow \quad \frac{x}{2} - \frac{y}{3} = 1 \Rightarrow 3x - 2y - 6 = 0$

31. Given line $2x - y + 16 = 0$

$\Rightarrow \quad \frac{2x}{-16} - \frac{y}{-16} = 1$

$\Rightarrow \quad \frac{x}{(-8)} + \frac{y}{16} = 1$

$A = -8$ and $B = 16$

$\therefore A + B = -8 + 16 = 8$

32. (i) $2x + y = 6 \Rightarrow y = -2x + 6$

$\therefore$ Gradient $= -2$

$2x + y = 6 \Rightarrow \frac{x}{3} + \frac{y}{6} = 1$

$\Rightarrow$ x intercept $= 3$

and y intercept $= 6$

(ii) $x - 9y = 22$

$\Rightarrow \quad y = \frac{x}{9} - \frac{22}{9}$

$\therefore$ Gradient $= \frac{1}{9}$

$x - 9y = 22$

$\Rightarrow \frac{x}{22} + \frac{y}{\left(\frac{-22}{9}\right)} = 1$

$\therefore$ x intercept $= 22$

and y intercept $= \frac{-22}{9}$

(iii) $11x - 4y = -43$

$\Rightarrow \quad y = \frac{11}{4}x + \frac{43}{4}$

$\therefore$ Gradient $= \frac{11}{4}$

$11x - 4y = -43$

$\Rightarrow \frac{x}{\left(\frac{-43}{11}\right)} + \frac{y}{\left(\frac{43}{4}\right)} = 1$

$\therefore$ x intercept $= \frac{-43}{11}$

and y intercept $= \frac{43}{4}$

(iv) $\sqrt{3}x + y = -2 \Rightarrow y = -\sqrt{3}x - 2$

$\therefore$ Gradient $= -\sqrt{3}$

$\sqrt{3}x + y = -2$

$\Rightarrow \frac{x}{\left(\frac{-2}{\sqrt{3}}\right)} + \frac{y}{(-2)} = 1$

$\therefore$ x intercept $= \frac{-2}{\sqrt{3}}$

and y intercept $= -2$

33. (d) Slope of joining points $A(2, 3)$ and $B(6, -5)$

$m_{AB} = -2$ and $m_{LM} = \frac{1}{2}$

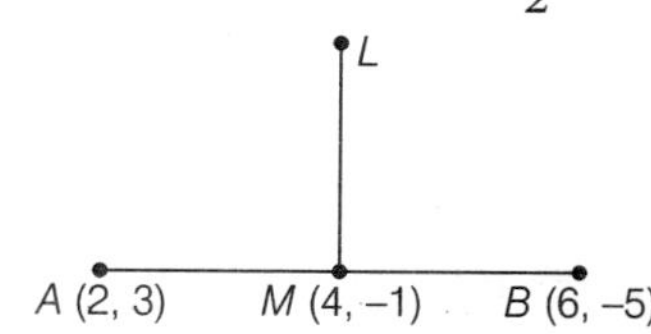

$\therefore$ Equation of LM is

$y - y_1 = m(x - x_1)$

$\Rightarrow \quad \frac{y - (-1)}{x - 4} = \frac{1}{2}$

$\Rightarrow \quad 2(y + 1) = x - 4$

$\Rightarrow x - 2y - 6 = 0$

34. (i) (True)

$AX + BY + C = 0$

$\Rightarrow \quad Y = -\frac{A}{B}X - \frac{C}{B}$

Hence, the given equation is slope intercept form.

(ii) (True)

$3x - 2y + 4 = 0$

$\Rightarrow 3x - 2y = -4$

$\Rightarrow \frac{3x}{-4} - \frac{2y}{-4} = 1$

$\Rightarrow \frac{x}{\left(\frac{-4}{3}\right)} + \frac{y}{(2)} = 1,$

which is intercept form.

35. (a) $\frac{1\times 0+2\times a}{1+2}=-5$

$\frac{1\times b+2\times 0}{1+2}=4$

$\Rightarrow a=-\frac{15}{2}$ and $b=12$

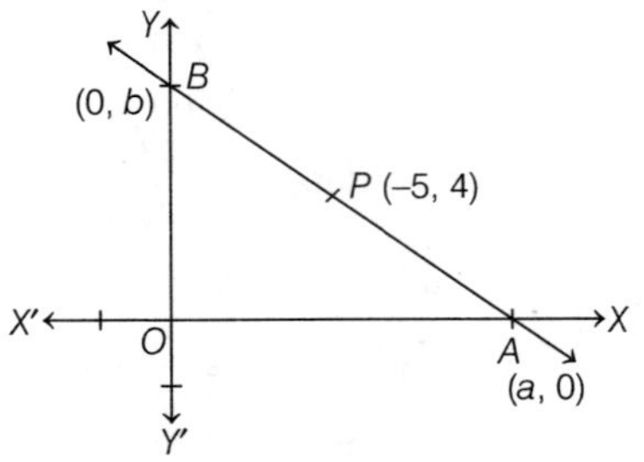

$\therefore$ Required equation of the line,

$$\frac{x}{\left(-\frac{15}{2}\right)}+\frac{y}{12}=1$$

$\Rightarrow \quad 8x-5y+60=0$

36. (a) Let the required equation be

$$y=-x+c$$

We know that perpendicular distance,

$$d=\frac{|Ax+By+C|}{\sqrt{A^2+B^2}}$$

$\Rightarrow \quad \frac{|0+0-c|}{\sqrt{1^2+1^2}}=5$

$\Rightarrow |c|=5\sqrt{2}\Rightarrow c=\pm 5\sqrt{2}$

Hence, the equation of the line is

$y=-x\pm 5\sqrt{2}$

i.e. $x+y+5\sqrt{2}=0$

or $x+y-5\sqrt{2}=0$

37. (i) (True)

$$d=\left|\frac{b\times a+a\times b-ab}{\sqrt{b^2+a^2}}\right|=\frac{|ab|}{\sqrt{a^2+b^2}}$$

(ii) (True)

$$d=\frac{12\times(-1)-5\times 1+82}{\sqrt{(12)^2+(-5)^2}}$$

$$=\frac{65}{\sqrt{169}}=\frac{65}{13}=5 \text{ units}$$

(iii) (True)

$5x-2y-1=0$

$\Rightarrow \quad y=\frac{5}{2}x-\frac{1}{2}$

$5x-2y-9=0$

$\Rightarrow \quad y=\frac{5}{2}x-\frac{9}{2}$

$5x-2y+7=0$

$\Rightarrow \quad y=\frac{5}{2}x+\frac{7}{2}$

$\therefore \; m=\frac{5}{2}, c=-\frac{1}{2}, c_1=\frac{-9}{2}$

and $c_2=\frac{7}{2}$

$$\therefore d_1=\frac{|c_1-c|}{\sqrt{1+m^2}}=\frac{\left|-\frac{9}{2}+\frac{1}{2}\right|}{\sqrt{1+\frac{25}{4}}}$$

$$=\frac{8}{\sqrt{29}} \text{ units}$$

$$\text{and } d_2=\frac{|c_2-c|}{\sqrt{1+m^2}}=\frac{\left|\frac{7}{2}+\frac{1}{2}\right|}{\sqrt{1+\frac{25}{4}}}$$

$$=\frac{8}{\sqrt{29}} \text{ units}$$

$\therefore \quad d_1=d_2\Rightarrow$ equidistant

$\Rightarrow$ Mid-parallel

38. (i) $d=\left|\frac{C_1-C_2}{\sqrt{A^2+B^2}}\right|$

$$=\left|\frac{-34-31}{\sqrt{(15)^2+8^2}}\right|$$

$$=\left|\frac{-65}{\sqrt{289}}\right|=\frac{65}{17} \text{ units}$$

(ii) $\because \quad y=\frac{3}{4}x+\frac{9}{4}$

and $y=\frac{3}{4}x-\frac{17}{8}$

$\Rightarrow \quad d=\frac{|c_2-c_1|}{\sqrt{1+m^2}}$

$$=\frac{\left|-\frac{17}{8}-\frac{9}{4}\right|}{\sqrt{1+\frac{9}{16}}}=\frac{7}{2} \text{ units}$$

Assertion Reason

1. (a) We know that slope of a line making angle θ with positive direction of X-axis is $\tan\theta$.

Here, $x=2$ is a vertical line making angle $90°$ with positive direction of X-axis i.e. $\theta=90°$.

$\Rightarrow \quad \tan 90°=$ undefined

$\therefore$ Slope of the line $x=2$ is not defined.

Both Assertion and Reason are correct but Reason is not the correct explanation of Assertion.

2. (b) We know that for a line $ax+by+c=0$, the slope is $-\frac{a}{b}$

Here, we have $2x+4y=5$

So, slope of the line $=-\frac{2}{4}=-\frac{1}{2}$

Also, we know that slopes of two parallel lines are equal.

Both Assertion and Reason are correct but Reason is not the correct explanation of Assertion.

3. (d) We have, lines $3x+5y=10$ and $5x+3y=9$

The slopes of the lines are $-\frac{3}{5}$ and $-\frac{5}{3}$.

Since, the slopes are not equal. Therefore, lines are not parallel.

$\therefore$ Assertion is incorrect.

We know that slope of the line joining two points (x_1, y_1) and (x_2, y_2) is $\frac{y_2-y_1}{x_2-x_1}$.

Here, $x_1=2, y_1=3, x_2=4$ and $y_2=-1$.

$\therefore \quad \frac{y_2-y_1}{x_2-x_1}=\frac{-1-3}{4-2}=\frac{-4}{2}=-2$

Hence, Reason is correct.

4. (b) If $\tan\theta$ is negative, then θ is obtuse and if $\tan\theta$ is positive, then θ is acute.

$\therefore$ The inclination of the line l may be acute or obtuse.

Also, slope of X-axis is zero and slope of Y-axis is not defined.

5. (c) We have, $x+y=8$

$\Rightarrow \quad \frac{x}{8}+\frac{y}{8}=1$

Here, $a=8=b$

$\therefore$ $x+y=8$ has equal intercepts on the axes.

Hence, Assertion is correct.

We know that distance between two parallel lines $a_1x+b_1y+c_1=0$ and $a_2x+b_2y+c_2=0$ is given by $\frac{|c_2-c_1|}{\sqrt{a_1^2+b_1^2}}$

We have, $a_1=3, b_1=4, c_1=-7$

$a_2=3, b_2=4, c_2=-5$

$\Rightarrow \quad \frac{|c_2-c_1|}{\sqrt{a_1^2+b_1^2}}=\frac{|-5-(-7)|}{\sqrt{3^2+4^2}}=\frac{2}{5}$

Hence, Reason is incorrect.

6. (d) We have, points (3, – 2) and (3, 4).

So, $\frac{y_2 - y_1}{x_2 - x_1} = \frac{4-(-2)}{3-3}$

$= \frac{6}{0}$ = undefined

∴ Assertion is incorrect and Reason is correct.

7. (c) The slope intercept form of a line is given by $\frac{x}{a} + \frac{y}{b} = 1$, where a and b are intercepts on X and Y-axis, respectively.

∴ Assertion is correct.

The slope of a line $ax + by + c = 0$ is $-\frac{a}{b}$.

∴ Reason is incorrect.

8. (d) We have, lines $ax + by + c = 0$ and $ax - by - \lambda = 0$

The slope of line $ax + by + c = 0$ is $-\frac{a}{b}$ and slope of line $ax - by - \lambda = 0$ is $\frac{a}{b}$.

∵ The slope of the lines are not equal.

∴Both the lines are not parallel.

Hence, Assertion is incorrect.

We have, lines $ax + by + c = 0$ and $bx - ay + \lambda = 0$

The slope of line $ax + by + c = 0$ is $-\frac{a}{b}$ and the slope of line $bx - ay + \lambda = 0$ is $\frac{b}{a}$.

$\Rightarrow -\frac{a}{b} \times \frac{b}{a} = -1$

∵ The product of the slope is – 1.

∴ Both the lines are perpendicular.

Hence, Reason is correct.

9. (a) Here, $A = 3, B = -4, C_1 = 9$ and $C_2 = -\frac{15}{2}$

$\therefore d = \frac{\left|-\frac{15}{2} - 9\right|}{\sqrt{9+16}} = \frac{\left|-\frac{33}{2}\right|}{5} = \frac{33}{10}$

Both Assertion and Reason are correct and Reason is the correct explanation of Assertion.

10. (b) We know that a horizontal line is parallel to X-axis.

So, equation of the horizontal line having distance a from the X-axis is $y = a$ or $y = -a$.

Also, a vertical line is parallel to Y-axis.

So, the equation of the vertical line having b from the Y-axis is $x = b$ or $x = -b$.

Both Assertion and Reason are correct but Reason is not the correct explanation of Assertion.

Case Based

Case 1 (i) (c) We have,

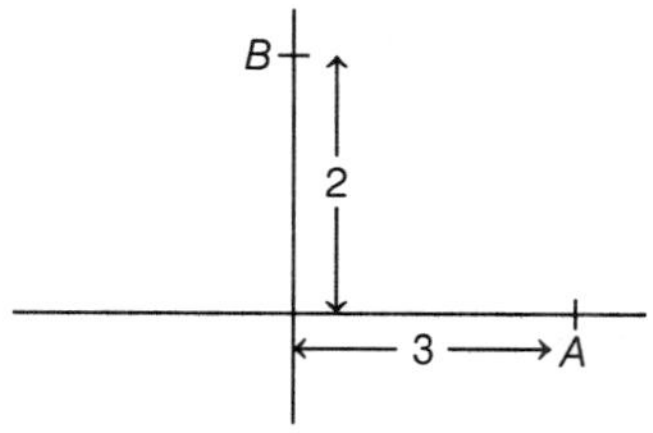

∵ Point A lies on X-axis at a distance of 3 km from origin.

∴ The coordinates of point A are (3, 0).

∵ Point B lies on Y-axis at a distance of 2 km from origin.

∴ The coordinates of point B are (0, 2).

(ii) (a) Using two points slope form of a line,

$y - y_1 = \frac{y_2 - y_1}{x_2 - x_1}(x - x_1)$

Here, $x_1 = 3, y_1 = 0, x_2 = 0, y_2 = 2$

$\therefore y - 0 = \frac{2-0}{0-3}(x-3)$

$\Rightarrow y = \frac{2}{-3}(x-3)$

$\Rightarrow -3y = 2x - 6$

$\Rightarrow 2x + 3y = 6$

(iii) (a) We have,

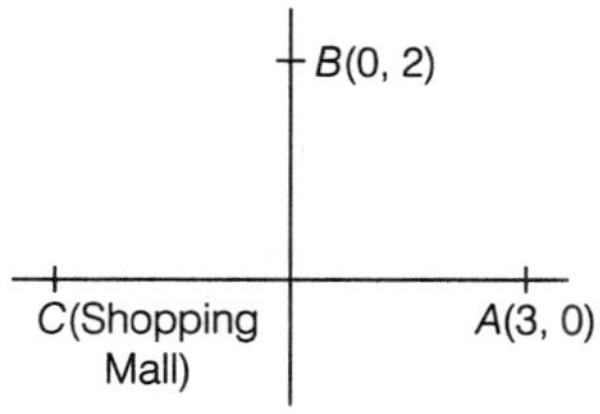

Using point slope form,

$y - y_1 = m(x - x_1)$

Here, $m = 1, x_1 = 0, y_1 = 2$

$\therefore y - 2 = 1(x - 0)$

$\Rightarrow y - 2 = x \Rightarrow x - y + 2 = 0$

Case 2 (i) We have, $\theta = 135°$

So, slope = $\tan\theta$

$= \tan(135°)$

$= \tan(90° + 45°)$

$\left[\because \tan\left(\frac{\pi}{2} + \theta\right) = -\cot\theta\right]$

$= -\cot 45°$

$= -1$

Hence, the slope of BE is – 1.

(ii) We have,

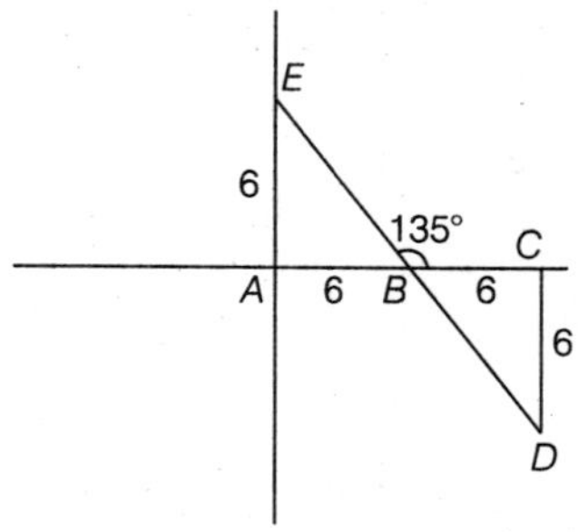

Slope intercept of line BE is

$\frac{x}{6} + \frac{y}{6} = 1$

$\Rightarrow x + y = 6$

∴ Equation of line BE is

$x + y = 6$.

(iii) The x-coordinate of point D

$= 6 + 6 = 12$

and y-coordinate of point D

$= -6$

∴ Coordinates of point D are (12, – 6).

(iv) The coordinates of point B and D are (6, 0) and (12, – 6), respectively.

Using two points slope form of a line

$y - y_1 = \frac{y_2 - y_1}{x_2 - x_1}(x - x_1)$

Here, $x_1 = 6, y_1 = 0, x_2 = 12$ and $y_2 = -6$

$\Rightarrow y - 0 = \frac{-6-0}{12-6}(x-6)$

$\Rightarrow y = -\frac{6}{6}(x-6)$

$\Rightarrow y = -1(x-6)$

$\Rightarrow y = -x + 6$

$\Rightarrow x + y = 6$

∴ Equation of the line BD is

$x + y = 6$

Competition Connect

1. $x\cos 15^\circ + y\sin 15^\circ = 3$

$$\Rightarrow \frac{x(\sqrt{3}+1)}{2\sqrt{2}} + \frac{y(\sqrt{3}-1)}{2\sqrt{2}} = 3$$

$$\Rightarrow (\sqrt{3}+1)x + (\sqrt{3}-1)y - 6\sqrt{2} = 0$$

2. (False)

$$y + 4 = 0 \Rightarrow -y = 4$$

$\Rightarrow x\cos\alpha + y\sin\alpha = p$,

where $\cos\alpha = 0$,

$\sin\alpha = -1$

and $p = 4$

$\therefore x\cos 270^\circ + y\sin 270^\circ = 4$

$\Rightarrow \alpha = 270^\circ$ and $p = 4$

3. (i) $\sqrt{3}x + y + 2 = 0$

$$-\sqrt{3}x - y = 2$$

$$\Rightarrow \left(-\frac{\sqrt{3}}{2}\right)x + \left(-\frac{1}{2}\right)y = 1$$

$$x\cos 210^\circ + y\sin 210^\circ = 1 \quad \text{...(i)}$$

(ii) On comparing Eq. (i) with

$x\cos\alpha + y\sin\beta = p$,

$\alpha = 210^\circ$ and $\beta = 210^\circ$

Competition Edge Up

1. (b) Let the point be (h, k)

According to the question,

$$\frac{\sqrt{(h-2)^2 + (k-1)^2}}{\sqrt{(h-1)^2 + (k-3)^2}} = \frac{5}{4}$$

By squaring and simplification,

$$16\,[(h-2)^2 + (k-1)^2]$$
$$= 25\,[(h-1)^2 + (k-3)^2]$$
$$\Rightarrow 16\,[h^2 + 4 - 4h + k^2 + 1 - 2k]$$
$$= 25\,[h^2 + 1 - 2h + k^2 + 9 - 6k]$$
$$\Rightarrow 9h^2 + 9k^2 + 14h - 118k + 170 = 0$$

Now, replace (h, k) with (x, y), so the locus is

$$9x^2 + 9y^2 + 14x - 118y + 170 = 0$$

Now, comparing it with

$ax^2 + by^2 + cxy + dx + ey + 170 = 0$,

we have

$$a = 9, b = 9, c = 0, d = 14$$

and $e = -118$

So, the value of

$$a^2 + 2b + 3c + 4d + e$$
$$= 81 + 18 + 0 + 56 - 118 = 37$$

2. (b) Given, $x^2 - y^2 + 2hxy + 2gx + 2fy + c = 0$ ...(i)

Locus of point (x, y) which is equidistant from $x + 2y + 7 = 0$ and $2x - y + 8 = 0$

$\therefore$ Equation will be

$$\frac{x + 2y + 7}{\sqrt{1+4}} = \pm\frac{2x - y + 8}{\sqrt{4+1}}$$

$$x + 2y + 7 = \pm(2x - y + 8)$$

Squaring both sides, we get

$$x^2 + 4y^2 + 49 + 4xy + 28y + 14x$$
$$= 4x^2 + y^2 + 64 - 4xy - 16y + 32x$$
$$\Rightarrow 3x^2 - 3y^2 - 8xy + 18x - 44y + 15 = 0$$
$$\Rightarrow x^2 - y^2 - \frac{8}{3}xy + 6x - \frac{44}{3}y + 5 = 0 \quad \text{...(ii)}$$

On comparing Eqs. (i) and (ii), we get

$2h = -\frac{8}{3}$ $\Rightarrow h = -\frac{4}{3}$	$2g = 6$ $\Rightarrow g = 3$	$2f = -\frac{44}{3}$ $\Rightarrow f = -\frac{22}{3}$	$c = 5$

$$\therefore g + c + h - f = 3 + 5 - \frac{4}{3} + \frac{22}{3}$$
$$= 8 + 6 = 14$$

3. (c) We have,

$A(a, -2)$, $B(a, 6)$ and $C\left(\frac{a}{4}, -2\right)$

and $O\left(5, \frac{a}{4}\right)$

$\therefore AO = BO$

$$\Rightarrow (a-5)^2 + \left(-2 - \frac{a}{4}\right)^2 = (a-5)^2 + \left(6 - \frac{a}{4}\right)^2$$

$$\Rightarrow a^2 + 25 - 10a + 4 + \frac{a^2}{16} + a = a^2 + 25 - 10a + 36 + \frac{a^2}{16} - 3a$$

$\Rightarrow a = 8$

$AB = 8$, $AC = 6$ and $BC = 10$

$\therefore \alpha = 5, \beta = 24$ and $\gamma = 24$

$\therefore \alpha + \beta + \gamma = 5 + 24 + 24 = 53$

4. (c) Given, ΔOPQ is isosceles triangle and $\angle POQ = 90^\circ$.

Here, $OP = OQ = a$

$\therefore PQ = \sqrt{2}a$

Let slope of OP be m_1

$\therefore$ Equation of line OP is $y = m_1 x$

and slope of $3x + 4y = 12$ is $-\frac{3}{4}$

i.e. $m_2 = -\frac{3}{4}$

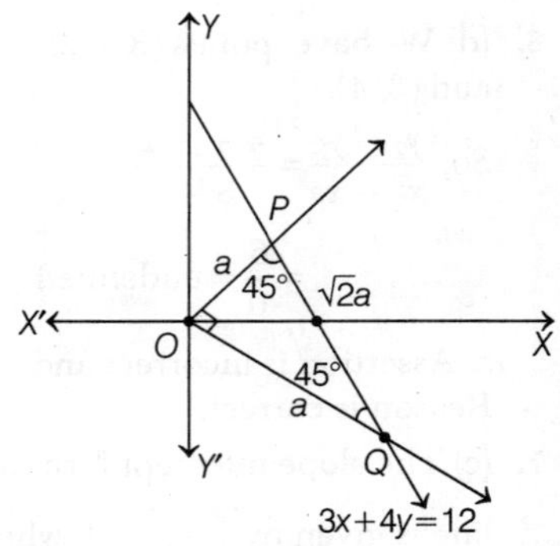

Now, $\tan 45^\circ = \left|\frac{m_1 - m_2}{1 + m_1 m_2}\right|$

$$\Rightarrow 1 = \left|\frac{m_1 + \frac{3}{4}}{1 - \frac{3}{4}m_1}\right|$$

$$\Rightarrow 1 - \frac{3}{4}m_1 = m_1 + \frac{3}{4}$$

$$\Rightarrow \frac{7}{4}m_1 = \frac{1}{4} \Rightarrow m_1 = \frac{1}{7}$$

$\therefore$ Equation of line OP is $y = \frac{1}{7}x$

Intersecting point of lines $y = \frac{1}{7}x$ and $3x + 4y = 12$ is $P\left(\frac{84}{25}, \frac{12}{25}\right)$

and $OP^2 = a^2 = \left(\frac{84}{25} - 0\right)^2 + \left(\frac{12}{25} - 0\right)^2$

$$\Rightarrow a^2 = \frac{7056}{625} + \frac{144}{625} = \frac{7200}{625} = \frac{288}{25}$$

$\therefore l = OP^2 + PQ^2 + OQ^2$

$$= a^2 + 2a^2 + a^2 = 4a^2$$
$$= 4 \times \frac{288}{25} = 46.08$$

$\therefore [l] = 46$

5. (d) The angle between two lines, whose slopes m_1 and m_2 is given by formula,

$$\tan\theta = \left|\frac{m_1 - m_2}{1 + m_1 m_2}\right|$$

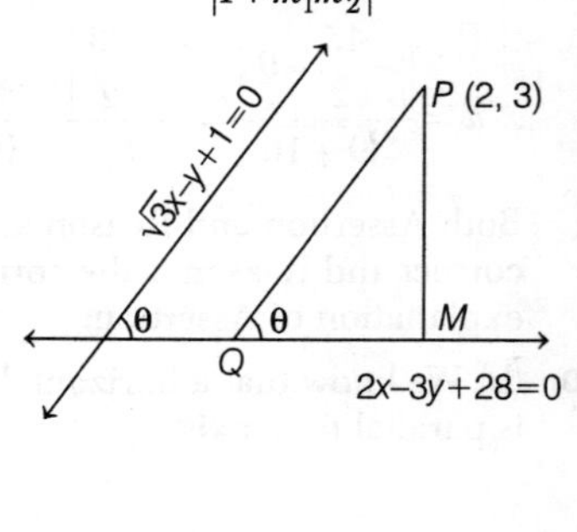

The distance of $P(2, 3)$ from the line $2x - 3y + 28 = 0$ measured parallel to the line $\sqrt{3}x - y + 1 = 0$ is PQ.

Let θ be the angle between two given lines

$$\tan\theta = \left|\frac{\frac{2}{3} - \sqrt{3}}{1 + \frac{2}{3}\sqrt{3}}\right|$$

$$\left(\because m_1 = \frac{2}{3} \text{ and } m_2 = -\sqrt{3}\right)$$

$$= \tan\theta = \left|\frac{2 - 3\sqrt{3}}{3 + 2\sqrt{3}}\right|$$

$$\tan\theta = \frac{3\sqrt{3} - 2}{2\sqrt{3} + 3}$$

Now,

$$PM = \left|\frac{2(2) - 3(3) + 28}{\sqrt{4 + 9}}\right| = \frac{23}{\sqrt{13}}$$

$$\because PQ = \frac{PM}{\sin\theta} = PM \operatorname{cosec}\theta$$

$$= \frac{23}{\sqrt{13}}\left[\frac{\sqrt{(2\sqrt{3} + 3)^2 + (3\sqrt{3} - 2)^2}}{3\sqrt{3} - 2}\right]$$

$$= \frac{23}{\sqrt{13}}\left(\frac{\sqrt{12 + 9 + 12\sqrt{3} + 27 + 4 - 12\sqrt{3}}}{3\sqrt{3} - 2}\right)$$

$$= \frac{23}{\sqrt{13}} \times \frac{\sqrt{52}}{(3\sqrt{3} - 2)}$$

$$= \frac{46}{3\sqrt{3} - 2} \times \frac{3\sqrt{3} + 2}{3\sqrt{3} + 2}$$

$$= \frac{46\,(3\sqrt{3} + 2)}{23} = 4 + 6\sqrt{3}$$

6. (d)

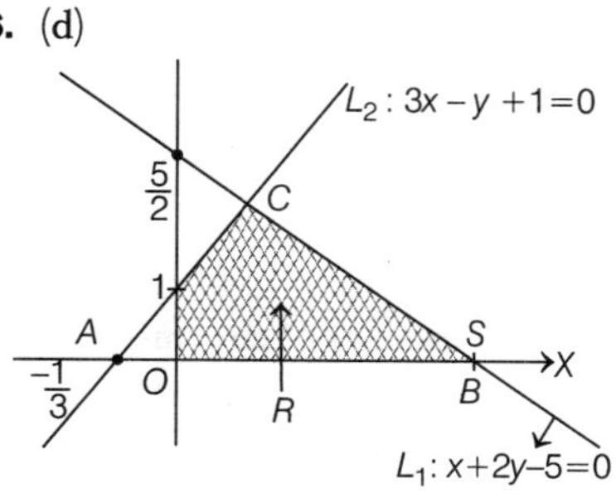

Let $L_1 : x + 2y - 5 = 0$

$L_2 : 3x - y + 1 = 0$

R = Shaded region, where $P(a^2, a + 1)$ should lie.

For line L_1 Origin and P lies same side w.r.t. L_1

$$L_1(O) \cdot L_1(P) < 0$$

$$\Rightarrow a^2 + 2(a + 1) - 5 < 0$$

$$\Rightarrow a^2 + 2a - 3 < 0$$

$$\Rightarrow (a - 1)(a + 3) < 0$$

$$\Rightarrow -3 < a < 1 \quad \text{...(i)}$$

For line L_2

$$L_2(O) \cdot L_2(P) > 0$$

$$\Rightarrow 3a^2 - a - 1 + 1 > 0$$

$$\Rightarrow 3a^2 - a > 0$$

$$\Rightarrow a(3a - 1) > 0$$

$$\Rightarrow a < 0 \text{ or } a > \frac{1}{3} \quad \text{...(ii)}$$

From Eqs. (i) and (ii), we have

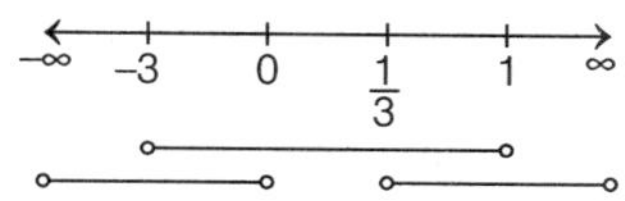

$$\Rightarrow a \in (-3, 0) \cup \left(\frac{1}{3}, 1\right)$$

7. (b) Let θ = angle between L_1 and L_2

According to the question,

$$PA = AB = BQ$$

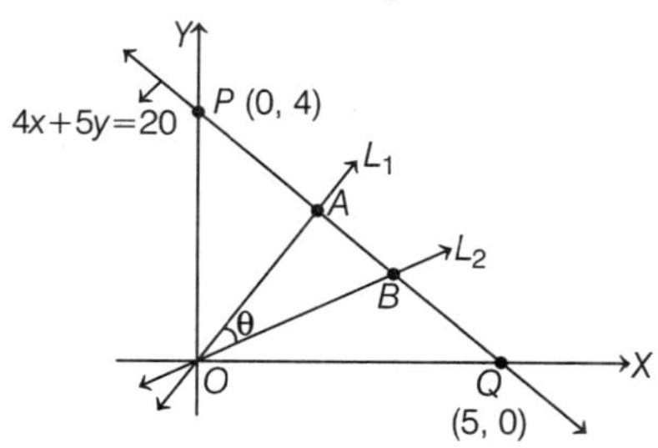

So, coordinates of $A \equiv \left(\frac{5}{3}, \frac{8}{3}\right)$

and coordinates of $B \equiv \left(\frac{10}{3}, \frac{4}{3}\right)$

$$\therefore m_{OA} = \text{slope of } OA = \frac{\frac{8}{3} - 0}{\frac{5}{3} - 0} = \frac{8}{5}$$

$$m_{OB} = \text{slope of } OB = \frac{\frac{4}{3} - 0}{\frac{10}{3} - 0} = \frac{2}{5}$$

$$\text{Now, } \tan\theta = \left|\frac{m_{OA} - m_{OB}}{1 + m_{OA} \times m_{OB}}\right|$$

$$= \left|\frac{\frac{8}{5} - \frac{2}{5}}{1 + \frac{8}{5} \times \frac{2}{5}}\right| = \left|\frac{\frac{6}{5}}{\frac{25 + 16}{25}}\right| = \frac{30}{41}$$

8. (1)

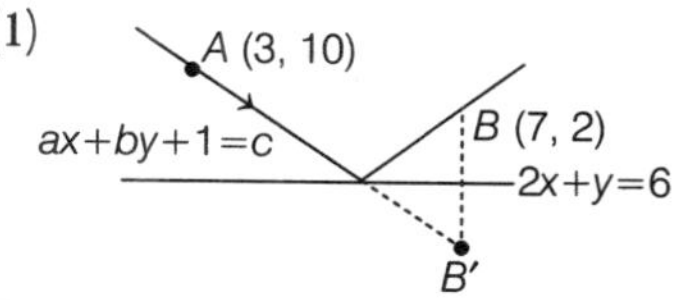

For B',

$$\frac{x - 7}{2} = \frac{y - 2}{1} = -2\left(\frac{14 + 2 - 6}{5}\right)$$

$$\Rightarrow \frac{x - 7}{2} = y - 2 = -4$$

$$\Rightarrow x = -1, y = -2$$

So, $B'(-1, -2)$; Slope $AB' = 3$

Equation of AB'

$$y + 2 = 3(x + 1) \Rightarrow 3x - y + 1 = 0$$

$$a = 3, b = -1$$

Therefore, $a^2 + b^2 + 3ab$

$$= 9 + 1 - 9 = 1$$

9. (36) We have,

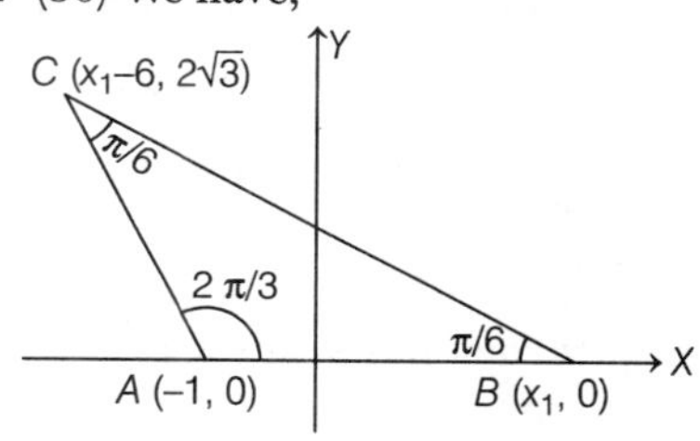

Coordinates of C are

$$\frac{x - x_1}{\cos\frac{5\pi}{6}} = \frac{y - 0}{\sin\frac{5\pi}{6}} = 4\sqrt{3}$$

$$\therefore \quad x = 4\sqrt{3}\cos\frac{5\pi}{6} + x_1$$

$$= 4\sqrt{3} \times \left(\frac{-\sqrt{3}}{2}\right) + x_1$$

$$= x_1 - 6$$

$$\Rightarrow y = 4\sqrt{3}\sin\frac{5\pi}{6}$$

$$\Rightarrow 4\sqrt{3} \times \frac{1}{2} \Rightarrow 2\sqrt{3}$$

$$C(x_1 - 6, 2\sqrt{3})$$

$$M_{AC} = -\sqrt{3}$$

$$\therefore \quad \frac{0 - 2\sqrt{3}}{-1 - x_1 + 6} = -\sqrt{3} \Rightarrow x_1 = 3$$

$$BC \Rightarrow x + \sqrt{3}y = 3, y = x + 3$$

$$\Rightarrow y - 3 + \sqrt{3}y = 3$$

$$\Rightarrow y = \frac{6}{\sqrt{3} + 1},$$

$$x = \frac{6}{\sqrt{3} + 1} - 3 = \frac{6 - 3\sqrt{3} - 3}{\sqrt{3} + 1}$$

$$x = \frac{3 - 3\sqrt{3}}{\sqrt{3} + 1} = \frac{-6}{(1 + \sqrt{3})^2}$$

$$\text{So, } \frac{\beta^4}{\alpha^2} = 36$$

10. (a)

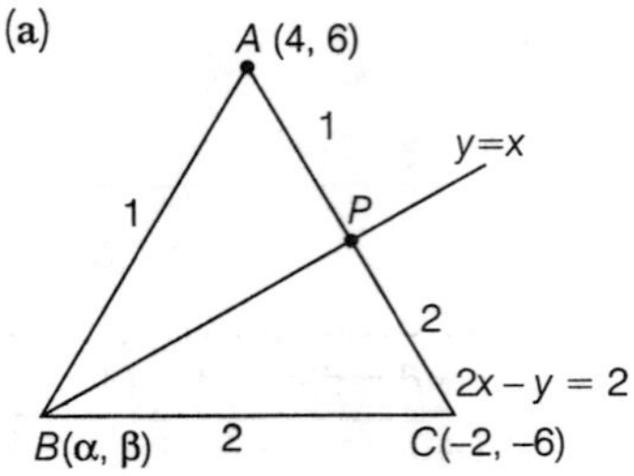

Given, $2AB = BC$

$\Rightarrow \quad \dfrac{AB}{BC} = \dfrac{1}{2}$

$\Rightarrow \quad AP = PC = 1 = 2$

We have, $y = x$ ...(i)

$2x - y = 2$ ...(ii)

On solving Eqs. (i) and (ii), we get point $P(2, 2)$

Let coordinates of C be (x, y)

$\therefore$ By section formula, we get

$$2 = \frac{1\times x + 2\times 4}{1+2} \Rightarrow x = -2$$

and $$2 = \frac{1\times y + 2\times 6}{1+2} \Rightarrow y = -6$$

$\therefore C \equiv (-2, -6)$

$\because$ Point B less on $y = x$

$\therefore (\alpha = \beta)$

$\because \dfrac{AB}{BC} = \dfrac{1}{2} \Rightarrow |BC| = 2|AB|$

$\Rightarrow \sqrt{(\alpha+2)^2 + (\alpha+6)^2} = 2\sqrt{(\alpha-4)^2 + (\alpha-6)^2}$

$\Rightarrow (\alpha+2)^2 + (\alpha+6)^2 = 4[(\alpha-4)^2 + (\alpha-6)^2]$

$\Rightarrow \alpha^2 - 16\alpha + 28 = 0 \Rightarrow \alpha = 2, 14$

$\alpha = 2$ given point P, $\Rightarrow \alpha = 14$

$\therefore \alpha + 2\beta = \alpha + 2\alpha = 3\alpha = 3\times 14 = 42$

11. (d)

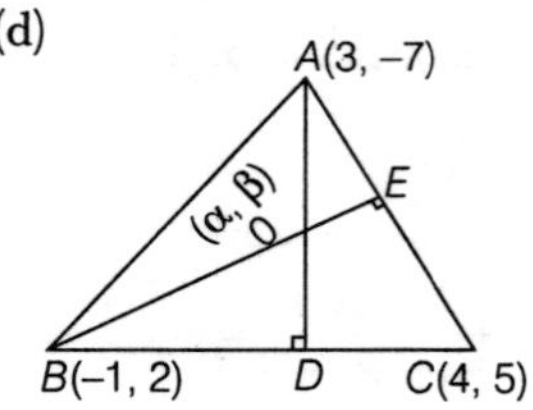

$$m_{AD} = \frac{-1}{m_{BC}} = \frac{-5}{3}$$

$$\left[\because m_{BC} = \frac{5-2}{4+1} = \frac{3}{5}\right]$$

$$m_{AC} = \frac{5+7}{4-3} = \frac{12}{1}; m_{BE} = -\frac{1}{12}$$

$$AD : (y+7) = \frac{-5}{3}(x-3)$$

$$3y + 21 = -5x + 15$$

$$5x + 3y + 21 - 15 = 0$$

$\Rightarrow \quad 5x + 3y + 6 = 0$ ...(i)

$BE : (y-2) = \dfrac{-1}{12}(x+1)$

$12y - 24 = -x - 1$

$x + 12y - 24 + 1 = 0$

$\Rightarrow \quad x + 12y - 23 = 0$ ...(ii)

$\Rightarrow \quad x = 23 - 12y$

On putting the value of x in Eq. (i), we get

$5(23 - 12y) + 3y + 6 = 0$

$\Rightarrow \quad 115 - 60y + 3y + 6 = 0$

$y = \dfrac{121}{57}$

$\Rightarrow \quad x = 23 - \dfrac{12\times 121}{57} = -\dfrac{141}{57}$

Orthocentre O,

$$(\alpha, \beta) = \left(\frac{-141}{57}, \frac{121}{57}\right)$$

$$= 9\alpha - 6\beta + 60$$

$$= 9\times\left(\frac{-141}{57}\right) - 6\left(\frac{121}{57}\right) + 60$$

$$= \frac{3\times(-141)}{19} - \frac{2\times 121}{19} + 60$$

$$= \frac{-423}{19} - \frac{242}{19} + 60 = 25$$

12. (b) We have, the line

$x\cos\theta + y\sin\theta = 7, \ \theta \in \left(0, \dfrac{\pi}{2}\right)$

$$\Rightarrow \quad \frac{x}{7\sec\theta} + \frac{y}{7\,\text{cosec}\,\theta} = 1$$

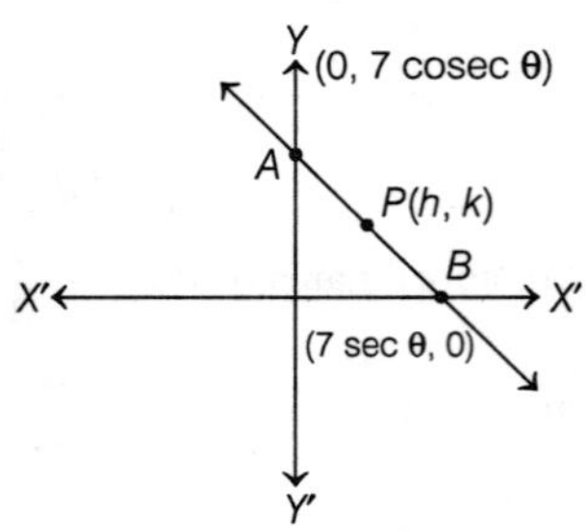

Let $P(h, k)$ be mid-point of the line segment AB.

$\therefore \quad h = \dfrac{7\sec\theta}{2}, k = \dfrac{7\,\text{cosec}\,\theta}{2}$

Since, $\theta \in \left(0, \dfrac{\pi}{2}\right) \Rightarrow h$ and k are positive.

Now, $\cos\theta = \dfrac{7}{2h}, \sin\theta = \dfrac{7}{2k}$

$$\Rightarrow \quad \left(\frac{7}{2h}\right)^2 + \left(\frac{7}{2k}\right)^2 = 1$$

Also, $\left(\alpha, \dfrac{7\sqrt{3}}{3}\right)$ lies on this curve

$$\Rightarrow \quad \left(\frac{7}{2\alpha}\right)^2 + \left(\frac{7\cdot 3}{2\cdot 7\sqrt{3}}\right)^2 = 1$$

$$\Rightarrow \quad \frac{49}{4\alpha^2} + \frac{3}{4} = 1$$

$$\Rightarrow \quad \alpha^2 = 49$$

$$\Rightarrow \quad \alpha = \pm 7$$

Since, $h > 0$ i.e. x-coordinate of points on curve are positive.

13. (b) Given, sides of triangle

$4x + 3y = 69$ ...(i)

$4y - 3x = 17$

$\Rightarrow \quad 3x - 4y = -17$ ...(ii)

$x + 7y = 61$ ...(iii)

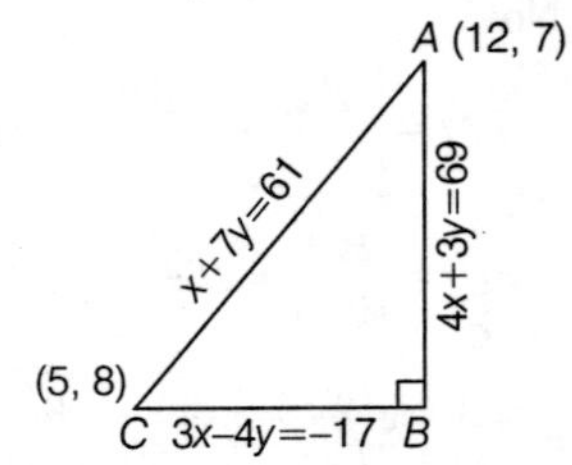

$\therefore$ Circumcentre of a right angled triangle is the mid-point of the hypotenuse.

On solving Eqs. (i) and (iii) after multiply by 4 in Eq (iii),

$$\begin{array}{r} 4x + 3y = 69 \\ 4x + 28y = 244 \\ - \quad - \quad - \\ \hline -25y = -175 \end{array}$$

$\Rightarrow \quad y = 7$ and $x = 12$

$A(12, 7)$

On solving Eqs. (ii) and (iii) for C,

$$\begin{array}{r} 3x - 4y = -17 \\ 3x + 21y = 183 \\ - \quad - \quad - \\ \hline -25y = -200 \end{array}$$

$\Rightarrow \quad y = 8$ and $x = 5$

$C(5, 8)$

Coordiantes of circumcentre

$= $ mid-point of AC

$$= \left(\frac{5+12}{2}, \frac{7+8}{2}\right)$$

$\therefore \quad \alpha = \dfrac{17}{2}, \beta = \dfrac{15}{2}$

$\therefore (\alpha - \beta)^2 + \alpha + \beta = 1 + 16 = 17$

14. (a)

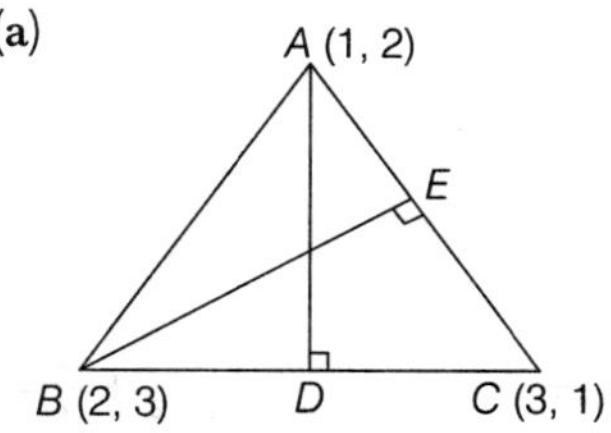

Slope of BC,

$$m_{BC} = \frac{1-3}{3-2} = \frac{-2}{1} = -2$$

$\therefore$ Slope of AD,

$$m_{AD} = \frac{-1}{m_{BC}} = \frac{-1}{-2} = \frac{1}{2}$$

So, equation of line AD is

$$y - 2 = \frac{1}{2}(x-1)$$

$$\Rightarrow \quad x - 2y + 3 = 0 \qquad \ldots(i)$$

Slope of AC, $m_{AC} = \frac{2-1}{1-3}$

$$= \frac{1}{-2} = \frac{-1}{2}$$

$\therefore$ Slope of BE,

$$m_{BE} = \frac{-1}{m_{AC}} = \frac{-1}{\left(-\frac{1}{2}\right)} = 2$$

So, equation of line BE is

$$y - 3 = 2(x-2)$$

$$\Rightarrow \quad 2x - y - 1 = 0 \qquad \ldots(ii)$$

On solving Eqs. (i) and (ii), we get

$$x = \frac{5}{3}, y = \frac{7}{3}$$

$\therefore$ Orthocentre of ΔABC is $\left(\frac{5}{3}, \frac{7}{3}\right)$.

$\therefore \quad \alpha = \frac{5}{3}$ and $\beta = \frac{7}{3}$

Now, Let $\alpha_1 = \alpha + 4\beta$

and $\beta_1 = 4\alpha + \beta$.

Then, $\alpha_1 = \alpha + 4\beta = \frac{5}{3} + 4 \times \frac{7}{3}$

$$= \frac{33}{3} = 11$$

and $\beta_1 = 4\alpha + \beta = 4 \times \frac{5}{3} + \frac{7}{3}$

$$= \frac{27}{3} = 9$$

Again, $\alpha_1 + \beta_1 = 11 + 9 = 20$

and $\alpha_1\beta_1 = 11 \times 9 = 99$

So, quadratic equation, whose roots are α_1 and β_1 is

$$x^2 - (\alpha_1 + \beta_1)x + \alpha_1\beta_1 = 0$$

$$\Rightarrow \quad x^2 - 20x + 99 = 0$$

Chapter-10

Conic Sections

1. (i) The equation of the circle is

$$(x-2)^2 + \{y-(-3)\}^2 = 4^2$$

[using $(x-h)^2 + (y-k)^2 = r^2$]

$$\Rightarrow \quad (x-2)^2 + (y+3)^2 = 16$$

$$\Rightarrow x^2 + y^2 - 4x + 6y - 3 = 0$$

(ii) $\left(x - \frac{1}{3}\right)^2 + \left(y - \frac{1}{2}\right)^2 = \left(\frac{1}{6}\right)^2$

$$\Rightarrow x^2 + \frac{1}{9} - \frac{2x}{3} + y^2 + \frac{1}{4} - \frac{2y}{2} = \frac{1}{36}$$

$$\Rightarrow \quad x^2 + y^2 - \frac{2x}{3} - y + \frac{1}{3} = 0$$

$$\Rightarrow 3x^2 + 3y^2 - 2x - 3y + 1 = 0$$

(iii) $(x - a\cos\theta)^2 + (y - a\sin\theta)^2 = (a)^2$

$$\Rightarrow x^2 + a^2\cos^2\theta - 2ax\cos\theta + y^2 + a^2\sin^2\theta - 2ay\sin\theta = a^2$$

$$\Rightarrow x^2 + y^2 + a^2(\cos^2\theta + \sin^2\theta) - 2ax\cos\theta - 2ay\sin\theta = a^2$$

$$\Rightarrow x^2 + y^2 - 2ax\cos\theta - 2ay\sin\theta = 0$$

(iv) Given, centre is $(-a, -b)$.

$\therefore h = -a, k = -b$ and radius,

$$r = \sqrt{a^2 - b^2}$$

$$\Rightarrow [x-(-a)]^2 + [y-(-b)]^2 = (\sqrt{a^2-b^2})^2$$

$$\Rightarrow (x+a)^2 + (y+b)^2 = a^2 - b^2$$

$$\Rightarrow x^2 + a^2 + 2ax + y^2 + b^2 + 2yb = a^2 - b^2$$

$$\Rightarrow x^2 + y^2 + 2ax + 2by + 2b^2 = 0$$

(v) Centre,

$$(h, k) = \left(\frac{a}{b}\cos\theta, \frac{a}{b}\sin\theta\right)$$

and radius $= \frac{a}{b}$

$\therefore$ Equation of the circle is

$$\left(x - \frac{a}{b}\cos\theta\right)^2 + \left(y - \frac{a}{b}\sin\theta\right)^2 = \left(\frac{a}{b}\right)^2$$

$$x^2 + y^2 - \frac{2a}{b}(x\cos\theta + y\sin\theta) = 0$$

2. (i) Given, equation of circle is

$$(x+3)^2 + (y-2)^2 = 16$$

On comparing with

$(x-h)^2 + (y-k)^2 = r^2$, we get

$$h = -3, k = 2 \text{ and } r = 4$$

$\therefore$ Centre $(h, k) = (-3, 2)$

and radius $= 4$

(ii) Given, equation of circle is

$$\left(x - \frac{1}{4}\right)^2 + \left(y + \frac{1}{5}\right)^2 = \frac{1}{9}$$

On comparing with

$(x-h)^2 + (y-k)^2 = r^2$, we get

$$h = \frac{1}{4}, k = -\frac{1}{5} \text{ and } r = \frac{1}{3}$$

$\therefore$ Centre $(h, k) = \left(\frac{1}{4}, -\frac{1}{5}\right)$

and radius $= \frac{1}{3}$

(iii) Given equation of circle is

$$x^2 + y^2 - 2x + 6y - 2 = 0$$

$$\Rightarrow x^2 - 2x + y^2 + 6y - 2 = 0$$

$$\Rightarrow x^2 - 2x + 1 - 1 + y^2 + 6y + 9 - 9 - 2 = 0$$

$$\Rightarrow (x-1)^2 + (y+3)^2 = (\sqrt{12})^2$$

$$\Rightarrow (x-1)^2 + (y+3)^2 = (2\sqrt{3})^2$$

$\therefore$ Centre $= (1, -3)$

and radius $= 2\sqrt{3}$

(iv) Given equation of circle is

$$2x^2 + 2y^2 - x = 0$$

When $2\left[x^2 - \frac{x}{2} + y^2\right] = 0$,

$$\left[x^2 - 2x\left(\frac{1}{4}\right) + \left(\frac{1}{4}\right)^2\right] + y^2 - \left(\frac{1}{4}\right)^2 = 0$$

$$\Rightarrow \left(x - \frac{1}{4}\right)^2 + (y-0)^2 = \left(\frac{1}{4}\right)^2$$

$\therefore$ Centre $= \left(\frac{1}{4}, 0\right)$

and radius $= \frac{1}{4}$

(v) Equation of the circle is

$$x^2 + y^2 - \frac{16}{5}x - \frac{4}{3}y - \frac{449}{225} = 0$$

or $\left(x - \frac{8}{5}\right)^2 + \left(y - \frac{2}{3}\right)^2 = (\sqrt{5})^2$

Thus, centre $= \left(\frac{8}{5}, \frac{2}{3}\right)$

and radius $= \sqrt{5}$

3. (True)

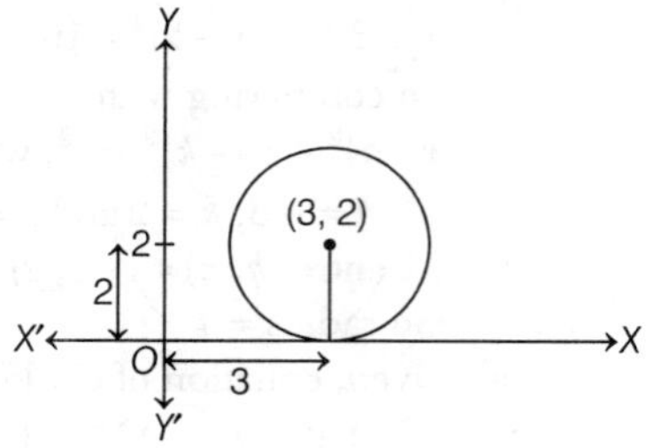

Radius = 2

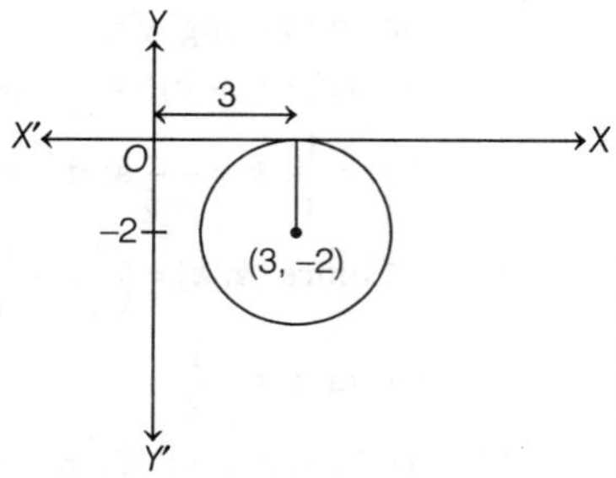

Radius $= |-2|$

Clearly, from the above figure, radius is equal to the absolute value of the y-coordinate of the centre.

4. (b) Given, centre, $(h, k) = (2, 0)$

$\therefore$ Radius = 2

So, equation of the circle is

$$(x-2)^2 + (y-0)^2 = 4$$

$$\Rightarrow \quad x^2 + y^2 - 4x = 0$$

5. (True)

Centre, $(h, k) = (a, a)$

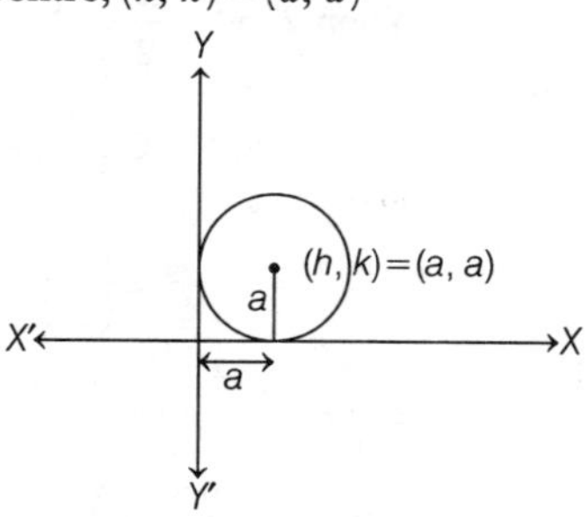

So, equation of the circle is

$$(x-a)^2 + (y-a)^2 = a^2$$

$$x^2 + y^2 - 2ax - 2ay + a^2 = 0$$

6. (True)

Let the equation of the circle be

$$(x-h)^2 + (y-k)^2 = r^2$$

Since, the circle passes through $(1, -2)$ and $(4, -3)$.

$$\therefore \quad (1-h)^2 + (-2-k)^2 = r^2 \quad \ldots\text{(i)}$$

$$\text{and } (4-h)^2 + (-3-k)^2 = r^2 \quad \ldots\text{(ii)}$$

Also, centre lies on the line

$$3x + 4y = 7$$

$$\therefore \quad 3h + 4k = 7 \quad \ldots\text{(iii)}$$

On solving Eqs. (i), (ii) and (iii), we get

$$h = \frac{47}{15}, \ k = -\frac{3}{5} \text{ and } r^2 = \frac{1465}{225}$$

$\therefore$ Required equation of circle is

$$\left(x - \frac{47}{15}\right)^2 + \left(y + \frac{3}{5}\right)^2 = \frac{1465}{225}$$

$$\Rightarrow (15x-47)^2 + 9(5y+3)^2 = 1465$$

$$\Rightarrow 15x^2 + 15y^2 - 94x + 18y + 55 = 0$$

7. Given, radius, $r = 5$

Since, centre of the circle is on X-axis i.e. $y = 0$

Let $(h, 0)$ be the centre of circle.

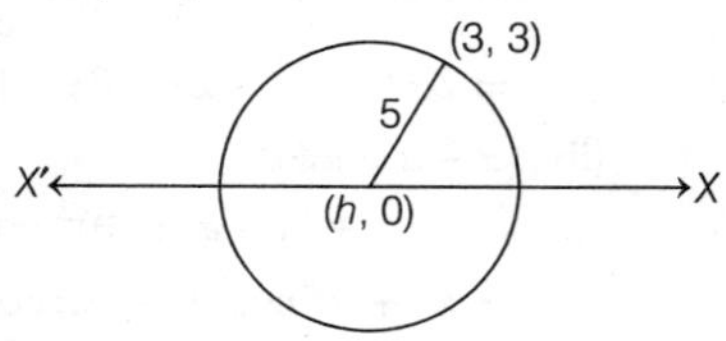

Now, by distance formula,

$$\sqrt{(h-3)^2 + (0-3)^2} = 5$$

$$h^2 + 9 - 6h + 9 = 25$$

$$\Rightarrow \quad h^2 - 6h - 7 = 0$$

$$\Rightarrow \quad h = -1, 7$$

So, centre of the circle is $(-1, 0)$ or $(7, 0)$.

Thus, the equation of the circle, when centre $= (-1, 0)$ and radius, $r = 5$

$$(x+1)^2 + (y-0)^2 = 25$$

$$\Rightarrow x^2 + y^2 + 2x - 24 = 0$$

When centre $= (7, 0)$ and radius, $r = 5$

$$(x-7)^2 + (y-0)^2 = 25$$

$$\Rightarrow x^2 + y^2 - 14x + 24 = 0$$

8. (True)

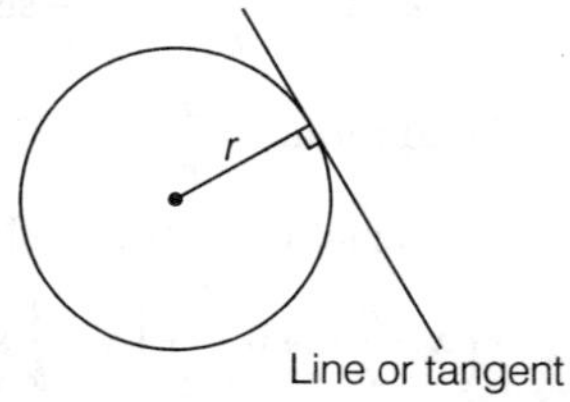

Clearly, from above figure when a circle touches a line, then length of the perpendicular from its centre on the given line is equal to the radius of the circle.

9. (a) Let the equation of the circle be $(x-h)^2 + (y-k)^2 = r^2$

Since, the circle passes through (1,1), (2, 0) and $(-6, -6)$.

Therefore,

$$(1-h)^2 + (1-k)^2 = r^2 \quad \ldots\text{(i)}$$

$$(2-h)^2 + (0-k)^2 = r^2 \ldots\text{(ii)}$$

$$\text{and } (-6-h)^2 + (-6-k)^2 = r^2 \ldots\text{(iii)}$$

On solving Eqs. (i), (ii) and (iii), we get

$$h = -2, \ k = -3 \text{ and } r^2 = 25$$

$\therefore$ Required equation of circle is

$$(x+2)^2 + (y+3)^2 = 25$$

$$\Rightarrow x^2 + 4 + 4x + y^2 + 9 + 6y = 25$$

$$\Rightarrow \quad x^2 + y^2 + 4x + 6y - 12 = 0$$

10. Given, centre of the circle is $(9, -4)$ and passes through the point $(2, 3)$.

$\Rightarrow$ Radius = Distance between the points $(9, -4)$ and $(2, 3)$

$$= \sqrt{(9-2)^2 + (-4-3)^2}$$

$$= \sqrt{7^2 + (-7)^2} = \sqrt{49 + 49}$$

$$= 7\sqrt{2} \text{ units}$$

$\therefore$ Required equation of circle

$$(x-9)^2 + (y+4)^2 = (7\sqrt{2})^2$$

$$\Rightarrow x^2 + 81 - 18x + y^2 + 16 + 8y = 98$$

$$\Rightarrow x^2 + y^2 - 18x + 8y + 97 - 98 = 0$$

$$\Rightarrow x^2 + y^2 - 18x + 8y - 1 = 0$$

11. (False)

Given, equation of the circle is

$$x^2 + y^2 + 6x + 2y = 0$$

$\therefore$ Centre $= (-3, -1)$

Since, the given line is

$$2x + 9y = 0$$

$$-6 - 9 \neq 0$$

$\Rightarrow$ Centre does not lie on the line

So, this line is not diameter of the circle.

12. Given equation of circle is

$$S \equiv x^2 + y^2 = 13$$

$$S \equiv x^2 + y^2 - 13 = 0 \quad \ldots\text{(i)}$$

Now, put $x = -3.5$ and $y = 3.5$ in Eq. (i), we get

$$S = (-3.5)^2 + (3.5)^2 - 13$$

$$S = 12.25 + 12.25 - 13$$

$$S = 11.5 > 0$$

$\therefore$ The given point $(-3.5, 3.5)$ lies outside the circle.

13. (a) **14.** (c)

15. (i) Given, equation of parabola

$$y^2 = 8x,$$

which is of the form $y^2 = 4ax$.

Here, $4a = 8 \Rightarrow a = 2$

$\therefore$ Focus $= (a, 0) = (2, 0)$

Axis = X-axis

Equation of the directrix,

$$x = -a \Rightarrow x = -2$$

and length of the latus rectum

$$= 4a = 4 \times 2 = 8$$

(ii) Given, equation of parabola

$$y^2 = -12x,$$

which is of the form

$$y^2 = -4ax$$

i.e. focus lies on the negative direction of X-axis.

Here, $4a = 12 \Rightarrow a = 3$

$\therefore$ Focus $= (-a, 0) = (-3, 0)$

Axis = X-axis

Equation of directrix,

$$x = a \Rightarrow x = 3$$

and length of latus rectum

$$= 4a = 4 \times 3 = 12$$

(iii) Given, equation of parabola

$$x^2 = 14y,$$

which is of the form

$$x^2 = 4ay$$

i.e. focus lies on the positive direction of Y-axis.

Here, $4a = 14 \Rightarrow a = \frac{7}{2}$

$\therefore$ Focus $= (0, a) = \left(0, \frac{7}{2}\right)$

Axis = Y-axis

Equation of directrix,

$$y = -a = -\frac{7}{2}$$

and length of latus rectum

$$= 4a = 4 \times \frac{7}{2} = 14$$

(iv) Given, equation of parabola

$$x^2 = -7y,$$

which is of the form

$$x^2 = -4ay$$

Here, $4a = 7 \Rightarrow a = 7/4$

$\therefore$ Focus $= (0, -a) = \left(0, -\frac{7}{4}\right)$

Axis = Y-axis

Equation of directrix,

$$y = a = \frac{7}{4}$$

and length of latus rectum

$$= 4a = 4 \times \frac{7}{4} = 7$$

16. (i) (True)

Given, focus = (4, 0)

and directrix, $x = -4$

Since, focus lies on the positive direction of X-axis.

$\therefore$ Equation of parabola will be of the form $y^2 = 4ax$ with

$$a = 4$$

$\therefore$ Required equation of parabola is

$$y^2 = 4ax = 4 \times 4x$$

$$\Rightarrow \quad y^2 = 16x$$

(ii) (False)

Given, focus $= (0, -5)$

and directrix, $y = 5$

Since, focus lies on the negative direction of Y-axis.

$\therefore$ Equation of parabola will be of the form $x^2 = -4ay$ with $a = 5$.

$\therefore$ Required equation of parabola is

$$x^2 = -4(5)y \Rightarrow x^2 = -20y$$

(iii) (False)

Given, vertex = (0, 0)

and focus = (6, 0)

Since, focus lies on positive direction of X-axis.

$\therefore$ Required equation of parabola is

$$y^2 = 4ax \Rightarrow y^2 = 4 \times 6 \times x$$

$$\Rightarrow y^2 = 24x$$

(iv) (True)

Given, vertex = (0, 0)

and focus $= (0, -8)$

Since, focus lies on negative direction of Y-axis.

$\therefore$ Required equation of parabola is

$$x^2 = -4ay = -4 \times 8 \times y$$

$$\Rightarrow x^2 = -32y$$

17. (i) Directrix is on the left hand side from the origin and parallel to Y-axis.

$\therefore$ Equation of directrix,

$$x = -2$$

(ii) We know that the distance from the directrix to the focus is $2a$.

$$\therefore \quad FM = 2a$$

$$\Rightarrow \quad 48 = 2a \Rightarrow a = 24$$

$\therefore$ The line of the directrix is

$$x = 24 \Rightarrow x - 24 = 0$$

18. Focal chord

19. Coordinates of the focus is (0, 4).

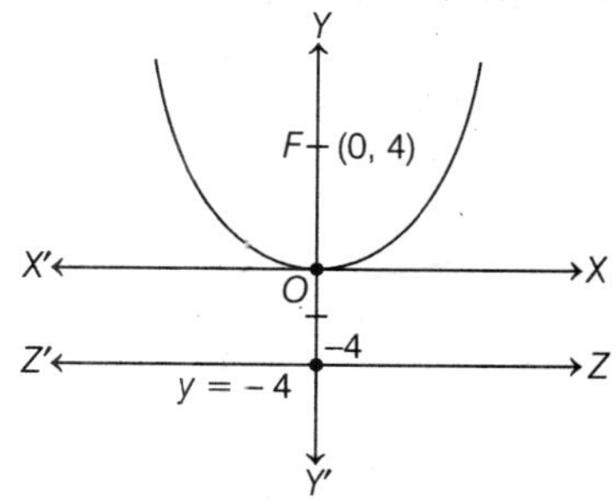

20. (c) Since, equation of directrix $y = 3$, then focus $= (0, -3)$

$$\Rightarrow \quad a = 3$$

and vertex = (0, 0)

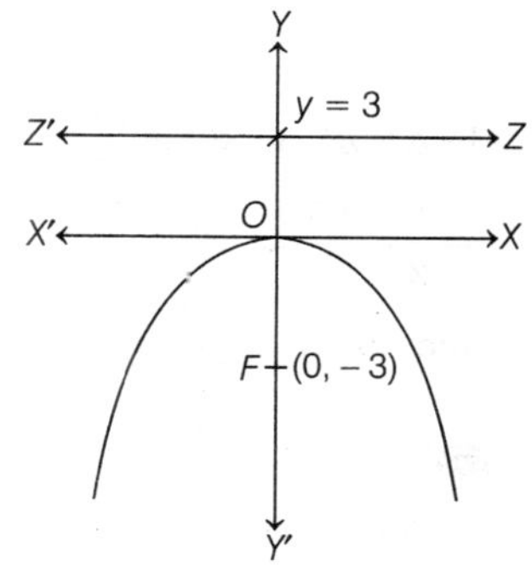

$\Rightarrow$ Equation of the parabola

$$x^2 = -4ay$$

$$= -4 \times (3)y = -12y$$

21. (True)

Given that parabola passes through the point $(\sqrt{8}, 5)$, then it satisfy the equation $x^2 = 4ay$

$$\Rightarrow \quad (\sqrt{8})^2 = 4a \times 5$$

$$\Rightarrow \quad 8 = 20a$$

$$\Rightarrow \quad a = \frac{2}{5}$$

$\therefore$ The focus is $\left(0, \frac{2}{5}\right)$.

22. Since, the point (9, 11) satisfying the equation $y^2 = 4ax$

$$\Rightarrow \quad 121 = 4a \times 9$$

$$a = \frac{121}{36}$$

Thus, the equation of the parabola is

$$y^2 = \frac{4 \times 121}{36} x$$

$$y^2 = \frac{121}{9} x$$

$$9y^2 = 121x$$

23. First, we draw the parabola in negative side of X-axis.

Let $OB = l = OA = AB$

[$\because$ equilateral triangle]

$\angle BOA = 60°$

$\Rightarrow \angle BOP = 30°$

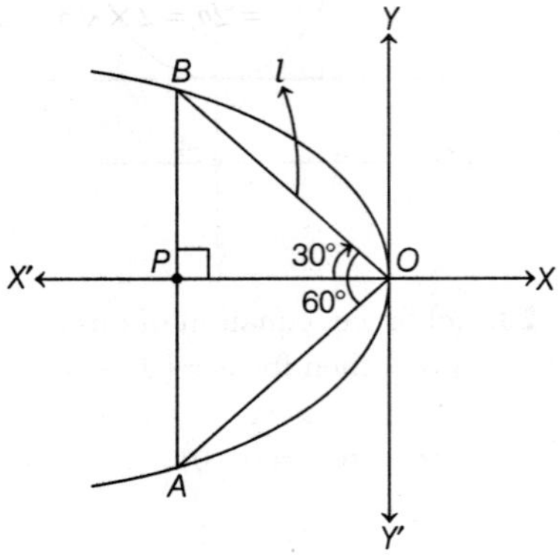

In ΔBOP, $\sin 30° = \frac{PB}{OB}$

$\Rightarrow \frac{1}{2} = \frac{PB}{l} \Rightarrow PB = \frac{l}{2}$

and $\cos 30° = \frac{OP}{OB} \Rightarrow \frac{\sqrt{3}}{2} = \frac{OP}{l}$

$\Rightarrow \quad OP = \frac{\sqrt{3}\,l}{2}$

$\therefore$ Coordinates of $B = (-OP, PB)$

$= \left(-\frac{\sqrt{3}}{2}l, \frac{l}{2}\right)$ will satisfy

$y^2 = -4ax$

i.e. $\left(\frac{l}{2}\right)^2 = -4a \times \left(-\frac{\sqrt{3}}{2}l\right)$

$l = 8\sqrt{3}\,a$

Hence, the length of side of the triangle is $8\sqrt{3}a$.

24. (a) We know that latus rectum $= 4a$

Given, $x^2 = -12y$

$\Rightarrow \quad 4a = 12$

$a = 3$

$\therefore$ Focus $F = (0, -3)$

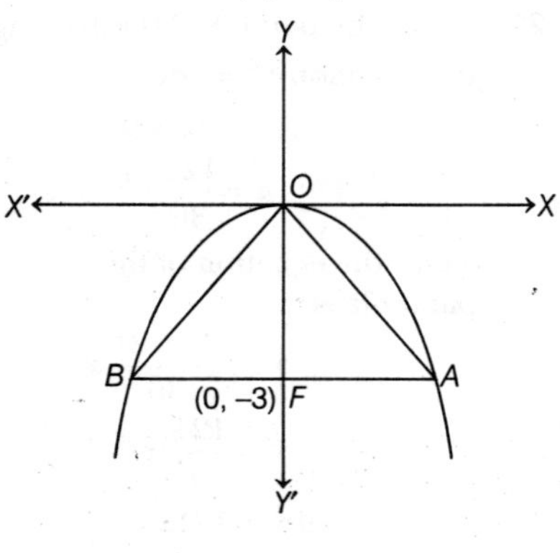

Now, area of $\Delta AOB = \frac{1}{2} \times AB \times OF$

$= \frac{1}{2} \times 12 \times (3)$

[$\because$ length is positive $= OF = 3$]

$= 18$ sq. units

25. (True)

Here, axis is vertical, so arch of parabola is $x^2 = 4ay$ ...(i)

Given, $OB = 10$ m

arch $AC = 5$ m

$\Rightarrow \quad AB = \frac{5}{2}$ m $\left[\because AB = BC = \frac{AC}{2}\right]$

Coordinates of $A = \left(\frac{5}{2}, 10\right)$ will satisfy Eq. (i),

$\left(\frac{5}{2}\right)^2 = 4a \times 10 \Rightarrow a = \frac{5}{32}$

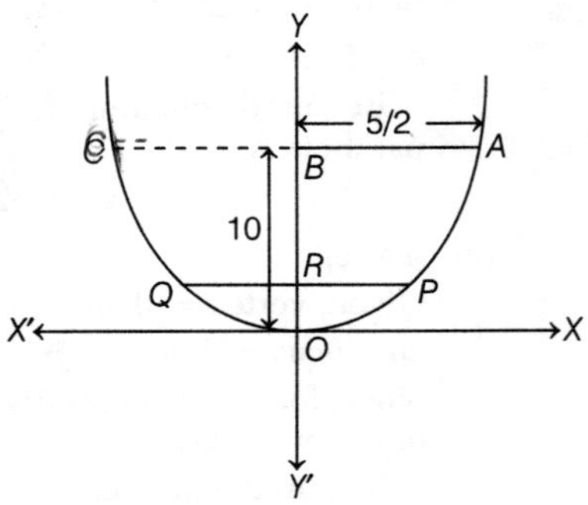

From Eq. (i),

$x^2 = 4 \times \frac{5}{32} y \Rightarrow x^2 = \frac{5}{8} y$

Let $OR = 2$ and $PQ = k$

$\Rightarrow RP = \frac{k}{2}$

$\therefore \quad P = \left(\frac{k}{2}, 2\right)$ will lies on parabola

$\Rightarrow \left(\frac{k}{2}\right)^2 = \frac{5}{8} \times 2 \Rightarrow k = \sqrt{5}$

26. (i) The major axis.

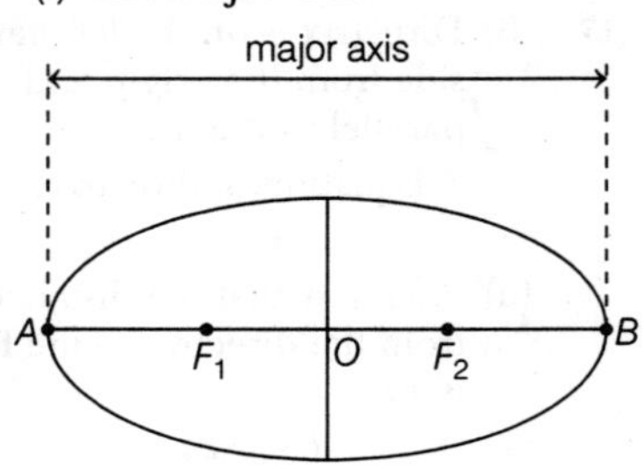

(ii) Minor axis

(iii) Vertices

27. (b) **Statement I** Let length of the semi-minor axis

$OQ = b$ [given]

$OF_2 = OF_1 = c$

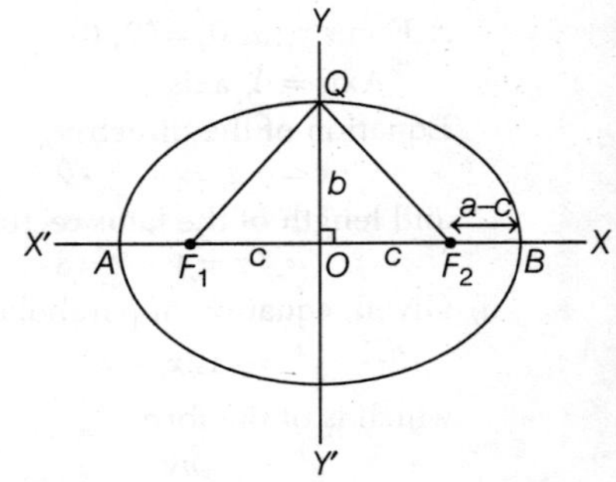

Length of the semi major axis $= a$

$OA = OB = a$

By the definition of ellipse,

$a^2 = b^2 + c^2$

$\Rightarrow \quad c = \sqrt{a^2 - b^2}$

Statement II In $c^2 = a^2 - b^2$, when $c = 0$, then both foci merge together with the centre of ellipse such that $a^2 = b^2$ and ellipse becomes circle.

Statement III When $c = a$, then $b = 0$, ellipse reduces to the line segment joining the two foci.

28. (a)

29. (i) Given, equation of ellipse

$\frac{x^2}{25} + \frac{y^2}{16} = 1$

Since, denominator of $\frac{x^2}{25}$ is larger than the denominator of $\frac{y^2}{16}$.

$\therefore$ Major axis is along X-axis.

On comparing with

$\frac{x^2}{a^2} + \frac{y^2}{b^2} = 1$, we get

$a^2 = 25, b^2 = 16$

$\Rightarrow \quad a = 5, b = 4$

Now, $c = \sqrt{a^2 - b^2}$

$= \sqrt{25 - 16} = 3$

$\therefore$ Foci $= (\pm c, 0) = (\pm 3, 0)$

Vertices $= (\pm a, 0) = (\pm 5, 0)$

Length of major axis

$= 2a = 2 \times 5 = 10$

Length of minor axis

$= 2b = 2 \times 4 = 8$

Eccentricity,

$$e = \frac{c}{a} = \frac{3}{5}$$

and length of latus rectum

$$= \frac{2b^2}{a}$$

$$= \frac{2 \times 16}{5} = \frac{32}{5}$$

(ii) Given, $\frac{x^2}{9} + \frac{y^2}{16} = 1$

Since, denominator of $\frac{y^2}{16}$ is larger than the denominator of $\frac{x^2}{9}$.

$\therefore$ Major axis is along Y-axis.

On comparing with

$\frac{x^2}{b^2} + \frac{y^2}{a^2} = 1$, we get

$b^2 = 9, a^2 = 16$

$\Rightarrow b = 3, a = 4$

Now, $c = \sqrt{a^2 - b^2}$

$= \sqrt{16 - 9} = \sqrt{7}$

$\therefore$ Foci $= (0, \pm c) = (0, \pm \sqrt{7})$

Vertices $= (0, \pm a) = (0, \pm 4)$

Length of major axis

$= 2a = 2 \times 4 = 8$

Length of minor axis

$= 2b = 2 \times 3 = 6$

Eccentricity,

$$e = \frac{c}{a} = \frac{\sqrt{7}}{4}$$

and length of latus rectum

$$= \frac{2b^2}{a} = \frac{2 \times 9}{4} = \frac{9}{2}$$

(iii) Given, $9x^2 + y^2 = 144$

$$\Rightarrow \frac{9x^2}{144} + \frac{y^2}{144} = 1$$

$$\Rightarrow \frac{x^2}{16} + \frac{y^2}{144} = 0$$

Here, $a^2 = 144, b^2 = 16$

$\Rightarrow a = 12, b = 4$

Now, $c = \sqrt{a^2 - b^2}$

$= \sqrt{144 - 16} = \sqrt{128}$

Foci $= (0, \pm c)$

$= (0, \pm \sqrt{128})$

$= (0, \pm 8\sqrt{2})$

Vertices $= (0, \pm a) = (0, \pm 12)$

Length of major axis

$= 2a = 2 \times 12 = 24$

Length of minor axis

$= 2b = 2 \times 4 = 8$

Eccentricity,

$$e = \frac{c}{a}$$

$$= \frac{8\sqrt{2}}{12} = \frac{2\sqrt{2}}{3}$$

and length of latus rectum

$$= \frac{2b^2}{a}$$

$$= \frac{2 \times 16}{12} = \frac{8}{3}$$

(iv) Given, $4x^2 + y^2 = 400$

$$\Rightarrow \frac{4x^2}{400} + \frac{y^2}{400} = 1$$

$$\Rightarrow \frac{x^2}{100} + \frac{y^2}{400} = 1$$

Here, $a^2 = 400, b^2 = 100$

$\Rightarrow a = 20, b = 10$

Now, $c = \sqrt{a^2 - b^2}$

$= \sqrt{400 - 100}$

$= \sqrt{300}$

$= 10\sqrt{3}$

$\therefore$ Foci $= (0, \pm c) = (0, \pm 10\sqrt{3})$

Vertices $= (0, \pm a) = (0, \pm 20)$

Length of major axis

$= 2a = 2 \times 20 = 40$

Length of minor axis

$= 2b = 2 \times 10$

$= 20$

Eccentricity,

$$e = \frac{c}{a}$$

$$= \frac{10\sqrt{3}}{20} = \frac{\sqrt{3}}{2}$$

and length of latus rectum

$$= \frac{2b^2}{a}$$

$$= \frac{2 \times 100}{20} = 10$$

(v) Given, $3x^2 + 27y^2 = 81$

$$\Rightarrow \frac{x^2}{27} + \frac{y^2}{3} = 1$$

Here, $a^2 = 27, b^2 = 3$

$\Rightarrow a = 3\sqrt{3}, b = \sqrt{3}$

Now, $c = \sqrt{a^2 - b^2}$

$= \sqrt{27 - 3}$

$= \sqrt{24} = 2\sqrt{6}$

$\therefore$ Foci $= (\pm c, 0) = (\pm 2\sqrt{6}, 0)$

Vertices $= (\pm a, 0) = (\pm 3\sqrt{3}, 0)$

Length of major axis

$= 2a = 2 \times 3\sqrt{3} = 6\sqrt{3}$

Length of minor axis

$= 2b = 2 \times \sqrt{3} = 2\sqrt{3}$

Eccentricity,

$$e = \frac{c}{a} = \frac{2\sqrt{6}}{3\sqrt{3}} = \frac{2\sqrt{2}}{3}$$

and length of latus rectum

$$= \frac{2b^2}{a} = \frac{2 \times 3}{3\sqrt{3}} = \frac{2}{\sqrt{3}}$$

30. (False)

Length of the major axis

= Distance between $\left(\frac{9}{2}, 0\right)$ and $\left(-\frac{9}{2}, 0\right)$

$$= \sqrt{\left(\frac{9}{2} + \frac{9}{2}\right)^2 + (0 - 0)^2}$$

$= \sqrt{(9)^2} = 9$ units

31. Given, $x^2 + 4y^2 = 52$

$$\Rightarrow \frac{x^2}{52} + \frac{y^2}{13} = 1$$

$a^2 = 52, b^2 = 13$

$\Rightarrow a > b$

$\therefore$ Major axis is along the X-axis.

32. (a) Clearly, major axis is along the Y-axis.

$\therefore a = 5, b = 3$

$\therefore$ Equation of ellipse is

$$\frac{x^2}{9} + \frac{y^2}{25} = 1$$

33. (a) Here, foci $(0, \pm c) = (0, \pm \sqrt{5})$

$\Rightarrow c = \sqrt{5}$

End points of the major axis

$(0, \pm a) = (0, \pm 9)$

$\Rightarrow a = 9$

$\therefore$ Eccentricity, $e = \frac{c}{a} = \frac{\sqrt{5}}{9}$

34. Given, length of the major axis

$= 2a$

$\Rightarrow 2a = 46 \Rightarrow a = 23$

Foci $(\pm c, 0) = (\pm 2, 0)$

$\therefore c = 2$

Thus, eccentricity $e = \frac{c}{a} = \frac{2}{23}$

35. (c)

36. (i) Given, $\frac{x^2}{36}+\frac{y^2}{16}=1$

On comparing the given equation with the standard equation of the ellipse, we get

$$a^2=36$$
$$\Rightarrow \quad a=6$$
and $\quad b^2=16$

$\therefore$ Latus rectum $=\frac{2b^2}{a}=\frac{2\times16}{6}=\frac{16}{3}$

(ii) Given, $\frac{x^2}{\left(\frac{1}{4}\right)}+\frac{y^2}{\left(\frac{1}{9}\right)}=1$

We have, $a^2=\frac{1}{4}\Rightarrow a=\frac{1}{2}$

$$b^2=\frac{1}{9}$$

$\therefore$ Latus rectum $=\frac{2b^2}{a}=\frac{2\times1\times2}{9\times1}=\frac{4}{9}$

(iii) Given, length of the major axis,

$$2a=25$$
$$\Rightarrow \quad a=\frac{25}{2}$$

and length of the minor axis,

$$2b=16$$
$$\Rightarrow \quad b=8$$

$\therefore$ Latus rectum $=\frac{2b^2}{a}=\frac{2\times64}{25}\times2=\frac{256}{25}$

37. (i) Since, the vertices are on X-axis, the equation of ellipse will be of the form

$$\frac{x^2}{a^2}+\frac{y^2}{b^2}=1,$$

where a is the semi-major axis.

Given, $a=13$ and $c=5$

From the relation

$c^2=a^2-b^2$, we get

$$25=169-b^2$$
$$\Rightarrow \quad b=12$$

Hence, the equation of the ellipse is

$$\frac{x^2}{169}+\frac{y^2}{144}=1$$

(ii) The ends of the major and minor axes are $(\pm 4, 0)$ and $(0, \pm 3)$, respectively.

$\therefore \ a=4$ and $b=3$

Thus, the equation of the ellipse is

$$\frac{x^2}{a^2}+\frac{y^2}{b^2}=1$$
$$\Rightarrow \frac{x^2}{16}+\frac{y^2}{9}=1$$

(iii) Given, $c=7$ and $a=10$

We know that

$$c^2=a^2-b^2$$
$$\Rightarrow (7)^2=(10)^2-b^2$$
$$\Rightarrow 49=100-b^2$$
$$\Rightarrow b^2=100-49$$
$$\Rightarrow b^2=51$$

Since, foci $(\pm 7, 0)$ lies on X-axis.

$\therefore$ Equation of ellipse is

$$\frac{x^2}{100}+\frac{y^2}{51}=1$$

(iv) Given, $b=4$ and $c=5$

We know that

$$c^2=a^2-b^2$$
$$\therefore \quad (5)^2=a^2-(4)^2$$
$$\Rightarrow 25=a^2-16$$
$$\Rightarrow a^2=25+16=41$$

Since, foci lies on X-axis.

$\therefore$ Equation of ellipse is

$$\frac{x^2}{41}+\frac{y^2}{16}=1$$

(v) Given, the major axis on X-axis.

The equation of ellipse

$$\frac{x^2}{a^2}+\frac{y^2}{b^2}=1 \quad \ldots(i)$$

Equation (i) passes through the points (4, 3) and (6, 2).

$$\therefore \quad \frac{16}{a^2}+\frac{9}{b^2}=1 \quad \ldots(ii)$$

and $\quad \frac{36}{a^2}+\frac{4}{b^2}=1 \quad \ldots(iii)$

On solving Eqs. (ii) and (iii), we get

$$a^2=52$$

and $\quad b^2=13$

Thus, the equation of the ellipse

$$\frac{x^2}{52}+\frac{y^2}{13}=1$$

38. (d) Let PQ be the rod $=12$ cm and $OP=x$, $OQ=y$

In ΔOPQ,

$\Rightarrow x^2+y^2=(12)^2$ [by Pythagoras theorem]

$$x^2+y^2=144 \quad \ldots(i)$$

Let $\quad AP=3$ cm

Then, $AQ=PQ-AP$
$=12-3$
$=9$ cm

$PA:AQ=3:9=1:3$

Let $A(h, k)$, for which locus to be found if $A(h, k)$ divides the points P and Q internally in the ratio $m:n$, then

$$\Rightarrow \quad h=\frac{1\times0+3\times x}{1+3}$$

and $\quad k=\frac{1\times y+3\times0}{1+3}$

$$\Rightarrow \quad h=\frac{3x}{4}$$

$$\Rightarrow \quad x=\frac{4h}{3} \text{ and } y=4k$$

From Eq. (i),

$$\left(\frac{4h}{3}\right)^2+(4k)^2=144$$
$$\Rightarrow \frac{x^2}{81}+\frac{y^2}{9}=1$$

39. Let equation of ellipse be

$$\frac{x^2}{a^2}+\frac{y^2}{b^2}=1 \quad \ldots(i)$$

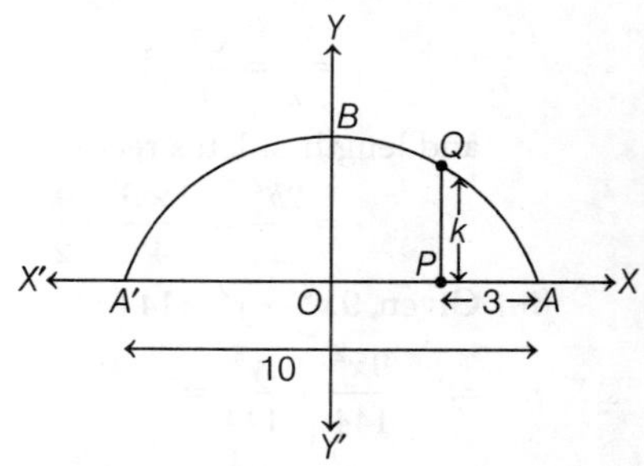

Here, $2a=10$

$$a=5 \text{ cm}$$

and $\quad b=4$ cm

Putting the values of a and b in Eq. (i), we get

$$\frac{x^2}{25}+\frac{y^2}{16}=1 \quad \ldots(ii)$$

Given, $AP=3$ cm

$OP=OA-AP$
$=5-3=2$ cm

Let $PQ = k$

$\therefore$ Coordinate $Q(2, k)$ will satisfy the Eq. (ii),

$$\frac{4}{25} + \frac{k^2}{16} = 1$$

$$\Rightarrow \quad k^2 = \frac{336}{25}$$

$$\Rightarrow \quad k^2 = 13.44$$

$$\Rightarrow \quad k = 3.7 \text{ m (approx.)}$$

40. (a) **41.** (b)

42. $\pm ae$

43. True

44. (i) Given, $\frac{x^2}{49} - \frac{y^2}{25} = 1$

On comparing the given equation with $\frac{x^2}{a^2} - \frac{y^2}{b^2} = 1$, we get

$$a^2 = 49, b^2 = 25$$

$$\Rightarrow \quad a = 7, b = 5$$

Now, $c^2 = a^2 + b^2$

$$= 49 + 25 = 74$$

$$\Rightarrow \quad c = \sqrt{74}$$

Here, in given equation coefficient of x^2 is positive. So, transverse axis is along X-axis.

$\therefore$ Foci $= (\pm c, 0) = (\pm \sqrt{74}, 0)$

Vertices $= (\pm a, 0) = (\pm 7, 0)$

Eccentricity,

$$e = \frac{c}{a} = \frac{\sqrt{74}}{7}$$

and length of latus rectum

$$= \frac{2b^2}{a}$$

$$= \frac{2 \times 25}{7} = \frac{50}{7}$$

(ii) Given, $\frac{y^2}{16} - \frac{x^2}{36} = 1$

On comparing the given equation with $\frac{y^2}{a^2} - \frac{x^2}{b^2} = 1$, we get

$$a^2 = 16, b^2 = 36$$

$$\Rightarrow \quad a = 4, b = 6$$

Now, $c^2 = a^2 + b^2$

$$= 16 + 36 = 52$$

$$\Rightarrow \quad c = 2\sqrt{13}$$

Here, in given equation coefficient of y^2 is positive, so transverse axis is along Y-axis.

$\therefore$ Foci $= (0, \pm c) = (0, \pm 2\sqrt{13})$

Vertices $= (0, \pm a) = (0, \pm 4)$

Eccentricity,

$$e = \frac{c}{a}$$

$$= \frac{2\sqrt{13}}{4} = \frac{\sqrt{13}}{2}$$

and length of latus rectum

$$= \frac{2b^2}{a} = \frac{2 \times 36}{4}$$

$$= 2 \times 9 = 18$$

(iii) Given, equation of hyperbola is

$$6y^2 - 4x^2 = 36$$

$$\Rightarrow \quad \frac{y^2}{6} - \frac{x^2}{9} = 1$$

Here, $a^2 = 6, b^2 = 9$

$$\Rightarrow \quad a = \sqrt{6}, b = 3$$

Now, $c^2 = a^2 + b^2$

$$= 6 + 9 = 15$$

$$\Rightarrow \quad c = \sqrt{15}$$

$\therefore$ Foci $= (0, \pm c) = (0, \pm \sqrt{15})$

Vertices $= (0, \pm a) = (0, \pm \sqrt{6})$

Eccentricity,

$$e = \frac{c}{a} = \frac{\sqrt{15}}{\sqrt{6}} = \sqrt{\frac{5}{2}}$$

and length of latus rectum

$$= \frac{2b^2}{a}$$

$$= \frac{2 \times 9}{\sqrt{6}} = 3\sqrt{6}$$

(iv) Given, equation of hyperbola is

$$9x^2 - 16y^2 = 144$$

$$\Rightarrow \quad \frac{x^2}{16} - \frac{y^2}{9} = 1$$

Here, $a^2 = 16, b^2 = 9$

$$\Rightarrow \quad a = 4, b = 3$$

Now, $c^2 = a^2 + b^2$

$$= 16 + 9 = 25$$

$$\Rightarrow \quad c = 5$$

$\therefore$ Foci $= (\pm c, 0) = (\pm 5, 0)$

Vertices $= (\pm a, 0) = (\pm 4, 0)$

Eccentricity,

$$e = \frac{c}{a} = \frac{5}{4}$$

Length of latus rectum

$$= \frac{2b^2}{a}$$

$$= \frac{2 \times 9}{4} = \frac{9}{2}$$

45. (True)

Since, the distance between the foci $(2c) = 26$

and transverse axis = X-axis

$$\therefore \quad c = \frac{26}{2} = 13$$

Therefore, the coordinates of the foci is $(\pm 13, 0)$.

46. Since, equation of the hyperbola is

$$\frac{x^2}{1600} - \frac{y^2}{81} = 1,$$

where $a^2 = 1600, b^2 = 81$

$$\Rightarrow \quad a = 40, b = 9$$

Then, $c = \sqrt{a^2 + b^2}$

$$= \sqrt{1600 + 81}$$

$$= \sqrt{1681} = 41$$

$\therefore$ Foci $= (\pm 41, 0)$

47. (d) The given equation is

$$\frac{x^2}{16} - \frac{y^2}{25} = 1$$

$$\Rightarrow \quad a^2 = 16 \Rightarrow a = \pm 4$$

Thus, the vertices are $(\pm 4, 0)$.

48. Given, foci $= (0, \pm \sqrt{27})$

$$\Rightarrow \quad c = \sqrt{27}$$

Vertices $= (0, \pm 4)$

$$\Rightarrow \quad a = 4$$

$\Rightarrow$ Eccentricity, $e = \frac{c}{a} = \frac{\sqrt{27}}{4}$

49. (i) Given, equation of the hyperbola is

$\frac{x^2}{48^2} - \frac{y^2}{14^2} = 1$, we get

Here, $a = 48$

and $b = 14$

Since, length of the latus rectum

$$= \frac{2b^2}{a} = \frac{2 \times 196}{48} = \frac{49}{6}$$

(ii) Given, equation of hyperbola is

$$5y^2 - 9x^2 = 36$$

$$\Rightarrow \quad \frac{y^2}{36/5} - \frac{x^2}{4} = 1 \quad \ldots(i)$$

Here, $a^2 = \frac{36}{5} \Rightarrow a = \frac{6}{\sqrt{5}}$

$$b^2 = 4 \Rightarrow b = 2$$

Thus, the latus rectum

$$= \frac{2b^2}{a}$$

$$= \frac{2 \times 4}{6} \times \sqrt{5} = \frac{4\sqrt{5}}{3}$$

50. (i) Since, the given foci is on Y-axis, the equation of the hyperbola is of the form

$$\frac{y^2}{a^2}-\frac{x^2}{b^2}=1$$

Since, vertices are $\left(0, \pm\frac{\sqrt{11}}{2}\right)$.

$$\Rightarrow \quad a=\frac{\sqrt{11}}{2}$$

and foci are $(0, \pm 3)$

$$\Rightarrow \quad c=3$$

Now, $b^2=c^2-a^2$

$$=\frac{25}{4}$$

$\therefore$ The equation of the hyperbola is

$$\frac{y^2}{\left(\frac{11}{4}\right)}-\frac{x^2}{\left(\frac{25}{4}\right)}=1$$

i.e. $100y^2-44x^2=275$

(ii) Since, foci $(\pm 10, 0)$ lies on X-axis.

$\therefore$ Equation of hyperbola will be of the form

$$\frac{x^2}{a^2}-\frac{y^2}{b^2}=1$$

Here, $c=10$, $2a=16$

$\Rightarrow \quad a=8$

Now, $c^2=a^2+b^2$

$\Rightarrow\ 100=64+b^2$

$\Rightarrow\ b^2=100-64=36$

$\therefore$ Equation of hyperbola

$$\frac{x^2}{64}-\frac{y^2}{36}=1$$

(iii) Since, foci $(\pm 3\sqrt{5}, 0)$ lies on X-axis.

$\therefore$ Equation of hyperbola will be of the form $\frac{x^2}{a^2}-\frac{y^2}{b^2}=1$

Here, $c=3\sqrt{5}$ and latus rectum,

$$\frac{2b^2}{a}=8 \Rightarrow b^2=4a$$

Now, $c^2=a^2+b^2$

$\Rightarrow 9\times 5=a^2+4a$

$\Rightarrow \quad a^2+4a-45=0$

$\Rightarrow a^2+9a-5a-45=0$

$\Rightarrow a(a+9)-5(a+9)=0$

$\Rightarrow \quad (a-5)(a+9)=0$

$\Rightarrow \quad a=5, -9$

Taking $a=5$, $b^2=4a$

$$=4\times 5=20$$

$\therefore$ Equation of hyperbola is

$$\frac{x^2}{25}-\frac{y^2}{20}=1$$

(iv) Since, vertices $=(\pm 7, 0)$

$$a=7$$

and $\quad e=\frac{4}{3}$

$\Rightarrow \quad \frac{c}{a}=\frac{4}{3} \quad \left[\because e=\frac{c}{a}\right]$

$\Rightarrow \quad \frac{c}{7}=\frac{4}{3}\Rightarrow c=\frac{28}{3}$

We know that

$$a^2+b^2=c^2$$

$\Rightarrow \quad 7^2+b^2=\left(\frac{28}{3}\right)^2$

$\Rightarrow \quad b^2=\frac{784}{9}-49$

$\Rightarrow \quad b^2=\frac{343}{9}$

Thus, the equation of the hyperbola is

$$\frac{x^2}{49}-\frac{9y^2}{343}=1.$$

(v) Given, vertices $(0, \pm 6)$

$\therefore \quad a=6$

and $\quad e=\frac{5}{3}$

Now, $c=ae=6\times\frac{5}{3}=10$

$\therefore \quad b^2=c^2-a^2$

$$=(10)^2-(6)^2=64$$

$\therefore$ Equation of the hyperbola is $\frac{y^2}{36}-\frac{x^2}{64}=1.$

Assertion Reason

1. (a) Given, end points of a diameter are $A(1, 5)$ and $B(-1, 3)$.

We know that the equation of circle, the end points of one of whose diameter are (x_1, y_1) and (x_2, y_2) is given by

$$(x-x_1)(x-x_2)+(y-y_1)(y-y_2)=0$$

Hence, the required equation of circle is

$(x-1)(x+1)+(y-5)(y-3)=0$

$\Rightarrow \quad x^2-1+y^2-8y+15=0$

$\Rightarrow \quad x^2+y^2-8y+14=0$

Both Assertion and Reason are true and Reason is the correct explanation of Assertion.

2. (d) We know that the distance between the directrices of the ellipse $\frac{x^2}{a^2}+\frac{y^2}{b^2}=1$ is $\frac{2a}{e}$.

Here, $a^2=16 \Rightarrow a=4$

$$b^2=8 \quad \Rightarrow b=2\sqrt{2}$$

So, $e=\sqrt{1-\frac{b^2}{a^2}}=\sqrt{\frac{1}{2}}=\frac{1}{\sqrt{2}}$

$\therefore \quad \frac{2a}{e}=\frac{2\times 4}{\frac{1}{\sqrt{2}}}=8\sqrt{2}$

$\therefore$ Assertion is false.

3. (a) The equation of the circle is

$$(x-2)^2+(y+5)^2=3^2$$

[using $(x-h)^2+(y-k)^2=r^2$, where (h, k) is the centre and r is the radius]

$\Rightarrow x^2+4-4x+y^2+25+10y=9$

$\Rightarrow \quad x^2+y^2-4x+10y+20=0$

Both Assertion and Reason are true and Reason is the correct explanation of Assertion.

4. (d) We have the general equation of circle,

$$2x^2+2y^2+4x+6y+1=0$$

$\Rightarrow \quad x^2+y^2+2x+3y+\frac{1}{2}=0$

Here, $g=1$ and $f=\frac{3}{2}$

$\therefore$ Centre $(-g, -f)=\left(-1, -\frac{3}{2}\right)$

and radius, $r=\sqrt{g^2+f^2-c}$

$$=\sqrt{1^2+\left(\frac{3}{2}\right)^2-\frac{1}{2}}$$

$$=\frac{\sqrt{11}}{2}$$

$\therefore$ Assertion is false.

Now, we have centre $(2, 1)$ and radius 2.

$\therefore$ The equation of circle is

$$(x-2)^2+(y-1)^2=2^2$$

$\Rightarrow \quad (x-2)^2+(y-1)^2=4$

$\therefore$ Reason is correct.

5. (b) We know that parabola $y^2=4ax$ is symmetrical about X-axis

$\therefore$ Parabola $y^2=12x$ is symmetrical about X-axis

Given, focus is $(0, 3)$, which lies on Y-axis.

$\therefore \quad a=3$

So, the equation of parabola is given by

$$x^2 = 4ay$$

$\Rightarrow \quad x^2 = 4 \times 3y \Rightarrow x^2 = 12y$

Both Assertion and Reason are true but Reason is not the correct explanation of Assertion.

6. (d) We have, $c = 3$, $2b = 4$

$\Rightarrow \quad b = 2$

So, $\quad c^2 = a^2 - b^2$

$\Rightarrow \quad a^2 = c^2 + b^2 = 9 + 4 = 13$

$\therefore$ The equation of ellipse is

$$\frac{x^2}{13} + \frac{y^2}{4} = 1$$

Hence, Assertion is false.

7. (a) Given, the focus $(0, -2)$ lies on negative Y-axis.

$\therefore$ The equation of parabola is given by $x^2 = -4ay$

We have, $a = 2$

$\therefore \quad x^2 = -4(2)y$

$\Rightarrow \quad x^2 = -8y$

Both Assertion and Reason are true and Reason is the correct explanation of Assertion.

8. (c) The foci of the hyperbola $\frac{x^2}{16} - \frac{y^2}{9} = 1$ lies on X-axis.

$\therefore$ Assertion is true.

Equation of the hyperbola whose centre is at origin and transverse axis is along X-axis is given by

$$\frac{x^2}{a^2} - \frac{y^2}{b^2} = 1.$$

$\therefore$ Reason is false.

9. (b) We know that eccentricity of conjugate hyperbola $\frac{y^2}{b^2} - \frac{x^2}{a^2} = 1$ is given by $e = \sqrt{\frac{b^2 + a^2}{b^2}}$.

Also, the equation of its directrix is given by $y = \pm \frac{b}{c}$.

Both Assertion and Reason are true but Reason is not the correct explanation of Assertion.

10. (a) We know that if the major axis is along Y-axis, the equation of ellipse is

$$\frac{x^2}{b^2} + \frac{y^2}{a^2} = 1$$

We have, points $(3, 2)$ and $(1, 6)$, which lie on the ellipse.

$$\therefore \quad \frac{9}{b^2} + \frac{4}{a^2} = 1 \quad \text{...(i)}$$

$$\text{and} \quad \frac{1}{b^2} + \frac{36}{a^2} = 1 \quad \text{...(ii)}$$

Solving Eqs. (i) and (ii), we get

$$a^2 = 40 \text{ and } b^2 = 10$$

$\therefore$ The equation of ellipse is

$$\frac{x^2}{10} + \frac{y^2}{40} = 1.$$

Both Assertion and Reason are true and Reason is the correct explanation of Assertion.

Case Based

Case 1 (i) (c) We know that

$$r = \sqrt{g^2 + f^2 - c}$$

Here, $g = 3, f = -2, c = 4$

$\therefore \quad r = \sqrt{3^2 + (-2)^2 - 4} = \sqrt{9 + 4 - 4} = 3$

Hence, the radius of the given circle is 3 units.

(ii) (b) We have,

$x^2 + y^2 - 4x + 6y - 96 = 0$

Here, $g = -2, f = 3$

$\therefore$ Centre of the circle is $(-g, -f)$

$\Rightarrow$ centre of the circle is $(-(-2), -3)$

i.e. $(2, -3)$

(iii) (a) We have,

$x^2 + y^2 - 8x - 6y + 16 = 0$

Here, $g = -4, f = -3,$

We know, $g = -h$ and $f = -k$

$\Rightarrow -4 = -h$ and $-3 = -k$

$\Rightarrow h = 4$ and $k = 3$

$\therefore h - k = 4 - 3 = 1$

Case 2 (i) Given, equation of parabola is $x^2 = 8y$,

which is the form of $x^2 = 4ay$ i.e. focus lies on the positive direction of Y-axis.

Here, $4a = 8 \Rightarrow a = 2$

$\therefore$ Focus $= (0, a) = (0, 2)$

(ii) Axis $= Y$-axis

$\therefore$ Directrix, $y = -a \Rightarrow y = -2$

(iii) Length of the latus rectum

$= 4a$

$= 4 \times 2 = 8$

Competition Edge Up

1. (c) Orthocentre is the intersection of altitudes.

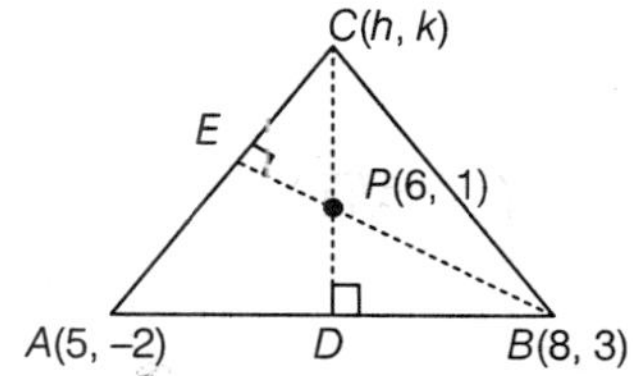

So, Slope of $BP \times$ Slope of $AC = -1$

$\Rightarrow \quad \left(\frac{3-1}{8-6}\right) \times \left(\frac{k+2}{h-5}\right) = -1$

$\Rightarrow \quad k + 2 = -h + 5$

$\Rightarrow \quad h + k = 3 \quad$ ...(i)

and slope of $CP \times$ slope of $AB = -1$

$\Rightarrow \quad \left(\frac{k-1}{h-6}\right) \times \left(\frac{3+2}{8-5}\right) = -1$

$\Rightarrow \quad 5k - 5 = -3h + 18$

$\Rightarrow \quad 3h + 5k = 23 \quad$ ...(ii)

On solving Eqs. (i) and (ii), we get

$h = -4, k = 7$

On checking, option (c) is correct

$x^2 + y^2 - 65 = 0$

2. (a) Common chord of two circles S_1 and S_2 can be found by $S_1 - S_2 = 0$.

$S_1 : x^2 + y^2 - 2x - 2y + 1 = 0$

$S_2 : x^2 + y^2 + 2x - 3 = 0$

$\Rightarrow \quad C_2(-1, 0)$ and $r = 2$

Equation of common chord

$\Rightarrow \quad S_1 - S_2 = 0$

$\Rightarrow -4x - 2y + 4 = 0 \Rightarrow 2x + y = 2$

At Y-axis $\Rightarrow P(0, 2)$

Distance between centre and

$P = \sqrt{(-1-0)^2 + (2-0)^2} = \sqrt{2}$

Its square $= 2$

3. (a) $C : x^2 + y^2 = 10$

$$AN = \frac{MN}{2} = 1$$

$\because$ In ΔOAN,

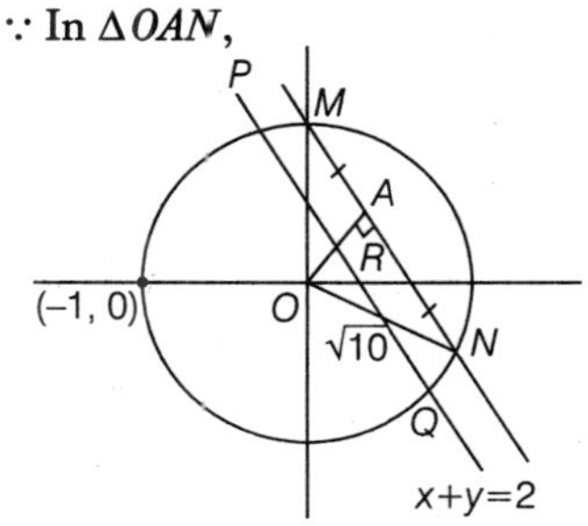

$\Rightarrow \quad ON^2 = OA^2 + AN^2$

$\Rightarrow \quad 10 = OA^2 + 1 \Rightarrow OA = 3$

Perpendicular distance of centre from $PQ = \left|\dfrac{0+0-2}{\sqrt{2}}\right| = \sqrt{2} = OR$

Perpendicular distance between MN and $P\ Q = AR = OA - OR$
$= 3 - \sqrt{2}$

4. (b) We have, circle with radius 1 cm and lines passing through the point (3, 2) and parallel to the coordinate axes.

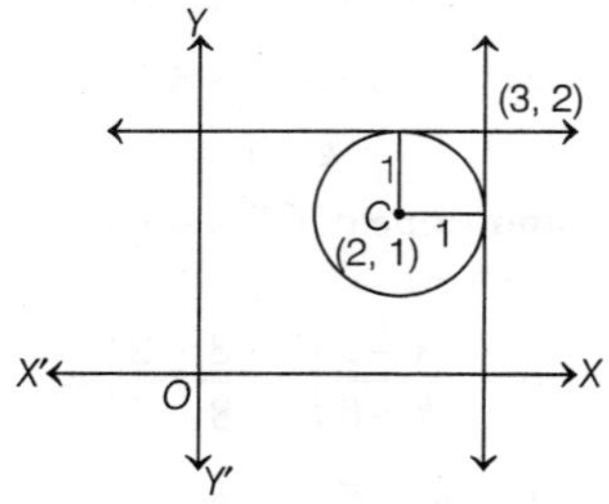

$\because$ Shortest distance of the circle C from the point (5, 5)

$= \sqrt{(5-2)^2 + (5-1)^2} - 1$

$\therefore$ Radius of circle

$= \sqrt{9+16} - 1 = 5 - 1 = 4$

5. (a) Circle : $x^2 + y^2 - 16x - 4y = 0$

Let line passing through centre of circle $C(8, 2)$ with slope m is
$y - 2 = m(x - 8)$

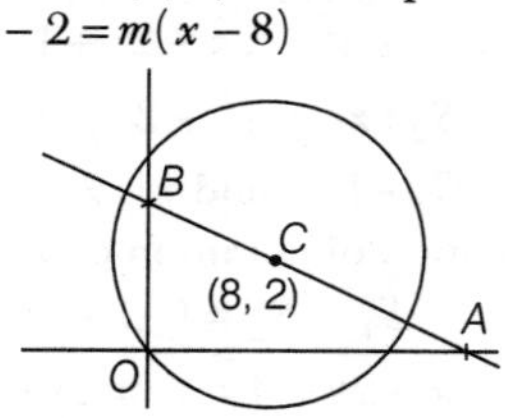

$$A = \left(8 - \frac{2}{m}, 0\right)$$

$$B = (0, 2 - 8m)$$

$$OA + OB = 8 - \frac{2}{m} + 2 - 8m$$

$$= 10 - \left(\frac{2}{m} + 8m\right)$$

AM $\geq$ GM

$$\frac{\frac{2}{m} + 8m}{2} \geq \sqrt{\frac{2}{m} \cdot 8m}$$

$$\frac{2}{m} + 8m \geq 8$$

Since, $m < 0$, $\left(\dfrac{2}{m} + 8m\right)_{\max} = -8$

Minimum value of

$$OA + OB = 10 - (-8) = 18$$

6. (d) $C_1 : (x - \alpha)^2 + (y - \beta)^2 = r_1^2$

$$C_2 : (x - 8)^2 + \left(y - \frac{15}{2}\right)^2 = r_2^2$$

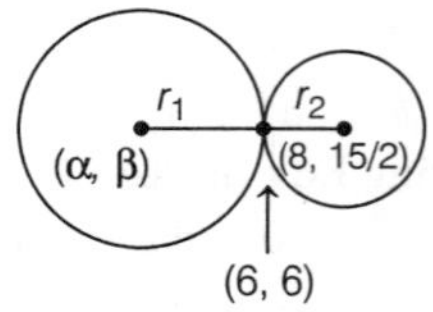

$$r_1 : r_2 = 2 : 1$$

So, $\dfrac{2 \times 8 + \alpha}{2 + 1} = 6 \Rightarrow \alpha = 2$

and $\dfrac{2 \times \frac{15}{2} + \beta}{2 + 1} = 6 \Rightarrow \beta = 3$

So, $\quad (\alpha, \beta) = (2, 3)$

Now, $\quad r_1 = \sqrt{(6-\alpha)^2 + (6-\beta)^2}$

$= \sqrt{(4)^2 + (3)^2} = 5$

$\Rightarrow \quad r_1^2 = 25$

and $r_2^2 = \left(\sqrt{(8-6)^2 + \left(\dfrac{15}{2} - 6\right)^2}\right)^2$

$= 4 + \dfrac{9}{4} = \dfrac{25}{4}$

Therefore, $(\alpha + \beta) + 4(r_1^2 + r_2^2)$

$= (2 + 3) + 4\left(25 + \dfrac{25}{4}\right)$

$= 5 + 4 \times \dfrac{125}{4} = 130$

7. (c) Since, (x_c, y_c) be the point of intersection of the lines

$3x + 5y = 1 \quad$ ...(i)

and $(2 + c)x + 5c^2y = 1 \quad$ ...(ii)

On solving Eqs. (i) and (ii), we get

$$(2 + c)x + 5c^2\left(\frac{1 - 3x}{5}\right) = 1$$

$$\Rightarrow \quad x = \frac{1 - c^2}{2 + c - 3c^2}$$

$$= \frac{(1-c)(1+c)}{(1-c)(2+3c)}$$

$$\Rightarrow \quad x = \frac{1+c}{2+3c} \quad \left(\because x_c = \frac{1+c}{2+3c}\right)$$

and $y = \dfrac{1 - 3x}{5} = \dfrac{-1}{5(3c+2)} = y_c$

Now, $h = \lim\limits_{c \to 1} x_c = \lim\limits_{c \to 1} \dfrac{(1+c)}{2+3c} = \dfrac{2}{5}$

$k = \lim\limits_{c \to 1} y_c = \lim\limits_{c \to 1} \left[\dfrac{-1}{5(3c+2)}\right] = \dfrac{-1}{25}$

$\therefore \quad$ Centre $= \left(\dfrac{2}{5}, \dfrac{-1}{25}\right)$,

Radius $= \sqrt{\left(2 - \dfrac{2}{5}\right)^2 + \left(0 - \dfrac{1}{25}\right)^2}$

$= \sqrt{\dfrac{64}{25} + \dfrac{1}{625}} = \dfrac{\sqrt{1601}}{25}$

So, equation of the circle is

$$\left(x - \frac{2}{5}\right)^2 + \left(y + \frac{1}{25}\right)^2 = \frac{1601}{(25)^2}$$

$$\Rightarrow \quad 25x^2 + 25y^2 - 20x + 2y - 60 = 0$$

8. (b)

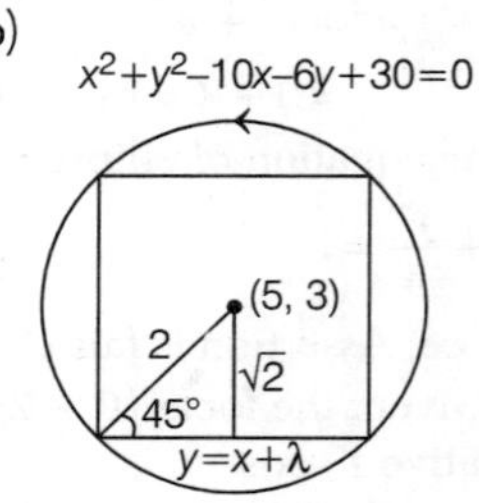

Given equation of circle is

$$x^2 + y^2 - 10x - 6y + 30 = 0$$

$\therefore$ Centre of the circle

$$= \left(-\frac{1}{2} \times (-10), -\frac{1}{2} \times (-6)\right)$$

$$= (5, 3)$$

Also, one side of square is parallel to the line $y = x + 3$.

So, equation of that side of square is given by, $y = x + \lambda$.

Now, distance of (5, 3) to the line $y = x + \lambda$ is $\sqrt{2}$.

$$\Rightarrow \quad \left|\frac{3 - 5 - \lambda}{\sqrt{2}}\right| = \sqrt{2}$$

$$\Rightarrow \quad |\lambda + 2| = 2$$

$$\Rightarrow \quad \lambda + 2 = \pm 2 \Rightarrow \lambda = 0, -4$$

So, the lines are $y = x$ and $y = x - 4$

Now, solving these lines with the circles as $y = x$ and

$x^2 + y^2 - 10x - 6y + 30 = 0$,

we get

$x = 3$, $y = 3$ and $x = 5$, $y = 5$

[by putting $y = x$ in the equation of circle]

and $y = x - 4$

and $x^2 + y^2 - 10x - 6y + 30 = 0$,

we get $x = 7$, $y = 3$ and $x = 5$, $y = 1$

So, vertices are (5, 5), (3, 3), (7, 3), (5, 1).

Hence, $\Sigma x_i^2 + y_i^2 = 9 + 9 + 25 + 25 + 25 + 1 + 49 + 9 = 152$

9. (b) $y^2 = 12x$

Equation of chord PQ, whose mid-point $(4, 1)$ is

$$\Rightarrow yy_1 - 12\left(\frac{n+x}{2}\right) = y_1^2 - 12x_1$$

$$T = S_1$$

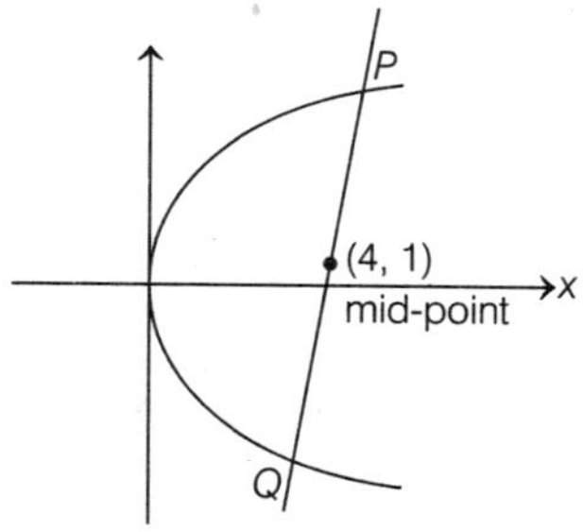

$$y(1) - \frac{12(x+4)}{2} = (1)^2 - 12(4)$$

$$\Rightarrow \quad y - 6(x+4) = 1 - 48$$

$$\Rightarrow \quad y - 6x - 24 = -47$$

$$\Rightarrow \quad 6x - y = 23$$

$\because \left(\frac{1}{2}, -20\right)$ satisfy above equation.

$\therefore$ Lines passes through $\left(\frac{1}{2}, -20\right)$.

10. (c) Given equation of parabola is $y^2 = 4x$

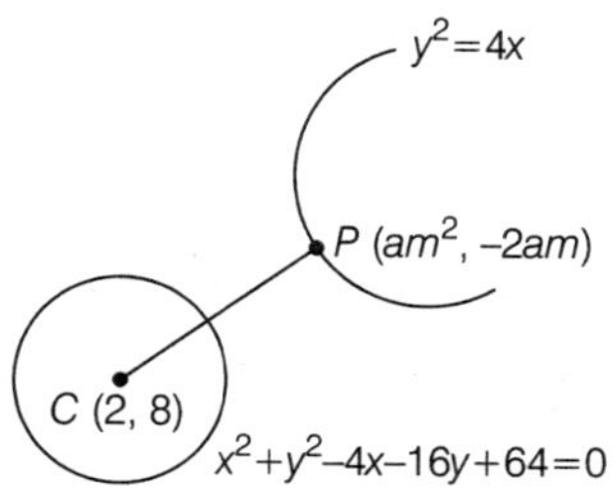

and equation of circle is

$$x^2 + y^2 - 4x - 16y + 64 = 0$$

Now, equation of normal to parabola is given by $y = mx - 2m - m^3$, where m = slope

This normal passing through centre of the circle which is $(2, 8)$.

So, $\quad 8 = 2m - 2m - m^3$

$$\Rightarrow \quad m^3 = -8 = (-2)^3 \Rightarrow m = -2$$

Coordinates of any point P taken on given parabola is of the form $(am^2, -2am)$ i.e $(4, 4)$

Now, $CP = \sqrt{(4-2)^2 + (4-8)^2}$

$= \sqrt{4+16} = \sqrt{20} = d \quad$ [given]

$\therefore \quad d^2 = 20$

11. **(c)** First use $e = \sqrt{1 - \frac{b^2}{a^2}}$, then

Length of latus rectum $= \frac{2b^2}{a}$

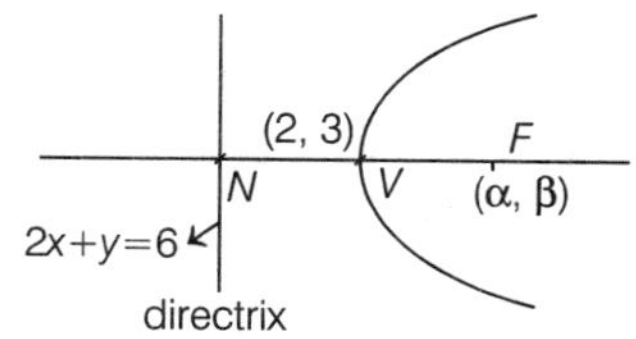

So, equation of axis is

$$y - 3 = \frac{1}{2}(x - 2)$$

$$\Rightarrow \quad x - 2y + 4 = 0$$

Solving $2x + y = 6$ and $x - 2y + 4 = 0$, $N\left(\frac{8}{5}, \frac{14}{5}\right)$

Since, V is the mid-point of N and F

$$\frac{\frac{8}{5} + \alpha}{2} = 2, \alpha = 4 - \frac{8}{5} = \frac{12}{5}$$

$$\Rightarrow \quad \frac{\frac{14}{5} + \beta}{2} = 3 \Rightarrow \beta = 6 - \frac{14}{5} = \frac{16}{5}$$

Given that ellipse passes through (α, β).

$$\therefore \quad \frac{\alpha^2}{a^2} + \frac{\beta^2}{b^2} = 1$$

$$\frac{(12/5)^2}{a^2} + \frac{(16/5)^2}{b^2} = 1 \quad \text{...(i)}$$

Also, eccentricity of ellipse is $\frac{1}{\sqrt{2}}$

$$\sqrt{1 - \frac{b^2}{a^2}} = \frac{1}{\sqrt{2}} \Rightarrow 1 - \frac{b^2}{a^2} = \frac{1}{2}$$

$$\Rightarrow \quad a^2 = 2b^2$$

Put in Eq. (i),

$$\frac{144/25}{2b^2} + \frac{256/25}{b^2} = 1$$

$$b^2 = \frac{72}{25} + \frac{256}{25} = \frac{328}{25}$$

Square of length of latus rectum

$$= \left(\frac{2b^2}{a}\right)^2 = \frac{4 \times b^4}{a^2}$$

$$= \frac{4b^4}{2b^2} = 2b^2 = \frac{656}{25}$$

12. (80) $C: x^2 + y^2 = 4$

$$P: y^2 = 8x$$

Equation of chord bisected at $(\alpha, 0)$, $T = S_1$

$$x(2t^2) + y(4t) - 4$$

$$= (2t^2)^2 + (4t)^2 - 4$$

$\because$ Lines passes through $(\alpha, 0)$

$$\alpha(2t^2) = 4t^4 + 16t^2$$

$$\alpha = 2t^2 + 8$$

$$\frac{\alpha - 8}{2} = t^2$$

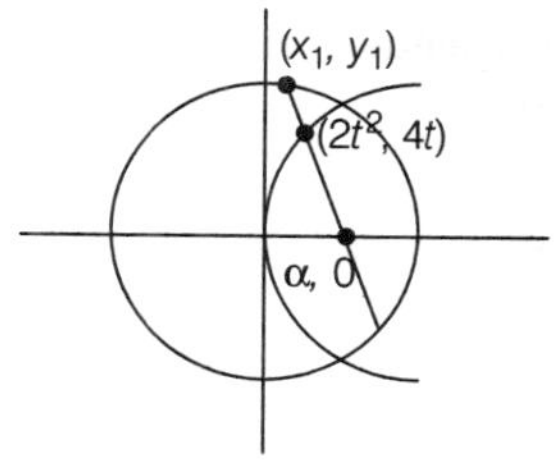

Also, $4t^4 + 16t^2 - 4 < 0$

$\therefore \quad t^2 = -2 + \sqrt{5}$

$\quad \alpha = 4 + 2\sqrt{5}$

$\therefore \quad \alpha \in (8, 4 + 2\sqrt{5})$

$\therefore \quad (2q - p)^2 = 80$

13. (10) $y^2 = 4(x - 9)$

Slope of tangent $= -\frac{1}{2}$

Point of contact

$$P\left[9 + \frac{1}{\left(-\frac{1}{2}\right)^2}, \frac{2 \times 1}{-1/2}\right] = (13, -4)$$

Centre of circle $C(7, 4)$

Distance

$$CP = \sqrt{(13-7)^2 + (-4-4)^2} = 10$$

14. (108) Given, equation of parabola $y^2 = 12x$

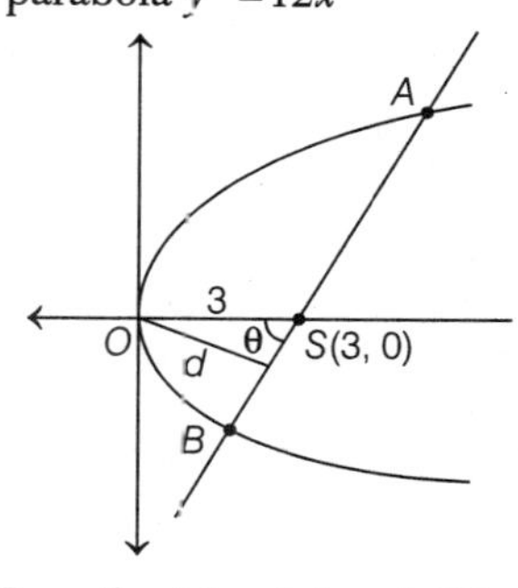

Length of focal chord AB,

$$l = 4a \operatorname{cosec}^2\theta$$

$$= 4 \times 3 \times \left(\frac{3}{d}\right)^2 = 12 \times \frac{9}{d^2}$$

$\therefore \quad ld^2 = 12 \times 9 = 108$

15. (b) If the minor axis is a and e is eccentricity. According to the question, $ae = 2b$

$$\Rightarrow \quad \frac{4b^2}{a^2} = e^2$$

$$\Rightarrow 4(1-e^2)=e^2 \quad \left[\because e=\sqrt{1-\frac{b^2}{a^2}}\right]$$

$$\Rightarrow \; 4=5e^2 \Rightarrow e^2=\frac{4}{5} \Rightarrow e=\frac{2}{\sqrt{5}}$$

Hence, the eccentricity $2/\sqrt{5}$.

16. (d) We have,

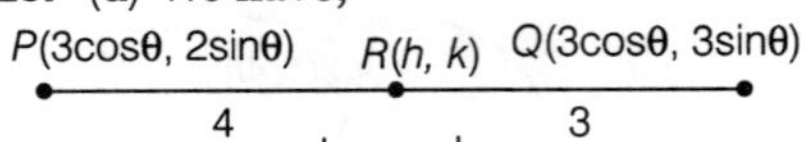

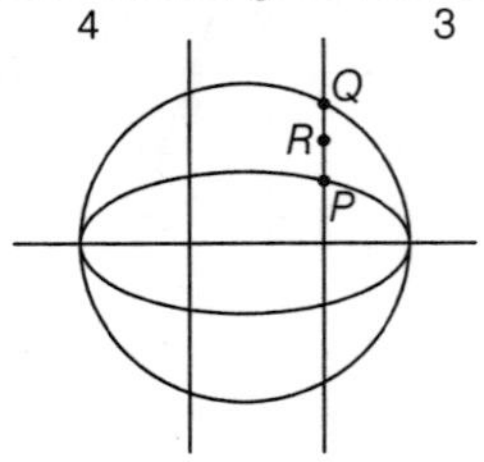

$$\therefore \quad h=\frac{12\cos\theta+9\cos\theta}{7}$$

$$\Rightarrow h=3\cos\theta$$

and $k=\dfrac{6\sin\theta+12\sin\theta}{7}$

$$\Rightarrow k=\frac{18}{7}\sin\theta$$

Hence, locus of the point R on PQ is

$$\frac{h^2}{3^2}+\frac{k^2}{\left(\frac{18}{7}\right)^2}=1$$

here, $a^2=3^2$ and $b^2=\left(\frac{18}{7}\right)^2$

Now, eccentricity, $e^2=\sqrt{1-\dfrac{b^2}{a^2}}$

$$=\sqrt{1-\frac{\left(\frac{18}{7}\right)^2}{3^2}}=\sqrt{1-\frac{36}{49}}=\sqrt{\frac{13}{49}}$$

So, $e=\dfrac{\sqrt{13}}{7}$

17. (c) Given equation of line $2x+3y-k=0$, which intersect the X-axis and Y-axis at the points A and B.

When $y=0$, then coordinate of A is $\left(\frac{k}{2},0\right)$ and when $x=0$, then coordinate of B is $\left(0,\frac{k}{3}\right)$.

Equation of circle with diameter AB is

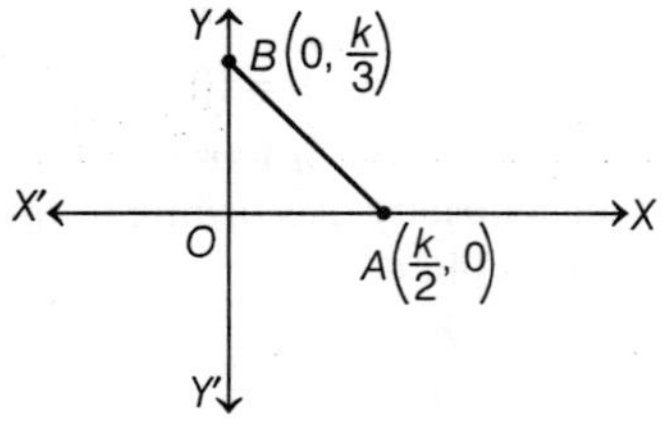

$$(x-0)\left(x-\frac{k}{2}\right)+\left(y-\frac{k}{3}\right)(y-0)=0$$

$$\Rightarrow \quad x^2+y^2-\frac{kx}{2}-\frac{ky}{3}=0$$

On comparing with

$x^2+y^2-3x-2y=0$, we get

$$\frac{k}{2}=3 \Rightarrow k=6$$

Now, equation of ellipse

$$x^2+9y^2=k^2=36$$

$$\Rightarrow \quad \frac{x^2}{36}+\frac{y^2}{4}=1$$

$$\text{Latus-rectum}=\frac{2b^2}{a}=\frac{2\times 4}{6}=\frac{4}{3}$$

$$\Rightarrow \quad m=4, n=3$$

$$\therefore \quad 2m+n=8+3=11$$

18. (c) $H:\dfrac{x^2}{9}-\dfrac{y^2}{4}=1$

Here, $a^2=9, b^2=4$

$$\therefore \quad a=3, b=2$$

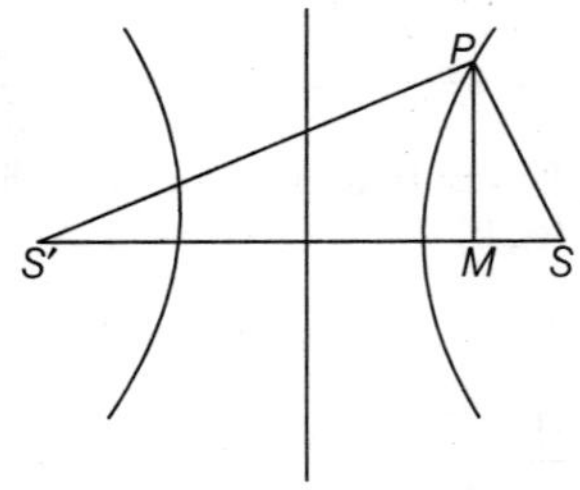

Let S and S' are focii of hyperbola.

$$\therefore \quad e=\sqrt{1+\frac{b^2}{a^2}}=\sqrt{1+\frac{4}{9}}=\frac{\sqrt{13}}{3}$$

$$\because \quad S=(ae,0) \text{ and } S'(-ae,0)$$
$$=(\sqrt{13},0) \text{ and } (-\sqrt{13},0)$$

$$\therefore \quad SS'=2\sqrt{13}$$

$$\therefore \quad \text{Area of } \Delta PSS'=2\sqrt{13}$$

$$\frac{1}{2}\times SS'\times PM=2\sqrt{13}$$

$$\Rightarrow \quad \frac{1}{2}\times 2\sqrt{13}\times PM=2\sqrt{13}$$

$$\Rightarrow \quad PM=2$$

Let coordinate of $P(h,k)$

$$\therefore \quad k=2 \qquad [\because PM=2]$$

P satisfies the equation of hyperbola.

$$\therefore \quad \frac{h^2}{9}-\frac{(2)^2}{4}=1 \Rightarrow h^2=18$$

$\therefore$ Square of distance of p from the origin

$$=h^2+k^2=18+4=22$$

19. (d) For ellipse use eccentricity, $e=\sqrt{1-\dfrac{a^2}{b^2}}$ and for hyperbola use eccentricity, $e=\sqrt{1+\dfrac{a^2}{b^2}}$

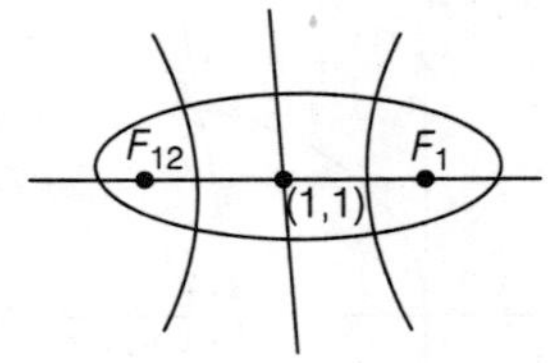

$$E:\frac{(x-1)^2}{100}+\frac{(y-1)^2}{75}=1$$

$$e_1=\sqrt{1-\frac{75}{100}}=\frac{1}{2}\Rightarrow e_2=2$$

$F_1(6,1)$ and $F_2(-4,1)$

$$2ae_2=10 \Rightarrow a=\frac{5}{2}\Rightarrow 2a=5$$

$$\therefore \quad \alpha=5$$

Now, $e_2^2=1+\dfrac{b^2}{a^2}\Rightarrow b^2=3a^2$

$$\Rightarrow \quad b=\frac{5\sqrt{3}}{2} \Rightarrow 2b=5\sqrt{3}=\beta$$

$$\therefore 3\alpha^2+2\beta^2=3\times 25+2\times 25\times 3=225$$

20. (c) $\dfrac{-x^2}{a^2}+\dfrac{y^2}{b^2}=+1$

$$e=\sqrt{1+\frac{a^2}{b^2}}=\sqrt{3}$$

$$\Rightarrow \; 1+\frac{a^2}{b^2}=3 \Rightarrow \frac{a^2}{b^2}=2 \qquad \ldots(\text{i})$$

and latus rectum $=\dfrac{2a^2}{b}=4\sqrt{3}$

By Eq. (i),

$$\frac{4b^2}{b}=4\sqrt{3} \Rightarrow b=\sqrt{3}$$

$$\Rightarrow \quad b^2=3 \text{ and } a^2=2\times 3=6$$

Now, $\dfrac{-x^2}{6}+\dfrac{y^2}{3}=1$

Put $(\alpha,6)$ on it

$$\frac{-\alpha^2}{6}+\frac{36}{3}=1$$

$$\Rightarrow \quad -\alpha^2=-66 \Rightarrow \alpha^2=66$$

For the given equation,

focal distances $=|ey_1-a|$, $|ey_1+a|$

So,

$$\beta=(ey_1+b)(ey_1-b)=e^2y_1^2-b^2$$
$$=3\times 6^2-3=105$$

So, $\alpha^2+\beta=66+105=171$

Chapter-11

Introduction to 3D

1. (i) II (ii) VIII (iii) IV (iv) I (v) III
2. (i) If a point lies on the Y-axis, then its x-coordinate is 0 and z-coordinate is also 0.
   (ii) If a point lies on the Z-axis, then its x-coordinate is 0 and y-coordinate is also 0.
3. (b) The point which has z-coordinate zero lies in XY-plane. $(3, -4, 0)$ has z-coordinate zero, so it lies in XY-plane. The point which has y-coordinate zero lies in XZ-plane. $(-5, 0, -6)$ has y-coordinate 0, so it lies in XZ-plane. The points which has x-coordinate zero lies in YZ-plane. $(0, 4, -2)$ has x-coordinate zero.
   So, it lies in YZ-plane.
4. (i) (True)
   The X-axis and Y-axis taken together determine a plane known as XY-plane.
   (ii) (False)
   The coordinate of a point in the XY-plane are of the form $(x, y, 0)$.
   (iii) (False)
   Coordinate plane divide the space into 8 octants.
   (iv) (False)
   Equation of a plane parallel to the XY-plane will have coordinate only through Z-axis.
   Hence, $z = 6$ represents a plane parallel to the XY-plane.
   (v) (True)
   Equation of a plane parallel to the YZ-plane will have coordinate only through X-axis.
   Hence, $x = 4$ represents a plane parallel to the YZ-plane.
5. Two distinct lines intersecting each other in a plane cannot have more than one point in common.
   Hence, the answer is one.
6. (b) Using distance formula,
   $$\sqrt{(a-0)^2+(0-1)^2+(1-2)^2} = \sqrt{27}$$
   $$\Rightarrow \sqrt{a^2+1+1} = \sqrt{27}$$
   $$\Rightarrow a^2+2 = 27$$
   $$\Rightarrow a^2 = 25$$
   $$\Rightarrow a = \pm 5$$
7. (i) Let l be the foot of perpendicular drawn from point P on Y-axis.
   Its x and z-coordinates are zero i.e. $(0, 7, 0)$.
   Distance between points $(0, 7, 0)$ and $(5, 7, 9)$
   $$= \sqrt{(5-0)^2+(7-7)^2+(9-0)^2}$$
   $$= \sqrt{25+0+81} = \sqrt{106}$$
   (ii) Let l be the foot of perpendicular drawn from point Q on X-axis.
   Its y and z-coordinates are zero i.e. $(1, 0, 0)$.
   $\therefore$ Distance between points $(1, 0, 0)$ and $(1, 2, 3)$
   $$= \sqrt{(1-1)^2+(2-0)^2+(3-0)^2}$$
   $$= \sqrt{0+4+9} = \sqrt{13} \text{ units}$$
   (iii) Let l be the foot of perpendicular drawn from point R on Z-axis.
   Its x and y-coordinates are zero i.e. $(0, 0, 6)$
   $\therefore$ Distance between points $(0, 0, 6)$ and $(5, 1, 6)$
   $$= \sqrt{(5-0)^2+(1-0)^2+(6-6)^2}$$
   $$= \sqrt{25+1+0}$$
   $$= \sqrt{26} \text{ units}$$
   (iv) $A = (1, 2, 3)$
   Let the point on Z-axis be $P(0, 0, z)$
   $$PA = \sqrt{21}$$
   $$\Rightarrow \sqrt{(1-0)^2+(2-0)^2+(3-z)^2} = \sqrt{21}$$
   On squaring both sides, we get
   $$1^2+2^2+(3-z)^2 = 21$$
   $$\Rightarrow 1+4+9+z^2-6z = 21$$
   $$\Rightarrow z^2-6z-7 = 0$$
   $$\therefore z = 7, -1$$
   Hence, the point on Z-axis are $(0, 0, 7)$ and $(0, 0, -1)$.
8. (a) The diameter end points are $(-1, 4, 3)$ and $(1, -2, 3)$.
   Length of diameter
   $$= \sqrt{(1+1)^2+(-2-4)^2+(3-3)^2}$$
   $$= \sqrt{(2)^2+(-6)^2+(0)^2}$$
   $$= \sqrt{4+36} = \sqrt{40}$$
   Radius is $d/2 = \dfrac{\sqrt{40}}{2} = \sqrt{10}$
9. (i) (True)
   The given points are $P(0, 7, -7)$, $Q(1, 4, -5)$ and $R(-1, 10, -9)$.
   Using distance formula,
   $$PQ = \sqrt{(1-0)^2+(4-7)^2+(-5+7)^2}$$
   $$= \sqrt{1+9+4} = \sqrt{14}$$
   $$RP = \sqrt{(0+1)^2+(7-10)^2+(-7+9)^2}$$
   $$= \sqrt{1+9+4} = \sqrt{14}$$
   $$RQ = \sqrt{(1+1)^2+(4-10)^2+(-5+9)^2}$$
   $$= \sqrt{4+36+16}$$
   $$= \sqrt{56} = 2\sqrt{14}$$
   $$\Rightarrow PQ + RP = RQ$$
   $$\Rightarrow \sqrt{14}+\sqrt{14} = 2\sqrt{14}$$
   $\therefore$ The points are collinear.
   (ii) (True)
   $$AB^2 = (-3-2)^2+(-2+4)^2+(1-1)^2$$
   $$= 25+4 = 29$$
   $$BC^2 = (-1+3)^2+(3+2)^2+(4-1)^2$$
   $$= 4+25+9 = 38$$
   $$CA^2 = (2+1)^2+(-4-3)^2+(1-4)^2$$
   $$= 9+49+9 = 67$$
   $$AB^2+BC^2 = 29+38 = 67 = CA^2$$
   So, ABC is a right angled triangle.
   (iii) (True)
   Given, $A(0, 1, 1)$, $B(1, 0, 1)$, $C(1, 1, 0)$ and $O(0, 0, 0)$
   Using distance formula,
   $$OA = \sqrt{(0-0)^2+(1-0)^2+(1-0)^2}$$
   $$= \sqrt{0+1+1} = \sqrt{2}$$
   $$OB = \sqrt{(1-0)^2+(0-0)^2+(1-0)^2}$$
   $$= \sqrt{1+0+1} = \sqrt{2}$$

$OC = \sqrt{(1-0)^2+(1-0)^2 + (0-0)^2}$
$= \sqrt{1+1+0} = \sqrt{2}$

$AB = \sqrt{(1-0)^2+(0-1)^2 + (1-1)^2}$
$= \sqrt{1+1+0} = \sqrt{2}$

$BC = \sqrt{(1-1)^2+(1-0)^2 + (0-1)^2}$
$= \sqrt{0+1+1} = \sqrt{2}$

$AC = \sqrt{(1-0)^2+(1-1)^2 + (1-0)^2}$
$= \sqrt{1+0+1} = \sqrt{2}$

$\therefore OA = OB = OC = AB = BC = AC = \sqrt{2}$

$\therefore$ *OABC* is a regular tetrahedron.

(iv) (True)

Let $A(-1, 2, 1)$, $B(1, -2, 5)$, $C(4, -7, 8)$ and $D(2, -3, 4)$

$AB = \sqrt{(1+1)^2+(-2-2)^2 + (5-1)^2}$
$= \sqrt{4+16+16} = \sqrt{36} = 6$

$BC = \sqrt{(4-1)^2+(-7+2)^2 + (8-5)^2}$
$= \sqrt{9+25+9} = \sqrt{43}$

$CD = \sqrt{(2-4)^2+(-3+7)^2 + (4-8)^2}$
$= \sqrt{4+16+16} = \sqrt{36} = 6$

$DA = \sqrt{(-1-2)^2+(2+3)^2 + (1-4)^2}$
$= \sqrt{9+25+9} = \sqrt{43}$

$AB = CD = 6$
$BC = DA = \sqrt{43}$

Since, opposite sides are equal.
So, it is a parallelogram.

(v) (True)

Let $A(5, -1, 1)$, $B(7, -4, 7)$, $C(1, -6, 10)$ and $D(-1, -3, 4)$

$AB = \sqrt{(7-5)^2+(-4+1)^2 + (7-1)^2}$
$= \sqrt{4+9+36} = \sqrt{49} = 7$

$BC = \sqrt{(1-7)^2+(-6+4)^2 + (10-7)^2}$
$= \sqrt{36+4+9} = \sqrt{49} = 7$

$CD = \sqrt{(-1-1)^2+(-3+6)^2 + (4-10)^2}$
$= \sqrt{4+9+36} = \sqrt{49} = 7$

$DA = \sqrt{(5+1)^2+(-1+3)^2 + (1-4)^2}$
$= \sqrt{4+9+36} = \sqrt{49} = 7$

$AC = \sqrt{(1-5)^2+(-6+1)^2 + (10-1)^2}$
$= \sqrt{16+25+81} = \sqrt{122}$

$BD = \sqrt{(-1-7)^2+(-3+4)^2 + (4-7)^2}$
$= \sqrt{64+1+9} = \sqrt{74}$

$\therefore AB = BC = CD = DA = 7$
$AC \neq BD$

$\therefore$ It is rhombus as it has all sides equal and diagonal are not equal.

10. Let the coordinates of point R be (x, y, z).

$RA^2 = (x+3)^2 + (y+2)^2 + (z-1)^2$
$RB^2 = (x-1)^2 + (y-4)^2 + (z+3)^2$
$RA^2 + RB^2 = 2K^2$

$\Rightarrow (x+3)^2 + (y+2)^2 + (z-1)^2 + (x-1)^2 + (y-4)^2 + (z+3)^2 = 2K^2$

$\Rightarrow 2x^2 + 2y^2 + 2z^2 + 4x - 4y + 4z = 2K^2 - 40$

$\Rightarrow x^2 + y^2 + z^2 + 2x - 2y + 2z = K^2 - 20$

11. Let $P(x, y, z)$ be the required point, then

$OP = PA = PB = PC$
$\Rightarrow OP = PA$
$\Rightarrow OP^2 = PA^2$
$\Rightarrow x^2 + y^2 + z^2 = (x-\alpha)^2 + (y-0)^2 + (z-0)^2$
$\Rightarrow 0 = -2\alpha x + \alpha^2$ [on simplifying]
$\therefore x = \frac{\alpha}{2}$

Similarly, $y = \frac{\beta}{2}$ and $z = \frac{\gamma}{2}$

Hence, the required coordinate is $\left(\frac{\alpha}{2}, \frac{\beta}{2}, \frac{\gamma}{2}\right)$.

12. (b) Let the coordinate of third vertex be (x, y, z). The distance of third vertex from above two vertices are same.

After equate distance between $(2, 1, 5)$ and (x, y, z) with distance between $(3, 2, 3)$ and (x, y, z).

On simplification,

$x^2 + y^2 + z^2 - 4x - 2y - 10z + 30 = x^2 + y^2 + z^2 - 6x - 4y - 6z + 22$
$\Rightarrow x + y - 2z + 4 = 0$

The point $(4, 0, 4)$ satisfy above equation.

13. Let (x, y, z) be the point equidistant from the given points by the distance d.

We have the equation,

$(x+1)^2 + (y-1)^2 + (z-3)^2 = d^2$ ...(i)
$(x-2)^2 + (y-1)^2 + (z-2)^2 = d^2$ ...(ii)
$x^2 + (y-5)^2 + (z-6)^2 = d^2$ ...(iii)
$(x-3)^2 + (y-2)^2 + (z-2)^2 = d^2$ ...(iv)

Using Eqs. (i) and (ii), we get
$z = 3x + 1$

Using Eqs. (ii) and (iv), we get
$y = 4 - x$

On substituting the values in Eqs. (i) and (iii), we get

$x^2 + 2x + 1 + 9 - 6x + x^2 + 9x^2 - 12x + 4 = x^2 + x^2 + 2x + 1 + 9x^2 - 30x + 25$

$\therefore x = 1$

Hence, the point is $(x, 4-x, 3x+1) = (1, 3, 4)$.

Assertion Reason

1. (a) The given points are $A(1, 2, -1)$, $B(3, 2, 1)$ and $C(-4, 0, 2)$.

Using distance formula,

$BC = \sqrt{(-4-3)^2+(0-2)^2 + (2-1)^2}$
$= \sqrt{(-7)^2 + (-2)^2 + (1)^2}$
$= \sqrt{49+4+1}$
$= \sqrt{54}$
$= \sqrt{9 \times 6}$
$= 3\sqrt{6}$ units

$\therefore$ Both Assertion and Reason are correct and Reason is the correct explanation of Assertion.

2. (a) The given points are $A(3, -1, 2)$, $B(1, 2, -4)$, $C(-1, 1, 2)$ and $D(1, -2, 8)$.

Using distance formula,

$$AB = \sqrt{(1-3)^2 + (2-(-1))^2 + (-4-2)^2}$$
$$= \sqrt{4+9+36}$$
$$= \sqrt{49} = 7$$

$$CD = \sqrt{(1-(-1))^2 + (-2-1)^2 + (8-2)^2}$$
$$= \sqrt{4+9+36}$$
$$= \sqrt{49} = 7$$

$$BC = \sqrt{(-1-1)^2 + (1-2)^2 + (2-(-4))^2}$$
$$= \sqrt{4+1+36} = \sqrt{41}$$

$$DA = \sqrt{(3-1)^2 + (-1-(-2))^2 + (2-8)^2}$$
$$= \sqrt{4+1+36} = \sqrt{41}$$

$$AC = \sqrt{(-1-3)^2 + (1-(-1))^2 + (2-2)^2}$$
$$= \sqrt{16+4} = \sqrt{20} = 2\sqrt{5}$$

$$BD = \sqrt{(1-1)^2 + (-2-2)^2 + (8-(-4))^2}$$
$$= \sqrt{0+16+144}$$
$$= \sqrt{160} = 4\sqrt{10}$$

Here, $AB = CD$, $BC = DA$ and $AC \neq BD$

$\therefore$ $ABCD$ is a parallelogram.

3. (a) $$AB = \sqrt{(2-(-1))^2 + (3-3)^2 + (5-2)^2}$$
$$= \sqrt{9+0+9} = \sqrt{18} = 3\sqrt{2}$$

$$CA = \sqrt{(-1-3)^2 + (3-5)^2 + (2-(-2))^2}$$
$$= \sqrt{16+4+16} = \sqrt{36} = 6$$

$$BC = \sqrt{(3-2)^2 + (5-3)^2 + (-2-5)^2}$$
$$= \sqrt{1+4+49} = 3\sqrt{6}$$

$$(AB)^2 + (CA)^2 = (BC)^2$$
$$\Rightarrow (\sqrt{18})^2 + (\sqrt{36})^2 = (\sqrt{54})^2$$
$$\Rightarrow 18 + 36 = 54 \Rightarrow 54 = 54$$

$\therefore$ Both Assertion and Reason are correct and Reason is the correct explanation of Assertion.

4. (c) The given points are $P(0, 0, 4)$, $Q(6, 2, 4)$ and $R(-9, -3, 4)$.

Using distance formula,

$$PQ = \sqrt{(6-0)^2 + (2-0)^2 + (4-4)^2}$$
$$= \sqrt{36+4+0} = \sqrt{40}$$
$$= 2\sqrt{10}$$

$$QR = \sqrt{(-9-6)^2 + (-3-2)^2 + (4-4)^2}$$
$$= \sqrt{225+25+0}$$
$$= \sqrt{250}$$
$$= 5\sqrt{10}$$

$$PR = \sqrt{(-9-0)^2 + (-3-0)^2 + (4-4)^2}$$
$$= \sqrt{81+9}$$
$$= \sqrt{90}$$
$$= 3\sqrt{10}$$

$QR = PQ + PR$

$\therefore$ Assertion is true but Reason is false.

5. (d) $$AB = \sqrt{(1-2)^2 + (8-9)^2 + (8-12)^2}$$
$$= \sqrt{1+1+16} = \sqrt{18} = 3\sqrt{2}$$

$$BC = \sqrt{(2-1)^2 + (11-8)^2 + (8-8)^2}$$
$$= \sqrt{1+9+0} = \sqrt{10}$$

$$CD = \sqrt{(1-2)^2 + (12-11)^2 + (12-8)^2}$$
$$= \sqrt{1+1+16}$$
$$= \sqrt{18} = 3\sqrt{2}$$

$$DA = \sqrt{(2-1)^2 + (9-12)^2 + (12-12)^2}$$
$$= \sqrt{1+9+0} = \sqrt{10}$$

$$AC = \sqrt{(2-2)^2 + (11-9)^2 + (8-12)^2}$$
$$= \sqrt{0+4+16}$$
$$= \sqrt{20} = 2\sqrt{5}$$

$$BD = \sqrt{(1-1)^2 + (12-8)^2 + (12-8)^2}$$
$$= \sqrt{0+16+16}$$
$$= 32 = 4\sqrt{2}$$

Here $AB \neq BC \neq CD$ and $AC \neq BD$

$\therefore$ $ABCD$ is not a rhombus.

$\therefore$ Assertion is false but Reason is true.

6. (a) Since, the point P is on Y-axis, therefore $x = 0$, $y = 4$, $z = 0$.

Hence, $y = 4$ represents a plane parallel to the ZX-plane.

$\therefore$ Both Assertion and Reason are correct and Reason is the correct explanation of Assertion.

7. (a) $(-3, 5, 4)$ and $(4, -5, 3)$ are different points as $(-3, 5, 4)$ lies in II octant and $(4, -5, 3)$ lies in IV octant.

$x \neq y \neq z$, $(x, y, z) \neq (z, y, x)$

$\therefore$ Assertion and Reason are both correct and reason is correct explanation of assertion.

8. (d) Equation of a plane parallel to the ZX-plane will have coordinate only Y-axis.

Hence, $y = 3$ represents a plane parallel to the ZX-plane.

Distance of the point $(2, 3, 5)$ from the ZX-plane is 3 units.

$\therefore$ Assertion is false but Reason is true.

9. (d) $(-5, 0, 0)$ lies on X-axis $(0, 0, -8)$ lies on Z-axis and $(0, -3, 0)$ lies on Y-axis.

$\therefore$ Assertion is false.

Every point on X-axis has zero unit distance from X-axis, every point on Y-axis has zero unit distance from Y-axis and every point on Z-axis has zero unit distance from Z-axis.

$\therefore$ Reason is true.

10. (b) Given point $(3, 1, 0)$

The points which have Z-coordinate zero lies in XY-plane.

$(3, 1, 1)$ has z-coordinate zero, so it lies in XY plane.

Given point $(0, 0, 2)$

The points which have x, y-coordinate zero lies on Z-axis.

$(0, 0, 2)$ has x and Y-coordinate zero, so it lies in Z-axis.

$\therefore$ Both Assertion and Reason are true but Reason is not the correct explanation of Assertion.

Case Based

Case 1 (i) (b) Given point, $P(3, 6, 5)$

$\because$ In YZ-plane, x-coordinate will be zero.

$x = 0, y = 6, z = 5$

$\therefore$ Point of $N(0, 6, 5)$

(ii) (c) Given point $(3, -2, -5)$

Sign of coordinate in VIII octant

x-coordinate $\Rightarrow +$ ve

y-coordinate $\Rightarrow -$ ve

and z-coordinate $\Rightarrow -$ ve

$\therefore$ Given point $(3, -2, -5)$ is in VIII octant.

(iii) (a) $\because$ Point B lies on Y-axis.

$\therefore$ x-coordinate $= 0$

z-coordinate $= 0$

(iv) (d) On Z-axis,

x-coordinate $= 0$

y-coordinate $= 0$

z-coordinate $= z$

Case 2 (i) (a) If we solve for t in one of the equations, such as $x = 3t$, we find that $t = \dfrac{x}{3}$

$$y = \frac{4}{3}x$$

This linear relationship betwen x and y suggests the missile is following a straight line path.

(ii) (c) Given euations are, $x = 3t$, $y = -4t$, $z = t$

put $t = 1$, $x = 3 \times 1$, $y = -4 \times 1$, $z = 1$, $x = 3$, $y = -4$, $z = 1$

Point $(3, -4, 1)$

put $t = 2$,

$x = 3 \times 2$, $y = -4 \times 2$, $z = 2$

$x = 6$, $y = -8$, $z = 2$

Point $(6, -8, 2)$

(iii) (b) Given equations, $x = 3t$, $y = -4t$, $z = t$

Given time, $t = 5$

$x = 3 \times 5$, $y = -4 \times 5$, $z = 5$

$x = 15$, $y = -20$, $z = 5$

Point $(15, -20, 5)$

Starting point $(0, 0, 0)$

Distance

$$= \sqrt{(15-0)^2 + (-20-0)^2 + (5-0)^2}$$

$$= \sqrt{225 + 400 + 25}$$

$$= \sqrt{650} \text{ km}$$

(iv) (d) Given, position of rocket $(5, -8, 10)$

$\because$ The ground is considered as XY-plane

$\therefore$ Height of rocket will in z-direction.

XY-plane is perpendicular to Z-axis.

Height of rocket $= 10$ km

Competition Connect

1. (i) $T(x, y, z)$ be the required point. If T divides PQ in the ratio 5 : 4.

$$\therefore \quad x = \frac{5 \times 2 + 4 \times 4}{5 + 4} = \frac{10 + 16}{9} = \frac{26}{9}$$

$$y = \frac{5 \times 3 + 4 \times (-3)}{5 + 4} = \frac{15 - 12}{9} = \frac{3}{9} = \frac{1}{3}$$

$$\text{and } z = \frac{5 \times (-4) + 4 \times 2}{5 + 4} = \frac{-20 + 8}{9} = \frac{-12}{9} = \frac{-4}{3}$$

Hence, the required coordinates are $\dfrac{26}{9}, \dfrac{1}{3}$ and $\dfrac{-4}{3}$.

(ii) Suppose $R(x, y, z)$ be the required point. R divides PQ externally in the ratio 3 : 4

$$\therefore x = \frac{mx_2 - nx_1}{m - n}, \; y = \frac{my_2 - ny_1}{m - n}$$

$$\text{and } z = \frac{mz_2 - nz_1}{m - n}$$

$$x = \frac{3 \times 4 - 4 \times 2}{3 - 4},$$

$$y = \frac{3 \times 3 - 4 \times (-1)}{3 - 4}$$

$$\text{and } z = \frac{3 \times 1 - 4 \times 4}{3 - 4}$$

$$x = \frac{12 - 8}{-1}, \; y = \frac{9 + 4}{-1} \text{ and}$$

$$z = \frac{3 - 16}{-1}$$

$x = -4$, $y = -13$ and $z = 13$

Hence, the coordinates are $(-4, -13, 13)$.

(iii) Suppose $S(x, y, z)$ be the required point. If S divides PQ internally in the ratio 3 : 2, then

$$\Rightarrow x = \frac{mx_2 + nx_1}{m + n}, \; y = \frac{my_2 + ny_1}{m + n}$$

$$\text{and } \quad z = \frac{mz_2 + nz_1}{m + n}$$

$$\Rightarrow \quad x = \frac{3 \times 1 + 2 \times (-3)}{3 + 2},$$

$$y = \frac{3 \times 4 + 2 \times 5}{3 + 2}$$

$$\text{and } \quad z = \frac{3 \times (-3) + 2 \times 2}{3 + 2}$$

$$\Rightarrow \quad x = \frac{3 - 6}{5}, \; y = \frac{12 + 10}{5}$$

$$\text{and } \quad z = \frac{-9 + 4}{5}$$

$$\Rightarrow x = -\frac{3}{5}, \; y = \frac{22}{5} \text{ and } z = -1$$

Hence, the coordinates of $S = \left(-\dfrac{3}{5}, \dfrac{22}{5}, -1\right)$.

2. Let P and Q be the points which trisect AB. Then, $AP = PQ = QB$.

$\therefore$ P divides AB in ratio 1 : 2 and Q divides in the ratio 2 : 1.

As, P divides AB in the ratio 1 : 2, so the coordinates of P are

$$\frac{1 \times 3 + \{2 \times (-3)\}}{1 + 2}, \; \frac{1 \times (-8) + 2 \times 1}{1 + 2}, \; \frac{1 \times 5 + 2 \times 2}{1 + 2}$$

$$= -\frac{3}{3}, \frac{-6}{3}, \frac{9}{3} = (-1, -2, 3)$$

Since, Q divides AB in the ratio 2 : 1, so the coordinates of Q are

$$\frac{2 \times 3 + 1 \times (-3)}{1 + 2}, \; \frac{2 \times (-8) + 1 \times 1}{1 + 2}, \; \frac{2 \times 5 + 1 \times 2}{1 + 2}$$

$$= \frac{6 - 3}{3}, \frac{-16 + 1}{3}, \frac{10 + 2}{3}$$

$$= 1, -\frac{15}{3}, \frac{12}{3} = (1, -5, 4)$$

Hence, the required points are $(-1, -2, 3)$ and $(1, -5, 4)$.

3. (b) Suppose R divides PQ in the ratio $\lambda : 1$. Then, the coordinates of R are

$$\frac{7\lambda + 1 \times 2}{\lambda + 1}, \; \frac{9\lambda + 1 \times (-3)}{\lambda + 1}, \; \frac{5\lambda + 1 \times 1}{\lambda + 1}$$

Since, x coordinate of R is 4.

$$\therefore \quad \frac{7\lambda + 2}{\lambda + 1} = 4 \Rightarrow \lambda = \frac{2}{3}$$

Hence, coordinates of R are

$$\frac{7\times\frac{2}{3}+2}{\frac{2}{3}+1}, \frac{9\times\frac{2}{3}-3}{\frac{2}{3}+1}, \frac{5\times\frac{2}{3}+1}{\frac{2}{3}+1}$$

$$=\frac{\frac{14+6}{3}}{\frac{2+3}{3}}, \frac{6-3}{\frac{2+3}{3}}, \frac{\frac{10+3}{3}}{\frac{2+3}{3}} = 4, \frac{9}{5}, \frac{13}{5}$$

4. (d) Let $D(x, y, z)$ be the required point. Mid-point of diagonal BD is

$$\frac{x+3}{2}, \frac{y+2}{2}, \frac{z-1}{2}$$

Mid-point of diagonal AC is

$$\frac{1+1}{2}, \frac{2+4}{2}, \frac{-4+3}{2} \text{ i.e. } 1, 3, -\frac{1}{2}$$

Mid-point of diagonal always coincide.

$$\therefore \frac{x+3}{2}=1, \frac{y+2}{2}=3 \text{ and } \frac{z-1}{2}=\frac{-1}{2}$$

$$x=-1, y=4 \text{ and } z=0$$

Hence, the required point is $-1, 4, 0$.

5. (i) (True)

Suppose the given points are collinear and C divides AB in the ratio $\lambda:1$. Then, the coordinates C are

$$\frac{3\lambda+5}{\lambda+1}, \frac{2\lambda+3}{\lambda+1}, \frac{\lambda-2}{\lambda+1}$$

But coordinates of C are given as $(-1, 0, 7)$

$$\therefore \frac{3\lambda+5}{\lambda+1}=-1, \frac{2\lambda+3}{\lambda+1}=0, \frac{\lambda-2}{\lambda+1}=7$$

On solving each, $\lambda=-\frac{3}{2}$

Since, each gives the same value of λ, so these points are collinear.

(ii) (True)

Suppose line joining the points $P(1, 2, 3)$ and $Q(-3, 4, -5)$ is divided at point R in the ratio $\lambda:1$ and lies in XY-plane. Thus, the coordinates of R are

$$\frac{-3\lambda+1}{\lambda+1}, \frac{4\lambda+2}{\lambda+1}, \frac{-5\lambda+3}{\lambda+1}$$

$\because$ R lies on XY-plane.

$$\therefore \quad z=0$$

$$\Rightarrow \frac{-5\lambda+3}{\lambda+1}=0 \Rightarrow \lambda=\frac{3}{5}$$

$\therefore$ Coordinates of R are

$$\frac{3\times(-3)+5\times1}{3+5}, \frac{3\times4+5\times2}{3+5}, \frac{3\times(-5)+5\times3}{3+5}=-\frac{1}{2}, \frac{11}{4}, 0$$

(iii) (False)

Given plane is

$$2x+3y+6z=1$$

$A(7, 0, 5)$ and $B(1, -3, 2)$

Let plane divides the line segment AB internally in the ratio $k:1$.

$$\therefore \quad P=\left(\frac{k+7}{k+1}, \frac{-3k}{k+1}, \frac{2k+5}{k+1}\right)$$

Since, P lies on given plane.

$$\therefore \frac{2(k+7)}{k+1}+3\left(\frac{-3k}{k+1}\right)+6\left(\frac{2k+5}{k+1}\right)=1$$

$$\Rightarrow 2k+14-9k+12k+30=k+1 \Rightarrow k=-\frac{43}{4}$$

Hence, the plane divide AB in the ratio of $43:4$.

6. (i) Let us assume that Q divides PR in the ratio $\lambda:1$.

Thus, the coordinates of Q are

$$\frac{7\lambda+1\times1}{\lambda+1}, \frac{8\lambda+2\times1}{\lambda+1}, \frac{9\lambda+3\times1}{\lambda+1}$$

Now, the coordinates of Q are $(4, 5, 6)$

$$\therefore \frac{7\lambda+1}{\lambda+1}=4, \frac{8\lambda+2}{\lambda+1}=5, \frac{9\lambda+3}{\lambda+1}=6$$

On solving, we get

$$\lambda=1$$

Thus, Q divides PR in the ratio of $1:1$.

(ii) Let the coordinates of C be (x, y, z) and the coordinates of the centroid G is $(1, 1, 1)$.

Now, the centroid of the triangle is given by

$$\frac{x_1+x_2+x_3}{3}, \frac{y_1+y_2+y_3}{3}, \frac{z_1+z_2+z_3}{3}$$

$$\frac{4+3+x}{3}, \frac{2-5+y}{3}, \frac{-6+8+z}{3}$$

$$\therefore \frac{7+x}{3}=1, \frac{-3+y}{3}=1, \frac{2+z}{3}=1$$

$$\therefore \quad x=-4, y=6 \text{ and } z=1$$

Hence, the coordinates of C are $(-4, 6, 1)$.

(iii) Let the coordinate of C be (x, y, z) and coordinate of centroid is $(2, 2, 2)$.

$$\therefore \frac{x+3+1}{3}=2, \frac{y-2+4}{3}=2,$$

$$x+4=6, y+2=6,$$

$$x=2, y=4,$$

$$\frac{z+3-5}{3}=2$$

$$z-2=6 \Rightarrow z=8$$

Hence, coordinates of C are $(2, 4, 8)$.

7. (i) (c) Let the required coordinates be (x, y, z) and coordinates of centroid G are $(1, 1, 1)$.

$$\therefore \quad \frac{x+2-1}{3}=1,$$

$$\frac{y-3-4}{3}=1 \text{ and } \frac{z+5+3}{3}=1,$$

$$x+1=3, y-7=3, z+8=3$$

$$\therefore x=2, y=10, z=-5$$

Hence, the coordinates of C are $(2, 10, -5)$.

(ii) (c) Suppose that the line joining the points $P(4, 5, 6)$ and $Q(-1, -2, -3)$ is divided by XY-plane at a point R in the ratio $\lambda:1$.

Then, the coordinates are

$$\frac{-\lambda+4}{\lambda+1}, \frac{-2\lambda+5}{\lambda+1}, \frac{-3\lambda+6}{\lambda+1}$$

$\because$ R lies on XY-plane.

$$\Rightarrow \quad z=0$$

$$\therefore \frac{-3\lambda+6}{\lambda+1}=0 \Rightarrow \lambda=2$$

Hence, the ratio is $2:1$.

(iii) (b) The given point is $(-8, 0, 0)$.

XY-plane is perpendicular to Z-axis. Image about XY-plane change the sign of z value of coordinate.

$$-8, 0, 0 \Rightarrow -8, 0, 0$$

Hence, image of given point is $(-8, 0, 0)$.

Chapter-12

Limits and Derivatives

1. $\lim_{x\to 0^-} f(x)=1$

2. (i) Let $f(x)=\dfrac{|10x|}{x}$

and let $h(x)=|10x|$

$$=\begin{cases}10x, & x>0\\ -10x, & x<0\\ 0, & x=0\end{cases}$$

Now,

$$\lim_{x\to 0^+} f(x)=\lim_{x\to 0^+}\frac{|10x|}{x}$$

$$=\lim_{x\to 0^+}\frac{10x}{x}=10$$

(ii) When $x\to -2^+$, x approaches -2 and $x>-2$.

$\therefore\ (x+2)\to 0^+$ [i.e. $x\to 0$ from right]

and when $x\to -2^+$, $(x^2-1)\to 3$

Now, $\lim_{x\to -2^+}\dfrac{x^2-1}{x+2}=\infty$

(iii) $\lim_{x\to 0^+}\dfrac{\sqrt{x^5}}{x^{1/2}}=\lim_{x\to 0^+}\dfrac{x^2\cdot x^{1/2}}{x^{1/2}}$

$$=\lim_{x\to 0^+}(x^2)=0$$

i.e. $\lim_{x\to 0^+}\dfrac{\sqrt{x^5}}{x^{1/2}}=0$

3. (i) (a) Given,

$$f(x)=\begin{cases}x^3+8x^2+3x+1, & \text{if } x\le 1\\ 16x+5, & \text{if } x>1\end{cases}$$

Now, $\lim_{x\to 1^+} f(x)$

$$=\lim_{x\to 1^+}[16x+5]$$

$$=16\cdot(1)+5=21$$

Hence, $\lim_{x\to 1^+} f(x)$ is 21.

(ii) (d) Given, $\lim_{x\to 0} f(x)$ exist.

Hence,

$$\lim_{x\to 0^+} f(x)=\lim_{x\to 0^-} f(x)$$

$\Rightarrow \lim_{x\to 0^+}(\cos x+1)=\lim_{x\to 0^-}(x+k)$

$\Rightarrow \cos 0+1=k$

$\therefore\ k=2$

(iii) (b) Given,

$$f(x)=\begin{cases}x^3+1, & 0<x<1\\ 2x+1, & 1\le x<2\end{cases}$$

$$\lim_{x\to 1^-} f(x)=\lim_{x\to 1^-}(x^3+1)=2$$

and $\lim_{x\to 1^+} f(x)$

$$=\lim_{x\to 1^+}(2x+1)=3$$

Now, the quadratic equation whose roots are 2 and 3, is

$$(x-2)(x-3)=0$$

$$\Rightarrow x^2-5x+6=0$$

(iv) (a) Given, $f(-x)=-f(x)$

$\therefore\ f(x)=-f(-x)$ ...(i)

Since, $\lim_{x\to 0} f(x)$ exists

$\therefore\ \lim_{x\to 0^-} f(x)$

$=\lim_{x\to 0^+} f(x)=l$ (let) ...(ii)

From Eq. (i),

$$\lim_{x\to 0^+} f(x)=-\lim_{x\to 0^+} f(-x)$$

$$=-\lim_{h\to 0^-} f(h)$$

[putting $h=-x$, so that when $x\to 0^+, h\to 0^-$]

$\Rightarrow\ l=-l$ [from Eq. (ii)]

$\Rightarrow\ 2l=0$

$\Rightarrow\ l=0$

Hence, $\lim_{x\to 0} f(x)=0$

(v) (d) Let $h(x)=|x-1|$

$$=\begin{cases}1-x, & x<1\\ 0, & x=1\\ x-1, & x>1\end{cases}$$

For the limit as x tends to 1,

$$\lim_{x\to 1^+} f(x)=\lim_{x\to 1^-} f(x)=f(1)$$

Now, $\lim_{x\to 1^+} f(x)=f(1)$

$\Rightarrow \lim_{x\to 1^+}[(x-1)+1]=a+b$

$\Rightarrow\ a+b=1$ ...(i)

Again, $\lim_{x\to 1^-} f(x)=f(1)$

$\Rightarrow \lim_{x\to 1^-}[(1-x)-1]=a+b$

$\Rightarrow a+b=-1$ ...(ii)

Eqs. (i) and (ii) are inconsistence.

Hence, no such values of a and b exist.

(vi) (b) Given,

$$f(x)=\begin{cases}ax^2+b, & x<0\\ 2 & x=0\\ a+b(x+1), & x>0\end{cases}$$

Since, limit exists, then

$$\lim_{x\to 0^+} f(x)=f(0)$$

Hence,

$$\lim_{x\to 0^+}[a+b(x+1)]=2$$

$\Rightarrow\ a+b(0+1)=2$

$\therefore\ a+b=2$ ...(i)

Also, $\lim_{x\to 0^-} f(x)=f(0)$

$\Rightarrow \lim_{x\to 0^-}(ax^2+b)=2$

$\Rightarrow\ b=2$ ...(ii)

From Eq. (i),

$a+b=2$

$\Rightarrow\ a+2=2$ [using Eq. (ii)]

$\Rightarrow\ a=0$

$\therefore\ a=0$ and $b=2$

Hence, the required value of $10-ab$ is equal to

$$(10-0\times 2)=10$$

(vii) (d) Given,

$$f(x)=\begin{cases}\dfrac{ax}{|x|-bx^2}, & x\ne 0\\ 0, & x=0\end{cases}$$

Now, $|x|=\begin{cases}-x, & x<0\\ x, & x>0\end{cases}$

So,

$$\lim_{x\to 0^-} f(x)=\lim_{x\to 0^-}\frac{ax}{-x-bx^2}$$

$$=\lim_{x\to 0^-}\frac{a}{-(1+bx)}=-a$$

and

$$\lim_{x\to 0^+} f(x)=\lim_{x\to 0^+}\frac{ax}{x-bx^2}=a$$

Here, $\lim_{x\to 0^+} f(x)\ne\lim_{x\to 0^-} f(x)$

Hence, $\lim_{x\to 0} f(x)$ does not exist.

(viii) (d) Given,

$$f(x)=\begin{cases}ax^3+b, & x<0\\ a+bx, & 0\le x<1\\ ax^2-bx+1, & x>1\end{cases}$$

Now, $\lim_{x\to 0} f(x)$ exist,

$\therefore\ \lim_{x\to 0^-} f(x)=\lim_{x\to 0^+} f(x)$

$\Rightarrow \lim_{x\to 0^-}(ax^3+b)=\lim_{x\to 0^+}(a+bx)$

$\Rightarrow\ b=a$

$\Rightarrow\ a=b$

and $\lim_{x\to 1} f(x)$ exist.

So, $\lim_{x \to 1^-} f(x) = \lim_{x \to 1^+} f(x)$

$\Rightarrow \lim_{x \to 1^-} (a + bx) = \lim_{x \to 1^+} (ax^2 - bx + 1)$

$\Rightarrow a + b = a - b + 1 \Rightarrow 2b = 1$

$\therefore b = \frac{1}{2}$

Hence, $a = b = \frac{1}{2}$

Therefore, the required values of a and b are, $a = \frac{1}{2}$ and $b = \frac{1}{2}$.

4. (i) (b) $\lim_{x \to -1} \sqrt{5}x^6 + \sqrt{3}x^3 + x^2 + x$

$$= \sqrt{5} - \sqrt{3} + 1 - 1$$

$$= \frac{(\sqrt{5} - \sqrt{3})(\sqrt{5} + \sqrt{3})}{(\sqrt{5} + \sqrt{3})} = \frac{2}{\sqrt{5} + \sqrt{3}}$$

(ii) (a) $\lim_{x \to \sqrt{3}} \frac{2}{3}x^2 + \sqrt{3}x - 5$

$$= \frac{2}{3}(3) + \sqrt{3}(\sqrt{3}) - 5$$

$$= 2 + 3 - 5 = 0$$

(iii) (b) $\lim_{x \to 5} (x^3 - 3x^2 + 5x + 1)$

$$= \lim_{x \to 5} x^3 - 3 \lim_{x \to 5} x^2 + 5 \lim_{x \to 5} x + \lim_{x \to 5} 1$$

$$= (5)^3 - 3(5)^2 + 5(5) + 1$$

$$= 125 - 75 + 25 + 1 = 76$$

(iv) (a) $\lim_{x \to -1} (x^4 + 3x^3 + 2x^2 + x - 1)$

$$= 1 - 3 + 2 - 1 - 1 = -2$$

5. (i) $\lim_{x \to 1} \frac{x^3 - 3x^2 + 3x - 1}{x - 1}$

$$= \lim_{x \to 1} \frac{(x-1)^3}{(x-1)} = \lim_{x \to 1} (x-1)^2 = 0$$

(ii) $\lim_{a \to 1} \frac{a^3 - 3a^2 + 2a}{a - 1}$

$\left[\equiv \frac{0}{0} \text{ form i.e. indeterminate form}\right]$

$$= \lim_{a \to 1} \frac{a[a^2 - 3a + 2]}{(a-1)} = \lim_{a \to 1} \frac{a(a-2)(a-1)}{(a-1)}$$

$$= \lim_{a \to 1} a(a-2)$$

$$= 1 \times (-1) = -1$$

(iii) $\lim_{x \to 1} \frac{x^3 - 6x^2 + 11x - 6}{x^2 - 3x + 2}$

$$= \lim_{x \to 1} \frac{(x-1)(x-2)(x-3)}{(x-1)(x-2)}$$

$$= \lim_{x \to 1} (x - 3) = 1 - 3 = -2$$

(iv) $\lim_{x \to 2} \frac{x^6 - 24x - 16}{x^3 + 2x - 12}$

$\left[\equiv \frac{0}{0} \text{ form i.e. indeterminate form}\right]$

$$= \lim_{x \to 2} \frac{(x-2)(x^5 + 2x^4 + 4x^3 + 8x^2 + 16x + 8)}{(x-2)(x^2 + 2x + 6)}$$

[applying factorisation method]

$$= \lim_{x \to 2} \frac{x^5 + 2x^4 + 4x^3 - 8x^2 + 16x + 8}{x^2 + 2x + 6}$$

$$= \frac{32 + 32 + 32 + 32 + 32 + 8}{4 + 4 + 6} = \frac{168}{14} = 12$$

6. (i) (True)

$\lim_{x \to 0} \frac{1}{\sqrt{x^2 + 1} - \sqrt{x^2 - 1}}$

$$= \lim_{x \to 0} \frac{(\sqrt{x^2+1} + \sqrt{x^2-1})}{(\sqrt{x^2+1} - \sqrt{x^2-1})(\sqrt{x^2+1} + \sqrt{x^2-1})}$$

$$= \lim_{x \to 0} \frac{(\sqrt{x^2+1} + \sqrt{x^2-1})}{(x^2 + 1 - x^2 + 1)}$$

$$= \frac{1}{2} \lim_{x \to 0} (\sqrt{x^2+1} + \sqrt{x^2-1})$$

$$= \frac{1}{2}(1 + \sqrt{-1})$$

$$= \frac{1}{2}(1 + i) \qquad [\because \sqrt{-1} = i]$$

(ii) (False)

$\lim_{x \to 0} \frac{\sqrt{1+x} - \sqrt{1-x}}{x} \qquad \left[\equiv \frac{0}{0} \text{ form}\right]$

$$= \lim_{x \to 0} \frac{(\sqrt{1+x} - \sqrt{1-x})(\sqrt{1+x} + \sqrt{1-x})}{x(\sqrt{1+x} + \sqrt{1-x})}$$

$$= \lim_{x \to 0} \frac{[1 + x - (1 - x)]}{x(\sqrt{1+x} + \sqrt{1-x})}$$

$$= \lim_{x \to 0} \frac{1 + x - 1 + x}{x(\sqrt{1+x} + \sqrt{1-x})}$$

$$= \lim_{x \to 0} \frac{2}{\sqrt{1+x} + \sqrt{1-x}} = \frac{2}{2} = 1$$

(iii) (True)

$\lim_{x \to 0} \frac{\sqrt{x^2 + a^2} - a}{\sqrt{x^2 + b^2} - b} \qquad \left[\equiv \frac{0}{0} \text{ form}\right]$

$$= \lim_{x \to 0} \frac{(\sqrt{x^2+a^2} - a)(\sqrt{x^2+b^2} + b)}{(\sqrt{x^2+b^2} - b)(\sqrt{x^2+b^2} + b)}$$

$$= \lim_{x \to 0} \frac{(\sqrt{x^2+a^2} - a)(\sqrt{x^2+b^2} + b) \times (\sqrt{x^2+a^2} + a)}{(x^2 + b^2 - b^2) \times (\sqrt{x^2+a^2} + a)}$$

$$= \lim_{x \to 0} \frac{(x^2 + a^2 - a^2)(\sqrt{x^2+b^2} + b)}{x^2 \cdot (\sqrt{x^2+a^2} + a)}$$

$$= \lim_{x \to 0} \frac{\sqrt{x^2+b^2} + b}{\sqrt{x^2+a^2} + a}$$

$$= \frac{b + b}{a + a} = \frac{b}{a}$$

7. (i) $\lim_{x\to 1}\frac{x^5-1}{x^3-1}=\lim_{x\to 1}\left[\frac{x^5-1}{x-1}\div\frac{x^3-1}{x-1}\right]$

$=\lim_{x\to 1}\left[\frac{x^5-1}{x-1}\right]\div\lim_{x\to 1}\left[\frac{x^3-1}{x-1}\right]$ $\left[\because \lim_{x\to a}\frac{x^n-a^n}{x-a}=n(a)^{n-1}\right]$

$=5(1)^4\div 3(1)^2=\frac{5}{3}$

(ii) We know, $\lim_{x\to a}\frac{x^n-a^n}{x-a}=na^{n-1}$

Now, $\lim_{x\to 2}\frac{x^n-2^n}{x-2}=192$

$\Rightarrow$ $n(2)^{n-1}=6\times(2)^{6-1}$

$\therefore$ $n=6$ [comparing both sides]

Therefore, the required value of n is 6.

(iii) $\lim_{x\to 0}\frac{(1+x)^n-1}{x}$

Let $1+x=t\Rightarrow x=t-1$

As, $x\to 0\Rightarrow t\to 1$

Now, $\lim_{t\to 1}\frac{t^n-1^n}{t-1}$

$=n(1)^{n-1}$ $\left[\because \lim_{x\to a}\frac{x^n-a^n}{x-a}=n(a)^{n-1}\right]$

$=n$

(iv) Given, $f(x)=x^6+x^5+2x^3+x^2+4$

$f(1)=1+1+2+1+4=9$

$f(0)=4$

Now, $\lim_{x\to 1}\frac{x^nf(1)-3[f(0)-1]}{x-1}=45$

$\Rightarrow$ $\lim_{x\to 1}\frac{x^n\times 9-3[4-1]}{x-1}=45$

$\Rightarrow$ $9\lim_{x\to 1}\frac{x^n-1^n}{x-1}=45$

$\Rightarrow$ $n(1)^{n-1}=5$

$\therefore$ $n=5$

8. (i) $\lim_{x\to 0}\frac{\sin 3x}{x}=3\lim_{x\to 0}\frac{\sin 3x}{3x}=3(1)=3$

(ii) $\lim_{x\to 0}\left[\frac{\sin mx}{x}+\frac{\sin^2 2x}{x^2}\right]$

$=\lim_{x\to 0}\frac{\sin mx}{x}+\lim_{x\to 0}\frac{\sin^2 2x}{x^2}$

$=m\lim_{x\to 0}\frac{\sin mx}{mx}+4\lim_{x\to 0}\left[\frac{\sin 2x}{2x}\right]^2$

$=m(1)+4(1)^2=m+4$

(iii) $\lim_{x\to 0}\left[\frac{1-\cos 2x}{x}+\cos^2 x+1\right]$

$=\lim_{x\to 0}\frac{1-\cos 2x}{x}+\lim_{x\to 0}\cos^2 x+\lim_{x\to 0}1$

$=\lim_{x\to 0}\frac{2\sin^2 x}{x}+(1)^2+1$

$=\lim_{x\to 0}2\cdot\left(\frac{\sin x}{x}\right)\sin x+1+1$

$=2(1)(0)+2=2$

9. (i) (a) We know,

$-1\le\cos\frac{1}{x}\le 1$

$\Rightarrow$ $-x\le x\cos\frac{1}{x}\le x$

Now, $\lim_{x\to 0}(-x)=0$ and $\lim_{x\to 0}x=0$

So, by Sandwich theorem, we have

$\lim_{x\to 0}\left(x\cos\frac{1}{x}\right)=0$

(ii) (b) $\lim_{x\to 0}\left(\frac{x}{\tan x}+\sqrt{x}+3\right)$

$=\lim_{x\to 0}\left(\frac{x\cdot\cos x}{\sin x}\right)+\lim_{x\to 0}(\sqrt{x})+\lim_{x\to 0}(3)$

$=\lim_{x\to 0}\left(\frac{1}{\frac{\sin x}{x}}\cdot\cos x\right)+\lim_{x\to 0}(\sqrt{x})+3\cdot\lim_{x\to 0}(1)$

$=1\cdot 1+0+3$ $\left[\because \lim_{x\to 0}\frac{\sin x}{x}=1\right]$

$=4$

Hence, the required limit is 4.

(iii) (a) Given, $f(x)=\frac{1}{x}\sqrt{\frac{1}{2}(1-\cos 2x)}$

Now, $\lim_{x\to 0}f(x)=\lim_{x\to 0}\frac{\sqrt{\frac{1}{2}(1-\cos 2x)}}{x}$

$=\lim_{x\to 0}\frac{\sqrt{\frac{1}{2}\times 2\sin^2 x}}{x}$

$=\lim_{x\to 0}\frac{\sqrt{\sin^2 x}}{x}$

$=\lim_{x\to 0}\frac{\sin x}{x}$

$=1$

(iv) (d) Given, $f(x)=\begin{cases}\frac{k\sin\left(x-\frac{\pi}{2}\right)}{\pi-2x}, & x\ne\frac{\pi}{2}\\ 2, & x=\frac{\pi}{2}\end{cases}$

Also given, $\lim_{x\to\frac{\pi}{2}}f(x)=f\left(\frac{\pi}{2}\right)$

Let $x-\frac{\pi}{2}=t$, as $x\to\frac{\pi}{2}$, so $t\to 0$

Now, $\lim_{t\to 0}f(x)=f\left(\frac{\pi}{2}\right)$

$$\Rightarrow \lim_{t \to 0} \frac{k \sin t}{-2t} = 2$$

$$\Rightarrow k \lim_{t \to 0} \frac{\sin t}{t} = -4 \Rightarrow k = -4 \quad \left[\because \lim_{t \to 0} \frac{\sin t}{t} = 1\right]$$

(v) (d) $\lim_{x \to 0} \frac{\sin ax - \sin bx}{\sqrt{1 - \cos cx}}$

$$= \lim_{x \to 0} \frac{2 \sin\left(\frac{ax - bx}{2}\right) \cdot \cos\left(\frac{ax + bx}{2}\right)}{\sqrt{2 \sin^2 \frac{cx}{2}}}$$

$$= \frac{2}{\sqrt{2}} \lim_{x \to 0} \left[\frac{\sin\left(\frac{a-b}{2}\right)x}{\left(\frac{a-b}{2}\right)x} \times \left(\frac{a-b}{2}\right) \times \frac{\frac{cx}{2}}{\sin\frac{cx}{2}} \times \frac{2}{c} \times \cos\left(\frac{a+b}{2}\right)x\right]$$

$$= \frac{2}{\sqrt{2}} \left[\lim_{x \to 0} \frac{\sin\left(\frac{a-b}{2}\right)x}{\left(\frac{a-b}{2}\right)x} \times \lim_{x \to 0} \frac{\frac{cx}{2}}{\sin\frac{cx}{2}} \times \lim_{x \to 0} \cos\left(\frac{a+b}{2}\right)x\right] \times \frac{a-b}{2} \times \frac{2}{c}$$

$$= \sqrt{2}\left(\frac{a-b}{c}\right)$$

(vi) (d) Given, $f(x) = \frac{1}{x}[\cos(a + x) - \cos(a - x)]$

Now, $\lim_{x \to 0} f(x) = \lim_{x \to 0} \frac{\cos(a + x) - \cos(a - x)}{x}$

$$= \lim_{x \to 0} \frac{-2 \sin a \cdot \sin x}{x}$$

$$= -2 \sin a \cdot \lim_{x \to 0} \frac{\sin x}{x}$$

$$= -2 \sin a \cdot 1 \quad \left[\because \lim_{x \to 0} \frac{\sin x}{x} = 1\right]$$

$\therefore \quad \lim_{x \to 0} f(x) = -2 \sin a$

(vii) (d) Given, $\lim_{y \to 0} \frac{(x + y) \sec(x + y) - x \sec x}{y}$

$$= \lim_{y \to 0} \frac{x \sec(x + y) - x \sec x + y \sec(x + y)}{y}$$

$$= \lim_{y \to 0} \frac{x[\sec(x + y) - \sec x]}{y} + \lim_{y \to 0} \sec(x + y)$$

$$= \sec x + \lim_{y \to 0} \frac{x}{y}\left[\frac{1}{\cos(x + y)} - \frac{1}{\cos x}\right]$$

$$= \sec x + \lim_{y \to 0} \frac{x}{y}\left[\frac{\cos(x) - \cos(x + y)}{\cos x \cdot \cos(x + y)}\right]$$

$$= \sec x + \lim_{y \to 0} \frac{x}{y}\left[\frac{\cos x(1 - \cos y) + \sin x \sin y}{\cos x \cdot \cos(x + y)}\right]$$

$$= \sec x + x \lim_{y \to 0} \frac{(1 - \cos y)}{y \cdot \cos(x + y)} + x \tan x \lim_{y \to 0}\left[\frac{\sin y}{y} \times \frac{1}{\cos(x + y)}\right]$$

$$= \sec x + x \times 0 + x \tan x \sec x \quad \left[\because \lim_{x \to 0} \frac{1 - \cos x}{x} = 0\right]$$

$$= \sec x + x \tan x \sec x$$

Therefore, $\lim_{y \to 0} \frac{(x + y) \sec(x + y) - x \sec x}{y}$

$$= \sec x + x \tan x \sec x$$

10. (i) Given, $\lim_{x \to 0} \tan\left(\frac{x}{\sqrt{3}}\right) \cdot \operatorname{cosec} mx = 2$

$$\Rightarrow \lim_{x \to 0} \frac{\sin\left(\frac{x}{\sqrt{3}}\right)}{\cos\left(\frac{x}{\sqrt{3}}\right)} \cdot \frac{1}{\sin mx} = 2$$

$$\Rightarrow \lim_{x \to 0}\left[\frac{\sin\left(\frac{x}{\sqrt{3}}\right)}{\frac{x}{\sqrt{3}}} \times \frac{x}{\sqrt{3}} \times \frac{mx}{\sin mx} \times \frac{1}{(mx)\cos\left(\frac{x}{\sqrt{3}}\right)}\right] = 2$$

$$\Rightarrow \lim_{x \to 0}\left(\frac{\sin\frac{x}{\sqrt{3}}}{\frac{x}{\sqrt{3}}}\right) \times \lim_{x \to 0}\left(\frac{mx}{\sin mx}\right) \times \lim_{x \to 0}\left(\frac{1}{\cos\frac{x}{\sqrt{3}}}\right) \times \frac{1}{m\sqrt{3}} = 2$$

$$\Rightarrow \frac{1}{m\sqrt{3}} \times 1 \times 1 \times 1 = 2 \quad \left[\because \lim_{x \to 0} \frac{\sin x}{x} = 1\right]$$

$$\Rightarrow \quad m = \frac{1}{2\sqrt{3}}$$

Hence, the required value of m is $\frac{1}{2\sqrt{3}}$.

(ii) Given, $f(x) = \frac{\cos x - \sin x}{\left(x - \frac{\pi}{4}\right)}$

Now, $\lim_{x \to \frac{\pi}{4}} f(x) = \lim_{x \to \frac{\pi}{4}} \frac{\cos x - \sin x}{x - \frac{\pi}{4}}$

Let $\quad x - \frac{\pi}{4} = t$

$\therefore \quad x = t + \frac{\pi}{4}$

and as $x \to \frac{\pi}{4} \Rightarrow t \to 0$

$$= \lim_{t \to 0} \frac{\cos\left(t + \frac{\pi}{4}\right) - \sin\left(t + \frac{\pi}{4}\right)}{t}$$

$$= \lim_{t \to 0} \frac{\left(\cos t \cdot \cos \frac{\pi}{4} - \sin t \cdot \sin \frac{\pi}{4}\right) - \left(\sin t \cos \frac{\pi}{4} + \cos t \cdot \sin \frac{\pi}{4}\right)}{t}$$

$$= \lim_{t \to 0} \frac{\frac{1}{\sqrt{2}}[\cos t - \sin t - \sin t - \cos t]}{t}$$

$$= -\frac{2}{\sqrt{2}} \lim_{t \to 0} \frac{\sin t}{t}$$

$$= -\sqrt{2} \quad \left[\because \lim_{t \to 0} \frac{\sin t}{t} = 1\right]$$

11. (i) Given, $f(x) = \left(1 + \frac{1}{x}\right)\left(1 - \frac{1}{x}\right) = \left(1 - \frac{1}{x^2}\right)$

On differentiating both sides w.r.t. x, we get

$$f'(x) = \frac{d}{dx}\left(1 - \frac{1}{x^2}\right)$$

$$= \frac{d}{dx}(1) - \frac{d}{dx}(x^{-2})$$

$$= 0 - (-2x^{-3}) = \frac{2}{x^3}$$

$$\therefore \quad f'(x) = \frac{2}{x^3}$$

(ii) Given, $f(x) = \frac{x^5}{5} - 2 \cdot \sqrt{x} + \frac{7}{x^2} + x$

On differentiating both sides w.r.t. x, we get

$$f'(x) = \frac{d}{dx}\left(\frac{x^5}{5}\right) - 2 \cdot \frac{d}{dx}\left(x^{\frac{1}{2}}\right) + 7 \cdot \frac{d}{dx}(x^{-2}) + \frac{d}{dx}(x)$$

$$= \frac{1}{5} \cdot 5x^4 - 2 \cdot \frac{1}{2} x^{-\frac{1}{2}} + 7(-2x^{-3}) + 1$$

$$= x^4 - \frac{1}{\sqrt{x}} - \frac{14}{x^3} + 1$$

Hence, $f'(x) = x^4 - x^{-\frac{1}{2}} - 14x^{-3} + 1$

(iii) $f(x) = \sqrt{x} + \frac{1}{\sqrt{x}}$

On differentiating both sides w.r.t. x, we get

$$f'(x) = \frac{d}{dx}\left(x^{\frac{1}{2}}\right) + \frac{d}{dx}\left(x^{-\frac{1}{2}}\right)$$

$$= \frac{1}{2} x^{-\frac{1}{2}} - \frac{1}{2}(x)^{-\frac{3}{2}} \quad \left[\frac{d}{dx}(x^n) = nx^{n-1}\right]$$

$$= \frac{1}{2}\left(x^{-\frac{1}{2}} - x^{-\frac{3}{2}}\right)$$

(iv) Given, $f(x) = x^{-m}(b + cx^{-n})$

On differentiating both sides w.r.t. x, we get

$$f' x = \frac{d}{dx}[x^{-m}(b + cx^{-n})]$$

$$= \left[\frac{d}{dx}(x^{-m})\right](b + cx^{-n}) + x^{-m}\left[\frac{d}{dx}(b + cx^{-n})\right]$$

$$= (-mx^{-m-1})(b + cx^{-n}) + x^{-m}(-cnx^{-n-1})$$

$$= x^{-m-1}[-mb - mcx^{-n} - cnx^{-n}]$$

$$= x^{-m-1}[-mb - cx^{-n}(m + n)]$$

(v) Given, $f(x) = \frac{1}{\sqrt{a^2 - x^2}}$

On differentiating both sides w.r.t. x, we get

$$f' x = \frac{d}{dx}\left(\frac{1}{\sqrt{a^2 - x^2}}\right)$$

$$= \frac{(\sqrt{a^2 - x^2})\frac{d}{dx}(1) - 1\frac{d}{dx}(\sqrt{a^2 - x^2})}{(\sqrt{a^2 - x^2})^2}$$

$$= \frac{\sqrt{a^2 - x^2} \cdot 0 - 1 \cdot \frac{1}{2}(a^2 - x^2)^{-\frac{1}{2}} \cdot (-2x)}{(a^2 - x^2)}$$

$$= \frac{x}{(a^2 - x^2)^{\frac{3}{2}}}$$

12. (i) (a) Given, $f(x) = 3x^2 + 6x$

$$\therefore \quad f'(x) = \frac{d}{dx}(3x^2 + 6x)$$

$$= \frac{3d}{dx}(x^2) + \frac{6d}{dx}(x) = 6x + 6$$

$$\therefore f'(-1) = -6 + 6 = 0$$

(ii) (b) Given, $f(x) = x^3 + 2x^2 + 3x$

$$\therefore \quad f'(x) = \frac{d}{dx}(x^3) + \frac{2d}{dx}(x^2) + \frac{3d}{dx}(x)$$

$$= 3x^2 + 4x + 3$$

$$\therefore \quad f'(1) = 3 + 4 + 3 = 10$$

(iii) (a) Given, $f(x) = x^3 - 4x^2 + 5x + 1$

On differentiating both sides w.r.t. x, we get

$$f'(x) = 3x^2 - 8x + 5 \quad \left[\because \frac{d}{dx}(x^n) = nx^{n-1}\right]$$

Now, $f'(0) = 5$, $f'(-1) = 3 + 8 + 5 = 16$

and $f'(1) = 3 - 8 + 5 = 0$

Therefore, $3f'(0) - f'(-1) + 2f'(1)$

$$= 3 \times 5 - 16 + 2 \times 0$$

$$= 15 - 16 = -1$$

(iv) (a) Given, $f(x) = x^3 + 5x^2 - 3x + 2$ ...(i)

Now, differentiating both sides w.r.t. x, we get

$$f'(x) = 3x^2 + 10x - 3$$

Now, putting $x = 0$, we get

$$f'(0) = -3$$

and in Eq. (i), putting $x = 2$, we get

$$f(2) = 8 + 5(4) - 3 \times 2 + 2$$

$$= 8 + 20 - 6 + 2 = 24$$

Therefore, $f'(0) + 3f(2)$

$$= -3 + 3 \times 24 = 69$$

(v) (a) Here, $f(x) = (1+ax)(1+bx^2)(1+cx^3)$

On differentiating both sides w.r.t. x, we get

$$f'(x) = \frac{d}{dx}[(1+ax)(1+bx^2)(1+cx^3)]$$
$$= (1+bx^2)(1+cx^3)\frac{d}{dx}(1+ax) + (1+ax)(1+cx^3)\frac{d}{dx}(1+bx^2) + (1+ax)(1+bx^2)\frac{d}{dx}(1+cx^3)$$
$$= a(1+bx^2)(1+cx^3) + 2bx(1+ax)(1+cx^3) + 3cx^2(1+ax)(1+bx^2)$$

Now, $f'(x)$ at $x=1$

i.e $\quad f'(x)|_{x=1} = a(1+b)(1+c) + 2b(1+a)(1+c) + 3c(1+a)(1+b)$

13. (i) Given, $y = \dfrac{x-1}{x^2-3}$

$$\therefore \frac{dy}{dx} = \frac{d}{dx}\left[\frac{x-1}{x^2-3}\right]$$
$$= \frac{(x^2-3)\frac{d}{dx}(x-1) - (x-1)\frac{d}{dx}(x^2-3)}{(x^2-3)^2}$$
$$= \frac{(x^2-3)(1) - (x-1)(2x)}{(x^2-3)^2}$$
$$= \frac{x^2 - 3 - 2x^2 + 2x}{(x^2-3)^2}$$
$$= \frac{-x^2 + 2x - 3}{(x^2-3)^2}$$

(ii) Given, $y = \dfrac{x}{\sqrt{1+x^2}}$ ...(i)

On differentiating both sides w.r.t. x, we get

$$\frac{dy}{dx} = \frac{d}{dx}\left(\frac{x}{\sqrt{1+x^2}}\right)$$
$$= \frac{\sqrt{1+x^2} - x\frac{1}{2}(1+x^2)^{-\frac{1}{2}}\cdot 2x}{(1+x^2)}$$
$$= \frac{(1+x^2) - x^2}{(1+x^2)(1+x^2)^{\frac{1}{2}}}$$
$$= \frac{1}{(1+x^2)\sqrt{1+x^2}}$$

(iii) Given, $y = \dfrac{1 + \frac{1}{\sqrt{x}}}{1 - \frac{1}{\sqrt{x}}}$

$$\Rightarrow \quad y = \frac{\sqrt{x}+1}{\sqrt{x}-1}$$

On differentiating both sides w.r.t. x, we get

$$\frac{dy}{dx} = \frac{(\sqrt{x}-1)\frac{d}{dx}(\sqrt{x}+1) - (\sqrt{x}+1)\frac{d}{dx}(\sqrt{x}-1)}{(\sqrt{x}-1)^2}$$
$$= \frac{(\sqrt{x}-1)\left(\frac{1}{2\sqrt{x}}\right) - (\sqrt{x}+1)\left(\frac{1}{2\sqrt{x}}\right)}{(\sqrt{x}-1)^2}$$
$$= \frac{-2}{2\sqrt{x}(\sqrt{x}-1)^2}$$
$$= -\frac{1}{\sqrt{x}(\sqrt{x}-1)^2}$$

Hence, $\dfrac{dy}{dx} = -\dfrac{1}{\sqrt{x}(\sqrt{x}-1)^2}$

(iv) Given, $y = \dfrac{ax^2 + bx + c}{rx^2 + sx + t}$

On differentiating both sides w.r.t. x, we get

$$\frac{dy}{dx} = \frac{(rx^2+sx+t)(2ax+b) - (ax^2+bx+c)(2rx+s)}{(rx^2+sx+t)^2}$$

Now, $\left.\dfrac{dy}{dx}\right|_{x=0} = \dfrac{tb - cs}{t^2}$

14. (i) Let $y = \sin x + \cos x$

$$\therefore \frac{dy}{dx} = \frac{d}{dx}(\sin x) + \frac{d}{dx}(\cos x)$$
$$= \cos x - \sin x$$

(ii) Let $y = 3\sec x + 2\tan x$

$$\therefore \frac{dy}{dx} = 3\frac{d}{dx}\sec x + 2\frac{d}{dx}\tan x$$
$$= 3\sec x \tan x + 2\sec^2 x$$
$$= \sec x(3\tan x + 2\sec x)$$

(iii) Let $y = 5\cot x + 2\sin x$

$$\therefore \frac{dy}{dx} = 5\frac{d}{dx}\cot x + 2\frac{d}{dx}\sin x$$
$$= -5\operatorname{cosec}^2 x + 2\cos x$$

(iv) Let $y = 3\operatorname{cosec} x + 2\tan x$

$$\therefore \frac{dy}{dx} = 3\frac{d}{dx}(\operatorname{cosec} x) + 2\frac{d}{dx}(\tan x)$$
$$= -3\operatorname{cosec} x \cot x + 2\sec^2 x$$

(v) Let $y = \sec x + \tan x - \sin x$

$$\therefore \frac{dy}{dx} = \frac{d}{dx}(\sec x) + \frac{d}{dx}(\tan x) - \frac{d}{dx}(\sin x)$$
$$= \sec x \tan x + \sec^2 x - \cos x$$

(vi) Let $y = \tan x \cdot \cot x$

$$\Rightarrow \quad y = 1 \qquad \left[\because \frac{\sin x}{\cos x} \times \frac{\cos x}{\sin x} = 1\right]$$

On differentiating both sides w.r.t. x, we get

$$\frac{dy}{dx} = 0$$

15. (i) (b) Here, $y = \dfrac{1}{\sqrt{1+\tan^2 x}} = \dfrac{1}{\sqrt{\sec^2 x}} = \dfrac{1}{\sec x}$

$$\therefore \quad y = \cos x$$

On differentiating both sides w.r.t. x, we get

$$\frac{dy}{dx} = -\sin x$$

(ii) (a) Here, $y=\sqrt{1+\sin 2x}$

$$=\sqrt{\sin^2 x+\cos^2 x+2\sin x\cos x}$$

$$=\sqrt{(\sin x+\cos x)^2}$$

$\therefore \quad y=\sin x+\cos x$

On differentiating both sides w.r.t. x, we get

$$\frac{dy}{dx}=\frac{d}{dx}(\sin x)+\frac{d}{dx}(\cos x)=\cos x-\sin x$$

(iii) (a) Here, $y=x^2\sin x$

On differentiating both sides w.r.t. x, we get

$$\frac{dy}{dx}=\frac{d}{dx}(x^2\sin x)$$

$$=\sin x\cdot\frac{d}{dx}(x^2)+x^2\cdot\frac{d}{dx}(\sin x)$$

$$=\sin x\cdot 2x+x^2\cdot\cos x$$

$$=2x\sin x+x^2\cos x$$

16. (i) Given, $f(x)=x\cos x$

On differentiating both sides w.r.t. x, we get

$$f'(x)=\frac{d}{dx}(x\cos x)=\cos x-x\sin x$$

Now, $f'(x)|_{x=\pi}=(\cos x-x\sin x)|_{x=\pi}$

$\Rightarrow \quad f'(\pi)=\cos\pi-\pi\sin\pi$

$$=-1-\pi\times 0=-1$$

$\therefore \quad f'(\pi)=-1$

(ii) Here, $f(x)=(3x^2+2x+5)(x\sin x+\tan x)$

On differentiating both sides w.r.t. x, we get

$$f'(x)=\frac{d}{dx}[(3x^2+2x+5)(x\sin x+\tan x)]$$

$$=(x\sin x+\tan x)\cdot\frac{d}{dx}(3x^2+2x+5)+(3x^2+2x+5)\frac{d}{dx}(x\sin x+\tan x)$$

$$=(x\sin x+\tan x)(6x+2)+(3x^2+2x+5)[\sin x+x\cos x+\sec^2 x]$$

$\therefore f'(x)=(6x+2)(x\sin x+\tan x)+(3x^2+2x+5)(\sin x+x\cos x+\sec^2 x)$

17. (i) (True)

Let $y=\sqrt{x\tan x}$

On differentiating both sides w.r.t. x, we get

$$\frac{dy}{dx}=\frac{d}{dx}(\sqrt{x}\cdot\sqrt{\tan x})$$

$$=\frac{1}{2\sqrt{x}}\sqrt{\tan x}+\sqrt{x}\cdot\frac{1}{2}(\tan x)^{-\frac{1}{2}}\cdot\frac{d}{dx}(\tan x)$$

$$=\frac{\sqrt{\tan x}}{2\sqrt{x}}+\frac{\sqrt{x}}{2\sqrt{\tan x}}\cdot\sec^2 x$$

$$=\frac{1}{2\sqrt{x\tan x}}\left(\tan x+x\cdot\frac{1}{\cos^2 x}\right)$$

$$=\frac{1}{2\sqrt{x\cdot\tan x}}(\tan x+x\sec^2 x)$$

(ii) (True)

Given, $f(x)=x^n\tan^2 x+\sec x+1$

On differentiating both sides w.r.t. x, we get

$$f'(x)=\frac{d}{dx}(x^n\tan^2 x)+\frac{d}{dx}(\sec x)+\frac{d}{dx}(1)$$

$$=nx^{n-1}\tan^2 x+x^n(2\tan x\cdot\sec^2 x)+\sec x\cdot\tan x+0$$

$$\therefore f'(x)=nx^{n-1}\tan^2 x+2x^n\sin x\cdot\sec^3 x+\sec x\cdot\tan x \quad \text{...(i)}$$

Now, putting $x=0$ in Eq. (i), we get

$$f'(0)=0$$

$\therefore \quad xf'(0)=0$

18. (i) (c) Here, $xy+1=-\cos(xy)$

On differentiating both sides w.r.t. x, we get

$$\frac{d}{dx}(xy+1)=(-1)\frac{d}{dx}[\cos(xy)]$$

$$\Rightarrow \quad \left[y+x\frac{dy}{dx}\right]=\sin(xy)\left[y+x\frac{dy}{dx}\right]$$

$$\Rightarrow \quad y+x\frac{dy}{dx}=y\sin(xy)+x\sin(xy)\cdot\frac{dy}{dx}$$

$$\Rightarrow \quad \frac{dy}{dx}(x-x\sin xy)=y[\sin(xy)-1]$$

$$\Rightarrow \quad \frac{dy}{dx}=-\frac{y}{x}$$

$$\text{Now, }\left[\frac{dy}{dx}\right]_{x=\frac{\pi}{2},\,y=0}=-\frac{0}{\frac{\pi}{2}}=0$$

(ii) (c) Given, $f(x)=\sin^2 2x\cos^4 4x+x^3+1$

On differentiating w.r.t. x, we get

$$f'x=\frac{d}{dx}(\sin^2 2x\cos^4 4x+x^3+1)$$

$$=\left[\frac{d}{dx}(\sin^2 2x)\right]\cos^4 4x+\sin^2 2x\cdot\frac{d}{dx}(\cos^4 4x)+\frac{d}{dx}(x^3)+\frac{d}{dx}(1)$$

$$=2\sin 2x\cdot\cos 2x\cdot(2)\cos^4 4x+\sin^2 2x\cdot 4\cos^3 4x\cdot(-\sin 4x)\cdot(4)+3x^2+0$$

$$=2\sin 4x\cos^4 4x-16\sin^2 2x\cdot\sin 4x\cos^3 4x+3x^2$$

(iii) (d) Let $y=\dfrac{x}{\sin x}$

On differentiating both sides w.r.t. x, we get

$$\frac{dy}{dx}=\frac{d}{dx}\left(\frac{x}{\sin x}\right)=\frac{\sin x\cdot\frac{d}{dx}(x)-x\cdot\frac{d}{dx}(\sin x)}{(\sin x)^2}$$

$$=\frac{\sin x-x\cos x}{\sin^2 x}$$

Hence, $\dfrac{d}{dx}\left(\dfrac{x}{\sin x}\right)=\dfrac{\sin x-x\cos x}{\sin^2 x}$

(iv) (c) Given, $y = \frac{\sin x + \cos x}{\sin x - \cos x}$

On differentiating both sides w.r.t. x, we get

$$\frac{dy}{dx} = \frac{d}{dx}\left(\frac{\sin x + \cos x}{\sin x - \cos x}\right)$$

$$= \frac{(\sin x - \cos x)\frac{d}{dx}(\sin x + \cos x) - (\sin x + \cos x) \times \frac{d}{dx}(\sin x - \cos x)}{(\sin x - \cos x)^2}$$

$$= \frac{(\sin x - \cos x)(\cos x - \sin x) - (\sin x + \cos x)(\cos x + \sin x)}{(\sin x - \cos x)^2}$$

$$= \frac{-(\sin x - \cos x)^2 - (\sin x + \cos x)^2}{(\sin x - \cos x)^2}$$

Now,

$$\left.\frac{dy}{dx}\right|_{x=\frac{\pi}{2}} = \frac{-\left(\sin\frac{\pi}{2} - \cos\frac{\pi}{2}\right)^2 - \left(\sin\frac{\pi}{2} + \cos\frac{\pi}{2}\right)^2}{\left(\sin\frac{\pi}{2} - \cos\frac{\pi}{2}\right)^2}$$

$$= \frac{-1-1}{1} = -2$$

Hence, the required value of $\frac{dy}{dx}$ at

$x = \frac{\pi}{2}$ is -2.

19. (i) Here, $y = (x + \sin x)(1 - \tan x)$

$$= (x + \sin x)\left(1 - \frac{\sin x}{\cos x}\right)$$

On differentiating both sides w.r.t. x, we get

$$\frac{dy}{dx} = \left[\frac{d}{dx}(x + \sin x)\right]\cdot\left(1 - \frac{\sin x}{\cos x}\right) + (x + \sin x)\frac{d}{dx}\left(1 - \frac{\sin x}{\cos x}\right)$$

$$= (1 + \cos x)\left(1 - \frac{\sin x}{\cos x}\right) + (x + \sin x)\left[0 - \frac{\cos x \cdot \cos x - \sin x(-\sin x)}{\cos^2 x}\right]$$

$$= (1 + \cos x)(1 - \tan x) + (x + \sin x)(-\sec^2 x)$$

(ii) Let $y = \frac{1 - \sin x}{\cos x}$

On differentiating both sides w.r.t. x, we get

$$\frac{d}{dx}(y) = \frac{d}{dx}\left(\frac{1 - \sin x}{\cos x}\right)$$

$$\Rightarrow \frac{dy}{dx} = \frac{\cos x \cdot \frac{d}{dx}(1 - \sin x) - (1 - \sin x)\frac{d}{dx}(\cos x)}{\cos^2 x}$$

$$= \frac{\cos x[-\cos x] - (1 - \sin x)(-\sin x)}{\cos^2 x}$$

$$= \frac{-(\cos^2 x + \sin^2 x) + \sin x}{\cos^2 x} = \frac{-1 + \sin x}{1 - \sin^2 x}$$

$$= \frac{-(1 - \sin x)}{(1 + \sin x)(1 - \sin x)} = \frac{-1}{1 + \sin x}$$

Hence, $\frac{d}{dx}\left(\frac{1 - \sin x}{\cos x}\right)$

$$= \frac{-1}{\sin x + 1}$$

20. (True)

Let $y = \frac{\sin ax}{1 + \cos bx}$

On differentiating both sides w.r.t. x, we get

$$\frac{d}{dx}(y) = \frac{d}{dx}\left(\frac{\sin ax}{1 + \cos bx}\right)$$

$$= \frac{(1 + \cos bx)(\cos ax)\cdot a - \sin ax(-\sin bx)\cdot b}{(1 + \cos bx)^2}$$

$$= \frac{a\cos ax + a\cos ax\cos bx + b\sin ax \cdot \sin bx}{(1 + \cos bx)^2}$$

Now, $\left.\frac{dy}{dx}\right|_{x=0} = \frac{a + a}{4}$

$$= \frac{2a}{4}$$

$\therefore \left.\frac{dy}{dx}\right|_{x=0} = \frac{a}{2}$

21. (i) Given, $y = \cos(\sqrt{\sin\sqrt{x}})$

On differentiating on both sides w.r.t. x, we get

$$\frac{dy}{dx} = \frac{d}{dx}(\cos\sqrt{\sin\sqrt{x}})$$

$$= -\sin(\sqrt{\sin\sqrt{x}})\cdot\frac{d}{dx}(\sqrt{\sin\sqrt{x}})$$

$$= -\sin(\sqrt{\sin\sqrt{x}})\left(\frac{1}{2}(\sin\sqrt{x})^{-\frac{1}{2}}\right)\cos\sqrt{x}\cdot\frac{d}{dx}(\sqrt{x})$$

$$= -\sin(\sqrt{\sin\sqrt{x}})\frac{1}{2\sqrt{\sin\sqrt{x}}}\cdot\cos\sqrt{x}\cdot\frac{1}{2}(x)^{-\frac{1}{2}}$$

Hence, $\frac{dy}{dx} = \frac{-1}{4\sqrt{x\cdot\sin\sqrt{x}}}\cos\sqrt{x}\cdot\sin\sqrt{\sin\sqrt{x}}.$

(ii) Given, $y = \sqrt{\frac{1 - \tan x}{1 + \tan x}}$

$$= \sqrt{\frac{\tan\frac{\pi}{4} - \tan x}{1 + \tan\frac{\pi}{4}\cdot\tan x}}$$

$\therefore y = \sqrt{\tan\left(\frac{\pi}{4} - x\right)}$

On differentiating on both sides w.r.t. x, we get

$$\frac{dy}{dx}=\frac{1}{2}\left[\tan\left(\frac{\pi}{4}-x\right)\right]^{-\frac{1}{2}}\cdot\sec^2\left(\frac{\pi}{4}-x\right)(-1)$$

$$=-\frac{\sec^2\left(\frac{\pi}{4}-x\right)}{2\sqrt{\tan\left(\frac{\pi}{4}-x\right)}}$$

$$=-\frac{1}{2}\frac{\left[\sec\left(\frac{\pi}{4}-x\right)\right]^{\frac{3}{2}}}{\sqrt{\sin\left(\frac{\pi}{4}-x\right)}}$$

Therefore, $\frac{dy}{dx}=-\frac{1}{2}\left[\frac{\left(\sec\left(\frac{\pi}{4}-x\right)\right)^{\frac{3}{2}}}{\sqrt{\sin\left(\frac{\pi}{4}-x\right)}}\right]$

(iii) Given, $y=\sqrt{1+\sin x}+\sqrt{\frac{1-x^2}{1+x^2}}$

$$=\sqrt{\sin^2\frac{x}{2}+\cos^2\frac{x}{2}+2\sin\frac{x}{2}\cdot\cos\frac{x}{2}}+\sqrt{\frac{1-x^2}{1+x^2}}$$

$$=\sin\frac{x}{2}+\cos\frac{x}{2}+\sqrt{\frac{1-x^2}{1+x^2}}$$

On differentiating both sides w.r.t. x, we get

$$\frac{dy}{dx}=\frac{d}{dx}\left(\sin\frac{x}{2}\right)+\frac{d}{dx}\left(\cos\frac{x}{2}\right)+\frac{d}{dx}\left(\sqrt{\frac{1-x^2}{1+x^2}}\right)$$

$$=\cos\frac{x}{2}\cdot\frac{1}{2}-\sin\frac{x}{2}\cdot\frac{1}{2}$$

$$+\frac{1}{2}\left(\sqrt{\frac{1+x^2}{1-x^2}}\right)\frac{(1+x^2)(-2x)-(1-x^2)(2x)}{(1+x^2)^2}$$

$$=\frac{1}{2}\left(\cos\frac{x}{2}-\sin\frac{x}{2}\right)-\frac{2x}{\sqrt{1-x^2}\,(1+x^2)^{\frac{3}{2}}}$$

$$\therefore\ \frac{dy}{dx}=\frac{1}{2}\left(\cos\frac{x}{2}-\sin\frac{x}{2}\right)-\frac{2x}{(1+x^2)(1-x^4)^{\frac{1}{2}}}$$

Assertion Reason

1. (a) Given, $\lim_{x\to 0}\frac{\cos 2x-1}{\cos x-1}$

At $x=0$, the value of given function takes a form $\frac{0}{0}$.

Now, $\lim_{x\to 0}\frac{\cos 2x-1}{\cos x-1}$

$$=\lim_{x\to 0}\frac{1-2\sin^2 x-1}{1-2\sin^2\frac{x}{2}-1}\qquad\left[\because \cos x=1-2\sin^2\frac{x}{2}\right]$$

$$=\lim_{x\to 0}\frac{\sin^2 x}{\sin^2\frac{x}{2}}$$

$$=\lim_{x\to 0}\frac{\left(\frac{\sin x}{x}\right)^2\cdot x^2}{\left(\frac{\sin\frac{x}{2}}{\frac{x}{2}}\right)^2\cdot\frac{x^2}{4}}$$

$$=4\cdot\frac{\left(\lim_{x\to 0}\frac{\sin x}{x}\right)^2}{\left(\lim_{x\to 0}\frac{\sin\frac{x}{2}}{\frac{x}{2}}\right)^2}\qquad\left[x\to 0\Rightarrow\frac{x}{2}\to 0\right]$$

$$=4\cdot\frac{(1)^2}{(1)^2}\qquad\left[\because \lim_{y\to 0}\frac{\sin y}{y}=1\right]$$

$$=4$$

$\therefore$ Both Assertion and Reason are true and Reason is the correct explanation of Assertion.

2. (b) $\lim_{x\to 0}\frac{(x+2)^3-8}{x}=12$

We know that $\lim_{x\to a}\frac{x^n-a^n}{x-a}=na^{n-1}$

$$\therefore\ \lim_{x\to 0}\frac{(x+2)^3-(2)^3}{(x+2)-(2)}$$

$$=\lim_{x+2\to 2}\frac{(x+2)^3-(2)^3}{(x+2)-(2)}$$

$$=3\times 2^{3-1}=3\times 2^2=12$$

Now, $\text{LHL}=\lim_{x\to 1^-}f(x)$

$$=\lim_{x\to 1^-}(3x-2)$$

$$=3-2=1$$

$\text{RHL}=\lim_{x\to 1^+}f(x)$

$$=\lim_{x\to 1^+}3(x-1)=0$$

$\because$ LHL $\neq$ RHL

$\therefore$ $\lim_{x\to 1}f(x)$ does not exist.

Assertion and Reason are true but Reason is not the correct explanation of the Assertion.

3. (d) We have, $\lim_{x\to 0}\frac{\sqrt{1-\cos x}}{x}$

$$=\lim_{x\to 0}\frac{\sqrt{1-\left(1-2\sin^2\frac{x}{2}\right)}}{x}$$

$$=\lim_{x\to 0}\frac{\sqrt{2\sin^2\frac{x}{2}}}{x}$$

$$=\lim_{x\to 0}\left(\frac{\sqrt{2}\sin\frac{x}{2}}{2\times\frac{x}{2}}\right)$$

$$=\frac{\sqrt{2}}{2}\lim_{x\to 0}\left(\frac{\sin\frac{x}{2}}{\frac{x}{2}}\right)$$

$$=\frac{1}{\sqrt{2}}\times 1$$

$$=\frac{1}{\sqrt{2}}$$

It is exist and Assertion is false.

Now, $\lim_{x\to 0}\frac{e^{\sin x}-1}{x}$

$$=\lim_{x\to 0}\frac{\left[1+x+\frac{x^2}{2}-\frac{x^4}{8}+\ldots-1\right]}{x}$$

$$\left[\because e^{\sin x}=1+x+\frac{x^2}{2}-\frac{x^4}{8}+\ldots\right]$$

$$=\lim_{x\to 0}\frac{x\left[1+\frac{x}{2}-\frac{x^3}{8}+\ldots\right]}{x}$$

$=1$

$\therefore$ Reason is true.

4. (c) We have, $\lim_{x\to 0}\frac{\sin 3x}{\sin 2x}$

$$=\lim_{x\to 0}(\sin 3x\div\sin 2x)$$

$$=\lim_{x\to 0}\left(\frac{\sin 3x}{3x}\times 3\div\frac{\sin 2x}{2x}\times 2\right)$$

$$=3\left(\lim_{x\to 0}\frac{\sin 3x}{3x}\right)\div 2\left(\lim_{x\to 0}\frac{\sin 2x}{2x}\right)$$

$$=3\times 1\div 2\times 1$$

$$=\frac{3}{2}$$

$\because \lim_{x\to 0}\frac{\sin 3x}{\sin 2x}=\frac{3}{2}$

$\therefore$ Assertion is true.

Now, $\lim_{x\to 0}\frac{\sin x}{x(1+\cos x)}$

$$=\left(\lim_{x\to 0}\frac{\sin x}{x}\right)\cdot\left(\lim_{x\to 0}\frac{1}{(1+\cos x)}\right)$$

$$=1\times\frac{1}{2}$$

$$=\frac{1}{2}$$

$\because \lim_{x\to 0}\frac{\sin x}{x(1+\cos x)}=\frac{1}{2}$

$\therefore$ It is defined.

$\therefore$ Reason is false.

5. (c) $\lim_{x\to 1}\frac{ax^2+bx+c}{cx^2+bx+a}$

$$=\frac{a(1)^2+b(1)+c}{c(1)^2+b(1)+a}$$

$$=\frac{a+b+c}{c+b+a}=1$$

$\because \lim_{x\to 1}\frac{ax^2+bx+c}{cx^2+bx+a}=1$

$\therefore$ Assertion is true.

Now, $\lim_{x\to -2}\frac{\frac{1}{x}+\frac{1}{2}}{x+2}$

$$=\lim_{x\to -2}\frac{\frac{2+x}{2x}}{x+2}$$

$$=\lim_{x\to -2}\frac{(x+2)}{(x+2)2x}$$

$$=\lim_{x\to -2}\frac{1}{2x}$$

$$=\frac{1}{2(-2)}$$

$$=-\frac{1}{4}$$

$\because \lim_{x\to -2}\frac{\frac{1}{x}+\frac{1}{2}}{x+2}\neq\frac{1}{4}$

Hence, Reason is false.

6. (d) If $\lim_{x\to a}f(x)=L$, then

$f(a)=L$

This Assertion is false. The limit of a function as x approaches a does not necessarily mean that the value of the function at a is equal to the limit. The function may not even be defined at a.

Reason the limit of a function as x approaches a is the value of the function at a.

This Reason is true. The limit of a function as x approaches as a is the value that the function approaches as x gets arbitrarily close to a.

$\therefore$ Assertion is false and Reason is true.

7. (a) $\lim_{x\to a}(x^3-a^3)$

We can use limit properties to break this

$$=\lim_{x\to a}x^3-\lim_{x\to a}a^3=a^3-a^3=0$$

Thus, the Assertion is true.

Now, $\lim_{x\to a}x^3=a^3$

This is a well-known limit property for polynomial functions, so the Reason is also true and Reason is correct explanation of Assertion.

8. (a) $f(x)=x^2$

$\Rightarrow\quad f'(x)=2x$

So, the Assertion is true.

Now, the Reason states that the derivative of x^n is nx^{n-1}. This is the power rule for differentiation, which is a fundamental rule in calculus.

The Reason is also true and Reason is correct explanation of Assertion.

9. (c) **Assertion** the derivative of $f(x)=x^2$ at $x=2$ is 4. This Assertion is true. The derivative of $f(x)=x^2$ is $f'(x)=2x$.

Therefore, at $x=2$,

$f'(2)=4$

$\therefore$ Assertion is true.

Reason the derivative of $f(x)=\sin x+\cos x$ is $\cos x-\sin x$.

$\therefore$ Reason is false.

10. (a) We have,

$$\lim_{x\to 1}=\frac{x^2-1}{x-1}$$

$$=\lim_{x\to 1}\frac{(x-1)(x+1)}{(x-1)}$$

$$=\lim_{x\to 1}(x+1)=2$$

$$\lim_{x\to 1}\frac{x^2-1}{x-1}=2$$

Assertion is true because the limit evaluates to 2.

Now, Reason is also true and Reason is the correct explanation of Assertion because we have shown that $\frac{x^2-1}{x-1}=x+1$.

Case Based

Case 1 (i) (b) $\lim_{x\to -1}\frac{x^{10}+x^5+1}{x-1}$

$$=\frac{(-1)^{10}+(-1)^5+1}{(-1)-1}$$

$$=\frac{1-1+1}{-1-1}=-\frac{1}{2}$$

(ii) (a) $\lim_{x\to -1}\frac{(x-1)^2+3x^2}{(x^4+1)^2}$

$$=\frac{(-1\ -1)^2+3(-1)^2}{[(-1)^4+(-1)]^2}$$

$$=\frac{4+3}{4}=\frac{7}{4}$$

(iii) (d) $\lim_{x\to 2}\left[\frac{x^2-4}{x^3-4x^2+4x}\right]$

Consider $f(x)=\frac{x^2-4}{x^3-4x^2+4x}$

On putting $x=2$, we get

$$f(2)=\frac{4-4}{8-16+8}=\frac{0}{0},$$

it is the form $\frac{0}{0}$.

So, $\lim_{x\to 2}\left[\frac{x^2-4}{x^3-4x^2+4x}\right]$

$$=\lim_{x\to 2}\frac{(x+2)(x-2)}{x(x-2)^2}$$

$$=\lim_{x\to 2}\frac{x+2}{x(x-2)}=\frac{2+2}{2(2-2)}=\frac{4}{0},$$

which is not defined.

$\therefore \lim_{x\to 2}\left[\frac{x^2-4}{x^3-4x^2+4x}\right]$ does not exist.

(iv) (b) Given,

$$\lim_{x\to 0}\frac{\sqrt{1+x^3}-\sqrt{1-x^3}}{x^2}$$

$$=\lim_{x\to 0}\frac{(1+x^3)-(1-x^3)}{x^2(\sqrt{1+x^3}+\sqrt{1-x^3})}$$

$$=\lim_{x\to 0}\frac{1+x^3-1+x^3}{x^2(\sqrt{1+x^3}+\sqrt{1-x^3})}$$

$$=\lim_{x\to 0}\frac{2x^3}{x^2\sqrt{1+x^3}+\sqrt{1-x^3}}$$

$$=\lim_{x\to 0}\frac{2x}{\sqrt{1+x^3}+\sqrt{1-x^3}}=0$$

Case 2 (i) (b) Given, $\lim_{x\to 0}\frac{\sin 4x}{8x}$

$$=\lim_{x\to 0}\frac{\sin 4x}{4x}\times\frac{4}{8}$$

$$=1\times\frac{1}{2}=\frac{1}{2}$$

(ii) (b) Given, $\lim_{\theta\to b}\frac{\tan(\theta-b)}{\theta-b}$

$[\theta-b\Rightarrow(\theta-b)\to 0]$

$$=\lim_{(\theta-b)\to 0}\frac{\tan(\theta-b)}{\theta-b}$$

$$\left[\because \lim_{x\to 0}\frac{\tan x}{x}=1\right]$$

$=1$

(iii) (a) $\lim_{x\to 0}\frac{\tan 2x-\sin 2x}{x^3}$

$$=\lim_{x\to 0}\frac{\frac{\sin 2x}{\cos 2x}-\sin 2x}{x^3}$$

$$=\lim_{x\to 0}\frac{\sin 2x}{x^3}\left(\frac{1-\cos 2x}{\cos 2x}\right)$$

$$=\lim_{x\to 0}\frac{\sin 2x}{x^3}\left(\frac{2\sin^2 x}{\cos 2x}\right)$$

$$=\lim_{x\to 0}2\left(\frac{\sin 2x}{2x}\right)\times 2\left(\frac{\sin x}{x}\right)^2\times\frac{1}{\cos 2x}$$

$$=2\times(1)\times 2\times(1)^2\times\frac{1}{1}$$

$=4$

(iv) (a) Given,

$$\lim_{x\to 0}\frac{2\sin x-\sin 2x}{x^2}$$

$$=\lim_{x\to 0}\frac{2\sin x-2\sin x\cdot\cos x}{x^2}$$

$$=\lim_{x\to 0}\frac{2\sin x(1-\cos x)}{x^2}$$

$$=2\cdot\lim_{x\to 0}\frac{\sin x}{x}\cdot\lim_{x\to 0}\left(\frac{1-\cos x}{x}\right)$$

$=2\times 1\times 0$

$=0$

Competition Edge Up

1. (b) $\lim_{x\to 0}\frac{e-(1+2x)^{1/2x}}{x}$

$$=\lim_{x\to 0}\frac{e-e^{\frac{1}{2x}\ln(1+2x)}}{x}$$

$$=\lim_{x\to 0}(-e)\frac{\left(e^{\frac{\ln(1+2x)}{2x}-1}-1\right)}{x}$$

$$=\lim_{x\to 0}(-e)\frac{e^{\frac{\ln(1+2x)}{2x}-1}-1}{\frac{\ln(1+2x)}{2x}-1},\ \frac{\frac{\ln(1+2x)-1}{2x}}{x}$$

$$=\lim_{x\to 0}(-e)\frac{\ln(1+2x)-2x}{2x^2}$$

$$=\lim_{x\to 0}(-e)\frac{\left[\left(2x-\frac{(2x)^2}{2}+\ldots\right)-2x\right]}{2x^2}$$

$=e\times 1=e$

2. (c) Let

$$L=\lim_{n\to\infty}\{(2^{\frac{1}{2}}-2^{\frac{1}{3}})(2^{\frac{1}{2}}-2^{\frac{1}{5}})\ldots(2^{\frac{1}{2}}-2^{\frac{1}{2n-1}})\}$$

Here, $(2^{\frac{1}{2}}-2^{\frac{1}{3}})^n<(2^{\frac{1}{2}}-2^{\frac{1}{3}})(2^{\frac{1}{2}}-2^{\frac{1}{5}})\ldots(2^{\frac{1}{2}}-2^{\frac{1}{2n-1}})<(2^{\frac{1}{2}}-2^{\frac{1}{2n-1}})^n$

$$\Rightarrow \lim_{n\to\infty}(2^{\frac{1}{2}}-2^{\frac{1}{3}})^n<L<\lim_{n\to\infty}(2^{\frac{1}{2}}-2^{\frac{1}{2n-1}})^n$$

Since, $\lim_{n\to\infty}(2^{\frac{1}{2}}-2^{\frac{1}{3}})^n=0$ and $\lim_{n\to\infty}(2^{\frac{1}{2}}-2^{\frac{1}{2n-1}})^n=0$

$\therefore \quad L=0$

3. (a) We have,

$$\lim_{x\to\alpha}([x-5]-[2x+2])=0$$

$$[\alpha-5]-[2\alpha+2]=0$$

$$[\alpha-5]=[2\alpha+2] \quad \ldots(i)$$

For algebraic calculation,

$\alpha-5=2\alpha+2\Rightarrow\alpha=-7$

So, its value will be around -7

For $\alpha=-7.5$ in Eq. (i), we get

$$[-7.5-5]=[-15+2]$$

$\Rightarrow [-12.5]=[-13]\Rightarrow -13=-13$

$\Rightarrow$ True

For $\alpha=-6.5$ in Eq. (i), we get

$$[-6.5-5]=[-13+2]$$

$\Rightarrow [-11.5]=[-11]\Rightarrow -12\neq -11$

$\Rightarrow$ Not satisfies.

$\therefore$ The required range will be $\alpha\in[-7.5,-6.5)$

4. (b) Given expansion can be written as

$$=\lim_{n\to\infty}\frac{\sum_{r=1}^{n-1}(r^2-r)(n-r)}{\sum_{r=1}^{n}r^3-\sum_{r=1}^{n}r^2}$$

$$=\lim_{n\to\infty}\frac{\sum_{r=1}^{n-1}(-r^3+r^2(n+1)-nr)}{\left(\frac{n(n+1)}{2}\right)^2-\frac{n(n+1)(2n+1)}{6}}$$

$$= \lim_{n\to\infty} \frac{\frac{-n^2(n-1)^2}{4} + \frac{(n+1)(n-1)n(2n-1)}{6} - \frac{n^2}{2}(n-1)}{\frac{n(n+1)}{2}\left(\frac{n(n+1)}{2} - \frac{2n+1}{3}\right)}$$

$$= \lim_{n\to\infty} \frac{\frac{-3n(n-1)^2 + 2(n+1)(n-1)(2n-1) - 6n(n-1)}{12}}{\frac{(n+1)}{2}\frac{[3n(n+1) - 2(2n+1)]}{6}}$$

$$= \lim_{n\to\infty} \frac{(n-1)[-3n(n-1) + 2(2n^2 + 2n - n - 1) - 6n]}{(n+1)[3n^2 + 3n - 4n - 2]}$$

$$= \lim_{n\to\infty} \frac{(n-1)[-3n^2 + 3n + 4n^2 + 2n - 2 - 6n]}{(n+1)(3n^2 - n - 2)}$$

$$= \lim_{n\to\infty} \frac{(n-1)[n^2 - n - 2]}{(n+1)[3n^2 - n - 2]} = \frac{1}{3}$$

5. (a) $$\lim_{n\to\infty} \frac{(1+2-3)+(4+5-6)+\ldots+(3n-2)+(3n-1)-3n}{\sqrt{2n^4+4n+3} - \sqrt{n^4+5n+4}}$$

$$= \lim_{n\to\infty} \frac{0+3+6+9+12+\ldots+(3n-3)}{\sqrt{2n^4+4n+3} - \sqrt{n^4+5n+4}}$$

$$= \lim_{n\to\infty} \frac{\sum_{r=1}^{n}(3r-3)}{(\sqrt{2n^4+4n+3} - \sqrt{n^4+5n+4})}$$

$$= \lim_{n\to\infty} \frac{\frac{3\cdot n(n+1)}{2} - 3}{n^2\left(\sqrt{2+\frac{4}{n^3}+\frac{3}{n^4}} - \sqrt{1+\frac{5}{n^3}+\frac{4}{n^4}}\right)}$$

$$= \lim_{n\to\infty} \frac{\frac{3}{2}\left(1+\frac{1}{n}\right) - \frac{3}{n^2}}{\left(\sqrt{2+\frac{4}{n^3}+\frac{3}{n^4}} - \sqrt{1+\frac{5}{n^3}+\frac{4}{n^4}}\right)}$$

Put $n = \infty$, $$\frac{\frac{3}{2}(1+0) - 0}{(\sqrt{2+0+0} - \sqrt{1+0+0})}$$

$$= \frac{3}{2(\sqrt{2}-1)} = \frac{3}{2}(\sqrt{2}+1)$$

6. (c) Let $L =$

$$\lim_{x\to\infty} \frac{(\sqrt{3x+1}+\sqrt{3x-1})^6 + (\sqrt{3x+1}-\sqrt{3x-1})^6}{(x+\sqrt{x^2-1})^6 + (x-\sqrt{x^2-1})^6}x^3$$

Now, we know that $(a+b)^6 + (a-b)^6$

$$= 2\,({}^6C_0a^6 + {}^6C_2a^4b^2 + {}^6C_4a^2b^4 + {}^6C_6b^6)$$

$\therefore L =$

$$\lim_{x\to\infty} x^3\left[\frac{2[{}^6C_0(3x+1)^3 + {}^6C_2(3x+1)^2(3x-1) + {}^6C_4(3x+1)(3x-1)^2 + {}^6C_6(3x-1)^3]}{2[{}^6C_0x^6 + {}^6C_2x^4(x^2-1) + {}^6C_4x^2(x^2-1)^2 + {}^6C_6(x^2-1)^3]}\right]$$

$$= \lim_{x\to\infty} \frac{x^6\left[\left(3+\frac{1}{x}\right)^3 + 15\left(3+\frac{1}{x}\right)^2\left(3-\frac{1}{x}\right) + 15\left(3+\frac{1}{x}\right)\left(3-\frac{1}{x}\right)^2 + \left(3-\frac{1}{x}\right)^3\right]}{x^6\left[1 + 15\left(1-\frac{1}{x^2}\right) + 15\left(1-\frac{1}{x^2}\right)^2 + \left(1-\frac{1}{x^2}\right)^3\right]}$$

$$= \lim_{x\to\infty} \frac{\left[\left(3+\frac{1}{x}\right)^3 + 15\left(3+\frac{1}{x}\right)^2\left(3-\frac{1}{x}\right) + 15\left(3+\frac{1}{x}\right)\left(3-\frac{1}{x}\right)^2 + \left(3-\frac{1}{x}\right)^3\right]}{\left[1 + 15\left(1-\frac{1}{x^2}\right) + 15\left(1-\frac{1}{x^2}\right)^2 + \left(1-\frac{1}{x^2}\right)^3\right]}$$

$$= \frac{(3)^3 + 15(3)^2(3) + 15(3)(3)^2 + (3)^3}{1+15+15+1}$$

$$= \frac{27 + 405 + 405 + 27}{32} = \frac{864}{32} = 27$$

7. (81) $$\lim_{x\to 0} \frac{ax^2e^x - b\log_e(1+x) + cxe^{-x}}{x^2\sin x} = 1$$

$$\lim_{x\to 0} \frac{ax^2\left(1+x+\frac{x^2}{2!}+\frac{x^3}{3!}+\ldots\right) - b\left(x - \frac{x^2}{2} + \frac{x^3}{3} - \ldots\right) + cx\left(1 - x + \frac{x^2}{2!} - \frac{x^3}{3!} + \ldots\right)}{x^3\left(\frac{\sin x}{x}\right)} = 1$$

$$\Rightarrow \lim_{x\to 0} \frac{(c-b)\,x + \left(\frac{b}{2} - c + a\right)x^2 + \left(a - \frac{b}{3} + \frac{c}{2}\right)x^3 + \ldots}{x^3} = 1$$

$$c - b = 0 \quad \ldots\text{(i)}$$

$$\frac{b}{2} - c + a = 0 \quad \ldots\text{(ii)}$$

$$a - \frac{b}{3} + \frac{c}{2} = 1 \quad \ldots\text{(iii)}$$

From Eqs. (i), (ii) and (iii), we get

$$a = \frac{3}{4},\ b = c = \frac{3}{2}$$

$$\therefore 16(a^2 + b^2 + c^2) = 16\left(\frac{9}{16} + \frac{9}{4} + \frac{9}{4}\right) = 9 + 72 = 81$$

8. (26) $$\sum_{n=0}^{\infty} \frac{n^3((2n)!) + (2n-1)(n!)}{(n!)((2n)!)}$$

$$= \sum_{n=0}^{\infty}\frac{1}{(n-3)!} + \sum_{n=0}^{\infty}\frac{3}{(n-2)!} + \sum_{n=0}^{\infty}\frac{1}{(n-1)!} + \sum_{n=0}^{\infty}\frac{1}{(2n-1)!} - \sum_{n=0}^{\infty}\frac{1}{(2n)!}$$

$$= e + 3e + e + \frac{1}{2}\left(e - \frac{1}{e}\right) - \frac{1}{2}\left(e + \frac{1}{e}\right)$$

$$= 5e - \frac{1}{e} = ae + \frac{b}{e} + c, \text{ where } a, b, c \in z$$

On comparing $a = 5, b = -1, c = 0$,

$$a^2 - b + c = 25 - (-1) - 0 = 26$$

9. (d) $$\lim_{x\to 0} \frac{e^{2|\sin x|} - 2|\sin x| - 1}{x^2}$$

$$\because\ e^x = 1 + x + \frac{x^2}{2!} + \frac{x^3}{3!} + \ldots$$

$$\therefore e^{2|\sin x|} = 1 + 2|\sin x| + \frac{(2|\sin x|)^2}{2!} + \frac{(2|\sin x|)^3}{3!} + \ldots$$

$$\therefore \lim_{x\to 0} = \frac{1 + 2|\sin x| + \frac{4|\sin x|^2}{2!} + \frac{8|\sin x|^3}{3!} + \ldots - 2|\sin x| - 1}{x^2}$$

$$= \lim_{x\to 0} \frac{|\sin x|^2}{x^2}\left[\frac{4}{2!} + \frac{8}{3!}|\sin x| + \ldots\right]$$

$$= \lim_{x\to 0} \frac{\sin^2 x}{x^2}\left[\frac{4}{2!} + \frac{8}{3!}|\sin x| + \ldots\right] = \frac{4}{2!} = 2$$

10. (c) $\lim_{x\to 0}\left[\left(\frac{1-\cos^2 3x}{\cos^3 4x}\right)\left(\frac{\sin^3 4x}{[\log_e(2x+1)]^5}\right)\right]$

$$= \lim_{x\to 0}\left[\frac{\sin^2 3x}{(3x)^2} \times \frac{\sin^3 4x}{(4x)^3} \times \frac{1}{\cos^3 4x} \times \frac{1}{\left[\frac{\log(1+2x)}{2x}\right]^5} \times \frac{3^2 \cdot 4^3}{2^5}\right]$$

$$= \frac{3^2 \cdot 4^3}{2^5} = 9 \times 2 = 18$$

11. (b) Let $L = \lim_{t\to 0}\left(1^{\frac{1}{\sin^2 t}} + 2^{\frac{1}{\sin^2 t}} + \ldots + n^{\frac{1}{\sin^2 t}}\right)^{\sin^2 t}$

$$= \lim_{t\to 0} n\left[\left(\frac{1}{n}\right)^{\operatorname{cosec}^2 t} + \left(\frac{2}{n}\right)^{\operatorname{cosec}^2 t} + \left(\frac{3}{n}\right)^{\operatorname{cosec}^2 t} + \ldots + \left(\frac{n-1}{n}\right)^{\operatorname{cosec}^2 t} + \left(\frac{n}{n}\right)^{\operatorname{cosec}^2 t}\right]^{\sin^2 t}$$

$$= \lim_{t\to 0} n \cdot [0 + 0 + 0 + 0 + \ldots + 0 + 1]^{\sin^2 t}$$

[$\because a^x \to 0$, when $x \to \infty$; $0 < a < 1$]

$= n$ [$\because$ (exact 1)$^{\text{(tends to zero)}}$ = always one]

12. (b) Given, $\lim_{x\to 0} \frac{3 + \alpha \sin x + \beta \cos x + \log_e(1-x)}{3\tan^2 x} = \frac{1}{3}$

$$\Rightarrow \lim_{x\to 0} \frac{3 + \alpha \sin x + \beta \cos x + \log e(1-x)}{\frac{3\tan^2 x}{x^2} \times x^2} = \frac{1}{3}$$

For limit to be exist, $\beta + 3 = 0 \Rightarrow \beta = -3$

$$\text{So, } \lim_{x\to 0} \frac{\alpha \cos x - \beta \sin x - \frac{1}{1-x}}{(2x)} = 1$$

[using L' Hospital rule and $\lim_{x\to 0}\left(\frac{\tan x}{x}\right)^2 = 1$]

For limit to be exist, numerator $\to 0$

$\Rightarrow \quad \alpha - 0 - 1 = 0 \Rightarrow \alpha = 1$

[for method (2) to solve this question is 'using expansion technique']

Hence, $2\alpha - \beta = 2 \times 1 - (-3) = 5$

13. (d) Given, $\lim_{x\to 0} \frac{e^{ax} - \cos(bx) - \frac{cxe^{-cx}}{2}}{1 - \cos 2x} = 17$

On expansion above, we get

$$\Rightarrow \lim_{x\to 0} \frac{\left(1 + ax + \frac{a^2x^2}{2!} + \ldots\right) - \left(1 - \frac{x^2b^2}{2!} + \ldots\right) - \frac{cx}{2}\left(1 - cx + \frac{c^2x^2}{2!}\ldots\right)}{1 - 1 + \frac{4x^2}{2!} + \ldots} = 17$$

[all the neighbour terms are negligible]

$$\Rightarrow \lim_{x\to 0} \frac{\left(a - \frac{c}{2}\right)x + x^2\left(\frac{a^2}{2} + \frac{b^2}{2} + \frac{c^2}{2}\right)}{2x^2} = 17$$

If above limit exist, then $a - \frac{c}{2} = 0$

$$a = \frac{c}{2} \Rightarrow c = 2a \text{ and } \frac{\frac{a^2}{2} + \frac{b^2}{2} + \frac{c^2}{2}}{2} = 17$$

$$\Rightarrow \frac{a^2 + b^2 + c^2}{4} = 17 \Rightarrow a^2 + b^2 + 4a^2 = 68 \; [\because c = 2a]$$

$$\Rightarrow \quad 5a^2 + b^2 = 68$$

14. (d) $x = 2$ is a root of $x^2 + px + q = 0$

$\Rightarrow \; 2^2 + 2p + q = 0 \Rightarrow q + 4 = -2p$ ...(i)

$\therefore \; q^2 + 8q + 16 = (q+4)^2 = 4p^2$ ...(ii)

and $x^2 - 4px + (q^2 + 8q + 16)$

$= x^2 - 4px + 4p^2 = (x - 2p)^2$ ...(iii)

$$f(x) = \begin{cases} \frac{1 - \cos(x^2 - 4px + q^2 + 8q + 16)}{(x-2p)^4}, & x \neq 2p \\ 0 & x = 2p \end{cases}$$

$$\Rightarrow f(x) = \begin{cases} \frac{1 - \cos(x-2p)^2}{(x-2p)^4}, & x \neq 2p \\ 0, & x = 2p \end{cases}$$

Now, as $x \to 2p^+$, $x - 2p \to 0^+$

$\therefore \lim_{x\to 2p^+} f(x) = \frac{1}{2}$ $\left[\because \lim_{y\to 0} \frac{1 - \cos y}{y^2} = \frac{1}{2}\right]$

Hence, $\lim_{x\to 2p^+} [f(x)] = 0$, where [.] is the greatest integer function.

Chapter-13

Statistics

1. (i) Mean $= \dfrac{2+9+5+6+4}{5} = \dfrac{26}{5} = 5.2$

(ii) Mean $= \dfrac{7+17+9+10+8+13+6}{7} = \dfrac{70}{7} = 10$

(iii) Mean $= \dfrac{9+13+4+11+20+16+10+5}{8} = \dfrac{88}{8} = 11$

(iv) Mean $= \dfrac{1+0+1+(-1)+2+3}{6} = \dfrac{6}{6} = 1$

2. (i) (True)

Arranging the following data in ascending order

56, 63, 72, 80, 124, 163, 180

Number of observation, $n = 7$ (odd)

Then, the median is $\left(\dfrac{n+1}{2}\right)$th observation

$= \left(\dfrac{7+1}{2}\right)$th observation

= 4th observation

Median = 80

(ii) (False)

Given, data 24, 69, 57, 102.

First, arranging the following data in ascending order

24, 57, 69, 102

Number of observations $(n) = 4$ (even)

Then, the median is mean of $\left(\dfrac{n}{2}\right)$th and $\left(\dfrac{n}{2}+1\right)$th observations.

$=$ mean of $\left(\dfrac{4}{2}\right)$th and $\left(\dfrac{4}{2}+1\right)$th observations

= mean of 2nd and 3rd observations

= mean of 57 and 69

[∵ 2nd observation = 57 and 3rd observation = 69]

$= \dfrac{57+69}{2} = 63$

Thus, the median of the following data is 63.

3. (b) Number of matches, $n = 5$ (odd)

Arranging the data in ascending order

21, 35, 44, 45, 55

Median $= \left(\dfrac{n+1}{2}\right)$th observation

$= \dfrac{5+1}{2} =$ 3rd observation

∵ 3rd observation is 44

So, median = 44

4. Arranging the data in ascending order

12, 14, 56, 60, 72, 80, 126

Mean $= \dfrac{12+14+56+60+72+80+126}{7}$

$= \dfrac{420}{7} = 60$

Number of observation, $n = 7$ (odd)

Median $= \left(\dfrac{n+1}{2}\right)$th observation

= 4th observation

$= 60$

Hence, the required sum $= 60 + 60 = 120$

5. (i) Yes, (ii) Yes, (iii) Yes, (iv) Yes

6. (False)

The range of a series is

= Maximum value – Minimum value

7. (i) We know that

Range = Maximum value – Minimum value

$= 4 - (-2)$

$= 6$

(ii) Range = Maximum value – Minimum value

Maximum value in data set = 96

Minimum value in data set = 2

Range $= 96 - 2 = 94$

(iii) Range $= 9 - (-1)$

$= 10$

(iv) Range $= 104 - 100 = 4$

8. (i) Mean of the data $= \dfrac{6+10+12+14+5+7}{6} = \dfrac{54}{6} = 9$

Absolute values of deviations are $|x_i - \bar{x}|$

$= |6-9|, |10-9|, |12-9|, |14-9|, |5-9|, |7-9|$

$= 3, 1, 3, 5, 4, 2$

(ii) Mean of the data $= \dfrac{15+8+7+4+6+11+5+16}{8}$

$= \dfrac{72}{8} = 9$

Absolute values of deviations are $|x_i - \bar{x}|$

$= |15-9|, |8-9|, |7-9|, |4-9|$
$|6-9|, |11-9|, |5-9|, |16-9|$

$= 6, 1, 2, 5, 3, 2, 4, 7$

9. (i) Mean of the given data is

$\bar{x} = \dfrac{2+5+2+3+(-4)+(-2)}{6} = \dfrac{6}{6} = 1$

Absolute values of the deviations are

$|x_i - \bar{x}| = 1, 4, 1, 2, 5, 3$

$\text{MD} = \dfrac{\sum_{i=1}^{6}(x_i - \bar{x})}{6}$

$= \dfrac{1+4+1+2+5+3}{6} = \dfrac{16}{6} = 2.67$

(ii) Mean of the given data is

$\bar{x} = \dfrac{-1+0+2+3+(-1)+1+0+2+3+1}{10}$

$= \dfrac{10}{10} = 1$

Absolute values of the deviations are

$|x_i - \bar{x}| = 2, 1, 1, 2, 2, 0, 1, 1, 2, 0$

$$MD = \frac{\sum_{i=1}^{10} |x_i - \bar{x}|}{10}$$
$$= \frac{2+1+1+2+2+0+1+1+2+0}{10}$$
$$= \frac{12}{10} = 1.2$$

(iii) Mean of the given data is
$$\bar{x} = \frac{5+8+10+13+4+6+9+17+18}{9}$$
$$= \frac{90}{9} = 10$$
Absolute values of the deviations are
$|x_i - \bar{x}| = 5, 2, 0, 3, 6, 4, 1, 7, 8$
$$\therefore \quad MD = \frac{\sum_{i=1}^{9} |x_i - \bar{x}|}{9}$$
$$= \frac{5+2+0+3+6+4+1+7+8}{9}$$
$$= \frac{36}{9} = 4$$

10. (i) Total number of observations = 6 (even)
First, arranging the data in ascending order
$-2, -1, 1, 1, 1, 2$
Median, M = Mean of $\left(\frac{6}{2}\right)$th and $\left(\frac{6}{2}+1\right)$th observations
= Mean of 3rd and 4th observations
$$= \frac{1+1}{2} = \frac{2}{2} = 1$$
Absolute values of the deviations are
$|x_i - M| = 3, 2, 0, 0, 0, 1$
$$\Rightarrow \quad MD = \frac{1}{6}\sum_{i=1}^{6} |x_i - M|$$
$$= \frac{1}{6} \times 6 = 1$$

(ii) Total number of observations = 11 (odd)
Arranging the data in ascending order
4, 6, 7, 8, 9, 10, 12, 14, 18, 19, 21
Median, $M = \left(\frac{11+1}{2}\right)$th observation
= 6th observation = 10
Absolute values of the deviations are
= 6, 4, 3, 2, 1, 0, 2, 4, 8, 9, 11
$$\sum_{i=1}^{11} |x_i - M| = 50$$
$$\therefore \text{ Mean deviation} = \frac{1}{11}\sum_{i=1}^{11} |x_i - M|$$
$$= \frac{1}{11} \times 50 = 4.55$$

11. (i) $N = \sum_{i=1}^{5} f_i = 4+3+9+2+2 = 20$
$$\bar{x} = \frac{\sum_{i=1}^{5} f_i x_i}{N}$$
$$= \frac{8+18+0+(-10)+4}{20} = \frac{20}{20} = 1$$

x_i	f_i	$\lvert x_i - \bar{x}\rvert$	$f_i\lvert x_i - \bar{x}\rvert$
2	4	1	4
6	3	5	15
0	9	1	9
–5	2	6	12
2	2	1	2
	$N = 20$		$\sum_{i=1}^{5} f_i\lvert x_i - \bar{x}\rvert = 42$

$$\text{Mean deviation about mean} = \frac{\sum_{i=1}^{5} f_i |x_i - \bar{x}|}{N}$$
$$= \frac{42}{20} = 2.1$$

(ii) $N = \sum_{i=1}^{6} f_i = 4+8+20+6+7+5$
$= 50$
$$\bar{x} = \frac{\sum_{i=1}^{6} f_i x_i}{N}$$
$$= \frac{4\times3+8\times5+20\times2+6\times8+7\times10+5\times18}{50}$$
$$= \frac{300}{50} = 6$$

x_i	f_i	$\lvert x_i - \bar{x}\rvert$	$\sum_{i=1}^{6} f_i\lvert x_i - \bar{x}\rvert$
3	4	3	12
5	8	1	8
2	20	4	80
8	6	2	12
10	7	4	28
18	5	12	60
	$N = 50$		$\sum_{i=1}^{6} f_i\lvert x_i - \bar{x}\rvert = 200$

$$\text{Mean deviation about mean} = \frac{\sum_{i=1}^{6} f_i |x_i - \bar{x}|}{N}$$
$$= \frac{200}{50} = 4$$

12. (i) (False)

Weight (x_i)	Items (f_i)	cf
1	6	6
2	2	8
3	3	11
4	4	15

$N = \Sigma f_i = 15$ (odd)

Median of the data, M = Value of $\left(\frac{15+1}{2}\right)$th observation i.e. 8th observation = 2 kg

$\|x_i - M\|$	1	0	1	2
f_i	6	2	3	4
$f_i\|x_i - M\|$	6	0	3	8

$$\sum_{i=1}^{4} f_i|x_i - M| = 17$$

Mean deviation about median $= \frac{1}{N}\sum_{i=1}^{4} f_i|x_i - M|$

$= \frac{1}{15} \times 17 = 1.13$

(ii) (True)

Height (in cm) (x_i)	Number of students (f_i)	Cumulative frequency
147	8	8
148	12	20
150	15	35
152	10	45
155	5	50
	$N = 50$ (even)	

Median of the data, M

= average of 25th and 26th observation

$= \frac{\text{25th observation + 26th observation}}{2}$

$= \frac{150+150}{2} = 150$ cm

$\|x_i - M\|$	3	2	0	2	5
f_i	8	12	15	10	5
$f_i\|x_i - M\|$	24	24	0	20	25

$$\sum_{i=1}^{5} f_i|x_i - M| = 93$$

Mean deviation about median $= \frac{1}{N}\sum_{i=1}^{5} f_i|x_i - M|$

$= \frac{93}{50} = 1.86$

13. (i)

Distance	Mid-values (x_i)	Number of people (f_i)	$f_i x_i$	$\|x_i - \bar{x}\|$	$f_i\|x_i - \bar{x}\|$
0-5	2.5	4	10	6.7	26.8
5-10	7.5	2	15	1.7	3.4
10-15	12.5	4	50	3.3	13.2
15-20	17.5	2	35	8.3	16.6
		$N = \Sigma f_i = 12$	$\Sigma f_i x_i = 110$		$\Sigma f_i\|x_i - \bar{x}\| = 60$

$\therefore \quad \bar{x} = \frac{\Sigma f_i x_i}{N} = \frac{110}{12} = 9.2$ (approx)

$\Rightarrow$ Mean deviation about mean $= \frac{1}{N}\Sigma f_i|x_i - \bar{x}|$

$= \frac{1}{12} \times 60 = 5$

(ii)

Classes	Mid-values (x_i)	Frequency (f_i)	$f_i x_i$	$\|x_i - \bar{x}\|$	$f_i\|x_i - \bar{x}\|$
30-40	35	2	70	16.7	33.4
40-50	45	4	180	6.7	26.8
50-60	55	3	165	3.3	9.9
60-70	65	2	130	13.3	26.6
70-80	75	1	75	23.3	23.3
		$N = \Sigma f_i = 12$	$\Sigma f_i x_i = 620$		$\Sigma f_i\|x_i - \bar{x}\| = 120$

$\therefore \quad \bar{x} = \frac{\Sigma f_i x_i}{N} = \frac{620}{12} = 51.7$

Mean deviation about mean $= \frac{1}{N}\Sigma f_i|x_i - \bar{x}|$

$= \frac{1}{12} \times 120 = 10$

14. (d) For the following data $h = 10$.

Let the assumed mean be $A = 35$

Age	Number of people (f_i)	Mid-points (x_i)	$d_i = \frac{x_i - A}{10}$	$f_i d_i$	$\|x_i - \bar{x}\|$	$f_i\|x_i - \bar{x}\|$
10-20	5	15	−2	−10	21	105
20-30	12	25	−1	−12	11	132
30-40	7	35 = A	0	0	1	7
40-50	8	45	1	8	9	72
50-60	6	55	2	12	19	114
60-70	2	65	3	6	29	58
	$N = \Sigma f_i = 40$			$\Sigma f_i d_i = 4$		$\Sigma f_i\|x_i - \bar{x}\| = 488$

$$\bar{x} = A + \left\{\frac{\Sigma f_i d_i}{N} \times h\right\}$$

$$= 35 + \left\{\frac{4}{40} \times 10\right\} = 36$$

$$\text{Mean deviation} = \frac{\Sigma f_i |x_i - \bar{x}|}{N}$$

$$= \frac{488}{40} = 12.2$$

15. (i)

Quantity of students	Mid-points (x_i)	School buses (f_i)	Cumulative frequency (c)	$\|x_i - M\|$	$f_i\|x_i - M\|$
0-10	5	3	3	10	30
10-20	15	2	5	0	0
20-30	25	1	6	10	10
30-40	35	1	7	20	20
40-50	45	1	8	30	30
		$N = \Sigma f_i = 8$			$\Sigma f_i\|x_i - M\| = 90$

$\therefore \frac{N}{2} = 4$

So, the median class 10-20

$\Rightarrow L = 10, f = 2, h = 10$ and $C = 3$

$$\therefore \text{Median, } M = L + \frac{\frac{N}{2} - C}{f} \times h$$

$$= 10 + \frac{4-3}{2} \times 10 = 15$$

$$\text{MD about median} = \frac{1}{N} \Sigma f_i |x_i - M|$$

$$= \frac{1}{8} \times 90 = 11.25$$

(ii)

Marks obtained	Number of students (f_i)	Cumulative frequency (c)	Mid-points (x_i)
15-25	9	9	20
25-35	13	22	30
35-45	25	47	40
45-55	30	77	50
55-65	13	90	60
65-75	10	100	70
	$N = \Sigma f_i = 100$		

$\because \quad N = 100$

$\Rightarrow \quad \frac{N}{2} = 50$

$\therefore$ Median class $= 45 - 55$, $L = 45$, $f = 30$, $h = 10$ and $C = 47$

$$\text{Median, } M = L + \frac{\left(\frac{N}{2} - C\right)}{f} \times h$$

$$= 45 + \frac{(50-47)}{30} \times 10$$

$$= 45 + 1 = 46$$

$\therefore \quad M = 46$

f_i	x_i	$\|x_i - M\|$	$f_i\|x_i - M\|$
9	20	26	234
13	30	16	208
25	40	6	150
30	50	4	120
13	60	14	182
10	70	24	240
$N = 100$			$\Sigma f_i\|x_i - M\| = 1134$

$$\therefore \text{Mean deviation} = \frac{\Sigma f_i |x_i - M|}{N}$$

$$= \frac{1134}{100} = 11.34$$

16. (i)

Age	Mid-points (x_i)	Students (f_i)	Cumulative frequency (C)	$\|x_i - M\|$	$f_i\|x_i - M\|$
0.5-5.5	3	2	2	6	12
5.5-10.5	8	5	7	1	5
10.5-15.5	13	1	8	4	4
15.5-20.5	18	3	11	9	27
		$N = \Sigma f_i$, $N = 11$			$\Sigma f_i\|x_i - M\| = 48$

$\therefore \frac{N}{2} = \frac{11}{2} = 5.5$

Median class = 5.5-10.5

Thus, $L = 5.5$, $f = 5$, $h = 5$ and $C = 2$

$$\therefore \text{Median, } M = L + \frac{\frac{N}{2} - C}{f} \times h$$

$$= 5.5 + \frac{5.5 - 2}{5} \times 5$$

$$= 5.5 + 3.5$$

$\Rightarrow \quad M = 9$

Mean deviation about median

$$= \frac{1}{N} \Sigma f_i |x_i - M|$$

$$= \frac{1}{11} \times 48$$

$$= 4.4$$

(ii)

Classes	Frequency (f_i)	Cumulative frequency (c)	Mid-points (x_i)
55.5-60.5	8	8	58
60.5-65.5	6	14	63
65.5-70.5	12	26	68
70.5-75.5	28	54	73
75.5-80.5	16	70	78
	$N = 70$		

Here, $N = 70$

So, $\frac{N}{2} = \frac{70}{2} = 35$

Median class $= 70.5 - 75.5$,

$L = 70.5, f = 28, h = 5$ and $C = 26$

$$\text{Median, } M = L + \frac{\frac{N}{2} - C}{f} \times h$$

$$= 70.5 + \frac{35-26}{28} \times 5$$

$$= 70.5 + 1.6$$

$$= 72.1$$

f_i	x_i	$\lvert x_i - M \rvert$	$f_i \lvert x_i - M \rvert$
8	58	14.1	112.8
6	63	9.1	54.6
12	68	4.1	49.2
28	73	0.9	25.2
16	78	5.9	94.4
$N = 70$			$\Sigma f_i \lvert x_i - M \rvert = 336.2$

$$\text{Mean deviation} = \frac{336.2}{70} = 4.8$$

17. True, because median $M >$ mean $\bar{x}$ so

$$\frac{\Sigma f_i | x_i - \bar{x}|}{N} > \frac{\Sigma f_i (x_i - M)}{N}$$

18. (i) First n natural numbers are 1, 2, 3, ..., n

$$\text{Mean, } \bar{x} = \frac{1 + 2 + 3 + ... + n}{n}$$

$$= \frac{1}{n} \cdot \frac{1}{2} n(n+1) = \frac{1}{2}(n+1)$$

$$\text{Variance, } \sigma^2 = \frac{1}{n} \sum_{i=1}^{n} (x_i - \bar{x})^2$$

$$= \frac{1}{n} \sum_{i=1}^{n} x_i^2 - \frac{1}{n} \cdot 2 \sum_{i=1}^{n} \left(\frac{n+1}{2}\right) x_i + \frac{1}{n} \sum_{i=1}^{n} \left(\frac{n+1}{2}\right)^2$$

$$= \frac{(n+1)(2n+1)}{6} - \frac{(n+1)^2}{2} + \frac{(n+1)^2}{4}$$

$$\left[\because \Sigma x_i^2 = \frac{n(n+1)(2n+1)}{6} \text{ and } \Sigma x_i = \frac{n(n+1)}{2}\right]$$

$$= \frac{(n+1)(2n+1)}{6} - \frac{(n+1)^2}{4}$$

$$= (n+1)\left[\frac{2n+1}{6} - \frac{n+1}{4}\right]$$

$$= \frac{(n+1)(n-1)}{12} = \frac{n^2-1}{12}$$

(ii) From the above part,

the variance of first n natural numbers is $\frac{n^2-1}{12}$.

$\therefore \quad \frac{n^2-1}{12} = 10$

$\Rightarrow \quad n^2 = 120 + 1 \Rightarrow n = 11$

Let m even natural numbers be 2, 4, 6, 8, ... , $2m$

$$\Rightarrow \text{Mean, } \bar{x} = \frac{2 + 4 + 6 + ... + 2m}{m}$$

$$= \frac{2m(m+1)}{2m} = m + 1$$

Variance of m even natural numbers,

$$\sigma^2 = \frac{2^2 + 4^2 + 6^2 + ... + (2m)^2}{m} - (m+1)^2$$

$$= \frac{1}{m} \times 2^2 [1^2 + 2^2 + ... + m^2] - (m+1)^2$$

$$= \frac{4}{m} \times \frac{m(m+1)(2m+1)}{6} - (m+1)^2$$

$$= \frac{m^2-1}{3}$$

$\Rightarrow \quad \frac{m^2-1}{3} = 16$ [given]

$m^2 - 1 = 48, m = 7$

$\therefore \quad m + n = 11 + 7 = 18$

19. (False)

Let $\bar{x}$ be the mean of $x_1, x_2, x_3 \dots x_n$

$$\bar{x} = \frac{1}{n}(x_1 + x_2 + x_3 + ... + x_n)$$

Let $y_i = x_i + a$ for each $i = 1, 2, 3, ..., n$

$\bar{y}$ be the mean of $y_1, y_2, y_3 \cdots y_n$

$$\bar{y} = \frac{1}{n}(y_1 + y_2 + y_3 + ... y_n)$$

$$= \frac{1}{n}(x_1 + a + x_2 + a + x_3 + a + ... + x_n + a)$$

$$= \frac{1}{n}(x_1 + x_2 + x_3 + ... + x_n) + \frac{1}{n}$$

$(a + a + ... + n \text{ times})$

$$= \bar{x} + \frac{1}{n} \times na = \bar{x} + a$$

$$\bar{y} = \bar{x} + a$$

Variance of new observation, $y_i\ (\sigma^2) = \frac{1}{n}\sum_{i=1}^{n}(y_i - \bar{y})^2$

$$= \frac{1}{n}\sum_{i=1}^{n}\{(x_i + a) - (\bar{x} + a)\}^2$$

$$= \frac{1}{n}\cdot\sum_{i=1}^{n}(x_i + a - \bar{x} - a)^2$$

Variance $y_i = \frac{1}{n}\cdot\sum_{i=1}^{n}(x_i - \bar{x})^2 =$ Variance x_i

From the calculation, the variance of new observation is same as original.

20. (False)

The observations are

4, 8, 12, 16, 20, 24, 28, 32, 36, 40

Here, $n = 10$

Mean, $\bar{x} = \frac{4 + 8 + \ldots + 40}{10}$

$$= \frac{4(1 + 2 + \ldots + 10)}{10} = \frac{4}{10}\times\frac{10(10+1)}{2} = 22$$

x_i	$x_i - \bar{x}$	$(x_i - \bar{x})^2$
4	– 18	324
8	– 14	196
12	– 10	100
16	– 6	36
20	– 2	4
24	2	4
28	6	36
32	10	100
36	14	196
40	18	324
	$\Sigma x_i - \bar{x} = 0$	$\Sigma(x_i - \bar{x})^2 = 1320$

Variance, $\sigma^2 = \frac{1}{n}\Sigma(x_i - \bar{x})^2$

$$= \frac{1}{10}\times 1320 = 132$$

21. Let the remaining two observations are x and y.

Mean $= \frac{7 + 8 + 12 + 13 + 17 + x + y}{7} = 10$

$\Rightarrow \quad 57 + x + y = 70 \Rightarrow x + y = 13 \quad \ldots(i)$

Given, variance $= 16$

$\therefore \frac{1}{7}(7^2 + 8^2 + 12^2 + 13^2 + 17^2 + x^2 + y^2) - 10^2 = 16$

$\Rightarrow \quad 715 + x^2 + y^2 = 812$

$\Rightarrow \quad x^2 + y^2 = 97$

Since, $(x + y)^2 + (x - y)^2 = 2(x^2 + y^2)$

$\Rightarrow \quad (x - y)^2 = 2\times 97 - (13)^2$ [by Eq. (i)]

$$= 194 - 169 = 25$$

$$x - y = \pm 5$$

So, when $x + y = 13$ and $x - y = 5$, then $x = 9$, $y = 4$

When $x + y = 13$ and $x - y = -5$, then $x = 4$, $y = 9$

Hence, the remaining two observations are 4 and 9.

22. (b) Let the given observations are

x_1, x_2, x_3, x_4, x_5 and x_6.

Mean = 7

$\Rightarrow \quad \frac{1}{6}(x_1 + x_2 + x_3 + x_4 + x_5 + x_6) = 7$

$$x_1 + x_2 + x_3 + x_4 + x_5 + x_6 = 42$$

Given, variance = 14

$\Rightarrow \frac{1}{6}(x_1^2 + x_2^2 + x_3^2 + x_4^2 + x_5^2 + x_6^2) - 7^2 = 14$

$$(x_1^2 + x_2^2 + x_3^2 + x_4^2 + x_5^2 + x_6^2) = 378$$

When each observation is multiplied by 3, then new observations are

$$3x_1, 3x_2, 3x_3, 3x_4, 3x_5 \text{ and } 3x_6$$

New mean $= \frac{1}{6}(3x_1 + 3x_2 + 3x_3 + 3x_4 + 3x_5 + 3x_6)$

$$= \frac{3}{6}(x_1 + x_2 + x_3 + x_4 + x_5 + x_6)$$

$$= \frac{1}{2}\times 42 = 21$$

New variance

$$= \frac{(3x_1)^2 + (3x_2)^2 + (3x_3)^2 + (3x_4)^2 + (3x_5)^2 + (3x_6)^2}{6} - (21)^2$$

$$= \frac{9}{6}(x_1^2 + x_2^2 + x_3^2 + x_4^2 + x_5^2 + x_6^2) - 441$$

$$= \frac{9}{6}\times 378 - 441$$

$$= 567 - 441 = 126$$

New mean = 21 and new variance = 126

23. Let the assumed mean $A = 12$, $h = 2$ and number of observations, $n = 10$

x_i	$d_i = \frac{x_i - A}{h}$	$x_i - \bar{x}$	$(x_i - \bar{x})^2$
4	– 4	– 9	81
6	– 3	– 7	49
8	– 2	– 5	25
10	– 1	– 3	9
12	0	– 1	1
14	1	1	1
16	2	3	9
18	3	5	25
20	4	7	49
22	5	9	81
	$\Sigma d_i = 5$		$\Sigma(x_i - \bar{x})^2 = 330$

$$\bar{x} = A + \frac{\Sigma di}{n} \times h$$
$$= 12 + \frac{5}{10} \times 2 = 13$$
$$\text{Variance, } \sigma^2 = \frac{1}{n}\sum_{i=1}^{10} (x_i - \bar{x})^2$$
$$= \frac{1}{10} \times 330 = 33$$
$$\text{SD, } \sigma = \sqrt{33} = 5.74$$

24. Let the assumed mean be $A = 7.5$

Size of item (x_i)	f_i	$d_i = x_i - A$	d_i^2	$f_i d_i^2$	$f_i d_i$
4.5	4	− 3	9	36	− 12
5.5	8	− 2	4	32	− 16
6.5	23	− 1	1	23	− 23
7.5	62	0	0	0	0
8.5	85	1	1	85	85
9.5	32	2	4	128	64
10.5	11	3	9	99	33
	$N = \Sigma f_i = 225$			$\Sigma f_i d_i^2 = 403$	$\Sigma f_i d_i = 131$

$$\text{Variance, } \sigma^2 = \left(\frac{1}{N}\Sigma f_i d_i^2\right) - \left(\frac{1}{N}\Sigma f_i d_i\right)^2$$
$$= \frac{1}{225} \times 403 - \left(\frac{131}{225}\right)^2 = 1.45$$
$$\text{SD, } \sigma = \sqrt{1.45} = 1.2$$

(i) False (ii) True (iii) False (iv) True

25. (d) $\bar{x} = \dfrac{66 + 68 + 58 + 46 + 48 + 55 + 60 + 72 + 80 + 37}{10}$

$$= \frac{590}{10} = 59$$

x_i	$x_i - \bar{x}$	$(x_i - \bar{x})^2$
66	7	49
68	9	81
58	− 1	1
46	− 13	169
48	− 11	121
55	− 4	16
60	1	1
72	13	169
80	21	441
37	− 22	484
		$\Sigma(x_i - \bar{x})^2 = 1532$

$$\text{Variance, } \sigma^2 = \frac{1}{N}\Sigma(x_i - \bar{x})^2 = \frac{1532}{10} = 153.2$$
$$\text{SD, } \sigma = \sqrt{153.2} = 12.38$$

26. (True)

Let the assumed mean be $A = 35.5$ and $h = 10$

x_i	f_i	$d_i = x_i - A$	$u_i = \frac{x_i - A}{h}$	$f_i u_i$	u_i^2	$f_i u_i^2$
5.5	2	− 30	− 3	− 6	9	18
15.5	6	− 20	− 2	− 12	4	24
25.5	13	− 10	− 1	−13	1	13
35.5	23	0	0	0	0	0
45.5	18	10	1	18	1	18
55.5	10	20	2	20	4	40
65.5	5	30	3	15	9	45
	$N = \Sigma f_i = 77$			$\Sigma f_i u_i = 22$		$\Sigma f_i u_i^2 = 158$

$$\text{Variance, } \sigma^2 = h^2\left[\left(\frac{1}{N}\Sigma f_i u_i^2\right) - \left(\frac{1}{N}\Sigma f_i u_i\right)^2\right]$$
$$= 100\left[\frac{1}{77} \times 158 - \left(\frac{22}{77}\right)^2\right]$$
$$= 197$$
$$\text{SD, } \sigma = \sqrt{197} = 14.03$$

27. (d) Let the assumed mean $A = 45$ and $h = 10$

Class interval	f_i	Mid-values (x_i)	$u_i = \frac{x_i - A}{h}$	$f_i u_i$	u_i^2	$f_i u_i^2$
10-20	4	15	− 3	− 12	9	36
20-30	7	25	− 2	− 14	4	28
30-40	12	35	− 1	− 12	1	12
40-50	16	45	0	0	0	0
50-60	14	55	1	14	1	14
60-70	6	65	2	12	4	24
70-80	5	75	3	15	9	45
	$N = \Sigma f_i = 64$			$\Sigma f_i u_i = 3$		$\Sigma f_i u_i^2 = 159$

$$\text{Variance, } \sigma^2 = h^2\left[\frac{1}{N}\Sigma f_i u_i^2 - \left(\frac{1}{N}\Sigma f_i u_i\right)^2\right]$$
$$= 100\left[\frac{159}{64} - \left(\frac{3}{64}\right)^2\right] = 248.23$$
$$\text{SD, } \sigma = \sqrt{248.23} = 15.75$$

28. Let the assumed mean $A = 6$, $h = 2$ and number of observations $(n) = 6$

x_i	$d_i = \frac{x_i - A}{h}$	$x_i - \bar{x}$	$(x_i - \bar{x})^2$
2	−2	−5	25
4	−1	−3	9
6	0	−1	1
8	1	1	1
10	2	3	9
12	3	5	25
	$\Sigma d_i = 3$		$\Sigma(x_i - \bar{x})^2 = 70$

(i) Mean, $\bar{x} = A + \frac{\Sigma d_i \times h}{n}$

$= 6 + \frac{3 \times 2}{6} = 7$

(ii) Variance, $\sigma^2 = \frac{1}{n}\Sigma(x_i - \bar{x})^2$

$= \frac{1}{6} \times 70$

$= 11.67$

(iii) SD, $\sigma = \sqrt{11.67}$

$= 3.4$

29. (i) Given, mean = 50

$\frac{\sum_{i=1}^{80} x_i}{80} = 50$

$\sum_{i=1}^{80} x_i = 4000$

Incorrect $\sum_{i=1}^{80} x_i = 4000$

Correct $\sum_{i=1}^{80} x_i = 4000 - 40 + 30 = 3990$

Correct mean $= \frac{3990}{80} = 49.8$

(ii) Given, SD $(\sigma) = 5$

$\therefore$ Variance, $\sigma^2 = 25$

$\frac{\sum_{i=1}^{80} x_i^2}{80} - (50)^2 = 25$ [given, mean = 50]

$\sum_{i=1}^{80} x_i^2 = 202000$

Incorrect $\sum_{i=1}^{80} x_i^2 = 202000$

Correct $\sum_{i=1}^{80} x_i^2 = 202000 - 40^2 + 30^2$

$= 201300$

Correct variance, $\sigma^2 = \frac{\text{Correct} \sum_{i=1}^{80} x_i^2}{80} - (\text{correct mean})^2$

$= \frac{201300}{80} - (49.8)^2$

$= 2516.25 - 2480.04$

$= 36.21 \approx 36$

SD $(\sigma) = \sqrt{36} = 6$

30. Given, mean $= 10 \Rightarrow \frac{\sum_{i=1}^{10} x_i}{10} = 10$

$\sum_{i=1}^{10} x_i = 100$ and SD $(\sigma) = 4$

$\therefore$ Variance, $\sigma^2 = 16$

$\frac{\sum_{i=1}^{10} x_i^2}{10} - (10)^2 = 16$

$\sum_{i=1}^{10} x_i^2 = 1160$

Thus, incorrect $\sum_{i=1}^{10} x_i = 100$

and incorrect $\sum_{i=1}^{10} x_i^2 = 1160$

On omitting 5, we are left with 9 observation

Correct $\sum_{i=1}^{9} x_i = \text{Incorrect} \sum_{i=1}^{10} x_i - 5$

$= 100 - 5 = 95$

Correct $\sum_{i=1}^{9} x_i = 95$

Correct mean $= \frac{95}{9} = 10.55$

Correct $\sum_{i=1}^{9} x_i^2 = \text{Incorrect} \sum_{i=1}^{10} x_i^2 - 25$

$= 1160 - 25 = 1135$

Correct variance, $\sigma^2 = \frac{1}{9} \text{correct} \sum_{i=1}^{9} x_i^2 - (\text{correct mean})^2$

$= \frac{1}{9} \times 1135 - (10.55)^2$

$= 126.11 - 111.36 = 14.75$

Correct SD $(\sigma) = \sqrt{14.75} = 3.83$

31. (False)

$$\text{Mean} = \frac{\sum_{i=1}^{n} (x_i - a)}{n} = \frac{n}{n} = 1$$

$$\text{Variance, } \sigma^2 = \frac{\sum_{i=1}^{n} (x_i - a)^2}{n} - (\text{mean})^2 = \frac{na}{n} - 1 = a - 1$$

32. (b) $\sum_{i=1}^{10} (x_i - P) = 3$ and $\sum_{i=1}^{10} (x_i - P)^2 = 9$

$$\text{Mean} = \frac{\sum_{i=1}^{10} (x_i - P)}{10} = \frac{3}{10}$$

$$\text{Variance, } \sigma^2 = \frac{\sum_{i=1}^{10} (x_i - P)^2}{10} - (\text{mean})^2$$

$$= \frac{9}{10} - \left(\frac{3}{10}\right)^2 = \frac{9}{10} - \frac{9}{100} = \frac{81}{100}$$

$$\text{SD}(\sigma) = \sqrt{\frac{81}{100}} = \frac{9}{10}$$

Assertion Reason

1. (a) The sum of the deviations of a given set of observations from their arithmetic mean is always zero. As the sum of positive deviations from the mean is equal to the sum of negative deviations.

2. (a) Mean of the given data is

$$\bar{x} = \frac{4 + 7 + 8 + 9 + 10 + 12 + 13 + 17}{8} = \frac{80}{8} = 10$$

Absolute values of the deviations are

$|x_i - \bar{x}| = 6, 3, 2, 1, 0, 2, 3, 7$

$$\therefore \quad \text{MD} = \frac{\sum_{i=1}^{8} |x_i - \bar{x}|}{8}$$

$$= \frac{6 + 3 + 2 + 1 + 0 + 2 + 3 + 7}{8} = \frac{24}{8} = 3$$

Both Assertion and Reason are true and Reason is correct explanation of Assertion.

3. (c) $N = \sum_{i=1}^{5} f_i = 7 + 4 + 6 + 3 + 5 = 25$

$$\bar{x} = \frac{\sum_{i=1}^{5} f_i x_i}{N} = \frac{35 + 40 + 90 + 60 + 125}{25} = \frac{350}{25} = 14$$

x_i	f_i	$\lvert x_i - \bar{x} \rvert$	$f_i \lvert x_i - \bar{x} \rvert$
5	7	9	63
10	4	4	16
15	6	1	6
20	3	6	18
25	5	11	55
	$N = 25$		$\sum_{i=1}^{5} f_i \lvert x_i - \bar{x} \rvert = 158$

$$\text{Mean deviation about mean} = \frac{\sum_{i=1}^{5} f_i |x_i - \bar{x}|}{N} = \frac{158}{25} = 6.32$$

Reason $N = \sum_{i=1}^{5} f_i = 4 + 24 + 28 + 16 + 8 = 80$

$$\bar{x} = \frac{\sum_{i=1}^{5} f_i x_i}{N} = \frac{40 + 720 + 1400 + 1120 + 720}{80} = \frac{4000}{80} = 50$$

x_i	f_i	$\lvert x_i - \bar{x} \rvert$	$f_i \lvert x_i - \bar{x} \rvert$
10	4	40	160
30	24	20	480
50	28	0	0
70	16	20	320
90	8	40	320
	$N = 80$		$\sum_{i=1}^{5} f_i \lvert x_i - \bar{x} \rvert = 1280$

$$\text{Mean deviation about mean} = \frac{\sum_{i=1}^{5} f_i |x_i - \bar{x}|}{N} = \frac{1280}{80} = 16$$

Assertion is true but Reason is false.

4. (a) In a distribution, where the degree of variability is very high, the median is not a representative central value. Thus, the mean deviation about median calculated for such series cannot be fully relied.
Both Assertion and Reason are correct and Reason is the correct explanation of Assertion.

5. (a) The sum of deviations from the mean is more than the sum of deviations from median. Therefore, the mean deviation about the mean is not very scientific, where degree of variability is very high.
Both Assertion and Reason are correct and Reason is the correct explanation of Assertion.

6. (c) **Assertion** Let the number of boys be x and number of girls be y.

Total marks obtained by all the boys

$= \text{Average marks} \times \text{Number of boys}$

$= 52x$

Total marks obtained by all the girls

$= \text{Average marks} \times \text{Number of girls}$

$= 42y$

The average marks of boys and girls combined

$$= \frac{\text{Total marks obtained by boys} + \text{Total marks obtained by girls}}{\text{Number of boys} + \text{Number of girls}}$$

$$= \frac{52x + 42y}{x + y}$$

$$\Rightarrow \frac{52x + 42y}{x + y} = 50 \quad \text{[given]}$$

$\Rightarrow 52x + 42y = 50x + 50y$

$\Rightarrow 2x = 8y$

$\Rightarrow x = 4y$

Hence, the percentage of boys in the class

$= \frac{4}{5} \times 100$

$= 80\%$

Reason Let number of boys are x and number of girls are y.

$\therefore \quad 53(x + y) = 55y + 50x$

$\Rightarrow \quad 3x = 2y$

$\Rightarrow \quad x = \frac{2y}{3}$

$\therefore$ Total number of students $= x + y = \frac{2y}{3} + y = \frac{5}{3}y$

Hence, required percentage $= \frac{y}{\frac{5y}{3}} \times 100\%$

$= \frac{3}{5} \times 100\% = 60\%$

Assertion is true, but Reason is false.

7. (a) **Assertion** Given numbers are

31, 35, 27, 29, 32, 43, 37, 41, 34, 28, 36, 44, 45, 42, 30

Arranging increasing order

27, 28, 29, 30, 31, 32, 34, 35, 36, 37, 41, 42, 43, 44, 45

$n = 15$ (odd)

$\therefore \quad \text{Median} = \left(\frac{n+1}{2}\right)^{\text{th}}$ value

$= \left(\frac{15+1}{2}\right)^{\text{th}}$ value

$= 8^{\text{th}}$ value

$= 35$ kg

If the weight 44 kg is replaced by 46 kg and 27 kg is replaced by 25 kg.

Then, new values in order be

25, 28, 29, 30, 31, 32, 34,35, 36, 37, 41, 42, 43, 45, 46

$n = 15$ (odd)

$\therefore \quad \text{Median} = \left(\frac{n+1}{2}\right)^{\text{th}}$ value $= \left(\frac{15+1}{2}\right)^{\text{th}}$ value $= 8^{\text{th}}$ value $= 35$ kg

Reason Total number of observations = 8 (even)

First, arranging the data in ascending order

40, 42, 45, 47, 50, 51, 54, 57

Median, M = Mean of $\left(\frac{8}{2}\right)^{\text{th}}$ and $\left(\frac{8}{2}+1\right)^{\text{th}}$ observations

= Mean of 4th and 5th observations

$= \frac{47 + 50}{2} = \frac{97}{2} = 48.5$

Absolute values of the deviations are

$|x_i - M| = 8.5, 6.5, 3.5, 1.5, 1.5, 2.5, 5.5, 8.5$

$$\Rightarrow \quad \text{MD} = \frac{1}{8}\sum_{i=1}^{8}|x_i - M|$$

$$= \frac{1}{8} \times 38 = 4.75$$

Both Assertion and Reason are correct and Reason is the correct explanation of Assertion.

8. (a) In the calculation of variance, we find that the units of individual observations x_i and the unit of their mean $\bar{x}$ are different from that of variance, since variance involves the sum of squares of $(x_i - \bar{x})$.

For this Reason, the proper measure of dispersion about the mean of a set of observations is expressed as positive square-root of the variance and is called standard deviation.

Both Assertion and Reason are correct and Reason is the correct explanation of Assertion.

9. (b)

x_i	f_i	$x_i f_i$
4	3	12
8	5	40
11	9	99
17	5	85
20	4	80
24	3	72
32	1	32
	$\Sigma f_i = 30$	$\Sigma x_i f_i = 420$

Mean, $\bar{x} = \frac{\Sigma x_i f_i}{\Sigma f_i}$

$\Rightarrow \quad \bar{x} = \frac{420}{30} \Rightarrow \bar{x} = 14$

x_i	f_i	$x_i - \bar{x}$	$(x_i - \bar{x})^2$	$f_i(x_i - \bar{x})^2$
4	3	$4 - 14 = -10$	$(-10)^2 = 100$	$3 \times 100 = 300$
8	5	$8 - 14 = -6$	$(-6)^2 = 36$	$5 \times 36 = 180$
11	9	$11 - 14 = -3$	$(-3)^2 = 9$	$9 \times 9 = 81$
17	5	$17 - 14 = 3$	$(3)^2 = 9$	$5 \times 9 = 45$
20	4	$20 - 14 = 6$	$(6)^2 = 36$	$4 \times 36 = 144$
24	3	$24 - 14 = 10$	$(10)^2 = 100$	$3 \times 100 = 300$
32	1	$32 - 14 = 18$	$(18)^2 = 324$	$1 \times 324 = 324$
	$\Sigma f_i = 30$			$\Sigma f_i(x_i - \bar{x})^2 = 1374$

Variance, $\sigma^2 = \dfrac{\Sigma f_i(x_i - x)^2}{\Sigma f_i}$

$= \dfrac{1374}{30} = 45.8$

Standard deviation, $\sigma = \sqrt{45.8} = 6.77$

Hence, the variance is 45.8 and the standard variance is 6.77

Both Assertion and Reason are correct but Reason is not the correct explanation of Assertion.

10. (b)

x_i	f_i	$x_i f_i$	$x_i - \bar{x}$, $(\bar{x} = 19)$	$(x_i - \bar{x})^2$	$f_i(x_i - \bar{x})^2$
6	2	12	−13	169	338
10	4	40	−9	81	324
14	7	98	−5	25	175
18	12	216	−1	1	12
24	8	192	5	25	200
28	4	112	9	81	324
30	3	90	11	121	363
	$\Sigma f_i = 40$	$\Sigma f_i x_i = 760$			$\Sigma f_i(x_i - \bar{x})^2 = 1736$

Mean, $\bar{x} = \dfrac{\Sigma f_i x_i}{\Sigma f_i}$

$= \dfrac{760}{40} = 19$

Variance, $\sigma^2 = \dfrac{\Sigma f_i(x_i - \bar{x})^2}{N}$

$= \dfrac{1736}{40} = 43.4$

Both Assertion and Reason are correct but Reason is not the correct explanation of Assertion.

11. (d)

x_i	f_i	$u_i = \dfrac{x_i - A}{h}$	u_i^2	$f_i u_i$	$f_i u_i^2$
60	2	−4	16	−8	32
61	1	−3	9	−3	9
62	12	−2	4	−24	48
63	29	−1	1	−29	29
64	25	0	0	0	0
65	12	1	1	12	12
66	10	2	4	20	40
67	4	3	9	12	36
68	5	4	16	20	80
Total	100			0	289

Here, $N = 100$, $h = 1$

Let mean $A = 64$

Mean, $\bar{x} = A + \dfrac{\sum_{i=1}^{9} f_i u_i}{N} \times h$

$= 64 + \dfrac{0}{100} \times 1 = 64 + 0 = 64$

Variance, $\sigma^2 = \dfrac{h^2}{N^2}\left[N\sum_{i=1}^{9} f_i u_i^2 - \left(\sum_{i=1}^{9} f_i u_i\right)^2\right]$

$= \dfrac{1}{100^2}[100 \times 286 - 0] = 2.86$

$\therefore$ Standard deviation, $\sigma = \sqrt{2.86} = 1.69$

Assertion is false but Reason is true.

12. (a) Let $\bar{x}$ be the mean of $x_1, x_2, x_3, \ldots, x_n$

$\bar{x} = \dfrac{1}{n}(x_1 + x_2 + x_3 + \ldots + x_n)$

Let $y_i = x_i + a$ for each $i = 1, 2, 3, \ldots, n$

$\bar{y}$ be the mean of $y_1, y_2, y_3, \ldots, y_n$

$\bar{y} = \dfrac{1}{n}(y_1 + y_2 + y_3 + \ldots.. y_n)$

$= \dfrac{1}{n}(x_1 + a + x_2 + a + x_3 + a + \ldots + x_n + a)$

$= \dfrac{1}{n}(x_1 + x_2 + x_3 + \ldots + x_n) + \dfrac{1}{n}(a + a + \ldots + n \text{ times})$

$= \bar{x} + \dfrac{1}{n} \times na = \bar{x} + a$

$\bar{y} = \bar{x} + a$

Variance of new observation, $y_i\ (\sigma^2) = \dfrac{1}{n}\sum_{i=1}^{n}(y_i - \bar{y})^2$

$= \dfrac{1}{n}\sum_{i=1}^{n}\{(x_i + a) - (\bar{x} + a)\}^2$

$= \dfrac{1}{n} \cdot \sum_{i=1}^{n}(x_i + a - \bar{x} - a)^2$

$$\text{Variance}(y_i) = \frac{1}{n}\cdot\sum_{i=1}^{n}(x_i-\bar{x})^2 = \text{Variance}(x_i)$$

From the calculation, the variance of new observation is same as original.

∴ Both Assertion and Reason are correct and Reason is the correct explanation of Assertion.

13. (d) Given that $n=18$, $\Sigma(x-5)=3$, $\Sigma(x-5)^2=43$

$$\therefore \text{Mean} = A + \frac{\Sigma(x-5)}{n} = 5 + \frac{3}{18} = \frac{93}{18} = 5.166 = 5.17$$

And $$\text{SD} = \sqrt{\frac{\Sigma(x-5)^2}{N} - \left[\frac{\Sigma(x-5)^2}{N}\right]^2}$$

$$= \sqrt{\frac{43}{18} - \left(\frac{3}{18}\right)^2}$$

$$= \sqrt{2.39 - (0.166)^2}$$

$$= \sqrt{2.39 - 0.27}$$

$$= 1.54$$

Hence, the required mean is 5.17 and SD = 1.54

∴ Assertion is false but Reason is true.

14. (d) First n natural numbers are 1, 2, 3, ..., n

$$\text{Mean, } \bar{x} = \frac{1+2+3+\ldots+n}{n} = \frac{1}{n}\cdot\frac{1}{2}n(n+1) = \frac{1}{2}(n+1)$$

$$\text{Variance, } \sigma^2 = \frac{1}{n}\sum_{i=1}^{n}(x_i-\bar{x})^2 = \frac{1}{n}\sum_{i=1}^{n}(x_i^2 - 2\bar{x}x_i + \bar{x}^2)$$

$$= \frac{1}{n}\sum_{i=1}^{n}x_i^2 - \frac{1}{n}\cdot 2\sum_{i=1}^{n}\left(\frac{n+1}{2}\right)x_i + \frac{1}{n}\sum_{i=1}^{n}\left(\frac{n+1}{2}\right)^2$$

$$= \frac{(n+1)(2n+1)}{6} - \frac{(n+1)^2}{2} + \frac{(n+1)^2}{4}$$

$$\left[\because \Sigma x_i^2 = \frac{n(n+1)(2n+1)}{6} \text{ and } \Sigma x_i \frac{n(n+1)}{2}\right]$$

$$= \frac{(n+1)(2n+1)}{6} - \frac{(n+1)^2}{4}$$

$$= (n+1)\left[\frac{2n+1}{6} - \frac{n+1}{4}\right] = \frac{(n+1)(n-1)}{12} = \frac{n^2-1}{12}$$

∴ Assertion is false but Reason is true.

15. (b) **Assertion**

Given, mean of n observations is $\frac{46n}{11}$.

Since, mean $\bar{x}$ is given by, $\bar{x} = \frac{\sum_{i=1}^{n} x_i}{n}$

$$\Rightarrow \frac{46n}{11} = \frac{1^2+2^2+3^2+\ldots+n^2}{n}$$

$$\Rightarrow \frac{46n}{11} = \frac{n(n+1)(2n+1)}{6n}$$

$$\Rightarrow \frac{46n}{11} = \frac{(2n^2+3n+1)}{6}$$

$$\Rightarrow 276n = 22n^2 + 33n + 11$$

$$\Rightarrow 22n^2 - 243n + 11 = 0$$

$$\Rightarrow (n-11)(22n-1) = 0$$

$$n = 11, \frac{1}{22}$$

Thus, the value of n is 11 or $\frac{1}{22}$.

Since, n cannot be a fraction.

Therefore, the value of n is 11.

Reason $\sigma_x^2 = 4$ and $\sigma_y^2 = 5$

Also, $\bar{x} = 2$ and $\bar{y} = 4$

Now, $\frac{\Sigma x_i}{5} = 2 \Rightarrow \Sigma x_i = 10$; $\Sigma y_i = 20$

and $\sigma_x^2 = \left(\frac{1}{5}\Sigma x_i^2\right) - (\bar{x})^2$, $\sigma_y^2 = \frac{1}{5}(\Sigma y_i^2) - 16$

$\Rightarrow$ $\Sigma x_i^2 = 40$ and $\Sigma y_i^2 = 105$

∴ Variance of the combined data set is

$$\sigma_z^2 = \frac{1}{10}(\Sigma x_i^2 + \Sigma y_i^2) - \left(\frac{\bar{x}+\bar{y}}{2}\right)^2$$

$$= \frac{1}{10}(40+105) - 9 = \frac{145-90}{10} = \frac{55}{10} = \frac{11}{2}$$

∴ Both Assertion and Reason are correct but Reason is not the correct explanation of Assertion.

Case Based

Case 1 You are given some observations as

34, 66, 30, 38, 44, 50, 40, 60, 42, 51.

(i) (c) Mean of the given data is

$$\bar{x} = \frac{34+66+30+38+44+50+40+60+42+51}{10}$$

$$= \frac{455}{10} = 45.5$$

(ii) (d) Absolute values of the deviation are $|x_i - \bar{x}|$ = 11.5, 20.5, 15.5, 7.5, 1.5, 4.5, 5.5, 14.5, 3.5, 5.5

$$\text{MD} = \frac{\sum_{i=1}^{10}|x_i-\bar{x}|}{10}$$

$$= \frac{11.5+20.5+15.5+7.5+1.5+4.5+5.5+14.5+3.5+5.5}{10} = \frac{90}{10} = 9$$

(iii) (c) Total number of observations = 10 (even)

First, arranging the data in ascending order

30, 34, 3?, 40, 42, 44, 50, 51, 60, 66

Median, M = Mean of $\left(\frac{10}{2}\right)^{\text{th}}$ and $\left(\frac{10}{2}+1\right)^{\text{th}}$ observations = Mean of 5th and 6th observations

$$= \frac{42+44}{2} = \frac{86}{2} = 43$$

(iv) (d) Absolute values of the deviations are

$|x_i - M|$ = 13, 9, 5, 3, 1, 1, 7, 8, 17, 23

$$\text{MD} = \frac{1}{10}\sum_{i=1}^{10}|x_i - M| = \frac{1}{10}\times 87 = 8.7$$

(v) (c) Mean deviation – Median deviation

$= 9 - 8.7 = 0.3$

Case 2 (i) (a) Mean, $\bar{x} = \frac{\Sigma f_i x_i}{\Sigma f_i}$

(ii) (a) $\sigma^2 = \frac{\Sigma f_i(x_i - \bar{x})^2}{N}$

x_i	f_i	$x_i f_i$	$x_i - \bar{x}$, $(\bar{x} = 14)$	$(x_i - \bar{x})^2$	$f_i(x_i - \bar{x})^2$
4	3	12	– 10	100	300
8	5	40	– 6	36	180
11	9	99	– 3	9	81
17	5	85	3	9	45
20	4	80	6	36	144
24	3	72	10	100	300
32	1	32	18	324	324
	$\Sigma f_i = 30$	$\Sigma f_i x_i = 420$			$\Sigma f_i(x_i - \bar{x})^2 = 1374$

(iii) (c) Mean, $\bar{x} = \frac{\Sigma f_i x_i}{\Sigma f_i} = \frac{420}{30} = 14$

(iv) (b) Variance, $\sigma^2 = \frac{\Sigma f_i(x_i - \bar{x})^2}{N}$

$= \frac{1374}{30}$

$= 45.8$

(v) (a) Standard deviation, $\sigma = \sqrt{\text{Variance}}$

$= \sqrt{45.8}$

$= 6.77$

Competition Connect

1. True
2. Yes
3. (d) The distribution which has the lowest coefficient of variation shows the lowest variability.
   Here, the coefficient of variation of IV is 14.8.
   Hence, distribution IV will show lowest variability.
4. (i) **Firm A**

   Number of employees, $n_1 = 300$

   Mean of monthly payout, $\bar{x}_1 =$ ₹ 7999

   Total monthly wages $= n_1 \times \bar{x}_1$

   $= 300 \times 7999 =$ ₹ 2399700

   Firm B

   Number of employees, $n_2 = 250$

   Mean of monthly payout, $\bar{x}_2 =$ ₹ 7999

   Total monthly wages $= n_2 \times \bar{x}_2$

   $= 250 \times 7999$

   $=$ ₹ 1999750

   Hence, firm A pays larger sum as monthly payout.

   (ii) Since, both firm have same means.

   So, the firm with greater variance will have more variability.

   Clearly, variance of firm $B >$ variance of firm A.
   Hence, firm B will have greater variability in individual payout.
5. (c) Given, variance $(\sigma^2) = 9$

   SD $(\sigma) = \sqrt{9} = 3$

   and $\bar{x} = 12$

   $\text{CV} = \frac{\text{Standard deviation}}{\text{Mean}} \times 100$

   $= \frac{3}{12} \times 100 = 25\%$
6. (True)

   $N = 2$ and $\Sigma(x_i - \bar{x})^2 = 28^2$

   Variance, $\sigma^2 = \frac{1}{N}\Sigma(x_i - \bar{x})^2$

   $= \frac{1}{2} \times 28 \times 28 = 392$

   SD, $\sigma = \sqrt{392} = 19.8$

   $\text{CV} = \frac{19.8}{10} \times 100 = 198$
7. (b) Standard deviation of Mathematics $= 12$
   Standard deviation of Physics $= 16$
   Standard deviation of Chemistry $= 15$
   Coefficient of variation is given by

   $\frac{\text{SD}}{\text{Mean}} \times 100$

   CV in Mathematics $= \frac{12}{48} \times 100 = 25$

   CV in Physics $= \frac{16}{80} \times 100 = 20$

   CV in Chemistry $= \frac{15}{45} \times 100 = 33.3$

   Subject with greater coefficient of variation is more variable than others.
   The highest variability in marks is in Chemistry and lowest variability in marks is in Physics.
8. $\text{CV}_1 = 80$, SD $(\sigma_1) = 40$

   $\text{CV}_2 = 90$, SD $(\sigma_2) = 18$

   Let $\bar{x}_1$ be the mean of first distribution, then

   $\text{CV}_1 = \frac{\sigma_1}{\bar{x}_1} \times 100$

   $\Rightarrow \quad 80 = \frac{40}{\bar{x}_1} \times 100 \Rightarrow \bar{x}_1 = 50$

   Let $\bar{x}_2$ be the mean of second distribution, then

   $\text{CV}_2 = \frac{\sigma_2}{\bar{x}_2} \times 100$

   $\Rightarrow \quad 90 = \frac{18}{\bar{x}_2} \times 100 \Rightarrow \bar{x}_2 = 20$

   Sum $= \bar{x}_1 + \bar{x}_2 = 50 + 20 = 70$
9. (b) Arranging the data in ascending order

   38, 40, 43, 44, 46, 47, 49, 53

   $\bar{x} = \frac{38 + 40 + 43 + 44 + 46 + 47 + 49 + 53}{8} = \frac{360}{8} = 45$

x_i	$d_i = x_i - \bar{x}$	d_i^2
38	−7	49
40	−5	25
43	−2	4
44	−1	1
46	1	1
47	2	4
49	4	16
53	8	64
	$\Sigma d_i = 0$	$\Sigma d_i^2 = 164$

$$\text{SD, } \sigma = \sqrt{\frac{\Sigma d_i^2}{n}} = \sqrt{\frac{164}{8}} = \sqrt{20.5} = 4.53$$

$$\text{CV} = \frac{\sigma}{\bar{x}} \times 100 = \frac{4.53}{45} \times 100 = 10.07\%$$

10. $\sum_{i=1}^{25} x_i = 169, \sum_{i=1}^{25} x_i^2 = 1150$

and $N = 25$

$$\bar{x}_i = \frac{\sum_{i=1}^{25} x_i}{N} = \frac{169}{25} = 6.76$$

$$\text{Variance, } \sigma_1^2 = \frac{1}{N} \sum_{i=1}^{25} (x_i - \bar{x})^2$$

$$= \frac{1}{25} \sum_{i=1}^{25} (x_i - 6.76)^2$$

$$= \frac{1}{25} \sum_{i=1}^{25} [x_i^2 - 13.52x_i + 45.69]$$

$$= \frac{1}{25} \left[\sum_{i=1}^{25} x_i^2 - 13.52 \sum_{i=1}^{25} x_i + 45.69 \times 25 \right]$$

$$= \frac{1}{25} [1150 - 13.52 \times 169 + 45.69 \times 25]$$

$$= 0.29$$

Also, given $\sum_{i=1}^{25} y_i = 225$ and $\sum_{i=1}^{25} y_i^2 = 2035$

$$\text{Mean, } \bar{y} = \frac{1}{N} \sum_{i=1}^{25} y_i = \frac{225}{25} = 9$$

$$\text{Variance, } \sigma_2^2 = \frac{1}{N} \sum_{i=1}^{25} (y_i - \bar{y})^2$$

$$= \frac{1}{25} \left[\sum_{i=1}^{25} y_i^2 - 18 \sum_{i=1}^{25} y_i + 81 \times 25 \right]$$

$$= \frac{1}{25} [2035 - 18 \times 225 + 81 \times 25]$$

$$= 0.4$$

So, variance of dollar is greater than the variance of rupee, so dollar vary more than the rupee.

11. To determine the consistency, we have to find coefficient of variation of two teams

Number of goals scored (x_i)	Number of matches (f_i)	$f_i x_i$	$f_i x_i^2$
0	3	0	0
1	8	8	8
2	6	12	24
3	6	18	54
4	2	8	32

Here, $N = \Sigma f_i = 25, \Sigma f_i x_i = 46$ and $\Sigma f_i x_i^2 = 118$

$$\bar{x}_A = \frac{\Sigma f_i x_i}{N} = \frac{46}{25} = 1.84$$

$$\sigma_A^2 = \frac{\Sigma f_i x_i^2}{N} - \left(\frac{\Sigma f_i x_i}{N} \right)^2$$

$$= \frac{118}{25} - \left(\frac{46}{25} \right)^2 = 1.34$$

$$\sigma_A = \sqrt{1.34} = 1.15$$

$$\bar{x}_B = 3 \text{ and } \sigma_B = 2.25$$

$$\text{CV by team } A = \frac{\sigma_A}{\bar{x}_A} \times 100$$

$$= \frac{1.15}{1.84} \times 100 = 62.5$$

$$\text{CV by team } B = \frac{\sigma_B}{\bar{x}_B} \times 100$$

$$= \frac{2.25}{3} \times 100 = 75$$

So, the coefficient of variation of goal scored by team B is greater than that of team A.

Hence, team A is more consistent.

12. (c) For determining we have to compute CV in both cases

Hospital *A*

Range	x_i	f_i	$u_i = \frac{x_i - 17.5}{5}$	$f_i u_i$	u_i^2	$f_i u_i^2$
5-10	7.5	3	−2	−6	4	12
10-15	12.5	8	−1	−8	1	8
15-20	17.5	30	0	0	0	0
20-25	22.5	53	1	53	1	53
25-30	27.5	12	2	24	4	48
30-35	32.5	4	3	12	9	36
		$N = \Sigma f_i = 110$	$\Sigma u_i = 3$	$\Sigma f_i u_i = 75$		$\Sigma f_i u_i^2 = 157$

$$\bar{x}_A = a + h\left(\frac{\Sigma f_i u_i}{N}\right)$$
$$= 17.5 + 5\times\frac{75}{110} = 20.9$$
$$\sigma_A^2 = h^2\left\{\frac{\Sigma f_i u_i^2}{N} - \left(\frac{\Sigma f_i u_i}{N}\right)^2\right\}$$
$$= 25\times\left\{\frac{157}{110} - \left(\frac{75}{110}\right)^2\right\}$$
$$= 25\{1.427 - 0.464\}$$
$$= 24.18$$
$$\sigma_A = \sqrt{24.18} = 4.9$$
$$\text{CV} = \frac{\sigma_A}{\bar{x}_A}\times 100$$
$$= \frac{4.9}{20.9}\times 100$$
$$= 23.44$$

Hospital *B*

Range	x_i	f_i	$u_i = \frac{x_i - 17.5}{5}$	$f_i u_i$	u_i^2	$f_i u_i^2$
5-10	7.5	10	−2	−20	4	40
10-15	12.5	12	−1	−12	1	12
15-20	17.5	17	0	0	0	0
20-25	22.5	31	1	31	1	31
25-30	27.5	28	2	56	4	112
30-35	32.5	13	3	39	9	117
		$N = \Sigma f_i = 111$		$\Sigma f_i u_i = 94$		$\Sigma f_i u_i = 312$

$$\bar{x}_B = a + h\left(\frac{\Sigma f_i u_i}{N}\right)$$
$$= 17.5 + 5\times\frac{94}{111} = 21.73$$
$$\sigma_B^2 = h^2\left\{\frac{\Sigma f_i u_i^2}{N} - \left(\frac{\Sigma f_i u_i}{N}\right)^2\right\}$$
$$= 25\times\left\{\frac{312}{111} - \left(\frac{94}{111}\right)^2\right\}$$
$$= 25\{2.81 - 0.71\} = 52.3$$
$$\sigma_B = \sqrt{52.3} = 7.23$$
$$\text{CV} = \frac{\sigma_B}{\bar{x}_B}\times 100$$
$$= \frac{7.23}{21.73}\times 100$$
$$= 33.3$$

∴ Average sampling of hospital *B* is higher. Coefficient of variation is less for hospital *A*, so hospital *A* has more uniform sampling.

Competition Edge Up

1. (d)

x	c	$2c$	$3c$	$4c$	$5c$	$6c$
f	2	1	1	1	1	1

$$\text{Variance, } X = \frac{\Sigma f_i x_i^2}{\Sigma f_i} - \left(\frac{\Sigma f_i x_i}{\Sigma f_i}\right)^2$$
$$160 = \frac{2c^2 + 4c^2 + 9c^2 + 16c^2 + 25c^2 + 36c^2}{7} - \left(\frac{2c + 2c + 3c + 4c + 5c + 6c}{7}\right)^2$$
$$\Rightarrow \quad 160 = \frac{92c^2}{7} - \frac{484c^2}{49} = \frac{160c^2}{49}$$
$$\therefore \quad c^2 = 49$$
$c = 7$ (taking only positive sign)

2. (a) From given information,

$$x + y = 10 \qquad \text{...(i)}$$

Age (x_i)	f	$\lvert x_i - M\rvert$	$f_i\lvert x_i - M\rvert$
15	5	3	15
16	8	2	16
17	5	1	5
18	12	0	0
19	x	1	x
20	y	2	$2y$

Median $= 18 = M$ (say)

$$\therefore \quad \text{MD} = \frac{\Sigma f_i\lvert x_i - M\rvert}{\Sigma f_i}$$
$$\Rightarrow \quad 1.25 = \frac{36 + x + 2y}{40}$$
$$\Rightarrow \quad x + 2y = 14 \qquad \text{...(ii)}$$

On solving Eqs. (i) and (ii), we get

$x = 6, y = 4$

Hence, $4x + 5y = 24 + 20 = 44$

3. (33) $a, b, c \in N, a < b < c$

$$\bar{X} = \text{Mean} = \frac{9 + 25 + a + b + c}{5} = 18$$
$$a + b + c = 56$$
$$\text{Mean deviation} = \frac{\Sigma\lvert X_i - \bar{X}\rvert}{n} = 4$$
$$\Rightarrow \quad 9 + 7 + \lvert 18 - a\rvert + \lvert 18 - b\rvert + \lvert 18 - c\rvert = 20$$
$$\Rightarrow \quad \lvert 18 - a\rvert + \lvert 18 - b\rvert + \lvert 18 - c\rvert = 4$$
$$\text{Variance} = \frac{\Sigma\lvert X_i - \bar{X}\rvert^2}{n} = \frac{136}{5}$$
$$\Rightarrow \quad 81 + 49 + \lvert 18 - a\rvert^2 + \lvert 18 - b\rvert^2 + \lvert 18 - c\rvert^2 = 136$$
$$\Rightarrow \quad (18 - a)^2 + (18 - b)^2 + (18 - c)^2 = 6$$

Possible values

$(18-a)^2=1, (18-b)^2=1, (18-c)^2=4a<b<c$

So, $18-a=1, 18-b=-1, 18-c=-2$

$a=17, b=19, c=20$

$\therefore 2a+b-c=2\times17+19-20$

$=34+19-20=33$

4. (b) According to the question,

Mean $\bar{x}=10$ and standard deviation $\sigma=2$

Now, $\bar{x}=\dfrac{x_1+x_2+x_3+\ldots+x_{20}}{20}=10$

$\Rightarrow \sum_{i=1}^{20} x_i=200$

Now, one entry was wrong, taken 8 instead of 12

So, correct sum = 200 − 8 + 12 = 204

Correct mean $=\dfrac{204}{20}=10.2$

We know,

Variance, $\sigma^2=\dfrac{\Sigma x_i^2}{n}-(\bar{x})^2=4$

$\Rightarrow \dfrac{\Sigma x_i^2}{20}-(10)^2=4 \Rightarrow \Sigma x_i^2=2080$

Now, the correct summation of square of observations

$\Rightarrow \Sigma x_i^2=2080-64+144=2160$

Correct variance,

$\sigma_n^2=\dfrac{2160}{20}-(10.2)^2$

$\sigma_n^2=3.96$

Correct standard deviation, $\sigma_n=\sqrt{3.96}$

5. (d) Given observations are $-3, 4, 7, -6, \alpha, \beta$

Mean = 2 and variance = 23

$\Rightarrow \dfrac{-3+4+7+(-6)+\alpha+\beta}{6}=2$

and $\dfrac{\Sigma x_i^2}{n}-(\mu)^2=23, \mu=\text{Mean}$

$\Rightarrow \alpha+\beta=10$ ...(i)

and $\Sigma x_i^2=n(23+\mu^2)=6\times(23+4)$

$=27\times6$

$\Rightarrow 9+16+49+36+\alpha^2+\beta^2=162$

$\Rightarrow \alpha^2+\beta^2=52$ ...(ii)

On solving Eqs. (i) and (ii), we get

$\alpha=4$ and $\beta=6$

So, mean deviation about mean

$=\dfrac{\Sigma|x_i-\bar{x}|}{n}$

$=\dfrac{|-3-2|+|4-2|+|7-2|+|-6-2|+|4-2|+|6-2|}{6}$

$=\dfrac{5+2+5+8+2+4}{6}=\dfrac{26}{6}=\dfrac{13}{3}$

6. (a) Given that $\bar{X}=\dfrac{\sum_{i=1}^{10} x_i}{10}=\dfrac{6}{5}$

and $\dfrac{x_i^2}{10}-(\bar{x})^2=\dfrac{84}{25}$

and $\sum_{i=1}^{10}(x_i-\alpha)=2, \dfrac{\sum_{i=1}^{10} x_i^2}{10}-\dfrac{36}{25}=\dfrac{84}{25}$

$\sum_{i=1}^{10} x_i-10\alpha=2, \dfrac{\sum x_i^2}{10}=\dfrac{120}{25}$

$\Rightarrow 12-10\alpha=2$ and $\sum x_i^2=48$

$\Rightarrow \alpha=1$

Now, $\sum_{i=1}^{10}(x_i-\beta)^2=40$

$\Rightarrow \sum_{i=1}^{10} x_i^2+10\beta^2-2\beta\sum_{i=1}^{10} x_i=40$

$\Rightarrow 48+10\beta^2-24\beta=40$

$\Rightarrow 10\beta^2-24\beta+8=0$

$\Rightarrow 5\beta^2-12\beta+4=0$

$\beta=2$ or $\beta=\dfrac{2}{5}$ (reject)

$\therefore \dfrac{\beta}{\alpha}=\dfrac{2}{1}=2$

7. (c) Use formula of mean deviation for simple distribution

$$\text{MD}=\frac{\sum_{i=1}^{n}|x_i-\bar{x}|}{n},$$

where n = number of terms

$\bar{x}$ = mean or median

Given data, 170, 125, 230, 190, 210, a, b

MD about median

$=\dfrac{|170-170|+|125-170|+|230-170|+|190-170|+|210-170|+|a-170|+|b-170|}{7}$

$\Rightarrow \dfrac{205}{7}=\dfrac{0+45+60+20+40+170-a+170-b}{7}$

$\therefore a+b=300$

Mean $=\dfrac{170+125+230+190+210+a+b}{7}$

$=\dfrac{170+125+230+190+210+300}{7}$

$=\dfrac{1225}{7}=175$

Mean deviation about mean

$$= \frac{|170-175|+|125-175|+|230-175| + |190-175|+|210-175|+|a-175| + |b-175|}{7}$$

$$= \frac{5+50+55+15+35+350-300}{7}$$

$$= \frac{5+50+55+15+35+50}{7} = \frac{210}{7} = 30$$

8. (a) Mean $= 55 \quad \frac{a+b+68+44+48+60}{6} = 55$

$\Rightarrow \quad a+b+220 = 330$

$\Rightarrow \quad a+b = 110$ ...(i)

Also, variance = 1.94

$$\Sigma \frac{(x_i - \bar{x})^2}{n} = 194$$

$$\Sigma \frac{(x_i - 55)^2}{6} = 194$$

$\Rightarrow \quad \Sigma (x_i - 55)^2 = 1164$

$$(a-55)^2 + (b-55)^2 + (68-55)^2 + (44-55)^2 + (48-55)^2 + (60-55)^2 = 1164$$

$\Rightarrow \quad a^2 - 110a + 3025 + b^2 - 110b + 3025 + 169 + 121 + 49 + 25 = 1164$

$$a^2 + b^2 - 110(a+b) = -5250$$

$$a^2 + b^2 - 110 \times 110 = -5250$$

$\Rightarrow \quad a^2 + b^2 = 6850$ ...(ii)

From Eq. (i), $b = 110 - a$ put in Eq. (ii),

$$a^2 + (110-a)^2 = 6850$$

$\Rightarrow \quad 2a^2 - 220a + 5250 = 0$

$\Rightarrow \quad a^2 - 110a + 2625 = 0$

$$a = 35, 75$$

If $a = 75, b = 35$

$$a + 3b = 75 + 105 = 180$$

9. (29)

x_i	f_i	$f_i x_i$	$f_i x_i^2$
0	3	0	0
1	2	2	2
5	3	15	75
6	2	12	72
10	6	60	600
12	3	36	432
17	3	51	867
Total	$\Sigma f_i = 22$	$\Sigma f_i x_i = 176$	$\Sigma f_i x_i^2 = 2048$

$\because$ Variance, $\sigma^2 = \left(\frac{\Sigma f_i x_i^2}{\Sigma f_i}\right) - \left(\frac{\Sigma f_i x_i}{\Sigma f_i}\right)^2$

$$= \frac{2048}{22} - \left(\frac{176}{22}\right)^2 = \frac{1024}{11} - 64$$

$$= 93.0909 - 64 = 29.0909$$

10. (d) We have,

x_i	0-4	4-8	8-12	12-16	16-20
f_i	3	9	10	8	6
cf	3	12	22	30	36

$\therefore \quad N = \Sigma f = 36$

$$\frac{N}{2} = \frac{36}{2} = 18$$

So, we have median lies in the class 8-12

$$l_1 = 8, f = 10, h = 4, cf = 12$$

So, here we apply formula,

$$M = l_1 + \frac{N/2 - cf}{f} \times h$$

$$= 8 + \frac{18-12}{10} \times 4$$

$\Rightarrow \quad M = 10.4$

So, $20M = 208$

11. (c) $\bar{X} = \frac{24}{5}$

$\Rightarrow \quad \frac{x_1 + x_2 + x_3 + x_4 + x_5}{5} = \frac{24}{5} = \Sigma x_i = 24$ ...(i)

Variance, $X = \frac{194}{25}$

$$n = 5$$

Mean of first four observation $= \frac{7}{2}$

$$\frac{x_1 + x_2 + x_3 + x_4}{4} = \frac{7}{2}$$

$$x_1 + x_2 + x_3 + x_4 = 14 \quad \text{...(ii)}$$

By Eqs. (i) and (ii), $x_5 = 10$

Now, variance, $X = \frac{194}{25}$

$\Rightarrow \quad \frac{\Sigma x_i^2}{5} - (\bar{X})^2 = \frac{194}{25}$

$\Rightarrow \quad \frac{x_1^2 + x_2^2 + x_3^2 + x_4^2 + x_5^2}{5} - \left(\frac{24}{5}\right)^2 = \frac{194}{25}$

$\Rightarrow \quad \frac{x_1^2 + x_2^2 + x_3^2 + x_4^2 + x_5^2}{5} = \frac{194}{25} + \frac{576}{26}$

$\Rightarrow \quad x_1^2 + x_2^2 + x_3^2 + x_4^2 = \frac{770}{5} - 100 = \frac{270}{5} = 54$

New variance $= \frac{\sum_{i=1}^{4} x_i^2}{4} - (\bar{X})^2 = \frac{54}{4} - \left(\frac{7}{2}\right)^2 = \frac{5}{4}$

12. (6344) Given, $\bar{x} = 56$ and $\sigma^2 = 66.2$

Variance, $\sigma^2 = \dfrac{\Sigma x_i^2}{n} - (\bar{x}_i)^2$

$$\Rightarrow 66.2 = \frac{65^2 + 68^2 + 58^2 + 44^2 + 48^2 + 45^2 + 60^2 + \alpha^2 + \beta^2 + 60^2}{10} - (56)^2$$

$$\Rightarrow \quad 66.2 = \frac{\alpha^2 + \beta^2 + 25678}{10} - (56)^2$$

$$\Rightarrow \quad 662 + 3136 \times 10 = \alpha^2 + \beta^2 + 25678$$

$$\Rightarrow \quad \alpha^2 + \beta^2 = 6344$$

13. (2521) Let μ' = incorrect mean,
μ = correct mean [given]
and σ' = standard deviation, σ = standard deviation (corrected) [given]

Now we have, $\mu' = \dfrac{\Sigma x_i}{15} = 12$ [given] $\Rightarrow \Sigma x_i = 180$

According to the question, corrected $\Sigma x_i = 180 - 10 + 12$

$$\Rightarrow \quad \mu \text{ (correct mean)} = \frac{182}{15}$$

Also, $\sigma' = \sqrt{\dfrac{\Sigma x_i^2}{15} - 144} = 3 \Rightarrow \Sigma x_i^2 = 2295$

Correct $\Sigma x_i^2 = 2295 - 100 + 144 = 2339$

[correct variance]

$$= \frac{2339}{15} - \frac{182 \times 182}{15 \times 15}$$

Hence, required value

$$= 15(\mu + \mu^2 + \sigma^2)$$

$$= 15\left(\frac{182}{15} + \frac{182 \times 182}{15 \times 15} + \frac{2339}{15} - \frac{182 \times 182}{15 \times 15}\right)$$

$$= 15\left(\frac{182}{15} + \frac{2339}{15}\right) = 2521$$

14. (b) Given, $\sum_{k=1}^{10} a_k = 50$

$$\Rightarrow a_1 + a_2 + a_3 + \ldots + a_{10} = 50 \quad \ldots\text{(i)}$$

and $\sum_{\forall k<j} a_k \cdot a_j = 1100 \quad \ldots$(ii)

On squaring Eq. (i), we get

$$(a_1 + a_2 + a_3 + \ldots + a_{10})^2 = (50)^2 = 2500$$

$$\Rightarrow \quad \sum_{i=1}^{10} a_i^2 + 2\sum_{k<j} a_k a_j = 2500$$

[when open whole square of LHS and written in Σ notation]

$$\Rightarrow \quad \sum_{i=1}^{10} a_i^2 = 2500 - 2(1100) \quad \text{[using Eq. (ii)]}$$

$$\Rightarrow \quad \sum_{i=1}^{10} a_i^2 = 300$$

Now, SD $= \sigma = \sqrt{\dfrac{\Sigma a_i^2}{10} - \left(\dfrac{\Sigma a_i}{10}\right)^2} = \sqrt{\dfrac{300}{10} - \left(\dfrac{50}{10}\right)^2}$

$$= \sqrt{30 - 25} = \sqrt{5}$$

Chapter-14

Probability

1. (i) $S_1 = \{H, T\}$
(ii) $S_2 = \{HH, HT, TH, TT\}$
(iii) $S_3 = \{HHH, HHT, HTH, THH, HTT, THT, TTH, TTT\}$
(iv) $S_4 = \{HHHH, HHHT, HHTH, HTHH, HHTT, HTHT, HTTH, HTTT, THHH, THHT, THTH, TTHH, THTT, TTHT, TTTH, TTTT\}$

2. (i) $S_1 = \{1, 2, 3, 4, 5, 6\}$
(ii) $S_2 = \{(1, 1), (1, 2), (1, 3), (1, 4), (1, 5), (1, 6), (2, 1), (2, 2), (2, 3), (2, 4), (2, 5), (2, 6), (3, 1), (3, 2), (3, 3), (3, 4), (3, 5), (3, 6), (4, 1), (4, 2), (4, 3), (4, 4), (4, 5), (4, 6), (5, 1), (5, 2), (5, 3), (5, 4), (5, 5), (5, 6), (6, 1), (6, 2), (6, 3), (6, 4), (6, 5), (6, 6)\}$

(iii)
$$x^2 - 5x + 6 = 0$$
$$\Rightarrow x^2 - 2x - 3x + 6 = 0$$
$$\Rightarrow \quad (x-2)(x-3) = 0$$
$$x = 2, 3$$

Therefore, $S_3 = \{2, 3\}$.

(iv) $x^3 + 3x^2 + 3x + 1 = 0$
$$\Rightarrow \quad (x+1)^3 = 0$$
$$\Rightarrow \quad x = -1$$

Therefore, $S_4 = \{-1\}$.

3. Here, two dice are thrown.
So, number of outcomes in sample space is $6^2 = 36$.
i.e. sample space $S = \{(x, y) : x, y \in \{1, 2, 3, 4, 5, 6\}\}$
Let E = {sum of faces equal to 7}
$= \{(x, y) : x + y = 7, (x, y) \in S\}$
Therefore, the required sample space is
$E = \{(1, 6), (6, 1), (2, 5), (5, 2), (3, 4), (4, 3)\}$

4. (d) The number of affected omicron cases in India, during a month can be either 0 or 1 or 2 or some positive integers. Therefore, the sample space associated with this experiment is
$S = \{0, 1, 2, 3, 4 \ldots\ldots\}$
$= \text{IN} \cup \{0\}$

5. For tossing a coin, either coin can turn up head (H) or tail (T), then the possible outcomes may be head $= H$ or tail $= T$,
i.e. sample space $= \{H, T\}$ and the sample space for rolling a die is $= \{1, 2, 3, 4, 5, 6\}$
Therefore, the sample space of the experiment is
$S = \{H1, H2, H3, H4, H5, H6, T\}$

6. (c) Let the 2 balls be taken as W for white and R for red.
If white ball is drawn, then again another ball is drawn.
So, the possible outcomes are (W, W), (W, R).
If the red ball is drawn, then a die is rolled.
So, the possible outcomes are
$(R, 1), (R, 2), (R, 3), (R, 4), (R, 5), (R, 6)$.

∴ Sample space is given by

$S = \{(W, W), (W, R), (R, 1), (R, 2), (R, 3), (R, 4), (R, 5), (R, 6)\}$

$\Rightarrow n(S) = 8$

7. Let red, black and white balls are denoted by R, B and W, respectively.

After rolling a die, we get $\{1, 2, 3, 4, 5, 6\}$ as a sample space.

If number on die is even i.e. $\{2, 4, 6\}$, then we draw a ball and if number on die is odd i.e. $\{1, 3, 5\}$, then a coin is tossed and the sample space for tossing a coin is $\{H, T\}$.

Now, the required sample space is

$\{2R, 2B, 2W, 4R, 4B, 4W, 6R, 6B, 6W, 1H, 1T, 3H, 3T, 5H, 5T\}$.

8. (b) For tossing a coin, two outcomes are possible

i.e. sample space S = {head, tail}

∴ The possible number of outcomes is

= (number of sample space)^n [n = number of times a coin tossed]

∴ The required number of outcomes is 2^6.

9. (d) In the experiment, either room X or room Y may come up on the first selection.

But in the second drawing, we have to select a cat and the cats are in the room Y.

So, we will choose room Y first, then select a cat.

Therefore, the sample space for the experiment is $\{YC_1, YC_2\}$.

10. (True)

Let us denote 2 red and 1 black balls by R_1, R_2 and B, respectively and faces on die by 1, 2, 3, 4, 5 and 6.

After tossing a coin, if we get tail T, then we draw a ball.

Hence, sample space

$S_1 = \{TR_1, TR_2, TB\}$

Again, after tossing coin, if it shows head H, then we throw a die.

∴ Sample space

$S_2 = \{H1, H2, H3, H4, H5, H6\}$

Total outcomes

$S = \{TR_1, TR_2, TB, H1, H2, H3, H4, H5, H6\}$

Let event A = event point contains black ball = $\{TB\}$

Let event B = event point contains the number 6 on the die = $\{H6\}$

$\Rightarrow A \cup B = \{TB, H6\}$

11. Let us denote white balls by W_1, W_2 and the black balls by B_1, B_2, B_3,

(i) Therefore, the sample space for the experiment, where 2 balls are drawn randomly, is

$= \{W_1W_2, W_1B_1, W_1B_2, W_1B_3, W_2B_1, W_2B_2, W_2B_3, B_1B_2, B_1B_3, B_2B_3\}$.

(ii) In this experiment second ball is drawn only, if black ball is drawn in the first case without replacement.

Hence, the sample space is

$= \{B_1B_2, B_1B_3, B_2B_1, B_2B_3, B_3B_1, B_3B_2, B_1W_1, B_1W_2, B_2W_1, B_2W_2, B_3W_1, B_3W_2\}$.

12. A die is thrown.

Then, $S = \{1, 2, 3, 4, 5, 6\}$

(i) $A = \{2, 3, 5\}$

(ii) $B = \{4\}$

(iii) $C = \{1, 3\}$

(iv) $D = \phi$

(v) $E = \{1, 2, 3, 6\}$

13. (True)

If a die is thrown, then the sample space = $\{1, 2, 3, 4, 5, 6\}$

The event E = A number less than or equal to 5.

Therefore, 1, 2, 3, 4 and 5 are the only element of the event space.

$\therefore E = \{1, 2, 3, 4, 5\}$

But this is not the only possibility for the event space.

It may be $\{4\}, \{5\}, \{4, 5\}, \{1, 2\}$ or $\{1, 2, 4\}$ or $\{1, 3, 5\}$ etc.

14. (Impossible event)

Because in a pack of cards only 4 kings exist.

15. (i) E_1 = 'Getting an even number' $= \{2, 4, 6\}$

E_1 is a compound event.

(ii) E_2 = 'Getting a number greater than 6' $= \phi$

E_2 is an impossible event.

(iii) E_3 = 'Getting an even prime number' $= \{2\}$

E_3 is a simple event.

(iv) E_4 = 'Getting a number more than 0 and less than 7' $= \{1, 2, 3, 4, 5, 6\}$

E_4 is sure event and also a compound event.

16. Let S be the sample space, then

$S = \{(x, y) : x, y \in \{1, 2, 3, 4, 5, 6\}\}$

and the number of elements

$= 6 \times 6 = 36$

(i) Clearly, no outcomes satisfy the condition because sum of the faces always ≤ 12.

Hence, A is an impossible event.

(ii) Event $B = \{(x, y) : x + y = 12, (x, y) \in S\} = \{(6, 6)\}$

Here, event B contains only one sample point.

Therefore, B is a simple event.

(iii) Event $C = \{(x, y) : 2 \mid (x + y), (x, y) \in S\}$

$= \{(1, 1), (1, 3), (1, 5), (2, 2), (2, 4) (2, 6), (3, 1), (3, 3), (3, 5), (4, 2), (4, 4), (4, 6), (5, 1), (5, 3), (5, 5), (6, 2), (6, 4), (6, 6)\}$

Here, C has more than one sample point.

Hence, C is compound event.

17. (False)

Sample space

$S = \{RRW, RRB, RWW, RWB, RBW, RBB, RWR, RBR, WWW, WWR, WWB, WRW, WRR, WRB, WBW, WBB, WBR, BBB, BBR, BBW, BRR, BRW, BRB, BWW, BWR, BWB\}$

Event 'A' $= \{RWW, RWB, RBW, RBB, WWR, WRW, WRB, WBR, BBR, BRW, BRB, BWR\}$

Event 'B' $= \{RBB, WBB, BBB, BBR, BBW, BRB, BWB\}$

Event B'

= Complementary event of B.

= Event points which are coming from S but not in B.

$= \{x : x \in S \text{ but } x \notin B\} \ne A$

As, $RRW \in B'$ but $RRW \notin A$.

Therefore, $A \ne B'$

18. (c) Let S be the sample space of tossing four coins.

Then,

$S = \{HHHH, HHHT, HHTH, HHTT, HTHH, HTHT, HTTH,$

$HTTT, THHH, THHT, THTH,$
$THTT, TTHH, TTHT,$
$TTTH, TTTT\}$

Event E = Three heads and one tail.

$= \{HHHT, HHTH, HTHH, THHH\}$

We know, event 'not E'
= Complementary event to E
= Evenly outcome which is not in E, 'not E' $= \{x : x \in S \text{ and } x \notin E\}$
$= S - E$

19. $A \cup B = \{1, 2, 3, 4, 5, 6\} \cup \phi$
$= \{1, 2, 3, 4,5, 6\}$

20. ϕ

21. (True)

Here, S is the sample space and A and B are two event of S.

Now, event $A - B$ = The set of all those sample points which are in A but not in B.

i.e. event $A - B = \{x : x \text{ is in } A \text{ but not in } B, x \in S\}$
$= \{x : x \in A \text{ and } x \notin B, x \in S\}$
$= \{x : x \in A \text{ and } x \in B'\}$
$= \{x : x \in A \cap B'\}$

Therefore, $A - B = A \cap B'$

22. Sample space

$S = \{WBB, WBW, WWB, BBB, BBW, BWB, BWW\}$

Now, event $A = \{WBB, WBW, WWB, BBW, BWB, BWW\}$

Event $B = \{WBW, WWB, BWW\}$

Event $C = \{WBB, WBW, WWB, BBW, BWB, BWW, BBB\}$

Therefore,

(i) $A' = \{BBB\}$

(ii) $A \cup B = \{WBB, WBW, WWB, BBW, BWB, BWW\}$

(iii) $A \cap C = \{WBB, WBW, WWB, BBW, BWB, BWW\}$

(iv) $A - C = A \cap C' = \phi$

(v) $A \cap B \cap C = \{WBW, WWB, BWW\}$

(vi) not $B = B' = \{WBB, BBB, BBW, BWB\}$

(vii) not $C = C' = \phi$

(viii) $A \cap B' \cap C' = \phi$

23. (False)

Event A : Sum of faces is multiple of 5.

$\therefore\ S(A) = \{(x, y) : 5 | x + y, x, y \in \{1, 2, 3, 4, 5, 6\}\}$
$= \{(1, 4), (4, 1), (2, 3), (3, 2), (4, 6), (6, 4)\}$

Event B : Sum of faces is greater than 5

$\therefore\ S(B) = \{(x, y) : x + y > 5, x, y \in \{1, 2, 3, 4, 5, 6\}\}$
$= \{(1, 5), (5, 1), (1, 6), (6, 1), (2, 4), (4, 2), ... (4, 6), (6, 4), ..., (6, 6)\}$

Now, $A \cap B = \{(4, 6), (6, 4)\} \neq \phi$

Hence, not mutually exclusive.

24. Let sample space

$S = \{(x, y) : x, y \in \{1, 2, 3, 4, 5, 6\}\}$

There are $36\ (= 6^2)$ elements in the sample space.

Then,

Event 'A' $= \{(2, 1), (2, 2), (2, 3), (2, 4), (2, 5), (2, 6), (4, 1), (4, 2), (4, 3), (4, 4), (4, 5), (4, 6), (6, 1), (6, 2), (6, 3), (6, 4), (6, 5), (6, 6)\}$

Event 'B' $= \{(x, y) : x + y \geq 9 \text{ and } 4 | x + y\} = \{(6, 6)\}$

Event 'C' $= \{(x, y) : x + y > 8 \text{ and } x + y = 2n, n \in N\}$
$= \{(4, 6), (5, 5), (6, 4), (6, 6)\}$

Event 'D' $= \{(1, 3), (1, 6), (3, 3), (3, 6), (5, 3), (5, 6)\}$

and $A' = \{(x, y) : (x, y) \notin A\}$

Again, we know, two events E and F are mutually exclusive, if $E \cap F = \phi$

(i) (No)

$A \cap C = \{(4, 6), (6, 4), (6, 6)\} \neq \phi$

A and C are not mutually exclusive.

(ii) (No)

$B \cap C = \{(6, 6)\} \neq \phi$

B and C are not mutually exclusive.

(iii) (Yes)

$A \cap D = \phi$

A and D are mutually exclusive.

(iv) (No)

$A' \cap D = D \neq \phi$

A' and D are not mutually exclusive.

25. (False)

The sample space of the experiment of tossing three coins is

$S = \{HHH, HHT, HTH, THH, HTT, THT, TTH, TTT\}$

Now, event A =

i.e. $A = \{HHT, HTH, THH\}$

and event B

i.e. $B = \{HTT, THT, TTH, TTT\}$

We know, two events A and B will be mutually exclusive, if both cannot occur simultaneously i.e. both are disjoints.

Here, $A \cap B = \phi$

and two events A and B will be exhaustive event, if $A \cup B = S$, i.e. one of them necessarily occurs whenever the experiment is performed.

Now, if $A \cap B = \phi$ and $A \cup B = S$, then the events A and B are called mutually exclusive and exhaustive events.

Here, $A \cap B = \phi$ but $A \cup B \neq S$,

Hence, A and B are not mutually exclusive and exhaustive.

26. When a coin is tossed three times, then

$S = \{HHH, HHT, HTH, THH, TTH, THT, HTT, TTT\}$

(i) A = Getting atleast two heads
$= \{HHH, HHT, HTH, THH\}$

B = Getting atleast two tails
$= \{TTH, THT, HTT, TTT\}$

$A \cap B = \phi$

(ii) A = Getting atmost two tails
$= \{HHH, HHT, HTH, THH, TTH, THT, HTT\}$

B = Getting no tails
$= \{HHH\}$

$A \cap B = \{HHH\} \neq \phi$

(iii) A = Getting no heads
$= \{TTT\}$

B = Getting exactly one head
$= \{TTH, THT, HTT\}$

C = Getting atleast two heads
$= \{HHH, HHT, HTH, THH\}$

$A \cap B = \phi, A \cap C = \phi,$
$B \cap C = \phi$ and $A \cup B \cup C = S$

(iv) A = Getting exactly one head
$= \{TTH, THT, HTT\}$

B = Getting exactly two heads
$= \{HHT, HTH, THH\}$

$A \cap B = \phi$ and $A \cup B \neq S$

27. Three coins are tossed once.

Sample space

$S = \{HHH, HHT, HTH, THH, TTH, THT, HTT, TTT\}$

$A = \{HHH\}$

$B = \{HHH, HHT, THH\}$

$C = \{TTH, THT, HTT\}$
$D = \{HHH, HHT, HTH, HTT\}$
Now, A contains only one outcomes.
Hence A is simple and B, C and D contain more than one outcomes.
$\therefore$ B, C and D are **compound**.
Also, $A \cap B \neq \phi$, $A \cap C = \phi$, and $A \cap D \neq \phi$
$\therefore$ A with C is **mutually exclusive** but not with B and D.
Again, $B \cap C = \phi$ and $B \cap D \neq \phi$.
$\therefore$ B with C is **mutually exclusive** but not with D.
$C \cap D \neq \phi$
$\therefore$ C and D are not mutually exclusive.
Also, $A \cup B \cup C \cup D$
$= \{HHH, HHT, THH, HTH, TTH, THT, HTT\} \neq S$
Hence, not **exhaustive event**.
Hence,
(i) event A
(ii) events B, C and D
(iii) events 'A and C' and 'B and C'.
(iv) A, B, C and D are not exhaustive events.

28. A coin is tossed thrice. Then,
$S = \{HHH, HHT, HTH, THH, TTH, THT, HTT, TTT\}$
$n(S) = 8$
$\therefore \quad P(E) = \dfrac{n(E)}{n(S)}$

(i) $E_1 = \{TTT\}$
$n(E_1) = 1 \Rightarrow P(E_1) = \dfrac{1}{8}$

(ii) $E_2 = \{TTH, THT, HTT\}$
$n(E_2) = 3 \Rightarrow P(E_2) = \dfrac{3}{8}$

(iii) $E_3 = \{TTH, THT, HTT, TTT\}$
$n(E_3) = 4 \Rightarrow P(E_3) = \dfrac{4}{8} = \dfrac{1}{2}$

(iv) $E_4 = \{TTT\}$
$n(E_4) = 1 \Rightarrow P(E_4) = \dfrac{1}{8}$

(v) $E_5 = \{HHH\}$
$n(E_5) = 1 \Rightarrow P(E_5) = \dfrac{1}{8}$

(vi) $E_6 = \{HHT, HTH, THH, TTH, THT, HTT, TTT\}$
$n(E_6) = 7$
$\Rightarrow P(E_6) = \dfrac{7}{8}$

29. After tossing four coins, the possible outcomes will be
$S = \{HHHH, HHHT, HHTH, HHTT, HTHH, HTHT, HTTH, HTTT, THHH, THHT, THTH, THTT, TTHH, TTHT, TTTH, TTTT\}$
which contains 2^4
$= 16$ event points.
Now, let event A = Getting atleast three heads
$A = \{HHHH, HHHT, HHTH, HTHH, THHH\}$
which contains 5 event points.
Therefore, the required probability $P(A) = \dfrac{5}{16}$.

30. (c) When a card is drawn from a well-shuffled pack, then the number of possible outcomes is 52.
A : One ace
$\therefore \quad P(A) = \dfrac{4}{52}$
[number of outcomes in A is 4]
$= \dfrac{1}{13}$
B : The card drawn is diamond
$P(B) = \dfrac{13}{52} = \dfrac{1}{4}$
So, the required probabilities are $\dfrac{1}{13}$ and $\dfrac{1}{4}$, respectively.

31. In leap year, there are 366 days in which 52 complete weeks and 2 days extra.
Clearly, from 52 weeks, 52 Mondays will be available.
If there are to be 53 Mondays in a randomly selected leap year, there must be one Monday in the extra two days.
Then, the sample space contains
(i) Sunday, Monday,
(ii) Monday, Tuesday,
(iii) Tuesday, Wednesday,
(iv) Wednesday, Thursday,
(v) Thursday, Friday,
(vi) Friday, Saturday,
(vii) Saturday, Sunday
Let event E = Probability of having 53 Mondays.
$\therefore$ Sample space E = {Sunday and Monday, Monday and Tuesday}
$\therefore \quad P(E) = \dfrac{2}{7}$

32. (i) Let event E_1 = A multiple of 4
$\therefore E_1 = \{4, 8, 12, 16, 20, 24, 28, 32, 36\}$
$\therefore n(E_1) = 9$ and $n(S) = 36$
$\therefore P(E_1) = \dfrac{9}{36} = \dfrac{1}{4}$

(ii) Let event E_2 = A number greater than 20
$\therefore E_2 = \{21, 22, 23, 24, 25, 26, 27, 28, 29, 30, 31, 32, 33, 34, 35, 36\}$
$\therefore n(E_2) = 16$
$\therefore P(E_2) = \dfrac{16}{36} = \dfrac{4}{9}$

(iii) Let event E_3 = A multiple of 13
$\therefore E_3 = \{13, 26\}$
$\therefore n(E_3) = 2$
$\therefore P(E_3) = \dfrac{2}{36} = \dfrac{1}{18}$

(iv) Let event E_4 = An odd number which is a multiple of 3
$\therefore E_4 = \{3, 9, 15, 21, 27, 33\}$
$\therefore n(E_4) = 6$
$\therefore P(E_4) = \dfrac{6}{36} = \dfrac{1}{6}$

(v) Let event E_5 = A number between 6 and 10
$\therefore E_5 = \{7, 8, 9\}$
$\therefore n(E_5) = 3$
$\therefore P(E_5) = \dfrac{3}{36} = \dfrac{1}{12}$

33. Sample space S is given by
S = {Anuj Amit Neha, Anuj Neha Amit, Amit Anuj Neha, Amit Neha Anuj, Neha Anuj Amit, Neha Amit Anuj}
(i) Let event E_1 = Anuj sits in the middle
$\therefore E_1$ = {Amit Anuj Neha, Neha Anuj Amit}
$\therefore n(E_1) = 2$ and $n(S) = 6$
$\therefore P(E_1) = \dfrac{2}{6} = \dfrac{1}{3}$

(ii) Let event E_2 = Anuj sits at the left end
$\therefore E_2$ = {Anuj Amit Neha, Anuj Neha Amit}
$\therefore n(E_2) = 2$
$\therefore P(E_2) = \dfrac{2}{6} = \dfrac{1}{3}$

(iii) Let event E_3 = Anuj sits at the right end

$\therefore E_3 = \{$Amit Neha Anuj, Neha Amit Anuj$\}$

$\therefore n(E_3) = 2$

$\therefore P(E_3) = \frac{2}{6} = \frac{1}{3}$

(iv) Let event E_4 = Amit and Neha are seated together

$\therefore E_4 = \{$Anuj Amit Neha, Anuj Neha Amit, Amit Neha Anuj, Neha Amit Anuj$\}$

$\therefore n(E_4) = 4$

$\therefore P(E_4) = \frac{4}{6} = \frac{2}{3}$

34. The experiment of 'examining three consecutive bulbs produced in a factory'.

Non-defective bulbs are denoted as G and defective bulbs are denoted as B. We may get 0, 1, 2 or 3 defective bulbs as result of examination.

Then, $S = \{BBB, BBG, BGB, GBB, BGG, GBG, GGB, GGG\}$

(i) Event A = Getting exactly one defective bulb

$= \{BGG, GBG, GGB\}$

$\therefore P(A) = \Sigma P(W_i)$, $\forall\ W_i \in A$

$= P(BGG) + P(GBG) + P(GGB)$

$= \frac{1}{8} + \frac{1}{8} + \frac{1}{8} = \frac{3}{8}$

(ii) Event B = Getting atleast two defective bulbs

$= \{BBG, BGB, GBB, BBB\}$

$\therefore P(B) = P(BBG) + P(BGB) + P(GBB) + P(BBB)$

$= \frac{1}{8} + \frac{1}{8} + \frac{1}{8} + \frac{1}{8} = \frac{4}{8} = \frac{1}{2}$

(iii) Event C = Getting no defective bulb

$= \{GGG\}$

$\therefore P(C) = P(GGG) = \frac{1}{8}$

35. The sample space of throwing two dice is $S = \{(x, y) : x, y \in \{1, 2, 3, 4, 5, 6\}\}$ which contains $6^2 = 36$ event points.

A = Event of getting equal faces

$= \{(x, x) : (x, x) \in S\}$

$= \{(1, 1), (2, 2), (3, 3), (4, 4), (5, 5), (6, 6)\}$

Hence, the required probability

$P(A) = \frac{6}{36} = \frac{1}{6}$.

36. (a) Let S be the sample space of tossing a coin three times in succession.

Hence, $S = \{HHH, HHT, HTH, THH, TTH, THT, HTT, TTT\}$

Let A = Event of 2 consecutive heads

$= \{HHT, THH, HHH\}$

$\therefore$ Therefore, $P(A) = \frac{3}{8}$

37. (b) Given, D denotes defective bulb and N denotes non-defective bulb.

After selecting 3 bulbs randomly from a lot, the sample space associated with this experiment is,

$S = \{NNN, NND, NDN, DNN, NDD, DND, DDN, DDD\}$

which contains atmost 3 defective bulbs.

and hence S has 8 event points.

Let event A = Getting atleast two defective bulbs.

$A = \{NDD, DND, DDN, DDD\}$

Therefore, the required probability

$P(A) = \frac{4}{8} = \frac{1}{2}$

38. (b) Event A = Sum of faces equal to 6

$P(A)$ = Probability of sum of faces equal to 6

$S(A) = \{(1, 5), (5, 1), (2, 4), (4, 2), (3, 3)\}$

$\therefore P(A) = \frac{5}{36}$

[$\because$ total number of outcomes $= 6^2 = 36$]

$P(B)$ = Probability of sum of faces is greater than 10

$S(B) = \{(5, 6), (6, 5), (6, 6)\}$

$P(B) = \frac{3}{36} = \frac{1}{12}$

$P(C)$ = Probability of sum of faces is even

$S(C) = \{(1, 1), (1, 3), (1, 5), (2, 2), (2, 4), (2, 6), (3, 1), (3, 3), (3, 5), (4, 2), (4, 4), (4, 6), (5, 1), (5, 3), (5, 5), (6, 2), (6, 4), (6, 6)]$

$\therefore P(C) = \frac{18}{36} = \frac{1}{2}$

Hence, A-II, B-I, C-III

39. (True)

Let R, B_1 and B_2 denote red, black and blue pens, respectively.

The outcomes will be $\{RB_1, RB_2\}$

Similarly, $\{B_1R, B_1B_2\}$, $\{B_2R, B_2B_1\}$

Thus, the sample space is

$S = \{RB_1, RB_2, B_1R, B_1B_2, B_2R, B_2B_1\}$

Event $A = \{RB_1, B_1R\}$

$\therefore$ Probability $P(A) = \frac{2}{6} = \frac{1}{3}$

40. In this random experiment, tail may come up on 1st toss or 2nd toss or 3rd toss and so on.

Hence, the sample space is

$= \{T, HT, HHT, HHHT, HHHHT, \ldots\}$

Now, for tossing a coin, we can assign the number $\frac{1}{2}$ to each of outcomes H and T

i.e. $P(H) = \frac{1}{2}$ and $P(T) = \frac{1}{2}$

Hence, the required probability

$P(S) = P(T) + P(HT) + P(HHT) + P(HHHT) + P(HHHHT) + \ldots$

$= \frac{1}{2} + \frac{1}{2}\cdot\frac{1}{2} + \frac{1}{2}\cdot\frac{1}{2}\cdot\frac{1}{2} + \frac{1}{2}\cdot\frac{1}{2}\cdot\frac{1}{2}\cdot\frac{1}{2} + \frac{1}{2}\cdot\frac{1}{2}\cdot\frac{1}{2}\cdot\frac{1}{2}\cdot\frac{1}{2} + \ldots$

$= \frac{1}{2}\left[1 + \frac{1}{2} + \left(\frac{1}{2}\right)^2 + \left(\frac{1}{2}\right)^3 + \left(\frac{1}{2}\right)^4 + \ldots\right]$

$= \frac{1}{2}\left(\frac{1}{1 - \frac{1}{2}}\right) = 1$

Therefore,

$P(S)$ = Total probability = 1.

41. $a^2 - b^2$ is divisible by 2 if a and b are both even or odd.

Now, the pair of numbers can be choosen from $\{1, 2, \ldots\ldots, 11\}$.

Both number of pairs will be even that can be chosen in $5 \times 5 = 25$ ways with replacement as $\{2, 4, 6, 8, 10\}$ is the set of even number.

Similarly, both odd can be chosen in $6 \times 6 = 36$ ways

Again, we can choose a and b from the set of first 11 positive integers in $11 \times 11 = 121$ ways.

Therefore, the required probability is

$= \frac{25 + 36}{121} = \frac{61}{121}$

42. After throwing a die, the sample space (outcomes) is

$$= \{1, 2, 3, 4, 5, 6\}$$

Let, event A = Getting a number greater than 4

$$= \{5, 6\}$$

and event B = Getting a number less than 3

$$= \{1, 2\}$$

Now event A or event B

$$= A \text{ or } B = A \cup B$$
$$= \{1, 2, 5, 6\}$$

Here, all the outcomes are equally likely, so the required probability is

$$P(A \cup B) = \frac{4}{6} = \frac{2}{3}$$

43. Let event A = 'A speaks the truth'

i.e. $P(A) = \dfrac{65}{100}$

and event B = 'B speaks the truth'

i.e. $P(B) = \dfrac{75}{100}$

Now, $P(A') = 1 - P(A)$

$$= 1 - \frac{65}{100} = \frac{35}{100}$$

$$P(B') = 1 - P(B) = 1 - \frac{75}{100} = \frac{25}{100}$$

Again, let

event E = They contradict to make the same information statement i.e.

event $E = (A \cap B') \cup (A' \cap B)$

Now,

$$P(E) = P(A \cap B') + P(A' \cap B)$$

Hence, $P(E) = P(A) \cdot P(B') + P(A') \cdot P(B)$

$$= \frac{65}{100} \times \frac{25}{100} + \frac{35}{100} \times \frac{75}{100}$$
$$= 0.425$$

In 42.50% cases, A and B contradict to make the same information statement.

44. Here, A and B are two events.

Given, $P(A) = \dfrac{2}{3}$, $P(B) = \dfrac{1}{6}$

and $P(A \cap B) = \dfrac{1}{3}$

Now, probability (not A and not B)

$$= P(A' \text{ and } B')$$

[$A' \equiv$ not A and $B' \equiv$ not B]

$$= P(A' \cap B')$$
$$= P(A \cup B)'$$

[by De-Morgan's law]

$$= 1 - P(A \cup B)$$
$$= 1 - [P(A) + P(B) - P(A \cap B)]$$
$$= 1 - \left[\frac{2}{3} + \frac{1}{6} - \frac{1}{3}\right]$$
$$= 1 - \left(\frac{5}{6} - \frac{1}{3}\right)$$
$$= 1 - \frac{3}{6}$$
$$= 1 - \frac{1}{2} = \frac{1}{2}$$

Therefore, probability (not A and not B) $= \dfrac{1}{2}$.

45. There are 6 fruits in a bag, in which 4 are mangoes and 2 are oranges.

Hence, total number of outcomes is 6.

Let event A = The fruit drawn is mango

Event B = The fruit drawn is orange

(i) Probability of choosing fruit which is mango

i.e. $P(A) = \dfrac{2}{3}$

(ii) Probability of choosing fruit which is orange

i.e. $P(B) = \dfrac{1}{3}$

(iii) The event 'either mango or orange' described by the event A or B.

As, A and B are mutually exclusive.

$\therefore \; P(A \cap B) = 0$

Now, $P(A \cup B) = P(A) + P(B) - P(A \cap B)$

$$= \frac{2}{3} + \frac{1}{3} - 0 = 1$$

(iv) The event 'not mango' denoted by 'not A' i.e. A'

Therefore, $P(A') = 1 - P(A)$

$$= 1 - \frac{2}{3}$$
$$= \frac{1}{3}$$

46. Given, $P(A - B) = \dfrac{1}{3}$, $P(A) = \dfrac{1}{2}$

and $P(B) = \dfrac{1}{3}$

Now we know, $A - B = A \cap B'$

Also, $A \cap B'$ and $A \cap B$ are mutually exclusive.

So, $A = (A \cap B) \cup (A \cap B')$

Hence,

$$P(A) = P(A \cap B) + P(A \cap B')$$

[$\because A \cap B$ and $A \cap B'$ are mutually exclusive]

$$\Rightarrow P(A \cap B) = P(A) - P(A \cap B')$$
$$= \frac{1}{2} - \frac{1}{3} = \frac{1}{6}$$

Hence, the value of $P(A \cap B)$ is $\dfrac{1}{6}$.

47. (True)

Total number lying from 1 to 500 is 500.

Let n_1 be the total numbers lying between 1 and 500 and also divisible by 4 is,

$$500 = 4 + (n_1 - 1) \cdot 4$$
$$\therefore \quad n_1 = 125$$

Let n_2 be the total numbers lying between 1 and 500 and divisible by 5 is,

$$500 = 5 + (n_2 - 1) \cdot 5$$
$$\therefore \quad n_2 = 100$$

Let n_3 be the total numbers lying between 1 and 500 and also divisible by 4 and 5 is,

$$500 = 20 + (n_3 - 1)\, 20$$
$$\Rightarrow \quad n_3 = 25$$

Let event A = The number is divisible by 4

$$\therefore \; P(A) = \frac{125}{500} = \frac{1}{4}$$

Event B = the number is divisible by 5

$$\therefore \quad P(B) = \frac{100}{500} = \frac{1}{5}$$

and $P(A \cap B) = \dfrac{25}{500} = \dfrac{1}{20}$

Therefore, the required probability i.e. probability (the number divisible by 4 or 5)

$$\Rightarrow P(A \cup B) = P(A) + P(B) - P(A \cap B)$$
$$= \frac{1}{4} + \frac{1}{5} - \frac{1}{20}$$
$$= \frac{9}{20} - \frac{1}{20}$$
$$= \frac{8}{20} = \frac{2}{5}$$

$\therefore$ The required probability is $\dfrac{2}{5}$.

48. Given, A and B are two events, where

$$P(A) = \frac{3}{4} \text{ and } P(B) = \frac{5}{8}$$

Again we know,

$$0 \le P(A \cup B) \le 1$$

Since, $P(A \cup B) \le 1$

$$\Rightarrow P(A) + P(B) - P(A \cap B) \le 1$$

$$\Rightarrow \quad \frac{3}{4} + \frac{5}{8} - P(A \cap B) \le 1$$

$$\Rightarrow \quad P(A \cap B) \ge \frac{3}{4} + \frac{5}{8} - 1 = \frac{3}{8}$$

$$\therefore \quad P(A \cap B) \ge \frac{3}{8} \quad \text{...(i)}$$

Again, $B \cap A$ and $B \cap A^C$ are mutually exclusive event.

and $B = (B \cap A) \cup (B \cap A^C)$

Now,

$$P(B) = P\{(B \cap A) \cup (B \cap A^C)\}$$
$$= P(B \cap A) + P(B \cap A^C)$$

[$\because B \cap A$ and $B \cap A^C$ are mutually exclusive]

$$\Rightarrow P(A \cap B) = P(B) - P(B \cap A^C)$$

$$\therefore P(A \cap B) = 5/8 - P(B \cap A^C)$$

Therefore, $P(A \cap B) \le 5/8$

[$\because P(B \cap A^C) \ge 0$] ...(ii)

Hence, from Eqs. (i) and (ii),

$$\frac{3}{8} \le P(A \cap B) \le \frac{5}{8}$$

Therefore, the statement is correct.

49. If a die is thrown once.

Then, sample space

$$S = \{1, 2, 3, 4, 5, 6\}$$

Probability of getting six $= \frac{1}{6}$

and getting no six $= \left(1 - \frac{1}{6}\right) = \frac{5}{6}$

Number of outcomes for throwing a die twice $= 6^2$

A = Atleast one six

A^C = Getting no six

$$P(A^C) = (5/6)^2$$

$$\therefore \; P(A) = 1 - \left(\frac{5}{6}\right)^2$$

$$= 1 - \frac{25}{36} = \frac{11}{36}$$

50. When a card is drawn from a well-shuffled pack of 52 cards, then the number of possible outcomes is 52.

Let event A = 1st card is diamond

Event B = 2nd card is diamond

Event C = 3rd card is diamond

The required probability of getting atleast one of them is diamond.

$$P(AB'C' + A'BC' + A'B'C + ABC' + AB'C + A'BC + ABC)$$
$$= P(AB'C') + P(A'BC') + P(A'B'C) + P(ABC') + P(AB'C) + P(A'BC) + P(ABC)$$

[$\because$ all events are mutually exclusive]

$$= \left(\frac{13}{52} \times \frac{39}{51} \times \frac{38}{50}\right) + \left(\frac{39}{52} \times \frac{13}{51} \times \frac{38}{50}\right) + \left(\frac{39}{52} \times \frac{38}{51} \times \frac{13}{50}\right) + \left(\frac{13}{52} \times \frac{12}{51} \times \frac{39}{50}\right) + \left(\frac{13}{52} \times \frac{39}{51} \times \frac{12}{50}\right) + \left(\frac{39}{52} \times \frac{13}{51} \times \frac{12}{50}\right) + \left(\frac{13}{52} \times \frac{12}{51} \times \frac{11}{50}\right)$$

$$= \frac{1}{132600} [19266 + 19266 + 19266 + 6084 + 6084 + 6084 + 1716]$$

$$= \frac{77766}{132600} = 0.59$$

[approximate value]

51. Let event A_i = Shivam throws 6 in the ith throw, $i = 1, 3, 5, ...$

and event B_j = Rishi throws 7 in the j th throw, $j = 2, 4, 6, ...$

Sample space of 'throwing 6 by two dice' is $\{(1, 5), (2, 4), (3, 3), (4, 2), (5, 1)\}$.

$$\therefore \quad P(A_i) = \frac{5}{36}$$

and the sample space of 'throwing 7 by two dice' is

$$\{(1, 6), (2, 5), (3, 4), (4, 3), (5, 2), (6, 1)\}$$

$$\therefore \quad P(B_j) = \frac{6}{36} = \frac{1}{6}$$

If Shivam begins, then Shivam wins, if atleast one of the events happens.

$A_1, A'_1 B'_2 A_3, A'_1 B'_2 A'_3 B'_4 A_5,$ .... all events are mutually exclusive and A' means 'not A'.

Hence, the probability that Shivam wins,

$$P(A_1 \cup A'_1 B'_2 A_3 \cup A'_1 B'_2 A'_3 B'_4 A_5 \cup ......)$$
$$= P(A_1) + P(A'_1 B'_2 A_3) + P(A'_1 B'_2 A'_3 B'_4 A_5) + \ldots$$
$$= \frac{5}{36} + \frac{31}{36} \cdot \frac{5}{6} \cdot \frac{5}{36} + \frac{31}{36} \cdot \frac{5}{6} \cdot \frac{31}{36} \cdot \frac{5}{6} \cdot \frac{5}{36}$$
$$= \frac{5}{36}\left[1 + \left(\frac{31}{36} \cdot \frac{5}{6}\right) + \left(\frac{31}{36} \cdot \frac{5}{6}\right)^2 + \ldots\right]$$
$$= \frac{5}{36} \times \frac{1}{1 - \left(\frac{31}{36} \cdot \frac{5}{6}\right)} = \frac{30}{61}$$

52. (b) Given, A and B are two independent events.

Now,

$$P(A) = P(A \cap B) + P(A \cap B')$$

[$\because A \cap B$ and $A \cap B'$ are mutually exclusive]

$$= P(A) \cdot P(B) + \frac{3}{25}$$

[$\because A$ and B are independent : $P(A \cap B) = P(A)\,P(B)$]

Let $P(A) = x$ and $P(B) = y$

$$\therefore \quad x = xy + \frac{3}{25} \quad \text{...(i)}$$

Similarly,

$$\therefore \quad y = xy + \frac{8}{25} \quad \text{...(ii)}$$

Subtracting Eq. (i) from Eq. (ii), we get

$$\therefore \quad y = x + \frac{1}{5} \quad \text{...(iii)}$$

Putting the value of y in Eq. (i), we get

$$x = x\left(x + \frac{1}{5}\right) + \frac{3}{25}$$

$$\Rightarrow \quad (5x - 3)(5x - 1) = 0$$

$$\therefore \quad x = \frac{3}{5}, x = \frac{1}{5}$$

By question, $P(A) > \frac{1}{2}$ i.e. $x > \frac{1}{2}$

So, $P(A) = \frac{3}{5}$

Now by Eq. (iii),

$$y = \frac{3}{5} + \frac{1}{5} = \frac{4}{5},$$

which is also $> \frac{1}{2}$.

53. (c) An event point is a permutation of 5 different balls, taken all at a time. Therefore, total number of sample point in the sample space is 5! and now the required event contains

$RWWRW = 2\times3\times2\times1\times1$
$= 12$ event points

Therefore, the required probability is

$$P(RWWRW) = \frac{12}{5!} = \frac{12}{5\times4\times3\times2\times1} = \frac{1}{10}$$

54. Total number of event points in the event space $= 10$ [7 boys + 3 girls]

Let event A = None of girls are together

The number of simple events favourable to A = Number of ways in which 10 members can be arranged, where the girls are placed in between and at the ends of 7 boys (i.e. 8 places)

$= {}^8P_3 \times 7!$

Assuming all the simple events are equally likely.

∴ The required probability

$$= \frac{{}^8P_3\times7!}{10!} = \frac{8!\times7!}{5!\times10!}$$

$$= \frac{8!\times7\times6\times5!}{10\times9\times8!\times5!} = \frac{7\times6}{10\times9} = \frac{7}{15}$$

55. If three cards are drawn from a well-shuffled pack, then number of possible outcomes is 52.

Event A = Atleast one card is spade.

Therefore, A' = None of them is spade.

Clearly, number of card (event points) in set $A' = 39$

$$\text{Therefore, } P(A') = \frac{\binom{39}{3}}{\binom{52}{3}} \qquad \left[\binom{a}{b} \equiv {}^aC_b\right]$$

$$= \frac{(39)!}{(36)!\times3!}\times\frac{(49)!\times3!}{(52)!} \qquad \left[\because {}^aC_b = \frac{(a)!}{(a-b)!\times b!}\right]$$

$$= \frac{39\times38\times37}{52\times51\times50}$$

$$= \frac{19\times37}{2\times17\times50} = \frac{703}{1700}$$

Hence, the probability (atleast one of them is spade)

$$= P(A) = 1 - P(\overline{A})$$

$$= 1 - \frac{703}{1700} = \frac{997}{1700}$$

56. A pack of card contains 52 cards. Hence, the number of possible outcomes is 52, of which 4 are king and 48 other cards.

Now, 13 cards are drawn from the pack, so there are $\binom{52}{13}$ ways of choosing. We have to find the probability among these 13 cards one is king.

Therefore, the required probability

$$= \frac{\binom{4}{1}\binom{48}{12}}{\binom{52}{13}}$$

$$= \frac{{}^4C_1\times{}^{48}C_{12}}{{}^{52}C_{13}}$$

$$= \frac{4!\times48!\times13!\times39!}{3!\times12!\times36!\times52!}$$

$$= \frac{13\times19\times37}{17\times25\times49} = \frac{9139}{20825} = 0.44$$

57. If two letters are chosen randomly from the word 'PROBABILITY', then there are

$${}^{11}C_2 = \frac{11!}{(11-2)!\times2!}$$

$$= \frac{11\times10}{2}$$

$= 55$ event points in the sample space.

Let event A = Atleast one letter is vowel

$= \{(P,O),(P,A),(P,I),(R,O),(R,A),(R,I),(B,O),(B,A),(B,I),(L,O),(L,A),(L,I),(T,O),(T,I),(T,A),(Y,O),(Y,A),(Y,I),(I,I),(O,A),(O,I),(A,I)\}$,

which contains 22 event points.

$$\therefore\quad P(A) = \frac{22}{55} = \frac{2}{5}$$

58. We can choose, 14 wrist watches randomly, from the packet of 20 wrist watches in ${}^{20}C_{14}$ way.

$$= \frac{20!}{(20-14)!\times14!}$$

$= 38760$

Let event E = Getting no defective watch

Event E' = Getting atleast one defective watch

Now, we can select 14 non-defective watches in ${}^{(20-5)}C_{14}$ ways $= 15$ ways

$P(E)$ = Probability of getting no defective watch

$$= \frac{15}{38760} = \frac{1}{2584}$$

$$P(E') = 1 - P(E)$$

$$= 1 - \frac{1}{2584}$$

$$= \frac{2583}{2584}$$

59. Total number of members

$= 3 + 2 = 5$

Out of which three members can be selected in ${}^5C_3$ ways.

(i) Exactly one boy in the group means one boy and two girls in the group.

∴The required probability is

P(exactly one boy)

$$= \frac{{}^3C_1\times{}^2C_2}{{}^5C_3} = \frac{3\times1}{10} = \frac{3}{10}$$

(ii) Atleast one boy in the group means one boy and two girls, two boys and one girl or three boys.

∴The required probability is

P (atleast one boy)

$$= \frac{{}^3C_1\times{}^2C_2}{{}^5C_3} + \frac{{}^3C_2\times{}^2C_1}{{}^5C_3} + \frac{{}^3C_3}{{}^5C_3}$$

$$= \frac{3\times1+3\times2+1}{10}$$

$$= \frac{3+6+1}{10} = \frac{10}{10} = 1$$

(iii) Atmost two girls in the group means 2 girls and one boy, one girl and two boys or three boys only (i.e. zero girl)

$= 1$ [same as part (ii)].

60. 13 cards are drawn from a well-shuffled pack of 52 cards. Then, number of event points in the sample space is ${}^{52}C_{13}$. A pack of 52 cards contain 4 aces.

Event A = Getting all the aces

$$P(A)=\frac{{}^4C_4\times{}^{48}C_9}{{}^{52}C_{13}}$$

Event B = Getting atleast one ace.

B' = Getting no ace

$$P(B^C)=\frac{{}^{48}C_{13}}{{}^{52}C_{13}}$$

Hence, $P(B)=1-P(B')=1-\dfrac{{}^{48}C_{13}}{{}^{52}C_{13}}$

$$P(A\cup B)=P(A)+P(B)-P(A\cap B)$$
$$=\frac{{}^4C_4\times{}^{48}C_9}{{}^{52}C_{13}}+\left(1-\frac{{}^{48}C_{13}}{{}^{52}C_{13}}\right)$$
$$=\frac{1\times{}^{48}C_9}{{}^{52}C_{13}}+\left(1-\frac{{}^{48}C_{13}}{{}^{52}C_{13}}\right)$$
$$P(A\cup B)=1+\frac{{}^{48}C_9-{}^{48}C_{13}}{{}^{52}C_{13}}$$

61. Let event A = a student reads Mathematics

Event B = a student reads Chemistry

and event C = a student reads Physics

Given, $P(A)=\dfrac{20}{100}$, $P(B)=\dfrac{16}{100}$

and $P(C)=\dfrac{14}{100}$

P (Mathematics and Chemistry)
$$=P(A\cap B)=\frac{8}{100}$$

P (Mathematics and Physics)
$$=P(A\cap C)=\frac{6}{100}$$

P (Chemistry and Physics)
$$=P(B\cap C)=\frac{4}{100}$$

and P (Mathematics, Chemistry and Physics)
$$=P(A\cap B\cap C)=\frac{2}{100}$$

$\therefore$ $P(A\cup B\cup C)=P(A)+P(B)+P(C)-P(A\cap B)-P(A\cap C)-P(B\cap C)+P(A\cap B\cap C)$
$$=\frac{20}{100}+\frac{16}{100}+\frac{14}{100}-\frac{8}{100}-\frac{6}{100}-\frac{4}{100}+\frac{2}{100}$$
$$=\frac{34}{100}$$

Now, the required probability that the students reads none is

P (the student reads none)

= Probability (the student reads other than Mathematics or Chemistry or Physics)

$$=P(A\cup B\cup C)'$$
$$=1-P(A\cup B\cup C)$$
$$=1-\frac{34}{100}=\frac{66}{100}=0.66$$

Hence, the required probability is 66%.

62. (a) Let Event A_i = ith letter is placed in the correct envelope (i = 1, 2, 3, 4)

Now, if the first letter is placed in the correct envelope, then remaining 3 letters can be placed in 3! ways and so on.

Therefore, the required probability of all letters are wrongly placed is, probability $(A_1'\cap A_2'\cap A_3'\cap A_4')$

$=P(A_1\cup A_2\cup A_3\cup A_4)'$ [by De-morgan's law]

$=1-P(A_1\cup A_2\cup A_3\cup A_4)$

$=1-[P(A_1)+P(A_2)+P(A_3)+P(A_4)-P(A_1\cap A_2)-P(A_1\cap A_3)-P(A_1\cap A_4)-P(A_2\cap A_3)-P(A_2\cap A_4)-P(A_3\cap A_4)+P(A_1\cap A_2\cap A_3)+P(A_1\cap A_3\cap A_4)+P(A_1\cap A_2\cap A_4)+P(A_2\cap A_3\cap A_4)-P(A_1\cap A_2\cap A_3\cap A_4)]$

$$=1-\left[\frac{3!}{4!}+\frac{3!}{4!}+\frac{3!}{4!}+\frac{3!}{4!}-\frac{2!}{4!}-\frac{2!}{4!}-\frac{2!}{4!}-\frac{2!}{4!}-\frac{2!}{4!}-\frac{2!}{4!}+\frac{1}{4!}+\frac{1}{4!}+\frac{1}{4!}+\frac{1}{4!}-\frac{1}{4!}\right]$$
$$=1-\left[4\times\frac{3!}{4!}-6\times\frac{2!}{4!}+3\frac{1}{4!}\right]$$
$$=1-\left[1-6\frac{1}{4\times3}+\frac{1}{4\times2}\right]$$
$$=1-\left[1-\frac{1}{2}+\frac{1}{8}\right]=\frac{3}{8}$$

63. (c) Given, $P(B)=\dfrac{5}{4}P(A)$ and

$P(C)=\dfrac{1}{5}P(B)$

Also A, B and C are mutually exclusive and exhaustive events

Now, $P(B)=5P(C)$ ...(i)

Again, $P(A)=\dfrac{4}{5}P(B)=\dfrac{4}{5}\cdot5P(C)$

$\therefore$ $P(A)=4P(C)$ ...(ii)

Since, A, B and C are mutually exclusive and exhaustive events of S.

Then, $A\cup B\cup C=S$

Therefore,
$$P(A\cup B\cup C)=P(S)=1$$
$\Rightarrow$ $P(A)+P(B)+P(C)=1$

[$\because$ A, B and C are mutually exclusive]

$\Rightarrow$ $4P(C)+5P(C)+P(C)=1$

$\therefore$ $P(C)=\dfrac{1}{10}$

Hence, $P(C)=\dfrac{1}{10}$

64. The assignment is valid.

Given, $P(A)=0.38$, $P(B)=0.30$ and $P(C)=0.32$

Since, events A, B and C are mutually exclusive and exhaustive, then $[P(A)+P(B)+P(C)]$ will be equal to 1.

Now, by given question,

$P(A)+P(B)+P(C)$

$=0.38+0.30+0.32$

$=1$, which satisfy the condition.

Hence, assignment of probabilities are valid.

65. (c) Given, $P(A)=0.4$, $P(B)=0.5$, $P(C)=0.3$, $P(A\cup B)=0.9$, $P(A\cap C)=0.2$ and $P(A\cap B\cap C)=0.1$

Now, for any three events A, B and C,

$P(A\cup B\cup C)=P(A)+P(B)+P(C)-P(A\cap B)-P(B\cap C)-P(C\cap A)+P(A\cap B\cap C)$

$=0.4+0.5+0.3-0-P(B\cap C)-0.2+0.1$

$\therefore$ $P(A\cup B\cup C)=1.1-P(B\cap C)$ ...(i)

Since, by given condition,
$$P(A\cup B\cup C)\geq0.65$$

By Eq. (i), $1.1-P(B\cap C)\geq0.65$

$\Rightarrow$ $1.1-0.65\geq P(B\cap C)$

$\therefore$ $P(B\cap C)\leq0.45$ ...(ii)

Again, $P(A\cup B\cup C)\leq1$

By Eq. (i), $1.1-P(B\cap C)\leq1$

$\Rightarrow$ $1.1-1\leq P(B\cap C)$

$\Rightarrow$ $0.1\leq P(B\cap C)$ ...(iii)

So, from Eqs. (ii) and (iii),
$$0.1\leq P(B\cap C)\leq0.45$$

Assertion Reason

1. (b) For a coin, there are two possible outcomes, $\{H, T\}$, and for a die, there are 6 possible outcomes $\{1, 2, 3, 4, 5, 6\}$.

$\therefore$ The sample space while a coin is tossed and a die is rolled at once is $\{H1, H2, H3, H4, H5, H6, T1, T2, T3, T4, T5, T6\}$.

Now, the sample space of throwing a die twice is

$\{(1, 1), (1, 2), (1, 3), (1, 4), (1, 5), (1, 6), (2, 1), (2, 2), (2, 3), (2, 4), (2, 5), (2, 6), (3, 1), (3, 2), (3, 3), (3, 4), (3, 5), (3, 6), (4, 1), (4, 2), (4, 3), (4, 4), (4, 5), (4, 6), (5, 1), (5, 2), (5, 3), (5, 4), (5, 5), (5, 6), (6, 1), (6, 2), (6, 3), (6, 4), (6, 5), (6, 6)\}$

i.e. $\{(a, b) : a, b \in \{1, 2, 3, 4, 5, 6\}\}$

2. (d) We have, sample space,

$S = [1, 2, 3, 4, 5, 6\}$

$A = \{2, 3, 5\}; B = \{2, 4, 6\}$

Here, $A \cap B = \{2\}$

$\therefore \quad P(A \cap B) \neq P(A) \cdot P(B)$

Hence, Assertion is false.

Now, when a coin is tossed twice, Sample space,

$S = \{HH, HT, TH, TT\}$

$A = \{HH\}$

$B = \{TT\}$

Here, $A \cap B = \phi$

$\therefore$ Reason is true.

3. (c) Here, $S = \{M, A, T, H, E, I, C, S\}$

$\therefore$ Total number of outcomes $= 8$

Hence, Assertion is correct.

Now, when a coin is tossed twice,

$S = \{HH, HT, TH, TT\}$

So, the probability of getting a single head $= \frac{2}{4} = \frac{1}{2}$

Hence, Reason is false.

4. (a) Here, $n(S) = 36$

$A = \{(6, 4), (5, 5), (4, 6)\}$

$\Rightarrow P(A) = \frac{3}{36} = \frac{1}{12}$

5. (d) Here, $P(A \cap B) > P(A), P(B)$

$\therefore$ Assertion (A) is false.

We have, $P(A) = \frac{1}{4}, P(B') = \frac{2}{5}$,

$P(A \cap B') = \frac{3}{20}$

$\Rightarrow \quad P(B) = 1 - P(B') = 1 - \frac{2}{5} = \frac{3}{5}$

$P(A \cap B') = P(A) - P(A \cap B)$

$\Rightarrow P(A \cap B) = \frac{1}{4} - \frac{3}{20} = \frac{2}{20} = \frac{1}{10}$

So, $P(A \cup B) = P(A) + P(B) - P(A \cap B)$

$= \frac{1}{4} + \frac{3}{5} - \frac{1}{10} = \frac{3}{4}$

6. (b) Here, when a coin is tossed, the sample space, $S = \{H, T\}$

$\therefore$ The probability of getting a head $= \frac{1}{2}$

When a coin is tossed twice, the sample space,

$S = \{HH, HT, TH, TT\}$

$\therefore$ Probability of getting no 'tails'

$= \frac{1}{4}$

7. (b) When tossing a coin, there are two exhaustive cases: heads and tails. When a pair of dice is thrown, then the number of exhaustive cases is $6 \times 6 = 36$

[$\because$ each die has 1 to 6 number on its faces]

8. (b) We have the word 'NAGATATION'.

Number of elements in the sample space, $n(S) = 10$

We have the word 'ASSASSINATION'.

Number of elements in the sample space, $n(S) = 13$

9. (d) If two dice are thrown simultaneously, then the total number of possible outcomes is 36 (6×6).

$\therefore$ Probability of each outcome

$= \frac{1}{36}$

Also, Probability of an event (E) is defined as

$$P(E) = \frac{\text{Number of favourable outcomes}}{\text{Total number of possible outcomes}}$$

Case Based

Case 1 (i) (a) We have, 3 men and 2 women

$\therefore$ Required probability

$= \frac{{}^3C_1 \times {}^2C_1}{{}^5C_2}$

$= \frac{3 \times 2 \times 2}{5 \times 4} = \frac{3}{5}$

(ii) (b) Required probability

$= \frac{{}^2C_2 \times {}^3C_0}{{}^5C_2}$

$= \frac{1 \times 1}{10} = \frac{1}{10}$

(iii) (d) Required probability

$= \frac{{}^3C_2 \times {}^2C_0}{{}^5C_2}$

$= \frac{{}^3C_1 \times 1}{{}^5C_2} = \frac{{}^3C_1 \times 1}{10} = \frac{3}{10}$

Case 2 (i) Let A be the event that Shikha will qualify the exam and B be the event that Kajal will qualify the exam.

$\therefore P(A) = 0.05, P(B) = 0.10$ and $P(A \cap B) = 0.02$

We know that

$P(A) + P(A') = 1$

[$\because 0 \leq P(A) \leq 1$]

$\Rightarrow \quad P(B') = 1 - P(B)$

$= 1 - 0.10$

$= 0.9$

Hence, the probability that Kajal will not qualify the exam is 0.9.

(ii) We know that

$P(A \cup B) = P(A) + P(B) - P(A \cap B)$

$\Rightarrow \quad P(A \cup B) = 0.05 + 0.10 - 0.02$

$= 0.13$

Hence, the probability that atleast one of them will qualify the exam is 0.13.

(iii) $P(A' \cap B') = P(A \cup B)'$

$\Rightarrow P(A' \cap B') = P(A \cup B)'$

$= 1 - P(A \cup B)$

[$\because (A \cup B)' = 1 - (A \cup B)$]

$= 1 - 0.13 \quad [\because P(A \cup B) = 0.13]$

$= 0.87$

Hence, the probability that both Shikha and Kajal will not qualify the exam is 0.87.

Edge Up

1. (d) Favourable cases $= {}^6C_3$

Total out comes $= 6^3$

$\therefore$ Probability of getting greater number than previous

$= \frac{{}^6C_3}{6^3} = \frac{20}{216} = \frac{5}{54}$

2. (b) $ax^2 + bx + c = 0$

One root bigger than other

$\therefore$ Roots are real and distinct

$D > 0 \Rightarrow b^2 - 4ac > 0$

$b = 3$, then $(a, c) = (1, 1), (1, 2), (2, 1)$

$b = 4$, then $(a, c) = (1, 1), (1, 2), (2, 1) (1, 7), (3, 1)$

$b = 5$, then $(a, c) = (1, 1), (1, 2), (2, 1) (1, 3), (3, 1), (1, 4), (4, 1), (1, 5), (5, 1), (1, 6), (6, 1), (2, 3), (3, 2), (2, 2)$

$b = 6$, then $(a, c) = (1, 1), (1, 2), (2, 1) (1, 3), (3, 1), (1, 4), (4, 1), (1, 5), (5, 1), (1, 6), (6, 1), (2, 3), (3, 2), (2, 2), (2, 4), (4, 2)$.

Favourable cases = 38

$$\therefore \quad p = \frac{38}{6 \times 6 \times 6} \Rightarrow 216p = 38$$

3. (b) Probability of tail $= \frac{1}{3}$

Probability of head $= \frac{2}{3}$

Two tails and one head $= TTH, THT, HTT$

Probability of getting 2 tails and 1 head

$$= \left(\frac{1}{3} \times \frac{1}{3} \times \frac{2}{3}\right) + \left(\frac{1}{3} \times \frac{2}{3} \times \frac{1}{3}\right) + \left(\frac{2}{3} \times \frac{1}{3} \times \frac{1}{3}\right) = \frac{2}{9}$$

4. (a) 10 red, 30 white, 20 blue and 15 orange marbles.

Probability of drawing first marble red and second marble white is

$$= P(R) \times P(W)$$

$$= \frac{10}{75} \times \frac{30}{75} = \frac{4}{75}$$

5. (a) We have,

$$P(2) = \frac{1}{6} \text{ and } P(\overline{2}) = \frac{5}{6}$$

$\therefore P$[2 obtained on even numbered toss]

$$= \frac{5}{6} \times \frac{1}{6} + \left(\frac{5}{6}\right)^3 \times \frac{1}{6} + \left(\frac{5}{6}\right)^5 \times \frac{1}{6} + \dots$$

$$= \frac{\frac{5}{6} \times \frac{1}{6}}{1 - \left(\frac{5}{6}\right)^2}$$

$$= \frac{5}{36} \times \frac{36}{11} = \frac{5}{11}$$

6. (b) Probability of required event

$$= \frac{{}^6C_4}{{}^{15}C_4} \times \frac{{}^9C_4}{{}^{11}C_4}$$

$$= \frac{15 \times 24}{15 \times 14 \times 13 \times 12} \times \frac{9 \times 8 \times 7 \times 6 \times 24}{24 \times 11 \times 10 \times 9 \times 8}$$

$$= \frac{1}{13 \times 7} \times \frac{7 \times 3}{11 \times 5} = \frac{3}{715}$$

7. (b) Let the numbers be x and y.

So, $x + y = 24$; $x, y \in N$

and $x \cdot y \geq \frac{3}{4}$ (maximum product)

Maximum product will be found.

When $x = y = \frac{24}{2} = 12$

So, $xy \geq \frac{3}{4}(12 \times 12)$

$\Rightarrow xy \geq \frac{3}{4} \times 144$

$\Rightarrow xy \geq 108$

Possible cases

x	y	xy
1	23	23
2	22	44
⋮	⋮	⋮
6	18	108
⋮	⋮	⋮
11	13	143
12	12	144
13	11	143
⋮	⋮	⋮
18	6	108

$\therefore$ Total combination = 13

So, $P(xy \geq 108) = \frac{13}{23} = \frac{m}{n}$

So, $n - m = 23 - 13 = 10$

8. (b) Since, x and y each can take values from 0 to 10, so the total number of ways of selecting x and y is

$11 \times 11 = 121$. Now, $|x - y| > 5$

$\Rightarrow x - y < -5$ or $x - y > 5$

When $x - y > 5$, we have following cases

When $x = 0, y = 0 \rightarrow 1$ case

$x = 7, y = 0, 1 \rightarrow 2$ cases

$x = 8, y = 0, 1, 2, \rightarrow 3$ cases

$x = 9, y = 0, 1, 2, 3 \rightarrow 4$ cases

$x = 10, 0, 1, 2, 3, 4 \rightarrow 5$ cases

Hence, the total number of cases 15.

Similarly, we have 15 cases for $x - y < 5$. There are 30 pairs values of x and y satisfying these two in equalities. So, favourable number of ways is 30.

Hence, required probability is $\frac{30}{121}$.

9. (19) $a, b, c \in \{1, 2, 3, 4\}$

Now, $ax^2 + bx + c = 0$ has all real roots, if $D \geq 0$.

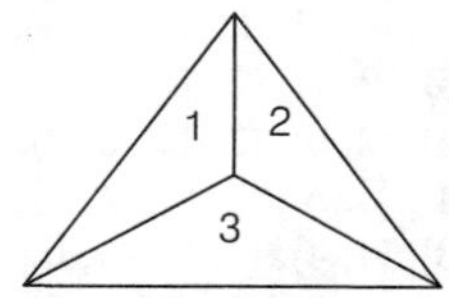

Tetrahedral dice

$\Rightarrow b^2 - 4ac \geq 0$

Let $b = 1 \Rightarrow 1 - 4ac \geq 0$ [not feasible]

$b = 2 \Rightarrow 4 - 4ac \geq 0$

$\Rightarrow 1 \geq ac \Rightarrow a = 1, c = 1$

$b = 3 \Rightarrow 9 - 4ac \geq 0 \Rightarrow \frac{9}{4} \geq ac$

$\Rightarrow (a = 1, c = 1), (a = 1, c = 2), (a = 2, c = 1)$

$b = 4 \Rightarrow 16 - 4ac \geq 0 \quad \Rightarrow 4 \geq ac$

$\Rightarrow (a = 1, c = 2), (a = 2, c = 1), (a = 1, c = 3)$

$(a = 3, c = 1), (a = 1, c = 4), (a = 4, c = 1), (a = 2, c = 2)$

$\therefore$ Required probability

$$= \frac{12}{4 \times 4 \times 4} = \frac{3}{16} = \frac{m}{n} \quad \text{[given]}$$

$$\therefore \quad m + n = 19$$

10. (a) Given, Ajay will not appear in exam $P(\overline{A}) = \frac{2}{7} \Rightarrow P(A) = \frac{5}{7}$

and both Ajay and Vijay will appear in the exam with probability

$$P(A \cap V) = \frac{1}{5} = P(A) \cdot P(V)$$

[$\because P(A)$ and $P(V)$ are independent]

$$\therefore \quad P(A) \cdot P(V) = \frac{1}{5}$$

$$P(V) = \frac{7}{25} \qquad \left[\because P(A) = \frac{5}{7}\right]$$

Now, probability that Ajay will appear in the exam and Vijay will not appear

$$P(A \cap \overline{V}) = P(A)\, P(\overline{V})$$

$$= \frac{5}{7} \times \left(1 - \frac{7}{25}\right) \quad [\because P(\overline{A}) = -P(A)]$$

$$= \frac{18}{35}$$

11. $U = \{1, 2, 3, \ldots, 50\}$
A = Set of integers which is multiple of 4
B = Set of integers which is multiple of 6
C = Set of integers which is multiple of 7
$n(A) = 12;\ n(B) = 8;\ n(C) = 7$
$n(A \cap B) = 4$
$n(B \cap C) = 1$
$n(C \cap A) = 1$
$n(A \cap B \cap C) = 0$
$\therefore n(A \cup B \cup C) = n(A) + n(B) + n(C) - n(A \cap B) - n(B \cap C) - n(C \cap A) + n(A \cap B \cap C)$
$= 12 + 8 + 7 - 4 - 1 - 1 + 0 = 21$
$\therefore$ Required probability $= \dfrac{21}{50}$

12. (a) Total number of outcomes
$= 6 \times 6 \times 6 = 216$
Number of outcomes getting different numbers on the three dice are
$${}^6P_3 = \frac{6!}{3!} = 120$$
$\therefore$ Required probability $= \dfrac{120}{216} = \dfrac{5}{9}$
$\therefore \quad p = 5$ and $q = 9$
$\therefore \quad q - p = 9 - 5 = 4$

13. (b) Given, Ω = sample space
A = an event such that $A \subseteq \Omega$
Now, as **S1** $P(A) = 0$, then A must be ϕ. So, **S1** is true.
Also, as **S2** $P(A) = 1$, then A must be equal to sample space (Ω). So, **S2** is also true.

14. Let N be the sum of numbers appeared when two fair dice are rolled.
Given, $N - 2, \sqrt{3N}, N + 2$ are in GP.
$[\because a, b, c$ are in GP, then $b^2 = ac]$
So, $(\sqrt{3N})^2 = (N - 2)(N + 2)$
$3N = N^2 - 4$
$N^2 - 3N - 4 = 0$
$(N - 4)(N + 1) = 0$
$N = 4$ and $N = -1$
$N = -1$ is rejected as it cannot be negative.
So, sum $= N = 4$
So, probability of getting sum 4 when two fair dice are rolled
$= \dfrac{\text{Favourable outcomes}}{\text{Total outcomes}}$
$\because$ Total outcomes $= 6 \times 6 = 36$
$\because$ Favourable outcomes
$= \{\text{sum} = 4\}$
$= \{(1, 3), (3, 1), (2, 2)\}$
So, probability $= 3/36 = 1/12$
But, it is given that the probability $= \dfrac{k}{48}$
So, $\dfrac{1}{12} = \dfrac{k}{48} \Rightarrow k = 4$

15. (10) Since, A fair $n (n > 1)$ faces die is rolled repeatedly until a number less than n appears. Thus, mean of the number of tosses
$$= 1 \cdot \left(\frac{1}{n}\right)^0 \left(\frac{n-1}{n}\right) + 2\left(\frac{1}{n}\right)^1 \left(\frac{n-1}{n}\right) + 3\left(\frac{1}{n}\right)^2 \left(\frac{n-1}{n}\right) + \ldots$$
$$= 1\left(\frac{n-1}{n}\right)\left(1 + \frac{2}{n} + \frac{3}{n^2} + \ldots\right)$$
$$= \left(\frac{n-1}{n}\right)\left(1 - \frac{1}{n}\right)^{-2}$$
$\{\because (1 - x)^{-2} = 1 + 2x + 3x^2 + \ldots\}$
$$= \left(\frac{n-1}{n}\right)\left(\frac{n-1}{n}\right)^{-2} = \frac{n}{n-1}$$
Again, the mean of number of tosses given $= \dfrac{n}{9}$
So, $\dfrac{n}{9} = \dfrac{n}{n-1} \Rightarrow n^2 - n - 9n = 0$
$\Rightarrow n^2 - 10n = 0 \Rightarrow n = 10 \quad [\because n > 1]$
Hence, the required value of n is 10.

16. (14) $\because$ Bag contains balls of different colours.
p = probability of both drawn balls are of same colour
$$= \frac{{}^6C_1}{6 \times 6} = \frac{1}{6}$$
q = probability that exactly three from four balls are of the same colour
$$= \frac{{}^6C_1 \times {}^5C_1 \times {}^4C_1}{6 \times 6 \times 6 \times 6} = \frac{6 \times 5 \times 4}{6 \times 6 \times 6 \times 6} = \frac{5}{54}$$
$$\frac{p}{q} = \frac{(1/6)}{(5/54)} = \frac{1}{6} \times \frac{54}{5} = \frac{9}{5} = \frac{m}{n}$$
So, $m = 9$ and $n = 5$
Therefore, $m + n = 9 + 5 = 14$

17. (10) Let the two real numbers be x and y. Then,
$|x - y| < a \Rightarrow -a < x - y < a$
$\Rightarrow \quad x - y < a$ and $x - y > -a$

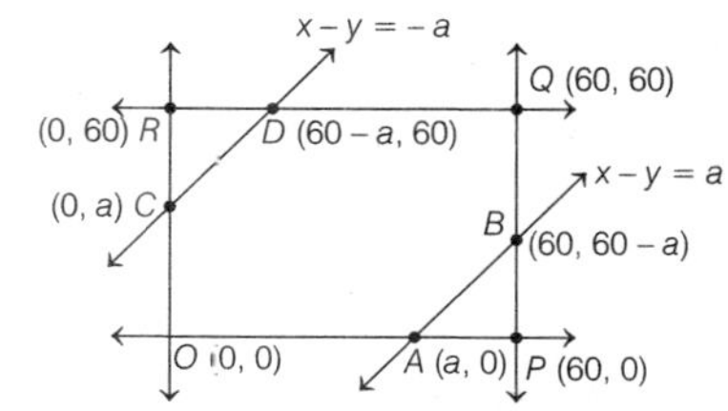

Required probability,
$$P(A) = \frac{\text{ar}(OABQDC)}{\text{ar}(OPQR)}$$
$$= \frac{\text{ar}(OPQR) - \text{ar}(\Delta APB) - \text{ar}(\Delta CDR)}{\text{ar}(OPQR)}$$
$$= \frac{(60)^2 - \frac{1}{2}(60 - a)^2 - \frac{1}{2}(60 - a)^2}{(60)^2}$$
$$= \frac{3600 - (60 - a)^2}{3600}$$
$$= \frac{3600 - 3600 - a^2 + 120a}{3600}$$
$$= \frac{120a - a^2}{3600}$$
It is given that $P(A) = \dfrac{11}{36}$
$\Rightarrow \quad \dfrac{120a - a^2}{3600} = \dfrac{11}{36}$
$\Rightarrow \quad 120a - a^2 = 1100$
$\Rightarrow \quad a^2 - 120a + 1100 = 0$
$\Rightarrow \quad (a - 10)(a - 110) = 0$
$\Rightarrow a = 10, 110 \Rightarrow a = 10\ [\because a \neq 110]$

18. (a) Required cases
= Total ways − All digits even − Exactly one digit odd
Total ways = 900 ways
All digits even $= 4 \times 5 \times 5 = 100$ ways
One digit odd $= \underset{\text{odd}}{5} \times 5 \times 5 = 125$ ways
$4 \times \underset{\text{odd}}{5} \times 5 = 100$ ways
$4 \times 5 \times \underset{\text{odd}}{5} = 100$ ways
$\therefore$ Required probability
$$= \frac{900 - 425}{900} = \frac{19}{36}$$

19. (c) Number of ways to select and arrange x_1, x_2, x_3, x_4, x_5 in increasing order selected from $1, 2, 3, \ldots, 18$.
$n(S) = {}^{18}C_5$
$x_1\ x_2\ x_3\ x_4\ x_5$
$n(E) = {}^6C_1 \times {}^3C_1 \times {}^7C_1$
(for $x < 7$) (for $x_3 \in \{8, 9, 10\}$) (for $x_5 > 11$)
$$P(E) = \frac{6 \times 3 \times 7}{{}^{18}C_5} = \frac{126}{8568} = \frac{1}{68}$$